BEGINNING MOBILE APPLICATION DEVELOPMENT IN THE CLOUD

W9-AHM-516

INTRODUCTION. xxi

CHAPTER 1   Introducing Cloud-Based Mobile Apps 1

CHAPTER 2   Mobilizing Your App. 31

CHAPTER 3   Building Mobile Web Apps. 71

CHAPTER 4   Enhancing Your App 111

CHAPTER 5   Building Apps in the Cloud. 135

CHAPTER 6   Use the Cloud! 177

CHAPTER 7   Enhancing the User Experience 211

CHAPTER 8   Working with the Cloud 235

CHAPTER 9   Creating Hybrid Apps that Run Natively 273

CHAPTER 10   Building a Photo-Blogging App. 315

CHAPTER 11   Working with Cloud Development Services 371

CHAPTER 12   Going Social!. 387

CHAPTER 13   App Stores 435

CHAPTER 14   Selling Your App. 455

APPENDIX   Exercise Solutions 471

INDEX. 505

BEGINNING

Mobile Application Development in the Cloud

BEGINNING

Mobile Application Development in the Cloud

Richard Rodger

WILEY

John Wiley & Sons, Inc.

Beginning Mobile Application Development in the Cloud

Published by
John Wiley & Sons, Inc.
10475 Crosspoint Boulevard
Indianapolis, IN 46256
www.wiley.com

Copyright © 2012 by John Wiley & Sons, Inc., Indianapolis, Indiana

Published simultaneously in Canada

ISBN: 978-1-118-03469-9
ISBN: 978-1-118-20333-0 (ebk)
ISBN: 978-1-118-20335-4 (ebk)
ISBN: 978-1-118-20334-7 (ebk)

Manufactured in the United States of America

10 9 8 7 6 5 4 3 2 1

Limit of Liability/Disclaimer of Warranty: The publisher and the author make no representations or warranties with respect to the accuracy or completeness of the contents of this work and specifically disclaim all warranties, including without limitation warranties of fitness for a particular purpose. No warranty may be created or extended by sales or promotional materials. The advice and strategies contained herein may not be suitable for every situation. This work is sold with the understanding that the publisher is not engaged in rendering legal, accounting, or other professional services. If professional assistance is required, the services of a competent professional person should be sought. Neither the publisher nor the author shall be liable for damages arising herefrom. The fact that an organization or Web site is referred to in this work as a citation and/or a potential source of further information does not mean that the author or the publisher endorses the information the organization or Web site may provide or recommendations it may make. Further, readers should be aware that Internet Web sites listed in this work may have changed or disappeared between when this work was written and when it is read.

For general information on our other products and services please contact our Customer Care Department within the United States at (877) 762-2974, outside the United States at (317) 572-3993 or fax (317) 572-4002.

Wiley also publishes its books in a variety of electronic formats and by print-on-demand. Not all content that is available in standard print versions of this book may appear or be packaged in all book formats. If you have purchased a version of this book that did not include media that is referenced by or accompanies a standard print version, you may request this media by visiting http://booksupport.wiley.com. For more information about Wiley products, visit us at www.wiley.com.

Library of Congress Control Number: 2011936907

Trademarks: Wiley, the Wiley logo, Wrox, the Wrox logo, Programmer to Programmer, and related trade dress are trademarks or registered trademarks of John Wiley & Sons, Inc. and/or its affiliates, in the United States and other countries, and may not be used without written permission. All other trademarks are the property of their respective owners. John Wiley & Sons, Inc., is not associated with any product or vendor mentioned in this book.

For Orla, Saorla, Lola and Ruadhán,
all my love.

ABOUT THE AUTHOR

RICHARD RODGER is the founder of Chartaca.com, a mobile analytics company built on the PhoneGap and Node.js technologies. He has led the successful development of several large scale enterprise mobile services, particularly in the news and media industry. He was previously CTO of FeedHenry.com, a JavaScript-focused cloud hosting platform for mobile apps, also based on PhoneGap and Node.js. As a senior researcher at the Telecommunications Software & Services Group at the Waterford Institute of Technology, Ireland, he led the research team that built the core platform that became FeedHenry. Richard is also the founder of Ricebridge.com, a company providing Java components for high volume data processing.

Richard has been a long-time participant in the Java open source community, and more recently in the Node.js community, contributing several modules for database integration and systems monitoring.

Richard has degrees in Computer Science from the Waterford Institute of Technology and Mathematics and Philosophy from Trinity College Dublin, Ireland.

CREDITS

ACKNOWLEDGMENTS

THERE IS AN ENORMOUS DIFFERENCE BETWEEN talking about technology and writing about it. It is surprisingly difficult to place your thoughts on paper in coherent form. I do not think anyone can ever claim to have a written a book by themselves. Behind every book is a broad and deep support structure, without which no author would ever make it to the finish line.

I am deeply grateful to my wife Orla, and my children, Saorla, Lola and Ruadhán. I missed you. You were always unconditionally there for me and gave me the strength to write this book. I am also very grateful to my parents, Hanish and Noreen, and Orla's parents, Noel and Kay. Thank you for helping us keep things together. Lauren, my sister, thank you for your words of encouragement. You are always thinking of us. And thank you, Alaister and Conor, you always believed in me.

I was delighted, in the Summer of 2010, to receive a call from Paul Reese at Wiley, inviting me to think about writing a book on the convergence of mobile apps and cloud computing. I've built two companies on this idea, and it's only getting started! Thank you, Paul, for that call and your patience as I juggled work and writing.

A very heartfelt thank you to Kelly Talbot, my editor and guide. It is an absolute pleasure to work with such a great professional. Thank you for getting me through my first book.

Thank you, too, to the other members of the team, Matthew Baxter-Reynolds and Dale Cruse, for your astute technical input, and Kitty Wilson for so much detailed work improving my prose. This book is far better for your efforts. All remaining errors in text and code are mine alone.

And thank you to all those in my professional life, colleagues and customers alike. You have helped me learn and grow. There would be nothing to write without you.

CONTENTS

INTRODUCTION   *xxi*

CHAPTER 1: INTRODUCING CLOUD-BASED MOBILE APPS   **1**

How to Build Mobile Apps in the Cloud   **2**
Using Your Existing Skill Set   2
Determining What Tools You Need   3
The Skills You'll Learn   4
Two Big Ideas About the App Industry   **4**
Web Apps and the Future   5
The Cloud as the Future   6
Getting Started   **7**
Using JavaScript Functions   7
The WebKit Browser Engine   20
A Colorful Little App   21
Introducing the nginx Web Server   25
Summary   **29**

CHAPTER 2: MOBILIZING YOUR APP   **31**

Building a Touch-Sensitive Drawing App   **32**
How to Draw on the Screen   32
Drawing in Response to Touch Events   39
Applying the DRY Principle to Your Code   46
Using the Amazon Cloud   **52**
How Geography Affects Amazon AWS   54
Using the Elastic Compute Cloud   54
Deploying Your Mobile Web App   61
Deploying Your Mobile App to the Instance   65
Summary   **67**

CHAPTER 3: BUILDING MOBILE WEB APPS   **71**

What You Can Do with Mobile Web Apps   **71**
Locating Your User   72
Responding to Device Orientation   74
More Features for Later   76
Installing Mobile Web Apps on iPhone Devices   76
Installing Mobile Web Apps on Android Devices   77

Introducing jQuery and jQuery Mobile	**78**
The jQuery Library	78
The jQuery Mobile Library	83
Building a To-Do List App	**91**
Summary	**108**

CHAPTER 4: ENHANCING YOUR APP	**111**

Using App Caching	**112**
Handling Touch Events	**115**
Touch Events	116
Gesture Events	118
Embedding an Interactive Map	**127**
The Google Maps API	127
Providing an Application Icon and a Startup Screen	**131**
Summary	**132**

CHAPTER 5: BUILDING APPS IN THE CLOUD	**135**

Server-Side JavaScript	**136**
Introducing Node	136
Installing Node	138
Using the Node Package Manager	141
Introducing the MongoDB Database	144
Cloud Analytics for Your To-Do List App	**150**
Doing the Math	150
Organizing Your System	152
Collecting the Usage Data	160
Submitting the Usage Data	164
Charting the Usage Data	167
Summary	**174**

CHAPTER 6: USE THE CLOUD!	**177**

The Classic Cloud Architecture	**177**
The REST Approach	178
Cloud Databases	179
Introducing Amazon SimpleDB	**180**
The SimpleDB Approach to Cloud Storage	180
The SimpleDB API	181
Putting the To-Do List App in the Cloud	**182**
Introducing the simpledb Library	182
Building a Command-Line Client	188

Working on Cloud Time 196
Running a Cloud Server 198
Synchronizing with the Cloud 203
Summary **209**

CHAPTER 7: ENHANCING THE USER EXPERIENCE **211**

Creating a Classic Tab Bar Interface **211**
Implementing the jQuery Mobile Solution 212
Using the iScroll Solution 216
Enabling Mobile Audio and Video **222**
Playing Audio in Your App 222
Playing Video in Your App 226
Launching Apps from Your App **230**
Launching a Web Browser from Your App 230
Launching a Phone from Your App 230
Launching SMS from Your App 230
Launching Mail from Your App 231
Launching Maps from Your App 231
Launching YouTube from Your App 231
Summary **232**

CHAPTER 8: WORKING WITH THE CLOUD **235**

Storing Content in Amazon S3 **236**
The Architecture of Amazon S3 236
Using Amazon S3 238
Signing In with the Cloud **247**
Building Large-Scale Apps **255**
Getting the Big Picture Right 256
Using the Cache! 258
Summary **271**

CHAPTER 9: CREATING HYBRID APPS THAT RUN NATIVELY **273**

Introducing Hybrid Apps **274**
The PhoneGap Project 274
Building Hybrid Apps **275**
Building an iPhone App 275
Understanding Code-Signing 276
Building an Android App 283
Using Device Features 288

Lifestream, a Photo-Blogging App	**294**
Uploading Pictures	295
Storing Pictures on Amazon S3	306
Summary	**310**
CHAPTER 10: BUILDING A PHOTO-BLOGGING APP	**315**
The Architecture of Lifestream	**316**
Building the Server	**317**
Laying the Foundation	317
Enabling User Following	333
Uploading and Posting Pictures	336
Completing the Lifestream App	**345**
Supporting User Accounts	346
Integrating Social Network Identity	357
Summary	**368**
CHAPTER 11: WORKING WITH CLOUD DEVELOPMENT SERVICES	**371**
Getting to Know the Mobile App Development Platforms	**372**
Using the FeedHenry Platform	**373**
FeedHenry Technology	374
The FeedHenry Development Environment	375
Deciding to Use FeedHenry	376
Using the Appcelerator Platform	**377**
Appcelerator Technology	378
The Appcelerator Development Environment	379
Deciding to Use Appcelerator	380
Using the appMobi Platform	**381**
appMobi Technology	382
The appMobi Development Environment	383
Deciding to Use appMobi	384
Summary	**384**
CHAPTER 12: GOING SOCIAL!	**387**
Using the Twitter API	**388**
Working with the Twitter API Usage Limits	390
Using the Entities that the Twitter API Exposes	390
The Parts You Need	391
An App for Direct Messages	**395**
The Design Process	395
Getting the Hygiene Factors Right	399

The Code Structure   404
OAuth Without a Server   413
Calling the Twitter API   421
Event Consumers and Producers   425
Summary   **431**

CHAPTER 13: APP STORES   435

What You Need to Publish Your App   **436**
Icons   436
Splash Screen   438
Screenshots and Orientations   439
App Metadata   440
Working with the App Stores   440
Building Your App for Release   **441**
Summary   **452**

CHAPTER 14: SELLING YOUR APP   455

Determining a Marketing Strategy   **456**
Building Apps for Others   457
Using Apps to Promote Your Business   458
Selling Your Own Apps   460
Choosing Tactics for Promoting Your App   **462**
Standard Tactics   463
Expensive Tactics   465
Guerrilla Tactics   466
Summary   **468**

APPENDIX: EXERCISE SOLUTIONS   471

INDEX   *505*

INTRODUCTION

YOU CAN BUILD HIGH-QUALITY MOBILE APPS using only HTML, CSS, and JavaScript. And you can use JavaScript to build the cloud services that support those apps. You don't need to learn Objective-C or Java to deliver production-quality iPhone and Android mobile apps.

This book shows you how to use the web development skills you already have to start working in the mobile app industry. With the support of new open source technologies like PhoneGap and Node.js, you can join the new industry momentum behind HTML5. With premium brands like Facebook and *The Financial Times* rolling out HTML5 mobile apps, the time is ripe to enter a new market with high demand for your development skills.

The move to standardize on HTML5 is one industry wave. The other is the move towards cloud computing. Cloud computing is the way most software services will be delivered in the near future. This book will show you how to work with cloud hosting services like Amazon, use cloud databases like MongoDB, authenticate against social media sites like Twitter and Facebook, and build large-scale high-uptime cloud APIs with Node.js to support your mobile app in production.

I wrote this book to give you the practical skills and tools you need to accelerate into this industry wave. The focus is on complete, fully working code samples (with error-handling!) that you can adapt for your own projects. During the course of this book, you will build three complete mobile apps, each covering key topics in mobile app development and cloud computing. I also wrote this book to communicate my genuine joy at rediscovering JavaScript, the oft-maligned language of the web. After years under the yoke of Java, programming is fun again!

WHO THIS BOOK IS FOR

This book is for two very different constituencies. The first is front-end web developers. You know your HTML, CSS, and JavaScript, but you'd really like to do more on the server-side. You know your way around Ruby, PHP, or Perl, but your first love is building fantastic user interfaces and web sites. You want to get into mobile app development, but you wonder if the time invested in learning Objective-C and Java is really worth it. This book shows you how to leverage your existing skills, letting you get started with mobile app development right away. And you can finally move beyond the client-side with JavaScript!

The second constituency is server-side developers. You've been stuck coding in Java or C# for years, and you need a change. You'd like to try your hand at mobile development, and of course you've already designed the cloud service to go with your app. This book shows you how to build the user interface of your app using standard web languages and how to structure your JavaScript at the level you're accustomed to with Java and C#. JavaScript may be a scripting language, but it's deeper than you think. This book also shows you how use JavaScript on the server-side. By doing this, you gain twice: There's no mental context switch between client and server coding, and you can use Node.js to build large-scale event-based servers. Your productivity will double (mine has!), and you'll be ready to build the next killer cloud service.

This material in this book is cumulative. Think of it as an in-depth extended tutorial that guides you step-by-step from first principles to happy clients and production apps. Each chapter takes you up another level. Most chapters cover client- and server-side topics, embracing their interdependence. Feel free to skip sections that introduce topics, like jQuery, that you might already be familiar with. But make sure you read the code. Often, old technologies are used in new ways.

The exercises are not written to test your knowledge of the material presented. Most of them will ask you to do something new, highlight something you need to think about, or take you off on an interesting tangent. While solutions are given, think of them more as suggestions. Trust your own instincts.

WHAT THIS BOOK COVERS

The client-side app code in this book uses the jQuery and jQuery Mobile open-source JavaScript libraries. These libraries are used to build complex, interactive user interfaces that demonstrate HTML structure manipulation, event handling, and animation effects. The latest versions of these libraries are used. These libraries are designed to work together and provide a solid basis for client-side development. They are widely used and well-tested by the community, and you are probably already familiar with at least jQuery.

To build mobile apps, this book introduces you to the latest features of HTML5 and then takes you further by showing you how to use the open-source PhoneGap project from Nitobi.com. You can deliver very substantial apps using just the web browser on your mobile device. Quite a lot of time is spent exploring how much you can do with HTML5. Eventually, of course, you'll need to build "real" apps that can be listed in the Apple App Store and Android Marketplace. This is where PhoneGap comes in. This ingenious project provides a way for you to run your web code inside a native container app, meaning you can still build everything using HTML, CSS, and JavaScript, but you can also access physical device features like the camera.

The server-side code uses the Node.js JavaScript application server. The 0.4 stable branch is used throughout the book. As Node.js is under an active initial development phase, it is likely that the 0.6 or higher stable branch may be available by the time you read this. The code in this book is conservative with respect to the Node.js API and sticks to common API use-cases that are unlikely to change. Feel free to use the latest stable version, but do check the Errata page at www.wrox.com and my blog (http://tech.richardrodger.com) in case there are any specific issues. The Node.js server was chosen as the underlying platform for this book because it is the primary example of the new generation of event-based cloud servers. And you can code in JavaScript!

For data storage, the examples in this book use "noSQL" systems. MongoDB is used extensively because it uses the JSON format natively, which is very convenient for JavaScript code. The examples were build against the 1.8 release family. An example is also given of the purely cloud-based SimpleDB service from Amazon. This service has a well-defined web API and feature set that is unlikely to change much over time. These schemaless databases show you how to free yourself from the restrictions of the traditional SQL databases.

As the complexity of the examples in this book increases, so does the need to structure your code more carefully. As the code bases get larger, you'll be given techniques to meet this challenge. You'll learn about the DRY principle (Don't Repeat Yourself), tracer bullets, unit and acceptance testing, use-case analysis, object-dependency mapping, and data structure design. All of these techniques are introduced in the context of a particular piece of code so that you have something concrete to help you understand how to apply them.

HOW THIS BOOK IS STRUCTURED

Each chapter in this book builds on the previous one. You'll get the most value out of the material if you read it in sequence. You'll build three apps in this book, each over the course of a few chapters:

➤ A classic To Do List app

➤ A Photo-blogging app

➤ A Twitter app

Each app is constructed piece by piece, just as you would code it yourself. At the end of each chapter, you'll have a working version of the app. It may not be feature-complete, but it will be a working app with a consistent code base.

Some chapters will take a detour to explore a key topic at a deeper level. You can skim this material if you just need to get your app built, returning later when you need some guidance on a particular topic.

Here are the topics covered by each chapter:

➤ Chapter 1, "Introducing Cloud-Based Mobile Apps," gets you up to speed with HTML5 and cloud servers, showing you how to deliver a simple mobile web app.

➤ Chapter 2, "Mobilize Your App!," starts to make your app behave more like a native app, and walks you through a deployment onto an Amazon cloud server.

➤ Chapter 3, "Building Mobile Web Apps," introduces the jQuery Mobile framework, giving your app a truly native look and feel, and starts the development of the To Do List app.

➤ Chapter 4, "Enhance Your App!," takes a closer look at touch and gesture events, and teaches you how to deal with them.

➤ Chapter 5, "Building Apps in the Cloud," introduces the Node.js server and builds a scalable event tracking system for the To Do List app.

➤ Chapter 6, "Use the Cloud!," converts the To Do List app to use the Amazon SimpleDB cloud database, showing you how to build on cloud services.

➤ Chapter 7, "Enhancing the User Experience," dives deeper into the features you'll need to build to create a native feel for you app, including momentum scrolling and audio-visual media playback.

➤ Chapter 8, "Working with the Cloud," lays the foundation for the photo-blogging app by showing you how to interact with the Amazon S3 cloud storage service and how to use the OAuth protocol to let your users log in with Twitter and Facebook.

➤ Chapter 9, "Creating Hybrid Apps that Run Natively," takes the photo-blogging app native, using PhoneGap, to create iPhone and Android apps built using HTML.

➤ Chapter 10, "Building a Photo-Blogging App" pulls together everything you've learned so far to deliver a complete photo-blogging app that can interact with the on-device camera and provide Twitter-like scalable follower/friend relationships for your users.

➤ Chapter 11, "Working with Cloud Services," takes you on a tour of the commercial cloud services that can make your life much easier as an HTML5 mobile app developer.

➤ Chapter 12, "Go Social!," builds a complete twitter client app that lets you manage your direct message conversations over multiple Twitter accounts.

➤ Chapter 13, "App Stores," takes you step-by-step through the app submission process for the Apple App Store and Android Marketplace

➤ Chapter 14, "Selling Your App," gives you a head start on your competitors by giving you some great ideas for promoting and selling your app.

➤ The Appendix, "Exercise Solutions," provides answers to the exercises found at the end of each chapter.

WHAT YOU NEED TO USE THIS BOOK

This book shows you how to build iPhone and Android mobile apps. You'll need Mac OS X to build both iPhone and Android apps. On Windows or Linux, you'll only be able to build Android apps. All the code in this book has been tested on both iPhone and Android, so you don't absolutely need a Mac, but it is highly recommended.

You will definitely need either an iPhone or Android mobile device (preferably both!). Mobile apps always need to tested on physical devices to be absolutely sure of how they will behave in the real world.

For the cloud computing material, you'll need to subscribe to various cloud services, like Amazon Web Services or MongoHQ.com. These are commercial services, and they generally require credit card details even if you do not intend to use the paid options. It is more than likely that you will end up paying some level of monthly charges if you begin to use these services seriously. That is in the nature of cloud services. Make sure you are ultimately making money from your clients to cover this!

CONVENTIONS

To help you get the most from the text and keep track of what's happening, we've used a number of conventions throughout the book.

Boxes with a warning icon like this one hold important, not-to-be-forgotten information that is directly relevant to the surrounding text.

 The pencil icon indicates notes, tips, hints, tricks, or asides to the current discussion.

As for styles in the text:

➤ We *highlight* new terms and important words when we introduce them.

➤ We show keyboard strokes like this: Ctrl+A.

➤ We show file names, URLs, and code within the text like so: `persistence.properties`.

We present code in two different ways:

```
We use a monofont type with no highlighting for most code examples.
We use bold to emphasize code that is particularly important in the present
context or to show changes from a previous code snippet.
```

SOURCE CODE

As you work through the examples in this book, you may choose either to type in all the code manually, or to use the source code files that accompany the book. All the source code used in this book is available for download at `www.wrox.com`. When at the site, simply locate the book's title (use the Search box or one of the title lists) and click the Download Code link on the book's detail page to obtain all the source code for the book. Code that is included on the website is highlighted by the following icon:

Available for download on Wrox.com

Listings include the filename in the title. If it is just a code snippet, you'll find the filename in a code note such as this:

code snippet filename

 Because many books have similar titles, you may find it easiest to search by ISBN; this book's ISBN is 978-1-118-03469-9.

Once you download the code, just decompress it with your favorite compression tool. Alternately, you can go to the main Wrox code download page at `www.wrox.com/dynamic/books/download .aspx` to see the code available for this book and all other Wrox books.

ERRATA

We make every effort to ensure that there are no errors in the text or in the code. However, no one is perfect, and mistakes do occur. If you find an error in one of our books, like a spelling mistake or faulty piece of code, we would be very grateful for your feedback. By sending in errata, you may save another reader hours of frustration, and at the same time, you will be helping us provide even higher quality information.

To find the errata page for this book, go to www.wrox.com and locate the title using the Search box or one of the title lists. Then, on the book details page, click the Book Errata link. On this page, you can view all errata that has been submitted for this book and posted by Wrox editors. A complete book list, including links to each book's errata, is also available at www.wrox.com/misc-pages/booklist.shtml.

If you don't spot "your" error on the Book Errata page, go to www.wrox.com/contact/techsupport.shtml and complete the form there to send us the error you have found. We'll check the information and, if appropriate, post a message to the book's errata page and fix the problem in subsequent editions of the book.

P2P.WROX.COM

For author and peer discussion, join the P2P forums at p2p.wrox.com. The forums are a Web-based system for you to post messages relating to Wrox books and related technologies and interact with other readers and technology users. The forums offer a subscription feature to e-mail you topics of interest of your choosing when new posts are made to the forums. Wrox authors, editors, other industry experts, and your fellow readers are present on these forums.

At p2p.wrox.com, you will find a number of different forums that will help you, not only as you read this book, but also as you develop your own applications. To join the forums, just follow these steps:

1. Go to p2p.wrox.com and click the Register link.

2. Read the terms of use and click Agree.

3. Complete the required information to join, as well as any optional information you wish to provide, and click Submit.

4. You will receive an e-mail with information describing how to verify your account and complete the joining process.

 You can read messages in the forums without joining P2P, but in order to post your own messages, you must join.

Once you join, you can post new messages and respond to messages other users post. You can read messages at any time on the Web. If you would like to have new messages from a particular forum e-mailed to you, click the Subscribe to this Forum icon by the forum name in the forum listing.

For more information about how to use the Wrox P2P, be sure to read the P2P FAQs for answers to questions about how the forum software works, as well as many common questions specific to P2P and Wrox books. To read the FAQs, click the FAQ link on any P2P page.

1

Introducing Cloud-Based Mobile Apps

WHAT YOU WILL LEARN IN THIS CHAPTER:

➤ Using your existing skills as a web developer to build mobile apps

➤ Understanding how HTML5 will be used as an app-development standard

➤ Learning how to dynamically create JavaScript functions

➤ Using the WebKit browser engine for app development

➤ Creating a mobile web app that responds to touch

➤ Installing and using the nginx web server

This book is for web developers who want to build mobile apps and cloud services. If you know HTML, CSS, and JavaScript, you already have the skills to build not only mobile apps but also the cloud services that power them.

The code examples in this book show you how to build complete apps. You are never left to put together the pieces yourself. The code is simple and includes error-handling logic, so you'll learn how to build production-ready apps and systems.

Over the course of this book, you will build three complete applications. You'll learn how to put together all the elements of the technology stack, and you'll learn about a wide range of technologies and services. This book will enable you to get to work but avoids unnecessary detail and theory.

This book is an accelerator for your skills. You can use it to efficiently make the leap into mobile and cloud development. Rather than attempting to be a reference for all the details, which you can find on the web anyway, it is a stepping stone for your skills.

HOW TO BUILD MOBILE APPS IN THE CLOUD

This book describes how to build apps that run on the new generation of smart mobile devices. It also shows how to build out the business logic behind these apps, and how to run that business logic in a cloud hosting environment, such as that provided by Amazon.

This book focuses on the two leading platforms: iPhone and Android. These two, between them, cover the vast majority of smartphones and provide access to the largest market.

> **NOTE** In this book, the term iPhone *should be taken as shorthand for any iOS-based device, including iPad and the iPod Touch devices. Similarly, the term* Android *refers to any device running Android version 2.1 or higher, including any of the Android tablets that are competing with the iPad.*

It's important to understand the types of apps that can run on mobile devices:

➤ **Mobile web apps** — These apps are really just websites, designed to function in an app-like way. They run in a web browser on a device.

➤ **Purely native apps** — These apps are written in a device-specific language, using a device-specific programming interface: Objective-C for iPhone apps or Java for Android apps. Native apps can access all the capabilities of the device and can take many forms, from simple utility apps to advanced 3-D games.

➤ **Hybrid native apps** — For these apps, you use HTML to build the user interface but wrap the HTML in a native container. Such apps can access some of the native capabilities of the device but can still be developed using HTML.

In this book you will learn how to build mobile web apps and hybrid apps.

The other component that many apps have is not something that lives on the mobile device at all. It is the business logic, data storage, and service integration that support the operation of the code on the mobile device. This element of app development is just as important as the visible part that you install on your device. Placing this code in a cloud-hosting environment is the best approach to developing a robust support system for your app, and this book shows you how to build the server elements of your app. You will learn how to do this by using your existing JavaScript skills. You'll run your code on the server using Node.js, a high-speed, high-capacity JavaScript server engine.

Using Your Existing Skill Set

As a web developer, you already possess all the skills you need to be a mobile app developer as well. If you can build websites, you can build mobile apps. If you are a web developer wanting to build mobile apps, you do not need to learn new languages such as Objective-C or Java. You do not even need to learn new languages to build the code for servers that support your app.

All you need to know is HTML, CSS, and JavaScript. This book assumes that you have a working knowledge of these three basic web languages. Even if you are more comfortable with design and graphics and are stronger in HTML and CSS than in JavaScript, you will still be able to follow the examples in this book and build your own apps.

This book takes a practical approach and shows you how to build real applications. The examples stick to common language features and avoid anything esoteric. The first set of code examples in this chapter lay the JavaScript ground work that will see you through to the end of the book.

You will use your existing skill set to build mobile web apps. You will then support those apps by using some server-side JavaScript, running on cloud servers, and you'll see all the steps needed to set this up. Then you'll learn how to create hybrid native apps using HTML, CSS, and JavaScript.

Determining What Tools You Need

You'll need some development tools in order to fully explore the examples in this book. You will certainly find a physical iPhone or Android device very useful for testing and development. You need to run mobile apps on an actual device to really understand how they will behave once users get hold of them.

To a certain extent, you can develop the apps and code examples in this book on any of the three major operating systems: Mac, Windows, or Linux. However, you will find that a Mac is the best choice, simply because the iPhone development tools from Apple can only run on a Mac. Your Mac can also run the server code quite easily. One thing you should do is upgrade to the latest version of the Mac OS X operating system, as this will support the most up-to-date versions of the iPhone development tools.

Windows and Linux are also acceptable, although you will have to do a little more configuration and setup work. In particular, on Windows, you will need to install the Cygwin UNIX environment so that you can run Node.js. Cygwin is available from www.cygwin.com. As discussed in Chapter, 11, you will also have to rely on third-party services to build hybrid native iPhone apps.

You can build mobile web apps and the necessary server code using your existing development tools. All you need is a good code editor, and I'm sure you've already chosen a favorite for coding websites. You'll also be using the command line quite a bit, especially for the server code. But don't worry if you're not comfortable with the command line; this book gives you exactly the commands you need to run.

Later in this book, you'll need to download and install the software development kits (SDKs) for iPhone and Android development. These SDKs are provided as part of the Xcode (for iPhone) and Eclipse (for Android) development environments. Xcode runs only on a Mac, but you can run Eclipse on all three operating systems.

The final development tool you'll use is the Safari web browser. You can download this directly from the Apple website: www.apple.com/safari. You will use Safari as a test and deployment tool because Safari is built with the open source WebKit browser engine. This browser engine is used on both iPhone and Android, and it is the web browser environment for which you need to develop. In your coding work cycle, you will use the desktop Safari browser as your test system.

The Skills You'll Learn

As you work through this book, you'll learn and enhance a wide range of skills. These skills will cover the entire mobile app technology stack, from the device, to the server, to the database. These will be practical skills, and theory will be kept to a minimum. All the code examples in this book create complete, fully working apps. You'll be able to use them as foundations for your own work.

You'll make good use of the new features in HTML5 when you build mobile web apps and HTML5-based native apps. The Safari browser and the WebKit engine have good support for many of the features of HTML5. You'll be able to use local on-device storage, app caching, geolocation, and even audio and video support.

You'll also learn about the special metatags and design considerations needed for mobile web app development. These allow you to deal with different screen sizes and device capabilities. They also allow you to define home screen icons and loading screens for your app.

To make the transition from a mobile web app to a hybrid native app, you'll use the open source PhoneGap project. This project provides a framework that allows you to embed your HTML in a native container. This is how you will build native apps using JavaScript. PhoneGap also provides you with an extended set of JavaScript functions that let you access the device camera and use the device accelerometer to detect movement.

The app on a device is only part of the story. The aim of this book is to teach you how to create mobile apps that provide complete services. This means you'll need to write server code that handles some of your business logic, such as user account management, user data storage, and integration with third-party cloud services. You'll also learn how to provide social media logins using Facebook and Twitter.

You will use JavaScript to build the server-side logic. You'll run your JavaScript in an application server known as Node.js (or more commonly, just "Node"), a JavaScript server created using the Google JavaScript engine from the Chrome web browser. Node is amazingly fast and designed to handle thousands of concurrent clients, so it's perfect for running a popular app.

You'll need a place to put your server-side code, so you'll learn how to host your code in the cloud, using Amazon Web Services (AWS). AWS is a full cloud-hosting system provided by Amazon that lets you create your servers and store images and files; it provides a nearly infinite database. You'll learn how to set up and configure an Amazon server and how to access the Amazon services over the web.

Finally, you'll learn how to work with next-generation databases that go beyond traditional tables, columns, and rows. You'll learn how to work with these schemaless database systems and how to synchronize them with the data on your mobile device.

TWO BIG IDEAS ABOUT THE APP INDUSTRY

This book is based on two predictions about where the app industry is going:

➤ **Cloud computing will be the primary way to build the service infrastructure for apps** — Most app developers accept this idea.

➤ **Using HTML5 is a great way to build apps and will only become better** — This view is still quite controversial.

The following sections take a closer look at these predictions and how they affect you, as a web developer and as a mobile app developer.

Web Apps and the Future

There are two types of web apps: mobile web apps and hybrid native apps. A mobile web app is delivered as a website and runs in a web browser on a mobile device. You can bookmark web apps on the home screen of the device, and you can give them icons and loading screens (as you'll see in Chapter 4). The user experience with mobile web apps is essentially different from that of native apps, but you can remove many of the differences.

The other type of web app, the hybrid native app, is actually a native app that runs a web browser inside itself. The entire app user interface is actually a web page that runs your HTML5 code. You use wrapper systems, such as the open source PhoneGap, to create a native wrapper. The native wrapper is a native app, but it only really does two things: create a `WebView` control (the native element that displays HTML) and provide access to device capabilities such as the camera via a JavaScript API.

This book will show you how to create both types of apps. You should carefully consider which approach is the best choice. The huge advantage of mobile web apps is that they are ultimately just websites, which means they do not have to be submitted to any app stores for approval. You can update them as frequently as you like, and they can be accessed from almost all smartphones (although functionality may be limited outside the iPhone and Android platforms).

However, hybrid native apps have the advantage of being proper apps that are listed in the app stores. They can use a device to its full potential, and you can extended these apps with native code, if necessary. You might be surprised to learn that a great many "purely" native apps actually make extensive use of HTML5 `WebView` controls. This is the main way to display rich text interfaces, even for purely native apps.

The following are the main reasons to develop an app using HTML5, whether as a mobile web app or within a hybrid native wrapper:

➤ **Cross-platform** — Your app is automatically cross-platform, and you have to develop it only once. The minor debugging required to handle device browser differences is inconsequential compared to the huge effort required to port an entire app from one platform language to another.

➤ **Standards compliant** — Long after the current set of mobile platforms have become historical entries in Wikipedia, your HTML5 app will still be running. HTML, as a technology choice, is a completely safe bet. It is quickly becoming the primary means of building user interfaces on any device, including tablet computers.

➤ **Lower-cost rapid development** — Developing your app with HTML, CSS, and JavaScript means that you can build and iterate extremely quickly. You have the advantage of many tools that support HTML, along with a wide pool of developer talent. Even if your ultimate goal is to create a native hybrid app, you can still do most of your development using a web browser, which means a much faster work cycle.

➤ **Low-friction deployment** — You can launch and update mobile web apps immediately, without waiting for a third-party approval process. You have complete control over content, user base, and commercial activities. No vendor is powerful enough to control the web.

➤ **Easy to learn** — You already have a good knowledge of web languages, so you can start building apps right away just by learning to deal with the particularities of mobile web app development. You do not need to invest any time in learning a new language such as Objective-C, which has limited use outside its own ecosystem.

➤ **JavaScript** — One important reason to build apps with HTML5 is that you will use JavaScript as your development language. Long-neglected as a toy scripting language and useful only for form validation and drop-down menus, JavaScript is emerging as the next big industry language. This change is happening because it is now possible to use JavaScript not only for websites but also for mobile apps and for server code. JavaScript is one of the few languages that can cover the entire technology stack.

JavaScript has certain weaknesses, including an unfortunate syntax inherited from the C language. But it is also capable of supporting advanced functional and object-oriented programming styles. You'll see examples of this power in many of the code examples in this book. With JavaScript, you need relatively few lines of code to quickly build complex apps, and you can easily debug those apps interactively in your web browser. As a result, when you adopt JavaScript as your primary language for mobile and cloud development, you will experience a huge increase in your software development productivity.

The Cloud as the Future

Cloud computing means many things. For mobile app developers, it provides the ability to build apps that millions of people can use. Cloud computing makes it easier to handle large and growing numbers of users.

This book shows you how to build your own cloud-based system from the ground up, using the Amazon cloud. You can use the same basic approach with other cloud vendors, such as Rackspace or Joyent. Chapter 11 covers the use of higher-level services that completely remove the need for any server configuration and just run your code for you.

You do not need to use traditional server-side languages such as Java or C# to build the cloud element of your app. You do not even need to know any of the existing scripting languages, such as Ruby, Python, or PHP. By using the Node server, you can run JavaScript on the server side. This means you can use a single language for all your development. You can stay focused on what you need to do, without being distracted by the differences between programming languages.

Using the cloud to build your server-side business logic has the following advantages:

➤ **Low cost** — It is easy to get started, as you pay only for what you use. There is no need to buy a server or sign up for a fixed monthly fee.

➤ **High capacity** — The cloud can provide you with as much bandwidth and storage as you need. You can grow your service easily as your user base grows.

➤ **Flexibility** — You can add and remove servers and databases very quickly, you can add capacity in the geographic regions where needed, and you can easily integrate with third-party services.

➤ **Low maintenance** — You do not need to worry about system administration or configuration. You can use prebuilt and preconfigured machines. You can use cloud databases that do not have to be tuned for performance.

By the end of Chapter 2, you'll be running a cloud-based mobile web app.

GETTING STARTED

This book contains many code examples. For the most part, each example is contained within its own folder, and you will be instructed to create these folders when needed. You do, however, need to decide on a place to keep all the sample code. The best thing to do is to create a `Projects` folder inside your home folder and store everything there. Of course, you are free to use a different folder structure if it suits you better.

All the code in this book is available for download. If you expand the downloadable zip file for each chapter into your `Projects` folder, you will end up with the full set of code examples in one easy-to-access location.

For the purposes of learning the material in this book, you may find it helpful to create some of the code by hand. The examples assume that you are doing everything manually, even if you are just running the downloadable code. The precise manual steps are explained so that you can follow along and understand not just the code but also how to put the mobile apps and cloud systems together end-to-end.

The instructions assume basic knowledge of the command line. They also assume that you are familiar with your code editor and know how to create folders and manipulate files.

Let's begin!

Using JavaScript Functions

In this book, you will use JavaScript as the primary language, on both the client and the server. JavaScript is a strange language, with some really great parts and some truly awful parts. If you've only used JavaScript for form validation or doing some HTML manipulation, then reading this book will help you get to the next level with JavaScript.

The most important part of JavaScript to understand is the way that functions work. This book makes liberal use of such things as dynamic functions, closures, and callbacks. This section is a primer on these aspects of JavaScript functions. If you already know your way around these concepts, feel free to skip to the next section. If not, try out these simple exercises to get a feel for some of the more advanced uses of functions in JavaScript.

 NOTE *Each of the JavaScript examples in this section is a self-contained HTML page that you can load directly into your web browser from the file system on your computer. The code in the examples inserts some output text into the blank HTML page so you can see what you are doing. These examples will work in all major browsers, but you should really use Safari or Chrome when doing mobile web app development, as these browsers use the same WebKit engine as iPhone and Android devices.*

JavaScript Literal Data Structures

One of the best things about JavaScript is that it is really easy to define data structures directly in code. The JavaScript syntax for doing this is so easy that it has inspired a data exchange format called JavaScript Object Notation, otherwise known as JSON. You'll be doing a lot of work with JSON in later chapters.

The following example shows the basic syntax for arrays and objects in JavaScript. If your JavaScript is a little rusty, or if you've just picked it up by copying random code snippets, then you'll find this example useful. If you already know your way around JSON, you might want to skip ahead to the next example.

The word *literal* used in this example means that you can type in the data structure directly, without executing any code to build it. As in many other languages, a literal JavaScript array is a comma-separated list of values, enclosed in square brackets:

```
["a", "b", "c"]
```

A literal JavaScript object is a list of key/value pairs, enclosed in braces:

```
{ ... }
```

The keys are strings, and the values can be anything from numbers to strings to literal arrays and objects themselves:

```
{"a":100, "b":"BBB", "c":["a", "b", "c"]}
```

The key/value pairs are separated by a : character, with the key on the left. As shorthand, you can remove the quotation marks from keys if they contain only letters and numbers:

```
{a:100, b:"BBB", c:["a", "b", "c"]}
```

TRY IT OUT Using Literal Data Structures in JavaScript

The code in this example shows you how to set and get values from arrays and objects, as well as how to print them in JSON format. Take a look:

1. Using your code editor, create a new file called `js-literals.html` in your `Projects` folder.

2. Insert the following HTML code into the new file and save it:

```
<!DOCTYPE html>
<html><head></head><body id="main"><script>
var main = document.getElementById('main');

var myarray = ['a','b'];
myarray.push('c');

var myobject = {
  a: 'AAA',
  b: 'BBB'
};
myobject.c = 'CCC';

main.innerHTML =
```

```
"<pre>" +
"myarray[0] is " + myarray[0] + "<br>"+
"myarray[1] is " + myarray[1] + "<br>"+
"myarray[2] is " + myarray[2] + "<br>"+

"myobject.a is " + myobject.a + "<br>"+
"myobject.b is " + myobject.b + "<br>"+
"myobject.c is " + myobject.c + "<br>"+

"myobject['a'] is " + myobject['a'] + "<br>"+
"myobject['b'] is " + myobject['b'] + "<br>"+
"myobject['c'] is " + myobject['c'] + "<br>"+

"myarray  is " + JSON.stringify(myarray) + "<br>"+
"myobject is " + JSON.stringify(myobject) + "<br>"+
"<pre>"
</script></body></html>
```

code snippet js-literals.html

To avoid typing all this code in by hand, you can instead use the downloadable code examples.

3. Open the `js-literals.html` file in your web browser. You can do this by double-clicking the file in your operating system's file explorer application. Or you can select File ➪ Open in your browser. Your web browser should display the following text:

```
myarray[0] is a
myarray[1] is b
myarray[2] is c
myobject.a is AAA
myobject.b is BBB
myobject.c is CCC
myobject['a'] is AAA
myobject['b'] is BBB
myobject['c'] is CCC
myarray  is ["a","b","c"]
myobject is {"a":"AAA","b":"BBB","c":"CCC"}
```

 WARNING *If you are using the Chrome browser, you'll find that there is no File ➪ Open command. Instead, you have to enter the full folder path to the* `js-literals.htm` *file in the address bar, prefixed with* `file://`. *Here's an example:* `file:///home/richard/Projects/js-literals.html`.

How It Works

For most of the examples in this book, the How It Works section goes through the code from top to bottom, showing how each feature is implemented. As you go through this book, you'll be able to understand larger sections of code in one go.

This example involves an HTML file. In fact, it is a HTML version 5 file, because you used the HTML5 document type at the start of the file:

```
<!DOCTYPE html>
```

Next, you define some boilerplate HTML to create an empty document. You'll reuse this boilerplate code in the other examples in this chapter. The boilerplate contains the standard HTML document tags: the html tag containing head and body tags. The body tag has an id attribute so that you can refer to it in the JavaScript code. Everything is squashed onto one line to keep it out of the way of the JavaScript code, which is the star of this show. At the end of this second line, an opening script tag means you can start to write some JavaScript:

```
<html><head></head><body id="main"><script>
```

The first line of JavaScript is also boilerplate. You need to get a reference to the body tag so that you can output some text to demonstrate various features of JavaScript literals. This line of code uses the built-in JavaScript document API provided by all browsers. This API, known as the Document Object Model (DOM), is standardized. You store the body tag reference in a variable called main:

```
var main = document.getElementById('main');
```

Now on to the actual sample code. First, you define a literal array:

```
var myarray = ['a','b'];
```

This array-building syntax is common to many languages and should feel quite comfortable to you. You can use either single or double quotes in JavaScript when you are providing literal string values. If you use single quotes, you do not need to escape double quotes (by using the \ character), and the same goes for single quotes inside double quotes. Thus the following are both acceptable:

```
var single = '"quoted"'
var double = "'quoted'"
```

To set an array value, you use the common square bracket syntax. For example, anarray[2] = "foo" sets the third element (array indexes start at 0) to the string value "foo".

In this book and in your own apps, you will often need to append values to the end of an array. You can do this by using the built-in push function, like so:

```
myarray.push('c');
```

In the code example, this means that the myarray array variable now contains three values, "a", "b", and "c". Every array object has a push function that you can use in this way.

The next lines of code define an object literal. The keys in the key/value pairs are referred to as the *properties* of the object. This object has two property keys, a and b. The a property key has the value AAA, and the b property key has the value BBB:

```
var myobject = {
  a: 'AAA',
```

```
    b: 'BBB'
};
```

The literal object syntax always follows this pattern:

```
{ <key1>:<value1>, <key2>:<value2>, ...}
```

Once the object is created, you can also set further values. In this line of code, you set the value of the c property key to CCC:

```
myobject.c = 'CCC';
```

This syntax, known as *dot notation*, lets you specify the properties of an object in an abbreviated manner. Dot notation is really just a shorthand for the full square bracket notation: myobject['d'] = 'DDD'. You can use dot notation when you already know the name of the property, and you can use the square bracket notation when you are using a variable whose value is the name of the property or when the property name contains non-alphanumeric characters that need to be inside quotes.

 NOTE *The examples in this book use the literal object notation a great deal, and it will become second nature to you very quickly.*

The final statement in the sample code is a multiline statement that displays a selection of syntax examples for accessing the values of array and object literals. The statement builds a string containing HTML code and then uses the innerHTML DOM property of the body tag (referenced by the main variable), to set the contents of the HTML page:

```
main.innerHTML =
  "<pre>" +
```

The pre tag is used to display the output as monospaced source code.

The first group of lines shows you how to access array values (no surprises here):

```
"myarray[0] is " + myarray[0] + "<br>"+
"myarray[1] is " + myarray[1] + "<br>"+
"myarray[2] is " + myarray[2] + "<br>"+
```

The second group of lines shows how dot notation works:

```
"myobject.a is " + myobject.a + "<br>"+
"myobject.b is " + myobject.b + "<br>"+
"myobject.c is " + myobject.c + "<br>"+
```

The next group of lines shows the same values, this time using square brackets to access the property values:

```
"myobject['a'] is " + myobject['a'] + "<br>"+
"myobject['b'] is " + myobject['b'] + "<br>"+
"myobject['c'] is " + myobject['c'] + "<br>"+
```

Finally, the last two lines display the `myarray` and `myobject` variables, using the JSON data format. Modern web browsers include a special JSON utility object. The `JSON.stringify` function converts a variable into a string containing the textual representation of the JSON encoding of the value of that variable. Of course, this looks almost exactly like the original object literal syntax you used at the top of the file:

```
"myarray  is " + JSON.stringify(myarray) + "<br>"+
"myobject is " + JSON.stringify(myobject) + "<br>"+
```

The last line of the statement closes the `pre` tag:

```
"</pre>"
```

At the end are the closing HTML tags:

```
</script></body></html>
```

Notice that the `script` tag in this example is not inside the `head` tag but rather inside the `body` tag. This means that the `script` tag code will run after the browser has prepared the DOM. And this means that the `document.getElementById` function will return an actual element rather than `null`. You can also use the `onload` event handler to the same end, but this example keeps the boilerplate code to a minimum.

The rest of the examples focus on the workings of the JavaScript code, and the boilerplate works in the same way for each example.

You now have enough knowledge of the JavaScript literal syntax to follow the rest of the examples in this book.

JavaScript Functions

JavaScript functions are both the same as and different from functions in other languages. You can create them before your code runs or while your code is running, and you can even create them without names. In this book, because you focus on Safari, you do not need to worry about cross-browser differences in the way that function definitions are handled. The examples in this book also stick to an easy-to-understand subset of all the ways you can use functions. This example covers the main things you need to know.

TRY IT OUT Writing JavaScript Functions

There are two main ways to create functions in JavaScript: by using function declarations or function expressions. You can use function declarations to create your functions ahead of time, before your code runs. You can use function expressions to create your functions on demand when your code is running. To see how these two methods are used, follow these steps:

1. Using your code editor, create a new file called `js-functions.html` in your `Projects` folder.

2. Insert the following HTML code into the new file and save it:

```
<!DOCTYPE html>
<html><head></head><body id="main"><script>
var main = document.getElementById('main');
var log = [];
log.push('<pre>');

log.push( declaration() );

function declaration() {
  return "declaration";
}


var expression = function() {
  return "expression";
}

log.push( expression() );


var myobject = {
  property: function() {
    return "property";
  }
}
log.push( myobject.property() );

log.push('</pre>');
main.innerHTML = log.join('<br>');
</script></body></html>
```

code snippet js-literals.html

If you prefer, you can use the downloadable code.

3. Open the `js-functions.html` file in your web browser by either double-clicking the file or using the File ➪ Open menu command in your browser. Your web browser will display the following text:

```
declaration
expression
property
```

How It Works

As in the previous example, this HTML file uses boilerplate code. The HTML tags are the same, as is the reference to the `body` tag stored in the `main` variable.

This time, you use the JavaScript array variable `log` to store the results of the code execution. `log` contains a list of strings that you build up over time by recording what happens in the code. You start with an empty array:

```
var log = [];
```

You use the `push` function to append strings to the array. Because you will want to display the output in a monospaced font when you are finished, you'll enclose the logging strings in a `pre` tag. The first push sets this up:

```
log.push('<pre>');
```

Next, you push the result returned from calling the `declaration` function onto the log:

```
log.push( declaration() );
```

But the declaration function has not been written yet! How can this work? It works because the `declaration` function is written using the syntax for function *declaration*. In this syntax, the name of the function appears after the `function` keyword, as highlighted below:

```
function declaration() {
  return "declaration";
}
```

This means that the `declaration` function is created before any code runs. By the time your code does run, the `declaration` function is already defined and is ready and waiting to be used.

The next function is defined using a function *expression*. You can tell it's an expression because the function is being treated like the value of a variable:

```
var expression = function() {
  return "expression";
}
```

Here, the `expression` variable is assigned a function as its value. This function is anonymous: There is no name after the `function` keyword. But you can still call the function by using the name of the variable that points at the function:

```
log.push( expression() );
```

In this line of code, you are again pushing the string value returned by the function onto the log array. You call the function by using the ordinary syntax:

```
<function_name>()
```

You call functions created using expressions the same way you call declared functions, except you use the name of the variable.

The other important point about function expressions is that you must define a function *before* you call it. In this example, the `expression()` call can work only after the `var expression = function() { ... }` lines.

There is a special case of function expressions that you will use quite a bit in this book. You can assign anonymous functions to the properties of an object. The function expression is the value of the property. The value just happens to be a function, and not a string or number:

```
var myobject = {
  property: function() {
    return "property";
  }
}
```

You call functions defined in this way by referencing them as object properties:

```
log.push( myobject.property() );
```

This line uses dot notation, but you could also write this:

```
log.push( myobject["property"]() );
```

The main reason for placing functions inside an object in this way is to put them together into logical groups. This makes object-oriented programming easier.

The last thing you need to do is display the results of all this function calling. First, you close the pre tag:

```
log.push('</pre>');
```

Then you use the innerHTML property of the body tag to set the textual content of the page. To turn the array into a string, you use the join function. This function is available on all arrays, and it joins up the values into one long string. You can provide an argument, such as "<br>", to the join function, and it will place the string value of the argument between the values in the final string. The br tag places each log entry on a new line.

This is not all there is to JavaScript functions. At the end of this section are some links to more detailed resources. However, the code examples in this book almost always use one of these three ways of creating functions, so you now know enough to follow the sample code.

Mastering the Power of Callback Functions

The most common function code pattern you will see in this book is the *callback* pattern. The idea is that when you ask a function to do something for you, instead of getting a result right away as a return value, you'll get a result later. This is useful when the function takes time to finish its job or only registers your interest in future events.

Consider the event-handling functions that web browsers provide, such as onclick or onkeypress. These can't return a click or keypress event to you as a return value because the click or key press only happens later, when the user performs those actions. If your code had to wait for a return value, it would be blocked, unable to proceed any further, and none of the rest of your code would run.

The solution that event handlers use is a callback function. You provide a function to the event handler when you set it up, and later, when the event happens, your callback function itself is called. This pattern is very easy to set up in JavaScript because you can create dynamic functions easily by using function expressions. In the most common form of this pattern, you pass an anonymous callback function directly as an argument to an event handler:

```
function eventHandler( function() {
  // body of your anonymous callback function
})
```

This pattern is also useful for things like database queries. You'll learn all about writing server-side JavaScript using the Node server later in this book, and you'll see many examples of this pattern in action. Because a database query takes some time to complete — you have to send data over the network between yourself and the database, and the database has to perform its own work — your query result will take time to come back to you. So you use the callback pattern and receive the query result via your callback function.

TRY IT OUT   Using Callback Functions

Callback functions are just like normal functions in that they have parameters that are used to receive the data they work on. In the case of callbacks, the parameters contain the results of the calling function's work. Here's a simple example to show how this works:

1. Create a new file called `js-callbacks.html` in your `Projects` folder.

2. Insert the following HTML into this file:

```
<!DOCTYPE html>
<html><head></head><body id="main"><script>
var main = document.getElementById('main');
var log = ['<pre>']

function waitForSomething( callback ) {
  callback('called')
}

waitForSomething( function( someText ) {
  log.push( someText )
})

log.push('</pre>')
main.innerHTML = log.join('<br>')
</script></body></html>
```

Code snippet js-callbacks.html

If you prefer, you can use the downloadable code.

3. View the `js-callbacks.html` file in your web browser. Your web browser should display the following:

```
called
```

How It Works

The boilerplate in this example is the same as the boilerplate in the preceding example. This example also uses the `log` variable as a string array to collect the output. The `innerHTML` element property and the array `join` function are used to display the logged output, as in the previous example.

In this example, the `waitForSomething` function is the function that will call the callback function. This code, because it is an example, just performs the call immediately and does not actually wait for anything:

```
function waitForSomething( callback ) {
  callback('called')
}
```

The `callback` parameter is a variable that points to your callback function. It is passed in as a variable name, `callback`, and called as a function, `callback()`. This callback function is passed an argument when it is called, a string with the value `'called'`. In the real world, this argument would be a mouse click event or database result set.

Now you use the `waitForSomething` function and pass in your callback function. To do this, you dynamically create an anonymous function and pass it in place as the first argument to `waitForSomething`. This is shown highlighted here:

```
waitForSomething( function( someText ) {
  log.push( someText )
})
```

The anonymous callback function takes in a single parameter, `someText`, and pushes this parameter onto the output log right away. To help you understand how this works, here is a list of the lines of code, in the order in which they are executed:

```
A: waitForSomething( callback )
B: callback('called')
C: function( someText ) // someText == 'called'
D: log.push( someText )
```

You'll get used to callbacks very quickly. The syntax is quite convenient because you can define the actions to take when an event happens right at the place in the code where you indicate your interest in that event.

> **NOTE** *Callback functions introduce a lot of brackets and braces into your code. Make sure your code editor helps you keep track of them (with some form of highlighting) and that you stick to a consistent coding and indentation style. It's easy to lose track of which closing bracket or brace matches which opening bracket or brace.*

Dynamic Functions

In JavaScript, you can create new functions at any time, using function expressions. This means you can create new functions when your code is running. This can be very useful for things like error handling, and you'll see examples of it in later chapters.

The other useful thing you can do with dynamic functions is to create functions that have some of their variables already set. This is useful because it means you have to write less code: You can drop any logic that has to figure out what the values should be.

Let's say you have a photo gallery app. Each time the user clicks on a photo, you pop up an expanded version of the photo. You write an `onclick` event-handling function, which you attach to each photo that first inspects the click event to determine which photo was clicked on and expands that photo.

But you could also create the photo click event handler dynamically. For each photo, you create a new event-handler function that already knows which photo it is meant to expand. Now you only have to write the photo expander code, and you can drop the event inspection code.

How does the dynamically created function know which photo to expand? It references a variable *outside* itself that has a reference to the right photo. Of course, this outside variable still has to be within the scope of the function; it could be a local variable or function parameter of the code that creates the dynamic function.

TRY IT OUT   **Using Dynamic Functions**

This simple example shows dynamic functions in action. Follow these steps:

1.   Create a new file called `js-dynamic.html` in your `Projects` folder.

2.   Insert the following HTML into this file:

```
<!DOCTYPE html>
<html><head></head><body id="main"><script>
var main = document.getElementById('main');
var log = ['<pre>']

function make( color ) {
  var dynamic = function( thing ) {
    return thing + ' is ' + color
  }
  return dynamic
}

var greenify  = make('green')
var blueify = make('blue')

log.push( greenify('grass') )
log.push( blueify('sky') )

log.push('</pre>')
main.innerHTML = log.join('<br>')
</script></body></html>
```

Code snippet js-callbacks.html

If you prefer, you can use the downloadable code.

3. View the `js-dynamics.html` file in your web browser. Your web browser should display the following:

```
grass is green
sky is blue
```

How It Works

The boilerplate in this example is the same as in the preceding examples. The `make` function is where the example begins. The `make` function creates another function *inside* itself. It first assigns the dynamically created function to the variable `dynamic` and then returns this variable. The dynamic function is shown highlighted:

```
function make( color ) {
  var dynamic = function( thing ) {
    return thing + ' is ' + color
  }
  return dynamic
}
```

The dynamic function creates a string that tells the color of something. The name of the thing is passed in as the `thing` parameter. However, the color of the thing is obtained from *outside* the dynamic function. It happens to be the value of the `color` parameter passed to the `make` function.

To aid your understanding of what happens when a JavaScript function is called, you need to be familiar with the concept of scope. The *scope* of a function is simply all the variables that the function can reach. A function can reach all its local variables and parameters, of course. But it can also reach any variables that were defined outside the function at a higher level, such as global variables or variables in any higher-level functions that the function is itself inside.

In this case, the function assigned to the `dynamic` variable is inside the `make` function and so can access the variables and parameters of the `make` function. When you return the newly created dynamic function, the value of the `color` parameter can still be accessed by the new dynamic function. You can think of the `color` variable as being carried around by the dynamic function.

You can now use the `make` function to create some functions with preconfigured colors. You call the `make` function, it returns the dynamic function, and you store a reference to the dynamic function in a local variable. In the sample code, `greenify` and `blueify` reference separate dynamic functions where the color variable has the value `'green'` or `'blue'`, respectively:

```
var greenify = make('green')
var blueify = make('blue')
```

In the case of the photo expander app, instead of a color, you would pass in the HTML `img` element that corresponds to each photo.

Finally, you use the dynamic functions to create the desired output:

```
log.push( greenify('grass') )
log.push( blueify('sky') )
```

There is a computer science term for dynamic functions (such as `greenify` and `blueify`) created in this way: They are known as *closures*.

Learning More About JavaScript

These introductory JavaScript examples have prepared you for the JavaScript used in the rest of this book. If you need a gentle but thorough introduction, try `http://eloquentjavascript`
`.net`. If you want to go deeper, try the best JavaScript reference on the web: `https://developer`
`.mozilla.org/en/JavaScript`. Even though this is focused on the Firefox browser, everything is still relevant to Safari. For Safari-specific information, visit `http://developer.apple.com/`
`devcenter/safari`. Finally, if you'd like to really understand JavaScript, visit
`http://crockford.com`, where Douglas Crockford, the inventor of JSON, waxes lyrical.

The WebKit Browser Engine

The built-in web browsers on the iPhone and Android use the open-source WebKit browser engine to display HTML. The WebKit project was launched in 2005 by Apple and has developers from many companies, including Google. The WebKit projects is descended from the KHTML project, which was one of the early Linux web browser engines, renowned for its small and clean code base. If you are interested, find more details at `http://webkit.org`.

In this book, you will use WebKit-based browsers on both your desktop development machine and your mobile device. On the Mac operating system, you will use the desktop version, in the form of the desktop Safari browser, which uses WebKit as its HTML engine. A version of Safari is also available for Windows, downloadable from `http://www.apple.com/safari`. On Linux, your easiest option is to use Chrome, which has some implementation differences from Safari but also uses WebKit — and it has virtually the same developer tools as Safari.

On your iPhone, you'll use the mobile version of WebKit, known as mobile Safari, and on Android, you'll also use WebKit, as the built-in browser is based on it.

The fact that your mobile apps will run on the WebKit engine on both desktop and mobile devices makes your life much easier. It means you can develop an app using the desktop version of Safari and see almost the same behavior there as you will see on a mobile device. There are differences, of course, and you will still need to test on a physical device.

You'll find that your development cycle will involve spending time testing in the desktop Safari browser, testing on the Safari running on the device simulators, and testing on the actual device using mobile Safari. Your code–test–debug cycle will be very fast when you are working with desktop Safari because you are just reloading a website. You'll find this is a great aid to productivity.

The other great thing about Safari is that the built-in developer tools are very good. If you have used the Firebug extension on the Firefox browser, you will feel right at home. To enable the developer tools, you open the Safari Preferences window, select the Advanced tab, and select the Show Develop Menu option. When a menu item titled Develop appears in the menu bar, you choose the Show Web Inspector menu item. The Web Inspector window should appear at the bottom of the page.

Figure 1-1 shows the Web Inspector with the previous code example file, `js-dynamic.html`, open. The tabs show various types of information about the page. The Elements tab is particularly useful; you can use it to review the HTML structure of the document when you make dynamic changes to it as you animate or alter the user interface of an app.

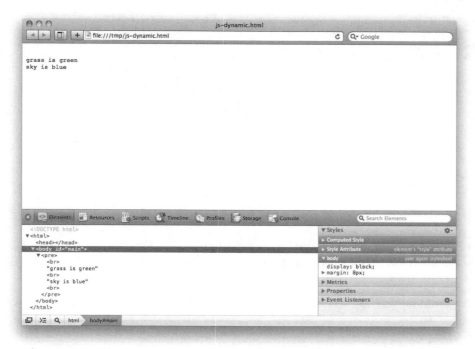

FIGURE 1-1

Apple provides copious volumes of documentation on every aspect of the Safari browser. You can find everything at the Safari Dev Center: `http://developer.apple.com/devcenter/safari`. In this book, you learn how to use Safari to develop and debug the various features in your app, such as HTML5 local storage.

A Colorful Little App

Now that you know some basics, in this section, you'll actually build an app! In this example, you will build an app that displays a box with a random color. Each time you click or tap the box, it will change to a new random color. Figure 1-2 shows the app in action, running on desktop Safari, with the developer console open.

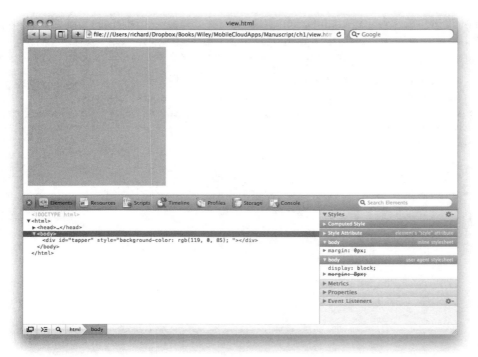

FIGURE 1-2

What do you need to do to create this app? You'll put everything in one HTML page. You'll need a square `div` tag to change color. You'll need some JavaScript to generate random colors and change the color of the `div` tag when the user click or taps it.

For now, you'll just build the desktop version of this app. In the following section, you'll learn how to view it on a mobile device.

TRY IT OUT Developing a Mobile Web App

You need to use the desktop Safari browser to view this example. You'll use Safari so that you can be sure you'll see the same results on your mobile device. As with all the other examples in this book, the code you see here is a full working example. Follow these steps:

1. Create a new subfolder called `view` in your `Projects` folder.

2. Create a new file called `view.html` in your `Projects/view` subfolder.

3. Insert the following HTML in the `view.html` file:

```
<!DOCTYPE html>
<html>
<head>
    <meta name="viewport"
          content="user-scalable=no,initial-scale=1.0,maximum-scale=1.0" />

    <style>
      body { margin: 0px; }
```

```
    #tapper {
      margin: 10px;
      width: 300px;
      height: 300px;
      background-color: #f00;
    }
  </style>

  <script>
    function hex() {
      var hexchars = "0123456789abcedf";
      var hexval = Math.floor(16 * Math.random());
      return hexchars[hexval];
    }
    window.onload = function() {
      var tapper = document.getElementById("tapper")
      tapper.onclick = function() {
        tapper.style.backgroundColor = "#"+hex()+hex()+hex();
      }
    }
  </script>
</head>
<body>
<div id="tapper"></div>
</body>
</html>
```

code view/view.html

If you prefer, you can use the downloadable code.

4. Open the view.html file in your desktop Safari browser. You should see 300-by-300–pixel square, filled with a random color.

5. Click the square several times and verify that the color changes to another random color each time you click.

How It Works

This HTML file introduces some of the boilerplate code that you will use throughout this book to define the user interface for your HTML5 mobile apps. The first line indicates to the browsers that this page uses HTML5:

```
<!DOCTYPE html>
```

Using this document type declaration is the standard way to start an HTML5 web page.

Next, you open the HTML file in the usual way, with the standard html and head tags. You use the viewport metatag to define the screen dimensions of the app:

```
<html>
<head>
  <meta name="viewport"
        content="user-scalable=no,initial-scale=1.0,maximum-scale=1.0" />
```

The mobile device's browser uses the `viewport` metatag to scale the page. When you visit a normal website on your mobile device, you use a two-finger pinch gesture to zoom in and out. This is not something you want to happen with your mobile app because it is not a website. To prevent this zooming behavior, you use the `viewport` metatag to specify a series of special settings for the mobile device. In this case, the `user-scalable=no` setting disables the zoom, the `initial-scale=1.0` setting makes your app occupy the entire width of the mobile device screen, and `maximum-scale=1.0` prevents any automatic scaling. These settings have no effect at the moment because you are working on the desktop version of Safari.

You define the user interface of this app by using HTML, so you can style it with CSS in the normal manner. The `style` tag sets the size and position of the square `div` that holds the color, which is initially set to red (`#f00`):

```
<style>
  body { margin: 0px; }
  #tapper {
    margin: 10px;
    width: 300px;
    height: 300px;
    background-color: #f00;
  }
</style>
```

Next comes the `script` tag. First, you need a little utility function to help generate random colors. The `hex` function generates a random number between 0 and 15 and then returns the hexadecimal digit for that number — one of the characters in the string "`0123456789abcdef`":

```
<script>
  function hex() {
    var hexchars = "0123456789abcdef";
    var hexval = Math.floor(16 * Math.random());
    return hexchars[hexval];
  }
```

The `hex` function uses the simple trick of listing the hex digits in ascending order in a string and using the random number as an index for the character position in that string. So if the random number is 8, the character at position 8, namely `"8"`, is returned. If the random is 15, the character at position 15, namely `"f"`, is returned.

Now you need to react to the click or tap on the color square. You use the `window.onload` event handler to make sure the page has fully loaded before you try to find any elements in it:

```
window.onload = function() {
```

Then you use the `document.getElementById` function to get the square color `div`, using the identifier you have given it: `'tapper'`:

```
var tapper = document.getElementById("tapper")
```

Once you have the color `div` in the `tapper` variable, you use the `onclick` event handler to detect clicks on the `div`:

```
tapper.onclick = function() {
```

Now you change the color. You use the `hex` function three times (once for each of the red, green, and blue color components) to generate a new random color and then set the background of the `div` to this new color:

```
tapper.style.backgroundColor = "#"+hex()+hex()+hex();
```

This is all the code logic you need. Now you can close your functions, the `script` tag, and the `head` tag:

```
      }
    }
  </script>
</head>
```

The body of the HTML page defines the color `div`, setting the identifier of the `div` to `"tapper"` so that you can find it by using `document.getElementById("tapper")`.

```
<body>
<div id="tapper"></div>
</body>
```

Finally, you close the HTML document:

```
</html>
```

Apart from the `viewport` metatag, this is all very standard HTML, CSS, and JavaScript. To view the app by using desktop Safari, you just load the `view.html` file directly. You can't do this with your mobile device because there is no way to load the file. You have to instead access the file by using a web server. The next section shows you how to do this.

Introducing the nginx Web Server

As you develop mobile apps, you'll need to test them on your mobile device. When you build HTML5-based apps, the device-testing process can actually be faster than the process of developing native apps. You can reload an app in the web browser on the device, which takes just a few seconds!

You can access an app on your mobile device by requesting it from a local web server running on your desktop development machine. To do this, you need to make sure that both your mobile device and your desktop machine are on the same local network. The easiest way to ensure this is to connect both to the same Wi-Fi router.

To deliver the HTML files for your app, you have to run a local web server. The web server used in this book is the nginx web server, available from `http://nginx.org`. This server is extremely fast and lightweight — perfect for cloud servers. It is also designed to handle large numbers of users. The nginx configuration file is also very easy to work with and has a simple syntax.

Installing nginx on a Mac

To install nginx on a Mac, you need to use the MacPorts installer system. The MacPorts installer lets you install UNIX command-line tools and servers on your Mac by using simple one-line commands. You can go to the `www.macports.org` site and click the Installing Mac Ports link on the left. Then you download the `dmg` file for your version of Mac OS X: Lion, Snow Leopard, or Leopard. Then you open the `dmg` file and install MacPorts by double-clicking its icon and following the onscreen instructions.

Next, you open the Terminal app, which you can find in the `Utilities` subfolder of the `Applications` folder. You need to make sure the MacPorts installer system knows about the latest version of nginx. To do this, you run this command (and then enter your password):

```
sudo port -d selfupdate
```

You see many lines of output, indicating the status of the update process. Then you can install nginx by running this command:

```
sudo port install nginx
```

Again, you see some lines of output that provide feedback on the installation process. When it completes, you are ready to start using nginx, and you can skip ahead to the "Starting and Stopping nginx" section.

Installing nginx on Windows

The nginx website, `http://nginx.org`, makes Windows binaries available for download. All you have to do is download the zip file from the site and unzip it into a convenient location. Then you can skip ahead to the "Starting and Stopping nginx" section.

Installing nginx on Linux

There are a number of different Linux distributions and a number of different ways to install server software on Linux. This book shows you how to use one of the most popular distributions, Ubuntu, which is available from `www.ubuntu.com`. When you set up your Amazon cloud servers, you will also use Ubuntu.

On Ubuntu, installing nginx is very simple: You use the built-in package manager. You run this command (and enter your root password):

```
sudo apt-get install nginx
```

Depending on the configuration of your machine, this installation process may start nginx for you. If it does not, you can follow the instructions in the next section.

Starting and Stopping nginx

Before you start nginx, you need to make sure there are no other web servers running. If there are, they will be occupying port 80 on your machine, the network port number used for HTTP, and nginx will not be able to run. To test whether there is a web server running on your desktop machine, you open a web browser (such as Safari) and visit `http://localhost`. If a web page appears, then you know you have another web server running, and you'll need to stop that web server first. If not, you can proceed to start nginx, as described below.

If the web server already running on your machine is Apache, then you can stop it on the command line by using this:

```
apachectl stop
```

If you are on a Windows machine, you can usually find an Apache administration application on the Start menu, and it should have a Stop button.

If you are using Windows, you might find that the Microsoft web server, known as Internet Information Server (IIS), is running. You can stop IIS by opening its administration application, which is in the Control Panel.

If you have previously installed a different web server, you should refer to its documentation to find the procedure to shut it down. You can always start it again after you have finished your app development.

To start nginx on your Mac or Windows machine, you go to the command line (on Windows you need to `cd` to the folder containing nginx) and run this command:

```
nginx
```

To stop nginx, you use the following command:

```
nginx -s stop
```

On Linux, the commands are slightly different. This is the start command:

```
sudo /etc/init.d/nginx start
```

And this is the stop command:

```
sudo /etc/init.d/nginx stop
```

And that's it! To verify that nginx has started, you should reload `http://localhost` in your web browser. You should see the text `"Welcome to nginx!"`.

Using nginx

You're going to use nginx to serve up the HTML files for your app. The nginx web server has a default `html` folder, where you can save HTML files. Any HTML files saved to this folder will be served by nginx. You'll copy your `view.html` file into your nginx `html` folder so that the URL `http://localhost/view.html` will deliver your `view.html` file.

The location of the nginx `html` folder depends on your system. On a Mac, it will be `/opt/local/share/nginx/html`. On Windows, it will be `C:\nginx\html` if you installed nginx in your `C:` drive. On Linux, it will `/var/www/nginx-default`.

Once you have located the nginx `html` folder, you need to copy your `view.html` file into it. Then you can access this file in your web browser by using `http://localhost/view.html`. You should do this now to verify that everything is working.

There is one last step to viewing the app on your device. From your device, you cannot use `localhost` as the website address because that would refer to the mobile device itself. Instead, you must use the Internet Protocol (IP) address of your desktop development machine. You'll need to determine your local IP address.

Your local IP address is not the same as your public address, which is the address your machine or network has on the public Internet. Rather, your local IP address is an address used internally on your local network. If you are on an IPv4 network, this IP address starts with `192.168.`, or `10.`, or `172.16.` If you are on an IPv6 network, this address starts with `fc00:.`

The approach to finding your local IP address depends on your system. On a Mac, you click the apple icon on the top-left of the menu bar and select About This Mac. Then you click the More Info button in the small summary window that appears. This opens a larger window with detailed information. Next, you click the Network item on the left and look for your IP address on the local Wi-Fi network in the AirPort item description.

On Windows, you open the list of network connections from the Start menu and double-click the Wireless Network Connection item. Then you click the Support tab of the small window that appears. Your local IP address will be shown.

On Linux, you use the `ifconfig` command to print out quite a few lines of information. You should look for the IP addresses that begin with the prefix numbers mentioned above, such as `192.168.`

Next, you load your app by using your local IP address. In your desktop Safari browser, you open the URL `http://YOUR_IP_ADDRESS/view.html`, replacing `YOUR_IP_ADDRESS` with your local IP address. You should see your app appear as before.

Now it's time to test the app on your device. On your iPhone or Android device, you open the built-in web browser app and enter `http://YOUR_IP_ADDRESS/view.html`. You should see your app appear as in Figure 1-3. As you can see from the figure, my local IP address is 192.168.100.112.

Tap the color square with your finger. It will change to a new random color. Congratulations! You have created your first mobile web app!

SUMMARY

This chapter introduced you to hybrid mobile apps, which are native apps built with an HTML5 container as their entire user interface. You were also introduced to JavaScript object literal syntax and the hidden power of JavaScript functions. Using these new skills you built a simple but complete mobile web app and debugged and tested this app using the Safari web browser. Finally, you installed the nginx web browser and delivered your mobile web app direct to your iPhone or Android device. At this point you have almost covered the complete mobile web app development cycle.

FIGURE 1-3

In the next chapter, you'll learn how to make your app respond to finger touch events, a critical feature of any mobile app. You'll learn how to give your app a more native look and feel. You'll also learn about "tracer bullets," a great technique for speeding up your development of new code. Finally, you create your first cloud service, live, on the Amazon cloud.

EXERCISES

1. In the sample code for the simple app you built in this chapter, you listened for a `click` event to change the color. Although this works on a mobile device, it is less responsive than using touch events. Modify the code to use the `ontouchstart` event instead.

2. Some of the apps you develop will need to be able to detect whether the mobile device is in portrait (vertical) or landscape (horizontal) orientation. You can use the `window.onresize` event to detect orientation changes. Add a listener for this event and turn the square into a rectangle when the device is moved into landscape orientation. Turn it back into a square when the device returns to portrait orientation.

3. When a user first visits your mobile web app, the address bar of the mobile browser remains visible, reducing the amount of space available for your user interface. For this exercise, overcome this by scrolling the page up by one pixel.

4. For the most part, you'll want your mobile apps to remain at the same fixed zoom level because this is how native apps behave. However, there are occasions when you might want to change this and take advantage of the native zooming behavior — for example, if you are displaying a large chart. Experiment with the scale setting in the `viewport` metatag to see if you can start the app zoomed out.

Answers to the Exercises can be found in the Appendix.

▶ WHAT YOU LEARNED IN THIS CHAPTER

TOPIC	KEY CONCEPTS
HTML5	The latest version of the HTML standard, produced by the World Wide Web consortium (W3C). This is the most important web standard to be released in recent years. It defines a new set of capabilities for applications built using HTML. You can now detect the location of your user, store data locally, and even generate complex graphics. The enhanced interactivity and dynamic interface features such as animation also enable you to build highly visual, user-friendly, and engaging user interfaces using HTML5.
Dynamic JavaScript Functions	The JavaScript language is more powerful than it might first appear. Because it supports a functional programming style through the use of dynamic functions, you can develop complex systems without code bloat. Learning the basics of the functional programming style can help you increase your code reuse significantly and enable you to become far more productive as a programmer.
WebKit	This open source browser engine has become the de facto standard for mobile web app development because it is used on both iPhone and Android, as well as other less popular platforms. The WebKit engine has string support for HTML5 and excellent support for debugging and app development. Because you can use the desktop version of WebKit, in the form of the Safari web browser, to test and develop your mobile app long before you reach for a physical device, your development work cycle is much faster and shorter.
nginx	This web server is specifically designed to handle large numbers of requests very efficiently. This makes it an excellent choice for cloud hosting. You'll use the nginx web server throughout this book to host mobile web apps and to provide a front end for your service interfaces.

2

Mobilizing Your App

WHAT YOU WILL LEARN IN THIS CHAPTER:

➤ Drawing graphics for your app by using the canvas element

➤ Using simple boilerplate code to give your app a native feel

➤ Creating a tracer bullet to test your app architecture end-to-end

➤ Building a simple drawing app that responds to finger movements

➤ Learning to refactor your code so that it is maintainable

➤ Understanding the cloud services that Amazon provides

➤ Using Amazon to create your own cloud server

➤ Configuring your cloud server to deliver mobile web apps

This chapter teaches you all the essentials of building a mobile cloud app. At the end of this chapter, you will be able to develop and deploy basic mobile web apps that live in the Amazon cloud.

The code in this chapter is brief and simple. You need to have only a basic understanding of JavaScript, and you'll put into practice concepts such as JSON and callback functions. If you are already comfortable with any of the concepts described here, feel free to skim over the explanations.

The focus of this chapter is to create a live, working app that is delivered from a public URL and that you can access anywhere. You'll even be able to ask your friends or colleagues to test it. Let's begin!

BUILDING A TOUCH-SENSITIVE DRAWING APP

In this section, you will build a complete mobile web app. This app will allow you to draw pictures on the screen of your mobile device, using your finger. Because you are just getting started, I'm going to ask you to trust me on some of the details and just cut and paste some of the code. This way, you can create a working app that's hosted in the cloud very quickly. Don't worry: You'll learn all the details in later chapters.

In this chapter, you'll develop a mobile web app on your local desktop machine, but you'll need to test it on your mobile device. That means your desktop machine has to deliver the HTML and JavaScript files to your mobile device, using a web server. In Chapter 1, you learned about the nginx web server, which you'll use in the rest of this book to deliver your mobile web apps. You'll use nginx locally and in the cloud. In Chapter 1 you set up nginx and placed your HTML files in the `html` folder so that nginx can easily find your HTML files.

How to Draw on the Screen

To create a touch-sensitive drawing app, you need a way to detect the movement of a finger across the screen. For this you can use special JavaScript event handlers that listen for finger touches and provide you with the position of a touch on the screen. These event handlers are called `ontouchstart` and `ontouchmove`, and they work in much the same way as traditional JavaScript event handlers such as `onclick` or `onmousemove`. Chapter 4 explores the details of touch events. For now, you're going to learn how to use them to draw pictures.

To draw a picture on the screen, you use the `canvas` HTML tag. This tag provides a pixel-based drawing rectangle on which you can draw lines and shapes by using JavaScript. The WebKit browser engine used on both the iPhone and Android has good support for the `canvas` tag, so your code will work equally well on both types of device. The `canvas` tag is similar to an `img` tag, except you can change the image. Here is an example:

```
<canvas id="mycanvas" width="300" height="300">
```

You need to set the width and height of the `canvas` tag, in pixels, so that the size of the drawing area is well defined. You also need to provide an `id` attribute so that you can get hold of the `canvas` element in JavaScript by using the `document.getElementById` function:

```
var canvas = document.getElementById('mycanvas');
```

The `canvas` tag allows you to create any image you like. This is an extremely useful ability, and many HTML5 games are created entirely with a `canvas` tag. You can use the `canvas` tag to create custom user interfaces, or to display generated graphics such as real-time charts, or even to use visual effects that enhance your app.

 NOTE *The* canvas *tag isn't the only way to draw images inside a web browser. You can also use Scalable Vector Graphics (SVG), an image drawing API that many browsers support. Unfortunately, Android does not support SVG (at least up to version 2.3), so it is not a practical option for mobile web apps.*

The `canvas` API uses the concept of a *context*. Instead of calling functions directly on the `canvas` object, you ask the `canvas` object for a `context` object. You use this `context` object to do the actual drawing. Why is a special `context` object designed into the API? To allow future support for 3-D graphics. At the moment, mobile browsers provide only a flat 2-D drawing surface, but in the near future, you will be able to use hardware-accelerated 3-D graphics. For now, you just ask for the 2-D `context` object, like so:

```
var context = canvas.getContext('2d');
```

The JavaScript `canvas` API gives you functions to draw straight lines, curved lines (called *arcs*), rectangular shapes, and shapes with many straight and curved sides. When you draw a line or shape with the `canvas` API, you can set properties of the context to control the appearance of the line or shape. For example, to set the width of a line, in pixels, you use the `lineWidth` property:

```
context.lineWidth = 5
```

Here are some common properties you can set:

➤ **strokeStyle** — The color used to draw lines and arcs

➤ **fillStyle** — The color used to fill in the inside of shapes

➤ **lineWidth** — The pixel width of lines

➤ **lineCap** — The shape used at the end of lines

➤ **lineJoin** — The way in which lines are joined together

You can use the `lineCap` and `lineJoin` properties to improve the appearance of lines and shapes. In this chapter's app, you'll set both of these properties to the value `round`, which means that lines will have nicely rounded ends and no sharp edges where they join.

You can't just draw with the `context` object. Instead, you have to define a path first. A *path* is a series of lines and other drawing actions all collected together into one unit. No pixels are changed on the screen while you are setting up the path. Only when you have defined the steps in the path do you ask the `context` object to draw pixels on the screen. While this might seem like extra complication, using a path is a useful way to organize your drawing logic and to write reusable code. Here are the functions on the `context` object that you use to set up the path and draw pixels:

➤ **beginPath** — Starts defining a path

➤ **closePath** — Finishes defining a path

➤ **stroke** — Draws the lines of the path defined so far

➤ **fill** — Fills in the area of the path defined so far

The `context` object offers lots of drawing functions. The following are the ones you need for this example.

➤ **rect** — Draws a rectangle defined by two points

➤ **arc** — Draws a curved line defined by starting and ending angles

➤ **lineTo** — Draws a line from the current pixel position to the position indicated

➤ **moveTo** — Moves the current pixel position without drawing anything

You can combine these basic functions in complex ways by using programmatic logic to draw complex objects. You can even create animations by clearing the entire canvas object and drawing a new animation frame.

> **NOTE** *This chapter covers only the part of the* canvas *API that you need to implement the drawing app. You can read more about the many properties and functions of the* canvas *API at* https://developer.mozilla.org/en/Canvas_tutorial.

In Chapter 1, you built a simple mobile web app that is completely contained within one HTML file. You did not have to integrate different files and components to get the app working. When you build more complex apps, you often need to connect different software components and services. You need to make sure that all these components can find and talk to each other properly.

It is a classic and traditional mistake in software engineering to build all the components separately and then integrate them all at the end of the project. This never works. Software, unlike mechanical components, is not subject to physical limitations and has multiple degrees of freedom. You need to integrate the software components first, before you build them out fully. You do this by using tracer bullets. In the physical world, *tracer bullets* help you see the stream of bullets from a gun. They are non-lethal bullets that burn up brightly and follow the same trajectory as normal bullets. You can apply a similar idea to software to verify that everything works end-to-end.

In the case of the drawing app, you need to integrate the canvas element in an HTML file with a separate JavaScript file that contains the programming logic. Then you need to deliver both HTML and JavaScript files from the nginx web server to your mobile device. You need to build a tracer bullet that works from top to bottom. It does not need to be functional, but it does need to prove that all the pieces of technology can talk to each other.

TRY IT OUT Using a Tracer Bullet

In this example, you'll create a tracer bullet — a small mobile web app that uses the canvas tag to display a line slanted at 45 degrees. You'll define the app interface in an HTML file, and you'll define the app logic in a separate JavaScript file. You'll deliver the app to your mobile device by using the nginx web server. Here's how you do it:

1. Create a new folder called draw inside your nginx html folder.

2. Start your code editor and create a new empty file called draw-tracer.html. Save this file in the draw subfolder of your nginx html folder, which also contains the view.html file from Chapter 1.

3. Insert the following HTML code into the draw-tracer.html file and save it:

```
<!DOCTYPE html>
<html>
<head>
  <meta name="viewport"
    content="user-scalable=no,initial-scale=1.0,maximum-scale=1.0" />

  <style>
  body { padding:10px; margin:0px; background-color: #ccc; }
  #main { margin: 10px auto 0px auto; }
  </style>

  <script src="draw-tracer.js"></script>
</head>
<body>
<canvas id="main" width="300" height="300"></canvas>
</body>
</html>
```

code snippet draw-tracer.html

4. Verify that nginx is delivering the file. To do so, open your desktop Safari browser and visit `http://localhost/draw/draw-tracer.html`. You should see a blank gray page.

5. Use your code editor to create a new empty file called `draw-tracer.js`. Save this file in you nginx `html` folder.

6. Insert the following JavaScript code into the `draw-tracer.js` file and save it:

```
window.onload = function() {

    var canvas  = document.getElementById("main");
    var context = canvas.getContext('2d');

    context.beginPath();
    context.lineWidth = 5;
    context.moveTo(50, 50);
    context.lineTo(250, 250);
    context.stroke();
    context.closePath();
```

code snippet draw-tracer.js

7. Verify that the code that uses the `canvas` tag is working correctly. To do so, reload `http://localhost/draw/draw-tracer.html` in your desktop Safari browser. You should see a black line slanted at 45 degrees on a gray background.

8. Open `http://localhost/draw/draw-tracer.html` on your mobile device, but use your desktop IP address instead of `localhost`. If you see the page shown in Figure 2-1, you know that the app works on your mobile device.

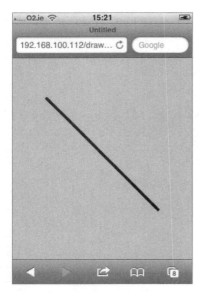

FIGURE 2-1

NOTE *When you're ready to test your app on your mobile device, you'll need to point the web browser on your mobile device at your local desktop machine. You should enter the IP address of your local machine into the address bar of the mobile Safari app. In order for this to work, you need to make sure that your desktop and your mobile device are both on the same Wi-Fi network. To find the IP address of your desktop machine, follow the instructions in Chapter 1.*

DEBUGGING YOUR APP DEVELOPMENT CONFIGURATION

The primary purpose of this example is to debug your app development configuration. It is common to encounter misconfigurations, network connection difficulties, syntax errors, and many other problems. By putting together the tracer bullet code, you have a very small code base to debug. Finding the cause of the problem is much simpler because your own code is so small and short.

If the app fails to display on your desktop browser, you can start by verifying your assumptions. Did you save the files in the right folder? Do they have the right file permissions? Is nginx running? Is it configured properly? Do not assume that anything is actually the way it is supposed to be; actually check it.

Another step you can take is to try other ways to interact with your code. For example, you can open the `draw-tracer.html` file directly by selecting Safari File ➪ Open File. Does it work then? If not, you can select View ➪ View Source to check that you have the right file. When accessing the file via the URL, you can open the Safari developer console by selecting Develop ➪ Show Web Inspector. Are there error reports? You can get also get a debug console on your iPhone.

To do this, you go to the settings for the mobile Safari browser. At the bottom of the list of settings, you touch the Developer item and then enable the Debug Console toggle switch.

Most of the time, you can solve integration problems by methodically verifying your assumptions. You should try to test each piece in isolation to confirm that it is all working correctly.

What if you are completely stuck? Don't head for Google just yet. You can try one more tactic, and it's a lot of fun: Break stuff! Yes, you can deliberately break things and verify that they fail in the right way. For example, you can introduce a syntax error and see if you get an error message. If you don't get one, perhaps you are looking at a different version of the file? Or maybe you're inadvertently editing a back-up version. We've all been there. By deliberately introducing errors, you can make sure that at least some parts of the system are working. You have a repeatable test. Something works. You break it. It doesn't work. You, not the bug, are now in control. You should keep breaking stuff until your assumptions are proven wrong. This is often a very quick way to find the real cause of an error.

If all these tactics fail, you must of course head for Google and any other online resources that can help. You should always try to search for the exact text of any error messages by cutting and pasting them into the Google search box. You're likely to quickly find an answer. Or you can head for social answer sites, such as `http://stackoverflow.com`. Don't forget that for many technology topics, you can find online chat communities that can provide direct help. Use Google to find them.

How It Works

If the slanted line appears on your mobile device, you can now examine the code to see how it works. If not, see the sidebar for some trouble-shooting advice.

The HTML document starts with the HTML5 document declaration:

```
<!DOCTYPE html>
```

All the examples in this book assume support for HTML5 and use this declaration. The WebKit browser engines on iPhones and Android devices provide good support for HTML5 features, and using this declaration makes your intentions clear.

The `head` element contains a special `viewport` metatag that controls the appearance and zoom level of the app. The `viewport` metatag is covered in more detail in Chapters 4 and 7. For now, you just use it as follows:

```
<meta name="viewport"
  content="user-scalable=no,initial-scale=1.0,
  maximum-scale=1.0" />
```

The head element also contains a small amount of CSS to lay out the canvas element on the screen:

```
<style>
body { padding:10px; margin:0px; background-color: #ccc; }
#main { margin: 10px auto 0px auto; }
</style>
```

Finally, the head element references a JavaScript file that contains the code that draws the slanted line on the canvas:

```
<script src="draw-tracer.js"></script>
```

The body of the HTML contains only one element, the canvas tag itself, with an id attribute with a value of "main". The app uses this id attribute to obtain a reference to the canvas element:

```
<canvas id="main" width="300" height="300"></canvas>
```

Note that the draw-tracer.js file is short and minimal — providing just enough code to be a good tracer bullet.

The first line of code is:

```
window.onload = function() {
```

This line of code sets an anonymous event handler function to the onload event of the window object. This anonymous function is called when the HTML page has finished loading. You need to do this to ensure that when the JavaScript code goes looking for the canvas element, it will find it. If you look for the canvas element too soon, before the document has finished loading, then it won't be found because it does not exist yet, and your code will fail.

You use the event handler function to get a reference to the canvas element:

```
var canvas  = documet.getElementById('main');
```

Once you have that, you can ask for the 2-D drawing context:

```
var context = canvas.getContext('2d');
```

Now you are ready to draw! First, you need to start a path:

```
context.beginPath();
```

Then you need to set the pixel width of the line. In this example, you set it to 5 pixels to get a nice wide line that is easy to see:

```
context.lineWidth = 5;
```

To draw the line, you move to a position 50 pixels from the top and left of the canvas:

```
context.moveTo(50, 50);
```

Canvas positions are calculated from the top-left corner, just like CSS positions. The top-left pixel of a canvas is thus always at position (0, 0).

To draw the line, you use the `lineTo` function, which takes as arguments the top and left positions of the end point of the line. Because the canvas is 300 by 300 pixels, you draw the line from position (50, 50) to position (250, 250), which gives you a line slanted at 45 degrees in the center of the screen:

```
context.lineTo(250, 250);
```

To draw the pixels and make the line visible, you call the `stroke` function on the `context` object:

```
context.stroke();
```

This draws all the elements of the path defined so far. There's only one, the line you just created.

Finally, you close the path:

```
context.closePath();
```

Drawing in Response to Touch Events

Now that you have a working mobile web app that uses the `canvas` tag to draw on the screen, it's time to add some interactivity and enable the app to respond to finger touches. In the following example, you'll turn your simple tracer bullet into a drawing app. You know that the end-to-end integration works, so you can now concentrate on the logic of the app.

When the user just taps the screen, you want to draw a dot. You'll use the canvas `arc` function to do this, by drawing a filled-in circle. You'll use the `ontouchstart` event handler to detect finger taps on the mobile device screen.

When the user drags a finger across the screen, you want to fill in the path the finger takes as closely as possible. The touch event gives you a continuous series of points that indicates the path of the user's finger. You will use the `lineTo` function to draw a line from the previous finger position to the latest finger position. You'll end up drawing lots of very short lines, and as a result, the user will see a continuous curve on the screen. You'll use the `ontouchmove` event handler to detect ongoing finger movement against the screen of the mobile device. You'll also add a Clear button to let the user erase the current drawing and start again.

TRY IT OUT Drawing with Your Finger

In this example, you'll turn your tracer bullet into a drawing app to enable the user to draw with his or her finger. Here's how you do it:

1. Inside the `draw` folder that you used for the previous example, copy the `draw-tracer.html` file and rename it `draw.html`.

2. Change two lines in the `draw.html` file, as shown boldfaced in the following code:

```
<!DOCTYPE html>
<html>
<head>
  <meta name="viewport"
    content="user-scalable=no,initial-scale=1.0,maximum-scale=1.0" />

  <style>
  body { padding:10px; margin:0px; background-color: #ccc; }
  #main { margin: 10px auto 0px auto; }
  </style>

  <script src="draw.js"></script>
</head>
<body>
<button id="clear">clear</button><br>
<canvas id="main" width="300" height="300"></canvas>
</body>
</html>
```

code snippet draw/draw.html

The first change, instead of loading the `draw-tracer.js` JavaScript file, loads a file called `draw.js`. The second change defines a Clear button.

3. Create new file called `draw.js` in the `draw` folder. Using your code editor, insert the following lines of code into the `draw.js` file:

```
window.onload = function() {

  document.ontouchmove = function(e){ e.preventDefault(); }

  var canvas   = document.getElementById('main');
  var canvastop = canvas.offsetTop;

  var context = canvas.getContext('2d');

  var lastx;
  var lasty;

  context.strokeStyle = "#000000";
  context.lineCap = 'round';
  context.lineJoin = 'round';
  context.lineWidth = 5;

  function clear() {
    context.fillStyle = "#ffffff";
    context.rect(0, 0, 300, 300);
    context.fill();
  }

  function dot(x,y) {
    context.beginPath();
    context.fillStyle = "#000000";
```

```
    context.arc(x,y,1,0,Math.PI*2,true);
    context.fill();
    context.stroke();
    context.closePath();
  }

  function line(fromx,fromy, tox,toy) {
    context.beginPath();
    context.moveTo(fromx, fromy);
    context.lineTo(tox, toy);
    context.stroke();
    context.closePath();
  }

  canvas.ontouchstart = function(event){
    event.preventDefault();

    lastx = event.touches[0].clientX;
    lasty = event.touches[0].clientY - canvastop;

    dot(lastx,lasty);
  }

  canvas.ontouchmove = function(event){
    event.preventDefault();

    var newx = event.touches[0].clientX;
    var newy = event.touches[0].clientY - canvastop;

    line(lastx,lasty, newx,newy);

    lastx = newx;
    lasty = newy;
  }


  var clearButton = document.getElementById('clear');
  clearButton.onclick = clear;

  clear();
}
```

code snippet draw/draw.js

4. Verify that nginx is delivering your new files. To do so, open your desktop Safari browser and visit `http://localhost/draw/draw.html`. You should see a blank gray page containing a 300-pixel white square, with a Clear button at the top.

5. Open `http://localhost/draw/draw.html` on your mobile device, but use your desktop IP address instead of `localhost`.

6. Draw something on the mobile device's screen. Verify that finger taps produce dots and that dragging your finger around the screen creates continuous lines. Figure 2-2 shows an example of a drawing.

7. Tap the Clear button to erase the drawing and start again.

How It Works

The HTML for this example is almost the same as for the previous example. Here you simply changed the JavaScript used to define the functionality of the app and added some HTML tags to define a Clear button.

The new JavaScript follows the same basic approach as the tracer bullet JavaScript. It waits for the `window.onload` event to get started, ensuring that all the HTML elements it needs will be ready in the document:

FIGURE 2-2

```
window.onload = function() {
```

The next line is a little bit of magic that keeps your app, which is really just an HTML page, from scrolling. You prevent the default scrolling behavior of the `ontouchmove` event. This is explained in greater detail in Chapter 4. For now, you use the following standard boilerplate code:

```
document.ontouchmove = function(e){ e.preventDefault(); }
```

Next, you grab the `canvas` element as you did in the tracer bullet code:

```
var canvas  = document.getElementById('main');
```

This time, you need the value of the `offsetTop` property of the canvas element:

```
var canvastop = canvas.offsetTop;
```

The canvas element appears about 50 pixels below the top of the browser window. When you get touch events, the `clientX` and `clientY` properties of the touch event give you the location of the touch on the browser window. But the `canvas` element is not directly at the top of the window, so you need to adjust the vertical Y value of the touch event position. The vertical Y value is currently 50 pixels too large because this value counts from the top of the browser window, not from the top of the `canvas` object.

As with the tracer bullet code, you need to get the 2-D context of the canvas, so that you can actually draw:

```
var context = canvas.getContext('2d');
```

To draw the continuous line, you need to keep track of the last-known touch position. Each time you get notification of a new touch position, you draw a line from the last-known position to the new position. The `lastx` and `lasty` variables store the last-known position.

```
var lastx;
var lasty;
```

You also need to set up the drawing context so that it draws the right type of line. To get a line that is colored black, you set the strokeStyle property to the color value #000000. To get a nice thick line, you set the width of the line to 5 pixels, using the lineWidth property. To make the start and end of the line smooth, you set the lineCap and lineJoin properties to the special string value 'round'. Here are the lines that set this all up:

```
context.strokeStyle = "#000000";
context.lineCap = 'round';
context.lineJoin = 'round';
context.lineWidth = 5;
```

You need to perform three high-level drawing operations: clear the canvas, draw a dot, and draw a line. These correspond to the user tapping the Clear button, tapping the screen, and moving a finger on the screen. These high-level operations are composed of low-level drawing context operations. If you place each high-level operation in its own function that performs the low-level function calls, your code will be reasonably well structured.

The clear function clears the canvas. It does this by drawing a white rectangle that covers the entire canvas, from the top-left corner (0, 0) to the bottom-right corner (300, 300). You set the fillStyle property to the color white. Then you use the rect function to specify a rectangular path and then draw the path by using the fill function:

```
function clear() {
  context.fillStyle = "#ffffff";
  context.rect(0, 0, 300, 300);
  context.fill();
}
```

You may have noticed that the clear function does not define a path explicitly using the beginPath and closePath functions. This is because there is always a current path to which you can add drawing operations. Calling the path drawing functions stroke or fill by themselves will draw the current path up to that point.

The dot function draws a small black circle on the canvas. It takes two parameters, x and y, that specify the location of the dot. This function uses an explicit path. You set the color with fillStyle and draw the dot using the arc function. The arc function takes a center point (x, y), a radius (1), the starting angle in radians (0), the ending angle in radians (2π), and a direction (counterclockwise). Remember from high school math that 360 degrees equals 2π radians. These low-level instructions define a complete circular path. You then call the fill function to fill in the inside of the circle, and you call stroke to draw the edge of the circle. Finally, you close the path with closePath:

```
function dot(x,y) {
  context.beginPath();
  context.fillStyle = "#000000";
  context.arc(x,y,1,0,Math.PI*2,true);
  context.fill();
  context.stroke();
  context.closePath();
}
```

The `line` function draws a straight line. Most of the time, your app will receive `ontouchmove` events so frequently that the user will never see perfectly straight lines but rather a continuous trace of the finger movement made up of many short lines. The user will notice straight lines only when moving a finger very fast.

The `line` function takes four parameters: `fromx` and `fromy` specify the starting point of the line, and `tox` and `toy` specify the ending point of the line. You use the `moveTo` function to move the path starting point, and you use the `lineTo` function to draw a line to the ending point. You call the `stroke` function to draw the line:

```
function line(fromx,fromy, tox,toy) {
  context.beginPath();
  context.moveTo(fromx, fromy);
  context.lineTo(tox, toy);
  context.stroke();
  context.closePath();
}
```

Because a line has no inside area, you do not need to call the `fill` function.

Now that your drawing functions are defined, you need to respond to finger taps and movements. You use the `ontouchstart` event handler to get notification that a finger has touched the screen. This notification just tells you that a touch event has started. The user may subsequently lift the finger off the screen or proceed to move it. For this drawing app, the difference is not that important because it will always draw a dot. If the user starts moving a finger, the dot simply becomes part of the continuous line.

In the `ontouchstart` event handler function, you again use the `preventDefault` function on the `event` parameter to disable any default browser actions, such as starting a copy-and-paste operation:

```
canvas.ontouchstart = function(event){
  event.preventDefault();
```

When you get a touch event, you always need to store the position of the touch in the `lastx` and `lasty` variables so the line can be drawn from the touch point if the user starts to move a finger. A touch event is a little more complex than a mouse click event, and Chapter 4 goes into all the details. For now, all you need to know is that the touch event object contains a special `touches` array. The first element of this array, `event.touches[0]`, contains an object that describes the finger position on the screen. The `clientX` and `clientY` properties of this object give the pixel position of the touch relative to the browser window. As noted earlier, you need to adjust the vertical pixel Y value because the `canvas` element is about 50 pixels below the top of the browser window. You subtract the `canvastop` value that you captured previously:

```
lastx = event.touches[0].clientX;
lasty = event.touches[0].clientY - canvastop;
```

Now that everything is ready, and the last touch position has been recorded, you draw the dot by calling the `dot` function:

```
  dot(lastx,lasty);
}
```

You also need to deal with finger movement. The `ontouchmove` event handler is called continuously as the user moves a finger across the screen, giving you near-real-time reports on the position of the finger. As with the `ontouchstart` event handler, you need to disable any default browser behaviors:

```
canvas.ontouchmove = function(event){
  event.preventDefault();
```

You also need to capture the position of the touch relative to the canvas. You don't store it in the `lastx` and `lasty` variables yet, though, as you still need those to draw the line:

```
var newx = event.touches[0].clientX;
var newy = event.touches[0].clientY - canvastop;
```

Then, you draw the line, from the last position recorded to the new position you have just received:

```
line(lastx,lasty, newx,newy);
```

Finally, you record the last position by updating the `lastx` and `lasty` variables:

```
lastx = newx;
lasty = newy;
}
```

One piece of the user interface remains: You need to make the Clear button work. You grab the button element by using its `id` and attach an `onclick` event handler, which is simply the `clear` function:

```
var clearButton = document.getElementById('clear');
clearButton.onclick = clear;
```

Finally, you prepare the canvas by calling the `clear` function directly, so that the user is presented with a blank white canvas before he or she starts drawing:

```
clear();
```

 NOTE In JavaScript, there is a difference between calling a function and using it as a variable. You call the `clear` function by putting brackets after the name. When you write `clear()` in your code, the `clear` function is called, and the statements inside it are executed right away. When you write `clear` without brackets, the `clear` function is not executed right away. The `clear` in this case is just a variable, the value of which happens to be a function! In JavaScript, functions are values, just like objects, strings, and numbers. This idea that you can work with functions as if they are normal values is part of the hidden power of JavaScript. When you wrote `clearButton.onclick = clear;`, you set the `onclick` property of the `clearButton` object equal a value, and that value is the `clear` function.

Applying the DRY Principle to Your Code

You have created a simple drawing app that covers quite a bit of ground. You can already see how the elements of a mobile web application are put together, from the HTML5 definition of the user interface to the JavaScript implementation of the functionality. You have met some of the functions specific to touch-sensitive interfaces, and you have seen some boilerplate code that makes your web app behave a little bit more like a native app than a web page.

As you progress through this book, you will build larger and more complex apps. When you use the techniques in this book to build production apps, they will almost certainly be large and complex as well. A good software engineer designs code in such a way that even large apps are as free of complication as possible. One of the most effective strategies is known as the Don't Repeat Yourself (DRY) principle. The basic idea is that you try to avoid repeating blocks of code. You try to ensure that you have one definitive function for each feature.

The benefit of the DRY principle is that when you a fix a bug, you have to fix it only once, and it is completely fixed. If you have to apply the same fix to multiple similar sections of code, it is very easy to forget individual sections or to make other mistakes. The same benefit applies when you enhance a feature: You must do it in only one place.

One of the best things about DRY code is that it is short code. By applying the DRY principle, you actually reduce the number of lines of code in your app. Not only does this improve performance, but it also reduces the effort required to build the app. You can deliver faster and earn more money!

In the following example, you'll refactor the drawing app code base from the preceding example. You'll take similar sections of code and replace them with a single definitive version. You'll take advantage of the fact that in JavaScript, you can treat functions like variables and give them to other functions to run. When you pass a function as an argument to another function, the function that you pass is often used as a *callback*. The function you called calls you back, using your function argument.

Here's an example. First, you create an anonymous function and store it in a variable called `callback`:

```
var callback = function() {
  alert("hello");
}
```

Then you pass `callback` as a parameter to another function called `callme`. The `callme` function does only one thing: It calls the function passed to it — in this case, `callback`:

```
function callme( callback ) {
  callback()
}
```

Another great way to refactor code, and achieve DRYness, is to use data structures rather than logic statements. To do so, you represent some of your logic as data. JavaScript makes this very easy, because it has a literal syntax for objects and arrays:

```
var myarray = ["a", "b", "c"];
var myobject = { a:1, b:2, c:3 };
```

This literal syntax allows you to define complex data structures where arrays can contain other arrays and objects, and objects can contain other objects and arrays:

```
var complex = { a:["a", "b", "c"], b:{c:3,d:4} };
```

This literal syntax is commonly known as JSON (JavaScript Object Notation). JSON is useful not only for defining data structures but also for representing data in string format for transmission over a network.

TRY IT OUT   **Don't Repeat Yourself**

In this example, you refactor the drawing app to use functions and JSON to avoid repetitive code and thus follow the DRY principle. Here's how you do it:

1. Inside the draw folder that you used for the previous example, copy the draw.html file and rename it draw-dry.html.

2. Change one line in the draw-dry.html file, shown boldfaced here:

```html
<!DOCTYPE html>
<html>
<head>
    <meta name="viewport"
      content="user-scalable=no,initial-scale=1.0,maximum-scale=1.0" />

    <style>
    body { padding:10px; margin:0px; background-color: #ccc; }
    #main { margin: 10px auto 0px auto; }
    </style>

    <script src="draw-dry.js"></script>
</head>
<body>
<button id="clear">clear</button><br>
<canvas id="main" width="300" height="300"></canvas>
</body>
</html>
```

code snippet draw/draw-dry.html

Instead of loading the draw.js JavaScript file as you did in the previous example, you now load a file called draw-dry.js.

3. Create a new file called draw-dry.js in the draw folder. Using your code editor, insert the following lines of code into the draw.js file:

```javascript
window.onload = function() {

    document.ontouchmove = function(e){ e.preventDefault(); }

    var draw = {
      fill: "#000000",
```

```
      stroke: "#000000",
      clear: "#ffffff",
      size: 5,
      cap: 'round',
      join: 'round',
      width: 300,
      height: 300
}

var canvas  = document.getElementById('main');
var canvastop = canvas.offsetTop

var context = canvas.getContext('2d');

var lastx;
var lasty;

function clear() {
  context.fillStyle = draw.clear;
  context.rect(0, 0, draw.width, draw.height);
  context.fill();
}


function path( moves ) {
  context.beginPath();
  context.strokeStyle = draw.stroke;
  context.fillStyle = draw.fill;
  context.lineCap = draw.cap;
  context.lineJoin = draw.join;
  context.lineWidth = draw.size;

  moves()

  context.fill();
  context.stroke();
  context.closePath();
}

function dot(x,y) {
  path(function(){
    context.arc(x,y,1,0,Math.PI*2,true);
  });
}

function line(fromx,fromy, tox,toy) {
  path(function(){
    context.moveTo(fromx, fromy);
    context.lineTo(tox, toy);
  });
}
```

```
function position(event,action) {
  event.preventDefault();

  var newx = event.touches[0].clientX;
  var newy = event.touches[0].clientY - canvastop;

  action(lastx,lasty, newx,newy)

  lastx = newx;
  lasty = newy;
}

canvas.ontouchstart = function(event){
  position(event,function(lastx,lasty, newx,newy){
    dot(newx,newy);
  })
}

canvas.ontouchmove = function(event){
  position(event,function(lastx,lasty, newx,newy){
    line(lastx,lasty, newx,newy);
  })
}


var clearButton = document.getElementById('clear');
clearButton.onclick = clear;

clear();
}
```

code snippet draw/draw-dry.js

4.   Verify that nginx is delivering your new files. To do so, open your desktop Safari browser and visit `http://localhost/draw/draw-dry.html`. You should see the same drawing interface as in the preceding example.

5.   Open `http://localhost/draw/draw-dry.html` on your mobile device, but use your desktop IP address instead of `localhost`.

How It Works

This drawing app has the same functionality as the previous one. However, it is far more easily extended and enhanced. If you try the exercises at the end of this chapter, you'll find that they are much more easily solved with this version.

You already know how the basic code works. Therefore, this section explains how the refactoring has changed the code and the reasoning behind the changes. You can use these techniques in your own work to deliver higher-quality apps faster.

The first big change is the use of JSON syntax to describe the properties of the drawing. You define a `draw` variable that contains these properties in an anonymous object. Think of the anonymous object as a bag of properties between an opening brace and a closing brace:

```
var draw = {
  fill: "#000000",
  stroke: "#000000",
  clear: "#ffffff",
  size: 5,
  cap: 'round',
  join: 'round',
  width: 300,
  height: 300
}
```

The purpose of these properties should be clear from the previous code examples. The `fill`, `stroke`, and `clear` properties specify the colors to use. The `size`, `cap`, and `join` properties specify the appearance of the line. The `width` and `height` properties specify the size of the canvas.

In the rest of the code, you can refer to these properties by using the syntax `draw.<name>`, where `<name>` is one of the property names, like `fill`. To get the fill color, for example, you use `draw.fill`. You may be more familiar with the syntax `draw["fill"]`, which is a style commonly seen in older online JavaScript tutorials. You can use either style, but the `draw.fill` form gives you clearer code as it has fewer characters.

In keeping with the DRY principle, the `draw` object is the only place where you keep the settings for the drawing. If you examine the previous code example, you'll notice that the `#000000` color value is repeated in the code. In this example, it appears only once.

The `clear` function needs to be updated to refer to the property values in the `draw` object. This is an easy change:

```
function clear() {
  context.fillStyle = draw.clear;
  context.rect(0, 0, draw.width, draw.height);
  context.fill();
}
```

Now you get to make some big changes. If you examine the dot and line functions, you see a lot of the same code. This repeated code begins and closes a drawing path, sets colors, and performs other housekeeping. Why not factor this common code out into its own function? Here is the code to do so, with the shared code shown highlighted:

```
function path( moves ) {
  context.beginPath();
  context.strokeStyle = draw.stroke;
  context.fillStyle = draw.fill;
  context.lineCap = draw.cap;
  context.lineJoin = draw.join;
```

```
        context.lineWidth = draw.size;

        moves()

        context.fill();
        context.stroke();
        context.closePath();
    }
```

How does this function work? First, it always uses a path by calling the `beginPath` and `closePath` functions. Second, it always sets up the appearance of the line or dot explicitly, every time. This means that if you make changes to the `draw` object properties in response to user input (for example, the user changing the drawing color), then those changes will be picked up automatically. Third, it uses a callback function, `moves`, to perform the drawing.

The callback function is the key to making the `path` function generic. The `path` function has one parameter — another function called `moves`. After the `path` function has done its housekeeping, it calls the `moves` function, using the syntax `moves()`. This is how a callback works. The `moves` function contains drawing instructions, but the `path` function doesn't need to know and doesn't care what they are. When the `moves` function is finished, the `path` function can call `fill` and `stroke` to make the drawing appear, and then it is done.

This might seem like a lot of work just to draw dots and lines. Here's what you get: The dot and line functions are now very short and simple! And if you want to add more drawing functions, such as squares or circles, those functions will be much shorter as well. You have made your code extensible and easy to maintain.

Here are the new dot and line functions. The boldfaced lines show how they use the `path` function:

```
        function dot(x,y) {
          path(function(){
            context.arc(x,y,1,0,Math.PI*2,true);
          });
        }

        function line(fromx,fromy, tox,toy) {
          path(function(){
            context.moveTo(fromx, fromy);
            context.lineTo(tox, toy);
          });
        }
```

The `dot` function still uses the `arc` function to draw the dot, and the `line` function still uses the `moveTo` and `lineTo` functions to draw the line. What is different is that they create a new anonymous function, using this syntax:

```
        function(){
          ...
        }
```

This is the `moves` function! It is passed to the `path` function, and the `path` function calls it to create the drawing.

You can apply the same refactoring to the handling of the touch events. The common code in this case should capture the finger position and record it. It should also call either the dot or line drawing functions, using a callback.

You need a new function, called position, to do the housekeeping work. This position function needs two things, the touch event, so that it can get the finger position, and a callback function, so that it can cause a drawing action to occur. Here is the code, with the callback logic highlighted:

```
function position(event,action) {
  event.preventDefault();

  var newx = event.touches[0].clientX;
  var newy = event.touches[0].clientY - canvastop;

  action(lastx,lasty, newx,newy)

  lastx = newx;
  lasty = newy;
}
```

The callback function is called action, and it has four arguments. The first two are the X and Y positions of the last touch event, and the next two are the X and Y positions of the new touch event. After the action function returns, the position function records the new touch position in the lastx and lasty variables.

As with the path function, the position function makes your event handlers much shorter. The benefit, again, is that when you extend the event handlers or create new ones, you have much less code to write. The use of the anonymous callback function is highlighted here:

```
canvas.ontouchstart = function(event){
  position(event,function(lastx,lasty, newx,newy){
    dot(newx,newy);
  })
}

canvas.ontouchmove = function(event){
  position(event,function(lastx,lasty, newx,newy){
    line(lastx,lasty, newx,newy);
  })
}
```

There is a lot more to writing large-scale maintainable apps. For example, you may want to make use of third-party software libraries to greatly reduce the amount of code you have to write. You'll learn more about that in Chapter 3.

USING THE AMAZON CLOUD

The Amazon cloud, more formally known as Amazon Web Services (AWS), is a collection of on-demand services for building websites and apps that can scale up to meet very high loads. In this book, you will learn how to use some of these services, of which there are many.

The primary Amazon service you will use in this section is the Elastic Compute Cloud (EC2). This service provides virtual servers known as *instances*. These server instances can be tiny virtual machines or large dedicated servers. You can boot up instances whenever you need them. The great thing about this is that you don't have to spend money buying servers up front. You may have a great idea for a mobile app, backed by an online service, but you don't know in advance how quickly you'll get users to sign up. Amazon's EC2 service lets you start with small services and pay for them as you use them.

Each instance is created from a prebuilt copy, known as an Amazon Machine Image (AMI). AMIs exist for all sorts of use cases. In this book, you'll use some prebuilt AMIs created by the Alestic blog community (see `http://alestic.com`). Instead of installing a new operating system each time, you can simply reuse a preconfigured copy that already has the right software installed. You can even create your own AMIs.

The EC2 service has many features, and like all the other Amazon services, it also has a web service API that you can use to automate the management of your servers. This book takes you through the basics required to get you up and running. If you intend to use AWS in a production capacity, you should make sure to read the detailed Amazon online documentation: `http://aws.amazon.com/ documentation`. (Follow the EC2 link for information about EC2.)

The EC2 service relies on the Elastic Block Service (EBS) to provide data storage. EBS provides virtual disk drives for a server. You will not need to use EBS directly in this book, but by using EC2, you will be relying on EBS indirectly. Each server that you create is "attached" to an EBS volume, which can be thought of as a virtual hard disk. The EBS service ensures that the data on this virtual disk is replicated and backed up. Nonetheless, you should not rely on EBS to store valuable data, as EBS volumes can and do become slow and unresponsive. The EBS service has considerable "rocket science" behind it, and Amazon is still working out some of the kinks.

 WARNING *If you have previously used server hosting services, then you'll need to adjust your expectations when it comes to AWS machines. They are individually unreliable. You may find that you need to reboot instances when EBS volumes become unresponsive and refuse to perform read/write disk operations. Amazon does also suffer from occasional large scale outages, just like any utility company. To work around this, plan to build your app using many small servers, rather than one big server.*

In this book, you will also encounter the SimpleDB service. This database lives in the Amazon cloud and provides a very simple key/value-based interface. You'll use SimpleDB to enhance one of the sample apps in Chapter 6.

In Chapter 8, you'll learn about the Simple Storage Service (S3). This service lets you store data in the cloud and access it via simple HTTP web requests. This was one of the first Amazon cloud services, and it is also one of the most successful. You can host entire websites by using S3.

How Geography Affects Amazon AWS

The AWS cloud is not provided as a single global service. Instead, the same service is offered in a number of AWS regions. These correspond to geographic regions where Amazon has set up data centers to provide the physical infrastructure for the AWS cloud. Each region has a code name that roughly corresponds to its location (for example, us-west-1, us-east-1, eu-west-1). The list of regions is expanding as Amazon sets up more facilities. There are cost differences between the regions, and in general, you should pick the region that is closest to your predicted user base. You might also want to deploy your service over multiple regions to ensure the highest levels of fault tolerance. Be aware that the cost of bandwidth between regions is much higher than the cost of bandwidth inside a region.

Inside each region, Amazon offers availability zones. It is commonly understood that each availability zone corresponds to a separate physical installation. However, it may actually just mean different physical rooms in the same data center. Amazon does not provide specific details. Also, availability zones are not the same for different users. Amazon does not release details about the way that availability zones are structured, so bear this in mind when you are planning your server deployments. All you can be sure of is that the cost of bandwidth between availability zones is much lower than the cost between regions. For good levels of fault tolerance, you can use multiple availability zones, but you should be aware that it is entirely possible to have outages of all zones in a region.

To access AWS, you need to prove you are who you say you are. You do this by using cryptographic keys rather than passwords. AWS requires you to cryptographically sign your requests with an access key and token. These are provided to you when you sign in to the AWS website using your Amazon account. You do not have to build the signing algorithms yourself (although doing so is not very difficult). In this book, you will use AWS API libraries to do the hard work for you.

To access EC2 instances, you need to use public/private key pairs. If you are familiar with SSH (the Secure Shell utility), you will not find this any different from the usual procedure for key-based login. If you are not familiar with SSH, then pay attention to the detailed instructions in the examples that follow. These instructions will show you how to log in to your server and run basic UNIX commands.

Using the Elastic Compute Cloud

In this book, you will use a server to run many of the examples. This server will run as an EC2 instance. You have to pay for the EC2 service, but Amazon offers a free usage tier. In this tier, you can use a low-powered very small virtual machine free for a year. This provides the perfect platform for experimentation.

In the following example, you'll deploy your drawing app to the Amazon cloud. To do this, you'll need to create a server instance that delivers your app to mobile devices. This server instance runs a web server that delivers the `draw.html` and `draw.js` files to mobile device web browsers.

This example walks you step-by-step through the server instance creation process. You'll use the free usage tier that Amazon provides. This allows you to run a very small server free for one year without paying for CPU time. However, you still need to pay for bandwidth and storage. For that reason, Amazon requires you to enter your credit card details to activate your account. You can choose to use one of your existing Amazon consumer accounts for this purpose. So that you can see how the process works without actually signing up, this example includes detailed screenshots.

I recommend that you do sign up with Amazon in any case, so that you can gain firsthand experience of a world-class cloud-based system. The bandwidth and storage costs for running this example amount to pennies per month, and you can of course shut down your test server at any time.

TRY IT OUT　Creating an Instance

In this example, you'll create an instance of the EC2 service. Here's how you do it:

1. Open your desktop Safari browser and visit `http://aws.amazon.com`. This is the home page of the AWS cloud system.

2. Click Create an AWS Account on the top right of the page. You are presented with the AWS sign-in page. This page looks almost exactly like the normal Amazon consumer sign-in page. Your AWS account is also a normal Amazon account and is handled by the same internal Amazon user authentication system.

3. Sign in using an existing Amazon account or create a new one especially for your AWS usage. The AWS management console appears. However, you are not able to do anything yet, as you have not signed up for any products.

4. Sign up for the EC2 product by clicking the yellow Sign Up button. As part of the sign-up process, you have to complete an account verification procedure. This is an additional security measure that all new AWS accounts must complete. An automated Amazon service will phone you, and you must enter a PIN code provided onscreen. Amazon will send you an email when the EC2 service has been activated for your account. This normally takes a few minutes, so grab a cup of coffee!

5. Once your account has been verified, click the EC2 tab of the AWS management console. Figure 2-3 shows the standard EC2 control panel interface, before you add any instances.

FIGURE 2-3

6. Open a new browser tab and visit `http://alestic.com`. Click the us-west-1 tab and choose the most recent version of Ubuntu from the list of AMI codes. This is usually the first entry at the top of the table, denoted "Ubuntu *version* EBS boot". The publisher should be Canonical, and you should select the 64-bit EBS instance. You can copy and paste the AMI code and enter it manually into the AWS management console. The Alestic blog also offers a shortcut link. If you click the arrow beside the AMI code, you are taken back to the AWS console, and, as shown in Figure 2-4, the Request Instances Wizard window appears; you can use it to set up your instance.

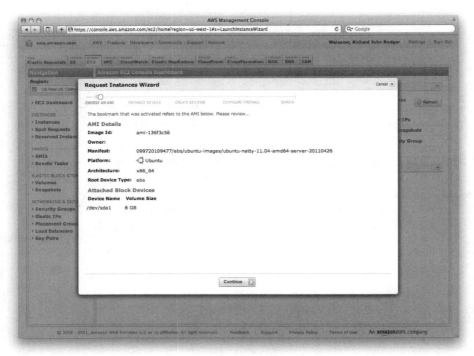

FIGURE 2-4

7. Go through the steps of the Request Instances Wizard. By using the shortcut link from the Alestic blog, you have already completed the first step, which is to choose the AMI. Click Continue.

8. Fill out the Instance Details step of the wizard, as shown in Figure 2-5. Choose the right size for the instance. You want to make sure you are on the free usage tier, so choose the Micro (t1.micro) option from the Instance Type drop-down list. Make sure you request only one instance and set your availability zone to us-west-1b. Also choose the Launch Instances option. Click Continue.

9. Complete the Create Key Pair step of the wizard, as shown in Figure 2-6. You need a secure cryptographic public/private key pair to actually log in to your instance. For this example, you can let Amazon do all the hard work and just create a new key pair. Choose the Create a New Key Pair option, call your key pair `yourkey`, and click the Create and Download Your Key Pair button. Save a file called `yourkey.pem` in a safe place.

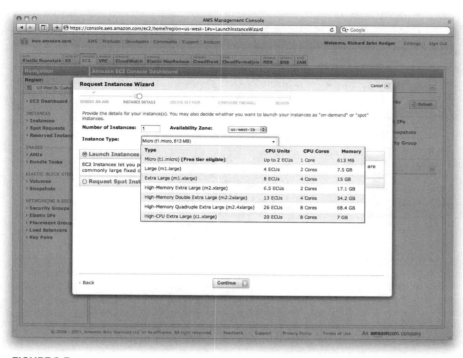

FIGURE 2-5

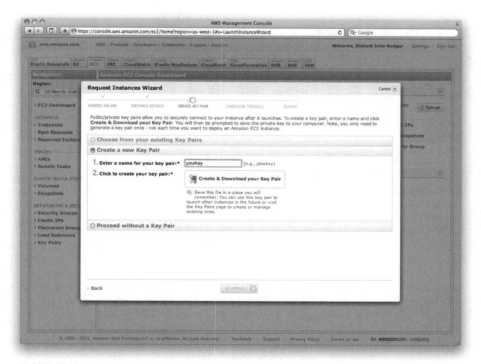

FIGURE 2-6

10. Complete the Configure Firewall step of the wizard, as shown in Figure 2-7, to make sure your instance is secure. Because this instance will be a web server, you want to allow HTTP traffic. You also want to allow SSH access so that you can log in. The best thing to do here is to create a security group that stores these web server firewall settings so that you can reuse them if you create new instances. Choose the Create a New Security Group option. Use the value web in the Group Name field. In the Inbound Rules box, choose SSH from the drop-down list, and leave the Source value as 0.0.0.0/0. Click the Add Rule button.

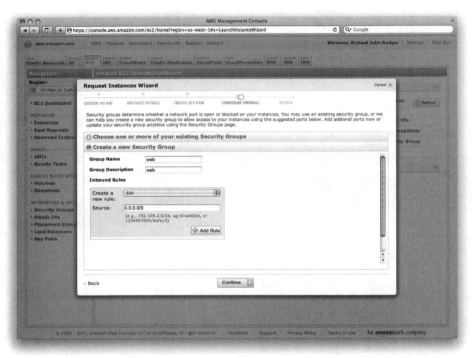

FIGURE 2-7

Add rules for HTTP and HTTPS by using the Inbound Rules box. When you are done, click Continue. Figure 2-8 shows these firewall settings.

11. Complete the Review step of the wizard. Your instance appears in the instances list on the main area of the EC2 tab, first with the state "pending" and then with the state "running." Right-click the instance and select Properties. The properties view for the instance appears, as shown in Figure 2-9.

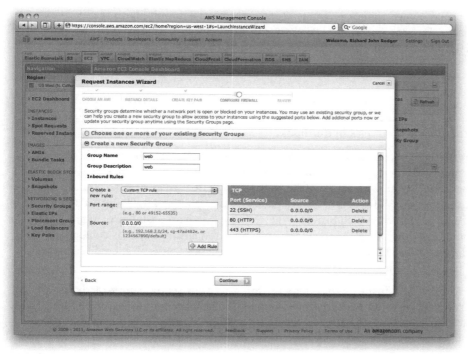

FIGURE 2-8

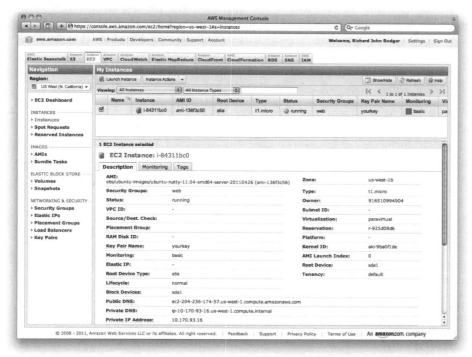

FIGURE 2-9

12. You are now the proud owner of an Amazon EC2 instance, so play around with the EC2 management console. Try stopping and starting your instance and take a look at the Monitoring tab in the properties view.

How It Works

The AWS management console is the graphical control panel for your Amazon cloud services. You can control all of your EC2 instances here. The Amazon AWS API also provides a programmatic interface, but you will not need that for the examples in this book.

There are thousands of AMIs to choose from. This book uses a 64-bit Ubuntu Linux AMI. The Ubuntu Linux distribution is one of the most common, and you will nearly always be able to find answers to any questions that you have about it on the web. It is updated frequently, so you can be sure you are running recent versions of server software packages that you install. Ubuntu also includes the Debian Advanced Packaging Tool, which provides the apt-get software installer command. This system utility can automatically install software on your machine and ensure that it is compatible with other, previously installed software libraries, upgrading them as necessary. It is an incredibly useful piece of software, and you will use it to quickly set up your instance in the next example.

In this example, you set up a 64-bit instance in order to ensure that your server can properly run the MongoDB database. (You'll learn about MongoDB in Chapter 5.) The maximum size of the MongoDB is restricted with a 32-bit instance, so it is better to go with the 64-bit option. This means that even though you're starting on a Micro instance, you can scale up to a large instance.

You selected an EBS-based instance. This means that disk space from Amazon EBS is allocated directly to this instance, in much the same manner as a normal hard disk is used by a traditional server. It is possible to create preconfigured instances that can run without individual dedicated disks. These types of instances are commonly used for CPU-intensive tasks such as video encoding. For this example, you need a normal server with a normal hard disk. Behind the scenes of the Amazon EC2 service, everything is virtual, but for your purposes, you can think of the instance as an ordinary server with its own hard disk. This abstraction is part of the value of cloud computing.

The security group configuration is an important part of using the Amazon cloud. Security groups allow you to set up firewall rules for groups of servers. All the servers inside a security group can talk to each other freely, but external servers, including other servers on the Amazon cloud, can access the group servers only via your configured ports. Because this example is a web application, the web security group opens up the standard web ports: 80 for HTTP and 443 for HTTPS. You also need port 22 for SSH access.

Once your instance is set up, you can review its properties and status by bringing up the properties view, as shown in Figure 2-9. There are many properties, and you should refer to the Amazon documentation for a full explanation. The Public DNS value is the most useful right now. This is the public name of your instance, and you will use this name to connect to your instance and to access the drawing app you created in the first part of this chapter.

The Monitoring tab in the properties view is particularly interesting. It allows you to view the performance characteristics of your server over different periods of time. You can review CPU usage, disk space, and bandwidth usage.

NOTE *When you are running a server in production, you should use external monitoring services to make sure everything is okay. You can configure these monitoring services to send you alerts when there is a problem with your server. Two great services with free options are* http://cloudkick.com *and* http://pingdom.com.

Deploying Your Mobile Web App

Now that you have a server up and running, it's time to deploy your mobile web app. The following example shows you how. To run the command-line utilities in the following example, you will need to use a command-line terminal. If you are using a Mac or Linux machine, you simply launch the Terminal application, and you are ready to go. If you are using a Windows machine, you can install the Cygwin environment, available from http://www.cygwin.com. This gives you a UNIX-like terminal that can run the commands in this example.

If you are not familiar with UNIX command-line utilities, you can still follow this example. Just make sure to enter the commands very precisely. It may help to do some background reading to become a little more familiar with these utilities, as you will need to use them to manage your cloud servers. http://www.linux.com is a good place to start.

TRY IT OUT Configuring an Instance

In this example, you'll upload the drawing application and access it directly from your Amazon instance. First, you'll need to log in and install a web server. Here's what you do:

1. Start the Terminal application. Use the `cd` command to go to the folder where you downloaded the `yourkey.pem` Amazon key file in the preceding example. On a Mac, you probably saved this file to your Downloads folder, so type this command:

```
cd Downloads
```

Alternatively, copy the `yourkey.pem` file into your home folder. You can use the `pwd` command to find your home folder. When you start the Terminal application, you start in your home folder:

```
pwd
/home/username
```

2. Open the AWS management console, open the properties view for your instance, and copy the public DNS name, which is a long string that looks something like this:

```
ec2-204-236-174-57.us-west-1.compute.amazonaws.com
```

3. In the Terminal application, enter the following command exactly as shown here:

```
chmod go-r yourkey.pem
```

This command ensures that the `yourkey.pem` file has the correct access permissions. Only you should be able to access this file. The `chmod` command removes read permission from other users on your machine. If you don't do this, the `ssh` command in the next step will refuse to run.

4. To log in to your instance, run the following command, replacing the highlighted text with the public DNS name of your instance:

   ```
   ssh -i yourkey.pem  -l ubuntu ec2...amazonaws.com
   ```

   You should now be logged in to your instance, and you should see something similar to Figure 2-10. This shows the `chmod` and `ssh` commands, executed locally, and then the connection to your instance. When you connect, a short message is displayed, showing usage statistics.

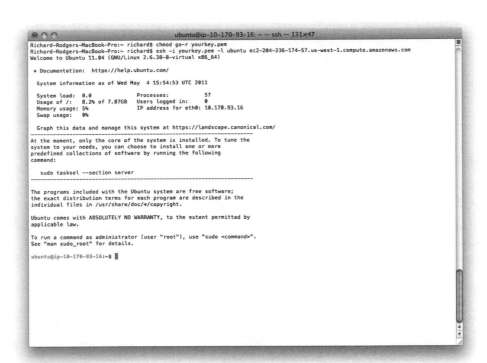

FIGURE 2-10

5. Install a web server on your instance to deliver the drawing application files to mobile device browser. In Chapter 1, you installed nginx on your local machine. Now you need to install nginx on your Amazon instance. Because you are using Ubuntu, this is very easy with the `apt-get` command, which is the command-line version of the Debian Advanced Packaging Tool. You need to be the root user to install nginx. Become root with this command:

   ```
   sudo -s
   ```

Then run the following command, and you should see the output shown in Figure 2-11:

```
apt-get install nginx
```

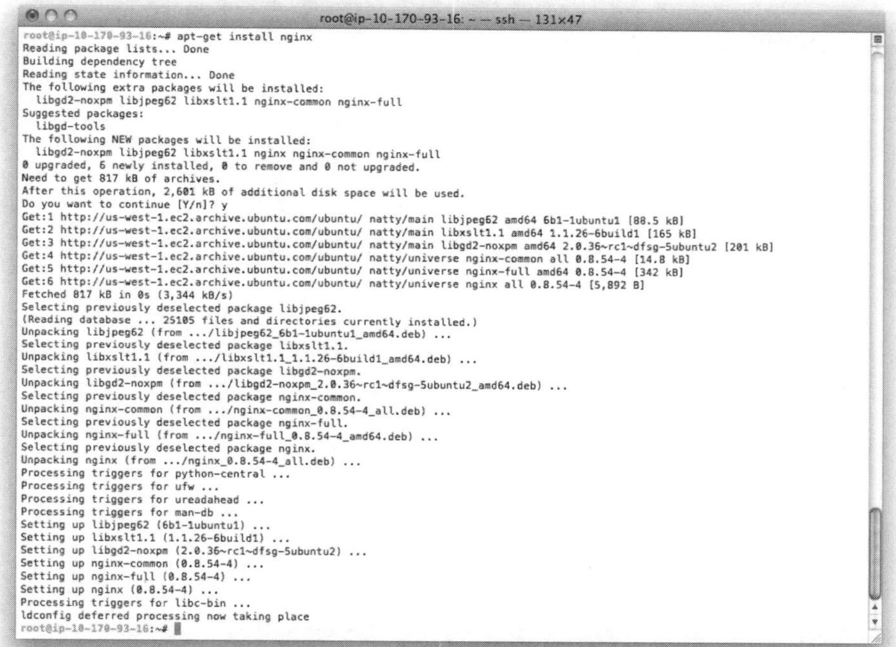

FIGURE 2-11

6. Still as root, start the nginx web server with this command:

```
nginx
```

The command prints no output. To check that nginx is indeed running, use this command:

```
ps -ef | grep nginx
```

This lists all processes with the name nginx that are running on the machine. You should see several lines of output that look similar to this:

```
... nginx: master process nginx
... nginx: worker process
... nginx: worker process
... nginx: worker process
... nginx: worker process
... grep --color=auto nginx
```

7. Verify that you have a working web server. Visit the public DNS name of your instance by using your desktop Safari browser. You should see a welcome message like the one shown in Figure 2-12.

FIGURE 2-12

How It Works

In this example, you use your Amazon public/private key file to gain access to your instance. Amazon uses key files because they are more secure than passwords. It is impossible for anyone to log in to your instance without the key file. For this reason, you should keep the key file stored safely and make sure to back it up as well. In this example, you place your key file in your home folder. Normally, you would store your key file in a special subfolder of your home folder called `.ssh`. To learn more about SSH, visit `www.openssh.com`. On a Windows machine, as an alternative to the Cygwin version of SSH, you can use an application called PuTTY. This is available from `www.chiark.greenend .org.uk/~sgtatham/putty`.

The `ssh` command takes many arguments. In this example, you use the `-i` argument to specify a key file and the `-l` argument to specify the name of the user to log in. For the Ubuntu AMI that you set up, this user is `ubuntu`. You do not log in directly as the root user, but you can become the root user if you need to by using the `sudo` command.

To install nginx, you use the `apt-get` command. This downloads, builds, configures, and installs nginx for you, all in one go. It does not start nginx automatically, so you need do this yourself, with this simple command:

```
nginx
```

This launches nginx as a UNIX daemon, which means it detaches itself from your login and will keep running in the background, even when you log off. This is what you want from a web server!

The ps command lists all the processes that are running on the instance. You run this command and then pipe its output, using the | character, as input to the grep command. The grep command searches for strings that match its arguments. The end result of this UNIX incantation is a list of any nginx processes that are running. This is a handy way to check that nginx is indeed running.

Finally, you visit your new website by accessing your Amazon instance in your web browser via its public DNS name. You see the default home page for nginx, which is a simple welcome message. The public DNS name is basically a website domain name that is inconveniently long and that you need to copy and paste in many places. It is possible to change this name and use a proper domain name by using the Amazon Elastic IP Service. This service is not covered by this book, but you can find details about it in the Amazon AWS documentation.

Deploying Your Mobile App to the Instance

Your Amazon instance is ready, and the next step is to deploy your mobile app to the instance. In a production scenario, you will want to use a version control system, such as Git or Subversion. In this example, you will simply copy the files onto the server. First, you'll need to configure nginx on the server. You'll need to edit the nginx configuration file. In order to do this, you will need to use a command-line text editor such as vi or Emacs. Because you can't use the mouse, these editors require you to use the Ctrl and Esc keys to enter commands such as copy and paste. You may already be familiar with one of these editors, in which case this example will be easy to complete. If not, you should first take a little time to learn the basics of either vi or Emacs. Here are some good places to start: www.wikihow.com/Learn-vi and www.wikihow.com/Program-Using-GNU-Emacs. These command-line editors may seem slightly prehistoric, but they are incredibly useful if you intend to build a cloud-based mobile app. You will need to be able to edit text files on your servers to configure and control the cloud-based elements of your app.

TRY IT OUT   Deploying Your Mobile App

In this example, you'll configure nginx to deliver the files for your mobile web app, and you'll copy those files onto your Amazon instance. Here's what you do:

1.   Open the Terminal application and log in to your instance as before, using the following command, where you replace the highlighted text with the public DNS name of your instance:

```
ssh -i yourkey.pem -l ubuntu ec2...amazonaws.com
```

2.   Open the nginx default configuration file using your command-line editor of choice. This file is located at /etc/nginx/sites-available/default.

WARNING *If you make a mistake with your nginx configuration, nginx will print a warning message and halt. When nginx is halted, no files are served, and your mobile web app is not available. As a general rule with UNIX configuration files, you should create a backup copy before you make changes. That way, you can always go back to a known good version of the file.*

3. Insert the following lines into the `server { ... }` section of the nginx configuration file, just after the `location / { ... }` subsection:

```
location /draw {
  alias /home/ubuntu/draw;
}
```

4. Save the file and exit the text editor.

5. In your home folder on the server, create a new folder called `draw` to hold the drawing app files. You are in your home folder just after you log in. To automatically return to your home folder if you have used `cd` to get to a different folder, use the command `cd` by itself, without any arguments. Here are the commands to create the `draw` folder:

```
cd
mkdir draw
```

6. To serve files from this folder, instruct nginx to reload its configuration by using this command:

```
sudo nginx -s reload
```

7. Open a new tab on the Terminal application and use `cd` to get to the `draw` folder you created for the drawing app you developed in the first part of this chapter. If you created the `draw` folder as a subfolder of your `Projects` folder, then this is the command:

```
cd Projects/draw
```

8. Copy the `draw.html` and `draw.js` files to the `draw` folder on the server. To do this, use the `scp` command from your local machine. This command has similar arguments to the `ssh` command, but it uses a special syntax (`<username>@<server>:<path>`) to indicate the remote destination of the file. Here are the commands, where you replace the highlighted text with the public DNS name of your instance:

```
scp -i yourkey.pem draw.html ubuntu@ec2...amazonaws.com:draw
scp -i yourkey.pem draw.js ubuntu@ec2...amazonaws.com:draw
```

Your mobile web app is now live in the cloud!

9. Verify that you can reach the app by using your desktop Safari browser. Visit the URL: `http://`**ec2...amazonaws.com**`/draw/draw.html` (where the boldfaced server name is the public DNS name of your instance). Your drawing app should appear.

10. Open the app on your mobile device browser, using the same URL. An easy way to do this is to email the URL to yourself and click on the link in the email on your mobile device. Your app should appear as in Figure 2-13.

How It Works

The nginx configuration in this example looks for a folder called `draw` in your home folder that contains all the files for the drawing application. In this book, you will create subfolders like this for most of the examples to keep your code organized. The same folder structure is used for the downloadable code. When you developed the drawing app on your local machine, you simply created a subfolder in the default nginx `html` folder. On the Amazon instance, you used a different location for the `draw` folder, and you had to configure nginx to tell it about this location.

This example shows you how to set up the configuration for nginx on a remote server, using only command-line utilities. This is an essential skill when it comes to developing and deploying your own cloud-based apps. To stay focused on the task of building cloud-based mobile apps, this example gives a minimum set of commands you can just type in to get the desired effect. There are many other ways to achieve the same results.

FIGURE 2-13

Once you have your app running on the EC2 service, you are ready to serve millions of users. With very little effort, you can change the size of your instance to a much larger-capacity machine; this gives you vertical scaling. You can also create multiple clones of the machine. This lets you scale your app by adding more and more machines, which gives you horizontal scaling. Combine both, and you can scale up to meet the huge success of your app!

SUMMARY

In this chapter you went step by step through the process of building and deploying a mobile web app. With just the knowledge in this chapter, you can already build quite complex and interesting mobile web apps. You also learned how to deploy these apps to the Amazon cloud service. You are therefore now in a position to scale up your app to millions of users when that time comes!

In the next chapter, you'll start learning more details, such as how to build apps that look like apps, not just websites. You'll also learn about the best third-party software libraries to use. You'll also learn how to provide features such as geolocation and how to respond to device orientation changes. The next chapter shows you how to build a fully functional interactive mobile web app with many features.

EXERCISES

1. Enable the user to draw using the colors red, green, and blue. Add three buttons at the top of the app. When the user taps a button for a given color, all subsequent dots and lines should be drawn using that color. Use the refactored DRY code example to make the modification easier.

2. Enable the user to save and restore the current drawing. You do not need to provide permanent storage, but you do need to be able to restore the canvas to a previous state while the app is running.

3. Very often when you start to build apps for clients, you will need to restrict access to the version that is under construction. You can do this by password-protecting the URL path using your nginx configuration file. The nginx wiki at `http://wiki.nginx.com` is a good place to start.

4. Using the `scp` command to deploy files to your server is going to be pretty painful on an ongoing basis. How can you use `http://github.com` to make deployments much easier?

Answers to the Exercises can be found in the Appendix.

▶ WHAT YOU LEARNED IN THIS CHAPTER

TOPIC	KEY CONCEPTS
The `canvas` element	This HTML5 element provides a pixel-based drawing surface that allows you to create arbitrary graphics for an app. The `canvas` API uses the concept of a path to describe complex images, using a collection of basic drawing steps. The `canvas` element is well supported in both iPhone and Android.
Mobile web app boilerplate code	Throughout this book, the sample code for mobile apps contains a certain amount of boilerplate code. This code declares that the app uses HTML5 and that certain default touch actions, such as scrolling, are disabled. The boilerplate also gives you control over the zoom level of the app and enables you to specify a standard look and feel across different devices.
Tracer bullet	A tracer bullet is an integrated code base that tests the end-to-end functionality of the app. It does not test the features of the app, but it tests whether all the different software components and dependencies are compatible and communicating properly with each other. Using a tracer bullet early on enables you to avoid complex debugging later on, when application logic is mixed in with integration code.
Touch events	You can react to the user's fingers touching the screen by using the same simple event handling code style that you use for reacting to mouse clicks in a traditional web browser. You receive touch events when the user's fingers first make contact with the screen, as they move, and when they leave the screen again.
Don't Repeat Yourself (DRY) principle	The DRY principle is a rule of thumb that is useful for software engineering. It stipulates that, within reason, you should avoid repeating sections of code or data. The opposite of the DRY approach is often derisively referred to as "cut-and-paste" coding. DRY code is far more maintainable and extensible, but it does require a slightly higher level of abstraction in the design.
Amazon AWS	The Amazon Web Services (AWS) platform is a collection of many different cloud services that help you scale and build apps more quickly. You pay for usage of the service on an as-needed basis, and you can pick and choose the services that you need.
Amazon EC2	The Amazon Elastic Compute Cloud is one of the primary AWS services. It offers the ability to quickly deploy new servers with almost no configuration and build time. You can specify the operating system and capacity of the new server and launch and control it — all from a user-friendly web interface. You still have full administrator access to the server and can configure it exactly as desired.

3

Building Mobile Web Apps

WHAT YOU WILL LEARN IN THIS CHAPTER:

➤ Building mobile web apps that look like native apps

➤ Using device geolocation to find a user's location

➤ Detecting the orientation of the mobile device screen

➤ Installing mobile web apps on the iPhone and Android home screens

➤ Using the jQuery JavaScript library

➤ Using the jQuery Mobile JavaScript library

➤ Building a to-do list mobile web app that provides the same user experience as a native app

You are now ready to learn the details of mobile web app development. In Chapter 2, as you built a working sample application, I asked you to accept some of the details on trust. This chapter goes into those details and shows you how to build a mobile web app from the ground up. First, you will see how to access some mobile device functions, such as location detection, from within your app. Then you'll be introduced to the jQuery Mobile library, which makes mobile web app development much easier. Finally, this chapter shows you how to build a fully working, cross-platform to-do list app with offline storage. At the end of this chapter, you will have this app installed on the home screen of your phone, and it will have the appearance and behavior of a native app.

WHAT YOU CAN DO WITH MOBILE WEB APPS

Mobile web apps are just web pages. You access them on your device, using a standard device web browser. In many cases, your experience with a mobile web app can be as good as your experience with the native installed app. Mobile web apps can support many, although not all, of the device functions available to native apps. These functions include geolocation, on-device storage, native app launching, and offline working. Google and Apple are continually enhancing the capabilities of mobile web apps, so keep an eye out for new capability announcements with each major iPhone or Android release.

Mobile web apps on iPhone and Android run on the built-in WebKit browser. This gives you a single web browser target for your apps, eliminating many cross-browser development issues. In developing web apps, your greatest challenge is dealing with different screen sizes. You can deal with this challenge by following this best-practice web design principle: Make sure your HTML uses a liquid layout that expands to fill the available space. The jQuery Mobile framework, which you will learn about in this chapter, makes layout very easy.

WebKit is an open-source browser engine, and many devices, including Android, use it. The WebKit developer community is committed to supporting the HTML5 web standard. By adopting WebKit as a development platform, you can future-proof yourself. New mobile device operating systems will replace iOS and Android in the future; it is guaranteed that those operating systems will have browsers supporting HTML5, because it is a W3C standard. While this book covers iPhone and Android, you will find that most of the material is also useful for Blackberry version 6 devices, as they use WebKit as well. Other mobile devices that do not use WebKit, such as Windows Phone 7, are nonetheless supporting the HTML5 standard.

Building HTML5 mobile web apps is easy! Instead of spending precious personal time learning Objective-C or Java, you can use your existing HTML, JavaScript, and Cascading Style Sheet (CSS) skills to build beautiful, highly interactive mobile apps. You also have a rapid development advantage over native coders because you can build apps much more quickly by using a scripting language such as JavaScript.

Next, you'll take a look at what you can do with mobile web apps.

Locating Your User

The HTML5 Geolocation API tells you the current position of the user's device. You can use it to build location-based services, such as taxi-hailing apps or restaurant finders. The Geolocation API also lets you track the user's location in real time. The device presents a pop up asking for the user's permission when you use the Geolocation API. Your app should always handle different cases, such as the user denying permission or an inability to determine the device's location.

To use the Geolocation API, you call functions on the `navigator.geolocation` built-in object. To determine the current position, call the `getCurrentPosition` function. This function expects you to provide two callback functions as arguments. The first function is called if the device position can be determined, and it gives you the latitude and longitude values of the current position. You can use the latitude and longitude values with services such as Google Maps to show a map to the user. The second function is called if the current position cannot be determined. The following is a fully working example that you can run using the `nginx` web server, as described in Chapter 1.

```
<!DOCTYPE html><html><head>
  <title>Geolocation</title>
  <meta name="viewport" content="initial-scale=1.0" />
</head><body>
<img id="map" />
```

```
<p id="msg"></p>
<script>
var img = document.getElementById('map');
var msg = document.getElementById('msg');
navigator.geolocation.getCurrentPosition(
  function(position){
    var latitude  = position.coords.latitude;
    var longitude = position.coords.longitude;
    var timestamp = new Date(position.timestamp);
    msg.innerHTML =
      'Latitude:  '+latitude+'<br />'+
      'Longitude: '+longitude+'<br />'+
      'Timestamp: '+timestamp;
    img.src =
      "http://maps.google.com/maps/api/staticmap?sensor=true&"+
      "center="+latitude+","+longitude+
      "&zoom=14&size=300x200&markers=color:red|"+
      latitude+","+longitude;
  },
  function(error){
    var txt;
    switch(error.code) {
      case error.PERMISSION_DENIED: txt = 'Permission denied'; break;
      case error.POSITION_UNAVAILABLE: txt = 'Position unavailable'; break;
      case error.TIMEOUT: txt = 'Position lookup timed out'; break;
      default: txt = 'Unknown position.'
    }
    msg.innerHTML = txt;
  }
);
</script>
</body></html>
```

code snippet geo.html

The bold lines in this example are the heart of the Geolocation API. Your callback function is invoked with a `position` parameter object. This `position` object has a `coords` sub-object that contains the actual latitude and longitude values, in decimal degrees. A timestamp for the position lookup is also provided. The rest of this example shows how to display a static map, using the Google Maps service, and how to handle any errors. You can trigger the error-handling code by refusing the page permission to get your location, when the permission pop-up appears.

The position information is not supplied immediately; it can take a few seconds to appear. The location information is not just determined by the satellite global positioning system (GPS). The W3C specification for geolocation says that the device may use any and all methods to determine location. This can include use of the GPS, cell tower triangulation, measurement of nearby Wi-Fi network strength, determination based on IP address, or use of previously cached locations. Geolocation may therefore be slow and inaccurate, depending on circumstances.

It is also possible to continuously track the user's location by using the `watchPosition` function. You use this function in exactly the same way you use the `getCurrentPosition` function. However, `watchPosition` calls your function every time the device position changes, so you can use it to track the user in (nearly) real time. When you want to stop tracking, you use the `clearWatch` function. The `watchPosition` function returns an identifier that you pass to the `clearWatch` function. When you watch the position in this manner, the device usually provides a visual indication to the user that his or her position is being watched continuously. For example, on the iPhone, a small purple arrow appears in the top bar when you use the following:

```
...
var watch = navigator.geolocation.watchPosition(
  function(position){
    ...

// some time later, stop tracking position
navigator.geolocation.clearWatch(watch);
```

 WARNING *Watching the user's position continuously reduces battery charge very quickly. Always provide a way for the user to turn off position tracking.*

Responding to Device Orientation

Users can hold Android and iPhone devices in either portrait or landscape orientation. In upright portrait orientation, the device is held vertically, with the home button at the bottom. This is by far the most common usage scenario. In landscape orientation, the device is held horizontally on its side, and the home button can be on the left or right. The device browser does not support upside-down portrait orientation, where the home button is at the top. You can verify this for yourself by loading a web page in the device browser and turning the device upside-down. The web page will not change. In practice, this limitation is not normally a problem as it is standard device behavior and users expect it. In addition, a user typically would not attempt to use a device upside down.

Although it is best to design the layout of your application so that it has a balanced appearance in both portrait and landscape orientations, you may need to change the user interface in some way when orientation changes occur. It is possible to detect orientation changes by using built-in JavaScript variables and events.

The browser sets the `window.orientation` variable to tell you the current orientation of the device. The values are 0 for upright portrait, 90 for landscape with the home button on the right, and -90 for landscape with the home button on the left. Unfortunately, if you are building a cross-platform and backward-compatible mobile web app, you cannot rely on this variable. You have to use the window width and height to determine the orientation. In portrait orientation, height is greater than width. In landscape orientation, width is greater than height. The code in this section shows you how to deal with this case.

You can use the `window.onorientationchange` event hook to get notifications of device orientation changes. Again, this is not fully cross-platform, so you need to use the `window.onresize` event hook as well.

In the following fully working example, the API functions names are in bold. This example provides a mini API for handling device orientation:

```html
<!DOCTYPE html><html><head>
  <title>Orientation</title>
  <meta name="viewport" content="initial-scale=1.0" />
</head>
<body>
<div id="orient"><div>
<script>
function getorientation() {
  var orientation = 'portrait';

  if( undefined != window.orientation ) {
    if( 90 == window.orientation
        || -90 == window.orientation )
    {
      orientation = 'landscape';
    }
  }
  else if( window.innerHeight < window.innerWidth ) {
      orientation = 'landscape';
  }

  return orientation;
}

function orientationchanged(callback) {
  if( 'onorientationchange' in window ) {
    window.onorientationchange = function() {
      callback(getorientation());
    }
  }
  else {
    window.onresize = function() {
      callback(getorientation());
    }
  }
}

var orient = document.getElementById('orient');
orient.innerText = getorientation();

orientationchanged(function(orientation){
  orient.innerText = orientation;
});
</script>
</body></html>
```

code snippet orient.html

Run this example by using `nginx` as described in Chapter 1. The `getorientation` method can be called at any time, and it returns a string value, which is either `'portrait'` or `'landscape'`. You can register your own event handler function by using the `orientationchanged` function. Your event handler with be called with one argument, a string value of either `'portrait'` or `'landscape'`, whenever the device orientation changes.

This code uses the `window.orientation` variable and the `window.onorientationchanged` event hook, if they are available, but it falls back to using the window dimensions and `window.onresize` event hook if they are not.

More Features for Later

So far, you've seen some of the things that are possible with mobile web apps. You can access even more device capabilities from a mobile web app, such as launching other apps, complex touch gestures, networking, and full SQL database storage. You'll take at look at these capabilities in later chapters. Once you start building hybrid apps with PhoneGap, you'll be able to access the full capabilities of the device, including taking pictures, measuring device movement, vibration alerts, and more.

Installing Mobile Web Apps on iPhone Devices

Now you will install an iPhone mobile web app. It's important to go through this process so that you understand the user experience thoroughly. Remember that you will be asking your users to follow this process. The iPhone has supported mobile web apps from very early in its history, and the mobile Safari browser makes the installation process relatively simple. Refer to Figure 3-1 as you follow these steps:

1. Open the mobile web app in the mobile Safari browser. For this example, you can use my Startup Death Clock mobile web app, which is available at `http://www.startupdeathclock.com`.

2. Tap the bookmark icon on the footer toolbar. The bookmark icon is the icon in the center of the toolbar. In iPhone versions before 3.0, this was a plus symbol, but it is now a forward symbol. An options menu slides up from the bottom of the screen.

3. Select the Add to Home Screen menu option. A simple form slides up from the bottom of the screen, showing the app icon and providing a suggested name for the App, which you can change.

4. Tap the Add button on the navigation bar at the top right. The page closes, and you see one of the pages on the home screen of your iPhone. The mobile web app has been installed as an icon.

5. Tap the mobile web app icon to launch the app.

FIGURE 3-1

Installing Mobile Web Apps on Android Devices

The process for installing web apps on Android devices is somewhat more complex than the iPhone process. The Android browser does not provide an option to directly add a mobile web app to a page of the home screen. Instead, the user must first create a bookmark and then add that bookmark to the home screen. Here's how it works (see Figure 3-2):

1. Open `http://www.startupdeathclock.com` in the Android browser.

2. Tap the bookmark button beside the URL address bar. The bookmarks page opens. A miniature faded version of the web app is shown in one of the free slots, with the word Add imposed over it.

3. Tap this free slot. A pop-up appears, showing the name of the app and its URL.

4. Tap the OK button. You have now saved the mobile web app as a bookmark.

5. To add the mobile web app bookmark to the home screen, press and hold your finger on the app bookmark for a few seconds. An option menu appears.

6. Tap the Add Shortcut to Home option. Exit the browser. You should now see an icon representing the app on the current page of your home screen.

FIGURE 3-2

INTRODUCING JQUERY AND JQUERY MOBILE

It's time to build a real application. In this section, you'll build a simple to-do list app. This type of app is very common in the iPhone and Android app stores. You should take a minute to install one of the free ones in order to gain an understanding of the basic user interface design. It doesn't really matter which to-do list app you try out; they are all very much alike. In order to build a to-do list app using HTML5, you need to use some utility libraries. If you tried to build the app using only the standard HTML5 JavaScript document API, you would have to write a lot of code. Instead, you can cut down on the number of lines of code you have to write and increase your productivity by reusing code from the libraries described in this section.

The jQuery Library

The jQuery JavaScript library is an essential item in your app development toolkit. It is by far the most popular library for web development. It also provides the underlying framework for the jQuery Mobile library, which you will learn about in the next section. While jQuery is not appropriate for all applications, and there are other excellent mobile-only JavaScript libraries, it is important to be familiar with jQuery. You will also find the jQuery Mobile library to be a significant productivity boost when building mobile web apps. This section provides a quick introduction to jQuery for beginners. If you are new to jQuery, it is well worth the time to learn, as it is a great resume enhancement. If you are already familiar with jQuery, feel free to skip ahead to the next section, on jQuery Mobile.

When a web browser loads your HTML, it constructs a Document Object Model (DOM). This is an internal data structure that maps out your HTML in a logical form. The standard JavaScript API provides many functions and objects that let you query and manipulate the DOM. This is how you create dynamic web apps that change their user interface in response to user actions.

The standard JavaScript DOM API is verbose and results in code that can be hard to read. The big idea with jQuery is that you can write short, easy-to-read code that gets the job done.

JavaScript allows you to use the dollar character, $, in your variable names, and jQuery exploits this by using $ as shorthand notation. The main idea with jQuery, and the reason the word *query* appears in the name of the library, is that it works by querying your HTML document for HTML elements. You then make changes to the set of elements that matched your query.

TRY IT OUT | Using jQuery

In this example, you will build a simple HTML page that shows off some of the features of jQuery. Follow these steps:

1. Download the latest development version of jQuery from `http://jquery.com`. It is provided as a single text file containing the JavaScript code of jQuery. The filename contains a version number. In this book, references to jQuery do not contain the version number, so rename the file `jquery.js`.

2. Create a new project folder called `jquery`. Copy the `jquery.js` file you downloaded in step 1 into this `jquery` project folder.

3. Using your code editor, create a new file called `jquery.html` in the `jquery` folder. This file will contain the entire code for this example.

4. Insert the following code into the `jquery.html` file and save it:

Available for download on Wrox.com

```
<!DOCTYPE html>
<html>
<head>
    <script src="jquery.js"></script>
</head>
<body>

<h1>Heading</h1>
<p id="para1">Paragraph 1</p>
<p id="para2">Paragraph 2</p>
<p id="para3">Paragraph 3</p>

<script>
$(function(){
  var para = $('<p>');
  para.attr('id','end');
  para.html('<i>The End</i>');
  $('body').append(para);

  $('p').css({color:'green'});
  $('#para2').css({color:'red'});

  $('h1').hide();
```

```
  $('h1').fadeIn(500);
  $('#para3').slideUp(500);

  $('#end').click(function(){
    var fontsize = parseInt( $(this).css('font-size'), 10 );
    $(this).css({'font-size':2+fontsize});
  });
});
</script>
</body>
</html>
```

Code snippet jquery.html

5. Start the Safari web browser. Select File ➪ Open File and then select the query.html file. You should see a page containing some colored text that animates when the page first loads.

6. Click on the final paragraph (with the text "The End"). The font size of the text in the paragraph will increase with each click.

> **NOTE** *This book asks you to remove the version number from the* jquery.js *file. This keeps the examples simple. When building a traditional website, it is often better for performance to load the* jquery.js *file from a Content Delivery Network (CDN), such as the one provided by Google:* http://code.google.com/apis/libraries/devguide.html. *The CDN provides high bandwidth and high performance content delivery. When building a mobile web app, things are different. If you need your app to continue working offline, then a CDN is not much use, and you'll need to provide all the files, including* jquery.js. *If your mobile web app is more like an interactive mobile web site and cannot function offline, then you should consider using a CDN.*

How It Works

The page you created in this example demonstrates the core features of jQuery. The first thing to notice is the way that jQuery lets you know that your HTML page is fully loaded and ready to be updated by your JavaScript code. Instead of using the document.onload event, in jQuery you use the following code:

```
$(function(){
  // your code goes here
});
```

The reason for doing things this way is that the document.onload event is not reliable in a cross-browser fashion. One of the advantages of jQuery is that it hides cross-browser issues from you and provides you with a safe interface for common browser events. Although this code may look slightly magical, it is easy to break down. The outer function call has the pattern:

```
$( ... )
```

This is a function call. You are calling the jQuery $ function. The jQuery $ variable is both a function *and* an object. As a function, you give it the code you want to run when your HTML page has fully loaded. You do this with a function definition:

```
function(){
  // your code goes here
);
```

This code goes inside the $(...) function call, as the first argument.

Once you've set your code up, you need to start using jQuery. Here is the general syntax for queries and operations on the DOM:

```
$( selector ).operation( callback )
```

selector is a specific DOM object or CSS selector string that identifies what you want jQuery to work on. *operation* is the type of work you want to perform, such as attaching an event handler or changing a HTML element. *callback* is your function. This function runs when something happens. It is known as a *callback* because jQuery *calls* it to go *back* to your code. Think of using the callback as leaving a voicemail for jQuery, instructing it to do something, and jQuery calls you back when it is done.

> **NOTE** *Callback functions are common in JavaScript code. They are used when a block of code has to run later. You don't know when the user will click a button, but you do know that you want your code to run when that click happens. Callback functions are passed to other functions as arguments, usually appearing as anonymous function definitions, such as* `function() { alert("This function has no name!")}`. *This can appear confusing. Just remember that the callback function does not run right away; it runs at a later time.*

When the HTML page has finished loading, your code finally starts to run. The first thing it does is insert a new paragraph at the end of the document:

```
var para = $('<p>');
para.attr('id','end');
para.html('<i>The End</i>');
$('body').append(para);
```

The bold parts of the code are jQuery API calls. The first jQuery API call is $('<p>'). This code follows the pattern $(*selector*). In this case, *operation* and *callback* are optional. The selector is a string value that looks exactly like an HTML paragraph p tag: It instructs jQuery to create a new HTML <p> element. This new element has not yet been inserted into the HTML document and is still invisible to the user.

The attr operation sets an attribute on an HTML element. Here, the attr operation sets the id attribute on the new <p> element. In ordinary HTML, this would look like <p id="end"></p>. The `html` operation injects HTML code inside the selected element. In ordinary HTML, the new element now looks like `<p id="end"><i>The End</i></p>`.

Finally, the new paragraph is inserted into the document and becomes visible. The code to do this follows the jQuery pattern:

➤ **`$('body')`** — Selects the `body` tag of the document.

➤ **`append(para)`** — Calls the `append` operation and appends the `para` element to the body. The `append` operation inserts an element into the final position inside the selected element.

You can do many things with jQuery. The following lines of code manipulate the CSS styles of the paragraph elements, using the `css` operation:

```
$('p').css({color:'green'});
$('#para2').css({color:'red'});
```

The selectors in this code are marked in bold. The first selector, `'p'`, selects all p elements in the document. This means that the `css` operation is applied to all of them. The result is that the text of all the paragraphs is colored green. This is an example of jQuery keeping your code short and sweet. You don't have to write a `for` loop to handle each paragraph individually. The `'#para2'` selector is an example of an `id` selector. This selector finds the single element in the document with the unique identifier `para2`. In this example:

```
<p id="para2">Paragraph 2</p>
```

The # character tells jQuery to look for an identifier that matches the `id` attribute of an element. In terms of the traditional JavaScript DOM API, `$('#foo')` is the same thing as `document .getElementById('foo')`. You can see that jQuery keeps your code short!

One of the most useful features of jQuery is its prebuilt set of animation effects. The following lines of code use these animation effects, which you can see when you load the page.

```
$('h1').hide();
$('h1').fadeIn(500);
$('#para3').slideUp(500);
```

The `hide` operation hides an element from view. The `fadeIn` operation is an animation that makes a transparent element visible by gradually making the element less and less transparent until it has no transparency. The `slideUp` operation inserts an element into your HTML document with an animated upward movement. The number `500` that is given as a argument to the `fadeIn` and `slideUp` operations tells jQuery to perform the animation over a 500-millisecond period (half a second).

 NOTE *The jQuery library has excellent documentation, tutorials, and FAQs. Go to* `http://docs.jquery.com` *to get the full list of animation effects.*

The last thing you need from jQuery to understand the app example provided later in this chapter is event handling. You want to be able to capture user actions, such as clicking a button or tapping a touch-sensitive screen. These are given to you as browser events, and the jQuery API makes it easy to capture them. The following code is an event handler for clicks on a given HTML element:

```
$('#end').click(function(){
  var fontsize = parseInt( $(this).css('font-size'), 10 );
  $(this).css({'font-size':2+fontsize});
});
```

This code increases the size of the end paragraph that you created earlier by increasing the font size by 2 pixels with every click. The `$(this).css('font-size')` operation gets the current font size of the element. The variable `this` is set by jQuery to be the DOM element that was clicked, in this case the end paragraph. The `parseInt` function converts this into an integer value. You then store this value in the `fontsize` variable. You set a new font size by adding 2 to the old font size: `2+fontsize`. Finally, you change the font size by using the jQuery `css` operation again, this time giving it a literal JavaScript object:

```
{'font-size':2+fontsize}
```

The property names of this object correspond to the CSS properties that you want to change, in this case, the `font-size`.

 WARNING *When writing callback functions, you need to be careful to get your brackets and braces in order. The pattern is always* `$.operation(function(){...})`. *You'll always end your callback function with* `})`. *It is easy to end up with code that has mismatched brackets or braces. This confuses the browser, which might give you an inappropriate line number as the location of the syntax error and can be tricky to correct. Always start by writing out* `$.operation(function(){})` *fully and then fill in the contents of the function afterward. This way, you'll never forget the final* `})`.

When you use jQuery in production, you need to consider your deployment options. During development, it is best to use the development version of jQuery, as instructed previously. The development version is normal, nicely formatted JavaScript code. Do not be afraid to open up `jquery.js` and look at the code. You'll learn a lot from it. For production, it is better to use the minimized version, generally named `jquery.min.js` (leaving out the version numbers). This is the production download on the jQuery site. The JavaScript code in this case has been programmatically compressed to reduce the size of the file, in a process known as "minification." The minified file can be sent more quickly over the network, and the browser can load and parse it more quickly.

The jQuery Mobile Library

The jQuery Mobile library extends jQuery to provide support for mobile devices. This cross-platform library works particularly well with iPhone and Android devices, which both use the same underlying WebKit browser engine. Unlike jQuery, which is designed to stay out of your way, jQuery Mobile modifies your HTML content to create a native-looking mobile app interface. You must use a prescribed set of HTML tags and attributes to create your desired user interface layout.

Most of the mobile web app frameworks use this approach, and it is an appropriate architecture for building user interfaces on small screens with limited user interaction models. If you want to create a custom or experimental interface, or a game, then jQuery Mobile is not an appropriate choice. If you want to quickly build a mobile web app that has a standard look and feel and operates in much the same way as a native app, then jQuery Mobile is a good choice.

In addition to the use of the $ character as the main entry point for its API, jQuery Mobile also makes use of the `data-*` custom attribute feature of HTML5. This feature allows you to add custom attributes to HTML elements while preserving the validity of your document. You can use any name after the `data-` prefix (for example, `<div data-foo="bar"></div>`). When you build your jQuery Mobile interface in HTML, you can add many of these `data-*` attributes to your HTML tags to tell jQuery Mobile how to display them. This approach is known as *declarative programming*, because you *declare* your user interface using literal tags, rather than executing code.

 NOTE *Using a declarative programming style means making your program as data driven as possible. Instead of defining the logic and behavior using code, you declare the logic and behavior using data. CSS style sheets are a good example. For jQuery Mobile, the declarative data is the HTML tags and* `data-*` *attributes that directly define the appearance of the app.*

TRY IT OUT **Using jQuery Mobile**

Now you will take a look at the wide range of user interface elements that jQuery Mobile provides by building a user interface that uses most of them. The elements will not trigger any actual functionality, but you will be able to see how they work. Follow these steps:

1. Download the latest uncompressed zip file version of jQuery Mobile from `http://jquerymobile.com`. The zip file contains a JavaScript file, a CSS file, and an images folder. Rename the files `jquery.mobile.js` and `jquery.mobile.css`, removing the version number. Because jQuery is a requirement of jQuery Mobile, ensure that you have a compatible version.

 WARNING *Using the uncompressed development versions of the jQuery Mobile files is even more essential in this case, as you will almost certainly run into unpredictable differences in behavior on different mobile devices.*

2. Create a new project folder called `jqmob`. Copy into your `jqmob` project folder the `jquery.js` file you downloaded in step 1.

3. Copy the `jquery.mobile.js` and `jquery.mobile.css` files, as well as the `images` folder into your `jqmob` project folder.

4. Using your code editor, create a new file called `jqmob.html`. This file will contain the entire code example.

5. Insert the following code into the `jqmob.html` file and save it:

Available for download on Wrox.com

```html
<!DOCTYPE html>
<html>
<head>
    <meta name="viewport"
          content="user-scalable=no,initial-scale=1.0,maximum-scale=1.0" />
    <meta name="apple-mobile-web-app-capable" content="yes" />

    <link rel="stylesheet" href="jquery.mobile.css" />

    <script src="jquery.js"></script>
    <script src="jquery.mobile.js"></script>
</head>
<body>

<div id="list" data-role="page">
  <div data-role="header" data-position="fixed">
    <h1>List Example</h1>
  </div>
  <div data-role="content">
    <ul data-role="listview">
      <li><a href="#content">Content Example</a></li>
      <li><a href="#button">Button Example</a></li>
      <li><a href="#form">Form Example</a></li>
    </ul>
  </div>
</div>

</body>
</html>
```

code snippet jqmob.html

6. Start Safari, Select *File* ➪ *Open File* and then select the `jqmob.html` file to open this file. You should see a page with a header containing an iPhone-style list. None of the list items are yet functional.

7. Edit the `jqmob.html` file by adding the following code before the closing `body` tag:

Available for download on Wrox.com

```html
<div id="content" data-role="page">
  <div data-role="header" data-position="fixed">
    <h1>Content Example</h1>
  </div>
  <div data-role="content">
    <h1>Heading</h1>
    <h2>Sub Heading</h2>
```

```
    <p>
        Lorem ipsum dolor sit amet, consectetur adipisicing elit.
    </p>

    <div data-role="collapsible">
      <h1>Collapsible</h1>
      <p>
        Sed do eiusmod tempor incididunt ut
        labore et dolore magna aliqua.
      </p>
    </div>

    <h3>Inset List</h3>
    <ul data-role="listview" data-inset="true">
      <li>Row One</li>
      <li>Row Two</li>
      <li>Row Three</li>
    </ul>

    <h3>Columns</h3>
    <div class="ui-grid-a">
      <div class="ui-block-a">
        Ut enim ad minim veniam, quis nostrud exercitation ullamco
        laboris nisi ut aliquip ex ea commodo consequat. Duis aute
        irure dolor in reprehenderit in voluptate velit esse
        cillum dolore eu fugiat nulla pariatur.
      </div>
      <div class="ui-block-b">
        Excepteur sint occaecat cupidatat non proident, sunt in
        qui officia deserunt mollit anim id est laborum.</p>
      </div>
    </div>
  </div>
</div>

<div id="button" data-role="page">
  <div data-role="header" data-position="fixed">
    <h1>Button Example</h1>
  </div>
  <div data-role="content">
    <a href="#list" data-role="button">Link</a>
    <a href="#list" data-role="button" data-icon="star">Icon</a>
    <a href="#list" data-role="button"
       data-inline="true">Small</a>

    <div data-inline="true">
    <a href="#list" data-role="button" data-inline="true">Same</a>
    <a href="#list" data-role="button" data-inline="true">Line</a>
    </div>

    <div data-role="controlgroup" data-type="horizontal">
      <a href="#list" data-role="button">Yes</a>
      <a href="#list" data-role="button">No</a>
      <a href="#list" data-role="button">Maybe</a>
```

```
      </div>
    </div>
</div>

<div id="form" data-role="page">
  <div data-role="header" data-position="fixed">
    <h1>Form Example</h1>
  </div>
  <div data-role="content">
    <div data-role="fieldcontain">
      <label for="input">Input:</label>
      <input type="text" id="input" placeholder="input" />

      <label for="textarea">Textarea:</label>
      <textarea rows="4" id="textarea"></textarea>

      <label for="slider">Slider:</label>
      <input type="range" id="slider" value="0"
             min="0" max="100"  />

      <div data-inline="true">
        <label for="toggle">Toggle:</label>
        <select id="toggle" data-role="slider">
          <option value="off">Off</option>
          <option value="on">On</option>
        </select>
      </div>

      <label for="select">Select:</label>
      <select id="select">
        <option>Option One</option>
        <option>Option Two</option>
        <option>Option Three</option>
      </select>
    </div>
  </div>
</div>
```

code snippet jqmob.html

8. Reload the `jqmob.html` file in Safari. The list items are now active. Click each one and verify that the relevant page appears. Click the *Back* button to return to the main list.

9. Open your `nginx.conf` file and add the following lines to the server configuration section. Refer to the "Setting Up Your Development Tools" section in Chapter 1 if you need a reminder about how to do this.

```
location /jqmob/ {
  alias   /path/to/your/jqmob/folder/;
}
```

10. Reload the `nginx` configuration by using the `nginx -s reload` command. Verify that you can access the `jqmob.html` file from your desktop Safari by opening the URL `http://localhost/jqmob/jqmob.html`.

11. Start the iPhone simulator, open the mobile Safari app, and open the same URL as in step 10 (`http://localhost/jqmob/jqmob.html`). You should see the jQuery Mobile interface in all its glory! Figure 3-3 shows you what it should look like. Verify that the user interface behaves correctly.

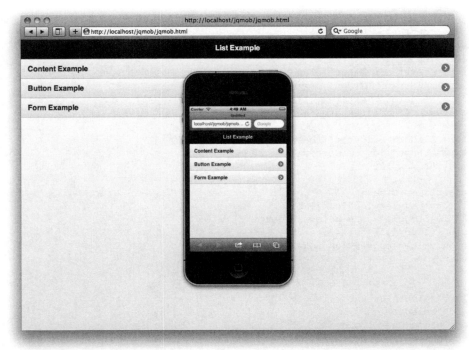

FIGURE 3-3

12. Open `http://localhost/jqmob/jqmob.html` in the Android emulator and verify that it looks and behaves the same as the iPhone version.

13. Open the `jqmob.html` file on your mobile device browser by visiting `http://YOUR_IP_ADDRESS/jqmob/jqmob.html`. As explained in Chapter 1, replace the `YOUR_IP_ADDRESS` placeholder with the IP address of your desktop machine. Verify that the user interface appears as expected and responds correctly to touch events.

How It Works

The demonstration application you just created, although built using jQuery Mobile, follows the standard approach introduced in Chapter 2. You begin the document with the `<!DOCTYPE html>` declaration to let the browser know that you are using HTML5. You also use the special header meta-tags that control the mobile browser view port.

To use jQuery Mobile, you need to make sure your page can access all the required files. This includes not only the standard `jquery.js` file but also the jQuery Mobile files, `jquery.mobile.js` and jquery.mobile.css, as well as the images folder from the jQuery Mobile distribution. The document references these documents using standard HTML header tags.

The basic structure that jQuery Mobile uses is a set of pages, described by top-level div elements. These pages contain the user interface definition. To create these pages, you give each top-level div element an id attribute and a data-role="page" attribute. data-role="page" turns the div into a top-level page. The first such div in the document will be shown when the app starts, and the others will be hidden. Any other elements at the top level will also be hidden by jQuery Mobile. The id attribute on each page uniquely identifies that page.

This app has four pages, and this is the basic structure, with all content removed:

```
<div id="list" data-role="page">
  <!-- content removed -->
</div>

<div id="content" data-role="page">
  <!-- content removed -->
</div>

<div id="button" data-role="page">
  <!-- content removed -->
</div>

<div id="form" data-role="page">
  <!-- content removed -->
</div>
```

You can see that jQuery Mobile provides a simple and clear logical structure for the different pages in your app.

The first page, with id="list" (call this the #list page), contains a header and a list of links to the other three pages. The header is unsurprisingly defined using the data-role="header" attribute. The function of most of the jQuery Mobile data-* attributes is quite clear as they have simple and direct names. You can place whatever you like inside the header element, but the convention is for mobile applications to show some title text and possibly buttons to the left and right of the title. As you will see when you run the app, jQuery Mobile provides you with an automatic back button on the left, so all you need to do for this app is provide the title, like so:

```
<div data-role="header" data-position="fixed">
  <h1>List Example</h1>
</div>
```

In this header, the data-position="fixed" attribute ensures that the header remains in a fixed position at the top of the screen. Different mobile web app libraries have taken different approaches to providing this functionality. In the case of jQuery Mobile, the header is faded back in if the user scrolls it out of view. This has an advantage in that native browser scrolling is used to scroll the contents of the page, but it also has the disadvantage of the header appearing to disappear temporarily, which is not normal for native apps. This may not be an issue if your app falls into the category of app-like mobile websites. One of the exercises at the end of this chapter points you to the iScroll library, which provides a better approach for native-like mobile web apps.

After the header, the contents of the page are placed within a new `div` with a `data-role="content"` attribute. All the pages in this app use this structure. For this first page, you need to show a clickable list of items that link to the other pages. This is where you can really start to leverage the facilities that jQuery Mobile provides. You won't need to write any JavaScript code to achieve this basic level of user interaction. The list is implemented as follows:

```
<ul data-role="listview">
  <li><a href="#content">Content Example</a></li>
  <li><a href="#button">Button Example</a></li>
  <li><a href="#form">Form Example</a></li>
</ul>
```

This code defines everything that jQuery Mobile needs to link up the pages. As usual, you use normal HTML tags to build the interface, and you use `data-*` attributes to turn them into mobile user interface components. You use the standard `ul` tag to build the list, and you apply the `data-role="listview"` attribute to turn the `ul` tag and its contents into a mobile app list view. Each list item is contained in a standard `li` tag, and the links to the other pages are standard `a` tags.

So how does jQuery Mobile link the pages? The value of the `href` attribute is the key to understanding this. You take the `id` of the page `div` you want to link to, prepend a `#` character, and you use this as the value of the `href` attribute. The jQuery Mobile library takes over at this point and performs the element manipulations that will hide the current page and make the new page appear. You can use this `#id` syntax with any `a` tag. You'll see how this works with buttons in a moment.

The content page is built using standard HTML tags. The jQuery Mobile library provides a few extra content elements, such as a collapsible section that opens and closes when you tap the section header, as well as support for column layouts. To create a collapsible section, use a `div` with `data-role="collapsible"` and place an `h1` tag inside this `div` to provide the text for the section name. Any other elements are contained with the collapsible section.

The jQuery Mobile library does not just use the `data-*` attributes exclusively. The library also provides a range of utility CSS style classes. In this example, the style classes allow you to build a two-column layout. You can cut and paste this `div` structure to replicate the layout.

The button page shows you how to create a variety of buttons. In jQuery Mobile, an ordinary button consumes as much horizontal space as it can. You can see this in the top Link button in the example, which fills the page from edge to edge. In the code for this button, you can see the same `href` linking style as used with the list view:

```
<a href="#list" data-role="button">Link</a>
```

Clicking this button returns you to the `#list` page. To create a button out of an `a` tag, you use the `data-role="button"` attribute.

In jQuery Mobile, you have many options for controlling the look and feel of button elements. You can use the `data-icon="star"` attribute to attach a star icon image to the button. A number of standard icons are provided with the library, such as `star`, `plus`, `minus`, `check`, and `refresh`. You can use these keywords as the value of the `data-icon` attribute. You can also use custom icons; refer to the jQuery Mobile documentation for more on this.

To prevent the button from taking up all the horizontal space, you can use the `data-inline="true"` attribute. This reduces the width of the button to the size of the text inside the button. To keep a number of buttons on the same line, you enclose them all with a `<div data-inline="true">` tag. Finally, to achieve the common mobile interface multi-button effect, where all the buttons are joined together on a single line, you use the following code:

```
<div data-role="controlgroup" data-type="horizontal">
  <a href="#list" data-role="button">Yes</a>
  <a href="#list" data-role="button">No</a>
  <a href="#list" data-role="button">Maybe</a>
</div>
```

This code groups the buttons together by using a `data-role="controlgroup"` div and by specifying with `data-type="horizontal"` that the controls are to be organized horizontally.

The final page of this example shows you how to construct HTML form elements. As a general principle, jQuery Mobile allows you to do this in the normal manner, using normal HTML tags. Make sure to follow best practice and use `label` tags to provide a text description of each form element. You connect each `label` to the correct form `input` element by setting the `for` attribute of the `label` to the value of the `id` attribute for the form `input` element. Connecting the elements in this manner gives jQuery Mobile enough information to lay out your form properly on different screen sizes.

A common mobile form element is the sliding toggle switch. You use the following code to create one:

```
<label for="toggle">Toggle:</label>
<select id="toggle" data-role="slider">
  <option value="off">Off</option>
  <option value="on">On</option>
</select>
```

The toggle switch is created using a normal HTML `select` input element. You need to add the attribute `data-role="slider"` to this `select` element and ensure that it has only two options. jQuery Mobile does the rest.

This example has given you a feel for what you can do with the jQuery Mobile library. In the next section, you will use jQuery Mobile to build a working mobile web app. However, there is much more to this library, and it has many more features to aid you in developing mobile web apps. Visit `http://jquerymobile.com` to see the complete reference documentation.

BUILDING A TO-DO LIST APP

Now that you know how to use jQuery and jQuery Mobile, it's time to build the To-Do List app. The code structure you will use for this app is something you can also use for more complex apps. This is why, in the examples that follow, the code is broken out into more than one file.

The jQuery code for this app is kept clean and simple. It consists almost entirely of event-handling code, as well as some utility methods. This structure will get you quite far. In later chapters, you will learn how to build much more complex apps and how to organize larger volumes of code. For now, dive right in!

TRY IT OUT The Basic Interface of the To-Do List App

The first task in building the To-Do List app is to create the app's basic user interface. You will build it in stages, so that you can verify that everything is working properly. The first step is to make sure that the HTML, JavaScript, and CSS files are all present and correct. After you open your code editor and start the Safari desktop browser, follow these steps:

1. Create a new project folder called `todo`. Using your code editor, create three files in the `todo` folder: `todo.html`, `todo.js`, and `todo.css`. The `todo.html` file will contain the HTML code defining the user interface of the app, the `todo.js` file will contain the JavaScript code defining the behavior of the app, and the `todo.css` file will contain the style sheet code defining the visual appearance of the app.

2. Copy the `jquery.js`, `jquery.mobile.js`, and `jquery.mobile.css` files into the `todo` folder.

3. Insert the following code into the `todo.html` file and save it. This step does not require jQuery Mobile, so the `jquery.mobile.js` file is not referenced yet.

```html
<!DOCTYPE html>
<html>
<head>
    <title>To Do App</title>
    <meta name="viewport"
          content="user-scalable=no,initial-scale=1.0,maximum-scale=1.0" />
    <meta name="apple-mobile-web-app-capable" content="yes" />

    <link rel="stylesheet" href="todo.css" />
    <script src="jquery.js"></script>
    <script src="todo.js"></script>
</head>
<body>

<p>hi css!</p>

</body>
</html>
```

code snippet todo.html

4. Insert the following code into the `todo.css` file and save it:

```css
p {
  color: red;
}
```

5. Insert the following code into the `todo.js` file and save it. This code will display a pop up alert message when the page loads.

```javascript
$(function(){
  alert('hi js!');
});
```

6. Select File ➪ Open File and then select the `todo.html` file to open this file in Safari. You should see a page containing the text "hi css!" in red and displaying an alert pop-up that says "hi js!" These tracer bullets verify that the `todo.html` page is working properly. Figure 3-4 shows you what you should see in Safari.

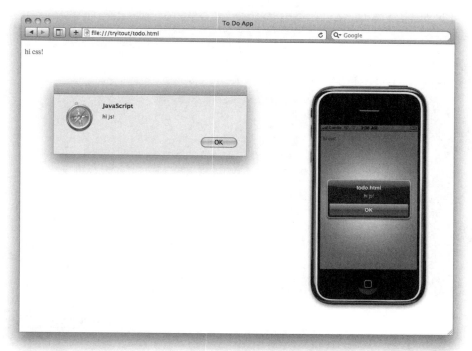

FIGURE 3-4

7. Edit the `todo.css` file by completely replacing its previous contents with the following code:

```
#cancel {
  display: none;
}

#newitem {
  display: none;
  height: 90px;
}

#save {
  font-size: 8pt;
}

#text {
  font-size: 8pt;
}

div.delete {
```

```
    font-size: 8pt;
    float: right;
    border: 1px solid #900;
    border-radius: 5px;
    padding: 5px;
    color: white;
    background: -webkit-gradient(
      linear,
      left bottom,
      left top,
      color-stop(0.18, rgb(173,0,0)),
      color-stop(0.57, rgb(250,120,120))
    );
}

li span.ui-icon-arrow-r {
  display: none;
}

span.check {
  border: 2px solid #333;
  line-height: 20px;
  font-size: 20px;
  width: 20px;
  height:20px;
  display: inline-block;
  margin-right: 10px;
}
```

code snippet todo.css

8. Edit the `todo.js` file by completely replacing its previous contents with the following code:

```
document.ontouchmove = function(e){ e.preventDefault(); }

$(function(){

    $('#add').tap(function(){
      $('#add').hide();
      $('#cancel').show();
      $('#newitem').slideDown();
    });

    $('#cancel').tap(function(){
      $('#add').show();
      $('#cancel').hide();
      $('#newitem').slideUp();
    });

});
```

code snippet todo.js

> **NOTE** *The jQuery library allows you to attach click event handlers to HTML elements using the* `click` *function. Your event handler is called when the user clicks on the associated element. When you are using jQuery Mobile, the equivalent is the* `tap` *function. Your event handler is called when the user taps on the associated element on their device. When you are viewing a jQuery Mobile interface on a desktop browser, the tap also handles clicks. This means you can use mouse clicks to simulate finger taps when testing on the desktop.*

9. Edit the `todo.html` file by adding the lines marked below in bold. jQuery Mobile uses these lines to build the user interface:

```html
<!DOCTYPE html>
<html>
<head>
  <title>To Do App</title>
  <meta name="viewport"
   content="user-scalable=no,initial-scale=1.0,maximum-scale=1.0" />
  <meta name="apple-mobile-web-app-capable" content="yes" />

  <link rel="stylesheet" href="jquery.mobile.css" />
  <link rel="stylesheet" href="todo.css" />

  <script src="jquery.js"></script>
  <script src="jquery.mobile.js"></script>
  <script src="todo.js"></script>
</head>
<body>

<div id="main" data-role="page">

  <div data-role="header" data-position="fixed">
    <h1>To Do List</h1>
    <a id="add" href="#" data-icon="plus"
       class="ui-btn-right">Add</a>
    <a id="cancel" href="#" data-icon="delete"
       class="ui-btn-right">Cancel</a>
  </div>

  <div data-role="content">
    <div id="newitem">
      <input type="text" id="text"
             placeholder="Enter To Do item"/>
      <a id="save" href="#"
         data-role="button" data-inline="true"
         data-icon='plus'>Save</a>
    </div>

    <ul id="todolist" data-role="listview">
      <li>
        <span class="check">&#10003;</span>
```

```
        <span class="text">test item</span>
        <div class="delete">Delete</div>
      </li>
    </ul>

  </div>

</div>

</body>
</html>
```

code snippet todo.html

10. Refresh the `todo.html` page in Safari. The basic interface of the To-Do List app appears, as shown in Figure 3-5. Click the Add button to get the item entry field to slide down.

FIGURE 3-5

11. Open your `nginx.conf` file and add the following lines to the server configuration section.

```
location /todo/ {
  alias   /path/to/your/todo/folder/;
}
```

12. Reload the `nginx` configuration by using the `nginx -s reload` command. Verify that you can access the `todo.html` file from your desktop Safari by opening the URL `http://localhost/todo/todo.html`.

13. Start the iPhone or Android simulator, start the browser app, and open `http://localhost/todo/todo.html`. You should see the mobile layout of the interface elements.

14. Open the `todo.html` file on your mobile device browser by visiting `http://YOUR_IP_ADDRESS/todo/todo.html`. Replace YOUR_IP_ADDRESS with the IP address of your desktop machine. Verify that the user interface appears as expected and responds correctly to touch events.

How It Works

The To-Do List app consists of a traditional iPhone-style navigation bar at the top and a main content pane. You can see that it is functionally similar to the pre-installed note-taking app on iPhone and Android devices. To achieve this app interface layout using jQuery Mobile, you place all the content in a single top-level page `div`:

```
<div id="main" data-role="page">
  <!-- page content goes here -->
</div>
```

jQuery Mobile recognizes the `data-role` attribute of the `div`, which marks the `div` as a top-level page in your application.

The main content of the app is the top navigation bar and the list of to-do items. The top bar is another `div`, with the `data-role="header"` attribute telling jQuery Mobile that the `div` is a top bar. The `data-position="fixed"` attribute means that the top bar will not scroll off the top of the screen if the content becomes longer than the mobile device screen.

The main content is a list of to-do items. In jQuery Mobile, you use ordinary HTML markup to build this list. The only extra thing is a `data-role="listview"` attribute on the `ul` tag. At this stage, the code has a single to-do item so that you can see what it will look like. Each to-do item consists of a check box, the text of the to-do item, and a Delete button, which is normally hidden. In the next section, you'll see how to reveal the Delete button with a swipe gesture. A swipe gesture occurs when the user drags his or her finger horizontally across the screen. The pre-installed apps on both iPhone and Android recognize this gesture, and users are familiar with it. Supporting this type of gesture gives your app a native feel.

The process you have used to construct this stage of the app is a good method to follow when first developing a new mobile application. It is important to get the screen layouts right and to verify that the app works on the desktop version of Safari, on the device simulators and emulators, and on your physical devices. You can do this without adding too much real functionality. Because jQuery Mobile uses declarative markup in the form of ordinary HTML tags, it is particularly suitable for this early stage of your projects.

WARNING *Do not be tempted to use jQuery Mobile for building prototypes that you will show to clients. Here is what will happen: They will think you are finished! Your clients will not understand why you have to bill them for a further month when, quite plainly, the app looks finished and even responds when they use the touch controls. Instead, use wireframes and hand-drawn layouts to subtly communicate that there is a lot more work to do to deliver a production-quality app.*

At this stage, the app contains one small piece of interactive behavior that is directly relevant to the user interface design. This is the slide-down animation that reveals the new item input field and Save button. You implement this behavior by using the jQuery API:

```
$('#add').tap(function(){
  $('#add').hide();
  $('#cancel').show();
  $('#newitem').slideDown();
});
```

This jQuery code selects the Add button in the top bar by its ID, `"add"`. Then it hides the Add button, makes the Cancel button visible, and the new item input field is revealed with a `slideDown` animation.

TRY IT OUT **The Basic Functionality of the To-Do List App**

Now that you have the basic To-Do List app interface ready, you can add the functionality. The user should be able to enter a to-do item and see it appear in the list. If a user taps the item or the check box, the item should be marked as done, with a checkmark in the check box and a line struck through the to-do item text. Here's how you make it happen:

1. Edit the `todo.css` file to hide the Delete button by default. To do this, search for the `div.delete` stylesheet rule in the `todo.css` file and add the line in bold inside the rule:

```
...
div.delete {
  display: none;
  font-size: 8pt;
...
```

2. Edit the `todo.css` file to hide the template `div` that defines the appearance of list items. Add the following lines to the end of the `todo.css` file:

```
#item_tm {
  display: none;
}
```

3. Edit the `todo.html` file to remove the hard-coded list item. The `ul` tag should be empty, as shown below:

```
<ul id="todolist" data-role="listview">
  <!-- hard-coded li tag was here but is now gone -->
</ul>
```

4. Edit the `todo.html` file to add the hidden list item template `div`. A hidden template is used because this is a declarative way to define the appearance of list items. Add the following lines to the end of the `todo.html` file, just before the closing `</body>` tag:

```
<div id="tm">

  <li id="item_tm">
    <span class="check"> </span>
    <span class="text"></span>
  </li>

</div>
```

5. Edit the `todo.js` file by completely replacing its previous contents with the following code:

```
document.ontouchmove = function(e){ e.preventDefault(); }
var saveon = false;

$(function(){

  $('#add').tap(function(){
    $('#add').hide();
    $('#cancel').show();
    $('#newitem').slideDown();
    saveon = false;
    activatesave();
  });

  $('#cancel').tap(function(){
    $('#add').show();
    $('#cancel').hide();
    $('#newitem').slideUp();
    $('div.delete').hide();
  });

  $('#text').keyup(function(){
    activatesave();
  });

  $('#save').tap(function(){
    var text = $('#text').val();
    if( 0 == text.length ) {
      return;
    }
    $('#text').val('');

    var id = new Date().getTime();
```

```
        var itemdata = {id:id,text:text,done:false};
        additem(itemdata);

        $('#newitem').slideUp();
        $('#add').show();
        $('#cancel').hide();
    });

});

function activatesave() {
    var textlen = $('#text').val().length;
    if( !saveon && 0 < textlen ) {
        $('#save').css('opacity',1);
        saveon = true;
    }
    else if( 0 == textlen ) {
        $('#save').css('opacity',0.3);
        saveon = false;
    }
}

function additem(itemdata) {
    var item = $('#item_tm').clone();
    item.attr({id:itemdata.id});
    item.find('span.text').text(itemdata.text);

    markitem(item,itemdata.done);
    item.data('itemdata',itemdata);

    item.tap(function(){
        var itemdata = item.data('itemdata');
        markitem(item,itemdata.done = !itemdata.done);
    });

    $('#todolist').append(item).listview('refresh');
}

function markitem( item, done ) {
    item.find('span.check').html( done ? '&#10003;' : ' ' );
    item.find('span.text').css({
        'text-decoration': done ? 'line-through' : 'none'
    });
}
```

code snippet todo.js

6. Refresh the todo.html page in Safari. You can now add to-do items to the main content area of
the app. Click items to mark them as done. Figure 3-6 shows this new functionality.

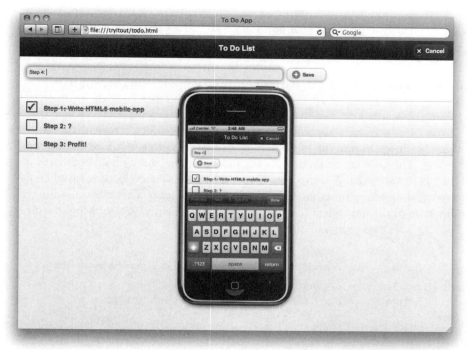

FIGURE 3-6

7. Refresh the `todo.html` page on your mobile device. Verify that you can tap items to mark them as done.

How It Works

Each time the user adds a new to-do item, the item template `div` is cloned and inserted into the list of to-do items. A template `div` is used because it lets you easily define the appearance of the list item in a declarative way. If you define the list item programmatically by creating element objects and setting their properties, your code will be harder to read and change.

The jQuery `clone` function creates a new copy of the item template `div`. The template `div` itself is very simple. It contains two `span` elements. One defines the check box, using the HTML character entity for the checkmark symbol (`&#10003;`). This avoids the need for an external image file to show the checkmark. The other `span` element holds the text of the to-do item:

```
<li id="item_tm">
  <span class="check"> </span>
  <span class="text"></span>
</li>
```

The Delete button will also go into the to-do item, as discussed in the next section.

When the user taps the Save button, the JavaScript code creates an `itemdata` object that describes the new to-do item. The `itemdata` object has three fields: The `id` field is a generated identifier based on the current time; the `text` field contains the text of the to-do item as entered by the user; and the `done` field marks the item as done, defaulting to `false` for new items. The `additem` function is then called to add the new to-do item to the list. Finally, the new item input field is cleared with an empty string and removed with a `slideUp` animation.

The `additem` function adds the new to-do item to the list of items. First, the item template `div` is cloned. Then the `id` attribute of the clone, which is still set to `item_tm`, is replaced with the `id` setting of the new to-do item. This makes the new item visible as the `display: none;` style applying to the template `div` with `id="item_tm"` no longer applying to the new item `div`, which now has its own `id`. The to-do item text is then inserted into the to-do item by using the jQuery text function on the `class="text"` span element. The `markitem` function is called to mark the item with a checkmark if it is done. New items start off as not done, but this function will be used when reloading saved items in the next section. A tap event-handling function is attached to the new item. This event-handling function toggles the done state of the item when the user taps the item. Finally, jQuery Mobile requires a call to the special `listview` function to update the item list properly.

> **NOTE** *jQuery has a feature called* function chaining *that is used in this example. It allows you to call more than one function on an HTML element. Instead of writing this:*
>
> ```
> var myitem = item.find('span.text');
> myitem.text(itemdata.text);
> ```
>
> *the proper convention when using jQuery is to write this:*
>
> ```
> item.find('span.text').text(itemdata.text);
> ```

The `markitem` function updates the to-do item by setting the text content of the check box and applying strikethrough to the to-do item text. There are two cases: done and not done. This code uses the `test ? true : false` syntax to keep the code clean. With an `if` statement, the two lines of the function would be repeated in the `else` clause. This breaks the DRY (Don't Repeat Yourself) principle introduced in Chapter 2. Here is the code:

```
function markitem( item, done ) {
  item.find('span.check').html( done ? '&#10003;' : ' ' );
  item.find('span.text').css({
    'text-decoration': done ? 'line-through' : 'none'
  });
}
```

To improve the usability of the app, the `activatesave` function uses a housekeeping `saveon` variable to disable the Save button if no text has been entered when adding a new item.

TRY IT OUT Saving the To-Do List

The To-Do List app currently does not save the to-do list to permanent storage, so the users will lose their to-do items if they close the app. You can fix that by following these steps:

1. Edit the `todo.html` file to add a hidden template `div` for the Delete button. Add the lines in bold below after the item template `div`:

```html
<div id="tm">

  <li id="item_tm">
    <span class="check"> </span>
    <span class="text"></span>
  </li>

  <div id="delete_tm" class="delete">Delete</div>

</div>
```

code snippet todo.html

2. Edit the `todo.js` file and add the lines marked here in bold. These lines implement the Delete button and the saving of the to-do list items:

```javascript
document.ontouchmove = function(e){ e.preventDefault(); }

var items = [];
var swipeon = false;
var saveon = false;

$(document).ready(function(){

  items = loaditems();
  for( var i = 0; i < items.length; i++ ) {
    additem(items[i]);
  }

  $('#add').tap(function(){
    $('#add').hide();
    $('#cancel').show();
    $('#newitem').slideDown();
    saveon = false;
    activatesave();
  });

  $('#cancel').tap(function(){
    $('#add').show();
    $('#cancel').hide();
    $('#newitem').slideUp();
    $('div.delete').hide();
    swipeon = false;
  });

  $('#text').keyup(function(){
```

```javascript
      activatesave();
    });

    $('#save').tap(function(){
      var text = $('#text').val();
      if( 0 == text.length ) {
        return;
      }
      $('#text').val('');

      var id = new Date().getTime();
      var itemdata = {id:id,text:text,done:false};
      items.push(itemdata);
      additem(itemdata);

      $('#newitem').slideUp();
      $('#add').show();
      $('#cancel').hide();

      saveitems(items);
    });
  });

  function activatesave() {
    var textlen = $('#text').val().length;
    if( !saveon && 0 < textlen ) {
      $('#save').css('opacity',1);
      saveon = true;
    }
    else if( 0 == textlen ) {
      $('#save').css('opacity',0.3);
      saveon = false;
    }
  }

  function additem(itemdata) {
    var item = $('#item_tm').clone();
    item.attr({id:itemdata.id});
    item.find('span.text').text(itemdata.text);

    var delbutton = $('#delete_tm').clone().hide();
    item.append(delbutton);

    delbutton.attr('id','delete_'+itemdata.id).tap(function(){
      for( var i = 0; i < items.length; i++ ) {
        if( itemdata.id == items[i].id ) {
          items.splice(i,1);
        }
      }
      item.remove();
      $('#add').show();
      $('#cancel').hide();
      saveitems(items);
```

```
      return false;
    });

  markitem(item,itemdata.done);
  item.data('itemdata',itemdata);

  item.tap(function(){
    if( !swipeon ) {
      var itemdata = item.data('itemdata');
      markitem(item,itemdata.done = !itemdata.done);
    }
  });

  item.swipe(function(){
    var itemdata = item.data('itemdata');
    if( !swipeon ) {
      markitem(item,itemdata.done = !itemdata.done);

      $('#delete_'+itemdata.id).show();
      $('#add').hide();
      $('#cancel').show();
      swipeon = true;
    }
    else {
      $('#add').show();
      $('#cancel').hide();
      $('div.delete').hide();
      swipeon = false;
    }
  });

  $('#todolist').append(item).listview('refresh');
}

function markitem( item, done ) {
  item.find('span.check').html( done ? '&#10003;' : ' ' );
  item.find('span.text').css({
    'text-decoration': done ? 'line-through' : 'none'
  });
  saveitems(items);
}

function saveitems(items) {
  localStorage.items = JSON.stringify(items);
}

function loaditems() {
  return JSON.parse(localStorage.items || '[]');
}
```

code snippet todo.js

3. Refresh the `todo.html` page in Safari. You can now delete to-do items by using the swipe gesture (see Figure 3-7).

4. Close and restart Safari, and you see that the state of your to-do items is preserved.

FIGURE 3-7

How It Works

The HTML5 `localStorage` API is used to store the to-do list items between uses of the To-Do List app. This API is very simple; you just use the `localStorage` object as if it were an ordinary JavaScript object, with the restriction that you can only set properties to string values. The easiest way to store objects like the to-do items is to serialize the object into a string in JSON (JavaScript Object Notation) format. The JSON format is very simple; it is the same as literal JavaScript code! Here's an example:

```
{
  propertyone:   'a string',
  propertytwo:   ['an', 'array'],
  propertythree: {sub: 'object'}
}
```

Modern browsers, and in particular the WebKit engine, provide a built-in JSON utility object. The `JSON.parse` function converts a string in JSON format into a JavaScript object. The `JSON.stringify` function converts a JavaScript object into a string. You can also obtain an implementation of the JSON utility from `http://crockford.com`.

When you are working with JavaScript, it is better to use JSON format for your data. While XML is an important industry standard, it is not as easy to work with.

This final version of the app uses a global items array variable to store the current state of the to-do list items. The saveitems and loaditems functions save and load the to-do list data. These functions do not access the items variable directly as that would be a brittle design. The items variable is passed in as an argument and returned as a result.

The loaditems function is called once when the app starts to load the previously saved to-do items. The additem function is called for each saved to-do item, and it in turn calls the markitem function to mark the to-do item as done or not done. The saveitems function is called whenever there is any change to the to-do items. This automatic saving of state is an established convention for mobile apps, and it helps to make the app feel more native for the user.

The remaining changes to the todo.js file implement the Delete button and the swipe gesture. To ensure that the app has good usability, there is some housekeeping code that uses the swipeon variable. This variable is set to true if the user has performed a swipe gesture and thus caused the Delete button to appear.

You can capture swipe gestures on elements by using the jQuery Mobile swipe function. Your event-handling function is called whenever the user drags his or her finger horizontally across the element to which the swipe gesture is attached. In this case, a swipe gesture is attached to each li HTML tag containing a to-do list item. When a swipe is detected, the Delete button for that to-do item is shown, and the top bar button is switched to a Cancel button so that the user can cancel the delete operation. There is an extra line in the event handler to call the markitem function to toggle the to-do item done state. This is needed because the tap event fires first, and the done state of the to-do item is incorrectly toggled and needs to be flipped back:

```
...
if( !swipeon ) {
  markitem(item,itemdata.done = !itemdata.done);
...
```

The Delete button is implemented by cloning an invisible template button and inserting the clone into each to-do item. When the Delete button is tapped, the to-do item li tag is removed from the ul list, using the jQuery remove function. The to-do item is also removed from the items array using the built-in JavaScript array splice function.

In order to determine which item was swiped, the code makes use of the jQuery data function. This function lets you store key-value data on an HTML element.

 WARNING *When you are removing items from an array in JavaScript, always use the* splice *function. This removes the element entirely and reduces the length of the array. If you use the* delete *keyword, you will simply replace the element at the given index in the array with a* null, *and the array will stay the same length.*

SUMMARY

This chapter introduces some of the device features that are available to mobile web apps directly via built-in JavaScript APIs. These include features such as geolocation, device orientation, and app launching. In this chapter, you also learned about the combination of jQuery and jQuery Mobile as an application-building framework for mobile web apps. Finally, you saw how to construct a working mobile web app from the ground up.

In the next chapter, you'll learn how to handle the full range of touch and gesture events in order to offer the best user interaction experience. You'll also learn how to cache your app locally on a device and work effectively offline. This breaks your dependency on having a network connection and gives your users an almost completely native experience.

EXERCISES

1. Add a timestamp to the to-do items so that the user can see when the items were created.

2. Use the `-webkit-transform` CSS property to animate the appearance of the Delete button so that it appears to slide in. This mimics the native behavior more closely. The Safari Visual Effects Guide link at the bottom of the `http://developer.apple.com/devcenter/safari` page can help.

3. Add a native scroll effect to the to-do item list by using the iScroll library. See `http://cubiq.org/iscroll` for help.

Answers to the Exercises can be found in the Appendix.

▶ **WHAT YOU LEARNED IN THIS CHAPTER**

TOPIC	KEY CONCEPTS
Geolocation	The iPhone and Android devices can provide you with the location of the device in terms of latitude and longitude. This position is calculated by the device using a number of different methods, such as GPS and cell-tower triangulation. You can get the position of the device using the HTML5 JavaScript Gelocation API. You can even register to get continuous updates as the location of the device changes. While the geolocation feature means you can build interesting apps, be careful not to overuse it, as you will drain the device battery.
Device Orientation	The physical orientation of a device screen, either vertical (portrait) or horizontal (landscape). You need to decide if your app works in only one orientation or both. If it supports both orientations, you need to make sure that your user interface layout reformats itself in an appropriate way. Using liquid CSS layouts can help with this.
Mobile Web Apps	Both the iPhone and Android provide a facility to save a link to your mobile web site on the home screen of the device. You use special HTML meta tags to define the icon you want to use. When you do this, your mobile web site becomes a mobile web app, and the user experience is similar to using a native app.
jQuery Library	This is a general purpose JavaScript library for the manipulation of the HTML page Document Object Model. This library also handles user interaction events. It is designed to be fast and avoids verbose code.
jQuery Mobile Library	This is a JavaScript library focused on mobile devices. It builds in the jQuery Library. An important additional feature is the provision of a declarative HTML tag syntax for building mobile user interfaces.

Enhancing Your App

WHAT YOU WILL LEARN IN THIS CHAPTER:

➤ Making your mobile app work when the device is offline

➤ Handling one-finger touch events

➤ Handling multitouch events with more than one finger

➤ Handling complex gestures

➤ Handling the two-finger pinch zoom gesture

➤ Handling the two-finger rotation gesture

➤ Providing a home screen icon for your app

➤ Providing a splash screen for your app

Your mobile web app should aim to provide the same level of user experience as a native app. In Chapter 3, you mastered the basic processes involved in building production-ready mobile web apps. Now it's time to start filling in the details and take your app to the next level.

In general, mobile web apps need an Internet connection. Or do they? In this chapter, you'll learn how to take your app offline. This is one of the most important things you can do to enhance your app, as mobile devices often have unreliable network connections. Your app should still work in underground rail tunnels, in the air, or in remote areas with weak coverage.

The users of your app will expect it to react to their fingers in the same way as native apps. You need to know how to respond to touch events involving one or more fingers. This chapter shows you how.

Finally, it would be nice to have your own icon for your app, instead of the default one. You'll learn how to provide one.

USING APP CACHING

HTML5 provides a way for web browsers to cache the files required for a web application. The files are stored locally, and the app can run even without an Internet connection. This works for desktop browsers as well as for mobile web apps. You can use this feature to "install" your web app on an iPhone or Android device. And you don't need App Store approval to do this.

Your users still have to follow the home screen bookmarking process described in Chapter 3, but after they do that, they can use and launch the app in the same way as they would a native app.

TRY IT OUT Caching Your To-Do List App

In this section, you will modify the To-Do List app from Chapter 3 to learn how to use the app-caching mechanism. In its Chapter 3 form, the app does not work if your mobile device has no network connection. Here's how you get the app to work offline:

1. Open the `todo` project folder that you created in Chapter 3. Open the `todo.html` file in your text editor.

2. Edit the `todo.html` file by adding the line in bold at the top of the file:

```
<!DOCTYPE html>
<html manifest="todo.manifest">
<head>
```

3. Open the `todo.js` file in your text editor. At the bottom of the file, add the following lines:

```
window.applicationCache.addEventListener('updateready',function(){
  window.applicationCache.swapCache();
  location.reload();
});
```

4. Create a new text file in the `todo` folder called `todo.manifest`.

5. Edit the `todo.manifest` file in your text editor by inserting the following contents:

Available for download on Wrox.com

```
CACHE MANIFEST
# version 1
todo.html
todo.js
todo.css
jquery.js
jquery.mobile.js
jquery.mobile.css
images/icons-18-white.png
```

Code snippet todo/todo.manifest

6. Open the top-level folder of your `nginx` installation. This is the folder that contains the `nginx .conf` file. Open the `mime.types` text file in that folder and add the following line in bold at the end of the file, before the closing brace:

```
    text/cache-manifest                    manifest;
}
```

WARNING *The* `mime.types` *file is not included in the downloadable code. This is an* `nginx` *configuration file that comes with your* `nginx` *installation.*

7. Reload your `nginx` configuration by executing the following command:

```
nginx -s reload
```

8. If you have installed a previous version of the To-Do List app by working through the examples in Chapter 3, delete this version from your iPhone or Android device by touching and holding the icon to activate the app delete option.

9. Reinstall the application by visiting `http://YOUR_IP_ADDRESS/todo/todo.html` in your mobile browser and performing the home screen installation procedure described in Chapter 3. Remember to replace the `YOUR_IP_ADDRESS` marker with the IP address of your desktop machine.

10. Verify that the To-Do List application works correctly. Close the app.

11. Open your device Settings application and place the device in Airplane or Flight mode. This turns off all network connectivity.

12. Start the To-Do List application again. The app should continue to function correctly. The mobile browser is now using files that it has cached on your device.

How It Works

To use the app-caching mechanism, you must do four specific things:

1. Tell the browser you want to use app caching by adding a `manifest` attribute to the `html` tag.

2. Provide a list of files to cache, using a manifest file.

3. Make sure your web server delivers the manifest file properly, with the MIME type `text/cache-manifest`.

4. Make sure your web server does not cause caching of the manifest file itself.

The first step is easy. Just make sure your `html` tag looks like this:

```
<html manifest="todo.manifest">
```

The value of the `manifest` attribute should point to the manifest file you created. The value of the manifest attribute is a URL path. In this example, the `todo.manifest` file is placed in the top-level folder.

 WARNING *Most browsers limit the total size of the cached files for an individual app to 5MB. Make sure you keep your app resources under this limit if you want app caching to work.*

The manifest file is the second item. In the example, this is the `todo.manifest` file. This is a simple list of the files you would like the browser to cache. Unfortunately, there are no shortcuts here, and you need to list every file, with its exact filename and relative URL path. The easiest way to get this list of files is to enable the Web Inspector console in Safari and open the Resources tab. You then see a list of all the files. Make sure to exercise all the functionality of your app so that you see all possible file requests. For the vast majority of apps, obtaining a list of files is all you'll ever need to do. If you'd like to know more, you can see the full details of the manifest file format in the W3C specification at `http://www.w3.org/TR/html5/offline.html`.

You might be asking "What if my app changes? How do I clear the cache?" There is a very specific way to do this, and you need to follow it exactly, or your app will not update. In your manifest file, add a comment line containing an arbitrary version number, like this:

```
# version 1
```

Any line in the manifest file that starts with a # character is considered to be a comment. The code example contains the above comment line with a version number. The rule is very simple: To clear the app cache, increase the version number and save the manifest file.

This works because of the way the browser uses the manifest file. When you start a cached app, the browser always tries to load the manifest file. If you are offline, this will not work, and the browser just runs the cached version of the app. If you are online, the browser downloads the manifest file. If the contents of the file have changed, the app cache is cleared, and the latest version of the app is downloaded. If the contents of the manifest file have not changed, the cached version of the app is used. Using a comment line in the manifest file containing a version number that you can change is the easiest way to clear the app cache. The version number in the comment can be anything you like, as long as you change it when you need to update your app.

To actually deliver the manifest file, you need to ensure that your web server does the job properly. This is the third step. You can't just serve it up as a text file, thanks to the requirements of the W3C specification. The file needs to be delivered with the correct MIME type. You can see the MIME type of a file by using the Safari Web Inspector console. Open the Resources tab, select a file on the left, and click the Headers tab. Look for a line similar to this:

```
Content-Type: text/html
```

In this case, `text/html` is the MIME type for HTML files. When you deliver the manifest file, you want it to say this:

```
Content-Type: text/cache-manifest
```

To get this to happen, you need to modify the configuration of your web server. In the case of `nginx`, you edit a configuration file called `mime.types`. The acronym MIME stands for Multipurpose Internet Mail Extensions, as the concept of content types was first used for email attachments. If you are not using `nginx`, you need to follow the instructions for your particular web server. You configure most of them the same way — by editing a text file containing a list of MIME types.

 WARNING *The MIME type configuration may be awkward, but it is absolutely necessary. The mobile Safari browser will not cache your app without the right MIME type for the manifest file. Don't forget that you have to do this not only on your local machine, but also on any servers that you deploy your app to.*

The fourth item is one that can easily trip you up. If your web server is configured to instruct browsers to cache the manifest file, your app will never update! Luckily, nginx does not do this by default, but other web servers may do it. Use the Safari Web Inspector to check the response headers returned when you request the manifest file. If you see a header called Expires with a date in the future, you need to modify your web server configuration to remove this header. You need to refer to your web server documentation for instructions to do this.

It is possible to track the status of the app cache by using the window.applicationCache object. The status property of this object tells you the current status of the cache. The values of this property are provided as constants on the window.applicationCache object:

➤ **UNCACHED** — The app is not cached.

➤ **IDLE** — The cache is up-to-date and in use.

➤ **CHECKING** — The browser is downloading the manifest file.

➤ **DOWNLOADING** — The browser is updating the cache files.

➤ **UPDATEREADY** — The cache update is complete.

➤ **OBSOLETE** — The cache is missing some files and is not in use.

You can use these status values to provide feedback to the user. To receive notifications of changes to the cache, you can register event handlers on the window.applicationCache object:

➤ **onchecking** — Fires when the browser is downloading the manifest file.

➤ **onnoupdate** — Fires when the manifest has not changed.

➤ **ondownloading** — Fires when files in the manifest begin downloading.

➤ **onprogress** — Fires as files in the manifest are downloading.

➤ **oncached** — Fires when cache downloading is complete.

➤ **onupdateready** — Fires when the cache is ready to use.

➤ **onobsolete** — Fires when the cache does not contain the full manifest and the caching fails.

➤ **onerror** — Fires when an error occurs and the caching fails.

To force an update of your app, you can call the update function on the window.applicationCache object. When the update is complete, you call the swapCache function to make the browser use the new cache. Finally, you call location.reload to show the new version of your app. When your app first starts, you can use the onupdateready event handler to perform an automatic reload if there is a new version. This is what the To-Do List code example does.

HANDLING TOUCH EVENTS

Touch events are at the core of the mobile app user experience. Your mobile web apps should provide the same tactile responsiveness as native apps. The mobile WebKit browser provides touch events that you can use to provide this enhanced experience.

Touch events are not like mouse events, and you need to think about them in a different way. The mouse is a continuous pointing device and is always present on the screen. Fingers touch the screen only to make something happen. They are like a mouse pointer that hops around the screen. This means that traditional mouse-oriented effects and events, such as hovering and `mouseover` and `mouseout`, are not usable on mobile devices. In fact, these effects and events do not even make sense.

The mobile WebKit browser must of course still display ordinary websites, so it provides all the standard mouse events. In the context of mobile web app development, these traditional mouse events are more useful as debugging aids when you are running your app in a desktop browser. If you use them as your primary event handlers in a mobile context, you will notice that your app is sluggish and does not respond as quickly as it could. Therefore, in this section, you will learn how to use the touch-oriented events provided by the mobile WebKit browser. You will also learn how to handle multitouch gestures involving more than one finger.

Touch Events

The jQuery Mobile library provides a number of high-level touch events that make dealing with touch interactions quite easy. But it's also important to understand the basic touch events provided by the WebKit browser. You met, briefly, the `touchstart` and `touchmove` events in Chapter 2. Now it's time to fill in the details. There are four basic touch events:

➤ **touchstart** — Fires when a finger first touches the screen.

➤ **touchmove** — Fires when a finger moves in contact with the screen.

➤ **touchend** — Fires when a finger leaves the screen.

➤ **touchcancel** — Fires when the device launches another app.

You register an event handler for these events in the usual manner, by calling the `ontouchevent` function of an HTML element:

```
document.getElementbyId('mydiv').ontouchstart(function(e){...})
```

All the touch event handlers are passed a touch event object as their first argument, which provides information about the finger or fingers that touched the screen.

 WARNING *If you are using jQuery, you need to use the original event object, not the jQuery event object. The original event is stored in the* `originalEvent` *property of the jQuery event object.*

The touch event object is an extension of the traditional mouse event object. It provides the following additional properties:

➤ **touches** — An array of separate touch details

➤ **targetTouches** — An array of touches that started on the same HTML element

➤ **changedTouches** — An array of touches that changed in this event

The `touches` array contains a list of objects that give you the details of each finger that is touching the screen. If more than one finger is touching the screen and some of the fingers are removed, those touches will not be in this list. You can detect up to five fingers simultaneously. The touch objects in this array have the following properties:

➤ **`clientX`** — Horizontal position with respect to the browser window

➤ **`clientY`** — Vertical position with respect to the browser window

➤ **`pageX`** — Horizontal position with respect to the HTML page

➤ **`pageY`** — Vertical position with respect to the HTML page

➤ **`screenX`** — Horizontal position with respect to the screen

➤ **`screenY`** — Vertical position with respect to the screen

➤ **`target`** — The HTML element that the touch hit

➤ **`identifier`** — A unique identifier for this touch

As you can see, a number of different X and Y position values are provided by the touch object. The `clientX` and `clientY` values are the most useful for mobile web app development because you usually have a fixed-size browser window.

The `targetTouches` array contains the subset of touches that began inside the HTML `target` element. As with the `touches` array, if a finger is not touching the screen, it won't be in this list. This list is useful if your user interface needs to know when two fingers touched the same HTML element.

The `changedTouches` array contains a list of the touch changes that caused this event. So if you remove a finger from the screen, its last position is in this array. If you add a finger to the screen, it appears here as well. You would normally access this array in the `touchend` event handler. Use the `identifier` property of each touch object to work out the changed touches.

One complication to bear in mind when dealing with touch events is that they may fire multiple times. For example, if you place two fingers on the screen, you may receive two `touchstart` events, one containing a single touch and the other containing both touches. This depends on the exact timing of the fingers hitting the screen.

You also need to prevent the default touch behaviors of the browser from interfering with your app. You do this by calling the `preventDefault` function on touch events. You encountered this function in Chapter 2. In particular, you should do this with the `touchmove` event on the HTML document object. Because this event is used for browser scrolling, it causes "rubber-banding" of your fixed-size mobile web app. When the user drags a finger over your app, its user interface will bounce up and down in an attempt to scroll. This is hardly a native app experience!

In the code example in this section, you will learn how to use the basic touch events to build an interactive app. The jQuery Mobile library provides high-level touch events that can make your life easier for common cases. Depending on the complexity of your app, you may need to use both the jQuery Mobile higher-level events and the basic events. The jQuery Mobile library provides the following high-level touch events:

➤ **`tap`** — A quick touch and release on an HTML element

➤ **`taphold`** — A touch and hold on an HTML element

➤ **swipe** — A swipe gesture in any direction

➤ **swipeleft** — A swipe gesture to the left

➤ **swiperight** — A swipe gesture to the right

To react to a `tap` event on a `div` element, for example, you would use this:

```
$('#mydiv').tap(function(){...})
```

Gesture Events

Gesture events provide an easy way to receive notification of two-finger gestures. There are three event handlers for gesture events:

➤ **gesturestart** — Fires when a two-finger gesture starts.

➤ **gesturechange** — Fires as a two-finger gesture proceeds.

➤ **gestureend** — Fires when a two-finger gesture ends.

To listen for these events, you use the *ongesturevent* function on an HTML element:

```
document.getElementbyId('mydiv').ongesturestart(function(e){...})
```

These handlers receive an event object that contains the standard touch properties, as above. In addition, this touch event also includes the following convenience properties:

➤ **scale** —The `scale` property tells you how much two-finger pinch zooming occurred. The decimal value of the property starts at 1.0 and changes in proportion to the zoom. If the user's fingers move toward each other, the value is below 1.0, and if they move apart, the value is above 1.0.

➤ **rotation** —The `rotation` property tells you how much two-finger rotation occurred. The two-finger rotation gesture occurs when the user places two fingers in contact with the screen and rotates both finger tips around a common central point. The value of the rotation is given in degrees, with positive values being clockwise.

Gesture events are merely abstractions of the underlying touch events. The underlying touch events are also fired, so you can listen for both.

Unfortunately, gesture events are not supported across all devices and versions. The iPhone supports gesture events fully, but Android has very inconsistent support, both in hardware and software. Therefore, you should use multitouch events only as an enhancement to your app, rather than as an essential feature.

When you are testing your app in the iPhone simulator, you can trigger multitouch events by holding down the Option key. Two small semi-transparent circles appear, indicating the simulated touch positions. You move the mouse pointer to input scaling or rotation events. The circles move as mirror images of each other.

TRY IT OUT An Interactive Image Viewer

This example shows you how to build a simple image viewer with interactive features. You can swipe left and right to browse through a predefined set of images. You can pinch zoom and rotate with two-finger touch gestures, and you can rotate the image in three dimensions by moving your finger or fingers on the screen. In this example, you'll learn how to capture all these touch events, and you'll get a preview of WebKit animation effects. Unfortunately, only the single finger interactions will work on your Android device.

1. Create a new file called `touch.html` for the HTML source code. Save this file to your `nginx html` folder, as described in Chapter 1.

2. Create a new file called `touch.js` for the JavaScript code. Save this file to your `nginx html` folder.

3. Follow the instructions in Chapter 3 to obtain jQuery if you have not done so already. Copy the `jquery.js` file into your `nginx html` folder.

4. Place three image files, `flower0.png`, `flower1.png`, and `flower2.png`, in the `nginx html` folder. They are available from the downloadable code at www.wrox.com. Alternatively, you can create your own images. Just remember to name them `flower0.png`, `flower1.png`, and `flower2.png`.

5. Insert the following code into the `touch.html` file:

```
<!DOCTYPE html>
<html>
<head>
    <meta name="viewport"
          content="user-scalable=no,initial-scale=1.0,maximum-scale=1.0" />
    <meta name="apple-mobile-web-app-capable" content="yes" />

    <link rel="stylesheet" href="jquery.mobile.css" />

    <style>
    #main { width:320px; height:480px; padding:0px; margin:0px }
    img.flower {
      display:block;
      width:128px; height:96px;
      position:absolute; top:166px; left:96px;
    }
    img.rightout { -webkit-transform: translate( 400%) }
    img.leftout  { -webkit-transform: translate(-400%) }
    </style>

    <script src="jquery.js"></script>
    <script src="jquery.mobile.js"></script>

    <script src="touch.js"></script>
</head>
<body><div id="main">

<img id="img0" src="flower0.jpg" class="flower">
<img id="img1" src="flower1.jpg" class="flower rightout">
<img id="img2" src="flower2.jpg" class="flower rightout">
```

```
        </div>
        </body>
        </html>
```

Code snippet touch.html

6. Insert the following code into the touch.js file:

```
document.ontouchmove = function(e){ e.preventDefault(); }

$(document).ready(function(){

    // index of current image
    var imgI = 0;

    var img  = $('#img'+imgI);
    var main = $('#main');

    var start = {active:false};
    var current = {
      xdeg:0, ydeg:0, zdeg:0,
      h:img.height(), w:img.width()
    };

    main.bind('touchstart',function(e){
      e.preventDefault();

      start.xdeg = current.xdeg;
      start.ydeg = current.ydeg;
      start.zdeg = current.zdeg;

      if( e.originalEvent.touches.length < 2 ) {
        start.x = e.originalEvent.touches[0].pageX;
        start.y = e.originalEvent.touches[0].pageY;
        start.when = new Date().getTime();
        start.active = true;
      }
    });

    main.bind('touchmove',function(e){
      e.preventDefault();
      current.x = e.originalEvent.touches[0].pageX;
      current.y = e.originalEvent.touches[0].pageY;

      if( start.active
          && !isSwipe(e)

          // single finger touch events only
          && e.originalEvent.touches.length < 2 )
      {
        var dr = 160;

        // distance finger has moved
        var dx = current.x - start.x;
        var dy = current.y - start.y;
```

```
        // damp the movement
        dx = Math.abs(1 + Math.sin((dx/dr)-(Math.PI/2))) * dx;
        dy = Math.abs(1 + Math.sin((dy/dr)-(Math.PI/2))) * dy;

        // map to degrees of rotation
        current.ydeg = start.ydeg + ( 180 * (dx / dr) );
        current.xdeg = start.xdeg + ( 180 * (dy / dr) );

        rotate();
      }
  });

main.bind('touchend',function(e){
    e.preventDefault();
    start.active = false;

    if( isSwipe(e) ) {
      var xdist    = current.x - start.x;
      var lastimgI = imgI;
      imgI = 0 < xdist ? imgI-1 : imgI+1;
      imgI = imgI < 0 ? 0 : 2 < imgI ? 2 : imgI;

      if( imgI != lastimgI ) {
        img = $('#img'+imgI);

        var css = {
          webkitTransform:'',
          webkitTransition: '-webkit-transform 1s'
        };

        $('#img'+lastimgI)
          .css(css)
          .addClass( imgI < lastimgI ? 'rightout' : 'leftout' );

        img
          .css(css)
          .removeClass( imgI < lastimgI ? 'leftout' : 'rightout' );

        current.ydeg = 0;
        current.xdeg = 0;
        current.zdeg = 0;
        current.h    = img.height();
        current.w    = img.width();

        setTimeout(function(){
          img.css({webkitTransition:''});
        },1000);
      }
    }
  });

main[0].ongesturechange = function(e) {
    var scale = e.scale;

    // damp zoom scale
    scale =
      scale <= 1
```

```
            ? Math.sin( scale * (Math.PI/2))
            : 1+( Math.pow(scale-1,2) );

      current.w = current.w * scale;
      current.h = current.h * scale;

      img.width( current.w );
      img.height( current.h );

      if( 2 < Math.abs(e.rotation) ) {
        current.zdeg = (start.zdeg + e.rotation) % 360;
        rotate();
      }
    };

    function isSwipe(e) {
      var duration = new Date().getTime()-start.when;
      var xdist     = current.x - start.x;
      return duration < 500 && 160 < Math.abs( xdist );
    }

    function rotate() {
      img.css(
        "-webkit-transform",
        'rotateX('+current.xdeg+'deg) '+
                  'rotateY('+current.ydeg+'deg) '+
                  'rotateZ('+current.zdeg+'deg)'
      );
    }
});
```

Code snippet touch.js

7. Make sure the nginx web server is running and open the touch.html file on your iPhone or Android device, using the URL http://YOUR_IP_ADDRESS/touch.html on your mobile browser. As always, replace YOUR_IP_ADDRESS with the IP address of your desktop machine. You can also open touch.html using the desktop Safari browser, but the touch events will not fire. (Refer to Chapter 1 if you need help opening the file in your mobile browser.) You should see the first image in the center of the screen. Try out some touch gestures, such as one-finger rotate, two-finger zoom and rotate, and left and right swipes. Figure 4-1 shows a rotated and scaled image after some touch manipulation.

How It Works

This image-manipulation example shows how to capture and use touch and gesture events. The HTML code for this app sets up three images to view:

```
<img id="img0" src="flower0.jpg" class="flower">
<img id="img1" src="flower1.jpg" class="flower rightout">
<img id="img2" src="flower2.jpg" class="flower rightout">
```

FIGURE 4-1

The `rightout` CSS style places the image far to the right, outside the viewable area. The `leftout` CSS style does the same thing but to the left. Instead of using the more traditional CSS `top` and `left` positioning properties, the `rightout` and `leftout` styles use the `-webkit-transform` property:

```
-webkit-transform: translate( 400% )
```

This property is provided by the WebKit browser engine to support animation effects, and it is hardware optimized. The swipe gesture, as you will see shortly, is implemented by adding or removing this property, causing an automatic animation to occur.

The HTML code uses a full-screen `div` with `id="main"` to capture touch events wherever they occur on the screen. If the events were only attached to the image, the user experience would be very poor because the reactive surface area would change, depending on the image size and rotation.

The JavaScript code for this example listens for touch events and manipulates the image accordingly. The app listens for swipe events to move back and forth between images, in much the same way as the pre-installed gallery app. The app listens for single-finger touch events to rotate the image in the X and Y dimensions, and it listens for two-finger touch events to rotate in the Z dimension and also to zoom the image.

The app needs to maintain some state variables to keep track of the current image and its orientation. The `imgI` variable stores the current image index — a value between 0 and 2 because there are three images in the example. The `img` variable stores a jQuery reference to the current `img` HTML element, and the `main` variable stores a jQuery reference to the full-screen `div` that captures the touch events.

The `start` object stores the screen location and time of the first point of a touch event sequence. Using jQuery, you bind the `touchstart` event to the main `div` and then you set the `start` object's properties based on this event:

```
main.bind('touchstart',function(e){
  e.preventDefault();

  start.xdeg = current.xdeg;
  start.ydeg = current.ydeg;
  start.zdeg = current.zdeg;

  if( e.originalEvent.touches.length < 2 ) {
    start.x = e.originalEvent.touches[0].pageX;
    start.y = e.originalEvent.touches[0].pageY;
    start.when = new Date().getTime();
    start.active = true;
  }
});
```

This captures the point at which the user's finger first touches the screen. The gesture events are used to handle the two-finger manipulations, so only the location of the first touch, provided by `e.originalEvent.touches[0]`, is stored. If there are two or more touches in the `e.originalEvent .touches` array, `touchstart` is ignored. Regardless of the number of touches, the `touchstart` handler always sets the start rotation of the current finger movement equal to the current rotation of the image. The rotation in the X, Y, and Z axes is stored. This is then used as the baseline for subsequent rotations with either one finger or two.

NOTE *Each of the event handler functions calls the* `preventDefault` *function on the event. This prevents any unwanted side effects from the touch event interfering with your own handling of the touch events.*

In addition to the starting position, the other state information you need to keep track of are the current orientation of the image and the current position of the user's finger as it drags across the screen. By using the difference between the starting position and the current position, you can calculate how much rotation to apply to the image. The `current` variable stores the degree of rotation of the image around the X, Y, and Z axes in three-dimensional space, as well as the current width and height of the image.

The three-dimensional rotation of the image is controlled in two ways. Single-finger movement causes rotation around the X and Y axes. The X axis is an imaginary line that goes horizontally across the middle of screen. The Y axis is an imaginary line that goes vertically down the center of the screen. The two-finger rotate gesture causes rotation around the Z axis. The Z axis is an imaginary line that goes right through the phone, extending directly out from the center of the screen and directly out from the back of the phone.

The three-dimensional rotation effects are performed by the `touchmove` event handler. The first thing this handler does is capture the current finger location. Remember that a `touchmove` event means that the user's finger has remained in contact with the screen. Here is how you record the position to which it has moved:

```
current.x = e.originalEvent.touches[0].pageX;
current.y = e.originalEvent.touches[0].pageY;
```

You want to perform the X and Y axis rotations only when the user has one finger on the screen. The event handler checks to make sure this is the case before proceeding. It also checks to make sure the touch event is not a swipe. You'll see how swipes are handled shortly.

The `touchmove` handler calculates the distance that the user's finger has moved by subtracting the starting position from the current position:

```
var dx = current.x - start.x;
var dy = current.y - start.y;
```

This then needs to be converted to an amount of rotation, in degrees. You need to use a bit of math here to make the conversion nice and smooth. You don't want the rotation to occur too quickly or too slowly. You also want the rotation to start slowly so the user can make small adjustments and then accelerate for large changes.

The trick to this math is to decide how far you have to move your finger to rotate a full 360 degrees. Actually, the user usually wants to rotate in only one direction at a time, so it's more useful to think in terms of 180 degrees. So how far should you move your finger to perform a 180-degree rotation? In this example, I opted for half the width of the iPhone screen, which is 160 pixels, stored in the `dr` variable.

NOTE *Mobile device web browsers allow you to specify pixel dimensions in your HTML and CSS. However these pixel values do not match the real physical device pixels! This is because the devices allow the user to scale web sites by zooming in and out with two fingers. The concept of a pixel on a mobile browser is thus not the same as on a desktop browser. When you set the* `initial-scale=1.0` *value using the* `viewport` *meta tag, the mobile browser gives you a screen width of 320 virtual pixels, even if you are using a phone that has a higher resolution display like the iPhone 4. Chapter 7 covers this in more detail.*

You need to use this same scale for vertical movement as well. Otherwise, the rotation will occur at different speeds around different axes. To convert from a finger-distance movement to a degree of rotation, you multiply 180 degrees by the *fraction* of 160 pixels that have been covered in the `touchmove` event. That's what this code does:

```
current.ydeg = current.ydeg + ( 180 * (dx / dr) );
current.xdeg = current.xdeg + ( 180 * (dy / dr) );
```

Just before you do this, though, you need to "damp" the motion. Damping adjusts the amount of motion so that it starts off slow and gets faster. Luckily, the *sin* function from math has exactly this property; it's a nice curve that starts slow and gets more curvy. The following lines of code adjust the finger distance to give you this effect:

```
dx = Math.abs(1 + Math.sin((dx/dr)-(Math.PI/2))) * dx;
dy = Math.abs(1 + Math.sin((dy/dr)-(Math.PI/2))) * dy;
```

This code multiplies the original distance by an adjusted fraction of itself. The distance comes in as a positive or negative number, meaning a movement left or right. The `Math.abs` function preserves the left or right nature of the movement. Without `Math.abs`, two negatives would make a positive, and you could never move left!

The distance starts from a value of 0, so you want values close to 0 to change slowly and values further away to change more rapidly. The `Math.sin` function does this for you, but you need to help it out a bit by moving the graph of the function so that the slow part starts at 0. This is why you add 1 to the *sin* function and subtract π/2 from its argument.

To apply the rotation, you can use the `-webkit-transform` property. Because you have three dimensions, you have three rotations. This is the syntax for the property value:

```
rotateX(30deg) rotateY(60deg) rotateZ(90deg)
```

The `rotate` utility function in the code example applies this property to the image. Because the `touchmove` event is fired in near real-time, the result of all this math is a nicely rotating image. Try it yourself now to understand how the motion works.

You still need to deal with rotation around the Z axis. You can use a gesture event to implement this, and you'll get zooming almost for free. The `gesturechange` event gives you an event object that has a `rotation` property. When the user places two fingers on the screen and rotates them around the center of the screen, this `rotation` property tells you how many degrees of rotation occurred. You can apply this to the image. In this case, damping is not necessary, as it is better if the image rotates at the same rate as your fingers move. This is because there is no translation from distance to degrees; you already have the degrees from the `rotation` property. The following code applies the rotation:

```
if( 2 < Math.abs(e.rotation) ) {
  current.zdeg = (start.zdeg + e.rotation) % 360;
  rotate();
}
```

This code ignores rotations of less than 2 degrees, which avoids spurious rotation when the user is just zooming. You offset the rotation reported by the event from the starting rotation (stored in the `start` object) recorded in the `touchstart` event handler.

Zooming is also performed in the `gesturechange` event handler. In this case, damping does give the user more control. The `gesturechange` event provides a `scale` property that tells how far the user's fingers have moved. Values under 1 indicate inward movement, and values above 1 indicate outward movement. To damp inward movement, you can use the `Math.sin` trick. To damp outward movement, you need to use a different mathematical function because sin works only with values between 0 and 1. A very simple solution is to use a parabolic curve: Just square the increase in scale (subtract 1 from the scale value to get this). This gives you the same sort of slow start effect as *sin* for values above 1. Here's how you implement it:

```
scale =
  scale <= 1
  ? Math.sin( scale * (Math.PI/2))
  : 1+( Math.pow(scale-1,2) );

img.width(  start.w * scale );
img.height( start.h * scale );
```

The swipe gesture is the last piece of the puzzle. A swipe left or right should cause the next image to the left or right to animate into view. You have to be careful here because the swipe gesture overlaps with X axis rotation. A swipe gesture is considered to be a fast horizontal movement over a long distance. You can use this definition to tell swipes and rotations apart: It's a swipe if it happens quickly (for example, under 500 milliseconds) and over at least half the screen. The `isSwipe` utility function puts this into practice:

```
function isSwipe(e) {
  var duration = new Date().getTime()-start.when;
  var xdist    = current.x - start.x;
  return duration < 500 && 160 < Math.abs( xdist );
}
```

The swipe action can be placed in the `touchend` event handler. If the touch motion is a swipe, you need to display the next image by animating it on to the screen. To determine if the touch motion is a swipe, you subtract the starting X position from the current X position. Movements to the right are positive, and movements to the left are negative. You can therefore tell whether to animate an image in from the left or right. To perform the animation, you first add the `rightout` or `leftout` CSS style to the current image, to get it to animate out of view. Then you remove the `rightout` or `leftout` style from the new image, which causes it to return to its normal position in the middle of the screen, effectively animating back into view. You do all this by using the `translate` value of the `-webkit-transform` CSS property. The `-webkit-transition` property is used to specify that the animation should take 1 second. After the animation is finished, the `-webkit-transition` property is cleared. Otherwise, it would interfere with the rotation and zooming animations by slowing them down.

EMBEDDING AN INTERACTIVE MAP

Providing your users with an interactive map is a common requirement when building mobile applications that make use of the user's current location. For example, a cab-hailing application can show you the location of nearby cabs, and a restaurant recommendation service can show you nearby restaurants. You don't have to build a mapping engine yourself, however. Google provides a JavaScript API that you can use, and this API has been tuned for use with mobile applications. The map that it provides supports interactive panning and multitouch pinch zooming. This section shows you how to get started.

 WARNING *The Google Maps API requires a license for certain types of commercial use. You'll need to review the terms of service on the Google Maps site* (`http://code.google.com/apis/maps`) *in the context of the type of app you are building.*

The Google Maps API

To use the Google Maps API, you need to include a script file from Google, and you need to write some JavaScript code to build the map and set its options. First, you create an empty HTML `div` tag with `id="mymap"` in your HTML document. Google will fill this `div` with the map contents. You should use CSS to set the width and height to your desired values:

```
<div id="mymap" style="width:300px;height:300px"></div>
```

Next, you set up a JavaScript object with your desired configuration. The most important property, which is also a required property, is the `center` property. This is the location of the center of the map when it first appears. The value of this property must be the special `google.maps.LatLng` object. You create this object by using latitude and longitude values. Here's a quick way to get these: Open `http://maps.google.com` and navigate to your desired location. Then paste the following code into your browser address bar:

```
javascript:void(prompt('',gApplication.getMap().getCenter()));
```

After you grab the values from the pop-up window, you can set up your map configuration:

```
var options = {
  zoom: 15,
  center: google.maps.LatLng(39.768376,-86.158042),
  };
```

The zoom property is an integer value between 1 and 18. The value 1 is the maximum zoom-out, and 18 is the maximum zoom-in.

You can display the map using one line of code:

```
new google.maps.Map(document.getElementById("mymap"), options);
```

Obviously, there's a lot more to the Google Maps API than is shown here. For all the details, you should visit http://code.google.com/apis/maps/documentation/javascript/. The following example shows you how to build a simple "find me" app.

> **NOTE** *The Google Maps API requires a connection to the Internet to function. Your app needs to retrieve the script file from Google, and it needs to access Google's servers to load the map image tiles.*

TRY IT OUT A Map That Can Pan and Zoom

This example is a complete, fully working map application that finds your current location and shows you the latitude and longitude of the center of the map, which is indicated by an overlaid marker. Because this example relies on the Google Maps API, you must have an active Internet connection to run it. Follow these steps:

1. Create a new file called map.html, which will contain all the code. Save this file in your nginx html folder, as described in Chapter 1.

2. Create a marker image that will be positioned over the center of the map. You can either copy the point.png file provided in the downloadable code for this chapter or create your own by using a graphics application. If you are creating your own image, remember to create a semi-transparent shadow around the marker image so that it stands out from the map surface. The marker image should be about 40 pixels high and about 55 pixels wide.

3. Insert the following code into map.html:

Available for
download on
Wrox.com

```
<html>
<head>
<meta name="viewport"
      content="initial-scale=1.0, user-scalable=no">

<style>
* { margin:0px; padding:0px; }
</style>

<script
  src="http://maps.google.com/maps/api/js?sensor=true"></script>

<script>
  var map;
```

```
function onload() {
  var locdiv = document.getElementById('loc');
  var mapdiv = document.getElementById('map')

  // center on Indianapolis, IN
  var latlng = new google.maps.LatLng(39.768376,-86.158042);
  var options = {
    zoom: 15,
    center: latlng,
    mapTypeId: google.maps.MapTypeId.ROADMAP,
    disableDefaultUI:true
  };

  map = new google.maps.Map(mapdiv, options);
  locdiv.innerHTML = map.getCenter();

  google.maps.event.addListener(map, 'center_changed',
    function() {
      locdiv.innerHTML = map.getCenter();
    });
}

function findme() {
  navigator.geolocation.getCurrentPosition(function(position) {
    var loc = new google.maps.LatLng(
      position.coords.latitude,
      position.coords.longitude );
    map.setCenter(loc);
  });
}

findme();
</script>
</head>
<body onload="onload()">
  <div id="map" style="width:320px; height:300px"></div>
  <img src="point.png"
      style="position:absolute;top:96px;left:140px">
  <input type="button" onclick="findme()" value="Find Me">
  <div id="loc"></div>
</body>
</html>
```

Code snippet map.html

4. Open the map.html file in Safari. You should see a small map with the marker image placed in the center. You should be able to pan and zoom the map, using your mouse or touchpad. The marker does not move and always remains at the center of the map.

5. Make sure the nginx web server is running and open the map.html file on your iPhone or Android device, using the mobile browser. The URL to open the file is http://YOUR_IP_

`ADDRESS/map.html`. Refer to Chapter 1 if you need help. The map should occupy most of the screen, as in Figure 4-2. Try panning and zooming, using your fingers. Tap the Find Me button to cause the map to display your current location.

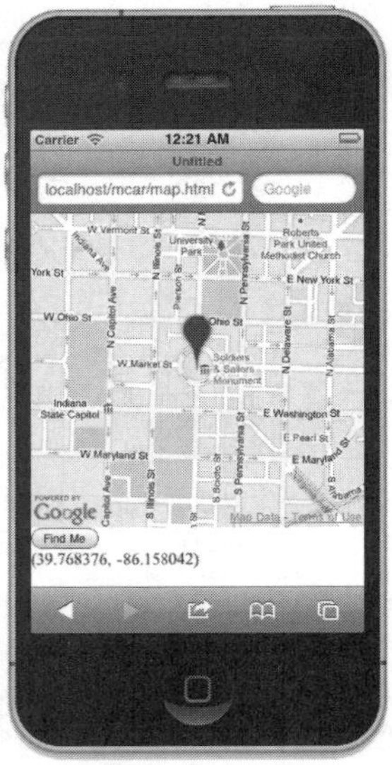

How It Works

This mobile web app relies on the Google Maps API for almost all of its functionality. The app prevents web page zooming by using a viewport meta-tag because the zoom action should only apply to the map:

```
<meta name="viewport"
      content="initial-scale=1.0, user-scalable=no">
```

To make use of the Google Maps API, you also need to include the required JavaScript file from Google. This is done with a HTML `script` tag in the `head` element. One very important thing to remember here is that you have to include the `sensor=true` parameter:

```
<script
   src="http://maps.google.com/maps/api/js?sensor=true"></script>
```

FIGURE 4-2

The API requires this, and it lets Google know that the user's device has a GPS sensor.

The HTML content of the app itself is quite sparse. There is a `div` to hold the map. Google will fill this `div` for you. There is also a `div` to hold the latitude and longitude values, so that the user can see them updating in real time. Finally, a Find Me button lets the user find his or her current location on the map, using the Geolocation API, which is covered in Chapter 3.

To mark the current location visually, a marker image is placed in an absolute position over the center of the map. An external marker is used to achieve the desired interface effect. Internal markers, provided by Google, would scroll with the map. Everything else is done using JavaScript.

To keep things simple, this example uses the standard Document Object Model (DOM) API and does not rely on libraries such as jQuery. First, you grab the map `div` and the location text `div` by using `getElementById`. Then you are ready to set up the Google map. The Google Maps API requires a fixed starting point. To provide this, you create a `LatLng` object, like so:

```
var latlng = new google.maps.LatLng(39.768376,-86.158042);
```

You need to choose the appropriate starting point based on your own app requirements. You can use `http://maps.google.com` to find the latitude and longitude values of any location.

With a starting point chosen, you can define the options for the map. In the sample code, this is done using the JavaScript Object Notation (JSON) syntax to create an `options` object with a set of map options. Your starting center point goes in here as the `center` property. You can also set the zoom level, the type of map, and the types of user interface control elements available to the user. The options in the sample code display a map with no additional controls, zoomed in to street map level. For a full list of options, and to keep up with new options available in future versions of the API, you should refer to the Google documentation at `http://code.google` `.com/apis/maps/documentation/javascript`.

Creating the map requires just a single line of code:

```
map = new google.maps.Map(mapdiv, options);
```

This line of code dynamically fills your map `div` with image tiles that build up the map view. It also adds touch event handlers that provide the panning and zooming functionality of the map.

To display the current location under the central marker image in real time as the user moves around the map, you can use one of the custom events that the Google Maps API provides. You listen for the `center_changed` event, get the new center location using the `map.getCenter` function, and insert the new location into the location `div` as text.

To implement the Find Me button, you use the HTML5 Geolocation API. Review the discussion of this API in Chapter 3 if you need some reminders of how it works. When you have the current location of the device, you set the center of the map by passing a `LatLng` object to the `map.setCenter` function.

PROVIDING AN APPLICATION ICON AND A STARTUP SCREEN

When the user installs a mobile web app from the browser by saving a bookmark icon to the home screen of his or her device, the default behavior, depending on the device, is to create the home screen icon from a screenshot of the app or to use a built-in bookmark icon. Neither approach is particularly satisfactory, especially if you would like your mobile web app to be as native as possible. There are, however, some `link` tags that you can use in your HTML `head` section to define your own home screen app icon. For newer devices, you can also specify a startup splash screen image.

The version of the To-Do List app provided in the downloadable code for this chapter includes the code for app icons. To use your own app icon, you first create a suitable image. For example, you can create a square `.png` image with a size of 57x57 pixels. The To-Do List app uses an image called `todo-icon.png`. Bear in mind that the device display will crop rounded borders off your icon and apply a shiny appearance. You add the following link tags to your HTML `head` element. The second line is needed to get the app icon to work on older Android devices:

```
<link rel="apple-touch-icon" href="todo-icon.png"/>
<link rel="apple-touch-icon-precomposed" href="todo-icon.png"/>
```

If you install the updated To-Do List application in this chapter, you should see the custom icon.

The iPhone also allows you to provide a startup splash screen. Android doesn't support this at present, but it might in future versions. Apple recommends, as part of its Human Interface Guidelines, that the splash screen be an "empty" version of the main app interface. This means the user first sees an almost empty page, with just the main navigation items for the app. This improves the user experience because it makes the app feel like it is launching faster. A traditional splash screen implicitly communicates a "Please wait…loading" message to the user, whereas the empty main screen approach gives the feeling of an instantaneous launch. To specify a splash screen, use the following link tag:

```
<link rel="apple-touch-startup-image" href="todo-startup.png" />
```

The downloadable To-Do List application for this chapter also provides an example of this approach. Figure 4-3 shows the application icon on the left and the loading screen on the right.

FIGURE 4-3

SUMMARY

This chapter covers some of the ways in which you can enhance your mobile web app to make it feel more native. By caching your app, you can allow it to work offline. Handling touches and gestures properly gives your app a very native feel. Adding an interactive map provides a high-value feature, and providing a proper app icon makes your user's experience far more native. All these techniques are useful for mobile web apps. And as you will see in Chapter 9, you can also use these techniques to enhance hybrid apps where you package up your web app into a native container.

In the next chapter, you'll learn how to build the other half of your application — the part that lives in the cloud. Most mobile apps, even games, need to talk to the outside world, and you'll learn how to use JavaScript on the server side to enable this.

EXERCISES

1. Add an online/offline indicator to the cached To-Do List application. You can use the `navigator .onLine` property to detect whether you are connected to the Internet. The `body` element has `online` and `offline` event handlers that fire when your device changes connectivity. Visit `http://www.w3.org/TR/html5/offline.html` to read the specification.

2. The sample code of the image viewer application you created in this chapter always resets the rotation of the image. Modify this app so that it remembers the previous orientation of an image. Hint: You need to change the definition of what a swipe is to prevent spurious rotation when swiping.

3. Add a new Mark button to the map example. When the user taps this button, the map should place a bouncing marker on the center of the map. The marker should remain on the same spot on the map as the user pans around the map. If the user taps the marker, it is removed. The Google Maps API documentation is a good place to start: `http://code.google.com/apis/maps/documentation/javascript`.

Answers to the Exercises can be found in the Appendix.

▶ WHAT YOU LEARNED IN THIS CHAPTER

TOPIC	KEY CONCEPTS
HTML5 Web App Caching	The HTML5 standard defines a web app caching feature that allows you to store your entire mobile web app on the user's mobile device. This means that when they start your app, it loads immediately without waiting for a web server to deliver the files and images in the app. It also means that your app can function without a network connection. The caching mechanism is controlled by a manifest file that lists all of the assets to cache.
Touch and Gesture events	Browser events that fire when the user touches the device screen and that you can capture with JavaScript event handlers. These events can be triggered by one or more simultaneous finger touches. The mobile Webkit browser provides you with custom touch and gesture events, although support is not uniform.
Google Maps API	A cloud services API provided by Google that lets you directly embed an interactive map inside your web application. Google has optimized this API to support mobile browsers, and the user experience is very fast and smooth. The Google Maps API provides many features and can be customized extensively. Care is needed if you are building a commercial application, as certain terms and conditions have to be met.
App icon and startup screen	You can define an icon which that represents your application on the device home screen, using special tags in your HTML. You can also provide a full-screen image that is shown before your app is ready to run.

5

Building Apps in the Cloud

WHAT YOU WILL LEARN IN THIS CHAPTER:

➤ Understanding event-based servers

➤ Installing the Node JavaScript server

➤ Learning the Node APIs

➤ Using the Node package manager

➤ Understanding document databases

➤ Installing the MongoDB database

➤ Developing efficient storage algorithms

➤ Designing a multi-process architecture

➤ Connecting nginx, Node, and MongoDB end-to-end

➤ Displaying real-time usage charts

In this chapter, you will connect your app to the cloud. You'll learn how to develop cloud-based applications using JavaScript and the JSON data format. You'll learn how to use the MongoDB database, which is perfect for cloud applications. And you'll learn how to reduce your data storage and keep your costs down.

MongoDB is one of the new generation of non-relational databases. These databases, sometimes referred to as noSQL databases, do not use the traditional SQL database language, do not provide transactions, and do not have standard table-based data models. Instead, a database like MongoDB is designed for building cloud services. MongoDB accepts very large numbers of read *and* write operations and supports JSON as its standard data format for input and output. This makes MongoDB one of the best choices when you are building mobile web apps in the cloud using JavaScript.

After you launch a mobile web app, you want to measure how people are using it. Web analytics solutions such as Google Analytics are much less helpful for mobile web apps than for traditional web apps. A mobile web app is usually just one highly dynamic and interactive page. You need to know how users are interacting with your application. This means you need to collect usage data, store it somewhere, analyze it, and display it. This is a perfect use case for cloud computing. In this chapter, you'll design, develop, and deploy a real-time analytics engine for your app.

The examples in this chapter are designed to run on an Amazon server. However, you will need to develop them locally first and then deploy them by copying the source code files to an Amazon server. When developing locally, you use the hostname `localhost` to access the examples from a web browser. When you deploy them to an Amazon server, you need to use the hostname of that server.

This chapter builds on the work in Chapter 2, where you set up an Amazon server instance. You can continue to use that instance here.

SERVER-SIDE JAVASCRIPT

To build the cloud applications in this book, you use server-side JavaScript. You write JavaScript code that runs on cloud servers, not on web browsers. This is a very powerful development strategy. JavaScript is emerging as a credible language for server-side development.

You may be forgiven for thinking that JavaScript is a strange choice for server-side development. Until recently, JavaScript wouldn't have been a good choice for server-side development. But in the past few years, production-quality toolkits and application platforms have become available that make it possible. If your only experience with JavaScript has been to use it as a simple language for HTML manipulation, it's time to embrace the hidden power in a language that many know but few know well. As a dynamic server-side language, JavaScript can compete admirably with Ruby, Python, Perl, and PHP.

The thing you will most appreciate when you start to build server-side applications in JavaScript is that all your code can be in the same language. This has huge productivity benefits. There is no need for a mental context switch when you start work on server-side code. You'll find that you can really crank out the code using the approach in this book.

Introducing Node

In this chapter, you will use the Node JavaScript application platform. The home page for Node is http://nodejs.org. There are other JavaScript platforms, but Node is one of the best. It is built using the Google V8 JavaScript engine, which the Google Chrome web browser uses. Google created the V8 engine from scratch so that online Google applications such as Gmail and Google Docs would be very fast when executed inside Google's Chrome browser.

The V8 engine is very fast for three reasons:

➤ Google V8 dynamically compiles your most frequently executed blocks of JavaScript into machine code instructions. This is the same way that Java's just-in-time compiler works. Google V8 JavaScript is not an "interpreted" language at all.

➤ Google wrote a generational garbage collector for V8. Garbage collection is a powerful programming language feature that prevents you from having to worry about removing old objects from memory. The problem with simple implementations of garbage collection is that they cause random delays in a program while the garbage collector looks for old objects. Google solves this problem by sorting objects into categories depending on how old the objects are. These categories are known as *generations*. As a result, your codes runs smoothly and predictably.

➤ V8 has hidden classes. This is a neat trick from the Google guys. JavaScript is object oriented, but it does not have classes; it has only objects. This is one of the things that sets it apart from other languages. Classes are very helpful for optimizing code, so Google V8 creates hidden classes, based on its analysis of your code. These hidden classes are used to avoid dynamic property lookups, which are relatively slow.

But here's the big reason for using Node: It does not use threads. It uses events. The Node engine is a state machine that reacts to bytes coming in from the network. Every time a new chunk of data arrives, Node fires an event. You work with Node by writing JavaScript functions that wait for events. This is exactly the same way that you write code for web browsers, where you wait for user events such as mouse clicks and finger gestures.

Traditional application servers create a new thread for each incoming client connection, or they share a pool of threads. This limits their maximum level of performance. Memory is needed to manage each thread, and processor time is needed to switch between threads. You also have to worry about all the horrible bugs that threads cause: deadlocks, race conditions, side effects, and inconsistent shared data. Node avoids all this. There is only one thread, and everything happens consecutively. You always know that the code you are looking at is the only code executing. This makes debugging and development much easier.

You might be wondering how Node handles multiple concurrent clients without threads. Let's look at an example in which a standard database-driven web page displays some product details:

1. The web browser sends an HTTP GET request for the page. The entire request, including headers, is 500 bytes long.

2. Node first receives 250 bytes, and the rest are delayed on the network. Node stores them in a temporary buffer and goes back to waiting for clients.

3. Several other web browsers make concurrent requests, with their data also arriving in pieces. Node buffers the requests. This is the same work that a threaded server would do, but without the threading overhead.

4. The second half of the request arrives — another 250 bytes. Node calls your event handler function with the full request. This is first event handler you have to write.

5. Your event handler function processes the request and parses a product identifier, and you make a database request to load the product details.

6. Node sends the request to the database and goes back to handling incoming clients. Node does *not* wait for the database to respond! This is how Node can handle multiple concurrent requests.

7. Some time later, the database sends back the product details. These arrive as incoming bytes and are handled in the same way as incoming bytes from web browsers. When all the data has been transferred, Node calls your database event handler. This is the second event handler you have to write.

8. You format the database results and send HTML back to the browser. Node has kept the HTTP connection to the browser open, even though there has been no data flowing. Node now sends your HTML back to the browser. All done!

Installing Node

You need to install Node on your Amazon instance. You can obtain the latest version from the Node home page, at `http://nodejs.org`. Node is still a young system, and its APIs are still subject to some change. In this book, I use version 0.4, but you should use the latest stable version to ensure that you have all the most recent bug fixes and performance improvements.

To get the latest version of Node running, you need to install it the old-fashioned way, by downloading and compiling the source code. These instructions should work on your local machine if you are using a Mac or Linux. On Windows, you will need to use the Cygwin environment to build and run Node. Refer to Chapter 2 for a reminder about how to run command line programs on the various operating systems.

1. Connect to your instance, using SSH as described in Chapter 2. You should see the standard shell prompt.

2. Use the `wget` command to download the Node distribution. Replace the X with the latest version shown on `http://nodejs.org`.

```
$ wget http://nodejs.org/dist/node-v0.4.X.tar.gz
```

3. Extract the Node archive:

```
$ tar -xzf node-v0.4.X.tar.gz
```

4. Go to the Node source folder and run the compilation commands:

```
$ cd node-v0.4.X
$ ./configure
$ make
$ make install
```

The `make` command takes about 10 minutes to complete. Go grab a coffee.

5. Check that Node installed correctly by using the following command to find the version number:

```
$ node -v
v0.4.X
```

These instructions will also work on the Amazon instance that you set up in Chapter 2, as that is an Ubuntu Linux machine. As your Amazon instance runs nginx as a web server, you will need to proxy HTTP requests through to Node, and you'll learn how to do that later in this chapter.

NOTE *You may encounter problems compiling Node. This can happen when the system you are using does not provide the Node build process with everything it needs. When this happens, copy and paste the exact text of the error message into Google. You may be able to find that other people have had the same problem, and someone else has provided a solution. If your search is not useful, try posting a question at* http://stackoverflow.com. *If you are really stuck, installing an earlier version of Node is often a good stopgap until someone answers your question.*

TRY IT OUT | Hello Node!

You need to get your "Hello World's" out of the way before going any further. Try out these short Node scripts to get a feel for how Node works:

1. Go to your /tmp folder. Create a file called helloworld.js and insert the following code into it:

Available for download on Wrox.com

```
console.log("Hello World!");
```

Code snippet helloworld.js

2. Run the following command:

```
node helloworld.js
Hello World!
```

3. Create a file called helloserver.js and insert the following code into it:

Available for download on Wrox.com

```
// import standard modules
var http = require('http');
var util = require('util');

var server = http.createServer(
  function(request, response){

    // print a debug message to standard output
    util.debug(request.method+' request, '+new Date());

    // send headers to HTTP client
    response.writeHead(
      200,
      { 'Content-Type': 'text/plain' }
    );

    // send final content to HTTP client
    response.end('Hi! Your request URL was: '+request.url);
  }
);

// start up the server!
server.listen(3000, "127.0.0.1");
util.debug('Server running at http://127.0.0.1:3000');
```

Code snippet helloserver.js

4. To run the script on your local development machine, use the following command:

```
node helloserver.js
```

DEBUG: Server running at http://127.0.0.1:3000

5. Open Safari and visit `http://localhost:3000/foo`. Safari displays this message:

```
Hi! Your request URL was: /foo
```

6. Go back to your shell terminal. The following log message has appeared:

DEBUG: Server running at http://127.0.0.1:3000
DEBUG: GET request, Sat Jan 08 2011 20:04:15 GMT+0000 (GMT)

How It Works

Node is a scripting language very much in the tradition of UNIX scripting languages. You run the `node` executable with the filename of your script as the first argument:

```
node myscript.js
```

However, unlike Ruby and similar products, Node brings along the JavaScript browser APIs. In the Hello World example, you used `console.log` to print some text. Familiar objects such as `Date`, `Array`, and `Math` are all available. The one thing you don't find out of the box is the `document` object; there is no browser on the server side!

Node is primarily used to build high-performance event-driven servers. The sample code shows you one. As with any other language, you need to bring in some external components to get stuff done. In Node, these are called *modules*, and you use the built-in `require` function to load them. The convention is to declare a variable with the same name as the module:

```
var util = require('util')
```

Node would not be much of a web server if it did not provide an HTTP module, and that's exactly what you get with `require('http')`. This module provides `Request` and `Response` objects that you can use to respond to HTTP client requests.

To write a web server, you provide the `http` module with a single JavaScript handler function. The `http` module calls your handler function each time an HTTP client request comes in. Node waits until all the HTTP headers have arrived, and then it calls your handler function. Remember that whenever anything happens, Node calls handler functions that you provide.

Your handler function should accept two arguments: the `Request` object and the `Response` object. Here is the basic code:

```
var server = http.createServer(

  // this is your handler function
  function(request, response){
    // do your stuff
  }
);
```

This form of code is very common for Node applications. Your handler function is a callback function. Any time you ask Node to perform an operation that will take some time (such as waiting for bytes from the network, or a file to load, or a database query to complete), you write a callback function to receive the results of the operation.

To create a debug log so that you can see what your server is doing, you load the `util` module using the `require` function. You can then use the `util.debug` function. In the sample code, you log the HTTP verb (for example, GET, POST) and the date and time of the request:

```
util.debug(request.method+' request, '+new Date());
```

Why don't you use `console.log`? Well, `console.log` works in the normal way for Node operations. You're asking Node to print some text, and Node will send the text to your command line terminal for printing. Node won't wait for the text to actually print, though; it'll just get right back to handling events. This is normally exactly what you want for high performance, but it's not what you want for debugging. You need debugging statements to print exactly at the point when they are called. The `util.debug` function is provided for this purpose. Node will block all code execution until your debugging text is printed. Just don't deploy that debug statement to production.

To send some data back to the web browser, you call functions on the `Response` object. The `writeHead` function lets you send back the HTTP status code and headers. In the example, you send a 200 status code to indicate that everything is okay, and you use a `text/plain` content-type header to let the browser know that you'll be sending plain text instead of HTML.

> **NOTE** *Node assumes that you know your way around HTTP. If you don't, or if you know only the basics, it's worth taking some time to learn the details. This is highly transferable and long-term knowledge; HTTP will around for a long time. Start here:* http://net.tutsplus.com/tutorials/other/ a-beginners-introduction-to-http-and-rest.

This example uses the `Response.end` function to send the entire response back to the web browser in one go. You can also send the response back in smaller pieces using the `Response.write` function. The `Response.write` function is more appropriate when you can generate partial results that are immediately useful. For example, if you have a database query that returns a large number of results, you can send them back a few at a time as they come in from the database, calling `Response.end` when you are finished to close the connection. Chapter 8 will walk you through this approach.

Finally, to kick-start your server, you call the `listen` method on the `server` object. Printing a debug message to indicate that things are running properly is also a good idea at this point.

Using the Node Package Manager

Node comes with quite a few built-in modules, such as the `http` and `util` modules you've already seen. It has modules for binary data, streaming data, process management, and more. Check out http://nodejs.org/docs/v0.4.X/api (remember to replace the X with the latest version number).

In addition to the built-in modules, you also need third-party modules to get real work done. You need modules to connect to your database, to organize complete server applications, and to interface with external web services. If you need to find a module to do something, the best place to look is the third-party module list page on Github: `https://github.com/joyent/node/wiki/modules`.

So how do you install modules? You can download each module manually and require the module directly. Or you can use the `npm` package manager. This Node tool is similar to `apt-get` for Ubuntu. It saves you the trouble of configuring and building modules by hand. The npm home page is `http://npmjs.org`.

In the next sections, you'll install modules, but at this point you need to install `npm`. On a test server, follow these steps:

1. Become root:

```
sudo -s
```

2. Run the following command:

```
curl http://npmjs.org/install.sh | sh
```

You should see multiple lines of output, indicating that `npm` is downloading and installing itself.

3. Run `npm` to confirm the installation. The version number will be displayed:

```
npm -v
1.X.Y-Z
```

4. Install the `connect` module, which provides a framework for web applications:

```
npm install connect
```

`npm` will display some output lines describing the installation.

5. Install the `mongodb` module, which provides a driver module for the MongoDB database that you'll use later in this chapter:

```
npm install mongodb
```

TRY IT OUT Using the connect Module

In the world of Node modules, `connect` is the Big Fish. It is a self-described "middleware" module, but don't let the enterprise-speak put you off. Node without `connect` is not a happy Node. You use `connect` to organize, control, and manage the pieces of your web application. Here's how:

1. Go to your `/tmp` folder. Create a file called `connectserver.js` and insert the following code into it:

Available for download on Wrox.com

```
var connect = require('connect');
var util    = require('util');

function sendjson(res,obj){
    res.writeHead(200,{
      'Content-Type': 'application/json',
    });
```

```
      var objstr = JSON.stringify(obj);
      util.debug('SENDJSON:'+objstr);
      res.end( objstr );
    }


    var server = connect.createServer(
      connect.router(function(app){

        app.get('/foo',function(req,res){
          sendjson(res,{path:'foo'});
        })

        app.get('/bar',function(req,res){
          sendjson(res,{path:'bar'});
        })
      })
    );


    server.listen(3000);
    util.debug('Server running at http://127.0.0.1:3000');
```

Code snippet connectserver.js

2. Run the server:

```
$ node connectserver.js
DEBUG: Server running at http://127.0.0.1:3000
```

3. Open Safari and visit `http://localhost:3000/foo`. Safari displays this message:

```
{"path":"foo"}
```

4. Go back to your shell terminal. A log message appears:

```
DEBUG: Server running at http://127.0.0.1:3000
DEBUG: SENDJSON:{"path":"foo"}
```

5. Visit `http://localhost:3000/bar`. A new log message appears:

```
DEBUG: SENDJSON:{"path":"bar"}
```

6. Visit `http://localhost:3000/woz`. There is no log message, and Safari displays the following:

```
Cannot GET /woz
```

How It Works

The `connect` module allows you to take a layered approach to your Node application development. You specify a series of layers that the HTTP client requests pass through. These layers can provide logging, authentication, caching, or whatever you like. The connect module provides a way to organize these middleware layers and make them reusable. Take a look at the connect home page to see the full list of built-in middleware layers: http://senchalabs.github.com/connect.

In the example, the only layer you are using is the router layer. Nonetheless, this is a very powerful component. It allows you to direct request processing to different parts of your application, based on the HTTP request method and URL. If you compare the connect code with the earlier plain HTTP server code, you can see that the code has a similar structure.

In true Node fashion, you use the router layer by providing a callback function. Your callback function has a single argument — an application object that lets you define request processing routes. You use the get and post methods of this application object to specify handlers for GET and POST requests, respectively. The first argument to these functions is the URL path prefix to match. Any HTTP request that starts with the specified URL prefix matches. The second argument is a callback to handle the requests. This request callback has the same form as the request callback for the plain server — two arguments, a Request object and a Response object. You should be noticing a familiar pattern with Node by now: It is simply a series of callbacks.

In the example, you define two URL endpoints, /foo and /bar, that respond with different JSON results. The example also shows what happens when you try to load an undefined URL /woz. In this case, connect displays a generic error message.

The example defines a JSON API. The server responds with JSON-formatted data. You used the sendjson function to handle the response. This function takes a Response object and a general JavaScript object. The JavaScript object is converted to a JSON-formatted string, which is then sent back to the client.

> **NOTE** When you are sending JSON back to the browser, remember that the only correct value of the Content-Type header for JSON data sent over HTTP is application/json. This is defined by the Internet standard RFC 4627, at http://www.ietf.org/rfc/rfc4627.txt.

Introducing the MongoDB Database

In order to build real applications, you need to store your data somewhere. Node has modules for traditional databases such as MySQL, but in this chapter you'll learn how to use MongoDB. MongoDB is a new type of database that speaks JSON natively, which makes it a perfect fit for Node. The MongoDB home page is http://mongodb.org.

So what makes MongoDB different from traditional databases? Instead of defining tables and columns in advance, you can use MongoDB to store new data entities on demand. MongoDB is a schema-less database. This means that you don't define a data schema (that is, tables and columns). You send JSON documents to MongoDB, and MongoDB stores them for you. You can then perform searches on the properties of these JSON documents. This is really convenient when you're coding in server-side JavaScript.

Of course, there has to be some sort of organization in MongoDB. MongoDB has the traditional concept of a named database, just like MySQL. You need to specify the name of the database when you connect to MongoDB. Inside the database, instead of tables, you have collections. Collections are just that — collections of JSON documents. There is no requirement that the JSON documents in a given collection have the same format, although they usually do. You can think of the top-level properties of the documents as being like traditional database table column names.

The schema-less nature of this design gives you a huge productivity boost. Schema changes are a non-issue. In the early days of your application, this is very valuable because you are still refining your data models, and you will need to modify them frequently as requirements become clear.

When you use a schema-less database like MongoDB, you are not constrained by a lot of traditional relational database ideas. For example, you can't perform join operations on collections. This seems crazy at first, but in practice, it is not a problem. Remember that you can embed documents inside documents. Whereas in a traditional database you might have a `ShoppingCart` table and a `CartItem` table, with MongoDB you store an array of cart items inside each shopping cart object. The diagram in Figure 5-1 shows this difference.

Traditional Database Schema

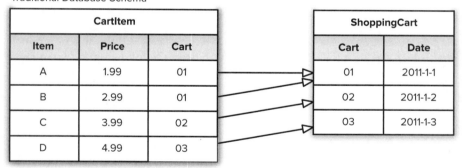

MongoDB Objects

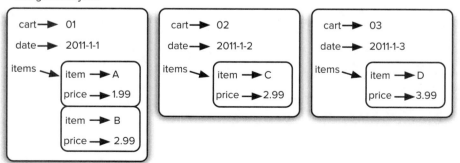

FIGURE 5-1

TRY IT OUT Using MongoDB

When you installed the npm package manager for Node, you also installed the mongodb module, so you should be all set up for this example. To use the mongodb module, you'll need to install the MongoDB database server. In this example, you'll see how to use the mongodb driver API to connect to the database from Node. Follow these steps:

1. On Linux, or your Amazon instance, use apt-get to download and install the latest version of MongoDB. On Mac and Windows, follow the download and install instructions on the MongoDB site.

```
apt-get install mongodb
```

2. To test that MongoDB is installed and running, run the following command. Your version numbers will probably be different.

```
mongod --version
db version v1.4.4, pdfile version 4.5
```

3. Connect to MongoDB by using the mongo command, which opens a command line database environment, and list the current set of databases by using the show dbs command:

```
mongo
Mongo shell version: 1.4.4
> show dbs
admin
local
```

4. Go to your /tmp folder. Create a file called mongo.js and insert the following code into it:

**Available for
download on
Wrox.com**

```
var util    = require('util');
var mongodb = require('mongodb');

var name   = "test";
var server = "localhost";
var port   = mongodb.Connection.DEFAULT_PORT;

var db =
  new mongodb.Db(
    name,
    new mongodb.Server(server, port, {}),
    {native_parser:true,auto_reconnect:true}
  );
util.debug('mongo:name='+name+',server='+server+',port='+port);

function res(win) {
  return function(err,result){
    if( err ) {
      util.debug('mongo:err='+err);
      db.close();
    }
    else {
      win(result);
    }
  }
}
```

```
db.open(res(function(){
  util.debug('mongo:ok');

  db.collection('fruit',res(function(fruit){
    util.debug('mongo:fruit:ok');

    fruit.insert(
      {name:'apple',price:0.99},
      res(function(apple){
        util.debug('mongo:insert:'+
                   JSON.stringify(apple));

        fruit.update(
          {name:'apple'},
          {$set:{price:1.99}},
          res(function(){
            util.debug('mongo:update');

            fruit.find(
              {name:'apple'},
              res(function(cursor){
                util.debug('mongo:cursor');

                cursor.each(
                  res(function(item){
                    if( item ) {
                      util.debug('mongo:item:'+
                                 JSON.stringify(item));
                    }
                    else {
                      db.close();
                    }
                  })
                )
              })
            )
          })
        )
      })
    )
  }))
}));
```

Code snippet mongo.js

5. Run the client script:

```
$ node mongo.js
DEBUG: mongo:name=test,server=localhost,port=27017
DEBUG: mongo:ok
DEBUG: mongo:fruit:ok
DEBUG: mongo:insert:[{"name":"apple","price":0.99,"_id":{"id":"..."}}]
DEBUG: mongo:update
DEBUG: mongo:cursor
DEBUG: mongo:item:{"name":"apple","price":1.99,"_id":{"id":"..."}}
```

6. Open the `mongo` shell and take a look at the contents of the `fruit` collection in the `test` database.

```
mongo
Mongo shell version: 1.4.4
> use test
switched to db test
> db.fruit.find()
{ "name" : "apple", "price" : 1.99, "_id" : ObjectId("...") }
```

How It Works

The MongoDB driver API provides a good example of the callback pattern that Node uses. Each callback represents a point at which Node has to wait on the database to do some work. Node never waits, of course; instead, it goes off and handles other events. When the database finally returns some data, your event handler code is called.

This callback pattern leads to a lot of code indentation, which can be uncomfortable at first. You can write helper functions to reduce the amount of indentation, and you can see an example of this in the `mongo.js` script. The `res` helper function deals with any errors that come back from the database and helps keep your code clean. You can be more aggressive about reducing indentation by using modules designed for this purpose (see `https://github.com/joyent/node/wiki/modules#async-flow`), but really, you're fighting the language. My advice: Learn to love the indent.

The `mongo.js` script opens a connection to MongoDB, uses a database called `test`, inserts an object into a collection called `fruit`, updates the object, and reloads it from the database. You don't need to predefine either the `test` database or the `fruit` collection; they are created dynamically on demand.

First, you need to configure your connection. You create a new `Db` object (provided by the `mongodb` module) and pass the name of your database and the hostname and port of the MongoDB database server. You don't need a username or password in the default configuration. MongoDB does support stricter access controls if you need them. You can find all the details on `http://mongodb.org`.

Next, you define the `res` helper function for handling database errors. To understand this function, you need to know how `mongodb` module callbacks work. After any operation, the `mongodb` module calls your result handler callback function and passes two arguments. The first is an error object that is `null` if there is no error. The second argument is the `result` object, which is what you are actually after. The `res` helper function creates a suitable callback function for the `mongodb` module. This is possible because JavaScript allows you to create functions as you need them. This new on-demand callback function understands the two-argument convention and can log errors if they occur. If there are no errors, the on-demand callback function calls the `win` function that you provided to the `res` function, handing over the `result` object. The upshot of all this dynamic function creation is that your callbacks don't need to worry about errors; you just get the `result` object. The dynamically created function is shown highlighted below:

```
function res(win) {
  return function(err,result){
    if( err ) {
      util.debug('mongo:err='+err);
      db.close();
    }
```

```
     else {
       win(result);
     }
   }
 }
```

To begin working with some data, you open the `test` database:

```
db.open(res(function(){ ...
```

Then you open the `fruit` collection:

```
db.collection('fruit',res(function(fruit){
```

Notice that you use the `res` function to cleanly deal with errors. You'll use this pattern from now on. Next, you insert an object into the `fruit` collection, just as you'd insert a table row in SQL:

```
fruit.insert(
   {name:'apple',price:0.99},
   res(function(apple){ ...
```

The property names `name` and `price` are completely arbitrary, and you do not need to define them in advance. In addition, you must place each subsequent piece of code into the callback function body. If you do not do this, your code will execute before the database operation completes, leading to incorrect results. This is the reason for all that indentation.

You can verify that the data has been saved by using the MongoDB shell:

```
mongo test
connecting to: test
> db.fruit.find()
{ "name" : "apple", "price" : 0.99, "_id" : ObjectId("...") }
```

Using this code is just like opening the MySQL client and performing a SELECT to view the data in your tables. For MongoDB, you use JavaScript code in the MongoDB shell to perform your queries. `db.fruit.find()` is JavaScript code that accesses the `fruit` collection and performs a `find` operation on it. This returns all the entries in the collection. Notice that MongoDB has given each entry a special unique identifier property called `_id`. You get this for free with objects you store.

To update data, you use the `update` function of the collection:

```
fruit.update(
   {name:'apple'},
   {$set:{price:1.99}},
   res(function(){
```

The `update` function takes three arguments. The first is a query. Think of the query as a sample object. All objects in the database that match the query object are returned. In this case, any objects that have a `name` property with the value `'apple'` are returned. The second argument is a set of commands that change the stored data objects. You specify these commands by using special properties that start with the $ character. The $set command sets an object property. In this case, you are changing the price of apples by setting the `price` property to a new value. The third argument is, not surprisingly, your callback function.

The next thing to do is to reload the updated data to see if has really changed:

```
fruit.find(
  {name:'apple'},
  res(function(cursor){
```

The `find` function does this for you. The first argument is again a query, as with the `update` function. The callback function does not get the result directly. There could be more than one object that matches the query. What you get instead is a `cursor` object. You may have come across the same thing with SQL databases. The `cursor` object does not actually have the result data. It goes back to the database to get it if you ask for it. This ensures better performance with large result sets.

Next, you ask the `cursor` for the result data:

```
cursor.each(
  res(function(item){
    if( item ) {
      util.debug('mongo:item:'+
                 JSON.stringify(item));
    }
    else {
      db.close();
    }
  })
```

What's happening here? Well, the `each` function calls your callback for each item in the result set, passing in the current item. The code prints out the item in JSON format. What happens when there are no more items? In this case, the `item` parameter is `null`. So you check for that and finish your data processing. In the code in the example, your script is now finished, so you can close the database connection.

CLOUD ANALYTICS FOR YOUR TO-DO LIST APP

Now you can return to the ultimate goal of this chapter: building a cloud-based analytics solution for your mobile app. You have all the pieces you need. The To-Do List app on your mobile device will send HTTP requests to your Amazon instance. The `nginx` web server will handle the requests, serving static files and passing functional requests to Node for processing. Node will connect to MongoDB to store and retrieve the analytics data. Finally, you'll use an open source charting library to display real-time analytics.

Doing the Math

After you've launched your To-Do List app, you may want to pitch it to some venture capitalists and get funded! You're going to need some numbers to prove that you're onto something big. Counting the number of app installs is relatively easy: You just increment a single counter each time a new app contacts your Amazon instance. But you'd also like to be able to talk about more interesting metrics that prove people are actually *using* your app. How about the total number of to-do items? Lots of to-do items means lots of actual use of your app.

The easiest way to get these numbers is to make the app report on them each time it launches and whenever the to-do list changes. For each app, you keep a log of the reports. Then all you have to do is add up all the most recent reports for each app, and then you will know the total number of to-do items and how many are done. That's great. But you need to run some back-of-the-envelope numbers with this approach. You always have to do this with cloud systems. You have to be sure your system can scale and that operational costs won't bankrupt you.

Let's say you get 1 million users. Well done. On average, each user adds a to-do item once a day. That's 1 million new log records you must store — *each day*, for each metric. Over time, that's a lot of cloud storage. And you have to execute a heavy database query to sum up all those records to come up with the total. Also, a friend told you that a venture capitalist his brother knows will only talk to people who have "real-time" analytics. So it looks like the easy road is also the road to nowhere. You need to take a different approach.

What you want is the real-time counts. You don't want to store all those records, and you don't want any heavy database queries. What's the minimum amount of information you need?

Imagine that you already know the current total count of to-do items. Then a new app appears and tells you it has 5 to-do items. You add 5 to the count. There's no need to store a log entry; just add 5 to the count, and you're done. What happens if it's not a new app, but an existing app? Imagine that you know that the existing app previously had 3 to-do items. Now it has 5. That's 2 new items. So you add 2 to the count and throw away the log record.

The trick is to apply the *changes* to the count in real-time, as they come in. To work out what the change is for any app, you need to know how many items it had previously. To do this, you store the previous number of items reported for each app. That's 1 million records — 1 for each app — but it's not 1 million *a day*. It's only 1 entry for each app, ever.

What about the total to-do items of all apps? If you can store that on a second-by-second basis, you can say "real-time" to that venture capitalist with a straight face. Yes, there are 86,400 (60 × 60 × 24) seconds in each day, but you don't need to store a count for every one of them. You need to store an entry only when the count changes. It's a fair assumption that usage times of your app will not be evenly distributed. Some periods of the day will see heavy use (for example, during office hours), and other periods will have almost no use (for example, late at night). So on any given day, quite a sizable chunk of those 86,400 second slots will be empty. It's even better on weekends.

You can fire up Excel and check that this works. Here's what some test data looks like, in Figure 5-2:

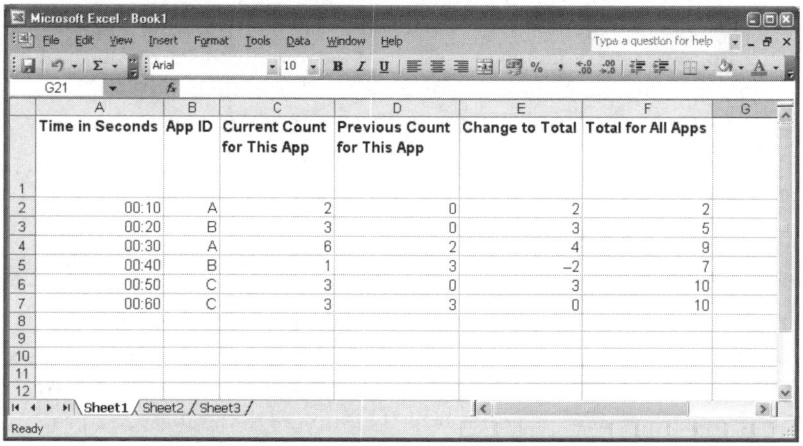

Time in Seconds	App ID	Current Count for This App	Previous Count for This App	Change to Total	Total for All Apps
00:10	A	2	0	2	2
00:20	B	3	0	3	5
00:30	A	6	2	4	9
00:40	B	1	3	−2	7
00:50	C	3	0	3	10
00:60	C	3	3	0	10

FIGURE 5-2

Given this data set, you need 3 entries for apps A, B, and C, to store the previous count of each. You also need to store only 6 entries for the total count over all apps over time. Let's say you want to display a nice chart for that venture capitalist. You plot a line chart, with the time along the bottom and the total for all apps as the value of the data points, as shown in Figure 5-3.

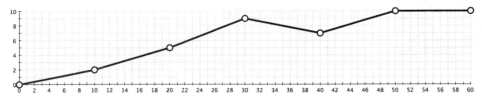

FIGURE 5-3

Feeling good? It's time for network reality to slap you in the face. Things are not as easy as all this. Apps out there in the wild will not report their to-do list counts in an orderly fashion. There will be network delays. Reports will arrive out of order. Besides, what is the "real" count? You'd like to know what the count was at the time the user entered the to-do item. By the time your Amazon instance gets the message, it's already out of date. So you need to get each app to send its local time along with the report. Then you can get the correct real-time count.

Or can you? Look at the figure again. Imagine that those reports all come in randomly after 00:60. Sure, you can still add up all the changes and get the correct result (10) at time point 00:60. But what about all the previous time points? You'll end up with incorrect intermediate totals because you'll be applying the changes out of order.

The solution? Don't store the total. *Instead, store the changes.* To do this, you store the Change to Total column. When you need to chart the data, you just apply the changes in order to get back to the total for each time point. And it doesn't matter what order the messages appear in, because you also store each change at the local time reported by the app. Your data is thus always as historically accurate as possible and completely real-time. Looks like you may get funding from that venture capitalist!

Organizing Your System

Before you start building a cloud-based Node application to handle your app usage data, you need to think about the design of your system. Collecting the usage data and charting that data are separate things. They should go in separate Node processes. That way, you can scale your app by running these processes on separate Amazon instances. For now, you'll run them both on the same server. You'll use the nginx web server to proxy HTTP requests to the two Node processes.

These two processes will certainly have some shared utility code. You'll need to put that somewhere, using Node's module mechanism.

TRY IT OUT   Using Tracer Bullets

You can use some tracer bullets to connect everything together and make sure it is all working properly before writing the functional code. This is the approach you learned in Chapter 2. You need to ensure that nginx is passing the HTTP requests to the correct Node process, that the Node processes are loading the shared code, that the Node processes can connect to the MongoDB database, and that the Node processes can respond to HTTP requests. This example will verify all of these connections. Follow these steps:

1. Create a new folder called `todostats`. You'll work in this folder for the rest of this example.

2. Create two subfolders under `todostats`: `lib` and `public`.

3. Create a file called `public/test.html` and insert the following contents:

```
public folder test
```

4. Become root by using `sudo -s`. Open the `nginx` configuration file `nginx.conf` in your text editor. (On your Amazon instance the file is `/etc/nginx/sites-enabled/default`.) Add the following lines inside the `server` directive section, modifying the line in bold to point to your `todostats` folder:

> **NOTE** *Note that all the entries except the* `init` *entry end with a* / *character.*

Available for download on Wrox.com

```
location /todo/stats/ {
  alias /path/to/your/todostats/public/;
}

location /todo/stats/data/ {
  proxy_pass http://127.0.0.1:3001/todo/stats/data/;
}

location /todo/stats/init {
  proxy_pass http://127.0.0.1:3000/todo/stats/init;
}

location /todo/stats/collect/ {
  proxy_pass http://127.0.0.1:3000/todo/stats/collect/;
}
```

Code snippet todostats/lib/nginx.conf.additions.txt

5. Reload your `nginx` configuration with the command:

```
$ nginx -s reload
```

6. Open Safari and visit `http://localhost/todo/stats/test.html`. Safari should respond with a page that says "public folder test." If it doesn't, review your `nginx` log files in `/var/log/nginx` for error messages.

7. Exit root with the `exit` command.

8. Create a new file called `lib/common.js`. Insert the following code in it:

Available for download on Wrox.com

```
var util    = exports.util    = require('util');
var connect = exports.connect = require('connect');
var mongodb = require('mongodb');
```

```javascript
// Time functions

exports.MINUTE = 60;
exports.HOUR   = 60 * exports.MINUTE;
exports.DAY    = 24 * exports.HOUR;

exports.SEC = {
  'second':1,
  'minute':exports.MINUTE,
  'hour':exports.HOUR,
  'day':exports.DAY,
}
exports.timesec = function(time) {
  return Math.floor( time / 1000 );
}
exports.second = function(second) {
  return second;
}
exports.minute = function(second) {
  return Math.floor( second / exports.MINUTE );
}
exports.hour = function(second) {
  return Math.floor( second / exports.HOUR );
}
exports.day = function(second) {
  return Math.floor( second / exports.DAY );
}
exports.sec = function(period,index) {
  return index * exports.SEC[period];
}

// JSON functions

exports.readjson = function(req,win) {
  var bodyarr = [];
  req.on('data',function(chunk){
    bodyarr.push(chunk);
  })
  req.on('end',function(){
    var bodystr = bodyarr.join('');
    util.debug('READJSON:'+req.url+':'+bodystr);
    var body = JSON.parse(bodystr);
    win && win(body);
  })
}

exports.sendjson = function(res,obj){
  res.writeHead(200,{
    'Content-Type': 'text/json',
  });
  var objstr = JSON.stringify(obj);
  util.debug('SENDJSON:'+objstr);
  res.end( objstr );
}
```

```
// MongoDB functions

var mongo = {
  mongo: mongodb,
  db: null,
}

mongo.init = function( name, server, port ){
  port = port || mongodb.Connection.DEFAULT_PORT;
  util.log('mongo:name='+name+',server='+server+',port='+port);
  mongo.db =
    new mongodb.Db(
      name,
      new mongodb.Server(server, port, {}),
      {native_parser:true,auto_reconnect:true});
}

// version of the res function from mongo.js that
// has a callback for both success (win), and
// failure (fail)
mongo.res = function( win, fail ){
  return function(err,res) {
    if( err ) {
      util.log('mongo:err:'+JSON.stringify(err));
      fail && 'function' == typeof(fail) && fail(err);
    }
    else {
      win && 'function' == typeof(win) && win(res);
    }
  }
}

mongo.open = function(win,fail){
  mongo.db.open(mongo.res(function(){
    util.log('mongo:ok');
    win && win();
  },fail))
}

mongo.coll = function(name,win,fail){
  mongo.db.collection(name,mongo.res(win,fail));
}

exports.mongo = mongo;
```

Code snippet todostats/lib/common.js

9. Use node to check the common.js module file for errors:

```
$ node common.js
```

There should be no output.

10. Create a new file called `lib/collect-tracerbullet.js`. Insert the following code in it:

```
var common  = require('./common.js');
var util    = common.util;
var connect = common.connect;
var mongo   = common.mongo;

var server = connect.createServer(
  connect.router(function(app){

    // POST {id:<string>}
    app.post('/todo/stats/init',function(req,res,next){
      common.readjson(req,function(json){
        common.sendjson(res,{ok:true,id:json.id});
      })
    })

    // POST {time:<UTC-millis>,total:<todos>,done:<done todos>}
    app.post('/todo/stats/collect/:id',function(req,res,next){
      var id = req.params.id;
      common.sendjson(res,{ok:true,id:id});
      common.readjson(req);
    })
  })
);

mongo.init('todo','localhost');
mongo.open()

server.listen(3000);
```

Code snippet todostats/lib/collect-tracerbullet.js

11. Run the data collection tracer bullet script:

```
$ node lib/collect-tracerbullet.js
9 Jan 14:33:22 - mongo:name=todo,server=localhost,port=27017
9 Jan 14:33:22 - mongo:ok
```

12. In a different shell window, use the `curl` command to post some data to the script:

```
$ curl http://localhost/todo/stats/init -d '{"id":"a"}'
{"ok":true,"id":"a"}
$ curl http://localhost/todo/stats/collect/a -d
  '{"time":1294424743926,"total":5,"done":2}'
{"ok":true,"id":"a"}
```

The `nginx` web server proxies these requests from the web browser to the Node server.

13. Review the command-line output from the `collect-tracerbullet.js` script to confirm that it has received the requests:

```
DEBUG: READJSON:/todo/stats/init:{"id":"a"}
DEBUG: SENDJSON:{"ok":true,"id":"a"}
DEBUG: SENDJSON:{"ok":true,"id":"a"}
DEBUG: READJSON:/todo/stats/collect/a:{"time":1294424743926,"total":5,
  "done":2}
```

14. Create a new file called `lib/view-tracerbullet.js`. Insert the following code in it:

```
var common = require('./common.js');
var util    = common.util;
var connect = common.connect;
var mongo   = common.mongo;

var server = connect.createServer(
  connect.router(function(app){

    // kind   = total,done,notdone;
    // period = day|hour|minute|second
    // time   = UTC millis
    app.get('/todo/stats/data/:kind/:period/:time',
      function(req,res,next){
      var kind   = req.params.kind;
      var period = req.params.period;
      var time   = req.params.time;

      common.sendjson(res,{
        kind:kind,period:period,step:0,start:0,end:0,points:[]
      });
    })
  })
)

mongo.init('todo','localhost');
mongo.open();

server.listen(3001);
```

Code snippet todostats/lib/view-tracerbullet.js

15. Run the data collection tracer bullet script:

```
$ node lib/view-tracerbullet.js
9 Jan 14:41:53 - mongo:name=todo,server=localhost,port=27017
9 Jan 14:41:53 - mongo:ok
```

16. In a different command line terminal window, use the `curl` command to get some data from the script:

```
$ curl http://localhost/todo/stats/data/total/second/1294424743926
{"kind":"total","period":"second","step":0,
"start":0,"end":0,"points":[]}
```

17. Review the command-line output from the `view-tracerbullet.js` script to confirm that it has received the request:

```
DEBUG:SENDJSON:{"kind":"total","period":"second",
  "step":0,"start":0,"end":0,"points":[]}
```

How It Works

This example sets up the infrastructure for your cloud app. The steps take you through each configuration setting and show you how to confirm that everything is working. You use tracer bullets to confirm everything end-to-end. The first thing you do is configure `nginx` so that it proxies requests for certain URLs to Node. This gives you a classic "web server talks to app server" configuration. The `nginx location` directives tell `nginx` to send requests onward to Node processes listening on ports `3000` and `3001`. There is also a `location` directive to serve up some HTML from the `todostats/public` folder. You use this to deliver a new version of the To-Do List app that reports on usage statistics.

The shared code for your Node processes lives in a script file called `common.js`. This is a Node module, which means you can use it in other Node scripts, like this:

```
var common = require('./common.js')
```

`common.js` is a local module, not a system module, so you need to provide a file path — `'./common.js'` — rather than just the name of the module. The `common` module loads the system `util` module, as well as the `connect` and `mongodb` modules that you downloaded and installed with `npm` earlier.

The `common` module provides some convenience functions for working with dates and times. These functions count the number of seconds, minutes, hours, or days since the start of January 1, 1970. You can use these counts to identify the time slots of the to-do item count changes for each time period, as you'll see shortly.

The module defines two utility functions — `readjson` and `sendjson` — for reading and sending JSON-formatted data. These functions also log the JSON data for easier debugging.

Finally, the module provides utility functions for dealing with MongoDB. You saw slightly simpler versions of these earlier in the chapter, in the Try It Out "Using MongoDB." In this version, the functions provide some additional convenience functionality.

The first Node process you write collects usage data from the To-Do List app. The version in this example, `collect-tracerbullet.js`, contains no actual functionality. Rather, it is a tracer bullet to confirm that the Node process can do the following:

1. Load the `common.js` module.

2. Connect to the MongoDB database.

3. Respond to HTTP requests proxied by `nginx`.

NOTE *If your Node processes are not receiving any requests, try pointing the* curl *commands in step 12 directly at the process ports rather than going through* nginx. *Replace* http://localhost/ *with* http://localhost:3000/ *in the* curl *commands. You should now be able to determine whether the Node processes are responding to direct requests.*

The `collect-tracerbullet.js` script pulls together the code that you've seen before in the `connectserver.js` script and the `mongo.js` scripts. A few things are new this time: the use of the `common.js` module and the sending and receiving of JSON data.

The first URL path that the `connect` module handles is `/todo/stats/init`. This will be used to tell the analytics system that a new app has been installed. In the tracer bullet code, you read in the JSON sent by the app and return some JSON yourself:

```
// POST {id:<string>}
app.post('/todo/stats/init',function(req,res,next){
  common.readjson(req,function(json){
    common.sendjson(res,{ok:true,id:json.id});
  })
})
```

You can't test this code directly with Safari. It's not an HTTP GET request. Instead, it's easier to create the required HTTP POST request by using the `curl` command. If you provide the `curl` command with some data using the `-d` argument, `curl` will send that data using a POST request. The response from the web server includes the output of the command:

```
curl http://localhost/todo/stats/init -d '{"id":"a"}'
{"ok":true,"id":"a"}
```

The second URL path that the script responds to starts with `/todo/stats/collect`. The code for this URL shows how `connect` provides you with access to parameters inside the URL. You use the special syntax `:name` inside the URL string and access the value by using `req.params.name`. In this case, you use this `connect` feature to get the identifier of the app that is submitting usage data:

```
// POST {time:<UTC-millis>,total:<todos>,done:<done todos>}
app.post('/todo/stats/collect/:id',function(req,res,next){
  var id = req.params.id;
  common.sendjson(res,{ok:true,id:id});
  common.readjson(req);
})
```

One other thing to notice about this code: You don't need to wait for any data to arrive from the client before sending your response. The `sendjson` function is called *before* the `readjson` function. This makes your data usage collection fast and ensures that it has no impact on the client. The client never has to wait for the server to confirm receipt of the data. When you collect usage data, this "fire-and-forget" approach is a reasonable design, trading off some data accuracy for an improved user experience.

The `view-tracerbullet.js` script is essentially the same as the `collect-tracerbullet.js` script. It responds to a different URL, of course. You will use this script to return the usage data for building that nice chart for the venture capitalist.

Collecting the Usage Data

Now it's time to add some functionality to the data collection script. You need to decide how to actually store the count changes and the last-known to-do item counts for each app. Also, it would be interesting to know how effective users are at completing their to-do lists. You should therefore store the done and not-done counts as well.

First, to handle the last-known to-do item counts, you use a MongoDB collection called `last`. The objects in this collection have the following properties:

➤ **id** — This is a unique identifier for the app.

➤ **kind** — This property can be set to `total`, `done`, or `notdone`.

➤ **sec** — This is the date and time of the last count received.

➤ **val** — This is the value of the last count received.

The `sec` property stores the time and date of the last known count. However, the date is not stored as an actual date but as the number of seconds since January 1, 1970. Thus, the `sec` property is an index for the unique second that the entry refers to. You need to ensure that each app has only one entry in the `last` collection. You'll see how to do this when you use the MongoDB "upsert" feature in the following example.

The app identifier is not the automatically generated `_id` MongoDB identifier. In this case, the To-Do List app generates its own unique identifier, and you use that instead. This way you can avoid scaling problems down the road because the app won't be dependent on a central server for its identifier.

Next, you need to store the total count history for the total count of to-do items and the total count of done and not-done items. If you store this data on a per-second basis, you still have to execute heavy queries to chart data on a per-minute, per-hour, or per-day basis. So why not precalculate those numbers, too?

How do you precalculate the totals for time periods greater than a second? You can use the same trick: Just store the changes to the total for each time period. There is nothing special about seconds. The counting algorithm works for any regular time period. You use a collection called `agg` (for aggregation) to store this data.

The objects in the `agg` collection have the following properties:

➤ **kind** — This property can be set to `total`, `done`, or `notdone`.

➤ **period** — This property can be set to `second`, `minute`, `hour`, or `day`.

➤ **index** — This is the number of periods since January 1, 1970.

➤ **val** — This is the amount of change in the total.

Again, with the `agg` collection you don't store normal dates. You store indexed dates. For each time period, you count the number of periods that have passed since January 1, 1970. The `val` property is not the total for the time period index; it's the amount of change since the last time period.

You might wondering at this stage how you turn this data into charts. After all, you are not storing the values that you will chart, but the changes to those values over time. To get back to the actual total for any given time period, you need to start from the beginning and add up all the changes. This gives you the actual value at a point in time.

TRY IT OUT   Collecting Usage Data

In this example, you'll extend the `collect-tracerbullet.js` script and add some real functionality. Follow these steps:

1. Copy the `collect-tracerbullet.js` script to a new file called `collect.js`.

2. Replace the `connect` router code in `collect.js` with the following:

Available for download on Wrox.com

```
connect.router(function(app){

    // POST {id:<string>}
    app.post('/todo/stats/init',function(req,res,next){
      common.sendjson(res,{ok:true});
      common.readjson(req,function(body){
        initEntry(body)
      })
    })

    // POST {time:<UTC-millis>,total:<todos>,done:<done todos>}
    app.post('/todo/stats/collect/:id',function(req,res,next){
      var id = req.params.id;
      common.sendjson(res,{ok:true,id:id});

      common.readjson(req,function(body){
        saveEntry(id,body)
      })
    })
  })
```

Code snippet todostats/lib/collect.js

3. Add the following functions to `collect.js`:

Available for download on Wrox.com

```
function initEntry(params,win) {
  mongo.coll('last',function(last){
    ['total','done','notdone'].forEach(function(kind){
      last.update(
        {id:params.id,kind:kind},
        {id:params.id,kind:kind,sec:0,val:0},
        {upsert:true},mongo.res(function(entry){
          util.debug('INIT:'+JSON.stringify(entry));
        }));
    })
  });
}
```

```
// params = {id:"a", time:UTC-millis, total:4, done:3}
function saveEntry(id,params) {
  var sec = common.timesec(params.time);
  params.notdone = params.total - params.done;

  ['total','done','notdone'].forEach(function(kind){
    var entry = {id:id,sec:sec,val:params[kind]};

    mongo.coll('last',function(last){
      var query = {id:entry.id,kind:kind,sec:{$lte:entry.sec}};

      last.findAndModify(
        query,
        [],
        {$set:{sec:entry.sec,val:entry.val}},
        {},

        mongo.res(function(lastentry){
          if( lastentry ) {
            var inc = entry.val - lastentry.val;

            mongo.coll('agg',function(agg){
              ['second','minute','hour','day'].forEach(function(period){
                var index = common[period](sec);

                agg.update(
                  {kind:kind,period:period,index:index},
                  {$inc:{val:inc}},
                  {upsert:true},
                  mongo.res()
                )
              })
            })
          }
        })
      )
    })
  })
```

Code snippet todostats/lib/collect.js

```
}
```

4. Run the `collect.js` script:

```
node lib/collect.js
```

5. Use `curl` to initialize a new app with identifier `"a"`:

```
curl http://localhost/todo/stats/init -d '{"id":"a"}'
{"ok":true}
```

6. Use the MongoDB command line environment to take a look at the data that has been inserted into the `last` collection:

```
mongo todo
> db.last.find()
{ "_id": ObjectId("..."), "id":"a", "kind":"total", "sec":0, "val":0 }
{ "_id": ObjectId("..."), "id":"a", "kind":"done", "sec":0, "val":0 }
{ "_id": ObjectId("..."), "id":"a", "kind":"notdone", "sec":0, "val":0}
```

7. Use `curl` to submit some usage data. First, get the current time in milliseconds (shown highlighted in the following code) and then use this value for the time property of the JSON data you submit. Node provides the `-e` option for executing JavaScript directly from the command line:

```
node -e "new Date().getTime()"
1294596640446
curl http://localhost/todo/stats/collect/a
  -d '{"time":1294596640446, "total":5, "done":2}'
{"ok":true,"id":"a"}
```

8. Review the data that has been inserted into the `agg` collection:

```
> db.agg.find().sort({index:1})
{_id:..., index:14983, kind:"total", period:"day", val:5}
{_id:..., index:14983, kind:"done", period:"day", val:2}
{_id:..., index:14983, kind:"notdone", period:"day", val:3}
{_id:..., index:359610, kind:"total", period:"hour", val:5}
{_id:..., index:359610, kind:"done", period:"hour", val:2}
{_id:..., index:359610, kind:"notdone", period:"hour", val:3}
{_id:..., index:21576610, kind:"total", period:"minute", val:5}
{_id:..., index:21576610, kind:"done", period:"minute", val:2}
{_id:..., index:21576610, kind:"notdone", period:"minute", val:3}
{_id:..., index:1294596640, kind:"total", period:"second", val:5}
{_id:..., index:1294596640, kind:"done", period:"second", val:2}
{_id:..., index:1294596640, kind:"notdone", period:"second", val:3}
```

This command also shows you how to sort data.

How It Works

The updated router functions call two new functions: `initEntry` and `saveEntry`. The `initEntry` function creates a new entry in the `last` collection for each metric (total, done, and not done) and ensures that there is only one such entry per client app. It does this by using the MongoDB "upsert" feature. An *upsert* is an update that can also insert data. If the query parameter of the update function does not find any matching entries, and the upsert option is used, it inserts a new entry. You can use an upsert to ensure that there is only one entry for each app and each kind of metric. An upsert will never duplicate an entry that already exists, but it will ensure that the entry is created if it does not already exist. In the example, you can also see how the `initEntry` function makes good use of the utility functions defined in the `common.js` module.

The `saveEntry` function saves new usage data as it arrives. It needs to store an entry for each time period — second, minute, hour, and day — and for each metric — total, done, and not done. The basic algorithm is as follows:

1. Find the last value.

2. Subtract the last value from the new value.

3. Save the result with the index for each time period.

MongoDB is designed for speed and while it does not provide traditional database transactions, it does provide a set of atomic operations that allow you to ensure data integrity. You use the special `findAndModify` function to update a matching entry atomically. This way, you can be sure that the update happens only if the matching conditions are met and that no other update will occur at the same time.

Using the `findAndModify` function allows you to satisfy a key requirement of the data storage algorithm: On a per-app basis, new updates need to occur *later* than the previous value. If, due to network delays, an earlier update arrives too late, after the one that followed it, that update needs to be discarded. You have no way of going back to the value before the last value. Yes, this does mean that sometimes fine-grained usage data for an individual app will be lost, but it does not affect data accuracy in the long run, as you always have the most recent count from the app. Note that this does not affect data from different apps; that data can arrive in any order because you store the last values for each app separately. So everything still works well enough to provide real-time analytics.

The way you use `findAndModify` to ensure that you update an individual app's count only in increasing time order is to search for a last entry that is earlier than the one you have just received. Hence this query:

```
var query = {id:entry.id,kind:kind,sec:{$lte:entry.sec}};
```

Because MongoDB accepts only JSON, you use the special property `$lte` to indicate that you want a value that is less than or equal to the specified value. In this case, you want to update the last collection only if there is an entry for the app where the seconds index, stored in the `sec` property, is less than the new entry that has just arrived. If such an entry exists in the collection, it means that the newly arrived entry is definitely more recent. If no such entry exists, the newly arrived entry is old, and you can discard it without saving.

Assuming that the new entry is the most recent, you need to update the change counts, which are stored in the `agg` collection. You need to call the `update` function for each time period to update the indexed time slot for that period. To perform this update, you use the `$inc` update command. This adds the specified value to the current stored value for the property. As per the storage algorithm, you increment the change value only by the change in the current app. Adding all the changes together gives you the full change amount for any time slot index.

It doesn't matter if multiple apps report data for the same time slot concurrently. Addition can happen in any order, and you still get the same answer.

With the storage algorithm, you now have real-time counts of to-do items, and you also have very low storage requirements. This makes your cloud application very cost-effective, as it won't require huge storage costs.

Submitting the Usage Data

Now you need to update the To-Do List app to send usage data back to the mother ship. You send the data in JSON format, using the jQuery `ajax` function. This works out well in terms of speed, as the JSON data is very small and is transmitted quickly.

TRY IT OUT Updating the To-Do List App

In this example, you will make some changes to the `todo.js` file. Follow these steps:

 NOTE *If you are using a cache manifest, you also need to increase the version number, as explained in Chapter 4.*

1. Copy all the files for the To-Do List app into the `todostats/public` folder.

2. Open the `todo.js` file and add to it the following highlighted line:

```
$(document).ready(function(){
  initapp();
```

3. Modify the `saveitemdata` and `loaditemdata` functions and add the following highlighted lines:

Available for download on Wrox.com

```
function saveitemdata(items) {
  localStorage.items = JSON.stringify(items);
  sendstats(items);
}

function loaditemdata() {
  var items = JSON.parse(localStorage.items || '[]');
  sendstats(items);
  return items;
}
```

Code snippet todostats/public/todo.js

4. Add the following functions to the end of the `todo.js` file. If you are running everything locally, replace the YOUR_IP_ADDRESS marker with the IP address of your local machine. If you are using your Amazon instance, use its public DNS Name instead.

Available for download on Wrox.com

```
function sendjson(urlsuffix,obj,win,fail) {
  $.ajax({
    url:'http://YOUR_IP_ADDRESS/todo/'+urlsuffix,
    type:'POST',
    contentType:'application/json',
    dataType:'json',
    data:JSON.stringify(obj),
    success:function(result){
      win && win(result);
    },
    failure:function(){
      fail && fail();
    }
  });
}
```

```
var appinfo = {};
function initapp() {
  appinfo = JSON.parse(localStorage.appinfo || '{}');
  if( !appinfo.id ) {
    var id = ''+Math.floor(Math.abs(1000000000 * Math.random()));
    sendjson('stats/init',{id:id},function(){
      appinfo.id = id;
      localStorage.appinfo = JSON.stringify(appinfo);
    })
  }
}

function sendstats(items) {
  if( navigator.onLine ) {
    var total = 0;
    var done  = 0;
    items.forEach(function(item){
      total++;
      done += item.done?1:0;
    })
    var time = new Date().getTime();
    var send = {time:time,total:total,done:done};
    sendjson('stats/collect/'+appinfo.id,send);
  }
}
```

Code snippet todostats/public/todo.js

5.   Open `http://YOUR_IP_ADDRESS/todo/stats/todo.html` in Safari. Add some to-do items. Open the Web Inspector window and take a look at the Resource tab. You should see usage data submissions being sent.

How It Works

The `initapp` function creates a new unique identifier for the app and calls the `/todo/stats/init` URL path. You simulated this with the `curl` command earlier in this chapter, when you wrote and tested the `collect.js` script. For your own apps, you'll probably want to define your own method for creating unique identifiers that fits your requirements.

 NOTE *You can generate production-quality unique identifiers using a number of different standards, conventions, and libraries. For Node, try the* `node-uuid` *module:* `https://github.com/broofa/node-uuid`, *which also has the advantage of working in web browsers.*

The `sendjson` function sends a JSON request back to the server, using the jQuery `ajax` function. The parameters are pretty obvious, but pay close attention to the `contentType` and `dataType` parameters. As you know, the `contentType` for JSON data is `application/json`, and you need to set this. The `dataType` parameter tells jQuery what sort of data you expect to get back, and jQuery then parses the data for you.

The `sendstats` function does the hard work. First, it checks whether the app is online, using the `navigator.onLine` property. There's no point trying to send data if there is no network connection.

For mobile apps, you have to assume that this is a frequent occurrence. Someone might be using your app on a plane or in an area with bad coverage. That's why the `loaditemdata` function always tries to send the latest updates to the server whenever the app launches; previous changes may not have been sent if there was no network availability.

The `sendstats` function works out the total number of to-do items and how many are done. It does not send the not-done amount. You can work out this number from the total and the done amounts; by handling it this way, you save some bandwidth. Remember that if you have a million users, little optimizations like this can have a big impact. The `sendstats` function also sends the current time on the device. This is the time that the storage algorithm will use.

Charting the Usage Data

Now it's time to generate some nice charts for that venture capitalist. There is a great open source charting library called Flot that you can use for this. It's very fast and easy to use. To calculate the data for the charts, you need to process the stored change counts.

This is the way it will work:

1. The user will send you the current time, in milliseconds, and the type of time period he or she is interested in.

2. You will return the previous 60 data points for that type of time period. For example, if the time period type is second, you return the totals for the past 60 seconds. If the time period type is day, you return the totals for the past 60 days.

So how do you calculate the totals from the change increments? You start from January 1, 1970, and add up all the increments, right up to the present second. This is easier than it sounds because you can take a shortcut. You add up all the days until yesterday. That's only a few hundred entries for each year that your startup survives. Then, starting from yesterday, you add up all the hours until the previous hour. Then, starting from the last hour, you add up all the minutes until the previous minute. Finally, you add up all the remaining seconds. This gives you the exact total at the present time. To go back 60 data points, you just stop counting 60 seconds before now (or 60 minutes, or 60 hours, or 60 days). Then you work forward to calculate the count for each data point. You send the 60 data points back to the web browser for charting. The following example shows how to do this. Here's the code.

TRY IT OUT   **Building the Charts**

In this example, you'll extend the `view-tracerbullet.js` script and add some real functionality. Follow these steps:

1. Copy the `view-tracerbullet.js` script to a new file called `view.js`.

2. Replace the `connect.router` code in `view.js` with the following:

```
connect.router(function(app){

    // kind   = total,done,notdone;
    // period = day|hour|minute|second
```

```
    // time    = UTC millis
    app.get('/todo/stats/data/:kind/:period/:time',function(req,res,next){
      var kind   = req.params.kind;
      var period = req.params.period;
      var time   = req.params.time;

      load(
        kind,period,time,
        function(start,end,step,points){
          common.sendjson(res,{
            kind:kind,period:period,step:step,start:start,end:end,points:points
          });
        }
      )
    })
  })
```

Code snippet todostats/lib/view.js

3. Add the following functions to `view.js`:

Available for download on Wrox.com

```
function total(kind,period,startindex,endindex,win){
  mongo.coll('agg',function(agg){
    agg.find(
      {kind:kind,period:period,
       index:{$gte:startindex,$lte:endindex}
      },
      {val:1},
      mongo.res(function(cursor){
        var totalres = 0;
        cursor.each(mongo.res(function(item){
          if( item ) {
            totalres += item.val;
          }
          else {
            win(totalres);
          }
        }));
      })
    )
  })
}

function load(kind,resultperiod,time,win) {
  var sec = common.timesec(time);
  var range = 60;
  var fromsec = sec - range * common.SEC[resultperiod];

  var startval = 0;
  var periods = ['day','hour','minute','second'];

  function totalinperiod(p,startsec,win) {
    var period = periods[p];
    var finalperiod = period == resultperiod;
```

```
    var startindex = common[period](startsec);
    var endindex = common[period](fromsec)-(finalperiod?0:1);

  total(kind,period,startindex,endindex,function(totalres){
    startval += totalres;

    if( finalperiod ) {
      win(startval,endindex);
    }
    else {
      totalinperiod(p+1,common.sec(period,endindex),win);
    }
  })
}

totalinperiod(0,0,function(startval,startindex){
  var runningtotal = startval;
  var endindex = common[resultperiod](sec);
  var points = [];

  mongo.coll('agg',function(agg){
    agg.find(
      {kind:kind,period:resultperiod,
       index:{$gte:startindex,$lte:endindex}
      },
      {val:1,index:1},
      mongo.res(function(cursor){
        cursor.each(mongo.res(function(item){
          if( item ) {
            runningtotal+=item.val;
            points[item.index-startindex] = 0+runningtotal;
          }
          else {
            var lastval = startval;
            for(var i = 0; i < range; i++) {
              if( !points[i] ) {
                points[i] = lastval;
              }
              else {
                lastval = points[i];
              }
            }

            var periodsec = common.SEC[resultperiod];
            win(1000*common.sec(resultperiod,startindex),
                1000*common.sec(resultperiod,endindex),
                1000*periodsec,
                points);
          }
        }));
      })
    )
  })
})
}
```

4. Run the `view.js` script:

```
node lib/view.js
```

5. Download the Flot charting library from `http://code.google.com/p/flot/`. Copy the `jquery.flot.js` file into the `public` folder.

6. Create a new file in the `public` folder called `charts.html`. Insert the following code in it:

```
<!DOCYPE html>
<html>
<head>

<style>
h1,h2,h3 {
  padding: 0px;
  margin:  5px 20px;
}
body > div {
  float: left;
  width:   220px;
  margin:  0px 0px 0px 20px;
}
div.chart {
  height:  150px;
  width:   200px;
  margin:  0px;
  padding: 0px;
}
.tickLabel {
  font-size: 9px;
}
</style>

<script src="jquery.js"></script>
<script src="jquery.flot.js"></script>
<script>
var timeformat = {
  second: '%S',
  minute: '%M',
  hour:   '%H',
  day:    '%b',
}
$(function(){
  var time = new Date().getTime();
  ['second','minute','hour','day'].forEach(function(period){
    ['total','done','notdone'].forEach(function(kind){
      $.ajax({
        url:'/todo/stats/data/'+kind+'/'+period+'/'+time,
        dataType:'json',
        success:function(data){
          console.log(JSON.stringify(data));
          var chartdata = [];
          for(var t = data.start,i=0; t <= data.end; t+=data.step,i++) {
            chartdata.push([t,data.points[i]]);
          }
```

```
                $.plot(
                   $('#'+kind+'_'+period),
                   [{data:chartdata}],
                   { xaxis: { mode:'time', ticks:6, timeformat:timeformat[period] },
                     yaxis: { min:0, ticks:5,
                              tickFormatter:function(val,axis){
                                return Math.floor(val)}}}
                )
              }
            });
         });
      });
</script>

</head>
<body>

<h3>To Do List App Usage Totals</h3>

<div
<h3>Last 60 Seconds</h3>
<h3>Total</h3>
<div class="chart" id="total_second"></div
<h3>Done</h3>
<div class="chart" id="done_second"></div
<h3>Not Done</h3>
<div class="chart" id="notdone_second"></div
</div>

<div>
<h3>Last 60 Minutes</h3>
<h3>Total</h3>
<div class="chart" id="total_minute"></div
<h3>Done</h3>
<div class="chart" id="done_minute"></div
<h3>Not Done</h3>
<div class="chart" id="notdone_minute"></div
</div>

<div>
<h3>Last 60 Hours</h3>
<h3>Total</h3>
<div class="chart" id="total_hour"></div
<h3>Done</h3>
<div class="chart" id="done_hour"></div
<h3>Not Done</h3>
<div class="chart" id="notdone_hour"></div
</div>

<div>
<h3>Last 60 Days</h3>
<h3>Total</h3>
<div class="chart" id="total_day"></div
<h3>Done</h3>
<div class="chart" id="done_day"></div
```

```
<h3>Not Done</h3>
<div class="chart" id="notdone_day"></div>
</div>

</body>
</html>
```

Code snippet todostats/public/charts.js

7. Open `http://localhost/todo/stats/charts.html` in Safari. Look at the lovely charts, which look as shown in Figure 5-4.

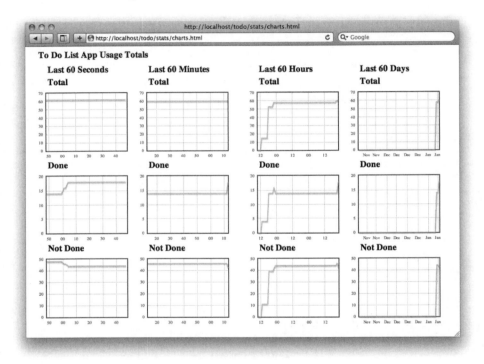

FIGURE 5-4

How It Works

The `view.js` script listens on port 3001, unlike the `collect.js` script, which listens on port 3000. These are separate processes, and you could run them on separate Amazon instances if you needed to handle a heavier load. If you need to handle even heavier loads, you can run multiple instances of each process, as they are stateless and do not use sessions.

The `view.js` script delivers the 60 data points prior to the time you specify, for the type of count you are interested in — total, done, or not done — and the time period type — second, minute, hour, or day. You specify this in the request URL. To make things easier for client applications, the time is given in milliseconds since January 1, 1970, which is the value you get from the `getTime` function of the JavaScript `Date` object.

Armed with these parameters, the load function first works out the starting second for the result set:

```
var sec = common.timesec(time);
var range = 60;
var fromsec = sec - range * common.SEC[resultperiod];
```

Then you have to divide up the work. First, you add up all the changes for the previous days. If days are the time period of interest, you can stop and return the results. If not, you continue with hours, and then minutes, and then seconds. This workflow naturally suggests a recursive function that calls itself.

But first, you need some utility code. The `total` function performs a MongoDB query to get all the change counts between two date indexes. It sums up the changes and returns the result via a callback. This is the function that does the job of adding up all the change counts prior to your 60-data-point period of interest. You need to do this to determine the starting value of your chart.

The `totalinperiod` function is the recursive function. It keeps calling the `total` function inside itself until it gets to the final period. It keeps track of the periods by using an array index `p` into a list of the periods, in decreasing size order:

```
var periods = ['day','hour','minute','second'];
```

You kick off the count by passing in a period index of 0, meaning day, and a start second of 0, meaning January 1, 1970. Don't be fooled by the callback function. This is the last function to be called, and it is called at the point highlighted below, inside `totalinperiod`, only when the recursion completes:

```
if( finalperiod ) {
    win(startval,endindex);
}
else {
    totalinperiod(p+1,common.sec(period,endindex),win);
}
```

This final callback function loads the actual 60 data points that you want to chart. You have the starting value of the chart from all that `totalinperiod` recursion. You load all the data points between the starting index and the end index of the required time period. This does not necessarily generate a return of a full 60 entries. Remember that some entries can be empty if no apps reported any activity. You place the entries that exist into a 60-element array at the position corresponding to their date index.

At the end of this process, you are left with an array that may contain empty elements. You loop through the array once and fill each empty element with the value of the previous element. You'll always have some value to fill with because you start with the starting value calculated by the `totalinperiod` recursion work.

To save bandwidth, you return the data points as an array of 60 elements, specifying the start and end times, in milliseconds. Again, you use milliseconds for the convenience of the client application.

The client is a single HTML page. This page, as you can see in Figure 5-3, shows a chart for each count type and each time period type. The code for this charting app is really just two `for` loops that loop through all the combinations of count and period:

```
['second','minute','hour','day'].forEach(function(period){
  ['total','done','notdone'].forEach(function(kind){
```

For each combination of count and period, you make an AJAX call to the `view.js` script, using the jQuery `ajax` function. This is a GET request, so you only need to specify a URL:

```
url:'/todo/stats/data/'+kind+'/'+period+'/'+time,
```

The data returned is in JSON format, and you let jQuery know this by using `dataType:"json"`. When the data comes back, you convert it into the form required by Flot. This charting library has many options, and you used some simple formatting for this example. For more details on Flot usage and the Flot API, you should take a look at the Flot home page: `http://code.google.com/p/flot`.

The Flot library needs your 60 data points as 60 two-element arrays, with the first element being the time in milliseconds and the second the value of the chart at the point. After the conversion is made, you call the `plot` function, and Flot looks after the rest, inserting a nice chart into the `div` element that you specify.

Remember to invite me to your IPO launch party.

SUMMARY

This chapter covers all the pieces of a full-scale cloud-based application. You learned how to set up the web server, the app server, and the database, and you learned how to run them all in the cloud. You are now ready to build complete cloud-based apps.

In the next chapter, you'll learn how to make use of the cloud services that Amazon provides beyond servers. You'll find out how to store your user's data efficiently, reliably, and cheaply in the cloud, as well as how to synchronize the cloud with your app.

EXERCISES

1. When you are debugging a Node application, it can be useful to print out the full description of an object in JSON format. The `util.debug` function will only print a string value. Review the Node documentation to find a way to do this.

2. Verify that your MongoDB database contains the correct analytics data. Start the To-Do List app, add some to-do items, and mark some as done. Use the `mongo` command to query the database.

3. The MongoDB database that stores your analytics data has two collections: `last` and `agg`. Both of these collections will be very large, probably with millions of entries. Configure an appropriate set of MongoDB indexes for these collections. For help, read this page of the MongoDB documentation: `http://www.mongodb.org/display/DOCS/Indexes`.

4. If you get the million users you're hoping for, you'll need to scale out your system. You can do this by spinning up a few more Amazon instances to run your Node processes. How do you distribute the load? Visit `http://wiki.nginx.org/HttpProxyModule` to read up on the `nginx` proxy module.

Answers to the Exercises can be found in the Appendix.

▶ WHAT YOU LEARNED IN THIS CHAPTER

TOPIC	KEY CONCEPTS
`Node.js` JavaScript server	An application server built using the Google Chrome V8 JavaScript engine that is optimized for event-driven activities. The `Node.js` engine is thus well suited to building server-side applications that must deal with many requests. The `Node.js` engine can handle very large volumes of concurrent requests as it uses this event-driven architecture to avoid the overhead of thread management and only executes code in response to event triggers. As this engine uses the JavaScript language, it is also ideally suited to building web applications, as the same language can be used on both the client and server-side.
JSON (JavaScript Object Notation) data format	A literal syntax in the JavaScript language for describing structured data. This syntax not only is a data format but is also valid code syntax in the JavaScript language. This makes it very easy to work with JSON-formatted data in JavaScript, especially when interacting with web service APIs.
noSQL Databases	An alternative database architecture to traditional relational databases. Instead of using the SQL language, these databases have custom query languages, hence the name. More importantly, the noSQL databases do not have the concept of tables storing well-defined data relations in rows and columns. Instead data is stored in a variety of structures, including hierarchical documents, schema-free tables, or even simple key-value pairs. The other significant difference is that these databases have a different approach to data integrity and do not provide traditional transactions. Rather, they tend to offer specific types of atomic operation and may require more than a single database server when run in production.
MongoDB document database	The MongoDB document database is a noSQL database that is particularly well-suited to the `Node.js` environment. All data going into or out of MongoDB uses the JSON data format. This means that there is very little conceptual friction between the database and your JavaScript code and objects. MongoDB is designed for fast data reads and writes and so is also suitable for modern web applications that can have a high write load.
Multi-process Architecture	A production deployment of a cloud system requires the use of multiple different kinds of servers that each perform a specific role. In this chapter the architecture consists of an `nginx` front-end server that accepts the connections from web browsers. The `nginx` server acts as a proxy to one or more `Node.js` servers. In larger scale deployments, `nginx` could also be used as a load balancer. The `Node.js` servers themselves delegate data storage to the MongoDB database. This architecture is just one variant of the many that are possible. In other scenarios you might configure `Node.js` to serve to web browsers directly, and also use `nginx` for static files on a different server.

Use the Cloud!

WHAT YOU WILL LEARN IN THIS CHAPTER:

➤ Understanding cloud services

➤ Understanding cloud databases

➤ Understanding the REST model for web services

➤ Learning to use the Amazon SimpleDB service

➤ Learning to use the `simpledb` Node module

➤ Developing a command-line interface for SimpleDB

➤ Dealing with time differences on clients and servers

➤ Developing a web service interface for SimpleDB

➤ Synchronizing local data with remote data

It's time to start using the cloud. In this chapter, you'll begin using cloud services as the building blocks for enhancing the functionality of your mobile applications. This chapter shows you how to store your application data in the cloud, using the Amazon SimpleDB cloud database. You'll also learn how to write a REST web service and how to synchronize local mobile application data with data in the cloud.

THE CLASSIC CLOUD ARCHITECTURE

When you start to build and use cloud-based services, you need to understand how all the pieces fit together. You need to understand these three participants: the clients, your service, and the third-party cloud services you use. It helps to have a simple picture in your head that drives your design decisions. Figure 6-1 shows such a picture.

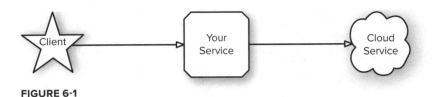

FIGURE 6-1

You may very well build the client apps yourself. But even if you provide client apps to your users, you will almost certainly want to provide a web service API as well, so that third-party developers can use your service as a platform. So you have to assume that the client is often external to your organization.

Your service itself may be based in the cloud. You might be running a set of virtual servers in Amazon, or you might be running a virtual app on Google or Heroku. Whatever the case may be, you need to consider how your cloud hosting will affect your use of other cloud services. For example, hosting on Amazon is a good idea if you plan to use Amazon cloud services such as the SimpleDB database, as data transfer internally within the Amazon cloud is free.

The other element of your service is the third-party cloud services that you will use to implement your service. Almost all online services interoperate in some way with a third-party web service. You need to consider what dependencies you will create and what services you want to outsource to the cloud. The advantage of using cloud databases, in particular, is that you do not have to worry about database server management. This means you have lower running costs, as the cloud database provider has to ensure reliable backups, scalability, and performance.

The REST Approach

One very important consideration when designing your cloud service is the type of API it offers. There are two major types of APIs:

➤ **Simple Object Access Protocol (SOAP)** — SOAP is an XML-based protocol that always uses the HTTP POST verb and includes many complex enterprise features. SOAP is focused on actions and virtual method calls on remote objects. It uses XML namespaces extensively. SOAP is generally regarded as being overly complex.

➤ **Representation State Transfer (REST)** — REST is an XML or JSON-based protocol that gets as much as it can out of the HTTP standard. REST focuses on resources and limits the actions on those resources. REST also uses the standard HTTP status codes and caching. It is much simpler than SOAP.

REST is really the way to go if you want quick and significant developer adoption of your service. SOAP is designed for enterprise systems and is not appropriate for mobile applications. Therefore, throughout this chapter and the book in general, you'll focus on the more practical use of REST.

For even more developer friendliness, choose JSON as your data format. JSON is much easier to work with than XML, particularly if you are coding in JavaScript.

To use the REST approach, you provide URLs that identify resources. For example, if your service is an online database of books, you might design URLs in this form: http://api.yourserver.com/

`book/ISBN`, where *ISBN* is the identifier of the book. A REST interface to this URL would work as follows:

1. HTTP GET — Return a JSON description of the book.

2. HTTP PUT — Create a new book and get an ISBN from the server.

3. HTTP POST — Update an existing book.

4. HTTP DELETE — Delete a book.

In general, these four HTTP verbs are all you need to manipulate a database. As you can see, REST is very simple — and this is why it's so popular.

The other key idea with REST is *idempotency*. This is a very simple idea with a fancy mathematical name. An *idempotent operation* is one you can perform again and again, without causing data to change each time. So you can GET a resource as many times as you like, and it will never change.

A web service interface that lets you use an HTTP GET to modify a resource is not a REST-style web service. For example, the following is not REST: GET /book/*ISBN*/delete. A GET can never modify a resource. The HTTP verbs GET, PUT, and DELETE are all idempotent within a REST interface. You can PUT a resource as many times as you like — it is only created once. You can DELETE a resource as many times as you like — it is only deleted once. You can GET a resource as many times as you like — it is not changed. The only operation that is not idempotent is POST because it updates an existing resource and thus changes data each time.

Cloud Databases

One of the most useful cloud services is a cloud database. Cloud databases provide a place to store your data remotely. These databases have the following attributes:

➤ **Reliable** — A cloud database is reliable because the cloud provider looks after backups.

➤ **Scalable** — A cloud database can handle very large volumes of data without impacting performance.

➤ **Low maintenance** — A cloud database does not require you to perform database administration.

➤ **Pay-as-you-go** — Storing data in the cloud means that you do not need to pay for storage in advance.

Most cloud databases offer access to data via an HTTP web service interface. This makes them easy to work with. It means that you can usually find several different client software libraries, so that you'll be able to choose the best one for your requirements. It means that you can easily understand your interactions with the database, because you can use command-line HTTP clients like `curl` to test the database API. It also means you can easily observe the HTTP traffic from your server to the database and use this to debug problems.

 NOTE *You use Wireshark an application that runs on Windows, Mac, and Linux, to observe HTTP traffic to and from your local machine as it happens. Wireshark is open source and available from* `http://www.wireshark.org`*.*

Cloud databases are highly scalable distributed systems. To achieve this scale, cloud databases have to make certain trade-offs. In particular, the traditional database concept of a *transaction* that guarantees data consistency is much harder to achieve in a highly distributed database. This, and other trade-offs, are made explicit by what is known as the CAP theorem. Eric Brewer, one of the co-founders of Inktomi, and a professor at UC Berkeley, developed the CAP theorem, which states that a highly scalable distributed system can provide only two of these three characteristics:

➤ **Consistency** — Consistency means that all clients see the same data.

➤ **Availability** — Availability means that clients can always access the database.

➤ **Partition tolerance** — Partition tolerance means that if any servers fail, the system keeps working.

The key reason you cannot have all three together is that the consistency characteristic requires you to wait for some form of transaction to complete on remote servers. If the remote servers do not answer, you don't know if they are down (the network is partitioned) or just slow. In order to be make the data available to clients right now, you'll just have to return the copy that you have right now and hope that it is up-to-date.

Different cloud databases emphasize different aspects of this choice. Amazon's SimpleDB database, which you'll look at next, sacrifices consistency so that it can provide high availability and partition tolerance. In practice, SimpleDB is said to be *eventually consistent*; you need to wait about 1 second in real time for all servers to be synchronized with your latest updates.

INTRODUCING AMAZON SIMPLEDB

Amazon SimpleDB is provided as one of the services under the Amazon Web Services (AWS) product list. To sign up for Amazon SimpleDB, you need to have an Amazon AWS account. If you do not have one, you should go to http://aws.amazon.com and sign up for one. Chapter 2 walks you through this process step-by-step. Once you have an account, you can click the Products tab and select Amazon SimpleDB. Then you simply click the Sign Up for Amazon SimpleDB button and provide the information Amazon asks for.

To authenticate with and use the SimpleDB service, you need your Amazon access key ID and secret key, which are strings of random alphanumeric characters. You can get these from your AWS account page by clicking the Account tab and then selecting Security Credentials. A page appears with your key details. Keep your keys safe!

 WARNING *SimpleDB is a service that you pay for. Amazon charges for data transmission and storage from the first byte. You can review the latest Amazon prices at* http://aws.amazon.com.

The SimpleDB Approach to Cloud Storage

All data in SimpleDB is organized into domains. A *domain* is a database table that can contain items. Items are the basic unit of storage, and each item consists of a set of attributes. Each attribute has one or more values. From a traditional SQL perspective, items are the rows of a database table, and attributes are the columns.

The really great thing about SimpleDB is that it is *schema-less*. This means that you do not have to define item attributes in advance. You can give any item any attributes you like. This is similar to the way that MongoDB works, as you saw in Chapter 5. The difference is that MongoDB lets you store complex tree-like documents. SimpleDB has only one attribute level. You cannot store attributes inside other attributes.

To keep things simple, SimpleDB can store only strings. If you want to store numbers or other types, you need to convert them to strings first. To store binary data you will also need to convert it to a string, using a suitable encoding such as Base64. SimpleDB allows you to store any kind of data you like, but you must handle the conversion to and from a string representation yourself.

All data in SimpleDB is sorted alphabetically. If you store numbers they will not be sorted correctly, because their string representations will sort differently to their proper numeric values. There is an easy trick to solve this problem. Prepend some zeros to the number so that it ends up looking like *0000123*. This way, you can still sort in numeric order, as the alphabetic sort gives the same ordering as a numeric sort.

SimpleDB places limits on the number of domains per account (100) and the number of attributes in a domain (1 billion). To get the full details on these and other limits, as well as the rest of the documentation on Simple, take a look at the SimpleDB Developer Guide, at `http://docs` `.amazonwebservices.com/AmazonSimpleDB/latest/DeveloperGuide/`.

The SimpleDB API

The SimpleDB API is an XML-based web service that is almost, but not quite, entirely unlike a REST API. It is not really a REST API because it uses named actions to perform data updates. While it is a well-designed API and relatively easy to work with, it uses XML. This means that you still have to do extra coding to interact directly with SimpleDB API, because you have to convert data to and from XML.

The SimpleDB web service is a great example of why you should use JSON for your service. The use of XML by SimpleDB introduces unnecessary complexity and means that you really have to use third-party modules to work with it. If SimpleDB used JSON, you could just make direct HTTP requests to it from your JavaScript code.

To avoid all this extra XML work, you can use the `simpledb` Node module to access the SimpleDB web service. This module hides all the complexity and lets you get straight to work. Despite the fact that you will be using a module, it is still important to understand the operations that SimpleDB offers.

SimpleDB provides the following operations:

➤   **CreateDomain** — Creates a domain.

➤   **ListDomains** — Lists domains.

➤   **DeleteDomain** — Deletes a domain.

➤   **DomainMetadata** — Provides statistics about the amount of data in a domain.

➤   **PutAttributes** — Uploads an item.

➤ **BatchPutAttributes** — Uploads multiple items at once.

➤ **GetAttributes** — Gets an item.

➤ **DeleteAttributes** — Deletes an item.

➤ **Select** — Performs a query on a domain.

You can use this short list of operations to create complex database-driven web services.

PUTTING THE TO-DO LIST APP IN THE CLOUD

To put your To-Do List app in the cloud, you need to provide a cloud API for the app. The mobile app will use this API to store and synchronize to-do items. More importantly, you can make the API public so that third-party developers can extend and enhance your service. To make this easy for third-party developers, you're going to build a JSON-format REST API. In this section, you'll see how to build this API.

Here you'll focus on the core functionality: user identity. This section doesn't discuss authentication and authorization, but in Chapters 8 and 10, you will learn how to hook up to the major social networking services to make use of their user authentication features.

To design a REST API, you need to think in terms of resources. *Resources* are the virtual entities that make up a service. In the case of the To-Do List app, the readily identifiable resources are the installed instances of the app and the to-do items that belong to each instance. For each to-do item resource, you'll support the four major REST verbs: GET, PUT, POST, and DELETE. For the installed app resource, you'll only implement GET and PUT, because apps, once registered, should not be able to remove themselves (with DELETE) or change their identifier (with POST).

For the server-side implementation, you will use the Node JavaScript server, and you will store your data in the Amazon SimpleDB database. You'll need to know how to hook everything up, so let's look at that now.

Introducing the simpledb Library

Accessing the SimpleDB REST API directly is not as easy as it might appear to be. The problem is that you have to sign each request. You do this by generating a signature value, using your AWS secret key. You can't really calculate this signature easily by hand, so using curl or a web browser to make test requests is not feasible.

The easiest way to access SimpleDB is via a software library designed for that purpose. Amazon provides several libraries for the major languages. However, Amazon does not provide one for Node. To access SimpleDB from Node, you need to use an open source module. In this book, you will use the simpledb module, which you can find at http://github.com/rjrodger/simpledb. I am a contributor to this module and have found it be very useful.

There is another reason for using the simpledb module: It provides fault-tolerant access to the Amazon SimpleDB service. Any given request to the Amazon SimpleDB service has a small chance of failing, and Amazon makes this quite clear. This is one of the trade-offs for the scalability of the system. Amazon recommends that you simply retry the request a number of times. After each failure, you should wait a longer and longer period of time before trying again; this is known as exponential back-off. The `simpledb` library handles exponential back-off for you, so you never need to worry about it, and your applications will be much more reliable as a result.

The best way to get started with the simpledb module is to build a tracer bullet. As you learned in Chapter 2, this lets you iron out any accidental configuration issues. Once you have the tracer bullet code working, you are free to concentrate your debugging time on the business logic of your code.

TRY IT OUT Coding a SimpleDB Tracer Bullet

This tracer bullet code verifies that you can perform basic database operations against the Amazon SimpleDB server. The code creates a SimpleDB *domain*, and then *puts* and *gets* a data item. Follow these steps:

1. Install the `simpledb` Node module by using `npm`:

```
sudo npm install simpledb
```

 NOTE *See Chapter 5 for a refresher on how use the* npm *package manager for Node.*

2. Install the `eyes` debugging module, which prints nicely formatted JSON:

```
npm install eyes
```

3. Create a folder called `todosync` that will contain the sample code for this chapter.

4. Create a file called `keys.js` in the `todosync` folder and insert the following code in it:

Available for
download on
Wrox.com

```
exports.keyid  = 'YOUR_AWS_KEY_ID'
exports.secret = 'YOUR_AWS_SECRET_KEY'
```

code todosync/snippet keys.js

5. Update the `keys.js` file with your Amazon key ID and secret key, which you can obtain from your Amazon AWS account as explained earlier in this chapter.

6. Create a file called `simpledb-tracerbullet.js` in the `todosync` folder and insert the following code in it:

Available for
download on
Wrox.com

```
var simpledb = require('simpledb')
var eyes     = require('eyes')

var keys = require('./keys.js')


var debug = 'debug' == process.argv[2]


var sdb = new simpledb.SimpleDB(
```

```
    {keyid:keys.keyid, secret:keys.secret},
    debug?simpledb.debuglogger:null
)


function error(win){
  return function(error,result,metadata){
    if( error ) {
      eyes.inspect(error)
    }
    else {
      eyes.inspect(result)
      win(result,metadata)
    }
  }
}


sdb.createDomain(
  'test',
  error(function(res,meta){

;sdb.putItem(
  'test',
  'item1',
  {attr1:'value1',attr2:'value2'},
  error(function(res,meta){

;sdb.getItem(
  'test',
  'item1',
  error(function(res,meta){

})) })) }))
```

code snippet todosync/simpledb-tracerbullet.js

7. Run the `simpledb-tracerbullet.js` script:

```
node simpledb-tracerbullet.js
{}
{}
{
    $ItemName: 'item1',
    attr2: 'value2',
    attr1: 'value1',
}
```

8. Run the `simpledb-tracerbullet.js` script again but in debug mode, by adding the argument value *debug* after the script name:

```
node simpledb-tracerbullet.js debug
...
multiple lines of debug output
...
```

NOTE *If the requests to SimpleDB fail for any reason, the error* Code *and* Message *attributes of the SimpleDB response will display. You can look them up in the SimpleDB Developer Guide to figure out the cause of the problem:* http:// docs.amazonwebservices.com/AmazonSimpleDB/latest/DeveloperGuide/.

How It Works

Using npm to install the simpledb and eyes modules ensures that you can use require('simpledb') and require('eyes') directly in your Node scripts, without knowing the full installation path of these modules.

The simpledb-tracerbullet.js script is designed to be run on the command line, and it takes one optional argument: the string 'debug'. If this optional argument is present, the script will print detailed information about its communication with the Amazon SimpleDB database. The process.argv variable is provided automatically by Node and holds a list of the command-line arguments. The first entry is 'node' itself, the second is the name of the script, 'simpledb-tracerbullet.js', and then the script arguments start at index 2. You set the debug variable to true if this argument has been specified.

To use Amazon SimpleDB, you need to specify your security credentials in order to gain access to the database. These credentials are your Amazon key ID and secret key, which are stored in the file keys.js. You use the require function to load this file as a local module:

```
var keys = require('./keys.js')
```

By using this approach, you don't have to store your sensitive keys directly in your code base.

After you load all the modules, you create a new instance of the simpledb.SimpleDB object, which is the main interface provided by the simpledb library:

```
var sdb = new simpledb.SimpleDB(
  {keyid:keys.keyid, secret:keys.secret},
  debug?simpledb.debuglogger:null
)
```

The simpledb.SimpleDB constructor takes two arguments. The first, which is required, is a set of options. You must supply your Amazon key ID and secret key. The second argument is optional and specifies the logging callback function. The module provides a simple debug logger that just prints logging events as they happen. If the 'debug' argument is used when running the script, you can use this simple logger to print debugging information.

The simpledb library follows the standard Node callback convention for operations that provide an error message if they fail. The convention is that the first argument to the callback function is an error object. If this error object is null, then there were no errors, and the operation succeeded. If the error object is not null, then the error object contains the details of the error. Depending on the module, the error object may be just a simple string message or a more complex object giving you additional context for the error. The second and subsequent arguments to the callback provide the results of the operation.

While this callback pattern is simple and easy to follow, it can make your code difficult to understand, as in this example:

```
doStuff( function( error, result ) {
  if( error ) {
    // handle error
  }
  else {
    doMoreStuff( function( error, result) {
      if( error ) {
        // and so on....
      }
    })
  }
})
```

To make the logic of the code easier to see at a glance, you can take advantage of the functional programming nature of JavaScript. You can create a function that prints errors for you and calls your result-handling code only if there is no error. How do you create this function? You write a function to do it, of course:

```
function error(win){
  return function() { ... } // the function you create dynamically
}
```

The idea here is that you provide a result-handling function, called win, that is called only if there are no errors. You used a similar approach in Chapter 5 to deal with MongoDB errors. The standard callback argument list for simpledb is always this:

```
function(error, result, metadata){ ... }
```

The error argument follows the normal convention: It returns null if everything is okay; otherwise, it contains a description of the error. The result argument returns the results of the operation — hopefully some data from SimpleDB. The metadata argument provides some additional information about the SimpleDB request. In particular, the metadata.BoxUsage field tells how much processing power Amazon used to execute the query. (Amazon charges you for this, so it's important information!)

So simpledb expects a function with the following three arguments:

```
function error(win){
  return function(error,result,metadata){
    ...
  }
}
```

The function you return should print out any errors and call the win function only if there are no errors:

```
function error(win){
  return function(error,result,metadata){
    if( error ) {
```

```
      eyes.inspect(error)
    }
    else {
      eyes.inspect(result)
      win(result,metadata)
    }
  }
}
```

You are now ready to create a domain in SimpleDB. You can call it `test`. Remember that domains are very much like SQL tables. You use the `createDomain` function to create the `test` domain in SimpleDB:

```
sdb.createDomain(
  'test',
  error(function(res,meta){
```

You can see the `error` function at work. The `win` function is marked in bold. At this point, the `simpledb` module sends a `CreateDomain` action to the SimpleDB service. You see the gory details if you use the `'debug'` option when you run the script. The output from this function is very exciting:

```
{}
```

The Amazon SimpleDB API is a very simple API. If it has nothing to say, it says nothing. If the `CreateDomain` action succeeds, there is nothing to say: It succeeded. The action will succeed even if the domain already exists. That's the way the API works.

If the domain was created, you can now proceed to store some data and read it back again. The `putItem` function stores data in SimpleDB, and the `getItem` function reads it back. The `simpledb` module uses consistent reads by default, so a `getItem` after a `putItem` will always work. You can turn this off if you specify the `consistent:false` option when you create the `simpledb.SimpleDB` object. You would turn off consistent reads to trade consistency for higher performance; they'll *eventually* be consistent anyway.

The arguments to the `putItem` and `getItem` functions specify the domain into which the item should be inserted and the unique identifier key for the item in that domain, which Amazon refers to as the item's `name`. The `putItem` function also takes a set of item attributes to save. The `result` object for the `getItem` function contains these attributes.

Again, the output from `putItem` is simply `{}`, but finally you see some results with the `getItem` function, which prints out the attributes that you saved:

```
{
    $ItemName: 'item1',
    attr2: 'value2',
    attr1: 'value1',
}
```

Notice that there's a special attribute called `$ItemName`. This provides you with the unique item name as a convenience. The `simpledb` module uses the `$` prefix for any special attributes like this.

Note that to avoid excessive indentation, the code makes use of a special formatting convention: Any line prefixed by a ; character can be shifted left to avoid further indentation. Thus, the indented code, which looks like this:

```
sdb.createDomain(
  'test',
  error(function(res,meta){

    sdb.putItem(
      'test',
      'item1',
      {attr1:'value1',attr2:'value2'},
      error(function(res,meta){

        sdb.getItem(
        'test',
        'item1',
        error(function(res,meta){

        }))
    }))
}))
```

changes to this:

```
sdb.createDomain(
  'test',
  error(function(res,meta){

;sdb.putItem(
  'test',
  'item1',
  {attr1:'value1',attr2:'value2'},
  error(function(res,meta){

;sdb.getItem(
  'test',
  'item1',
  error(function(res,meta){

})) })) }))
```

This code is much easier to scan vertically than the first version, which is indented more. As noted in Chapter 5, it is best to accept that JavaScript code will contain a lot of indentation. Sometimes, as in this case, you can take steps to mitigate the level of indentation.

Building a Command-Line Client

Before you build the web service for the To-Do List app, you need to be able to test and verify that the functions it provides work correctly. One way to do this is to provide an alternate way to access these functions. You can do so by building a command-line script. The other advantage of doing this is that you can test and develop in a very direct manner, without worrying about setting up HTTP requests.

TRY IT OUT Creating a Command-Line API

The `api-cmdline.js` script builds on the tracer bullet script you created in the preceding Try It Out. The command-line script you create in this example will form the basis for the web service script. The command-line API follows this format:

```
node api-cmdline.js api cmd arg1 arg2 ...
```

In this case, `cmd` is one of the API commands, such as `getapp` or `listapp`.

1. In the `todosync` folder, create a file called `api-cmdline.js` and insert the following code in it:

```
var util     = require('util')
var simpledb = require('simpledb')
var eyes     = require('eyes')

var keys = require('./keys.js')


function Api(keyid, secret) {
  var self = this

  var sdb = null
  function getsdb() {
    if( !sdb ) {
      sdb = new simpledb.SimpleDB({keyid:keyid, secret:secret},
                              self.debug?simpledb.debuglogger:null)
    }
    return sdb
  }


  function sdberr(win,fail) {
    return function(err,res,meta){
      if( err ) {
        if( !fail ) {
          console.log('ERROR:')
          eyes.inspect(err)
        }
        else {
          fail(err,meta)
        }
      }
      else {
        win && win(res,meta)
      }
```

```
    }
  }


  self.create = function( jsonout, what ) {
    if( 'all' == what ) {
      var created = []
      getsdb().createDomain('todo_app',sdberr(function(res){
        created.push('todo_app')

      ;getsdb().createDomain('todo_item',sdberr(function(res){
        created.push('todo_item')

        jsonout({created:created})
      })) }))
    }
  }


  self.metadata = function( jsonout, what ) {
    if( 'all' == what ) {

      var metadata = {}
      getsdb().domainMetadata('todo_app',sdberr(function(res){
        metadata.todo_app = res

      ;getsdb().domainMetadata('todo_item',sdberr(function(res){
        metadata.todo_item = res

        jsonout(metadata)
      })) }))
    }
  }


  self.listapp = function( jsonout, what ) {
    if( 'all' == what ) {
      getsdb().select(
        "select * from todo_app",sdberr(function(res){
          jsonout(res)
        }))
    }
  }


  self.getapp = function( jsonout, appid ) {
    getsdb().getItem('todo_app',appid,sdberr(function(appres){
      if( appres ) {
        getsdb().select(
          "select * from todo_item where app = '?'",[appid],
          sdberr(function(itemres){
            appres = appres || {}
            appres.id = appres.$ItemName || null
            delete appres.$ItemName

            itemres.forEach(function(item){
```

```
            delete item.$ItemName

            item.created = parseInt(item.created,10)
            item.updated = parseInt(item.updated,10)
            item.done   = 'true' == item.done
          })
          appres.items = itemres

          jsonout(appres)
        }))
    }
    else {
      jsonout({code:'not-found'})
    }
  }))
}

self.putapp = function( jsonout, appid ) {
  var attrs = {created:new Date().getTime()}
  getsdb().putItem(
    'todo_app', appid,
    attrs,
    {'Expected.1.Name':'created', 'Expected.1.Exists':'false'},
    sdberr(function(res){
      attrs.id = appid
      jsonout(attrs)
    })
  )
}


self.getitem = function( jsonout, appid, itemid ) {
  var itemname = appid+'_'+itemid
  getsdb().getItem('todo_item',itemname, sdberr(function(itemres){
    if( itemres ) {
      delete itemres.$ItemName

      // simpledb only works with strings
      itemres.created = parseInt(itemres.created,10)
      itemres.updated = parseInt(itemres.updated,10)
      itemres.done    = 'true' == itemres.done

      jsonout(itemres)
    }
    else {
      jsonout({code:'not-found'})
    }
  }))
}


self.putitem = function( jsonout, appid, itemid, jsonin, isnew ) {
  // simpledb only works with strings
  jsonin.created = ''+jsonin.created
```

```
      jsonin.updated = ''+jsonin.updated
      jsonin.done    = ''+jsonin.done

    var itemname = appid+'_'+itemid
    getsdb().getItem('todo_item',itemname, sdberr(function(itemres){
      var created  = new Date().getTime()
      var updated  = created
      var expected = {}
      if( itemres ) {
        if( isnew ) {
          jsonout({code:'item-exists'})
          return
        }

        if( parseInt(itemres.updated,10) < parseInt(jsonin.updated,10) ) {
          created = itemres.created
          updated = jsonin.updated
          expected =
            {'Expected.1.Name':'updated',
             'Expected.1.Value':itemres.updated}
        }
        else {
          jsonout({code:'item-old'})
          return
        }
      }

      var attrs = {
        id:itemid,
        app:appid,
        created:created,
        updated:updated,
        text:jsonin.text,
        done:jsonin.done
      }

      getsdb().putItem(
        'todo_item',
        itemname,
        attrs,
        expected,
        sdberr(function(res){
          jsonout(res)
        })
      )
    }))
  }


  self.delitem = function( jsonout, appid, itemid ) {
    var itemname = appid+'_'+itemid
    getsdb().deleteItem('todo_item',itemname, sdberr(function(res){
      jsonout()
    }))
  }
```

```
  }

  var api = new Api( keys.keyid, keys.secret )


  var numargs = process.argv.length
  var cmd = process.argv[2]


  function printUsageAndExit() {
    console.log(
      [ ""
        ,"Usage: node api-cmdline.js cmd arg\n"
        ,"Options:"
        ," api func args...:  call api function func with arguments"
        ,"    args are strings or JSON (enclose with single quotes):"
        ,"    api func foo '{\"bar\":123}'"
        ,"\n"
      ].join("\n")
    )
    process.exit(0)
  }

  function printjson(json) {
    eyes.inspect(json)
  }


  if( numargs < 4 ) {
    printUsageAndExit()
  }
  else if( 'api' == cmd || 'debug' == cmd ) {
    api.debug = 'debug' == cmd

    var func = process.argv[3]

    var arg = null, aI = 4, args = [printjson]
    while( arg = process.argv[aI++] ) {
      if( '{' == arg.charAt(0) ) {
        arg = JSON.parse(arg)
      }
      else if( 'false' == arg ) {
        arg = false
      }
      args.push(arg)
    }

    api[func].apply(api,args)
  }
  else {
    printUsageAndExit()
  }
```

code snippet todosynx/api-cmdline.js

2. Run the script with no arguments to verify that it works and can print a help message:

```
node api-cmdline.js
Usage: node api-cmdline.js cmd arg

Options:
  api func args...:  call api function func with arguments
    args are strings or JSON (enclose with single quotes):
    api func foo '{"bar":123}'
```

3. Run the following sequence of commands to create some test data:

```
node api-cmdline.js api create all
{
    created: [ 'todo_app', 'todo_item' ]
}

node api-cmdline.js api putapp app1
{ created: 1295921107614, id: 'app1' }

node api-cmdline.js api getapp app1
{
    created: '1295921107614',
    id: 'app1',
    items: []
}

node api-cmdline.js api putitem app1 item1
  '{"text":"todo1","done":true,"created":1000,"updated":1000}'
{}

node api-cmdline.js api getitem app1 item1
{
    id: 'item1',
    app: 'app1',
    text: 'todo1',
    created: 1295921270524,
    updated: 1295921270524,
    done: true
}
```

How It Works

The api-cmdline.js script builds on the tracer bullet script you created in the preceding Try It Out. You renamed the error-handling function sdberr and extended it to accept both win and fail functions. If no fail function is provided, the default behavior is to print the error.

You encapsulated the API commands in an Api object. Each command is implemented by an appropriately named function and uses the simpledb module to perform its task. In addition, each API function takes a jsonout function as its first parameter. In this command-line version of the API, the jsonout function just prints the results of the API command. In the web service version that you will see shortly, the jsonout function sends JSON data back to the client.

The create function makes sure that two domains — todo_app for registered To-Do List apps and todo_item for to-do items — exist.

The metadata function gets the SimpleDB-reported metadata for each domain. You want to keep track of this on your production services because Amazon charges you for data storage.

The listapp function returns a list of all the apps stored in the todo_app domain. This function uses a SimpleDB SELECT query:

```
select * from todo_app
```

SimpleDB does not provide you with the traditional SQL language. It does, however, copy the SQL SELECT query syntax. Just remember that this is not a SQL SELECT statement, and the syntax is only superficially similar.

The getapp function gets the details of a particular app and all the items for that app. Again, you use a SELECT query. This time, you use the replacement parameter feature of the simpledb module to ensure that the app ID string is properly escaped. (In a query string literal, each apostrophe must be escaped by placing another apostrophe before it.) The replacement parameter feature replaces each question mark in the query string with the value of the corresponding array element:

```
"select * from todo_item where app = '?'",[appid]
```

The getapp function must also make sure to execute its operations in the correct order. That is why the query for to-do items occurs inside the callback of the getItem function.

Because SimpleDB can store only string values, it is necessary to parse these back into native JavaScript values:

```
item.created = parseInt(item.created,10)
item.updated = parseInt(item.updated,10)
item.done    = 'true' == item.done
```

The putapp function registers a new app in the SimpleDB database. To make sure this happens only once per app, you use a conditional put operation. You provide an expected value for an attribute, and SimpleDB performs the operation only if the expected value matches. If the value does not match, the operation should not proceed because it is either out-of-date or invalid. You specify conditional puts by using the override feature of the simpledb module. This way, you can provide a set of SimpleDB attributes that are applied to the request and override any attributes that have been set automatically:

```
{'Expected.1.Name':'created', 'Expected.1.Exists':'false'},
```

These attributes specify that an attribute called Name must *not* exist for the specified item. Of course, this is the case if the item itself does not exist! So this is an existence test for an app registration entry.

The getitem function returns a single item from SimpleDB. Notice that the unique name of each item is created by concatenating the app ID and the item ID:

```
var itemname = appid+'_'+itemid
```

The `putitem` function inserts a to-do item into the SimpleDB database. The `isnew` boolean argument indicates whether the item is a new item to insert into the database. If the item is supposed to be new but it is found to exist already, then the `jsonout` callback function is called with an error object:

```
if( isnew ) {
  jsonout({code:'item-exists'})
  return
}
```

The script must also check that the item is the most recent update. If a more recent update exists in the database, then this update is old and will not be applied. This can happen if an update is delayed in transit over the network. You use a conditional `put` to implement this check:

```
if( parseInt(itemres.updated,10) < parseInt(jsonin.updated,10) ) {
        created = itemres.created
        updated = jsonin.updated
        expected =
          {'Expected.1.Name':'updated',
           'Expected.1.Value':itemres.updated}
```

Finally, the `delitem` function deletes a to-do item from the SimpleDB database.

The remainder of the script is some simple logic to implement the command-line interface. This logic matches the name of the command to the name of the function implementing the command. So using the command `getapp` will cause the `Api.getapp` function to be called. One item of interest is the input of JSON data, required for the `putitem` function. Any argument that starts with a `{` character is considered to be JSON-formatted data. Actually entering this data on the command line requires some care: You need to enclose the entire JSON data in apostrophes and use quotation marks for all property names, or `JSON.parse` will complain.

Working on Cloud Time

You want to use the To-Do List API to save your to-do items in the SimpleDB cloud database. But there's a catch: The local time on the mobile device running the To-Do List app and the time on your Amazon server are almost certainly different, possibly differing by several minutes. You therefore need to be careful about using update times to determine which to-do items have changed. If your iPhone clock is ahead of your server, for example, more recent updates from other clients might be obliterated because the iPhone items look like they are more recent. You need to compensate for this type of time difference.

When it comes to time synchronization, your most accurate option is to use a third-party reference clock, such as one of the atomic clocks run by the U.S. Naval Observatory. Luckily, this is not a requirement for your To-Do List app. All you need to know is that the time updates are ordered correctly. Given that it takes a few seconds to actually type in and save a to-do item, this is the level of accuracy that you need. You could go for higher accuracy, but that wouldn't be a good use of time or money in this case. An important principle in cloud computing is to accept the inherent constraints and move on. These consistency compromises are a good example.

So what options do you have? As it turns out, there's a very simple formula you can use to estimate the clock difference between two systems. From the perspective of the client, the clock difference is an offset that needs to be added to the local client time to get the server time. This difference is therefore called the *server offset*. To get the server offset, you send a request from the client to the server. You record four times:

➤ t_0 — When the request leaves the client.

➤ t_1 — When the request arrives at the server.

➤ t_2 — When the response leaves the server.

➤ t_3 — When the response arrives at the client.

If you assume that the network latency and transmission rate are stable (in practice latency and bandwidth have random variations that make this formula less accurate), the request interval will be equal to the response interval. So you can add them up, divide by 2, and then add this result to the client time to get the server time, like so:

$$\text{Server offset} = \tfrac{1}{2} \left((t_1 - t_0) + (t_2 - t_3)\right)$$

Figure 6-2 shows the formula in action. In this example, the server is 10 seconds ahead of the client. When you plug the numbers from this example into the preceding formula, this is what you get:

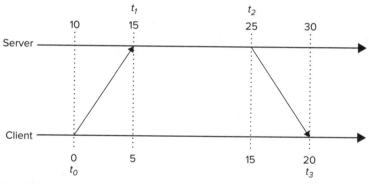

FIGURE 6-2

$$\text{Server offset} = \tfrac{1}{2} \left((15 - 0) + (25 - 20)\right)$$
$$= \tfrac{1}{2} \left(15 + 5\right)$$
$$= 10$$

You might be wondering why it's $t_2 - t_3$ and not $t_3 - t_2$. Remember that t_0 and t_2 are client times, and t_1 and t_3 are server times. When you do a direct subtraction between client and server times, the result is not the actual number of seconds. The result includes the offset value, because the client and server clocks are different. You don't know what the offset value is, but you can "cancel" it out — just turn the second subtraction around. That way $t_1 - t_0$ overshoots, and $t_2 - t_3$ undershoots. You can see this in the example numbers above.

You can use this formula in the To-Do List app to calculate a server offset value before you synchronize the to-do items. The clients apply the offset. The server does not modify time values at all but trusts the clients to report the corrected values. This keeps the example straightforward.

Running a Cloud Server

To provide a web service for the To-Do List app, you can use the `nginx` and Node architecture developed in Chapter 5. In this case, though, instead of using the MongoDB database, you use SimpleDB. The web service itself will provide a REST interface to the To-Do List service. This means that the web service will offer a standard format for resource URLs, where the resources are apps and to-do items.

TRY IT OUT   Creating a Web Service API

The Node script that implements the web service builds on the command-line script that you have already developed and tested. You'll keep the command-line option and add an option to listen for requests on a given port. You'll then configure the `nginx` web server to proxy API requests to this port. Follow these steps:

1. In the `todosync` folder, create a new file called `common.js`. Insert the following code in it:

Available for download on Wrox.com

```
var util     = exports.util     = require('util');
var connect  = exports.connect  = require('connect');
var simpledb = exports.simpledb = require('simpledb');
var eyes     = exports.eyes     = require('eyes');


// JSON functions

exports.readjson = function(req,win) {
  var bodyarr = [];
  req.on('data',function(chunk){
    bodyarr.push(chunk);
  })
  req.on('end',function(){
    var bodystr = bodyarr.join('');
    util.debug('READJSON:'+req.url+':'+bodystr);
    var body = JSON.parse(bodystr);
    win && win(body);
  })
}

exports.sendjson = function(code,res,obj,sendtime){
  res.writeHead(code,{
    'Content-Type': 'text/json',
  });
  if( sendtime ) {
    obj.sendtime = new Date().getTime()
  }
  var objstr = JSON.stringify(obj);
```

```
util.debug('SENDJSON:'+objstr);
res.end( objstr );
}
```

2. Open the `nginx.conf` file in your `nginx` installation folder and add the following lines to the server section:

Available for download on Wrox.com

```
location /todo/sync/ {
  alias /path/to/your/todosync/public/;
}

location /todo/sync/api {
  proxy_pass http://127.0.0.1:3000/todo/sync/api;
}
```

3. Reload the `nginx` configuration with this command:

```
sudo nginx -s reload
```

4. Copy the `api-cmdline.js` file to a new file called `api.js`. Add the following functions to the `Api` object in `api.js`:

Available for download on Wrox.com

```
function err500(jsonout,win){
  return sdberr(win,function(err,meta){
    jsonout(500)
  })
}


function errcond(jsonout,errcode,win){
  return sdberr(win,function(err,meta){
    var out = {}, status = 500
    if( 'ConditionalCheckFailed' == err.Code ) {
      status = 400
      out.code = errcode
    }
    jsonout(out,status)
  })
}


self.timesync = function( jsonout, clienttime ) {
  var arrivaltime = new Date().getTime()
  jsonout({clienttime:parseInt(clienttime,10),arrivaltime:arrivaltime},true)
}
```

5. In `api.js`, replace all occurrences of `jsonout({code:'not-found'})` with `jsonout(404)`.

6. At the bottom of the `api.js` file, add the following additional `else if` statement to the command-line parsing code:

```
else if( 'run' == cmd ) {
  var port = parseInt(process.argv[3],10)

  function sendjson(res){
    return function(json,status){
      var sendtime = false
      if( 'object' != typeof(json) ) {
        status = json
        json = {}
      }
      status = status || 200

      if( 'boolean' == typeof(status) ) {
        sendtime = status
        status = 200
      }

      common.sendjson( status, res, json, sendtime )
    }
  }

  var server = connect.createServer(
    connect.router(function(app){

      app.get('/todo/sync/api/app/:appid',function(req,res,next){
        api.getapp( sendjson(res), req.params.appid )
      })

      app.put('/todo/sync/api/app/:appid',function(req,res,next){
        api.putapp( sendjson(res), req.params.appid )
      })


      app.get('/todo/sync/api/app/:appid/item/:itemid',function(req,res,next){
        api.getitem( sendjson(res), req.params.appid, req.params.itemid )
      })

      app.put('/todo/sync/api/app/:appid/item/:itemid',function(req,res,next){
        common.readjson(req,function(input){
          api.putitem( sendjson(res),
                       req.params.appid, req.params.itemid, input, true )
        })
      })

      app.post('/todo/sync/api/app/:appid/item/:itemid',function(req,res,next){
        common.readjson(req,function(input){
          api.putitem( sendjson(res),
                       req.params.appid, req.params.itemid, input, false )
        })
```

```
    })

  app.del('/todo/sync/api/app/:appid/item/:itemid',function(req,res,next){
    api.delitem( sendjson(res), req.params.appid, req.params.itemid )
  })

  app.get('/todo/sync/api/time/:clienttime',function(req,res,next){
    api.timesync( sendjson(res), req.params.clienttime )
  })
  })
  )

  server.listen( port )
  console.log('To Do List API server listening on port '+port)
  api.metadata(printjson,'all')
}
```

code snippet api.js

7. Start the Node server. The server prints the results of the metadata command when it starts:

```
node api.js run 3000
To Do List API server listening on port 3000
{
    todo_app: {
        ItemCount: 9,
        ItemNamesSizeBytes: 65,
        AttributeNameCount: 1,
        AttributeNamesSizeBytes: 7,
        AttributeValueCount: 9,
        AttributeValuesSizeBytes: 117,
        Timestamp: 1295880912
    },
    todo_item: {
        ItemCount: 4,
        ItemNamesSizeBytes: 62,
        AttributeNameCount: 6,
        AttributeNamesSizeBytes: 27,
        AttributeValueCount: 22,
        AttributeValuesSizeBytes: 166,
        Timestamp: 1295880912
    },
    $status: 200
}
```

Your usage numbers will be different from the ones in this example.

8. To test the server, run the following curl commands, which test first a direct connection to Node and second a proxied connection via nginx:

```
curl http://127.0.0.1:3000/todo/sync/api/app/app1
{"created":"1295921107614","id":"app1",
 "items":[{"app":"app1",
```

```
          "text":"todo1",
          "updated":1295921270524,
          "created":1295921270524,
          "done":true,
          "id":"item1"}]}

curl http://127.0.0.1/todo/sync/api/app/app1
{"created":"1295921107614","id":"app1",
 "items":[{"app":"app1",
          "text":"todo1",
          "updated":1295921270524,
          "created":1295921270524,
          "done":true,
          "id":"item1"}]}
```

The results shown here assume that you have run the command-line tests shown earlier in this chapter.

How It Works

The common.js file is a modification of the common.js file from Chapter 5. You've added references to the simpledb and eyes modules. There's also a new special option in the sendjson function to insert the time at which a response is sent. You will use this for the time synchronization algorithm explained earlier in this chapter. The util.debug statements that show the incoming and outgoing JSON are still there, and you can use them to help understand the message flow between the server and client.

The api.js script is an extension of the api-cmdline.js script. It provides an HTTP server using the connect module. You implement this server in the same manner you implemented the server in Chapter 5 — by providing the connect module with a list of routes that map to implementation functions. In this case, you are also routing on the HTTP PUT and DELETE verbs in addition to the more traditional GET and POST.

The Api object has some new functions. The additional error-handling functions err500 and errcond return the correct HTTP status code if an error occurs. You use the same function-building tactic here that you use with the sdberr function. Because you have cleanly separated the interface from the implementation by using this technique, there are almost no changes to the command functions, except for some minor edits to the jsonout calls.

The timesync function is a new command function for the API. It implements the time synchronization algorithm discussed earlier. Clients can call this command to calculate the server offset. Note that this command does not identify a REST resource but is more like a remote procedure call. The REST philosophy does not exclude this type of interface, where it is appropriate, as it is in this case.

You implement the server by using the connect module. Based on the specification of the API URLs and the HTTP verbs, this is a REST interface.

You have the app resource answering to GETs and PUTs on /todo/sync/app/appid. By design, the verbs POST and DELETE are not supported.

Each app resource contains a list of to-do item resources, so you have item resources with each app resource. The verbs GET, PUT, POST, and DELETE all operate on /todo/sync/app/appid/itemid. To get an initial list of to-do items, you issue a GET on the app identifier, and the list is included in the response.

The `sendjson` function contains some housekeeping logic to handle the case where there is no result data and the case where a `timesync` command is used.

Finally, you modified the code to return an HTTP status code of 404 when an item is not found. This is also part of the REST API approach. You are using the HTTP protocol as designed.

Synchronizing with the Cloud

Now you're ready to update the To-Do List app to synchronize with the cloud service you have developed. To minimize clutter, you'll update the version of the To-Do List app from Chapter 4 rather than the one from Chapter 5. (However, the analytics code in Chapter 5 is quite orthogonal to the changes here and is relatively easy to merge in if you want it.)

TRY IT OUT   Synchronizing Your To-Do List App with Your Cloud Service

To synchronize your To-Do List app with the cloud, you need to add a set of functions to handle the network communication. You need the app to synchronize whenever a to-do item changes or is created. You also need to add a function to do a full synchronization with the server whenever the app starts up so that a list of changes can be exchanged between the client and server. Finally, you need to handle the case where the app is offline, such as when the user is using the app on a flight and will reconnect only after landing. To do all this, follow these steps:

1. Copy the To-Do List app files — `todo.js`, `todo.html`, and `todo.css` — into the `todosync` folder. Also copy the `jquery.js`, `jquery.mobile.js`, and `jquery.mobile.css` files and the jQuery Mobile `images` folder into the `todosync` folder.

2. Open the `todo.js` file and replace the to-do item save event handler with this new version (where the highlighted lines show some of the significant changes):

```
$('#save').tap(function(){
    var text = $('#text').val()
    if( 0 == text.length ) {
        return
    }
    $('#text').val('')

    var created = new Date().getTime() + serveroffset
    var updated = created
    var itemdata =
      { id:makeid(),
        text:text,
        done:false,
        created:created,
        updated:updated }

    items.push(itemdata)
    additem(itemdata)
    uploaditem(itemdata, true)

    $('#newitem').slideUp()
```

```
    $('#add').show()
    $('#cancel').hide()
  })
```

3. Add the following functions to the bottom of the `todo.js` file, replacing the YOUR_SERVER place-holder with the IP address or domain name of your server:

```
function sendjson(method,urlsuffix,obj,win,fail) {
  $.ajax({
    url:'http://YOUR_SERVER/todo/'+urlsuffix,
    type:method,
    contentType:'application/json',
    dataType:'json',
    data:'GET'==method?null:JSON.stringify(obj),
    success:function(result){
      win && win(result)
    },
    error:function(xhr){
      fail && fail(xhr.status)
    }
  })
}


var appinfo = {}
function initapp() {
  appinfo = JSON.parse(localStorage.appinfo || '{}')
  if( !appinfo.id ) {
    var id = makeid()
    appinfo.id = id
    localStorage.appinfo = JSON.stringify(appinfo)
  }


  function putapp(status){
    if( 404 == status ) {
      sendjson(
        'PUT','sync/api/app/'+appinfo.id,{},
        function(result){
          // app created
        },
        function(status){
          // app not created
        }
      )
    }
  }


  if( navigator.onLine ) {
    var clienttime = new Date().getTime()
```

```
    sendjson(
      'GET','sync/api/time/'+clienttime,null,
      function(result){
        result.clientreturn = new Date().getTime()
        handletime(result)
        sendjson(
          'GET','sync/api/app/'+appinfo.id,null,
          function(result){
            syncitems(result.items)
          },
          putapp
        )
      }
    )
  }
}


function makeid() {
  return ''+Math.floor(Math.abs(1000000000 * Math.random()))
}

function handletime(timesync) {
  serveroffset =
    Math.floor(
      0.5 *
        ( ( timesync.arrivaltime - timesync.clienttime ) +
          ( timesync.sendtime    - timesync.clientreturn ) ) )
}


function uploaditem(itemdata) {
  if( navigator.onLine ) {
    sendjson(
      isnew?'PUT':'POST',
      'sync/api/app/'+appinfo.id+'/item/'+itemdata.id,itemdata
    )
  }
  else {
    var uploads = JSON.parse(localStorage.uploads || '[]')
    uploads.push(itemdata)
    localStorage.uploads = JSON.stringify(uploads)
  }
}


function syncitems(serveritems) {
  if( !navigator.onLine ) {
    return
  }

  var localitems = items
  var localmap = {}
  localitems.forEach(function(item){
```

```
    localmap[item.id] = item
})

var servermap = {}
serveritems.forEach(function(item){
  servermap[item.id] = item
})

serveritems.forEach(function(serveritem){
  var localitem = localmap[serveritem.id]
  if( localitem ) {
    if( localitem.updated < serveritem.updated ) {

      localmap[serveritem.id].created = serveritem.created
      localmap[serveritem.id].updated = serveritem.updated
      localmap[serveritem.id].done = serveritem.done
      localmap[serveritem.id].text = serveritem.text

      var itemelem = $('#'+serveritem.id)
      itemelem.find('span.text').text(serveritem.text)
      markitem(itemelem,serveritem.done)
    }
  }
  else {
    items.push(serveritem)
    additem(serveritem)
  }
})


var uploads = JSON.parse(localStorage.uploads || '[]')
var newitems = []
var existingitems = []

uploads.forEach(function(upload){
  if( servermap[upload.id] ) {
    if( servermap[upload.id].updated < upload.updated ) {
      existingitems.push(upload)
    }
  }
  else {
    newitems.push(upload)
  }
})

newitems.forEach(function(item){
  sendjson(
    'PUT','sync/api/app/'+appinfo.id+'/item/'+item.id,upload
  )
})

existingitems.forEach(function(item){
  sendjson(
    'POST','sync/api/app/'+appinfo.id+'/item/'+upload.id,upload
```

```
        )
    })

    localStorage.uploads = '[]'

}
```

code snippet todo.js

4. Add a call to the `initapp` function at the top of the `todo.js` file:

```
$(document).ready(function(){
    initapp()
```

5. Open the To-Do List app on your mobile device, by visiting the URL `http://YOUR_SERVER/todo/sync/todo.html`. Add some to-do items. Observe the debug output from the `api.js` script. You can use this output to manually simulate the same user accessing his or her data on multiple devices.

6. Using the debug output of the `api.js` script, copy the app ID string. You can identify it by looking for the `app` attribute of any item, like this:

```
DEBUG: SENDJSON:{...,"items":[{ "app":"123..." ,...
```

7. Open your desktop Safari browser and open the To-Do List app. Use the Safari Web Inspector tool to manually edit the value of the app ID in your local storage: Click the Storage tab, double-click the `appinfo` item, and edit the JSON to set the ID to the ID of your mobile app:

```
{"id":"123..."}
```

8. Refresh the To-Do List app in your desktop Safari browser. You should see the same to-do items as on your mobile device.

9. Add some more items and observe the HTTP traffic by using the Safari Web Inspector tool.

10. Stop the `api.js` briefly, add some items, restart the `api.js` server, and refresh the app. Use the Web Inspector to observe the startup synchronization traffic.

How It Works

To implement the synchronization of the to-do items with the server, there are two cases you need to deal with. First, you need to upload any immediate changes to individual items. Second, when the app starts, you need to upload any changes that have accumulated locally and apply any changes that have happened remotely in the meantime.

Uploading any immediate changes to individual items is easy. You execute an HTTP PUT or POST on the item resource url `/todo/sync/appid/itemid` and send the item attributes as JSON. You do this whenever an item changes. Because this is a REST API, you use PUT for new items and POST for existing ones. What happens if the mobile device is offline? You can detect this by using the `navigator.onLine` property, which is `false` when the device is not connected to a network. You store the changes and wait for the next synchronization. To store the changes, you use the `localStorage` API.

You handle this logic with the `uploaditem` function, which you call from the save event handler:

```
function uploaditem(itemdata, isnew) {
  if( navigator.onLine ) {
    sendjson(
      isnew?'PUT':'POST',
      'sync/api/app/'+appinfo.id+'/item/'+itemdata.id,itemdata
    )
  }
  else {
    var uploads = JSON.parse(localStorage.uploads || '[]')
    uploads.push(itemdata)
    localStorage.uploads = JSON.stringify(uploads)
  }
}
```

This function uses the `sendjson` utility function to send the data to the server. You saw a similar function in Chapter 5. As in Chapter 5, this `sendjson` function also uses the `jQuery.ajax` function to do the hard work.

Now you need to consider the full synchronization workflow. When the app starts, the `initapp` function needs to do the following:

1. Determine the server time offset.

2. Register the app, if necessary.

3. Synchronize the to-do items.

If you follow the logic flow on the `initapp` function, you can see these steps unfolding.

The `/todo/sync/api/time` URL calculates the server time offset. The `handletime` function then applies the server offset formula described earlier in this chapter and stores the time offset in the `serveroffset` variable. This variable is then added to the `created` and `updated` time attributes of each item.

App registration is performed if the server returns a "404 Not Found" status from the `Api.getapp` function. The app then attempts a `PUT` on the app resource, which results in a call to the `Api.putapp` function on the server.

Finally, you call the `syncitems` function. This function iterates through the list of items from the server. If an item fetched from the server is not found locally, it is inserted into the local list of items. If a server item has a more recent `updated` time attribute than the corresponding local item, the server version is considered more recent and replaces the local version.

Then the local app gets its chance. The local app reviews the list of pending uploads. If any item updates are entirely new and unknown to the server, they are uploaded. If a pending update is known to the server, and the local update is more recent, then it is also uploaded. If the server version is more recent, the local update is discarded.

This synchronization procedure implements a basic version of the "most recent wins" algorithm. This is sufficient for to-do items maintained by a single user across multiple devices.

SUMMARY

This chapter shows how to build an end-to-end web service using cloud services. You learned how to integrate the SimpleDB cloud database into a Node server. You also addressed problems related to client/server synchronization, adjusting for time differences and remote data changes.

In the next chapter, you'll return to the mobile device and learn how to provide an enhanced user experience. You will learn how to control the appearance of your mobile web app, make full use of the enhanced features of HTML5, launch native applications, and provide a full audiovisual experience.

EXERCISES

1. The example code uses a simple random number to generate app and to-do item identifiers. In a production app you'll have to use something more robust. Review Chapter 5 for clues!

2. There's one little thing missing from your REST API. If you issue a GET request against a resource and you don't specify an identifier, your API should return a list of all items of that resource type. Modify the api.js script to handle this situation.

3. In the To-Do List app, the only change that can be made to the to-do items is to mark them as done or not done. It would be useful to be able to change the text of the to-do item as well and have this text synchronize via the cloud. You should therefore modify the To-Do List app so that when the user taps the text of an item, the text becomes editable. When the user taps again or taps elsewhere, the text changes should be saved and synchronized.

4. The synchronization code in this chapter does not support delete operations. You should now provide support for them. The sample code in the chapter incorrectly restores deleted items that exist on the server. You'll need to find a way to record which items have been deleted. But beware: You should not delete an item if it has a more recent update on the server! You'll also need to handle delete operations that occur offline.

Answers to the Exercises can be found in the Appendix.

▶ WHAT YOU LEARNED IN THIS CHAPTER

TOPIC	KEY CONCEPTS
Cloud Service Architecture	When you build a cloud service, you have to take into account all the constituents of that service. There are the clients of the service, your service itself, and then the third-party cloud services that your service uses. You need to design your system so that it offers the optimal capacity in a cost-effective way. You will often find that the best way to do this is to outsource as many functions as possible to the cloud. In particular, outsourcing the database can be a big win in terms of cost savings.
Web Services APIs	A web service API is a well-defined set of operations that a web service (typically hosting in the cloud) offers to clients. Web services are delivered over the HTTP protocol. There are two primary types of web service APIs: SOAP and REST. SOAP is XML-based and uses HTTP merely as a transport layer. REST can be XML- or JSON-based and tries to work with HTTP, reusing the HTTP request verbs such as GET, PUT, POST and DELETE and also making use of HTTP status code. For example, a result with a 404 status code means that the specific item requested was not found in the web service database.
Amazon SimpleDB	A cloud database service offered by Amazon. This cloud database is a highly simplified data store that offers effectively unlimited storage capacity without suffering from performance loss. On the other hand, the SimpleDB database does not offer traditional relational database transactions, and data can only be assumed to be consistent after a small period of elapsed time. Values stored in the SimpleDB database must be encoded as strings, and the encoding must be done by the client.
Cloud Time Synchronization	It will always be the case that the local time on clients and servers will vary to a certain extent. To deal with this random time difference, you can use a simple formula to calculate an adjustment, known as the *server offset*, which clients add to their local time. This technique allows you to handle time-sensitive logic effectively.

Enhancing the User Experience

WHAT YOU WILL LEARN IN THIS CHAPTER:

➤ Building a tab bar–style app

➤ Using the built-in jQuery Mobile scrolling feature

➤ Using the iScroll library for near-native content scrolling

➤ Playing audio files in your app

➤ Playing video files in your app

➤ Launching other apps from your app

In this chapter, you'll learn how to provide an improved user experience by making your app look and feel like native apps. You'll also learn how to play multimedia content and how to interact with other apps on the device.

By building your app using HTML5, you get to reach the widest audience possible because your app is cross-platform out of the box. The challenge is to avoid giving your app a lowest-common-denominator interface that is obviously implemented using HTML. This chapter looks at a few techniques you can use to avoid this.

CREATING A CLASSIC TAB BAR INTERFACE

Mobile web apps built using HTML5 are usually productivity-style apps. If you go to the iPhone App Store or the Android Marketplace and take a look at the apps in the productivity category, you'll notice that many of them have a tab bar at the bottom. This layout style presents a row of tabs at the bottom of the screen. Tapping a tab opens a new page of the app. Each tab corresponds to a logical grouping of app features. Most apps have between four and six tabs.

This layout style is so common that the native code libraries provide preconfigured classes that make it easy for developers to build tab bars. You can do this in HTML. But it's not as simple as just positioning a tab bar at the bottom of the screen. You also need to solve a tricky problem: scrolling the content above the tab bar. The user needs to be able to scroll this content in the same way as in any native app. With a one-finger touch, a user should be able to flick the content up and down at high speed and see it "rubber-band" at the start and end of the scroll.

Generally, in a mobile web app, scrolling applies to the whole app, not just your content element. But you don't want a user to be able to scroll your entire interface, including the tab bar! You want the tab bar to say in place and the rest of the app to scroll. The To Do List app in the previous chapters side-stepped this problem by having no tab bar at the bottom. But this is not an option if your client wants one.

In a non-mobile context, the way that you make the content of an HTML element scrollable is by adding the CSS style `overflow:scroll`. If you do this in a mobile context, you will make the content scrollable, but only with two fingers. This is still not what you want.

There are two solutions. One is the jQuery Mobile solution, which involves making the tab bar fade out while the user is scrolling and making it fade it back in when the scrolling is done. This solution has the advantage of using the mobile browser's built-in page scrolling, which is always going to be fast. The disadvantage is that this is not the same as native scrolling behavior. It is an acceptable solution for a mobile web app that will remain in a browser window. For full-screen mobile web apps, however, you need another solution. This is where the iScroll library comes into play. The iScroll library is a custom JavaScript library for mobile scrolling that intercepts touch events over a given element and uses those events to control the scrolling of the element. The scrolling effect is carefully tuned using hardware-accelerated CSS3 transitions to closely replicate the feel of native scrolling. The iScroll library is not quite as fast as native scrolling, but it does work very well for small- to medium-sized scrolling lists.

In the following sections, you'll see how to implement both of these solutions.

Implementing the jQuery Mobile Solution

The scrolling effect is built into the jQuery Mobile library and is thus very easy to use. By setting custom properties on the jQuery Mobile elements, you can control which elements remain in place when the user scrolls the page. In the following example, you'll create a small demonstration app to learn how to achieve the effects described in this and the remaining code examples in this chapter. The tab bar you create here will have pages that correspond to the other code examples in this chapter.

TRY IT OUT Scrolling with jQuery Mobile

You can use the code in this example as a template for your own tab bar–style apps. Here's what you do:

1. Create a new folder called `enhanced`. Copy the `jquery.js`, `jquery.mobile.js`, and `jquery .mobile.css` files as well as the jQuery Mobile `images` folder into the `enhanced` folder.

2. Open your `nginx.conf` file in your nginx installation folder and add the following lines to the server section:

```
location /enhanced/ {
  alias /path/to/your/enhanced/;
}
```

code snippet nginx.conf.additions.txt

3. Reload the nginx configuration file with this command:

```
sudo nginx -s reload
```

4. Create a file called `scroll-jqm.css` and insert the following code in it:

```
#main, #footer {
  padding: 0px;
}
div.content {
  display:none;
}
```

code snippet scroll-jqm.css

5. Create a file called `scroll-jqm.html` and insert the following code in it:

```
<!DOCTYPE html>
<html>
<head>
  <title>Enhanced App</title>
  <meta name="viewport"
    content="user-scalable=no,initial-scale=1.0,maximum-scale=1.0" />
  <meta name="apple-mobile-web-app-capable" content="yes" />

  <link rel="stylesheet" href="jquery.mobile.css" />
  <link rel="stylesheet" href="scroll-jqm.css" />

  <script src="jquery.js"></script>
  <script src="jquery.mobile.js"></script>
  <script src="scroll-jqm.js"></script>
</head>
<body>

<div id="main" data-role="page">

  <div data-role="header" data-position="fixed">
    <h1>Enhanced App</h1>
  </div>

  <div data-role="content">
    <div id="content_scroll" class="content">
      <ul data-role="listview">

        <li>a</li><li>b</li><li>c</li><li>d</li>
        <li>e</li><li>f</li><li>g</li><li>h</li>
        <li>i</li><li>j</li><li>k</li><li>l</li>
```

```
          <li>m</li><li>n</li><li>o</li><li>p</li>
          <li>q</li><li>r</li><li>s</li><li>t</li>
          <li>u</li><li>v</li><li>w</li><li>x</li>
          <li>y</li><li>z</li>

          <li>A</li><li>B</li><li>C</li><li>D</li>
          <li>E</li><li>F</li><li>G</li><li>H</li>
          <li>I</li><li>J</li><li>K</li><li>L</li>
          <li>M</li><li>N</li><li>O</li><li>P</li>
          <li>Q</li><li>R</li><li>S</li><li>T</li>
          <li>U</li><li>V</li><li>W</li><li>X</li>
          <li>Y</li><li>Z</li>

      </ul>
    </div>

    <div id="content_audio" class="content">
      <p>audio example</p>
    </div>

    <div id="content_video" class="content">
      <p>video example</p>
    </div>

    <div id="content_launch" class="content">
      <p>launch example</p>
    </div>

  </div>

  <div id="footer" data-role="footer" class="ui-bar" data-position="fixed">
    <div data-role="navbar" class="ui-navbar">
      <ul class="ui-grid-b">
        <li class="ui-block-b">
          <a id="tab_scroll"
             href="javascript:void(0)">scroll</a></li>
        <li class="ui-block-c">
          <a id="tab_audio"
             href="javascript:void(0)">audio</a></li>
        <li class="ui-block-d">
          <a id="tab_video"
             href="javascript:void(0)">video</a></li>
        <li class="ui-block-e">
          <a id="tab_launch"
             href="javascript:void(0)">launch</a></li>
      </ul>
    </div>
  </div>

</div>


</body>
</html>
```

code snippet scroll-jqm.html

6. Create a file called `scroll-jqm.js` and insert the following code in it:

```
$(function(){

function handletab(tabname) {
  return function(){
    $("div.content").hide()
    $("#content_"+tabname).show()
  }
}

  $("#tab_scroll").tap(handletab('scroll')).tap()
  $("#tab_audio").tap(handletab('audio'))
  $("#tab_video").tap(handletab('video'))
  $("#tab_launch").tap(handletab('launch'))
})
```

code snippet scroll-jqm.js

7. Open the application by visiting `http://YOUR_IP_ADDRESS/enhanced/scroll-jqm.html` in your mobile browser.

8. To install the example as a mobile web app, perform the home screen installation procedure described in Chapter 3.

9. Verify that you can scroll the list of items on the first page and that the header and tab bar fade in and out when you stop and start scrolling, as shown in Figure 7-1.

10. Verify that the tab bars function correctly. Tapping on each tab should show the content for that tab.

How It Works

The code in this example follows the basic HTML mobile template you have been using for all the examples in this book.

This example uses a single jQuery Mobile page (`div id="main"`) to display the full user interface of the app. You don't use separate pages as that would require cutting and pasting the header and footer content for each page.

FIGURE 7-1

The scrolling behavior is very simple to activate. You simply add the `data-position="fixed"` attribute to the header and footer. Now, whenever you scroll the page, these elements reposition themselves so that they always appear at the top and bottom of the page. Because it would be impossible to match the speed of the page scrolling, the elements are faded out while the scroll animates, and they're faded back in when it is finished.

Tapping on a tab causes the content for that tab to appear. You enable this functionality manually, by attaching a tap event handler to each tab. The event handler is built dynamically using a generator function:

```
function handletab(tabname) {
  return function(){
    $("div.content").hide()
    $("#content_"+tabname).show()
  }
}
```

The generator function takes the name of the tab, dynamically creates a tap function just for that tab, and returns the new dynamically created function (shown boldfaced here). This returned function (not the `handletab` function itself!) is then attached to the tab. Dynamic function generation prevents you from having to work out the ID of the tapped element by using the `event` object. You'll see more examples of dynamic function generation in later chapters. It's a feature of the JavaScript language that you can often use to your advantage.

The tap handler itself is very simple. It just hides all content and then shows the content for the tapped tab.

This tab bar solution is best used when you have a mobile website with an app-like interface. In the next section, you'll learn about a better solution for mobile web apps that need a more native feel.

 NOTE *jQuery Mobile supports automated page transitions, which can make writing your own tap event handlers unnecessary. However, the jQuery Mobile page transition feature is more suitable for mobile web sites that have multiple physical pages, and it is not as useful for single page sites that are really app interfaces.*

Using the iScroll Solution

To give a more native feel to content scrolling, you need to use a supporting JavaScript library. Several of them are available. The one you'll use here is called iScroll, and it is available at `http://cubiq .org/iscroll-4`. You should download this library now because you will need it for this example.

iScroll works by tracking finger movements over the content to be scrolled. The library listens for touch events and converts them into scroll actions that mimic the native scrolling behavior. The library is very well implemented and re-creates the feel of native scrolling quite effectively. It even enables the flick effect, where a user can scroll faster by flicking a finger over the content. It also enables the "rubber band" effect, which allows the user to temporarily scroll the content above or below its natural limit and have the content bounce back as soon as he or she lets go.

How does a JavaScript library manage to get near-native performance? By using CSS3 animation properties such as `-webkit-translate3d`. You learned about these CSS3 properties in Chapter 4. This 3-D translation property is hardware accelerated, which means it delivers near-native performance. The iScroll library looks after the math and works out the correct transitions for you.

The iScroll library requires you to include some extra markup in your HTML. Because of the way the library is implemented and because the library needs to know the exact size of the scrollable area, you need to provide an additional `div` that wraps your content. You always use the following pattern:

```
<div class="wrapper">
  <div class="scroller">
    <p> your content that scrolls </p>
  </div>
</div>
```

You must also give the wrapper element an exact height value. This is important. Without an exact height, iScroll will fail to function properly.

Inside the wrapper, the first element becomes the one that will be scrollable. In the above example code, this first element is the `div` with `class="scroller"`, shown in the boldfaced text.

TRY IT OUT   Scrolling with iScroll

In this example, you'll upgrade the previous example to use the iScroll library. You already have nginx set up, so you can just create a new set of files with the new functionality. Follow these steps:

1. Copy the `iscroll.js` file from your download of the iScroll library into the `enhanced` folder.

2. Create a file called `scroll-is.css` and insert the following code in it:

Available for
download on
Wrox.com

```
div {
   padding: 0px !important;
}

ul, p {
  margin: 0px !important;
}

div.content {
  display: none;
}
```

code snippet scroll-is.css

3. Copy the `scroll-jqm.html` file and save it as `scroll-is.html`. In the new file, as shown in the following boldfaced code, replace the references to `scroll-jqm.css` and `scroll-jqm.js` with `scroll-is.css` and `scroll-is.js`, respectively. Insert a `script` statement to load the `iscroll.js` file:

Available for
download on
Wrox.com

```
...
    <link rel="stylesheet" href="jquery.mobile.css" />
    <link rel="stylesheet" href="scroll-is.css" />

    <script src="jquery.js"></script>
    <script src="jquery.mobile.js"></script>
    <script src="iscroll.js"></script>
```

```
<script src="scroll-is.js"></script>
</head>
<body>
...
```

code snippet scroll-is.css

4. Create a file called `scroll-is.js` and insert the following code in it:

```
document.ontouchmove = function(e){ e.preventDefault(); }

$(function(){

    var current = 'scroll'
    var scrollers = {}

    var header  = $("#header")
    var footer  = $("#footer")

    header.css({zIndex:1000})
    footer.css({zIndex:1000})


    function handletab(tabname) {
      return function(){
        $("#content_"+current).hide()
        current = tabname
        $("#content_"+tabname).show()
        refresh()
      }
    }

    $("#tab_scroll").tap(handletab('scroll')).tap()
    $("#tab_audio").tap(handletab('audio'))
    $("#tab_video").tap(handletab('video'))
    $("#tab_launch").tap(handletab('launch'))


    function refresh() {
      var content = $("#content_"+current)
      if( !scrollers[current] ) {
        scrollers[current] = new iScroll("content_"+current,{hscroll:false})
      }

      content.height(
        $('body').height() - header.height() - footer.height() - 4
      )
      scrollers[current].refresh()
    }

    window.onresize = function() {
      refresh()
    }
}
```

code snippet scroll-is.js

5. Open the application by visiting `http://YOUR_IP_ADDRESS/enhanced/scroll-is.html` in your mobile browser.

6. Install the app onto your home screen as a mobile web app to get the full effect.

7. Verify that you can scroll the list of items on the first page and that the header and tab bar remain in place when you scroll. Also ensure that you can perform native scrolling actions such as flicking and rubber-banding, as shown in Figure 7-2.

FIGURE 7-2

 WARNING *The iScroll library is designed to provide scrolling for touchscreen devices. When you review or debug your app using a desktop browser and a mouse, you may notice inconsistent scrolling behavior.*

How It Works

In this example, you use JavaScript to set up the user interface so that it has the characteristics of a native app. Because you will be handling content scrolling yourself, you need to prevent the default web browser scrolling behavior of scrolling the entire page. If you don't deactivate this in the browser, your entire app will rubber-band. This line of code intercepts and disables the standard touch move event that causes scrolling:

```
document.ontouchmove = function(e){ e.preventDefault(); }
```

As an experiment, try commenting out this line, reloading the app, and seeing what happens when you press and hold one of the tabs and then move upward. Your whole app moves up! So you can see that this line prevents that from happening.

The remaining code executes when the web app HTML document has fully loaded. You use a jQuery shortcut here: $(function(){...}). This passes a function directly to the $ jQuery object. The function will be called when the document is ready. You need to use this standard jQuery code pattern to make sure that the browser has properly created and set up all the HTML elements before you modify them and attach your event listeners.

Because there are multiple tabs, you need to keep track of which one is currently being shown; you do this by using the current variable. This is not very important for this example because the other tabs have no content. But you will use this app template for the rest of the chapter, and keeping track of which tab is being shown will become more important as you build the rest of the complete tab bar app.

Each content section for each tab needs to be scrollable, so you need to create an iScroll object for each one. The scrollers variable keeps track of the iScroll objects, using the name of the tab.

In order to calculate the proper height of the content area so that you can give it to iScroll, you need to get the heights of the header bar at the top and the tab bar at the bottom. Then you add these together and subtract that number from the total body height. For now, you can just store jQuery references to these elements in the variables header and footer:

```
var header  = $("#header")
var footer  = $("#footer")
```

To make sure that the header and footer are always visible above anything else on the page, you set their z-index CSS property by using jQuery:

```
header.css({zIndex:1000})
footer.css({zIndex:1000})
```

The handletab function from the previous example needs some additional logic. You need to record the name of the tab that was just tapped and also refresh the iScroll object that controls the content for that tab. You do this by calling a refresh function; you will see the code for this shortly. This refresh enables iScroll to work again. When the user taps on a different tab and moves away from this tab, the content is hidden using CSS. Now that the user has returned to this tab, the content is made visible again, and iScroll needs to know about it. The lines to store the current tab and call the refresh function are shown boldfaced:

```
function handletab(tabname) {
  return function(){
    $("#content_"+current).hide()
    current = tabname
    refresh()
    $("#content_"+tabname).show()
  }
}
```

You attach the tab handlers as in the previous example, using the handletab generator function to create a new tap handler function for each tab.

The `refresh` function does the work of setting up the iScroll objects if they do not already exist or refreshing them if they do. This is an example of "lazy initialization," which is a strategy for improving performance. According to this strategy, you create only the objects you need, when you need them. You don't create them all at once when the app starts up.

The refresh function first gets the content `div` for the current tab. A sensible naming convention helps you here. Giving each content `div` an identifier in the form `content_`*tabname* makes it easy to construct the string value of the `id` attribute of the element you want:

```
function refresh() {
    var content = $("#content_"+current)
```

Next, you check whether you have a scroller already. If not, you need to create one. The iScroll object constructor takes the value of the `id` attribute of the element that contains content to scroll, as well as a set of options. You use the `hscroll:false` option to disable horizontal scrolling because you only want vertical scrolling:

```
if( !scrollers[current] ) {
    scrollers[current] = new iScroll("content_"+current,{hscroll:false})
}
```

The iScroll website provides an up-to-date list of the available configuration options that you can specify in the second parameter.

Once you have your iScroll object, you can proceed with the refresh. You recalculate the height of the content section each time because the device orientation may have changed. To get the height of the content section, you subtract the height of the header and footer from the height of the body. You also need to subtract an additional 4 pixels to account for the 1-pixel borders on the header and footer `div`s:

```
content.height(
    $('body').height() - header.height() - footer.height() - 4
)
```

After you have the height set, you can refresh the scroller:

```
    scrollers[current].refresh()
}
```

The last little piece of housekeeping is to make sure you call the refresh function when the user changes the device orientation:

```
window.onresize = function() {
    refresh()
}
```

The iScroll library always requires you to refresh if there are any changes to the content or the layout. If you don't refresh, the scroll will behave incorrectly. If in doubt, refresh!

WARNING *The first argument to the iScroll constructor is the identifier of the element that contains the content to scroll. This value is not a jQuery selector, so you don't put a # in front of it. It is just the plain element identifier string. Also, if you give iScroll the identifier of the wrong element, especially the parent of the content element, you may see behavior that is almost, but not quite, right. Double-check your element identifiers!*

 NOTE *Version 5 of the iPhone platform (known as iOS 5) introduces support for* overflow:scroll. *That's the good news. Actually it gets better: Add a* -webkit-overflow-scrolling: touch *property to the scrollable element, and you get native speed and scrollbars! The bad news? This is iOS 5 only. You'll still need to use something like iScroll for full cross-platform support. There can be no doubt that iScroll will be updated to hand over scrolling to the native implementation on iOS 5 devices, so it is still your best option for cross-platform, and multiple-version supporting code.*

ENABLING MOBILE AUDIO AND VIDEO

It is possible to play audio and view video within your mobile web app. HTML5 provides a range of new capabilities in this area. Unfortunately, it is also an area with many challenges, both technical and legal.

In this section, you'll learn how to get simple embedded players working, on both iPhone and Android devices. You'll learn about simple use cases where you just need to play the content as part of your app.

Playing Audio in Your App

In theory, playing audio files in a mobile web app should be as easy as displaying an image. The new HTML5 audio tag is meant to be used in much the same way as the traditional img tag. You have a src element that you point to your media file:

```
<audio src="audio.mp3" controls="yes">
```

In practice, using the audio tag directly is not yet feasible. While the iPhone has a solid implementation, many Android phones, even up to version 2.3 of Android, do not support the audio tag correctly. Therefore, you need a workaround. You can use Flash. Or, rather, you can use a third-party library that uses Flash. Once you reach the stage where your code requires multiple hacks based on browser and device versions, it is best to delegate that logic to a component library. There are quite a few audio and video JavaScript libraries out there that can help. In this book, you'll use the jPlayer library. This library is a jQuery plug-in, which makes life even easier.

The jPlayer library is available at www.jplayer.org. You need to download this library to complete the examples in this chapter. You also need to download the Blue Monday theme stylesheet files from the same download page.

Before you start coding, you also need to consider the file formats that you'll need for your audio file. There are many audio file formats. Not all of them are free. Some are patented and require the payment of royalties. You will find, however, that both iPhone and Android can handle MP3 files, so this is a good format to use. If you need to convert from other formats, you might need to install a utility to do so. The open source Audacity sound-editing application is adequate for this purpose. You can download Audacity at http://audacity.sourceforge.net.

You need some sound files to run the code examples in this chapter. If you do not have any MP3 files available, you can use Audacity to create some. Or you can download some files from www.pdsounds.org, which is a library of free public domain sound files.

If you are building an app that relies heavily on audio, you need to conduct further research to determine the best audio formats and quality levels to use. The example in this book will get you started, in the sense that it will give you just enough rope to hang yourself!

In the following example, you'll add an audio player to the audio tab section of your app. You'll need to take care of a complication: Each tab section is hidden, shown only when the user taps on it. However, the jPlayer library requires that its player HTML tags remain visible at all times. The solution is simply to place the audio player offscreen and move it onscreen when the audio tab is displayed.

TRY IT OUT   Embedding Audio in Your App

In this example, you'll embed audio in your app. Here's how:

1. Copy the jquery.jplayer.js file from the jPlayer download into the enhanced folder. Also copy the Jplayer.swf file.

2. Copy the Blue Monday theme stylesheet files into the enhanced folder as well:

```
jplayer.blue.monday.*
```

3. Copy the scroll-is.html file from the preceding example and save it as scroll-audio.html.

4. Modify the scroll-audio.html file by inserting or modifying the following boldfaced lines:

```
...
    <link rel="stylesheet" href="jquery.mobile.css" />
    <link rel="stylesheet" href="scroll-full.css" />

    <link type="text/css" href="jplayer.blue.monday.css" rel="stylesheet" />

    <script src="jquery.js"></script>
    <script src="jquery.mobile.js"></script>
    <script src="iscroll.js"></script>
    <script src="jquery.jplayer.js"></script>

    <script src="scroll-audio.js"></script>
</head>

...
```

```
      <div id="content_audio" class="content">
        <p> </p>
      </div>
...
</div>


<div id="audio" style="position:absolute;top:9999px;overflow:hidden">
  <div id="jquery_jplayer_1" class="jp-jplayer"></div>
  <div class="jp-audio">
    <div class="jp-type-single">
      <div id="jp_interface_1" class="jp-interface">
        <ul class="jp-controls">
          <li><a href="#" class="jp-play" tabindex="1">play</a></li>
          <li><a href="#" class="jp-pause" tabindex="1">pause</a></li>
          <li><a href="#" class="jp-stop" tabindex="1">stop</a></li>
          <li><a href="#" class="jp-mute" tabindex="1">mute</a></li>
          <li><a href="#" class="jp-unmute" tabindex="1">unmute</a></li>
        </ul>
        <div class="jp-progress">
          <div class="jp-seek-bar">
            <div class="jp-play-bar"></div>
          </div>
        </div>
        <div class="jp-volume-bar">
          <div class="jp-volume-bar-value"></div>
        </div>
        <div class="jp-current-time"></div>
        <div class="jp-duration"></div>
      </div>
      <div id="jp_playlist_1" class="jp-playlist">
        <ul>
          <li>Audio</li>
        </ul>
      </div>
    </div>
  </div>
</div>

</body>
</html>
```

code snippet scroll-audio.html

5. Copy the `scroll-is.js` file from the preceding example and save it as `scroll-audio.js`.

6. Modify the `scroll-audio.js` file by inserting or modifying the following boldfaced lines:

```
var audio = null

function refresh() {
  var content = $("#content_"+current)
  if( !scrollers[current] ) {
    scrollers[current] = new iScroll("content_"+current,{hscroll:false})
```

```
    }

    if( 'audio' == current ) {
      if( !audio ) {
        $("#jquery_jplayer_1").jPlayer({
          ready: function () {
            $(this).jPlayer("setMedia", {
              mp3: "audio.mp3",
            });
          },
          swfPath:'',
          supplied: "mp3"
        });
        audio = true;
      }

      $('#audio').css({top:header.height()})
    }
    else {
      $('#audio').css({top:9999})
    }

  content.height(
    $('body').height() - header.height() - footer.height() - 4
  )
  scrollers[current].refresh()
}
```

code snippet scroll-audio.js

FIGURE 7-3

7. Copy an MP3 file into the enhanced folder. Rename the file audio.mp3.

8. Open the application by visiting http://YOUR_IP_ADDRESS/ enhanced/scroll-audio.html in your mobile browser.

9. Install it as a mobile web app.

10. Verify that you can see the audio control box when you tap the audio tab. Press play to start the audio track. Verify that the control works as expected. Your screen should look as shown in Figure 7-3.

How It Works

The jPlayer library is quite easy to use. You just include the jquery .jplayer.js script file and provide some skinning CSS. The code in this example creates a simple audio player box with standard controls.

You can't hide the jPlayer HTML tags in the normal manner, so you simply position them offscreen:

```
<div id="audio" style="position:absolute;top:9999px;overflow:hidden">
```

The HTML tags inside this positioning `div` construct the player audio controls. You can get these tags — consisting of multiple elements styled with the `jp-*` family of CSS classes — from the jPlayer website. You can customize this view to create your own player.

The audio content page `div` itself contains a filler paragraph: `<p> </p>`. This ensures that iScroll continues to function correctly.

The JavaScript code for this example consists of extra logic executed when the audio tab is viewed. The `audio` variable keeps track of the existence of the jPlayer library object. You want to create it only once — but lazily. This is the same performance optimization you used for the iScroll library. You configure the jPlayer object with a set of properties that specify the media files to play, the location of supporting files, such as the `Jplayer.swf` Flash file, and various other options:

```
$("#jquery_jplayer_1").jPlayer({
  ready: function () {
    $(this).jPlayer("setMedia", {
      mp3: "audio.mp3",
    });
  },
  swfPath:'',
  supplied: "mp3"
});
```

Finally, you need to ensure that the audio player is moved in and out of view, as needed. You do this by placing it just below the header if the audio tab is active or moving it far down the page, below the visible section, when the audio tab is not active:

```
if( 'audio' == current ) {
  ...
  $('#audio').css({top:header.height()})
}
else {
  $('#audio').css({top:9999})
}
```

Playing Video in Your App

Playing video in your app involves many of the same challenges as playing audio. The HTML5 `video` tag, like the `audio` tag, does not work reliably on Android versions up to 2.3. Here's what the tag looks like:

```
<video srv="video.m4v" controls="yes">
```

As with audio, you have to use a third-party library to play videos if you want a practical solution. Luckily, the jPlayer library can also do this, and the code is very similar.

The main challenge with video is not so much getting it to play as getting it into the right format. To have video play on iPhone and Android, you need to use the MPEG4 video container format.

Inside, this uses the H.264 video codec. You need to use a video converter utility or service, such as www.zencoder.com, to convert your videos to this format.

The H.264 codec is patent-protected, so you can't use it freely. In many cases, you can transmit H.264-encoded content over the Internet without incurring a charge. However, the licensing details are rather complex, and you should obtain legal advice if you plan to deliver video in a commercial context.

In the future, other options for video encoding may become more widespread (for example, Ogg Theora, Google WebM). It remains to be seen whether Apple will support these. Until it does, you're stuck with H.264.

In the following example, you will continue to extend the tab bar app by filling out the video content tab.

TRY IT OUT **Embedding Video in Your App**

Like the audio example, this example uses the jPlayer library. You again need to make sure that the video player tags are not hidden but rather pushed off the visible area. Follow these steps:

1. Copy the `scroll-audio.html` file from the last section and save it as `scroll-video.html`.

2. Modify the `scroll-audio.html` file by inserting or modifying the following boldfaced lines:

Available for download on Wrox.com

```
...
      <div id="content_video" class="content">
         <p> </p>
      </div>
...
   </div>

<div id="video" style="position:absolute;top:9999px;overflow:hidden">
  <div class="jp-video jp-video-270p">
    <div class="jp-type-single">
      <div id="jquery_jplayer_2" class="jp-jplayer"></div>
      <div id="jp_interface_2" class="jp-interface">
        <div class="jp-video-play" ></div>
        <ul class="jp-controls">
          <li><a href="#" class="jp-play" tabindex="1">play</a></li>
          <li><a href="#" class="jp-pause" tabindex="1">pause</a></li>
          <li><a href="#" class="jp-stop" tabindex="1">stop</a></li>
          <li><a href="#" class="jp-mute" tabindex="1">mute</a></li>
          <li><a href="#" class="jp-unmute" tabindex="1">unmute</a></li>
        </ul>
        <div class="jp-progress">
          <div class="jp-seek-bar">
            <div class="jp-play-bar"></div>
          </div>
        </div>
        <div class="jp-volume-bar">
          <div class="jp-volume-bar-value"></div>
        </div>
        <div class="jp-current-time"></div>
```

```
            <div class="jp-duration"></div>
        </div>
        <div id="jp_playlist_1" class="jp-playlist">
          <ul>
            <li>Video</li>
          </ul>
        </div>
      </div>
    </div>
</div>

</body>
</html>
```

code snippet scroll-video.html

3. Copy the scroll-video.js file from the preceding example and save it as scroll-video.js.

4. Modify the scroll-video.js file by inserting or modifying the following boldfaced lines:

```
var video = null
var audio = null

function refresh() {
  var content = $("#content_"+current)
  if( !scrollers[current] ) {
    scrollers[current] = new iScroll("content_"+current,{hscroll:false})
  }


  ...
  else {
    $('#audio').css({top:9999})
  }


  if( 'video' == current ) {
    if( !video ) {
      $("#jquery_jplayer_2").jPlayer({
        ready: function () {
          $(this).jPlayer("setMedia", {
            m4v: "video_h264aac.m4v",
            poster: "poster.png"
          });
        },
        swfPath: "",
        supplied: "m4v",
        cssSelectorAncestor: '#jp_interface_2'
      });
      video = true;
    }

    $('#video').css({top:header.height()})
  }
```

```
else {
  $('#video').css({top:9999})
}


content.height(
  $('body').height() - header.height() - footer.height() - 4
)
scrollers[current].refresh()
}
```

code snippet scroll-video.js

5. Copy an MPEG4 video file into the `enhanced` folder. Rename the file `video_h264aac.m4v`. The jPlayer library is quite sensitive to the name format, so make sure you include the `h264aac` part. If you have a still image that you want to use as the initial content of the video box before it starts playing, you should also copy it into the `enhanced` folder and call it `poster.png`.

6. Open the application by visiting `http://YOUR_IP_ADDRESS/enhanced/scroll-video.html` in your mobile browser.

7. Install it as a mobile web app.

8. Verify that you can see the video control box when you tap the video tab. Press play to start the video. Verify that the control works as expected.

 WARNING *On the iPhone, the video does not play embedded in your app. Instead, the app launches a full-screen video player. Tapping the Done button returns to your app.*

How It Works

As in the preceding example, the jPlayer library does all the hard work for you. For a production app, you need to adjust the styling on the `jp-*` classes to get the sizing, look, and feel you want.

The video control exists side-by-side with the audio control from the preceding example. In order to make it work, jPlayer requires that you provide a different set of HTML tags as the control template. You do so by pointing the `cssAncestorSelector` property at the HTML tags for the video controls:

```
$("#jquery_jplayer_2").jPlayer({
  ready: function () {
    $(this).jPlayer("setMedia", {
      m4v: "video_h264aac.m4v",
      poster: "poster.png"
    });
  },
  swfPath: "",
```

```
      supplied: "m4v",
        cssSelectorAncestor: '#jp_interface_2'
    });
```

The jPlayer library has many more controls and options. There isn't enough space to cover them all in this book. Check out the jPlayer site for details and more examples: `http://jplayer.org`.

LAUNCHING APPS FROM YOUR APP

You can run other apps from your own app. To do so, you just need to use specially formatted URLs. You replace the `http://` part of the URL with a code string known as a *URL scheme*. When the user taps a link with one of these URLs, the associated application opens. iPhone and Android phones recognize a standard set of URLs, and you'll learn how to use them in this section.

Installed native applications can also register their own custom URL schemes. You'll learn how to do this yourself in Chapter 10. A number of sites keep a registry of custom URL schemes. One of the most comprehensive is `http://applookup.com`. You can use this site to find the URL schemes of apps that you might want to launch from your own app.

The standard URL schemes allow you to launch a number of apps, as described in the following sections.

Launching a Web Browser from Your App

Any normal `a` tag link will work as usual when your app is running inside the mobile browser. When you install your app as a mobile web app on the home screen, the link will instead open the browser app separately, maintaining the illusion that your web app is a native app. The URL scheme has the following formats (replace `www.example.com` with the URL of the website you want to display):

```
http://www.example.com
https://www.example.com
```

Launching a Phone from Your App

You can start phone calls by using this URL scheme:

```
tel:123456789
```

To prevent malicious use, the phone number can contain only digits and hyphens. This prevents an app from activating special functions using the # and * characters. The iPhone simulator does not contain a phone application, so you need a real device to test this.

Launching SMS from Your App

You can start an SMS messaging application from your app. When you do this, you can enter the phone number to SMS, but again, as a security measure, you cannot set the text of the message. This scheme has the following format:

```
sms:123456789
```

Launching Mail from Your App

You can open the mail application and create a new email message for the user to send. Unlike with the SMS scheme, you can set some parameters here. This scheme has the following basic format:

```
mailto:richard@example.com
```

You can set the subject and body of the email like this:

```
mailto:richard@example.com?subject=Hello&body=How+are+things%3F
```

The text in the URL must be URL encoded, or it will not work. You use the JavaScript `escape` function to URL encode a string.

Launching Maps from Your App

To send a user directly to a maps application, you use a special form of the standard Google Maps URL. In this case, there is no URL scheme, but the mobile device browser will nonetheless recognize the URL as a special case. You use this format:

```
http://maps.google.com/maps?q=Dublin,Ireland
```

Launching YouTube from Your App

You can link directly to YouTube videos from your app. As with maps, there is no URL scheme, but the browser will recognize URLs if you use this format:

```
http://www.youtube.com/watch?v=Xzhlrggtesg
```

TRY IT OUT Launching Apps

The code in this example displays a list of links that each open a separate app, placing your mobile web app in the background. Follow these steps:

1. Copy the `scroll-video.html` file from the preceding example and save it as `scroll-launch .html`.

2. Open the `scroll-launch.html` file and insert the following boldfaced HTML content into its launch content section:

Available for
download on
Wrox.com

```
<div id="content_launch" class="content">
  <div>
    <h3>Launchers</h3>
    <ul>
      <li><a href="http://google.com">http://google.com</a><br><br></li>
      <li><a href="tel:123456789">tel:123456789</a><br><br></li>
      <li><a href="sms:123456789">sms:123456789</a><br><br></li>
      <li><a href="mailto:richard@example.com">
        mailto:richard@example.com</a><br><br></li>
      <li><a href="http://maps.google.com/maps?q=Dublin,Ireland">
```

```
        http://maps.google.com/maps?q=Dublin,Ireland</a><br><br></li>
      <li><a href="http://www.youtube.com/watch?v=Xzhlrggtesg">
        http://www.youtube.com/watch?v=Xzhlrggtesg</a><br><br></li>
    </ul>
  </div>
</div>
```

code snippet scroll-launch.html

3. Install the application as a web app from `http://YOUR_IP_ADDRESS/enhanced/scroll-launch.html`.

4. Start the app and tap the launch tab. You should see a list of links, as shown in Figure 7-4. Tap each link in turn to launch the different apps.

FIGURE 7-4

How It Works

In this example, the mobile browser does all the hard work for you. All you have to do is make sure to follow the correct URL syntax for each type of app.

SUMMARY

In this chapter, you learned a number of techniques that you can use to enhance your mobile web app. It is quite possible to replicate many native features through innovative use of HTML5 and by using some of the excellent third-party JavaScript libraries that are available.

In the next chapter, you'll take a break from the client side and learn how to build the server-side logic of your app. You'll also learn how to make good use of cloud hosting to accelerate your development and ensure that the service your app provides is scalable to large numbers of users.

EXERCISES

1. The transitions between tabs in the example applications in this chapter are instantaneous. Use CSS transforms to create a sliding animation that animates the tab content by sliding it upwards when the user taps on a tab. Consider using the CSS `keyframe` syntax.

2. By default, the iScroll library provides you with a scrolling area that mimics native scrolling as closely as possible. Sometimes this is not what you want, either for performance reasons or to provide a custom user interface selection control. Adjust the iScroll code to hide the simulated scrollbar and prevent momentum-based scrolling.

3. You can also launch the iTunes application from your iPhone app. However, iTunes links are quite complex to construct. Is there an automated way to "make iTunes links"?

4. Many apps that feature scrollable content also let you refresh that content by pulling down on the scrollable area. For example, the official Twitter mobile app loads new tweets whenever you pull down on the list of tweets. Replicate this feature by using iScroll.

Answers to the Exercises can be found in the Appendix.

▶ WHAT YOU LEARNED IN THIS CHAPTER

TOPIC	KEY CONCEPTS
Tab bar apps	The tab bar style is a very common app interface layout, where the app content appears above a fixed navigation bar that contains a number of tabs. The tabs can contain text or icons. Tapping a tab opens the content page for that tab.
jQuery Mobile scroll support	The jQuery Mobile project enables you to use the native scrolling behavior of the mobile browser by handling the placement of fixed page elements automatically. Due to performance limitations, this placement can only be achieved by fading the fixed elements out when scrolling occurs and fading them back in when scrolling ceases.
iScroll library	iScroll is an open source JavaScript library that replicates the native scrolling interaction by listening for touch events on a particular HTML element and then moving the element's contents to mimic native scrolling. By using hardware-accelerated CSS3 transforms, you can achieve near-native performance.
HTML5 media tags	The HTML5 standard introduces the `audio` and `video` tags. These tags provide a standard set of controls for playing media files. Unfortunately, due to inconsistent implementations and media format support issues, these tags are not yet ready for cross-platform production use.
jPlayer library	jPlayer is an open source JavaScript library that hides the complexity of embedding audio and video in your app. It supports multiple formats and enables a number of workarounds for browsers that do not properly support the HTML5 media tags.
Custom URL scheme	Native apps installed on a device can register a code string that can be used as a URL in the mobile browser. Tapping on a link with this code string launches the app. You can use a number of standard URL schemes to launch some of the standard device apps, such as email or the phone.

Working with the Cloud

WHAT YOU WILL LEARN IN THIS CHAPTER:

➤ Working with the Amazon S3 service

➤ Streaming data efficiently

➤ Understanding the OAuth protocol

➤ Signing in to your app with Twitter

➤ Signing in to your app with Facebook

➤ Designing a large-scale system

➤ Designing a shared-nothing architecture

➤ Using a `memcached` server

➤ Using the consistent hashing algorithm

➤ Dealing with complex cache invalidation

It's time to move on from the To Do List application and build something more exciting. In this chapter, you'll build a social networking app called Lifestream. It will be similar to Twitter for photos. Instead of posting 140-character messages, your users will post photos direct from their mobile phones using your app. Your Lifestream app will allow users to follow each other in the same way Twitter does.

To build the Lifestream app, you'll need to pull together some cloud services, extend your existing knowledge of server-side JavaScript, and work out how handle a truly large-scale application. You want to build an app that can handle millions of users and millions of photos. The techniques you'll learn in putting together the Lifestream app are applicable to a wide range of apps and services. After you've build this app, you'll be ready to build the next revolutionary cloud and mobile startup!

In this chapter, you'll find out how to answer some big questions:

➤   How do you store millions of photos?

➤   How do you link a service to social networking sites?

➤   How do you handle millions of users?

STORING CONTENT IN AMAZON S3

The Lifestream application you'll build in this chapter will let you take photos on your phone and upload them to the Lifestream service. Other users can follow you. They will see a stream of your most recent photos, mixed in with the photos of all the other people they are following.

You need a place to store all those photos. You also need a way to deliver the photos when people want to look at them. You could build your own custom photo storage system, perhaps even using Amazon Elastic Compute Cloud (EC2) for the servers. Sounds like a lot of work.

There is an easier solution: You can use Amazon S3. The S3 stands for Simple Storage Service. The S3 service is one of the original cloud services first offered by Amazon, and has a proven track record. It allows you to store an unlimited number of files and is perfect for storing mobile photos. The service can also deliver your photos directly to users over the web, so you don't even have worry about writing a web service to do that.

The way that Amazon makes money from S3 is by charging you for storage and transfer costs. You pay for as much as you use. This means that you can start off small and grow bigger over time. In a startup context, it means that you can bootstrap your service for very little cash down when you have only a few thousand users, and then you can really ramp things up when you get funding. This is one of the big advantages of cloud services: You no longer need to spend large amounts of money up-front on high-end servers to handle large user volumes. This is especially important for mobile apps, where an app can easily "go viral" if you design and execute well. It would be terrible to have your service crash just when you're beginning to taste victory.

The Architecture of Amazon S3

The Amazon S3 service is a key-value store for data files. This means that each file that you upload to S3 is identified by a unique *key* string that you specify. The files that you upload are known as data *objects* when they are inside S3. As far as S3 is concerned, files are just objects, and objects are just collections of bytes. Thus keys and objects are at the heart of the service, and most operations involve working with them.

To help organize your objects, S3 provides *buckets*. These are named collections of objects. You can store as many objects as you like in a bucket, but you can create only up to 100 buckets. Each object can be up to 5 terabytes in size. Each key is limited to 255 characters.

You can store your buckets in different geographic regions. You might want to do this in order to store your data near your users or for legal reasons, such as to comply with privacy legislation.

When you upload a data file to S3, Amazon copies the data to multiple different physical machines, using a proprietary algorithm. This means that S3 data storage is not quite like a traditional database. If you save a file to S3 and then read it back out again right away, you might get old data because the new data has not yet propagated to all the relevant servers. As explained in Chapter 6, this property is known as *eventual consistency*.

Eventual consistency is not as bad as it sounds. The positive side is that you get almost infinite storage capacity with predictable download times. This is great news for storing lots of photos — exactly what you need!

Amazon provides free introductory offers for S3, but for the most part, you will be a paying customer. As with other for-a-fee services, Amazon provides a service-level agreement for S3. This means that if the service falls below certain performance levels, you get a refund. It also means that Amazon has an incentive to make sure that the service stays up, which is a good thing.

Amazon S3 is a web service provided over HTTP. The web service API is available in Representation State Transfer (REST) and Simple Object Access Protocol (SOAP) variants. As explained in Chapter 6, you'll find the REST variant much easier to work with. The core REST operations can be broken down as follows:

➤ Service-level operations:

➤ **GET** — Returns a list of all your buckets

➤ Bucket-level operations:

➤ **PUT** — Creates a bucket

➤ **GET** — Returns a list of all your objects

➤ **DELETE** — Deletes a bucket

➤ Object-level operations:

➤ **GET** — Downloads a data file

➤ **PUT** — Uploads a data file

➤ **HEAD** — Gets the details for a data file

➤ **DELETE** — Deletes a data file

In addition, more detailed operations deal with access control and other S3 features. This book does not cover those operations, but you can find the full documentation for S3 at http://aws.amazon .com/documentation/s3.

You can access the web service API directly from your web browser, and S3 provides unique URLs for each of your data files. This means that you can use S3 to deliver photos directly to the users of the Lifestream application without transferring them through your own servers. Not only is this much faster, as you are using the full might of Amazon's infrastructure, but it also saves you money, because you don't have to consume bandwidth and CPU delivering the photos yourself.

To perform operations that change data, such as uploading or deleting a photo, the S3 web service requires you to use your Amazon Web Services (AWS) developer keys. These are the same keys that you used in Chapter 6 for access to the Amazon SimpleDB database. The key-signing process works exactly the same way. Due to this signing requirement, the easiest way to perform operations on S3 is by using a software library.

Using Amazon S3

In this section, you'll learn how to create an S3 bucket, upload a file, and download a file. Later in this book, you'll integrate these core operations into the complete Lifestream service.

TRY IT OUT   Setting Up Amazon S3

You can configure the Amazon S3 service from the Amazon AWS Administration Console website. You click on the Amazon S3 tab to view the S3 section. Using the interface you find in the S3 section, you can review the status of your buckets and manually upload and download files. To build an application and a service that uses S3, you need to access S3 programmatically, using the HTTP API that Amazon provides. However, it is much easier to set up your application buckets manually when your application uses only a few buckets. In the case of the Lifestream application, the users' photos are stored in a single bucket. You can now create this bucket by following these steps:

1. Open the AWS S3 console by visiting `https://console.aws.amazon.com/s3/home`.

2. If you're not already signed in to AWS, sign in with your Amazon account. The AWS S3 console shows a list of your existing buckets. If you have not created any buckets yet, you see the page shown in Figure 8-1.

FIGURE 8-1

3. Click the Create Bucket button at the top of the Buckets sidebar. A dialog appears, asking you to enter the details of your bucket.

4. Enter a name for your bucket. Bucket names must be globally unique and can be in one of several geographic regions. Figure 8-2 shows my settings for the Lifestream app. You need to use your own bucket name, however, as you will not have write permission on the bucket I used for the Lifestream app.

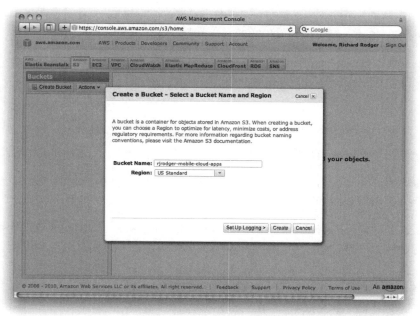

FIGURE 8-2

5. Click the Create button. Amazon takes a short time to process your request and then presents you with a brand-new shiny bucket, as shown in Figure 8-3. If you click on this bucket in the sidebar, Amazon shows you a list of the content files in the bucket. But because this is a new bucket, it won't have any content files yet.

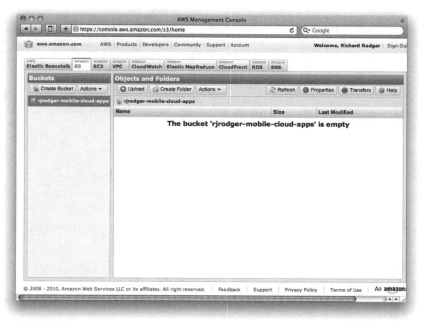

FIGURE 8-3

> **NOTE** *Make sure you select the best region for your bucket. The examples in this book use the US Standard setting for the region. In general, you pay for data transfers across Amazon regions, so the most cost-effective strategy is to keep all your EC2 instances and S3 data in the same region.*

How It Works

When you create a bucket, Amazon checks that the name of the bucket is globally unique across all bucket names in S3. You need to plan ahead and choose a naming scheme that keeps you out of trouble by avoiding name clashes. One quick and easy strategy is simply to prefix each bucket name with the name of your company or your own name. To be even more sure you have a unique name, you can generate universally unique identifier (UUID) values by using a software library and use these values as part of the bucket name. Just remember that you can use a maximum of 255 characters for bucket names, and for the names you can use only lowercase letters, numbers, dots (.), dashes (-), and underscores (_).

Each Amazon account is limited to 100 buckets. You can request more buckets, but it is probably better to design your system to use a limited number of buckets. You can store as many files as you like inside each bucket. There is no limit here except your wallet (you pay for all the bytes!).

One great feature of Amazon S3 as a content store is that unlike with a traditional database, there is no performance difference between a bucket containing one item and a bucket containing a million items. One of the underlying advantages of cloud storage systems like Amazon S3 is that they are architected for reliable scale increases. So when your next project goes viral, your app will keep working as user numbers increase exponentially.

> **NOTE** *This book does not cover the advanced features of the S3 service, such as access control, data redundancy settings, data versioning, and notifications. The best place to read up on these features is the* Amazon S3 Developer Guide, *which is available at* http://aws.amazon.com/documentation/s3.

TRY IT OUT **Putting Content into Amazon S3**

You want the Lifestream application to allow users to store their mobile photos in the cloud, with Amazon S3. You therefore need to implement a web service that can accept a photo upload and then store the photo content in S3. You'll learn how to do this end-to-end in Chapters 9 and 10. For now, you just want to get the photos into S3.

You'll be using Node as your server platform and the knox library as your interface to S3. You could write all your S3 code from scratch, but it's a lot of work to handle all the HTTP flows and cryptographic request signing. To see the nitty-gritty details, you can check out the knox library, which is open source and available at https://github.com/LearnBoost/knox. This example shows you how to create a command-line Node script to perform the upload; you will reuse this code later in the book. Follow these steps:

1. Choose a file to upload. You can use one of your own photos or the public domain image Ireland_circa_900.png, which is included with the code download for this example.

2. Install the knox library by using npm:

```
npm install knox
```

3. Create a folder and subfolder called lifestream/server to contain the code for this chapter.

4. Create a file called keys.js in lifestream/server and insert the following code in it. Replace YOUR_AWS_KEY_ID and YOUR_AWS_SECRET_KEY with your Amazon AWS key ID and key secret values respectively.

```
exports.keyid  = 'YOUR_AWS_KEY_ID'
exports.secret = 'YOUR_AWS_SECRET_KEY'
```

Code snippet keys.js

5. Create a file called s3-put.js in lifestream/server and insert the following code in it:

```
var fs   = require('fs')
var knox = require('knox')

// amazon keys
var keys = require('./keys.js')

var testfile = 'Ireland_circa_900.png'


var client = knox.createClient({
  key:    keys.keyid,
  secret: keys.secret,
  bucket: 'rjrodger-mobile-cloud-apps',
})


fs.stat(testfile, function(err, stat){
  if (err) return console.dir(err);

  var filesize = stat.size
  var instream = fs.createReadStream(testfile)

  var req = client.put(
    testfile,
    {
      'Content-Length':filesize,
```

```
      'x-amz-acl': 'public-read'
    }
  )

  instream.on('data',function(chunk){
    console.log('sending: '+chunk.length)
    req.write(chunk)
  })

  instream.on('end',function(){
    req.end()
    console.log('waiting for amazon...')
  })

  req.on('error',function(err){
    console.log('error: '+err)
  })

  req.on('response',function(res){
    console.log('response: '+res.statusCode)
  })
})
```

Code snippet s3-put.js

6. Run the `s3-put.js` script:

```
$ node s3-put.js
sending: 40960
sending: 40960
sending: 40960
sending: 40960
sending: 40960
sending: 40960
sending: 14323
waiting for amazon...
response: 200
```

 WARNING *Running this example will cost you money! It will cost a very small amount of money, but money all the same. No interaction with Amazon S3 is free. Check out* `http://aws.amazon.com/s3/pricing` *for the latest pricing information.*

How It Works

You will build out this code example into the full Lifestream app. It's therefore important that you organize your files properly. You want all the server-side code to go into the `server` subfolder of the `lifestream` project folder.

The `s3-put.js` script is a command-line script that uploads a photo to S3 and then exits. The script needs access to the file system, so you use the built-in `fs` module for that part of the task. And you use the `knox` module for the S3 upload:

```
var fs   = require('fs')
var knox = require('knox')
```

As with the Amazon SimpleDB code in Chapter 6, you need your Amazon developer access keys to run this code. The keys are stored in the `keys.js` file, and you load this file into your script by using the `require` function:

```
var keys = require('./keys.js')
```

The next step is to create a `knox` client object to talk to S3. The `knox` module needs your Amazon keys and the name of your bucket. Make sure to use the name of the bucket that you created in the previous example. The code in the example uses my bucket name, which is shown highlighted:

```
var client = knox.createClient({
  key:    keys.keyid,
  secret: keys.secret,
  bucket: 'rjrodger-mobile-cloud-apps',
})
```

The S3 service is quite picky in some ways. One of the things you must provide is the size of the file you are uploading. The Node `fs` module lets you get this information. The functions in the `fs` module are quite close to the underlying UNIX C functions that perform the actual work for you inside the Node engine. If you are not familiar with C, the function names can seem a little strange. (Remember that these names are artifacts from the 1970s!) To get the size of the file, you use the `stat` function. This gives you all the details about a particular file, including its size in bytes. As always with Node, the result is not given as a return value from the function but rather via callback function. Node does not block waiting for the disk to find your file and read its details. This nonblocking design is used for everything in Node, and it's what gives Node the ability to handle so many concurrent clients. Here's the call to the `stat` function:

```
fs.stat(testfile, function(err, stat){
  if (err) return console.dir(err);

  var filesize = stat.size
```

There's one other thing to note about the above code. If there's an error, it means the file to be uploaded could not be read. This could happen due to an incorrect file path or a missing file permission. When an error occurs in a callback function, you cannot just throw the error in the traditional manner using the JavaScript `throw` statement. Your thrown error will disappear into the Node event stack, and you'll never know about it! Instead, you should always either pass the error onwards to another callback or simply log it and return. The `return` statement in the code has the effect of exiting from the callback, preventing further processing when you have an error. The code also uses the fact that the value returned from a callback is conventionally ignored. This means you can sneak in a call to `console.dir` by making it the return value. Of course, `console.dir` just prints a description of the error and returns nothing. You will see this idiom used in some of the Node modules.

Assuming the file is readable, you now need to create a PUT request to upload the file to Amazon. In this case, you want to call the `put` function of the `knox` client object. This function needs the name of the file, as it will be named inside S3 (which can be different from its local file name) and also some HTTP headers to send to S3. You control the many features of Amazon S3 by using special HTTP headers. For the Lifestream app, you need only one of these:

```
x-amz-acl: public-read
```

This header tells Amazon to make the photo publicly readable but allow only you, the owner, to change it. The `x-amz-acl` header shows you an example of the format of these special headers. The `x-amz-` prefix indicates that it is for Amazon, and the `acl` part specifies that this header is setting the Access Control List (ACL) for the file. This permission setting is exactly what you need for the Lifestream app, where users publish public photos but your server application controls the photo storage on S3. The other header is a standard HTTP `Content-Length` header, which you use to specify the size of the file, as required by S3. These headers are shown in bold here:

```
var req = client.put(
  testfile,
  {
    'Content-Length':filesize,
    'x-amz-acl': 'public-read'
  }
)
```

Now that everything is set, the next step is to stream the contents of the photo file to Amazon. Streaming the data is very important. It is not a good idea to load the entire file into memory and then send it to Amazon. Doing so would quickly overload your servers. Memory is the most important resource for a server. The most efficient approach is to load the file a little piece at a time and send that to Amazon. The disk can only provide you with chunks of the file at a time anyway. And the network can only transport the file in chunks. The other big advantage of this method is that it is quite robust and can upload very large files.

To set up the stream of chunks, you need to read the file in as a stream and write out to Amazon each time you get a new piece of the file. Node makes this all very easy. The `fs` module provides a `createReadStream` function that loads a file as a stream. Each time there is a new data chunk available, a `data` event is fired. You register a callback function to deal with this. When the end of the file is reached, an `end` event is fired.

The `knox` module returns a standard `http` request object from the `http` built-in Node module. You call the `write` function of this object to send data down the pipe to the remote server. You call the `end` function when you are done.

You can now put this all together to stream the data up to Amazon. The event handlers and request functions are shown here in bold:

```
var instream = fs.createReadStream(testfile)

...

instream.on('data',function(chunk){
```

```
      console.log('sending: '+chunk.length)
      req.write(chunk)
  })

  instream.on('end',function(){
    req.end()
    console.log('waiting for amazon...')
  })
```

TRY IT OUT **Getting Content from Amazon S3**

Getting photo data out of Amazon S3 is almost the same as putting photo data in. You use the same libraries and streaming algorithm, just in reverse. Follow these steps:

1. Create a file called s3-get.js in the lifestream/server folder and insert the following code in it:

Available for
download on
Wrox.com

```
var fs   = require('fs')
var knox = require('knox')
var util = require('util')

// amazon keys
var keys = require('./keys.js')

var testfile = 'Ireland_circa_900.png'
var savefile = 'Ireland_circa_900-saved.png'


var client = knox.createClient({
  key:    keys.keyid,
  secret: keys.secret,
  bucket: 'rjrodger-mobile-cloud-apps',
})


var outstream = fs.createWriteStream(savefile)

var req = client.get(testfile)
req.end()

req.on('response',function(res){
  console.log('response: '+res.statusCode)

  res.on('data',function(chunk){
    console.log('get: '+chunk.length)
    outstream.write(chunk)
  })

  res.on('end',function(){
    console.log('done')
    outstream.end()
```

```
    })
})

req.on('error',function(err){
  console.log('error: '+err)
})
```

Code snippet s3-get.js

2. Run the s3-get.js script:

```
$ node s3-get.js
response: 200
get: 1103
get: 5840
get: 1700
get: 1460
...
get: 1460
get: 1800
done
```

3. Compare the original image file (Ireland_circa_900.png) to the downloaded image file (Ireland_circa_900-saved.png). They should both be the same size.

 WARNING As with the SimpleDB service in Chapter 6, Amazon does not guarantee that calls to S3 will succeed every time. This is due to the distributed, eventually consistent design of the service. The recommended way to deal with this is to retry the request. If your file download from S3 fails in any way or takes too long to respond, you should restart the download.

How It Works

The s3-get.js script uses the same modules and configuration as the s3-put.js script. However, it does not to overwrite the original image file, and it saves the downloaded image with a different filename:

```
var testfile = 'Ireland_circa_900.png'
var savefile = 'Ireland_circa_900-saved.png'
```

The data is transferred as a stream. In this case, you use the createWriteStream function to save data to a file. The event handling is driven by the response from the Amazon S3 server. You listen for data events on the response object (the res variable). Each time you get one, you save the chunk to the local data file by using the write function of the stream object (the outstream variable). The relevant lines are shown here in bold:

```
var outstream = fs.createWriteStream(savefile)

var req = client.get(testfile)
```

```
req.end()

req.on('response',function(res){
  console.log('response: '+res.statusCode)

  res.on('data',function(chunk){
    console.log('get: '+chunk.length)
    outstream.write(chunk)
  })

  res.on('end',function(){
    console.log('done')
    outstream.end()
  })
})
```

SIGNING IN WITH THE CLOUD

For the full Lifestream app, you will need to provide a way for your users to sign in with the major cloud services. You could provide your own stand-alone user account system and require your users to register with you directly, but it is a much better idea to use major cloud services, such as Facebook and Twitter. Most users already have accounts with these services and are accustomed to signing in to smaller third-party apps by using their Facebook or Twitter accounts.

The protocol you use to enable this third-party sign-in is OAuth, an independent web standard that specifies the communication flow between your service and, for example, Facebook's servers. Most major cloud services use some version of the OAuth protocol.

The OAuth protocol can seem quite intimidating if you start with the OAuth specification document. However, it is actually quite easy to work with if you use software libraries to do the heavy lifting. The oauth Node module can handle OAuth versions 1.0, 1.0A, and 2.0. In this section you'll focus on Twitter and Facebook, but the same techniques can be used for LinkedIn, FourSquare, Meetup.com, and many others.

It is important to understand the OAuth flow. Here's how it works, using the Twitter OAuth version 1.0A implementation as an example:

1. The user clicks a Sign In with Twitter button on your site.

2. This click calls a script on your web server that makes a background request to Twitter.

3. The background request asks Twitter for a request token.

4. Twitter responds to the background request by giving you a request token.

5. Your web server redirects the user's browser to the Twitter sign-in page, passing along the request token as a query parameter.

6. The user signs in to Twitter.

7. Twitter redirects the user back to your site, passing you a verifier token.

8. Your site accepts the redirect and then makes a background request to Twitter for an access token, using the verifier token. This token will enable you to make authorized requests to Twitter to get the user's details.

9. Your site displays a confirmation page to your user.

As you can see, there is a lot of back-and-forth between your server and the OAuth provider. Version 2.0 of OAuth, used by Facebook, is only a slight simplification. And some of this communication flow needs to be cryptographically signed. That is why it is essential to use a supporting software library to manage this process. If you would like to get the full details of this process, the Twitter documentation is a good place to start; see `http://dev.twitter.com/pages/auth`.

TRY IT OUT   Signing In with Twitter

To let your users sign in with Twitter, you need to register your app with Twitter. Visit `http://dev .twitter.com`, click the Your Apps link at the top of the page, and fill in the form. That's all there is to it! Once your app is registered, Twitter gives you an app ID and a secret key that you can use to communicate securely with Twitter.

You can run the code in this example by using a local web server. You do not need to deploy this to a public machine. However, you do need to set your local IP address in this code. Replace the YOUR_IP_ADDRESS marker in the code with your own local IP address. The example does not require a public web server because the HTTP redirects are sent back to your local web browser, which then makes requests to your local web server.

You run this example from your desktop web browser. In Chapter 10, you'll learn how to integrate this code into the Lifestream mobile app. For now, follow these steps:

1. Install the `oauth` Node module, using npm:

```
npm install oauth
```

2. Create a subfolder called `public` under the `lifestream` folder.

3. Create a file called `twitter.html` in the `public` subfolder and insert the following code in it:

Available for download on Wrox.com

```
<a href="http://YOUR_IP_ADDRESS:3003/oauth/twitter/login?1">
  <img src="twitter.png">
</a>
```

Code snippet twitter.html

The `twitter.png` image file you use here is available in the code download for this book.

4. Add the following line to the `keys.js` file. Replace the markers with the key and secret Twitter has assigned to your app. You can obtain these from your Twitter app details page.

```
exports.twitter  = {
  keyid:'YOUR_TWITTER_KEY_ID',
  secret:'YOUR_TWITTER_SECRET'
}
```

5. Create a file called `twitter.js` in the `lifestream/server` folder and insert the following code in it:

```
var connect = require('connect')
var oauth   = require('oauth')
var url     = require('url')

var keys = require('./keys.js')

var oauthclient = new oauth.OAuth(
  'http://twitter.com/oauth/request_token',
  'http://twitter.com/oauth/access_token',
  keys.twitter.keyid,
  keys.twitter.secret,
  '1.0',
  'http://YOUR_IP_ADDRESS:3003/oauth/twitter/callback',
  'HMAC-SHA1',
  null,
  {'Accept': '*/*', 'Connection': 'close', 'User-Agent': 'twitter-js'}
)

var state = {}

var server = connect.createServer(
  connect.router(function(app){

    app.get('/oauth/twitter/login',function(req,res,next){

      oauthclient.getOAuthRequestToken(
        function(
          error,
          oauth_token,
          oauth_token_secret,
          oauth_authorize_url,
          additionalParameters)
        {
          if (!error) {
            state[oauth_token] = oauth_token_secret;

            res.writeHead( 301, {
              "Location":
                "http://api.twitter.com/oauth/authorize?oauth_token="
                +oauth_token
            })
            res.end()
          }
          else {
            res.end( JSON.stringify(error) )
          }
        }
      )
    })

    app.get('/oauth/twitter/callback',function(req,res,next){
```

```
        var parsedUrl = url.parse(req.url, true);

        oauthclient.getOAuthAccessToken(
          parsedUrl.query.oauth_token,
            state[parsedUrl.query.oauth_token],
          parsedUrl.query.oauth_verifier,

          function(
            error,
            oauth_token,
            oauth_token_secret,
            additionalParameters)
          {
            if (!error) {
              res.writeHead( 301, {
                "Location":
                  "http://YOUR_IP_ADDRESS:3003/oauth/twitter/launch"
              })
              res.end()
            }
            else {
              res.end( JSON.stringify(error) )
            }
          }
        )
      })

    app.get('/oauth/twitter/launch',function(req,res,next){
      res.writeHead(200)
      res.end( 'Signed in with Twitter!' );
    })
  }),
  connect.static('../public')
)
server.listen(3003)
```

Code snippet twitter.js

6. Run the `twitter.js` script:

```
node twitter.js
```

7. Open your desktop web browser and visit
`http://YOUR_IP_ADDRESS:3003/twitter`
`.html`. You should see a Twitter sign-in
button, as shown in Figure 8-4.

8. Click the sign-in button. You are taken to the
Twitter sign-in page, as shown in Figure 8-5.
This page will show the user the name of your
app (in the figure, the name is Chartaca, which
is one of my apps), and ask for the user's
permission to log in.

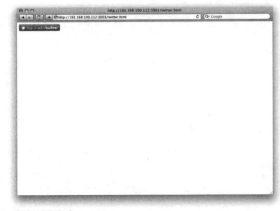

FIGURE 8-4

9. Click the Allow button. Twitter redirects you back to your own local site and displays the message "Signed in with Twitter!"

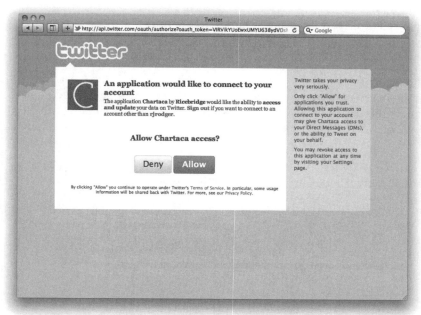

FIGURE 8-5

 NOTE *When you test this code, you need to manually change the request counter (. . . /login?1) at the end of the login URL in the* twitter.html *file. Just keep incrementing the number. If you don't do so, your requests will be stale and will not authenticate. In the real Lifestream application this will be done automatically.*

How It Works

The OAuth module provides a client object that you initialize by providing a set of configuration parameters:

```
var oauthclient = new oauth.OAuth(
  'http://twitter.com/oauth/request_token',
  'http://twitter.com/oauth/access_token',
  keys.twitter.keyid,
  keys.twitter.secret,
  '1.0',
  'http://YOUR_IP_ADDRESS:3003/oauth/twitter/callback',
  'HMAC-SHA1',
  null,
  {'Accept': '*/*', 'Connection': 'close', 'User-Agent': 'twitter-js'}
)
```

Most of this is boilerplate. The important elements for you to fill out are your Twitter keys and your callback URL. Your Twitter keys are available from the settings page for your app, at `http://dev.twitter.com`. Your callback URL is something that you specify. The sample code uses the pattern `oauth/<service>/callback`.

The sample code implements a simple HTTP server listening on port 3003, using the `connect` Node module to handle the request routing. (Take a quick look at Chapter 5 if you need a reminder of how this works.)

The first step in the authentication process is to get your request token. When the user clicks the Sign In with Twitter button, he or she submits a request to your site. The `/oauth/twitter/login` end point handles this request. The handler for this end point calls the `getOAuthRequestToken` function of the `oauthclient` object. The `oauthclient` object then makes a background request to Twitter to get your request token for you. Your callback function is executed when this is complete. The request token is the value of the `oauth_token_secret` parameter.

Your callback then redirects the user to the Twitter site, ready to sign in (shown here in bold):

```
state[oauth_token] = oauth_token_secret;

res.writeHead( 301, {
  "Location":
    "http://api.twitter.com/oauth/authorize?oauth_token="
    +oauth_token
})
res.end()
```

You also need to keep a record of the request token so that you can use it later. In this example code you just store it in memory. Take a look at the exercises at the end of this chapter to see a more robust approach that can scale to multiple servers. This completes the request token stage. Now you have to wait for the user to sign in on the Twitter site. Once the user has signed in, Twitter redirects the user back to your site, calling your callback endpoint: `/oauth/twitter/callback`.

The handler for the callback endpoint then moves on to the access token stage. The handler calls the `getOAuthAccessToken` function of the OAuth client, passing in the token that it has just received from Twitter.

Again, a background request is made to Twitter, this time to get the access token. Here, you use the request token, which you previously stored, to validate the request. Once this completes, the user has signed in to your service, using Twitter, and you can display a welcome message.

 WARNING *The OAuth process can go wrong in many weird and wonderful ways. Keep your cool and log everything carefully. One tool that you will find very helpful is the Wireshark network analyzer. Wireshark can eavesdrop on your network connection and show you the traffic between your machine and the outside world. In this way, you can see the messages that are flowing. This is very useful for debugging OAuth interactions. You can find Wireshark at* `www.wireshark.org`.

TRY IT OUT Signing In with Facebook

As with Twitter, you may want your users to be able to sign in to your app with Facebook. Visit http:// facebook.com/developers to get started. Once you have registered your app, you need to make sure your app settings are configured to support the code in this example. To do this, you go to your developer page, select your app from the list on the right, click the Edit Settings link, click the Web Site link on the left, and enter the following value in the Site URL field: http://YOUR_IP_ADDRESS:3003 (but using your own local IP address). For a live app, you use the URL of the live web server. Also on this page you will find your application ID and secret key. Follow these steps:

1. Create a file called facebook.html in the lifestream/public subfolder and insert the following code in it:

Available for download on Wrox.com

```
<a href="http://YOUR_IP_ADDRESS:3003/oauth/facebook/login?1">
  <img src="facebook.png">
</a>
```

Code snippet facebook.html

The facebook.png image file is available in the code download for this book.

2. Add the following line to the keys.js file:

```
exports.facebook  = {
  keyid:'YOUR_FACEBOOK_KEY_ID',
  secret:'YOUR_FACEBOOK_SECRET'
}
```

3. Create a file called facebook.js in the lifestream/server folder and insert the following code in it:

Available for download on Wrox.com

```
var connect = require('connect')
var oauth   = require('oauth')
var url     = require('url')

var keys = require('./keys.js')

var oauthclient = new oauth.OAuth2(
  keys.facebook.keyid,
  keys.facebook.secret,
  'https://graph.facebook.com'
)


var server = connect.createServer(
  connect.router(function(app){

    app.get('/oauth/facebook/login',function(req,res,next){
      var redirectUrl =
        oauthclient.getAuthorizeUrl(
          {redirect_uri:
            'http://YOUR_IP_ADDRESS:3003/oauth/facebook/callback',
```

```
            scope:'' })

        res.writeHead( 301, {
          'Location':redirectUrl
        })
        res.end()
      })

    app.get('/oauth/facebook/callback',function(req,res,next){
      var parsedUrl = url.parse(req.url, true);

      oauthclient.getOAuthAccessToken(
        parsedUrl.query.code ,
        {redirect_uri:
          'http://YOUR_IP_ADDRESS:3003/oauth/facebook/callback'},
        function( error, access_token, refresh_token ){

          if (!error) {
            res.writeHead( 301, {
              'Location':
                "http://YOUR_IP_ADDRESS:3003/oauth/facebook/launch"
            })
            res.end()
          }
          else {
            res.end( JSON.stringify(error) )
          }
        }
      )
    })

    app.get('/oauth/facebook/launch',function(req,res,next){
      res.writeHead(200)
      res.end( 'Signed in with Facebook!' )
    })

  }),
  connect.staticProvider('../public')
)
server.listen(3003)
```

Code snippet facebook.js

4. Run the facebook.js script:

```
node facebook.js
```

5. Open your desktop web browser and visit http://YOUR_IP_ADDRESS:3003/facebook.html. You should see a Facebook sign-in button, similar to the Twitter button.

6. Click the sign-in button. You are taken to the Facebook sign-in page.

7. Authorize your app to sign you in to Facebook. Facebook redirects you to your own site and displays the message "Signed in with Facebook!"

How It Works

The Facebook OAuth flow is similar to the Twitter flow, but it uses version 2 of the protocol. The setup with your application keys is the same. As you can see, OAuth version 2 is simpler than OAuth version 1, and it does not require as many configuration parameters:

```
var oauthclient = new oauth.OAuth2(
  keys.facebook.keyid,
  keys.facebook.secret,
  'https://graph.facebook.com'
)
```

Instead of having a secret request token, OAuth version 2 just uses the request token itself as a verifier, so there is no need to store any state during the sign in process. The `oauth` module does the hard work for you with the `getAuthorizeUrl` function.

Once the user has signed in with Facebook, he or she is redirected back to your callback end point: `/oauth/facebook/callback`. From here, you need to get the access token, as before:

```
oauthclient.getOAuthAccessToken(
  parsedUrl.query.code ,
  {redirect_uri:
    'http://YOUR_IP_ADDRESS:3003/oauth/facebook/callback'},
```

You need to include your callback URL as a validity check (shown in bold above).

Once you have the token, you can display your welcome message.

 WARNING *Facebook uses your redirect URL as a validity check. Make sure that you always use exactly the same characters for this field, or the authentication will fail. The redirect URL also needs to match the value you entered into your app settings on Facebook.*

BUILDING LARGE-SCALE APPS

Hosting your app in the cloud will solve most of your scaling problems. Need to store lots of photos? Use Amazon S3! Need to store lots of data records? Use Amazon SimpleDB, or perhaps a MongoDB hosting provider such as MongoHQ.com. Need to add more servers quickly? Use Amazon EC2, or go up a layer of abstraction and use a platform host such as Heroku. Once you take the cloud as the starting point, you can generally solve your scaling problems by outsourcing the hard computer science to a service provider. This way, you can concentrate on your app and your business goals.

However, using a cloud provider is not always the solution. You need to get your own house in order. It doesn't matter if you are configuring your own Amazon servers or using a platform host; you still need to make sure the logic of your application can handle high usage volumes. In this section, you'll learn about some strategies to adopt, and you'll see a particularly useful but simple caching algorithm that can make a big difference in your processing costs.

Getting the Big Picture Right

What's the easiest way to handle more users? Buy a bigger server. This can get you quite far. On Amazon, you can deploy your server-side functionality on one of the extra-large instance options, and you'll certainly get more capacity. This type of scaling is known as *vertical scaling*. When you scale vertically, you do so by using bigger machines and spending more money.

The problem with vertical scaling is that it costs more and more for less and less. There's a limit to the physical power you can buy. Your costs increase exponentially. A new machine twice as powerful as your old server is not twice as expensive. It is often many times more expensive. Eventually, you reach a hard limit on the number of users you can handle on one machine. The next step in this case is to split your database, application server, and other components onto their own machines. This will buy you time, but it won't solve the problem.

In the world of social networking, your app may have only one chance at the big time, and if you can't keep all those new users, you'll be forgotten for tomorrow's new app. What you need is *horizontal* scalability. You want to be able to keep adding new cheap commodity machines — as many as you need. Or in the case of Amazon, you want to be able to keeping adding new instances. These small, cheap machines all handle the load together. But how do you achieve horizontal scalability?

Building a system that can scale horizontally can quickly get deeply technical. A few core components need to be part of such systems:

 NOTE *This book does not cover the specifics of systems that can scale horizontally, but it is important that you know what to look out for. While you may not need to implement all these components from day one, you need to design your app so that it can continue to work as the network becomes more complex.*

➤ **Load balancer** — Fronting your app, you need a load balancer. This a networking component that shares incoming requests between a set of machines. This is the most basic way to share the load between multiple machines. Amazon, of course, has a load-balancing product you can use: Elastic Load Balancer. If you host using a platform provider, then load balancing will probably be built in.

➤ **Asynchronous messaging system** — For efficient communication between the machines in your system, you need to use an asynchronous messaging system. It is very important that your machines do not hang around waiting for each other. Rather, units of work should be sent on a fire-and-forget basis, so that each machine can get back to serving users.

➤ **In-memory cache** — To reduce the load on your data stores, traditional or otherwise, you need to use an in-memory cache. Instead of loading data from the database, you can more quickly pull it directly from memory. In terms of scaling, providing in-memory caching is the single most effective thing you can do.

➤ **Other considerations** — Other things you need to consider are monitoring systems that notify you when things are going wrong, automated scaling in response to the load (spinning up more machines as needed), activity logging for your system, and fault-tolerant systems that can survive one or more machines crashing.

There's a lot of complexity here. Cloud vendors are solving more and more of these problems for you, which is good news. The bad news? You can't pretend these issues don't exist. You need to write your code so that it can run on multiple machines at the same time.

And that means you're going to have to give up on user sessions. If you have used any of the mainstream server-side languages and frameworks for building web sites, then you will have used user sessions at some point. The HTTP protocol does not maintain any state between requests, and user sessions were quickly introduced by the early web frameworks as a way to get around this. Most web frameworks today still work in the same way. A user session is the period of time when a user is directly interacting with a web site, making ongoing requests. The state information associated with the user session is stored in the memory of the web server, and an HTTP cookie is used as a key to find the session for each request.

If the user stops making requests, then after a given period of time (usually 30 minutes), the session is considered closed and the web server dumps the data from memory. Because each session needs to store data in memory, you can see how this can lead to problems when you have lots of users, and not enough memory. Not only that, but a lot of the sessions are not even active anymore and are just waiting for their 30-minute timeout!

When you start to add more servers to handle higher loads, you have to decide how you are going to deal with user sessions. Your load-balancer will typically distribute HTTP requests to each server using a "round-robin" algorithm. Each server in turn gets the next request. This means that one user sending many requests over a period of time will end up on different servers.

How is each request going to get hold of the right session data, which is stored in the memory of only one server? Perhaps your load balancer can keep track of which server first started talking to which user, and then always send the user's requests to that server. This approach is known as *sticky sessions*.

Hopefully the idea of sticky sessions is giving you a bad feeling. What happens if too may sessions end up on one machine? What happens if a machine dies, taking all its sessions with it? And load-balancers with that sticky-session feature are also more expensive.

Another idea is to move sessions around. The server that is handling the request can copy the session data from the server that had it previously. This is workable. And very complex. Some enterprise application architectures can do this well, but that's probably not what you are looking for.

The simplest way to make sure your application can scale is to not use sessions. This is called a *shared-nothing architecture*. In such an architecture, for *every* request, if you need some user data, you get it from the database. This may not sound very efficient, but if you also use an in-memory cache, it can be very efficient. The data for active users will tend to end up in the cache, and you won't hit the database as much as you think you might. Because each machine has no session state, you can easily add new machines or remove old ones. The load balancer keeps doling out work to whatever machines are available.

Using the Cache!

The shared-nothing architecture is the key to building an app that can handle huge popularity. To use this architecture to best advantage, you need to know how to make effective use of memory caches. In this section, you'll learn how to do just that.

TRY IT OUT Using memcached

The most commonly used in-memory cache is the `memcached` server. Many high-profile sites have used this cache server and proved its ability to work with a heavy load. It is very simple and easy to use because it is basically a big key-value store. The obvious operations are supported: You can get, set, and delete a value by using that value's key. You can also increment or decrement a numeric value. You can visit `http://memcached.org` to read up on the details of these operations. The code examples in this book explain how `memcached` is used. To get started, follow these steps:

1. Use `apt-get` to download and install the latest version of `memcached`:

   ```
   apt-get install memcached
   ```

   If `app-get` is not available, follow the manual installation instructions on the `memcached` site.

2. The `memcached` executable should now be available. To test it, run the following command (but note that your version may be different from what is shown here):

   ```
   memcached -i
   memcached 1.4.5
   ...
   ```

3. The `memcached` executable is not normally installed as a system service in the same way as a database like MongoDB. You might want to run several instances of `memcached` on each of your servers, for example. The exact configuration will therefore depend on the details of your app. For development purposes, you can simply start `memcached` from the command line, specifying the port on which it is to listen for requests (using -p), and asking for verbose output to help with debugging (using -vv):

   ```
   memcached -vv -p 11211
   ```

4. Install the `memcached` Node module, which allows you to connect to `memcached`:

   ```
   sudo npm install memcached
   ```

5. Create a file called `memcache.js` in the `lifestream/server` folder and insert the following code in it:

   ```
   var Memcached = require( 'memcached' )

   var memcached = new Memcached("127.0.0.1:11211")
   var expires   = 3600

   memcached.set( "foo", 'bar', expires, function( err, result ){
   ```

Available for download on Wrox.com

```
      if( err ) return console.error( err );
      console.dir( result );

      memcached.get( "foo", function( err, result ){
        if( err ) return console.error( err );
        console.dir( result );
      })
   })
```

Code snippet memcache.js

6. Run the `memcache.js` script:

```
node memcache.js
bar
```

7. Because the script keeps a connection to `memcached` open, use Ctrl+C to exit.

How It Works

The `memcached` module takes a list of `memcached` servers from you and uses all of them to store your cached data. In this script, only one `memcached` server is used — the one you started in step 3:

```
var memcached = new Memcached("127.0.0.1:11211")
```

This tells the module that a `memcached` server is available locally at port 11211. If you look at the console output of the `memcached` server, you see logging messages printing as the script runs.

To store data in `memcached`, you use the `set` function. This takes several arguments: the key string for the value (`"foo"`), the value itself (`"bar"`), an expiration time, in seconds, and a callback function. The key string is a unique name for the value. If a previous value was stored under that key, it will be overwritten. The value itself can be anything you like, including binary data. The expiration time tells `memcached` to drop the value when it is older than the number of seconds specified. The example uses a value of 3600 seconds. This means that after one hour, you cannot assume that `memcached` still stores data for the `"foo"` key.

Finally, the callback tells you whether the operation succeeded. This follows the standard Node pattern, with the first argument being an `error` object that is `null` if everything is okay and the `set` operation succeeded. The second argument contains the result data, if any:

```
memcached.set( "foo", 'bar', lifetime, function( err, result ){
```

Once you have the data stored, you can get it back by using the `get` function:

```
memcached.get( "foo", function( err, result ){
```

It is important to remember that in both cases, the data is transferred over the network from the `memcached` server to your application. While this is a lot faster than getting data from a database, you still need to be careful not to make your data values too large or to make unnecessary requests.

How should you use memcached? There's a simple rule: If the data is stored safely somewhere else, or if you can easily recompute it, you can store it in memcached. It should not matter if memcached has your data (called a *cache hit*), or does not have your data (called a *cache miss*). In fact, it should not matter if all the memcached servers are down; your app should continue to function normally — but it won't be very fast. Never use memcached as the original source of data. And don't be tempted to try to simulate old-style user sessions. Your app will become unreliable when memcached dumps your sessions to make way for new data.

The most common usage pattern is known as the *write-through cache*. In this pattern, when you save anything to the database, you also put it into memcached. Whenever you need to read anything out of the database, you first check memcached, and you use the memcached value if it exists. Otherwise, you use the database.

The write-through cache pattern works quite well in practice, but beware of the "thundering herd" problem, which can bring down your whole app. If you clear all your caches, and your app is under heavy load, then all your app servers will simultaneously try to get data from the cache, find that it is not there, and then all head for your database at the same time, with devastating effect. The thundering herd can be so bad that your app never gets a chance to "warm" its cache with data, and you can't bring your app live again. The solution to this problem is to carefully design your cache usage such that you almost never need to clear the entire cache. This is easier said than done, of course. You'll learn one technique that uses versioned keys, later in this chapter.

TRY IT OUT Running Multiple Cache Servers

You can use memcached to scale very effectively by running multiple cache servers. Certain large-scale social networking sites run massive memcached clusters that store data temporarily, using large quantities of RAM. These machines do nothing else.

The trick to running multiple memcached servers is to know which one has your data. The easiest way to solve this problem is to use the "phone book" algorithm. To do this, you run 26 memcached servers and assign a letter of the alphabet to each one. Then you take the first letter of each key, and that tells you where to store the value.

Or you can use a slightly more sophisticated algorithm known as "consistent hashing." Consistent hashing is more efficient because it spreads your data more evenly than the phone book algorithm. Luckily, the memcached module supports consistent hashing. Before going into the details of the algorithm, this example shows you how to talk to multiple memcached servers. Follow these steps:

1. Set up three memcached servers — one each on ports 11211, 11212, and 11213. Start each one in a separate console window. Arrange your console windows as shown in Figure 8-6. This way, you can observe the sample code in action.

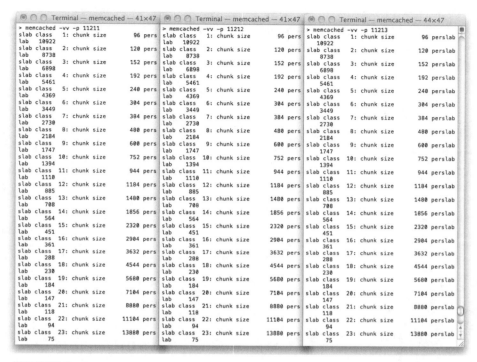

FIGURE 8-6

2. Create a file called `memcache-multi.js` in the `lifestream/server` folder and insert the following code in it:

```
var util       = require('util')
var Memcached = require( 'memcached' )

var memcached =
    new Memcached(
        ["127.0.0.1:11211","127.0.0.1:11212","127.0.0.1:11213"],
        {reconnect:2000,timeout:2000,retries:2,retry:2000,remove:false}
    )

var expires = 3600
var itemcount = 0


function setcount(count,win) {
  memcached.set(
    'name'+count,
    'value'+count,
    expires,
    function(err) {
      if( err ) {
        console.error( err )
      }
```

```
          else {
            win()
          }
        }
      )
    }

function getcount(count,win) {
  memcached.get(
    'name'+count,
    function(err,result) {
      if( err ) {
        console.error( err )
      }
      else {
        win(result)
      }
    }
  )
}


function setitem(count) {
  setcount(count,function(){
    util.debug('set '+count)
    itemcount++

    function getitem(count) {

      if( count < itemcount ) {
        getcount(count,function(result){
          util.debug('get '+count+'='+result)

          if( !result ) {
            setcount(count,function(){
              getitem(count+1)
            })
          }
          else {
            getitem(count+1)
          }
        })
      }
    }
    getitem(0)
  })

  setTimeout(function(){
    setitem(count+1)
  },2000)
}
setitem(0)
```

Code snippet memcache-multi.js

3. Run the `memcache-multi.js` script. (Use Ctrl+C when you're ready to exit, or the script will run forever.) Figure 8-7 shows the output of the script overlaid over the output of the `memcached` servers.

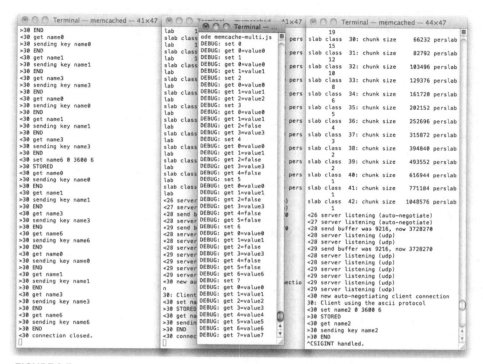

FIGURE 8-7

4. While the script is running, kill one of the `memcached` servers and restart it a few seconds later. In Figure 8-7, you can see that the `memcached` server on the far right was killed and restarted. This server was responsible for key value 2. You'll notice in the output of the `memcached-multi.js` script in the foreground terminal window that the state of key value 2 changes to `false` for a while, indicating that it could not be found, before returning to `true` when the far right `memcached` server comes back online.

How It Works

In this example, you run three `memcached` servers locally. In a production environment, you will run multiple `memcached` servers on multiple machines. You run more than one `memcached` server per machine to take advantage of multiple processors, as `memcached` is single-threaded.

To connect to the `memcached` servers, you give the `memcached` module the IP address and port of each of three servers. The module then distributes your keys evenly over the servers, ensuring that they each store about one-third of your cached data:

```
var memcached =
  new Memcached(
```

```
["127.0.0.1:11211","127.0.0.1:11212","127.0.0.1:11213"],
{reconnect:2000,timeout:2000,retries:2,retry:2000,remove:false}
)
```

As noted above, the algorithm used to do this is known as a "consistent hashing" algorithm. To understand how it works, you first need to understand how a simple direct hashing algorithm works.

Direct hashing solves a rather severe issue with the 26-letter phone book approach. The letter z, for example, does not have many keys, but the letter a probably does. The keys will be unevenly distributed, and the load will not be distributed evenly. You need even load distribution in order to scale properly.

Instead of using the text value of the key, direct hashing uses the *hash* of the key text. A hash is a scrambling algorithm that generates nonsense values from a given piece of text. The most important thing about a hash algorithm is that the same piece of text should always generate the same piece of nonsense. There are numerous hashing algorithms, and the good ones are designed to generate nearly unique hashes for each input text. You can use a hash value as a key. If you interpret the hash as a large number, you can divide it by the number of memcached servers you have and use the remainder as an index number that identifies the server to use; in other words, you can take the modulo of the number of servers. Mathematically, this guarantees an even distribution of keys.

Direct hashing works very well. But what happens when you need to add a new server or when an existing server dies? Somehow, you need to dynamically redistribute the keys among the current set of servers. It would be nice if the algorithm to do this also kept keys pointing at their original servers as much as possible. That way, cached data would mostly remain accessible. If you just took a new direct hash, you would effectively clear the entire cache, as nothing could be found, leaving you open to the thundering herd problem.

Consistent hashing prevents this. Imagine a 12-hour clock, with four servers — one each at 12, 3, 6, and 9 o'clock. Now, instead of hashing for 4 servers, you hash for 12. If you get a hash value of 1 or 2, you use the server at 3 o'clock. If you get 4 or 5, you use the server at 6 o'clock. You continue in this manner for the other servers. This scheme ensures that all keys find a server by going clockwise from where they land on the clock circle until they get to a server.

What happens when the server at 6 o'clock dies? You just send all the hashes from 4, 5, and 6 o'clock onward in a clockwise direction. They'll end up at the 9 o'clock server, and your system keeps running! What happens when the server at 6 o'clock comes back? Then you can go back to the old assignment, with 4 and 5 o'clock hashes stopping when they hit 6.

There is one little problem left: This method does not redistribute the hashes evenly. When the 6 o'clock server dies, the 9 o'clock server gets all of its workload, and the 12 and 3 o'clock servers get no extra work.

To make sure hashes are distributed evenly over all the servers, you can use more than use 12 points; you can instead use 2^{32} or even 2^{64} points. And you can assign more than one point to each server; you can assign thousands, and you can assign them randomly. But the same clockwise rule applies: You stop when you hit a server. Assigning the points randomly means that when a server dies, the hashes moving forward clockwise will hit many different servers randomly, so that, on average, they are equally redistributed. It also means that only the points from a dead server have to move.

The code in this example shows assigning points randomly in action. The script starts up an infinite loop that keeps adding keys to the cache. You can observe the distribution of keys by keeping the `memcached` terminal windows in view. If you manually kill a `memcached` server, you can then see that the script starts reporting that key as missing.

In the code in this example, the remove option of the `memcached` module is set to `false`, which means the keys are not redistributed because the module expects the failing server to eventually return. You can set this option to `true` and run the script again to see the key redistribution in effect.

The code in this script keeps adding new keys to the cache by counting upward. You can't just use a simple `for` loop to do this, however, because you need to be able to handle the callbacks from the `memcached` module. Therefore, you use a recursive loop. Each time the `setitem` function is called, it sets a new key. It then waits 2 seconds before calling itself again, incrementing the key count by 1.

Inside the `setitem` function, the `getitem` function loops over all the existing keys in the same way. This gets the script to print out the current values of all the keys every 2 seconds, and it also allows you to see the state of the cache. When you kill one of the `memcached` servers, some of the keys start reporting that they are missing.

TRY IT OUT **Caching Complex Objects**

The real power of caching comes into force when you cache complex objects. Complex objects, in this case, are things that take a lot of processing or database activity to create. A product description page on a dynamic website would fall into this category. For the Lifestream application, the followers of a user and all those the user follows form a complex object that would be great to cache. When you have millions of users, working out the follower graphs is an expensive operation due to the many-to-many relationships that exist between users.

You can't rebuild such an object only when a user changes who he or she follows. You also need to change it when someone who follows that user stops following the original user. With millions of users, you can see how this can get out of hand very fast.

 NOTE *As the late Phil Karlton, one of the original programmers at Netscape, was fond of saying, "There are two hard things in computer science: cache invalidation, naming things, and off-by-one errors."*

There is a rather neat solution to this particular caching problem that uses versioned keys. The following example shows you how it works:

1. Start a `memcached` server as follows:

```
memcached -vv -p 11211
```

2.   Create a file called `memcache-followers.js` in the `lifestream/server` folder and insert the following code in it:

```
var Memcached = require( 'memcached' )

var memcached = new Memcached("127.0.0.1:11211")
var expires  = 3600


function FollowDB() {
  var users = {}

  this.follow = function(user,follower) {
    users[user] = ( users[user] || {name:user} )
    users[user].followers = ( users[user].followers || [] )
    users[user].followers.push(follower)

    users[follower] = ( users[follower] || {name:follower} )
    users[follower].following = ( users[follower].following || [] )
    users[follower].following.push(user)
  }

  this.user = function(user){
    return users[user]
  }
}


function FollowAPI( followdb ) {

  function error(win) {
    return function( err, result ) {
      if( err ) {
        console.log(err)
      }
      else {
        win && win(result)
      }
    }
  }

  function incr(user,win){
    memcached.incr( user+'_v', 1, error(function(res){
      if( !res ) {
        memcached.set( user+'_v', 0, expires, error(function(){
          win()
        }))
      }
      else {
        win()
      }
    }))
  }
```

```
    this.follow = function(user,follower,win) {
      followdb.follow(user,follower)
      incr(user,function(){
        incr(follower,win)
      })
    }

    this.user = function(user,win) {
      memcached.get( user+'_v', error(function( user_v ){
        user_v = user_v || 0
        var user_f_key = user+'_'+user_v+'_f'

        memcached.get( user_f_key, error(function( user_f ){
          if( user_f ) {
            user_f.cache = 'hit'
            win(user_f)
          }
          else {
            user_f = followdb.user(user)
            memcached.set( user_f_key, user_f, expires, error(function(){
              user_f.cache = 'miss'
              win(user_f)
            }))
          }
        }))
      }))
    }
}


var followdb = new FollowDB()
var followapi = new FollowAPI(followdb)

function printuser(next){
  return function(user) {
    console.log(user.name+':'+JSON.stringify(user,null,2))
    next && next()
  }
}

followapi.follow(,alice','bob',function(){

  followapi.user(,alice',printuser(function(){
    followapi.user(,alice',printuser(function(){

      followapi.follow(,jim','alice',function(){

        followapi.user(,alice',printuser())
      })
    }))
  }))
})
```

Code snippet memcache-followers.js

3. Run the `memcache-followers.js` script:

```
node memcache-followers.js
alice:{
  "name": "alice",
  "followers": [
    "bob"
  ],
  "cache": "miss"
}
alice:{
  "name": "alice",
  "followers": [
    "bob"
  ],
  "cache": "hit"
}
alice:{
  "name": "alice",
  "followers": [
    "bob"
  ],
  "cache": "miss",
  "following": [
    "jim"
  ]
}
```

How It Works

This example simulates a data store that keeps track of the followers and followees of a given user. The `FollowDB` object is a stub that is used to provide a simple in-memory implementation. In the real Lifestream application, this data will be stored in MongoDB. The `follow` function takes two usernames as arguments, and it sets up the data store so that the second user is a follower of the first. The `user` function returns a description of the user, including two lists. One list contains the user's followers, and the other list contains the users that the user follows. This is the complex, expensive object that you need to cache.

The `FollowAPI` object implements the API that you will use to build the Lifestream application. It has the same functions as the data store but includes support for caching. The `error` convenience function should be familiar from Chapter 6.

To understand this example, start at the bottom. The API is used to set up some follow relationships with the `alice` user. The description of the `alice` user is also printed each time, so that you can see the current state of the system.

After the first `follow` is set up (bob follows alice), the code loads `alice` twice:

```
followapi.follow('alice','bob',function(){

  followapi.user('alice',printuser(function(){
    followapi.user('alice',printuser(function(){
```

As you can see in the output from the script, the first time `alice` is loaded from the database because she is not in the cache; this is a cache miss. The second time, she is in the cache; this is a cache hit:

```
alice:{
  "name": "alice",
  "followers": [
    "bob"
  ],
  "cache": "miss"
}
alice:{
  "name": "alice",
  "followers": [
    "bob"
  ],
  "cache": "hit"
}
```

Next, the test code sets up `alice` to follow `jim`. Now the version of `alice` in the cache is out-of-date, and you should see a cache miss. And this is just what happens:

```
alice:{
  "name": "alice",
  "followers": [
    "bob"
  ],
  "cache": "miss",
  "following": [
    "jim"
  ]
}
```

So how does it work? The trick is to use two cache entries. One entry stores the `alice` object. But the key for this object includes a version number, and this version number is incremented each time `alice` changes in any way. That way, when `alice` changes, the old data is not returned because it does not have the current key.

So how do you get the version number? You store it in the cache! It's not important what the version number is — just that it changes whenever `alice` changes. You can use the memcached incr operation to increment a version counter. This version number does not need to be persistent. If it drops out of the cache, you just start again from 0.

The sequence then works as follows: When you are looking for `alice`, you first get her version number, stored in the cache under the key alice_v, and then you use the version number to construct the key for the complex `alice` object, like this: alice_<version>_f.

The important thing is that you must increment `alice`'s version number whenever she changes in any way. This strategy will work even with multiple dependent objects. If any of them change, the version is bumped, and the cache is invalidated, ensuring that a new, correct version of `alice` is built and returned. Next, take a look at how this is implemented in the code.

The incr function is used to increment a user counter in the cache. In order to support any surrounding callback flow, the incr function also takes a win argument, which it calls as a function when it is finished. If the counter for a given user does not already exist, it needs to be created (as shown here in bold):

```
function incr(user,win){
  memcached.incr( user+'_v', 1, error(function(res){
    if( !res ) {
      memcached.set( user+'_v', 0, lifetime, error(function(){
        win()
      }))
    }
    else {
      win()
    }
  }))
}
```

To follow a user, you call the `follow` function, and this increments the counter for both the follower and the followee (as show here in bold) because both have now changed:

```
this.follow = function(user,follower,win) {
  followdb.follow(user,follower)
  incr(user,function(){
    incr(follower,win)
  })
}
```

To load a user, you first get the version number for that user and then construct the key for the complex object describing the user (as shown in bold):

```
this.user = function(user,win) {
  memcached.get( user+'_v', error(function( user_v ){
    user_v = user_v || 0
    var user_f_key = user+'_'+user_v+'_f'
```

Then you use the constructed key to find the user in the cache:

```
memcached.get( user_f_key, error(function( user_f ){
  if( user_f ) {
    user_f.cache = 'hit'
    win(user_f)
  }
```

However, if the user is not in the cache, you need to load the user from the database and put the user back in the cache with the appropriate new version number:

```
else {
  user_f = followdb.user(user)
  memcached.set( user_f_key, user_f, lifetime, error(function(){
    user_f.cache = 'miss'
    win(user_f)
  }))
}
```

This technique is useful in many contexts, and it is particularly useful for reducing processing costs on cloud servers.

SUMMARY

This chapter lays the foundation for the Lifestream app. In this chapter, you learned how to store photos in the cloud, how to integrate a user's identity with the major social networking sites, and how to handle large volumes of users. This chapter covers a lot of ground, and you are now ready to build out the server side of the Lifestream app.

But first, in Chapter 9, you'll build the client side of the app. In order to capture photos from a mobile device, you need to build a native mobile app. You can do so by using PhoneGap open source toolkit. You'll learn how to package up and deploy a native app so that your users can install it from the Apple App Store or the Android Marketplace.

EXERCISES

1. The Amazon S3 examples in this chapter showed you how to perform get and put operations on files stored in S3. Modify the examples to perform a delete operation as well.

2. In this chapter you were shown example code to perform an OAuth based sign in to Twitter and Facebook. The social networking site LinkedIn also provides an OAuth version 1.0A API. Modify the Twitter sign in code to work with LinkedIn. You can find out more about the LinkedIn developer API at `http://developer.linkedin.com`.

3. In the example "Signing In with Twitter," you store the token returned by Twitter as a state variable in the server. This won't work when you have more than one server because requests would end up at servers that do not have the token stored. Update the example to store the token in `memcached` instead.

4. There's one little problem with the solution to exercise 3. While the solution shows you how to use `memcached`, it is not a solution that will be fault tolerant under high load. Modify the solution to exercise 3 so that it uses the Redis key-value database instead. The Redis key-value database is just like `memcached`, except that it also stores data persistently on disk. Download Redis from `http://redis.io` and use the redis-node module from `https://github .com/bnoguchi/redis-node`.

Answers to the Exercises can be found in the Appendix.

▶ WHAT YOU LEARNED IN THIS CHAPTER

TOPIC	KEY CONCEPTS
Cloud storage using Amazon S3	When you need to store large volumes of data objects, it makes sense to outsource this requirement to a large-scale cloud provider such as Amazon. This saves you from the complex effort required to implement a reliable and scalable system yourself, as well as the cost involved in deploying high-end hardware. Cloud storage providers give you an HTTP interface to your data, so working with them is natural and easy. The Amazon S3 service is one of the most effective, and has may supporting software libraries, including the knox library for Node.
Streaming data transfer	When you are working with large data objects, especially media files like photos or videos, you need to be careful how you manage your available system RAM. Just loading entire files into memory will lead to capacity problems. It is much better to send files piece by piece when you upload or download them. This reduces the overall memory consumption and means you can handle more files. The data in the files is streamed in small pieces from one location to another, and this places a much lower load on the sending and receiving systems.
Third-party authentication using OAuth	The number of websites that require user accounts continues to increase. It is common for sites to make their sign-in requirements easier on users by outsourcing user identity and sign-in to the cloud. The major social networking sites, including Twitter and Facebook, provide implementations of the OAuth protocol that make this possible. When the user logs in to your app, he or she is temporarily redirected to the social networking site, which handles the login. Your system needs to participate in a data exchange flow defined by the OAuth standard. As this flow can be quite complex, it is easiest to use a third-party library. For Node, you can use the `oauth` module.
Shared-nothing architecture	Shared-nothing architecture is a scaling pattern for large systems. To allow these systems to scale linearly by adding new machines, you must reduce the interdependence between machines. In the shared-nothing architecture, each application server is completely independent from all the others and is unaware of their existence. Each app server interacts with the cache and the data store independently.
Versioned cache invalidation	Making sure the data objects stored in your cache are not stale is an important requirement for building reliable systems. One way to address this problem is to version the data in the cache. When a dependent data item changes, you increment the versions of all the other data items it affects. Subsequent cache requests will use the new version number and avoid pulling in the old data.

Creating Hybrid Apps that Run Natively

WHAT YOU WILL LEARN IN THIS CHAPTER:

➤ Understanding web, hybrid, and native apps

➤ Understanding the PhoneGap project

➤ Setting up the iPhone development environment

➤ Setting up the Android development environment

➤ Building hybrid iPhone apps

➤ Building hybrid Android apps

➤ Accessing device features from JavaScript

➤ Using the device camera

➤ Streaming data uploads for efficiency

➤ Streaming data onto Amazon S3

In this chapter, you will learn how to build apps that you can publish to the Apple App Store and the Android Marketplace. These apps are different from web apps. The user can download these apps as binary packages. It is your job, as a developer, to build this package and upload it to the App Store or Marketplace.

In this chapter, you'll learn how to create these downloadable apps, using HTML, JavaScript, and CSS. It is not necessary to learn Objective-C or Java. Instead, you can use the open source PhoneGap project, which wraps your web app in a native package. PhoneGap does this by running an embedded version of the WebKit browser inside the native package. This is a standard technique, and many native apps use it to display rich content. Apps that use an embedded WebKit browser for their entire user interface are known as *hybrid apps*.

You will learn how to set up your development environment to produce hybrid iPhone and Android apps, how to run hybrid apps in a device simulator, and how to deploy hybrid apps to physical devices. You will also learn how to access native device features such as the camera and how to stream picture data from the camera to cloud services such as Amazon S3.

INTRODUCING HYBRID APPS

You've constructed mobile web apps in the earlier chapters of this book. Those apps, however, are limited by the scope of HTML5. For example, although mobile web apps can use geolocation, the device accelerometer, orientation, and local storage, they are incapable of using extended device features such as the camera and alerting. They also can't integrate with advanced device features or third-party plug-ins that require custom code.

To build hybrid apps, you need to use the development environments that native app developers use. For iPhone, you use the Xcode environment, and for Android, you use the Eclipse environment. This chapter assumes that you have some familiarity with the way that modern integrated development environments (IDEs) such as these work.

The PhoneGap Project

To build hybrid apps, you can use the PhoneGap project. This open source project provides a wrapper framework for hybrid apps. The framework embeds the WebKit browser engine inside a native app, and it uses this embedded browser to run your HTML, JavaScript, and CSS code. The embedded browser engine is the same one that is used for mobile Safari and the Android browser. This means that your code environment is effectively the same one as for mobile web apps.

You can download PhoneGap from `www.phonegap.com`. This chapter focuses on building an app and does not cover the installation instructions for Xcode, Eclipse, or PhoneGap, which tend to vary between versions in any case. However, the PhoneGap project itself has an excellent and up-to-date online guide, with detailed step-by-step instructions and many screenshots. This is especially helpful if you have not used or installed Xcode or Eclipse previously. Always make sure that you install the most recent versions of Xcode and Eclipse. As the project is under active development and the installation procedures are still subject to change, this is the best place to get up-to-date instructions: `www.phonegap.com/start`.

 NOTE *The rest of this chapter assumes that you have Xcode or Eclipse installed.*

 NOTE *To run apps on an iPhone, you need to sign up for the Apple Developer program, pay the $99 annual subscription fee, and create a developer certificate for code-signing your apps. Follow the PhoneGap instructions carefully to get this right. For Android, you do not need to worry about this, as your development apps can be installed on your device without code-signing.*

BUILDING HYBRID APPS

In this section, you will learn how to build hybrid apps. You'll start with a simple example and work all the way up to a complex app that can take pictures and store them in the Amazon cloud. This app will work on both iPhone and Android devices.

Building an iPhone App

In this section, you will use the Xcode development environment provided by Apple to develop, test, and build iPhone apps. The Xcode environment is well designed and quite easy to use as it follows the common customs for development environments: It provides a project window with a tree menu on the left; editor windows for writing source code; output windows for build results; and settings windows for configuration. There are no real surprises with Xcode, and you should actively experiment with all the options, using a test project. A Mac is required, of course.

To build an iPhone app, you can use a template provided by PhoneGap. This template enables you to code the app using HTML, JavaScript, and CSS. Your files are then included in the native app binary package, which presents them using an embedded web browser.

Your files are stored in the www subfolder of the project. You can treat the files in the www folder as if they were a mobile website. The PhoneGap library provides an additional JavaScript API for accessing native device features, and you will learn how to use that API shortly. For now, enjoy the ability to create actual iPhone apps using nothing more than HTML!

The development process for hybrid apps has three testing cycles. The first cycle is the one you are already familiar with: creating a mobile web app and testing using the desktop Safari browser. Developing a hybrid app that runs natively introduces two new testing cycles.

The second cycle is the simulator cycle. In this testing cycle, you have completed the main work for a feature and are verifying that it behaves correctly in the simulator environment, which is much closer to the final version that will run on a device. The advantage of the simulator test cycle is that it is fast. It's not quite as fast as the web-based cycle, but it's still much faster than deploying to a physical device. You should be happy with your app in the simulator before you go anywhere near running your app in an actual device.

The third cycle is the device cycle. Here, you compile, install, and run the app on the device for each change you make to the source code. This can be tedious and slow. This testing is necessary for final verification, but if you find yourself using this third cycle to debug your app, you should return to an earlier cycle to work things out.

Some things, like the camera, can be tested only on a physical device. In these cases, it is worth investing some time in writing stub code to simulate device features.

The Xcode development process compiles your code twice: once for the simulator and once for the device. This is done because your computer and your iPhone use different CPU architectures — Intel for the computer (whether Mac or PC) and ARM for the iPhone. Be aware that the simulator doesn't accurately reflect how an app will perform on a device. An app runs much more slowly on a device than in the simulator, and you need to design for this.

Understanding Code-Signing

You cannot just compile an iPhone app, install it on a physical device, and run it. Your iPhone will refuse to run an app that has not been cryptographically signed. Apple uses this "code-signing" procedure as a security mechanism to ensure that only validated and trusted apps are available to the general public.

If you have not used a code-signing system before, the process and terminology can be confusing. It can be even harder to debug errors, and if you search online, you'll see developer forums full of questions about code-signing problems.

The easiest way to avoid trouble is to understand the key concepts and how they fit together. The first concepts are the *development phase* and *distribution phase*. In the development phase, you install frequent new binary builds of your app onto your own iPhone. As you fix bugs or test new features, you generate a new binary build of your app using Xcode and then install it onto your iPhone. Xcode copies the binary build onto your iPhone. In the distribution phase, you create a special, code-signed version of your app and upload it to the Apple App Store. This is the version the end users will download and run.

In order for the development version of your app to run on a physical device, you need to sign it with a *development certificate*. You obtain your development certificate from the iOS Provisioning Portal, which is a sub-website of the main Apple developer website. The process of obtaining a development certificate is itself somewhat involved and subject to change by Apple. The best way to obtain a certificate is to go to the iOS Provisioning Portal (follow the link from `http://developer.apple .com`), click the Certificate tab on the menu on the left, and then click the How To sub-tab on the far right. Here you will find the most up-to-date step-by-step instructions direct from Apple.

After you download your development certificate file from the iOS Provisioning Portal, you double-click on it to install the certificate. The Keychain Access application (this is a Mac system application) will appear, showing you a list of installed certificates.

You also need a special Apple certificate as part of the code-signing process. This is known as the *WWDR intermediate certificate*. It is available for download from the Certificates tab on the iOS Provisioning Portal. Download, double-click, and it will install itself. You only need to do this once.

The next concept is the *app ID*. This is a unique string, like a domain name, that identifies your app. There is an App ID tab on the left menu of the iOS Provisioning Portal, and this also has a How To sub-tab to guide you in creating an app ID. For development, your easiest option is to create a *wildcard* ID. A wildcard ID can be used for many apps, which means you don't have to set up a new app ID each time. The wildcard is really a prefix string, and to make it unique for each app you build, you provide a unique suffix. This is shown in in step 9 in the following Try It Out.

The next concept is that of a *registered device*. You need to tell Apple which devices you want to install your development app on. Apple only allows you a maximum of a 100 development devices, and you need to enter the unique identifier of each one on the Provisioning tab of the portal. The unique identifier of each iPhone, iPad, and iPod Touch is known as a UDID. Again, the How To sub-tab will guide you through the most up-to-date method of finding the UDID of your device.

You're not done yet! The next thing you need is a *provisioning profile*. This is a small cryptographic file that Apple generates for you. You download the provisioning profile file, and you install it on each development device. Development apps will not run without a matching provisioning profile on the device. If you are sending a development app to a client for review, remember to send them the provisioning profile as well. Follow the How To sub-tab of the Provisioning tab to learn how to create one.

When you create a provisioning profile, you'll notice that it ties together three things:

➤ Your development certificate

➤ Your list of registered devices

➤ Your app identifier (the UDID)

When you build an app using Xcode, all of these three things have to match for the app to build and install successfully. Normally, you'll have your development certificate installed on your Mac already, and you'll have installed the provisioning profile on your development devices (the How To guides you through this).

NOTE *Your development provisioning profile is valid for only three months. After that, you have to renew by logging in to the iOS Provisioning Portal. If you find yourself unable to demo an app to a client because your profile has run out, a temporary fix is to send your iPhone back in time by setting the date on the device to a date in the past. Your app will magically start working again, and you can write that invoice!*

The tricky thing is configuring Xcode. For each iPhone app project, you need to tell Xcode which development certificate and which app ID to use. This is done in the project settings, as explained in the Try It Out below.

There's one final concept: the *developer profile*. Xcode does not refer to your developer certificate directly. Rather it associates the developer certificate with a developer profile. You need to make sure that the developer profile used by Xcode for your project is the one that contains the correct developer certificate. You can end up with lots of these if you have lots of clients.

You can get an overview of all these items in Xcode by selecting the Window ⇨ Organizer menu option. This opens the Organizer window, which shows you all of your installed developer and provisioning profiles.

Once you have finished coding, debugging, and testing your iPhone app, you'll need to publish it on the Apple App Store. Chapter 13 discusses how to go about doing this.

TRY IT OUT A Simple iPhone App

This example takes you through the process of building an iPhone app and running it — first in the simulator and then on a device. This example shows you how to complete the development phase of building an iPhone app.

1. Start the Xcode development environment. Once it has opened, choose File ⇨ New Project from the top menu bar. You should see the New Project dialog, as shown in Figure 9-1.

FIGURE 9-1

2. On the left sidebar in the New Project dialog, click PhoneGap in the User Templates section. Then click the PhoneGap-Based Application icon on the right to create a new PhoneGap project.

3. In the file selection dialog that appears, enter `lifestream` as the name of your project. Save the project to a folder, such as the `Projects` folder in your home folder.

4. When the project window appears, showing all the items in your `lifestream` project, expand the www item. You see the `index.html` file, as shown in Figure 9-2.

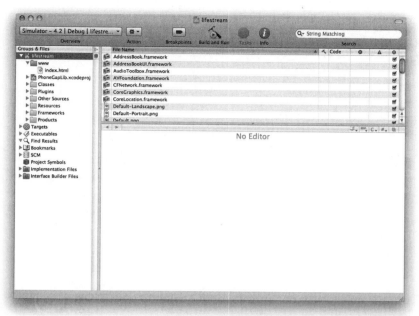

FIGURE 9-2

5. Open the `index.html` file by double-clicking it. A code editor window appears, showing the default contents of the `index.html` file. PhoneGap provides some boilerplate code to get you started. To verify that everything works, you can modify this file and run the app in the simulator, so add the word `lifestream` to the body of the HTML, as shown near the bottom of Figure 9-3.

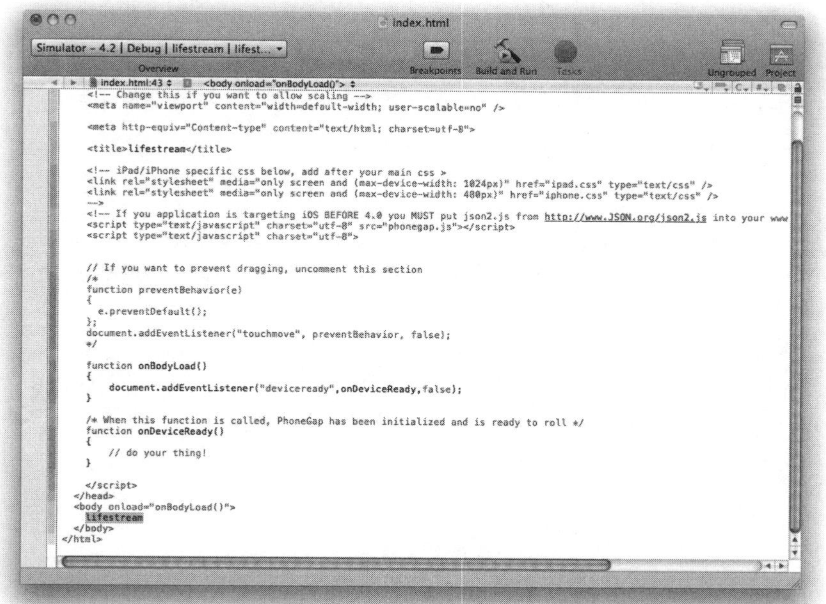

FIGURE 9-3

6. Click the Build and Run icon at the top of the code editor window. Xcode compiles your app, runs the PhoneGap scripts, and launches the iPhone simulator. Your new app appears in the simulator, as shown in Figure 9-4.

FIGURE 9-4

NOTE *An out-of-the-box PhoneGap installation should not encounter any issues running in the simulator. If you do run into problems, it is likely that Xcode has a stale cache. In this case, the best option is to close Xcode completely, restart, and open your project again.*

7. To install and run your app on an iPhone, make sure your iPhone is connected via USB to your Mac. Select Window ➪ Organize and verify that your iPhone appears in the sidebar, in the Devices section, and has a green dot beside it.

8. Select Project ➪ Edit Project Settings. The Project Info window appears. Select the Build tab at the top. Ensure that the Base SDK setting has the value Latest iOS and that the Code Signing Identity setting is set to your certified developer profile. Figure 9-5 shows how this window should look.

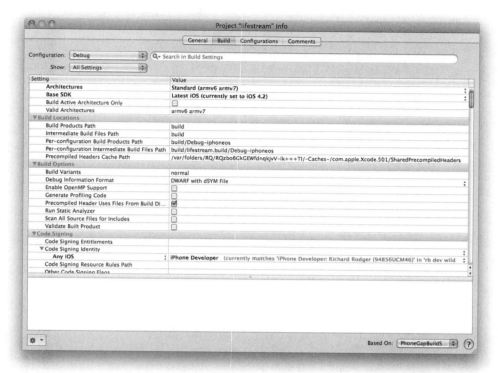

FIGURE 9-5

 WARNING *You need a valid developer identity and provisioning profile to actually run your apps on a physical device. It is extremely easy to tie yourself in knots trying to get this right. Make sure to document your actions as you take them. Work slowly and carefully. Avoid the temptation to start making random changes in the hope that things will just work.*

9. Return to the project window (by clicking on it), which shows all the items in your project. Click the Resources item and open the `lifestream-Info.plist` file. A plist editor window appears. Edit the Bundle Identifier setting and enter your wildcard app identifier by replacing the * character with the string `lifestream`. This setting points your iPhone at your developer provisioning profile, which gives your app permission to run. For example, in Figure 9-6, you can see my `ricebridge` wildcard.

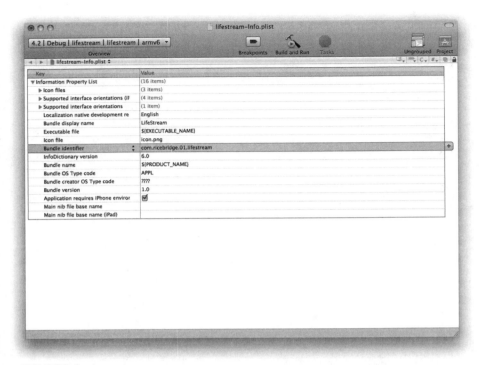

FIGURE 9-6

10. Return to the project window. Select the Device entry from the drop-down menu at the top right. (It was previously set to Simulator.)

11. Click the Build and Run icon at the top of this window. Xcode recompiles your app, runs the PhoneGap scripts, installs the app on your connected iPhone, and runs the app. The app will appear on your iPhone exactly as it appeared in the simulator, except that the startup time will be slower.

How It Works

The HTML, JavaScript, and CSS source code files for your app are all located in the www folder. Apart from icon files and plist settings files, you do not need to modify any other files in the project. This means that you do not need to worry about all the Objective-C files in the project. Take a look at them if you are curious, but in day-to-day work with PhoneGap, there is no need to have any familiarity with the Objective-C language.

When you create a new project with Xcode, you can base that project on a set of template files. This gets you started more quickly. Apple provides a number of templates for native app developers. The PhoneGap project uses this template system to create a ready-made app for you, with all the Objective-C code already in place.

You will do most of your work on the files in the www folder. The index.html file is created by PhoneGap and provides you with a template to get started. In the example, you just make a small change to the index.html file to verify that your changes will make it onto the simulator and the device.

The simulator is the default destination when a project is first created. When you click the Build and Run icon, Xcode runs a build procedure in the background to create your app binary package. This procedure consists of multiple steps, and various command line programs are run in the background for you, including compilers and script generators. Xcode will also install your app binary onto the simulator, launch the simulator itself, and run your app in the simulator, so you can start testing right away.

 NOTE *You can run the simulator by itself. This is very useful if you want to test mobile web apps using the simulator's mobile Safari browser. The simulator app lives in the subfolder of the top level Developer folder on your Mac (which Xcode installed). The easiest way to find it is to use the Spotlight search application; use the query text "iOS Sim" and you should see the Simulator appear as one of the application results. A Spotlight search can be run by clicking on the magnifying glass icon on the top right of the screen.*

To get your PhoneGap app running on your physical device, you need to ensure that all the code-signing paraphernalia is in place and that your Xcode project settings are correct. In the instructions above, you are shown how to set these. The Bundle Identifier setting needs to match the app ID that is contained in your provisioning profile. This must be an exact match, or, as in the example, if the app ID is a wild card, then the Bundle Identifier prefix must match the wildcard app ID.

Building an Android App

To create an Android app, you use the Eclipse development environment. The Android SDK is a separate download which you integrate into Eclipse. As the installation procedure is subject to change, you should follow the instructions on `www.phonegap.com/start` as these will be the most up-to-date. This example assumes you have Eclipse and the Android SDK installed and configured.

Setting up a project for an Android app is a more manual process than for an iPhone app, and the device emulator is more clunky. However, you do not need to worry about code signing at all to put your Android apps on a physical device for testing, and that's a big plus. You do still need to sign your Android apps in order to submit them to the Android Marketplace. Chapter 13 will show you how to do this.

PhoneGap for Android works exactly the same way as for iPhone. This time, the binary application consists of compiled Java source code rather than Objective-C. Your HTML, CSS, and JavaScript files are again included in the package and displayed using a browser component. You should aim to use the same HTML, CSS, and JavaScript source code files for both Android and iPhone versions of your app. This will make you life much easier in the long run. One way to do this is by using symbolic links to ensure that your Xcode and Android projects both use the same www folder.

You may still need to deal with differences between the two platforms. You can approach this challenge in the same manner as you do when building a website that works in multiple browsers: Use JavaScript to dynamically detect the environment and make adjustments. This is a slight annoyance, but it is a much lower maintenance cost than having separate code bases.

The Android emulator is much slower than the iPhone simulator, and thus it is closer to the actual performance of your app on a physical device. One important thing to understand is that the Android device emulator is not a device simulator. The emulator emulates the system infrastructure and hardware of your Android device, meaning that it can run the same binary code as your physical device. The iPhone simulator on the other hand does not run the same binary code, providing instead a simulated environment that happens to have the same APIs.

To put it another way, you only compile once with Android, and the same binary app package can run on the emulator and on your device. You need to compile separate binary packages for the iPhone device itself, and the iPhone simulator.

TRY IT OUT   **A Simple Android App**

This example shows you how to set up an Android project and get your app running on the emulator and on your Android device. As with the iPhone, you'll use the PhoneGap open source project to create a native wrapper that displays your HTML. Unlike the template PhoneGap app for iPhone, which is just an empty HTML page, the template PhoneGap app for Android gives you example code for most of the PhoneGap API. This inconsistency seems to be simply due to the fact that different open source developers have worked on different parts of the PhoneGap project.

Follow these steps to build your first Android app:

1.   Copy the `Sample` Android project from your unzipped PhoneGap download. You'll create a copy of this folder for each new Android app project. Paste the folder into a folder such as the `Projects` folder on your computer. Rename the folder `android-lifestream`.

2.   Start the Eclipse development environment. Select File ⇨ New ⇨ Project from Eclipse menu bar. The New Project dialog appears, as shown in Figure 9-7.

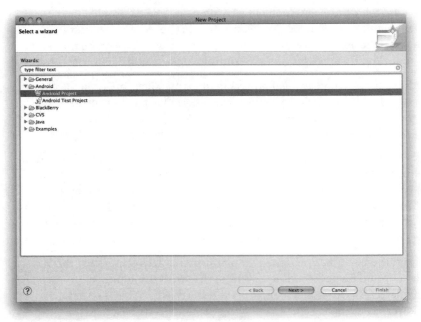

FIGURE 9-7

3. Select Android Project and click the Next button.

4. On the project details page that appears (see Figure 9-8), enter the string `lifestream` for your project name. Choose the Create Project from Existing Source option and point the Location field at your `android-lifestream` folder. Select the most recent version of Android as your build target.

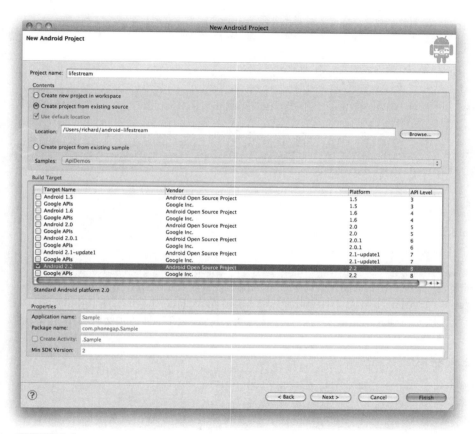

FIGURE 9-8

5. Click the Finish button. Your project opens in Eclipse, but it does not build at first and instead reports an error (see Figure 9-9).

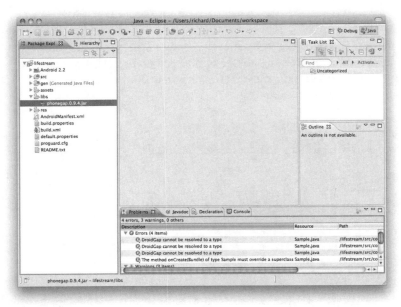

FIGURE 9-9

6. Open the `libs` subfolder of the project. Right-click the `phonegap.jar` file and select the Add to Build Path option. Your project should rebuild without errors.

7. Open the `assets/www` subfolder, which stores the HTML, JavaScript, and CSS files for Android projects. Right-click the `index.html` file and select the Open in Text Editor option. You see that the Android sample project contains a large amount of boilerplate code. Find the first `h1` tag, just after the opening `body` tag, and modify its contents to be the string `lifestream`, as shown in Figure 9-10.

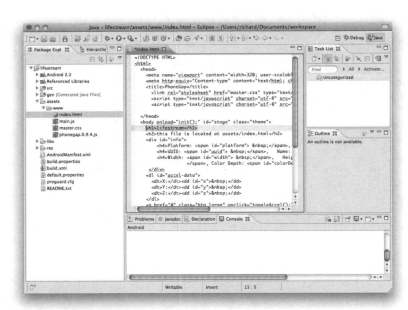

FIGURE 9-10

8. Before connecting your Android phone to your computer, run the app in the Android emulator by clicking the green run arrow in the top icon bar of Eclipse. In the dialog that appears, choose the Android Application option to launch the Android emulator. The emulator installs and runs your app, but it can be slow to start, so go grab a cup of coffee. Eventually, the screen shown in Figure 9-11 appears.

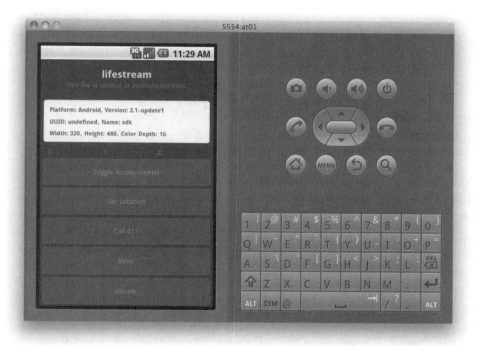

FIGURE 9-11

 NOTE *You can speed up the emulator (and its start-up time) in various ways. The easiest is to keep a snapshot of the emulator state and start from that. Select the Snapshot option when you are creating an Android Virtual Device. Giving the emulated device plenty of RAM, at least 1024Mb, will also help. Finally, having large amounts of physical RAM (at least 8Gb) on your development machine can have a significant impact on the emulator. There are other configuration changes that depend upon your specific versions of Eclipse and Android.* `stackoverflow.com` *is your best bet to find them.*

9. Connect your Android device to your computer. Make sure to select the "debugging" option on your device once it notifies you that it has connected. Run your app again. This time, you are offered a choice of running the app on either the emulator or your device. Choose your device. The app is installed and launched on your device. It should look exactly the same as in the emulator. You'll notice that the Android device deployment is much faster than the iPhone deployment.

NOTE *Eclipse has some strange ideas about managing files inside projects. If you modify any files using another editor, such as Xcode, Eclipse will not notice that you made any changes. You must manually refresh your project. Do this by selecting the project and then pressing the F5 key.*

How It Works

When you create a new Android PhoneGap project, you do so by manually cloning a sample application that the PhoneGap project provides. PhoneGap does not provide an actual plug-in for Eclipse, which is why you have to do this manually.

When you create a new Android project, you select your copy of the sample app as the existing source code from which to create the project. You do this in the Eclipse New Project dialog window.

Once the project is created, you need to ensure that the build path is set up correctly. For Android projects, PhoneGap comes in the form of a `phonegap.jar` file that includes all the PhoneGap functionality. You need to ensure that this `jar` file is in the build path for the project so that the Java code of the wrapper classes (which are included in the sample app) can find its PhoneGap dependencies. As with the iPhone and PhoneGap, you do not need to write any Java code, and once you are set up, you will normally not need to make any changes to the Java code.

To run your app in the Android emulator, you click on the standard Eclipse run icon (the green arrow in the top icon bar). In order to run an emulator, you will first have to create a virtual Android device. The `phonegap.com` website always has the most up-to-date instructions for doing this. The process of creating a suitable Android virtual device for PhoneGap is not covered here because these instructions tend to change frequently, typically with each release of PhoneGap. You'll need to check for changes after each update.

When you run your app in the emulator, you will find that it can be rather slow. Remember that the emulator is attempting to simulate the hardware of a physical device. The advantage of this approach is that you can be sure that you will find and resolve more bugs and issues via the emulator. Although the emulator is slow to start and slow to run your app, it can accept redeployments quite quickly once it is up and running. It is very feasible to make continuous small changes and redeploy to the emulator multiple times for testing. You'll find this is much faster than deployment to the iPhone simulator.

To run your app on your Android device, simply connect it to your machine via USB. Eclipse will detect the presence of your device and offer it as a deployment option when you next run your app. As you do not have to worry about code-signing at this stage, it is much easier to get a test version up and running on Android.

To share pre-release test versions of your Android app with clients, simply email them the `apk` file that you'll find in the `bin` folder of your Eclipse project. This is the Android binary package of your app, equivalent to the iPhone `ipa` file. Your clients simply have to copy the `apk` file onto their Android devices, and by opening the file in the Android file manager, the install process runs automatically.

Using Device Features

It's time to try out some device features. You need to know how to access native device features that you can't get to from a mobile web app. The PhoneGap project provides you with a uniform API to these features, and in the following example, you'll start to use them. You'll create an app that displays native notifications, can beep at the user, and can vibrate the phone.

The PhoneGap JavaScript API consists of a set of feature-specific objects. Most of these objects are available as properties of the built-in `navigator` object (which all web browsers have), but some are standalone. A full list can always be found at `docs.phonegap.com`. Here are some of the most useful PhoneGap objects:

➤ `navigator.camera`: provides access to the device camera, so you can capture pictures.

➤ `navigator.compass`: provides access to the device compass, so you can tell which direction the user is facing. Try Exercise 3 at the end of the chapter for an example of the compass in use.

➤ `navigator.accelerometer`: indicates the amount of three-dimensional acceleration the device is experiencing. Because gravity is always present as a downward acceleration, this can be used to determine the orientation of the device in three-dimensional space. You could also implement a shake gesture by detecting sudden changes in acceleration.

➤ `navigator.notification`: alerts the user in various ways, including vibrating the device. You'll learn more about this object in the next example.

➤ `device`: gives you details about the device, such as the phone type, version number, and unique identifier.

PhoneGap also provides a full API to read and write files on the device file system. The file API is not covered in this book, but you will be able to find all the details in the PhoneGap documentation. Start with the `FileEntry` object and work from there.

Finally, PhoneGap also fires a set of custom events. These inform you of changes to device state, use of physical buttons, and device readiness. You register your interest in a PhoneGap event in the same way as for other browser events, like so:

```
document.addEventListener("deviceready", function(){ ... } );
```

The events you can listen for are as follows:

➤ `deviceready`: fires when the HTML document is ready and PhoneGap has completed its own initialization. In a complex app you should always start your script by listening for this event.

➤ `pause` and `resume`: fires when your app is placed into the background on the device, and when your app is brought back into the foreground.

➤ `backbutton`, `menubutton`, `searchbutton`: fire when the respective Android physical device buttons are pressed. They will not fire on the iPhone.

TRY IT OUT   Making a Device Dance and Sing

In this example, you'll extend the `lifestream` app project you created in the preceding section. Your work in Chapter 8 laid the foundation for the Lifestream application. In the following examples, you'll return to that folder structure and add in some more components as you build toward a complete app. Follow these steps:

1. Go to your `lifestream` project folder. Copy your existing downloads of the jQuery and jQuery Mobile files into this folder. (You'll use these libraries to help build your app, just as you did in

Chapter 6.) Copy the `jquery.js`, `jquery.mobile.js`, and `jquery.mobile.css` files and the jQuery Mobile `images` folder.

2. Ensure that you have a sound file called `beep.wav` to provide the sound for the beep function. Either create or download your own beep sound or use the version in the source code download available for this chapter.

3. Open the `index.html` file and replace its contents with the following code:

Available for
download on
Wrox.com

```html
<!DOCTYPE html>
<html>
<head>
  <title>Lifestream App</title>
  <meta name="viewport"
        content="user-scalable=no,initial-scale=1.0,maximum-scale=1.0" />

  <link rel="stylesheet" href="jquery.mobile.css" />
  <link rel="stylesheet" href="lifestream.css" />

  <script src="phonegap.js"></script>
  <script src="jquery.js"></script>
  <script src="jquery.mobile.js"></script>
  <script src="lifestream.js"></script>
</head>
<body>
<div id="main" data-role="page">

  <div data-role="header" data-position="fixed">
    <div data-role="navbar">
      <ul>
       <li><a id="nav_alert">Alert</a></li>
       <li><a id="nav_confirm">Confirm</a></li>
       <li><a id="nav_beep">Beep</a></li>
       <li><a id="nav_vibrate">Vibrate</a></li>
      </ul>
    </div>
  </div>

  <div data-role="content">
    <p id="msg">device features</p>
  </div>

</div>
</body>
</html>
```

Code snippet lifestream/app-www-features/index.html

Note the reference to the `phonegap.js` file, which is highlighted in this example. PhoneGap automatically provides this file, and you do not need to copy it in. Some versions of PhoneGap add a version number suffix to this filename, and you will see a file of the form `phonegap-x.y.z.js` in your project www folder. If your version of PhoneGap adds a version number, make sure to include it the `script` tag `src` attribute.

4. Create a `lifestream.css` file and insert the following lines in it:

```css
#main {
  width: 320px;
}
```

Code snippet lifestream/app-www-features/lifestream.css

5. Create a `lifestream.js` file and insert the following lines in it:

```js
document.addEventListener("deviceready", ondeviceready)

function ondeviceready(){
  document.ontouchmove = function(e){ e.preventDefault(); }

  var msg = $('#msg')

  $('#nav_alert').tap(function(){
    navigator.notification.alert(
      'Alerting...',
      function(){
        msg.text('alert')
      },
      'My Alert',
      'DONE')
  })

  var colors = ['Red','Green','Blue','Dismiss']
  $('#nav_confirm').tap(function(){
    navigator.notification.confirm(
      'Pick a Color',
      function(index){
        msg.text(colors[index-1])
      },
      'Colors',
      colors.join(','))
  })

  $('#nav_beep').tap(function(){
    msg.text('beep')
    navigator.notification.beep(1);
  })

  $('#nav_vibrate').tap(function(){
    msg.text('vibrate')
    navigator.notification.vibrate(1000);
  })
}
```

Code snippet lifestream/app-www-features/lifestream.js

6. Open the `lifestream` project in Xcode. Deploy it to the iPhone simulator by selecting the Simulator option from the drop-down on the top right on the project window. Your app will appear in the Simulator.

7. Click the Alert tab in the app. The alert dialog shown in Figure 9-12 appears. As you'll see shortly, you can fully specify all the text elements of the alert dialog that appears. This is not possible using the basic JavaScript `alert` function.

8. Click the Confirm tab in the app. The dialog shown in Figure 9-13 appears. Again you can control the content of the dialog.

FIGURE 9-12   **FIGURE 9-13**

9. It's more fun to try out the beep and vibrate functions on a real device than in the simulator, so select the Device Deployment option from the project window to deploy the app to an iPhone that's connected to your computer.

10. On the iPhone, with the volume turned up, tap the Beep tab. You should hear a beep.

11. Tap the Vibrate tab. The iPhone should shake.

12. Open the `lifestream` project in Eclipse and deploy it to your Android device. Remember to refresh the project before you deploy the project to get Eclipse to recognize your changes. Verify that the features also work on an Android device by repeating steps 10 and 11 with that device.

How It Works

The code base you've created so far will form the basic framework for the Lifestream app. The `index.html` file follows the code you developed for the To-Do List app. Hybrid apps are really just mobile web apps packaged to run natively, so you can reuse all your mobile web app skills when building hybrid apps.

The head element of the index.html file is mostly the same as for the To-Do List app. It is not necessary, however, to include the meta tags specifying the icons. You'll learn how to specify icons for hybrid apps in Chapter 13.

In addition to the jQuery scripts, and your own lifestream.js script, there is also a tag referencing the "magic" phonegap.js script. This is the JavaScript API layer provided by the PhoneGap project. The project build scripts include it automatically and ensure that it's correctly versioned. On the native side, in Objective-C for iPhone and Java for Android, PhoneGap has registered JavaScript objects that provide access to native device features. These special objects are exposed as a pure JavaScript API in the phonegap.js file. This is the cross-platform PhoneGap JavaScript API, as documented fully at http://docs.phonegap.com.

The user interface of the Lifestream app is built using the tagging conventions specified by jQuery Mobile. The data-role attributes indicate the layout of each element. In this app, you are using data-role="header" with data-role="navbar" to display a set of tabs across the top of the app:

```
<div data-role="header" data-position="fixed">
  <div data-role="navbar">
    <ul>
     <li><a id="nav_alert">Alert</a></li>
     <li><a id="nav_confirm">Confirm</a></li>
     <li><a id="nav_beep">Beep</a></li>
     <li><a id="nav_vibrate">Vibrate</a></li>
    </ul>
  </div
</div>
```

The style sheet for this app is very simple:

```
#main {
  width: 320px;
}
```

This ensures that the main content of the app takes up the entire width of the device screen. All WebKit-based mobile browsers simulate a screen width of 320 pixels for mobile web apps, regardless of their true pixel dimensions. This is the case because most modern mobile sites are designed for iPhones, and this simulation is the standard behavior of the mobile Safari browser. You can use this simulated width to write cross-platform hybrid apps.

The JavaScript that implements the hybrid app is the most interesting part of this example. Here is the standard way to initialize a hybrid app:

```
document.addEventListener("deviceready", ondeviceready)

function ondeviceready(){
  document.ontouchmove = function(e){ e.preventDefault(); }

  // your code
}
```

The `deviceready` event is a PhoneGap event. This event is fired by the native PhoneGap code when the device is ready to run your app and the Document Object Model (DOM) in the embedded browser is ready. This replaces the more familiar jQuery code `$(function(){ ... });`.

By default, the embedded browser supports the standard "rubber-band" web page scrolling behavior. You can see this rubber-band effect if you try to scroll a web page in the mobile Safari browser beyond the top or bottom of the page content. The web page animates as if a rubber-band is holding it back. Sometimes, you'll want to keep this behavior, especially for efficient scrolling of large amounts of content. But if you want your app interface to remain fixed, you can capture the `ontouchmove` event, as shown in the highlighted code in the `ondeviceready` function above, and prevent this default scrolling.

The main body of code in this example sets up some standard jQuery event handlers that fire when the user taps on the tabs. Each event handler uses a device feature exposed by PhoneGap.

The `navigator.notification.alert` function displays a more native-looking alert than the plain JavaScript `alert` function. The arguments are the title of the dialog window, the callback function, the text content, and the name of the button.

The `navigator.notification.confirm` function displays a quick options dialog. You can specify the title, the callback, the text, and the list of options. As with the `navigator.notification.alert` function, this function calls your callback with the user's response.

The `navigator.notification.beep` function does exactly what you think it does. The single argument is the number of times to beep. On Android a system beep sound is used, but on iPhone you need to supply your own, in the form of a `beep.wav` file.

Finally, the `navigator.notification.vibrate` function makes the phone vibrate. The single argument is the duration, in milliseconds.

From this example, you can see that there is no special coding needed to access native device features. You call standard JavaScript functions, and PhoneGap provides the bridge to the native code that performs the requested action.

LIFESTREAM, A PHOTO-BLOGGING APP

The Lifestream app is a social photo-blogging application. You can take pictures of the things that happen to you during the day and post them to your lifestream. Your friends can subscribe to your lifestream and see your latest photos. It is very similar to Twitter, except with photos. You will build this app in stages over the course of the next few chapters. There's a lot to do, and you'll have some technical challenges to overcome: How can you capture a photo using the camera? How do you send the photo back to the server? What does the server do with it? You'll learn the answers to these questions here.

Answers to other questions, such as how to store the followers of a user and how to enable a user to login, will be answered in other chapters. Stay tuned!

Here's the technical problem you need to solve:

1. Take a picture using the device camera. Your app needs to launch the camera app and then return to the foreground after the picture is taken.

2. Upload the picture data, in some format, to the server. Because the picture is a large file, you need to be concerned about memory consumption on the server when lots of users are uploading lots of photos.

3. Store the picture data somewhere so that it can easily be displayed. You'll have to think about bandwidth usage and storage capacity, especially if your app becomes popular.

You can reuse your Amazon S3 code from Chapter 8 for the picture storage functionality. You'll need to modify that code, but the basic foundation is all there.

Uploading Pictures

To enable picture taking in the Lifestream app, you can use the PhoneGap API. The `navigator` `.camera.getPicture` function launches the standard device camera app. It also returns the user to your app after the picture is taken. This function takes three arguments: a success function, a failure function, and an options object. You'll see how to use these functions in the following example.

The picture data is not provided as binary data. Rather, it is provided in *base64* format. This encoding format represents binary data using only 64 ASCII characters: uppercase and lowercase letters, numerals, and two punctuation characters (usually + and /). The = character is used as padding at the end so that the number of characters in any message is always divisible by 4. Every four base64 characters represent 3 bytes.

In your JavaScript code running on the device, your success function (which you passed to `navigator` `.camera.getPicture` as the first argument) will receive a base64 string. It makes no sense to convert this string to binary on the device, as the image file needs to be stored in the cloud on Amazon S3. So you'll use a Node server to do the conversion and storage. You still need to send the base64 data to Node, and you can do this using the jQuery `ajax` function, as you'll see shortly in the example code.

When Node receives the base64 data, it should convert it to an ordinary image file in binary format and then store this image file on Amazon S3. To convert between base64 and binary with Node, you can use the built-in `Buffer` object, which encapsulates binary data. You can create a Buffer object from a string encoding data in a particular format by specifying the format as the second argument to the object constructor function. For base64, this looks like:

```
var binary = new Buffer("...your base64 string...","base64")
```

The above line of code assumes you have the entire base64 string in memory. When you are using Node, you will not be given the entire base64 string. Instead, as pieces of the string are transmitted over the network, you will receive randomly-sized sequential chunks of the base64 string. This is how Node works. You receive data in the form of events. In this case, an event is the arrival of another little piece of the entire string.

In your Node server code, you'll need to do some housekeeping in order to keep everything synchronized. If you get it right, your memory consumption will be very low because you'll only need to keep small chunks of an image in memory.

Being very conservative with server resources is the essential philosophy of cloud computing. Remember that you pay for CPU, memory, and disk usage. The more efficient your server-side code, the more money you make.

TRY IT OUT   Taking a Picture and Uploading it to a Server

In this example, you'll modify the app from the previous example. That example provides you with the basic HTML structure for the Lifestream app. You'll add a Lifestream logo to one of the tabs, in preparation for the full app interface, and you'll also refactor the JavaScript into a more structured form that can grow as the functionality of the app expands. Follow these steps:

1. Open your `lifestream` folder. Copy the `lifestream.png` file from the downloadable code package for this chapter into the www subfolder. This file is the logo for your app and appears on one of the tabs at the top of the page.

2. Edit the `index.html` file by replacing the HTML code inside the `div` tag as follows:

```html
<div id="main" data-role="page">

  <div data-role="header" data-position="fixed">
    <div data-role="navbar">
      <ul>
        <li>
          <a id="nav_lifestream">
            <img id="logo" src="lifestream.png"> 
          </a>
        </li>
        <li><a id="nav_post">Post</a></li>
      </ul>
    </div
  </div>

  <div id="con_lifestream" data-role="content">
    <p>photo stream</p>
  </div>

  <div id="con_post" data-role="content">
    <a id="btn_takepic" data-role="button">Take Picture</a>
    <img id="post_pic" />
    <a id="btn_upload" data-role="button">Upload Picture</a>
    <p id="post_msg"></p>
  </div>

</div>
```

Code snippet lifestream/app-www-upload/index.html

3. Edit the `lifestream.css` file and append the following CSS rules to it:

```css
#logo {
  position: absolute;
  top:7px;
  left:44px;
}

#con_post {
  display:none;
}
```

```css
#post_pic {
  display: block;
  margin: 0px auto;
  width:  200px;
  height: 200px;
  border: 1px solid #ccc;
}

#post_msg {
  text-align: center;
  font-weight: bold;
}
```

Code snippet lifestream/app-www-upload/lifestream.css

4.   Replace the entire `lifestream.js` file with the following code (replacing the `YOUR_IP_ADDRESS` marker at the top of the file with the IP address of your machine):

Available for download on Wrox.com

```javascript
document.addEventListener("deviceready", ondeviceready)

var server = 'YOUR_IP_ADDRESS:3009'
var app = null


function ondeviceready(){
  app = new App()
}


function App() {
  var imagedata = null
  var con = $('#con_lifestream')

  var post_pic = $('#post_pic')
  var post_msg = $('#post_msg')

  var btn_upload = $('#btn_upload')


  $('#nav_lifestream').tap(function(){
    showcon('lifestream')
  })

  $('#nav_post').tap(function(){
    showcon('post')
  })

  $('#btn_takepic').tap(picTake)
  $('#btn_upload').tap(picUpload)


  function picTake(){
    navigator.camera.getPicture(
```

```
            function(base64) {
              imagedata = base64
              post_pic.attr({src:"data:image/jpeg;base64,"+imagedata})
            },
            function(){
              post_msg.text('Could not take picture')
            },
            { quality: 50 }
          )
        }

        function picUpload(){
          if( imagedata ) {
            post_msg.text('Uploading...')

            $.ajax({
              url:'http://'+server+'/lifestream/api/upload',
              type:'POST',
              contentType:'application/octet-stream',
              data:imagedata,
              success:function(){
                post_msg.text('Picture uploaded.')
              },
              error:function(err){
                console.log(err)
                post_msg.text('Could not upload picture')
              },
            })
          }
          else {
            post_msg.text('Take a picture first')
          }
        }

        function showcon(name) {
          if( con ) {
            con.hide()
          }
          con = $('#con_'+name)
          con.show()
        }
      }
```

Code snippet lifestream/app-www-upload/lifestream.js

5. Open Xcode and deploy the Lifestream app to your physical iPhone by choosing the Device option and clicking Build and Run. You should see the app interface, as shown in Figure 9-14.

6. Click the Post tab. You should see the picture posting page, as shown in Figure 9-15.

7. Click the Take Picture button. When you are taken to the device camera app, snap a random picture and then click the Use button to return to the Lifestream app. Your picture will appear on the picture posting page, as shown in Figure 9-16.

FIGURE 9-14

FIGURE 9-15

FIGURE 9-16

8. Now you need to configure the server. Edit your `nginx conf` file by adding the following directive to the `server` section:

Available for download on Wrox.com

```
location /lifestream/api {
    proxy_pass http://127.0.0.1:3009/lifestream/api;
}
```

Code snippet lifestream/upload/nginx-conf-additions.txt

This is the same style of proxy directive as you used for the To Do List app.

9. Go to the `lifestream/server` folder that you created in Chapter 8. Your server-side Node code will continue to live in this folder. Refactor the Amazon key lines so that they are in the following format and consistent with the key entries for Twitter and Facebook:

Available for download on Wrox.com

```
exports.amazon   = {
  keyid:'YOUR_AWS_KEY_ID',
  secret:'YOUR_AWS_SECRET'
}
```

Code snippet lifestream/upload/keys.js

10. Run the following npm install commands as root to ensure that the required Node modules are installed:

```
sudo -s
npm install connect
npm install knox
npm install simpledb
npm install uuid
```

11. Create a new file called common.js in the lifestream/server folder. This file will contain shared code. Insert the following lines in it:

```
var util      = exports.util    = require('util')
var fs        = exports.fs      = require('fs')

var connect   = exports.connect = require('connect')
var knox      = exports.knox    = require('knox')
var simpledb  = exports.simpledb = require('simpledb')
var uuid      = exports.uuid    = require('node-uuid')

var keys = exports.keys = require('./keys.js')
```

Code snippet lifestream/upload/common.js

12. Create a new file called upload.file.js in the lifestream/server folder. This is the Node server that will listen on port 3009 and handle the picture file uploads. Insert the following lines in it:

```
var common = require('./common.js')

var connect = common.connect
var util    = common.util
var fs      = common.fs

var bs = 48

var server = connect.createServer(
  connect.router(function(app){

    app.post('/lifestream/api/upload',function(req,res) {
      util.debug('upload start')

      var w = fs.createWriteStream('pic.jpg')
      var remain = ''

      req.on('data', function(chunk) {
        var ascii = remain + chunk.toString('ascii')
        var bslen = bs * Math.floor( ascii.length / bs )

        var base64    = ascii.substring(0,bslen)
        var binary    = new Buffer(base64,'base64')
        var newremain = ascii.substring(bslen)
```

```
        util.debug('in='+ascii.length+' out='+binary.length')

        remain = newremain
        w.write(binary)
      });

      req.on('end', function() {
        if( 0 < remain.length ) {
          w.write(new Buffer(remain,'base64'))
        }
        w.end()

        util.debug('upload end')

        res.writeHead(200, "OK", {'Content-Type': 'application/json'});
        res.end('{"ok":true}')
      });

    })
  }),
  connect.static('../public')
)

server.listen(3009)
```

Code snippet lifestream/upload/upload.file.js

13. Run the Node server by using this command:

```
node upload.file.js
```

14. Return to the Lifestream app on your iPhone. Tap the Upload Picture button. An "Uploading..." message appears, and after a few seconds, a "Picture Uploaded" message appears.

15. Examine the output from the Node server. You see a long stream of debug messages, one for each chunk of data transferred, showing the bytes received, decoded from base64, and saved:

```
DEBUG: upload start
DEBUG: bytelen:450541
DEBUG: in=1448 out=1080
DEBUG: in=1456 out=1080
DEBUG: in=1464 out=1080
...
DEBUG: in=1472 out=1080
DEBUG: in=1480 out=1080
DEBUG: in=380 out=252
DEBUG: bytes:481353
DEBUG: upload end
```

16. Open the `pic.jpg` file that has appeared in your `lifestream/server` folder. Confirm that it is the same as the picture you took on your iPhone.

How It Works

This example introduces new code on both the client and server sides. Let's take a look at the client code first. The client code retains the same basic structure as in Chapter 8, which is the Lifestream foundation that you are building on. The index.html file has two tabs: one for the photo stream, titled Lifestream, and one for taking pictures and uploading them, titled Post. The Lifestream tab does double-duty as the logo for the app, which is the reason it is a logo image. Space is in short supply when you build mobile apps, and using this method prevents wasting vertical space on a title bar.

There are two content divs in the HTML, with identifiers con_lifestream and con_post, one for each of the tabs. You'll notice that like most of the other HTML element identifiers in this app, these are prefixed with a three-letter namespace prefix: con. As you start to build larger apps, you'll need to take a more structured approach to the code to keep it under control. Namespacing is a good way to do this.

In the content for each tab, you use the data-role="button" attribute on each a tag so that jQuery Mobile will know to style it as a button. You also use the btn namespace for the button IDs:

```
<a id="btn_takepic" data-role="button">Take Picture</a>
```

The CSS for this app sets up the basic layout and assumes the standard iPhone screen width of 320 pixels. As explained earlier, this assumption is safe because devices with more pixels use these dimensions, too, as a virtual size for mobile web apps, and also for embedded browsers in hybrid apps.

The JavaScript code for this app is also more structured. All the logic for the app is contained in a new App object. This object-oriented approach will help you to organize your code as the app grows. The deviceready event handler function creates an instance of the App object:

```
function ondeviceready(){
    app = new App()
}
```

The first thing the App object does is to find all the HTML elements it needs, by using jQuery. These element references are then cached into local variables within the scope of the App object. When you are writing mobile apps using JavaScript, it is important to keep performance considerations in mind, and one easy way is to use caching like this whenever you can.

The element references are stored as local variables inside the App object; this way, only functions inside the App object can access them. This means that they are like the private member variables in more formal object-oriented languages, such as Java. The local variables are also namespaced. All this structure might seem like too much for such a small app, but remember that you'll be adding a lot more code soon. Here is the code that creates the element references:

```
function App() {
    var imagedata = null
    var con = $('#con_lifestream')

    var post_pic = $('#post_pic')
    var post_msg = $('#post_msg')

    var btn_upload = $('#btn_upload')
```

Next, you need to handle the swapping of the content `divs` when the user taps on the navigation tabs. You do this by using jQuery to bind functions to `tap` events on these tabs. The `showcon` function manages the transition by hiding and showing the relevant content `divs`:

```
$('#nav_lifestream').tap(function(){
  showcon('lifestream')
})

$('#nav_post').tap(function(){
  showcon('post')
})
...
function showcon(name) {
  if( con ) {
    con.hide()
  }
  con = $('#con_'+name)
  con.show()
}
```

Next, you work with the code that takes a picture. First, you bind the Take Picture button to the `picTake` function. The `picTake` function calls the PhoneGap API directly, using the `navigator.camera.getPicture` function. This function takes three arguments: a success callback function, a failure callback function, and an options object.

When the user taps the Take Picture button, your app is placed in the background, and the device camera app launches. The user takes a picture in the usual manner and is then asked to accept or reject the image. If the user accepts, the success callback is called; otherwise, the failure callback is called.

The image data is passed to the success callback in base64 format. It is passed as a string variable containing the ASCII characters encoding the binary data. You need to store a reference to this string by using the `imagedata` private variable so that you can upload the data later. You also need to display the picture to the user. You do this by using the special `data:` syntax for the `img` tag `src` attribute.

To reduce the size of the images, the quality is set to 50%, using the options argument. You can change the quality level to suit the requirements of your app. Here is the picture-taking code, with the success callback highlighted:

```
$('#btn_takepic').click(picTake)
...
function picTake(){
  navigator.camera.getPicture(
    function(base64) {
      imagedata = base64
      post_pic.attr({src:"data:image/jpeg;base64,"+imagedata})
    },
    function(){
      post_msg.text('Could not take picture')
    },
    { quality: 50 }
  )
}
```

Next, you upload the picture. You bind the Upload Picture button to the `picUpload` function. When the button is tapped, the `picUpload` function uses the jQuery `ajax` function to send the image data to the server, using an HTTP POST request. You need to be very careful with this request. It has to be set up in the right way. You are not sending JSON or HTML form data, which are more difficult to stream in chunks. You are just sending the plain base64 stream of characters. Therefore, you set `contentType` to have the value `application/octet-stream` to prevent the data from being modified or escaped. The settings for the jQuery `ajax` function are shown highlighted below:

```
$('#btn_upload').click(picUpload)
...
function picUpload(){
  if( imagedata ) {
    post_msg.text('Uploading...')

    $.ajax({
      url:'http://'+server+'/lifestream/api/upload',
      type:'POST',
      contentType:'application/octet-stream',
      data:imagedata,
      success:function(){
        post_msg.text('Picture uploaded.')
      },
      error:function(err){
        console.log(err)
        post_msg.text('Could not upload picture')
      },
    })
  }
  else {
    post_msg.text('Take a picture first')
  }
}
```

At this point, the app can take pictures and display them to the user. However, it cannot yet upload them because there is no server for it to talk to. You now need to look at the server code.

The `common.js` script file is used to store common code. It also uses the Node `require` function to load all the modules you need. By placing all the modules in a central location, you can keep things under control as the size of the code base grows.

The `upload.file.js` server implements the server side of the picture-uploading equation. This is a standard `connect` module server that works in the same manner as the ones you created in earlier chapters. It listens on port 3009 and responds to only a single URL path: `/lifestream/api/upload`.

The server code receives the image data when the user uploads a picture. The data does not all arrive at once. Instead, it arrives in small chunks of base64 ASCII character strings. You register a callback function on the request object (pointed to by the `req` variable) to listen for these chunks as they arrive:

```
req.on('data', function(chunk) {
```

What do you do with the chunks? You could store them all in memory and then concatenate them all together when the upload is finished. This code would be quite simple because you could convert the full base64 string to binary at one time, using the built in `Buffer` object. The problem is that you need to store all the data in memory first. With lots of users, this approach won't scale.

Instead, you can open an output file on the server to store the binary image data:

```
var w = fs.createWriteStream('pic.jpg')
```

As the chunks arrive, you convert them immediately to binary and save them out to the file, concatenating as you go. This means you need to store only one chunk in memory at a time.

Converting the chunks to binary is not an easy operation, however. You cannot break up base64 strings into arbitrary chunks and then convert each chunk. This is because base64 encodes every 3 bytes using 4 ASCII characters, and if you split those 4 character segments, you get corrupt data. You need to rearrange the chunks slightly to end up on four character boundaries.

Consider the first chunk that comes in. If you divide its length by four, it will probably have some leftover characters at the end. So you convert all the characters, except the leftover ones. Then you keep them until you get another chunk. When the next chunk arrives, you prepend the leftovers to the start of this new chunk and then continue in the same way: Divide by 4 and store the remainder until the next chunk.

This algorithm gets you all the way to the end of the data stream, converting it a chunk at a time. This is the exactly what you want — streaming data. You still need to be careful how you implement this code, though, because you need to account for padding characters in the base64 string, and you want to make sure it is performant. Allowing the block size of the remainder string to be up to 48 characters in size (48 is divisible by 4) gives good performance. You specify this by using the `bs` variable in the code. You may need to tune this for your server. But be careful: If the remainder block size is too large, and the chunk is smaller than the block size, the algorithm will fail. The block size is used as follows: You divide the chunk length by the block size and ignore the remainder. Then you multiply the answer by the block size. This gives you the length, in characters, of the part of the chunk that can be converted safely. You keep the remainder for the next chunk.

Let's take a concrete example. Let's say you have 6 bytes encoded as 8 characters. The characters arrive in chunks: first 5 characters, and then 3. Let's use a block size of 4.

With the first 5 character chunk, you break it into blocks of 4 characters. This gives you one block, the first 4 characters, and a remainder, of 1 character. So you can convert the first 4 character block into 3 bytes. You still have a 1-character remainder left over.

Now the next three characters arrive. Prepend the remainder character, giving you a block of 4 characters. This you can again convert to 3 bytes, and you're done! This is the calculation that the formulas in the code example perform.

You use the built-in Node `Buffer` object to perform the base64 conversion. As each block is converted, you write the binary data out to the file. The code implementing this algorithm is highlighted below:

```
req.on('data', function(chunk) {
  var ascii = remain + chunk.toString('ascii')
  var bslen = bs * Math.floor( ascii.length / bs )

  var base64    = ascii.substring(0,bslen)
  var binary    = new Buffer(base64,'base64')
  var newremain = ascii.substring(bslen)

  util.debug('in='+ascii.length+' out='+binary.length )
```

```
        remain = newremain
        w.write(binary)
    });
```

When all the data has been uploaded, you need to convert the final remainder and return an answer to the app by using JSON:

```
    req.on('end', function() {
      if( 0 < remain.length ) {
        w.write(new Buffer(remain,'base64'))
      }
      w.end()

      util.debug('upload end')

      res.writeHead(200, "OK", {'Content-Type': 'application/json'});
      res.end('{"ok":true}')
    });
```

You can try out this server by taking a number of different pictures with the app on your phone. Pay attention to the debugging output to see how the chunk conversion sizes work.

Storing Pictures on Amazon S3

The previous example stores the uploaded picture straight to the server disk. This is not a good strategy for building a scalable service. Individual disks are unreliable and they fill up quickly. To accommodate the millions of users you're aiming to have, you'll need use Amazon S3 storage for the pictures.

Your code will work in the same manner as the previous example. You take a stream of data chunks from the app, convert them to binary, and send them on to Amazon S3.

There is just one little problem. Amazon S3 needs to know the binary size of the file in advance. Because you get the data in chunks, you don't know the final size until you've converted it all. Does this mean you still have to write it to disk first and then stream it? That would not be an optimal solution. It turns out that you can compute the binary size in advance and then stream directly to Amazon. The following example shows you how.

TRY IT OUT   Using Amazon S3 to Store a Picture in the Cloud

You can use the knox module, introduced in Chapter 8, to upload binary picture data to Amazon S3 (refer to Chapter 8 for a reminder of how Amazon S3 works). The basic upload algorithm is no different from that for saving the data to disk. The tricky part is calculating the binary size in advance for Amazon. You'll see in this example how you can get the app to do some of the size calculation work for the server. Follow these steps:

1.   Modify the lifestream.js file in the lifestream app project. Replace the picUpload function with the following code:

Available for
download on
Wrox.com

```
function picUpload(){
    if( imagedata ) {
        post_msg.text('Uploading...')

        var padI = imagedata.length-1
        while( '=' == imagedata[padI] ) {
          padI--
        }
        var padding = imagedata.length - padI - 1

        $.ajax({
          url:'http://'+server+'/lifestream/api/upload',
          type:'POST',
          contentType:'application/octet-stream',
          data:imagedata,
          headers:{'X-Lifestream-Padding':''+padding},
          success:function(){
            post_msg.text('Picture uploaded.')
          },
          error:function(err){
            console.log(err)
            post_msg.text('Could not upload picture')
          },
        })
    }
    else {
      post_msg.text('Take a picture first')
    }
}
```

Code snippet lifestream/app-www-s3/lifestream.js

2. Use Xcode to redeploy the app to your iPhone.

3. Kill the `upload.file.js` script, if it is still running. Create a new script file called `upload.s3.js` in the `lifestream/server` folder (replacing the `YOUR_S3_BUCKET` marker with the name of your S3 bucket):

Available for
download on
Wrox.com

```
var common = require('./common.js')

var connect = common.connect
var knox    = common.knox
var util    = common.util
var uuid    = common.uuid

var keys    = common.keys

var bs = 48

var server = connect.createServer(
  connect.router(function(app){

    app.post('/lifestream/api/upload',function(req,res) {
      util.debug('upload start')
```

```
var bytes = 0

var s3client = knox.createClient({
  key:    keys.amazon.keyid,
  secret: keys.amazon.secret,
  bucket: 'YOUR_S3_BUCKET',
})

var conlen  = parseInt( req.headers['content-length'], 10 )
var padding = parseInt( req.headers['x-lifestream-padding'], 10 )
var bytelen = Math.floor( ((conlen-padding)*3)/4 )
util.debug('bytelen:'+bytelen)

var picid = uuid()

var s3req = s3client.put(
  picid+'.jpg',          {
    'Content-Length':bytelen,
    'x-amz-acl': 'public-read'
  }
)

s3req.on('error',function(err){
  util.debug('error: '+err)
})

s3req.on('response',function(res){
  util.debug('response: '+res.statusCode)

  res.on('data',function(chunk){
    util.debug(chunk)
  })
})

var remain = ''

req.on('data', function(chunk) {
  var ascii = remain + chunk.toString('ascii')
  var bslen = bs * Math.floor( ascii.length / bs )

  var base64     = ascii.substring(0,bslen)
  var binary     = new Buffer(base64,'base64')
  var newremain  = ascii.substring(bslen)

  util.debug('in='+ascii.length+' out='+binary.length )
  bytes+=binary.length

  remain = newremain
  s3req.write(binary)
});

req.on('end', function() {
  if( 0 < remain.length ) {
    var binary = new Buffer(remain,'base64')
```

```
                    bytes+=binary.length
                    s3req.write(binary)
                }
                s3req.end()

                util.debug('bytes:'+bytes)
                util.debug('upload end')

                res.writeHead(200, "OK", {'Content-Type': 'application/json'});
                res.end( JSON.stringify({ok:true,picid:picid}) )
            });
        })
    }),
    connect.static('../public')
)

server.listen(3009)
```

Code snippet lifestream/upload/upload.s3.js

4. Run this new Node server by using the following command:

```
node upload.s3.js
```

5. Take some pictures and observe the output from the script.

6. Open the Amazon Web Services (AWS) management console (http://aws.amazon.com) in your browser and take a look at the contents of your bucket. You should see your uploaded image files. They will have long unique identifier strings for filenames.

How It Works

The following formula (which you can derive from the definition of the base64 format: 4 characters for every 3 bytes) gives you the length of the binary decoding of a base64 string:

Binary size = (Base64 length – Padding) * 3 / 4

You can use this formula to calculate the file size that Amazon needs. On the app, you are given the entire base64 string. When you submit it to the server, the browser sets the Content-Length header to the length of the base64 string. The server can get the total length of the base64 string from this header.

To get the amount of padding, you get the app to count the number of = characters at the end of the base64 string. To send this information back to the server, you use a custom HTTP header. You can't send it as part of the body of the request, because that is taken up with the base64 string. The highlighted lines below show the calculation of this custom header value:

```
var padI = imagedata.length-1
while( '=' == imagedata[padI] ) {
  padI--
}
var padding = imagedata.length - padI - 1
```

```
$.ajax({
  url:'http://'+server+'/lifestream/api/upload',
  type:'POST',
  contentType:'application/octet-stream',
  data:imagedata,
  headers:{'X-Lifestream-Padding':''+padding},
  success:function(){
    post_msg.text('Picture uploaded.')
  },
  error:function(err){
    console.log(err)
    post_msg.text('Could not upload picture')
  },
})
```

On the server, you need to take two values, the content length and the padding length, and plug them in to the formula to get the binary length, and then use this when you submit the data to Amazon. The highlighted code shows the formula at work on the server:

```
var conlen  = parseInt( req.headers['content-length'], 10 )
var padding = parseInt( req.headers['x-lifestream-padding'], 10 )
var bytelen = Math.floor( ((conlen-padding)*3)/4 )
util.debug('bytelen:'+bytelen)

var picid = uuid()

var s3req = s3client.put(
  picid+'.jpg',          {
    'Content-Length':bytelen,
    'x-amz-acl': 'public-read'
  }
)
```

You also need to provide a unique name for each picture. The Node uuid module does the job for you, generating standards-compliant universally unique identifier (UUID) tokens that you can use as the picture names.

From this point, the code streams the data up to Amazon in the same way the data was streamed to disk in the previous example. What you have here is a highly efficient upload server that stores pictures in the cloud and can handle large numbers of clients.

SUMMARY

In this chapter, you learned how to build iPhone and Android apps that users can install as native apps on physical devices. In this way, you can deliver your cloud service directly to mobile devices. This chapter shows how to work with the development environments for iPhone and Android to build and deploy apps to physical devices. You used the PhoneGap project to provide access to device features via a JavaScript API. You also learned how to build a mobile app that can take pictures and save them to the cloud.

In the next chapter, you'll learn how to integrate the Twitter and Facebook login example from Chapter 8 into your hybrid app. You'll also implement the followers logic that provides the social networking aspect of the app. Instead of using a local database, the followers database will be stored in the cloud, using the MongoHQ cloud service.

EXERCISES

1. As you develop your app, you'll want to release test versions to your clients. This is not an issue for Android, as you can send them the same version that you use. But for iPhone apps, they won't have Xcode and will probably be running on Windows. Review the Apple developer documentation on Ad Hoc distribution to find out how to send easy-to-install test versions to your clients. In particular, try to find how to create and use `ipa` files.

2. When you build apps using PhoneGap, desktop Safari is your best debugging option for the main part of your development work. On the simulator and devices, the best you can hope for is to view the debug log when you enable it in the Safari settings menus. Or is it? Take a look at `http://pmuellr.github.com/weinre`, and see if you can get it running.

3. When the user takes a picture with the Lifestream app, no additional information is stored about the image. Add an annotation function to the app that writes the current data and time into the photo. You can use the `canvas` element to manipulate the image. In addition to the time, also insert the direction that the user is facing when they took the photo. Use the PhoneGap `navigator.compass` object to do this.

4. The Lifestream application you've built so far can only upload pictures. Extend the app so that it (locally) stores a list of the photos that have been uploaded and displays them under the Lifestream tab, as shown in Figure 9-17.

FIGURE 9-17

Answers to the Exercises can be found in the Appendix.

▶ WHAT YOU LEARNED IN THIS CHAPTER

TOPIC	KEY CONCEPTS
Mobile web apps	A mobile web app is an app that is delivered exclusively over the web to a mobile device. While it may be cached locally, it is still ultimately a website and suffers from the security restrictions that apply to all websites. This means that many physical devices features, such as vibration and the camera, are not available to mobile web apps. Nonetheless, mobile web apps can be performant, and are suitable for a wide range of functionalities.
Native apps	A native app is written in the preferred development language of the mobile platform (that is, Objective-C for iPhone, Java for Android). A native app has access to all the features of the device, can use the standard user interface libraries, and is generally faster than a mobile web app. On the other hand, native apps must be separately developed for each platform, which becomes expensive very quickly when you need to support more than one device type.
Hybrid apps	A hybrid app combines the best features of mobile web apps and native apps. It is an HTML, JavaScript, and CSS app embedded inside a native container. The entire user interface of the app is built using web code. However, a hybrid app also has access to physical device features, usually by means of a JavaScript API.
PhoneGap	PhoneGap is an open source project that allows you to easily build hybrid apps without having to write your own wrapper code. PhoneGap also provides a convenient JavaScript API for accessing physical device features that are not available to mobile web apps.
Xcode and Eclipse Development Environments	To create hybrid and native apps, you will need to use the appropriate developer tools. In the case of the iPhone, this means that you will need a Mac. You will use the Xcode development environment provided by Apple, which supports the Objective-C language. You'll need to integrate PhoneGap into Xcode to produce hybrid apps. In addition, you will need to register with Apple as a developer, pay a fee, and create and install code signing certificates. Xcode provides you with an iPhone and iPad simulator to test your apps.
	To build Android apps, you will need to use the Eclipse development environment. This supports the Java language, which Android uses. You'll need a number of additional components: PhoneGap, the separately downloaded Android SDK, and the Android Eclipse plug-in. The Android SDK provides you with an emulator to test your apps.

TOPIC	KEY CONCEPTS
Hybrid App Development	You can use the same HTML, CSS, and JavaScript code base to create hybrid apps that will run on both iPhone and Android. PhoneGap provides you with a common abstraction API to the device features such as the camera. In your development work cycle, you will first use the desktop Safari during initial development, then the simulator or emulator for initial testing, and then finally a physical device for final testing. The physical device deployment procedures have higher friction for the iPhone as you will need to cryptographically sign your app before copying it onto your device.
Data streaming	To efficiently handle a large number of users with large numbers of large files, you need to stream data from client to server and from server to server. With data streaming, you break the data into small pieces and handle one piece at a time. TCP already breaks the data into packets, so all data is actually transferred this way anyway. You just need to ensure that your code deals with the data in this way. One of the benefits of the Node platform is that it makes this very easy.

10

Building a Photo-Blogging App

WHAT YOU WILL LEARN IN THIS CHAPTER:

➤ Using the MongoHQ cloud database

➤ Defining a production architecture for Node applications

➤ Defining a web API for your service

➤ Using acceptance testing to verify your API

➤ Defining a database schema for followers

➤ Handling a mixture of JSON and streaming data

➤ Connecting a mobile app to your API

➤ Using Facebook and Twitter sign-in from a mobile app environment

In this chapter you'll build on the work you did in Chapters 8 and 9. Here you'll combine all the features you've previously explored into one complete, fully functional app — including the cloud element on the server side. You can use the structure of this app as the foundational structure for your own services. It will include the cross-platform mobile client, the highly scalable and performant cloud server, and examples of implementations of all the major features you need.

In earlier chapters you learned how to use the MongoDB database to store your data in a JavaScript-friendly way. In this chapter you'll also use MongoDB, but this time you'll host your database in the cloud, using the MongoHQ service: http://mongohq.com. This means you won't have to worry about maintaining a MongoDB installation, scaling your own MongoDB cluster, or running backups. Instead, you'll simply point your Node server at the MongoHQ service and get back to building your app.

THE ARCHITECTURE OF LIFESTREAM

The Lifestream app is a photo-sharing mobile app that works like Twitter. Instead of sharing short messages with your followers, you share photos. Your photo stream shows the photos of the people you follow, with the most recent photos first.

To build this app, you need to create a user database that can store the follower/following relationships — and do so in a scalable way. You also need a place to store all photos. And you need to build an Android and iPhone app, to get the widest possible user base.

You already solved the storage issue in Chapter 8: Amazon S3 will do the job nicely. And you solved the cross-platform issue in Chapter 9: PhoneGap can help you build an Android and iPhone app, using the same code base. You will solve the remaining issue by using MongoDB to store the follower/following relationships.

The data schema you'll use in this chapter is remarkably simple. You need only one collection (a "table," in traditional terms), which you can call the `user` collection. In it you'll need the following fields:

➤ **username** — The unique username

➤ **token** — A login token for authentication

➤ **stream** — A list of recently posted images

➤ **followers** — A list of users that follow this user

➤ **following** — A list of the users that this user follows

And that's it. The great thing about MongoDB is that it lets you store lists inside a document (a "row," in traditional terms). This means you can store all the details about a user, including the follower/following relationships, in one place.

This book is all about building mobile apps using cloud services. One key idea is that the mobile app is just one type of client for your cloud service. Your service should have a proper web API that any client can access. That way, you can support a third-party ecosystem, which is a great way to build a substantial fan base for your service and app.

As you build out the Lifestream app and service, you'll also define a stand-alone API for the service that can do everything the app can do. This API will have URLs mostly in this form:

```
http://YOUR_SERVER/lifestream/api/user/:username/:action
```

In this case, `:username` is the username of the user, and `:action` is an optional action. Some actions, such as searching, do not need a username, and so that is optional as well. Your API will support these actions:

➤ **register** — Register a new user

➤ **oauth** — Handle Twitter and Facebook logins via the OAuth protocol

➤ **search** — Search for users

➤ **:username** — With no action, get the user's details

➤ **:username/follow** — Follow a user

- ➤ **`:username/unfollow`** — Unfollow a user

- ➤ **`:username/upload`** — Upload image data but don't publish it yet

- ➤ **`:username/post`** — Publish an image to your followers

- ➤ **`:username/stream`** — Get your latest image stream

The full application stack starts with the mobile app on the physical mobile device, which talks to an nginx proxy server, which talks to your Node server, which talks to the MongoHQ service.

BUILDING THE SERVER

You'll use the Node JavaScript server to implement the server side of the Lifestream application, which will live in the cloud. You can host this server on Amazon or Rackspace. You can run multiple instances on multiple servers and handle load balancing with nginx or a proprietary load balancer.

The server code itself consists of three files: `server.js`, which contains the business logic; `common.js`, which contains utility functions; and `config.js`, which contains your configuration details.

NOTE *When you build a public-facing API, as you will do in this chapter, it is especially important to validate the correctness of your implementation. You can do this using acceptance testing. Acceptance tests, unlike unit tests, are performed against a running version of your server. They simulate the expected behaviors of client apps.*

Laying the Foundation

The MongoHQ service is a cloud service similar to Amazon S3, except it is focused exclusively on cloud-hosted MongoDB instances. You can sign up for the service at `http://mongohq.com`. There is a free option for small databases under 16MB, and you can use it to run the examples in this chapter. The online user interface is easy to use and allows you to get a quick view of your data.

When you have your MongoHQ account set up, you should create a new database, called `lifestream`, using the online interface. You'll be given the database server name and port number, which are different for each MongoHQ database. You'll also have to enter a username and password for database access. The online interface will give you your database login details.

In the following example, you'll put together all the files needed to deliver the full Lifestream app. First, you'll need to get your configuration in order, test your connection to the MongoHQ service, and verify that a minimal feature set actually works. In Chapter 9, you built the picture upload feature. You'll set that aside for now and concentrate on supporting user registration. Introducing the basic concept of adding users to the system is essential for bootstrapping the rest of the features.

TRY IT OUT Developing and Testing a User Registration Server

So that you can focus on the core functionality, in this example, you'll work with a very simple user registration feature. Instead of a password, you'll use a unique token for each physical device. Ultimately you'll use OAuth tokens for user registration, but a unique device token will do for now. Here are the steps to get this running:

1. Go to your `lifestream/server` folder. (You'll continue to work in the same folder as in Chapters 8 and 9.) Run the following `npm` module installation commands:

```
npm install connect
npm install mongodb
npm install knox
npm install uuid
npm install oauth
npm install url
npm install request
npm install cookies
```

If you have some of these modules already installed from previous chapters, `npm` will either report the version you have installed or upgrade to the latest version.

2. Create a new file called `config.js` to store your server configuration and insert the following code in it, replacing the boldfaced items with your own settings:

```
exports.mongohq   = {
  username: 'YOUR_DB_USERNAME',
  password: 'YOUR_DB_PASSWORD',
  name:     'YOUR_DB_NAME',
  host:     'YOUR_DB_HOST',
  port:     YOUR_DB_PORT
}

exports.amazon   = {
  s3bucket: 'YOUR_S3_BUCKET_NAME',
  keyid:    'YOUR_AWS_KEY_ID',
  secret:   'YOUR_AWS_SECRET'
}

exports.twitter   = {
  keyid:  'YOUR_TWITTER_KEY_ID',
  secret: 'YOUR_TWITTER_SECRET'
}

exports.facebook = {
  keyid:  'YOUR_FACEBOOK_KEY_ID',
  secret: 'YOUR_FACEBOOK_SECRET'
}

exports.server = 'YOUR_IP_ADDRESS'
exports.max_stream_size = 100
```

code snippet lifestream/server/config.js

3. Replace your `common.js` file in the `lifestream/server` folder with the following updated version:

```javascript
var util     = exports.util     = require('util')
var connect  = exports.connect  = require('connect')
var knox     = exports.knox     = require('knox')
var uuid     = exports.uuid     = require('node-uuid')
var oauth    = exports.oauth    = require('oauth')
var url      = exports.url      = require('url')
var request  = exports.request  = require('request')
var Cookies  = exports.Cookies  = require('Cookies')

var config = exports.config = require('./config.js')


// JSON functions

exports.readjson = function(req,win,fail) {
  var bodyarr = [];
  req.on('data',function(chunk){
    bodyarr.push(chunk);
  })
  req.on('end',function(){
    var bodystr = bodyarr.join('');
    util.debug('READJSON:'+req.url+':'+bodystr);
    try {
      var body = JSON.parse(bodystr);
      win && win(body);
    }
    catch(e) {
      fail && fail(e)
    }
  })
}

exports.sendjson = function(res,obj){
  res.writeHead(200,{
    'Content-Type': 'text/json',
    'Cache-Control': 'private, max-age=0'
  });
  var objstr = JSON.stringify(obj);
  util.debug('SENDJSON:'+objstr);
  res.end( objstr );
}


// mongo functions

var mongodb = require('mongodb')

var mongo = {
  mongo: mongodb,
```

```
    db: null,
}

mongo.init = function( opts, win, fail ){
  util.log('mongo: '+opts.host+':'+opts.port+'/'+opts.name)

  mongo.db =
    new mongodb.Db(
      opts.name,
      new mongodb.Server(opts.host, opts.port, {}),
      {native_parser:true,auto_reconnect:true});

  mongo.db.open(function(){
    if( opts.username ) {
      mongo.db.authenticate(
        opts.username,
        opts.password,
        function(err){
          if( err) {
            fail && fail(err)
          }
          else {
            win && win(mongo.db)
          }
        })
    }
    else {
      win && win(mongo.db)
    }
  },fail)
}

mongo.res = function( win, fail ){
  return function(err,res) {
    if( err ) {
      util.log('mongo:err:'+JSON.stringify(err));
      fail && 'function' == typeof(fail) && fail(err);
    }
    else {
      win && 'function' == typeof(win) && win(res);
    }
  }
}

mongo.open = function(win,fail){
  mongo.db.open(mongo.res(function(){
    util.log('mongo:ok');
    win && win();
  },fail))
}

mongo.coll = function(name,win,fail){
  mongo.db.collection(name,mongo.res(win,fail));
}

exports.mongo = mongo
```

code snippet lifestream/server/common.js

This updated version of common.js supports MongoDB authentication, which you need to use the MongoHQ cloud database service.

4. Create a new file in lifestream/server called server.mongo.js and insert the following code in it:

```
var common   = require('./common.js')
var config   = common.config
var mongo    = common.mongo

var util     = common.util
var connect  = common.connect
var knox     = common.knox
var uuid     = common.uuid
var oauth    = common.oauth
var url      = common.url
var request  = common.request
var Cookies  = common.Cookies


// API functions

function search(req,res){
  var merr = mongoerr400(res)

  mongo.coll(
    'user',
    function(coll){
      coll.find(
        {username:{$regex:new RegExp('^'+req.params.query)}},
        {fields:['username']},
        merr(function(cursor){
          var list = []
          cursor.each(merr(function(user){
            if( user ) {
              list.push(user.username)
            }
            else {
              common.sendjson(res,{ok:true,list:list})
            }
          }))
        })
      )
    }
  )
}

function loaduser(req,res) {
  var merr = mongoerr400(res)

  finduser(true,['username','name','following','followers','stream'],
           req,res,function(user)
  {
    var userout =
      { username:  user.username,
```

```
          name:      user.name,
          followers: user.followers,
          following: user.following,
          stream:    user.stream
        }
      common.sendjson(res,userout)
    })
}


function register(req,res) {
  var merr = mongoerr400(res)

  mongo.coll(
    'user',
    function(coll){

      coll.findOne(
        {username:req.json.username},

        merr(function(user){
          if( user ) {
            err400(res)()
          }
          else {
            var token = common.uuid()
            coll.insert(
              { username:  req.json.username,
                token:     token,
                followers: [],
                following: [],
                stream:    []
              },
              merr(function(){
                common.sendjson(res,{ok:true,token:token})
              })
            )
          }
        })
      )
    }
  )
}


// utility functions

function finduser(mustfind,fields,req,res,found){
  var merr = mongoerr400(res)

  mongo.coll(
    'user',
    function(coll){
```

```
        var options = {}

        if( fields ) {
          options.fields = fields
        }

        coll.findOne(
          {username:req.params.username},
          options,
          merr(function(user){
            if( mustfind && !user ) {
              err400(res)
            }
            else {
              found(user,coll)
            }
          })
        )
      }
    )
  }
}

function mongoerr400(res){
  return function(win){
    return mongo.res(
      win,
      function(dataerr) {
        err400(res)(dataerr)
      }
    )
  }
}

function err400(res,why) {
  return function(details) {
    util.debug('ERROR 400 '+why+' '+details)
    res.writeHead(400,''+why)
    res.end(''+details)
  }
}


function collect() {
  return function(req,res,next) {
    if( 'POST' == req.method ) {
      common.readjson(
        req,
        function(input) {
          req.json = input
          next()
        },
        err400(res,'read-json')
      )
    }
```

```
      else {
        next()
      }
    }
  }


function auth() {
  return function(req,res,next) {
    var merr = mongoerr400(res)

    mongo.coll(
      'user',
      function(coll){

        coll.findOne(
          {token:req.headers['x-lifestream-token']},
          {fields:['username']},
          merr(function(user){
            if( user ) {
              next()
            }
            else {
              res.writeHead(401)
              res.end(JSON.stringify({ok:false,err:'unauthorized'}))
            }
          })
        )
      }
    )
  }
}


var db     = null
var server = null

mongo.init(
  {
    name:     config.mongohq.name,
    host:     config.mongohq.host,
    port:     config.mongohq.port,
    username: config.mongohq.username,
    password: config.mongohq.password,
  },
  function(res){
    db = res
    var prefix = '/lifestream/api/user/'
    server = connect.createServer(
      connect.logger(),
      collect(),

      connect.router(function(app){
        app.post( prefix+'register', register)
```

```
          ,app.get(  prefix+'search/:query', search)
        }),

        auth(),

        connect.router(function(app){
          app.get(  prefix+':username', loaduser)
        })
      )
      server.listen(3009)
    },
    function(err){
      util.debug(err)
    }
  )
```

code snippet lifestream/server/server.mongo.js

5. Create a new file in `lifestream/server` called `accept.mongo.js` and insert the following code in it:

```
var common   = require('./common.js')
var config   = common.config
var util     = common.util
var request  = common.request

var assert   = require('assert')
var eyes     = require('eyes')


var urlprefix = 'http://'+config.server+':3009/lifestream/api'
var headers   = {}


function handle(cb) {
  return function (error, response, body) {
    if( error ) {
      util.debug(error)
    }
    else {
      var code = response.statusCode
      var json = JSON.parse(body)
      util.debug('  '+code+': '+JSON.stringify(json))

      assert.equal(null,error)
      assert.equal(200,code)

      cb(json)
    }
  }
}

function get(username,uri,cb){
  util.debug('GET '+uri)
```

```
  request.get(
    {
      uri:uri,
      headers:headers[username] || {}
    },
    handle(cb)
  )
}

function post(username, uri,json,cb){
  util.debug('POST '+uri+': '+JSON.stringify(json))
  request.post(
    {
      uri:uri,
      json:json,
      headers:headers[username] || {}
    },
    handle(cb)
  )
}


module.exports = {

  api:function() {
    var foo = (''+Math.random()).substring(10)
    var bar = (''+Math.random()).substring(10)


    // create and load

    ;post(
      null,
      urlprefix+'/user/register',
      {username:foo},
      function(json){
        assert.ok(json.ok)
        headers[foo] = {
          'x-lifestream-token':json.token
        }

    ;get(
      foo,
      urlprefix+'/user/'+foo,
      function(json){
        assert.equal(foo,json.username)
        assert.equal(0,json.followers.length)
        assert.equal(0,json.following.length)


    ;post(
      null,
      urlprefix+'/user/register',
      {username:bar},
```

```
    function(json){
      assert.ok(json.ok)
      headers[bar] = {
        ,x-lifestream-token':json.token
      }
  ;get(
    bar,
    urlprefix+'/user/'+bar,
    function(json){
      assert.equal(bar,json.username)
      assert.equal(0,json.followers.length)
      assert.equal(0,json.following.length)


  // search
  ;get(
    null,
    urlprefix+'/user/search/'+foo.substring(0,4),
    function(json){
      assert.ok(json.ok)
      assert.equal(1,json.list.length)
      assert.equal(json.list[0],foo)


  ;})   // search
  ;})   // get
  ;})   // post
  ;})   // get
  ;})   // post

  }
}
```

code snippet lifestream/server/accept.mongo.js

This is an acceptance test that you will use to test the running server. Each test case runs inside the callback of the previous test case, ensuring that the tests run one by one, in order.

6. Install the expresso testing framework, which you'll need in order to run the accept.mongo.js script:

```
npm install expresso
```

7. Open a new terminal window and start the server:

```
node server.mongo.js
21 Mar 13:39:47 - mongo: flame.mongohq.com:27044/lifestream
```

8. Open another new terminal window and run the acceptance test:

```
expresso accept.mongo.js
DEBUG: POST http://192.168.100.112:3009/
  lifestream/api/user/register: {"username":"707915425"}
DEBUG:    200: {"ok":true,
```

```
    "token":"0C257205-AB94-4768-9FCC-A1B1321AD2A5"}
DEBUG: GET http://192.168.100.112:3009/
  lifestream/api/user/707915425
DEBUG:    200: {"username":"707915425",
  "followers":[],"following":[],"stream":[]}
...
```

Both the server and the acceptance test generate debugging output, showing you the exact sequence of HTTP requests and responses.

9. Go to the MongoHQ website and review the contents of the user collection. You should see two documents in the user collection.

 WARNING *The acceptance test requires a live network connection because the server has to talk to the remote MongoHQ service to store and retrieve data. This is why it is called an* acceptance *test rather than a* unit *test. Acceptance tests, by definition, have external dependencies.*

How It Works

The app in this chapter is a full app with many different functions, and it depends on quite a few npm modules. You've already met most of these modules in previous chapters. The ones you haven't seen before — url, request, cookies — are helper modules for dealing with HTTP requests.

This chapter also introduces the notion of using a config.js file to store your server configuration. This is really just an extension of the keys.js file used in previous chapters. When you are building a production app, it is a good idea to separate configuration from implementation and not embed configuration settings in your code.

Earlier in this chapter, you signed up with MongoHQ, and you should also have keys from Amazon, Twitter, and Facebook from previous chapters. You use these keys to fill in your settings.

The common.js file in this chapter includes all the utility functions you have seen in earlier chapters. These utility functions make it easy for you to deal with JSON requests and responses in your HTTP API and to work with the MongoDB API. There is one additional piece of functionality. In order to use the MongoHQ service, you need to log in to your database. To do so, you use the following code:

```
mongo.db.open(function(){
  if( opts.username ) {
    mongo.db.authenticate(
      opts.username,
      opts.password,
      function(err){
        ...
```

To make things easier to follow as you add new functionality in this chapter, the server-side code is stored in separate server.*.js files. The file for this example is called server.mongo.js. You can compare these files as you work through the chapter to aid your understanding. The server-side code follows the structure used in earlier chapters. First, it has the main API functions, then some utility functions, and then the connect module configuration.

In this example, you implement a search function, user registration, and a function to get the user's details. The search function uses MongoDB's regular expression search feature to look for usernames that match a given prefix. This is just a simple way to implement the user search function in the app. The code uses the mongoerr400 utility function to deal with MongoDB errors gracefully by returning the HTTP 400 status code to any clients if there is a problem. How this works is explained later in this section. This is how the search function works:

```
coll.find(
  {username:{$regex:new RegExp('^'+req.params.query)}},
  {fields:['username']},
  merr(function(cursor){
    var list = []
    cursor.each(merr(function(user){
      if( user ) {
        list.push(user.username)
      }
      else {
        common.sendjson(res,{ok:true,list:list})
      }
```

The first boldfaced line in this code shows how you can use a regular expression query against MongoDB. This follows the standard MongoDB query syntax. The value of the query is provided as a parameter of the HTTP request, which is exposed by the req object that was passed into the function.

The second boldfaced line shows how you can restrict the fields returned by a result from MongoDB. This way, you can avoid returning all the data for each user, which is a waste of resources when all you want is a list of matching usernames.

The result of the query is provided as a cursor object. To use this object, you provide a callback for its each function. Your callback is called once for each item in the result set. This is quite similar to the way traditional SQL database cursors work. When all the items have been returned, you are given a null object. This is your signal to stop. An if statement checks whether the user parameter is null and returns the JSON result if that is the case. Otherwise, it keeps appending usernames to the JSON result.

The loaduser function hands off most of its work to the finduser utility function. This function does not return the pure database result because doing so might expose internal system details, such as the MongoDB id field. Instead, the loaduser function returns only a specific set of data. Explicitly sanitizing data in this way may seem a little paranoid, but it is a good rule-of-thumb security practice.

The finduser utility function, further down the script file, in the utility functions section, does the work of actually finding the user in the database. The key lines are calls to the findOne function of the collection object, which performs the search for the user:

```
coll.findOne(
  {username:req.params.username},
```

The username is specified as an HTTP request parameter. In the URL structure that is used for the API, the username must be part of the URL path for user-specific requests.

The register function is very similar to the `finduser` function, except that it performs an action if the user does not exist. If the given username cannot be found, the user does not yet exist and can be registered. The registration is performed by the following `insert` operation:

```
var token = common.uuid()
coll.insert(
  { username:  req.json.username,
    token:     token,
    followers: [],
    following: [],
    stream:    []
  },
```

`token` is a special field that is used to validate the identity of a user. The `uuid` module gives you a way to generate long, random, and unique strings that are perfect as tokens. Because this example focuses on building an app rather than user management features, there is no implementation of a password system. Rather, the code takes a shortcut. Registrations are given out on a first come, first served basis. The token is given back to the client app, and the client stores it permanently. This token can then be used to access the API. It is effectively a permanent login token. You would not use this design in production, but you can use it here to simulate enough of the user management logic to demonstrate registration and authentication and, later on, integration with Facebook and Twitter. During development you'll need to remove any existing logins. Do this by deleting and reinstalling the app. If you're testing the example in a browser, just delete the `user` item in the local storage system.

The value of the username comes from the rather strange-looking `json` property of the standard Node request object. This a custom property that the `collect` utility function has injected into the request object, and it contains the parsed value of any JSON content submitted with the request. The `collect` function intercepts HTTP `POST` requests, sucking in their content by using the `common.readjson` function:

```
function collect() {
  return function(req,res,next) {
    if( 'POST' == req.method ) {
      common.readjson(
        req,
        function(input) {
          req.json = input
          next()
        },
        err400(res,'read-json')
      )
    }
    else {
      next()
    }
  }
}
```

The `collect` function is special for another reason. It is actually a `connect` module *middleware* function. A middleware function is a function that does some processing on an HTTP request and then passes the request onward to the rest of the server. Hence the name: It sits in the middle of requests. The `connect` module is a stack of middleware functions, each one doing some work on the request. In earlier chapters, you used the standard `router` middleware to define your own URL end points. In this example, you get to build your own middleware!

To define a `connect` middleware function, you write a function that takes some configuration parameters (`collect` does not have any yet) and returns a function that accepts three parameters: the request, the response, and a special `next` function. This is another example of the power of JavaScript: You can use functions to build other functions dynamically.

The real work of the `collect` middleware function occurs inside this dynamic function. You check for POST requests, read in the JSON, and set the custom `json` property of the `req` object. When you are done, you call the special `next` function. This lets `connect` know that your middleware is finished, and it can pass on the request to the next stage of processing.

What happens when there are errors? Because you are building an API that can be used independently of the app, you need to make sure that you are a good HTTP citizen. This means you need to return a 400 Bad Request status code if something goes wrong because you were given bad input. You use the `err400` utility function to perform this task, and this function creates a function to do the actual work. This way, you can define appropriate error messages for different places in your code. In particular, the `mongoerr400` function creates an error-handling function for the special case of MongoDB errors. As you can see from the code, you use these functions by calling them to create a custom error function for each top-level API function, like so:

```
var merr = mongoerr400(res)
```

 NOTE The error handling code in this example always returns a status code of 400 Bad Request. Strictly speaking, you should return a status code of 500 Internal Server Error if the error is your fault (for example, if the database connection goes down).

The `collect` middleware function is not the only middleware function in this server code. There is also an `auth` middleware function to handle user authentication. Certain API calls should work only for signed-in users. This prevents other users from accessing someone's private details. The `auth` middleware function sits in front of these API calls and checks whether the request is from a signed-in user. This is why the `connect` section of the code is split into two router sections: The first is for unauthenticated actions, such as registration and searching, and the second is for authenticated actions, such as getting user details or following other users.

The `auth` function is similar to the `finduser` function in that it has to search for a user by their username. It also requires a custom HTTP header, X-Lifestream-Token, containing the registration token that must match the token stored against the user. If authentication fails, an HTTP 401 status code is returned, indicating unauthorized access. Otherwise, the special `next` function is called, and the request proceeds. Here is the code that performs the token search:

```
coll.findOne(
  {token:req.headers['x-lifestream-token']},
  {fields:['username']},
  merr(function(user){
```

```
        if( user ) {
          next()
        }
        else {
          res.writeHead(401)
          res.end(JSON.stringify({ok:false,err:'unauthorized'}))
        }
      })
    )
```

The final section of code sets up the `connect` middleware stack after creating a connection to the MongoDB database. The ordering of the middleware functions implements the API structure you are putting together.

You should not just test this server manually. You should also use a set of standard tests to verify that the API operates correctly. You can do this by building acceptance tests. You can use the Node `expresso` module for building both unit and acceptance tests. Although you should create both unit and acceptance tests, this example focuses on the acceptance tests. What is the difference between unit and acceptance tests? Acceptance tests depend on external resources, and unit tests do not. To test that your server works properly with MongoHQ, which is an external resource, you need acceptance tests.

The acceptance test code is in the `accept.mongo.js` script. You run this script in a separate terminal while the main server is running. The `expresso` module will run, as tests, any functions that are placed in the special `exports` variable. In the code in this example, there is only one main test: the `api` function. This function contains a set of tests that run in sequence and exercise the operations of the API.

You use the `common.js` file here to avoid duplicating code. The `handle`, `get`, and `post` functions are utility functions to track the HTTP requests and print the results as they come in. You can therefore run the test and see what happens directly, which is very useful for debugging.

The tests themselves are a sequence of calls to the API. When you run them, two users are registered, their data is requested, and a search is performed:

```
;post(
  null,
  urlprefix+'/user/register',
  {username:foo},
  function(json){
    ...
    headers[foo] = {
      'x-lifestream-token':json.token
    }

;get(
  foo,
  urlprefix+'/user/'+foo,
  function(json){
    ...

;post(
  null,
  urlprefix+'/user/register',
  {username:bar},
  function(json){
    ...
```

```
      headers[bar] = {
        'x-lifestream-token':json.token
      }

  ;get(
    bar,
    urlprefix+'/user/'+bar,
    function(json){
      ...

  // search
  ;get(
    null,
    urlprefix+'/user/search/'+foo.substring(0,4),
```

The code is formatted using a convention that avoids lots of annoying indentation. Because each test must execute inside the callback of the previous test, you would normally end up with code indenting off the screen to the right. To avoid this, you can use a ; character at the start of the line. This gives you permission to reset the indentation level. You need to make sure you close all the brackets properly, so they are listed in reverse order at the end, with comments. There are other ways to solve this formatting problem using various utility libraries. They are useful in more complex scenarios, but in this case, there is a simple linear execution flow, and the ; convention keeps the code relatively clean with very little effort.

Enabling User Following

The next major piece of functionality you need to implement in the Lifestream app is user following. This works the same way as with Twitter: Users can follow each other independently. For each user, you need to maintain a list of the followers of that user and those users that the user is following. The MongoDB document for each user stores the list of users that person follows, as well as the list of those who follow this user. Storing this information separately for each user introduces redundancy into the system because the follower/following relationship is stored in two places. However, the performance gain is enormous, as you need to perform only one database query to find all the information for one user.

TRY IT OUT   Extending the Server with User Following

In the following example, you'll extend the server code with operations that support following and unfollowing users. You'll also extend the acceptance test to confirm that everything is working. Follow these steps:

1. Copy the `server.mongo.js` script to a new file called `server.follow.js`. Insert the following new API functions in it, just after the `// API functions` comment near the top of the file:

```
// API functions


function follow(req,res){
```

```
    followop('$addToSet',req,res)
}

function unfollow(req,res){
  followop('$pull',req,res)
}


function followop(opname,req,res) {
  var merr = mongoerr400(res)

  var op = {}
  op[opname] = { following: req.json.username }

  mongo.coll(
    'user',
    function(coll){

      coll.update(
        { username: req.params.username },
        op,
        merr(function(){

          var op = {}
          op[opname] = { followers: req.params.username }

          coll.update(
            { username: req.json.username },
            op,
            merr(function(){
              common.sendjson(res,{ok:true})
            })
          )
        })
      )
    }
  )
}
```

code snippet lifestream/server/server.follow.js

2. Scroll down to the end of the file to the URL path definitions for the connect module. After the auth() middleware setup call, add the following boldfaced lines, which provide the URL end points in the Lifestream API for the follower/following functionality:

```
auth(),

connect.router(function(app){
  app.get(  prefix+':username', loaduser)

  ,app.post( prefix+':username/follow', follow)
  ,app.post( prefix+':username/unfollow', unfollow)
})
```

code snippet lifestream/server/server.follow.js

3. Copy the `accept.mongo.js` script to a new file called `accept.follow.js`. Insert the following additional test cases just after the existing test cases:

```
// follow
;post(
  foo,
  urlprefix+'/user/'+foo+'/follow',
  {username:bar},
  function(json){
    assert.ok(json.ok)

;get(
  foo,
  urlprefix+'/user/'+foo,
  function(json){
    assert.equal(0,json.followers.length)
    assert.equal(1,json.following.length)
    assert.equal(bar,json.following[0])

;get(
  bar,
  urlprefix+'/user/'+bar,
  function(json){
    assert.equal(1,json.followers.length)
    assert.equal(0,json.following.length)
    assert.equal(foo,json.followers[0])


// unfollow
;post(
  foo,
  urlprefix+'/user/'+foo+'/unfollow',
  {username:bar},
  function(json){
    assert.ok(json.ok)

;get(
  foo,
  urlprefix+'/user/'+foo,
  function(json){
    assert.equal(0,json.followers.length)
    assert.equal(0,json.following.length)

;get(
  bar,
  urlprefix+'/user/'+bar,
  function(json){
    assert.equal(0,json.followers.length)
    assert.equal(0,json.following.length)


;})  // get
;})  // get
;})  // unfollow
```

```
;})  // get
;})  // get
;})  // follow
```

4. Shut down the `server.mongo.js` script if it is still running. Start up the `server.follow.js` script:

```
node server.follow.js
```

You should see debugging output from this script, as before, when you run the acceptance test.

5. Run the `accept.follow.js` acceptance test in a new terminal window:

```
node accept.follow.js
```

6. Review the debugging output from the acceptance test and the server and trace the logic of the operations.

How It Works

In this example, you add two API end points: `follow` and `unfollow`. Only an authenticated user can perform these actions. The `followop` function performs both the actual work for both following and unfollowing.

MongoDB provides two operations that make implementing this example very easy. The `$addToSet` operation adds an item to an array, but only if the item is not already in the array. This is exactly what you need for the `follow` function. The `$pull` operation removes matching items from an array. This is exactly what you need for the `unfollow` function.

The processing is quite simple. First, for the user performing the `follow` or `unfollow` function, you update the `following` property in the user's MongoDB document. For the user being followed or unfollowed, you update the `followers` property. There is no need to make this transactional. Scaling to millions of users is more important. You use the `update` function of the `collection` object of the MongoDB API to perform the update.

You also need to update the acceptance test to make sure everything so far works. You add the `follow` and `unfollow` API calls after the initial set of user registration calls.

Uploading and Posting Pictures

When a Lifestream app user takes a pictures and uploads it, the picture should appear on that person's Lifestream photo stream. The picture should also appear on the photo stream of all the users who follow this user. The easiest way to implement this is to update each user's photo stream each time a new photo from a user he or she follows is posted. This makes the server application write-heavy, in that a lot of database writes are needed to keep up with the stream of photos. However, this is exactly the use case that MongoDB was designed for. MongoDB will store these writes in memory at first, avoiding the traditional slowdown of writing data to disk transactionally.

In the following example, you'll see that there are two parts to posting a picture. First, you upload the picture and store it on Amazon S3. Second, you update the user's picture stream by pushing the new picture to the front of the stream. You need to do this for each user who follows the user posting a picture.

TRY IT OUT Streaming Uploads and Updating Streams

In this example, you will reuse and modify the Amazon S3 code you developed in Chapter 9. Here's how you do it:

1. Copy the `server.follow.js` script to a new file called `server.post.js`. Insert the following new API functions in it, just after the `// API functions` comment near the top of the file:

```
// API functions

function upload(req,res) {

    var bs = 48
    var bytes = 0

    var s3client = knox.createClient({
      key:    config.amazon.keyid,
      secret: config.amazon.secret,
      bucket: config.amazon.s3bucket,
    })

    var conlen  = parseInt( req.headers['content-length'], 10 )
    var padding = parseInt( req.headers['x-lifestream-padding'], 10 )
    var bytelen = Math.floor( ((conlen-padding)*3)/4 )

    var picid = uuid()

    var s3req = s3client.put(
      picid+'.jpg',
      {
        'Content-Length':bytelen,
        'x-amz-acl': 'public-read'
      }
    )

    s3req.on('error',function(err){
      err400(res,'S3')(''+err)
    })

    var remain = ''

    req.streambuffer.ondata(function(chunk) {
      var ascii = remain + chunk.toString('ascii')
      var bslen = bs * Math.floor( ascii.length / bs )

      var base64   = ascii.substring(0,bslen)
      var binary   = new Buffer(base64,'base64')
```

```javascript
      var newremain  = ascii.substring(bslen)

      bytes+=binary.length

      remain = newremain
      s3req.write(binary)
    })

    req.streambuffer.onend(function() {
      if( 0 < remain.length ) {
        var binary = new Buffer(remain,'base64')
        bytes+=binary.length
        s3req.write(binary)
      }
      s3req.end()
      common.sendjson(res,{ok:true,picid:picid})
    })
  }

function stream(req,res) {
  finduser(true,['stream'],req,res,function(user,coll){
    common.sendjson(res,{ok:true,stream:user.stream})
  })
}


function post(req,res) {
  var merr = mongoerr400(res)

  var picid    = req.json.picid
  var username = req.params.username

  finduser(true,['followers'],req,res,function(user,coll){
    append(username,username,picid,coll,merr,function(){
      common.sendjson(res,{ok:true})

      var followers = user.followers
      function appendfollower(fI) {
        if( fI < followers.length ) {
          append(followers[fI],username,picid,coll,merr,function(){
            appendfollower(fI+1)
          })
        }
      }
      appendfollower(0)

    })
  })

}
```

code snippet lifestream/server/server.post.js

2. Insert the following new utility functions just after the `// utility functions` comment near the middle of the `server.post.js` file:

```
// utility functions
function StreamBuffer(req) {
    var self = this

    var buffer = []
    var ended  = false
    var ondata = null
    var onend  = null

    self.ondata = function(f) {
      for(var i = 0; i < buffer.length; i++ ) {
        f(buffer[i])
      }
      ondata = f
    }

    self.onend = function(f) {
      onend = f
      if( ended ) {
        onend()
      }
    }

    req.on('data', function(chunk) {
      if( ondata ) {
        ondata(chunk)
      }
      else {
        buffer.push(chunk)
      }
    })

    req.on('end', function() {
      ended = true
      if( onend ) {
        onend()
      }
    })

    req.streambuffer = self
}


function append(touser,fromuser,picid,coll,merr,cb) {
  coll.findOne(
    {username:touser},
    {fields:['stream']},

    merr(function(user){
      var stream = user.stream

      coll.update(
        {username:touser},
```

```
        {$push:{stream:{picid:picid,user:fromuser}}},
      merr(function(){

        if( config.max_stream_size < stream.length ) {
          coll.update(
            {username:touser},
            {$pull:{stream:stream[stream.length-1]}},
            merr(function(){
              cb()
            })
          )
        }
        else {
          cb()
        }
      })
    )
  })
  )
}
```

Code snippet lifestream/server/server.post.js

3.   Replace the `collect` function near the end of the `server.post.js` file with the following code:

```
function collect(streamurl) {
  var streamregexp = new RegExp(streamurl)

  return function(req,res,next) {
    if( 'POST' == req.method ) {
      if( streamregexp.exec(req.url) ) {
        new StreamBuffer(req)
        next()
      }
      else {
        common.readjson(
          req,
          function(input) {
            req.json = input
            next()
          },
          err400(res,'read-json')
        )
      }
    }
    else {
      next()
    }
  }
}
```

Code snippet lifestream/server/server.post.js

4. To provide the URL end points in the Lifestream API for the picture-posting functions, add the following boldfaced lines after the `connect` middleware setup section:

Available for
download on
Wrox.com

```
server = connect.createServer(
  connect.logger(),
  collect('/upload$'),

  connect.router(function(app){
    app.post( prefix+'register', register)
    ,app.get(  prefix+'search/:query', search)
  }),

  auth(),

  connect.router(function(app){
    app.get(  prefix+':username', loaduser)

    ,app.post( prefix+':username/follow', follow)
    ,app.post( prefix+':username/unfollow', unfollow)

    ,app.post( prefix+':username/upload', upload)
    ,app.post( prefix+':username/post', post)
    ,app.get(  prefix+':username/stream', stream)
  })
)
```

code snippet lifestream/server/server.post.js

In this code, you're also configuring the new `collect` function to buffer data uploaded via the `upload` end point.

5. Copy the `accept.follow.js` script to a new file called `accept.post.js`. Replace the `post` function at the top of the file with the following code:

Available for
download on
Wrox.com

```
function post(username,uri,json,cb){
  util.debug('POST '+uri+': '+JSON.stringify(json))
  var opts = {
    uri:uri,
    headers:headers[username] || {}
  }

  if( json.__raw__ ) {
    opts.body = json.__raw__
    opts.headers['x-lifestream-padding'] = 2
  }
  else {
    opts.json = json
  }


  request.post(
    opts,
```

```
      handle(cb)
    )
  }


var base64img = '/9j/4A...KAP/2Q=='
```

code snippet lifestream/server/accept.post.js

The boldfaced line contains a base64 encoding of the binary data of a test image that the acceptance test will upload. The full encoding is not shown here because it is too long, but is in the downloadable code for this example.

6. To use your own test image, get the base64 encoding string by running the following code using Node:

```
console.log(
  require('fs').readFileSync('YOUR_PICTURE.JPG').toString('base64')
)
```

7. Insert the following additional test cases between the existing `follow` and `unfollow` test cases:

```
// post and stream
;post(
  bar,
  urlprefix+'/user/'+bar+'/upload',
  {__raw__:base64img},
  function(json){
    assert.ok(json.ok)
    var picid = json.picid

;post(
  bar,
  urlprefix+'/user/'+bar+'/post',
  {picid:picid},
  function(json){
    assert.ok(json.ok)

;get(
  bar,
  urlprefix+'/user/'+bar+'/stream',
  function(json){
    assert.ok(json.ok)
    assert.equal(1,json.stream.length)
    assert.equal(picid,json.stream[0].picid)
    assert.equal(bar,json.stream[0].user)

;get(
  foo,
  urlprefix+'/user/'+foo+'/stream',
  function(json){
    assert.ok(json.ok)
    assert.equal(1,json.stream.length)
```

```
        assert.equal(picid,json.stream[0].picid)
        assert.equal(bar,json.stream[0].user)


// unfollow
```

8. Insert the closing braces for these new tests after the closing brace for the `unfollow` tests, as shown in the boldfaced lines:

```
;})   // unfollow
;})   // stream
;})   // stream
;})   // post
;})   // upload
```

9. Run the `server.post.js` server and `accept.post.js` acceptance test in the same manner as before. Again, observe the debugging output to trace the operations.

How It Works

In this example, you add three new end points to the API: `upload`, `post`, and `stream`. They all require authentication, so they appear after the `auth()` middleware call.

The `stream` function is the easiest. It simply returns the contents of the `stream` property of the `user` document in MongoDB. This property stores the list of photos that the user should see.

The `post` function updates all the `stream` properties for each relevant user. The process is pretty simple: You load the `followers` property for the user who is posting. For each follower, you append the new photo to his or her photo stream. You are not actually moving around image data — just the image name — so there is very little processing overhead. However, you need to perform an update for each follower. Node helps you here, as you do not need to wait for all the updates to return a result. The first boldfaced line below shows how the `post` function returns an HTTP result first, and only then proceeds to update the followers:

```
function post(req,res) {
  var merr = mongoerr400(res)

  var picid    = req.json.picid
  var username = req.params.username

  finduser(true,['followers'],req,res,function(user,coll){
    append(username,username,picid,coll,merr,function(){
      common.sendjson(res,{ok:true})

      var followers = user.followers
      function appendfollower(fI) {
        if( fI < followers.length ) {
```

```
                    append(followers[fI],username,picid,coll,merr,function(){
                       appendfollower(fI+1)
                    })
                }
            }
         appendfollower(0)

      })
   })

}
```

Notice how the follower updates are done. Instead of using a traditional for loop, you define a recursive function called appendfollower, and you perform each follower update sequentially. If you used a for loop, all the updates would be sent at the same time. The effect of this would be to create large numbers of open HTTP connections for Node to manage at the same time, but this would not be a scalable solution. By instead updating each follower one after the other, you reduce the overhead on the Node server. There is no need for the updates to occur instantly.

The append utility function performs the actual append of the photo to the stream property. This function includes some extra logic to prevent the streams from growing too large. If the stream length exceeds the config.max_stream_size setting, the oldest photo is dropped by using the MongoDB $pull operation to remove it from the list, as shown in the boldfaced code:

```
function append(touser,fromuser,picid,coll,merr,cb) {
  coll.findOne(
    {username:touser},
    {fields:['stream']},

    merr(function(user){
      var stream = user.stream

      coll.update(
        {username:touser},
        {$push:{stream:{picid:picid,user:fromuser}}},
        merr(function(){

          if( config.max_stream_size < stream.length ) {
            coll.update(
              {username:touser},
              {$pull:{stream:stream[stream.length-1]}},
              merr(function(){
                cb()
              })
            )
          }
          else {
            cb()
          }
        })
      )
    })
  )
}
```

The `upload` function performs the image data upload. This is the same function you saw in Chapter 9 but with some refinements. When you are building full applications, you need to account for the different types of requests that the system must deal with. In this case, there are standard JSON requests, where data is exchanged in JSON format, and there are image uploads, where the data is streamed in chunks of base64 content.

This requirement to handle different types of requests creates a problem when you combine it with the requirement to query the MongoDB database to check the user's identity. As soon as you send a database request, the code stops, and Node starts dealing with other network events. Of course, once the database responds, the callback is called, and everything proceeds as normal. The problem arises if you are also expecting to receive streamed data. Because the `upload` function has not even been called yet, the code to deal with data events on the request object has not yet been hooked into Node. So the data handler will never be called, and Node will drop the image data!

To solve this problem, you need to register a handler for the data events on the request object before you pass control back to Node. You use the `StreamBuffer` utility object to do this. It temporarily caches any data that arrives before Node gets to the `upload` function. Once the `upload` function executes, the cached data chunks are drained, and the stream proceeds as normal.

Because these are API functions, you need to make sure they work by using acceptance tests. You insert them into the list of acceptance tests just before the `unfollow` tests so that there are some followers to work with. To test the upload function, a hard-coded base64 data stream is provided in the acceptance test script.

 WARNING *Running this acceptance test will upload data to Amazon S3, and Amazon will charge you for the privilege of storing your data. Remember to delete the test uploads when you are done.*

COMPLETING THE LIFESTREAM APP

It is time to complete the Lifestream app! This section walks you through how to create a fully working cross-platform mobile app that uses cloud services to deliver its functionality. Startups have been funded based on demos that do less than this example. You should be able to reuse this app code, and the server code, as a starting point for your own mobile cloud apps.

Because you have already verified the Lifestream API using acceptance tests, connecting the app to the API is quite easy. The benefit of running the tests is that you do not have to laboriously debug the API by repeatedly deploying the app. If there are bugs at this stage, you can be quite confident that they are in the app code, not the server code.

In this section, you'll build on the basic app structure that you created in Chapter 9:

> **Lifestream tab** — This tab is used for registration, and after a user is registered, for showing the photo stream.

➤ **Post tab** — This tab remains the same as in Chapter 9, allowing users to take a picture and upload it.

➤ **Follow tab** — On this new tab, a user can find other users to follow and see his or her followers.

Supporting User Accounts

In the following example, you'll extend the existing Lifestream app to provide support functions and user interface elements so that users can register, follow other users, post pictures, and view their picture streams. Because you'll be performing many different API calls, you also need to introduce some utility functions to handle HTTP GET and POST requests.

TRY IT OUT   Connecting the Lifestream App to the API

In this example, you'll expand the Lifestream app in a number of ways and connect it to the API. Follow these steps:

1. Start the Xcode development environment and open the Lifestream project.

2. Open the index.html file in the www folder and replace its contents with the following code:

Available for download on Wrox.com

```
<!DOCTYPE html>
<html>
<head>
    <title>Lifestream App</title>
    <meta name="viewport"
      content="user-scalable=no,initial-scale=1.0,maximum-scale=1.0" />
    <meta name="apple-mobile-web-app-capable" content="yes" />

    <link rel="apple-touch-icon" href="lifestream-icon.png"/>
    <link rel="apple-touch-icon-precomposed" href="lifestream-icon.png"/>
    <link rel="apple-touch-startup-image" href="lifestream-startup.png" />

    <link rel="stylesheet" href="jquery.mobile.css" />
    <link rel="stylesheet" href="lifestream.css" />

    <script src="phonegap.0.9.4.min.js"></script>
    <script src="jquery.js"></script>
    <script src="jquery.mobile.js"></script>
    <script src="lifestream.js"></script>
</head>
<body>
<div id="main" data-role="page">

  <div data-role="header" data-position="fixed">
    <div data-role="navbar">
      <ul>
        <li><a id="nav_lifestream">
          <img id="logo" src="lifestream.png"> </a></li>
        <li><a id="nav_post">Post</a></li>
        <li><a id="nav_follow">Follow</a></li>
      </ul>
    </div>
  </div>
```

```
      </div>

      <div id="con_lifestream" data-role="content">
        <div id="lifestream_register">
          <h2>Registration</h2>

          <label>Username:</label><br/>
          <input id="lifestream_username"><br/>
          <a id="btn_register" data-role="button">Register</a>
        </div>

        <ul id="lifestream_images">
        </ul>
        <li id="lifestream_image">
          <span></span><br/>
          <img/>
        </li>

      </div>

      <div id="con_post" data-role="content">
        <a id="btn_takepic" data-role="button">Take Picture</a>
        <img id="post_pic" />
        <a id="btn_upload" data-role="button">Upload Picture</a>
        <p id="post_msg"></p>
      </div>

      <div id="con_follow" data-role="content">
        <h3 id="follow_user"></h3>

        <h2>Followers</h2>
        <ul id="follow_followers">
        </ul>

        <h2>Following</h2>

        <div data-role="collapsible" data-collapsed="true">
        <h3>Search:</h3>
        <input id="follow_search"><br/>
        <a id="btn_search" data-role="button">Search</a><br/>
        <ul id="follow_results">
        </ul>
        </div>

        <ul id="follow_following">
        </ul>
        <li id="follow_followee">
          <p class="username">username</p>
          <a class="follow" data-role="button"></a>
        </li>

      </div>

    </div>
```

code snippet lifestream/app-www-basic/index.html

3. Open the `lifestream.css` file and replace its contents with the following code:

```css
#main {
  width: 320px;
}
#logo {
  position: absolute;
  top:7px;
  left:18px;
}

#con_post {
  display:none;
}
#con_follow {
  display:none;
}

#lifestream_images {
  width: 100%;
}

#lifestream_images li {
  display: block;
  margin:  8px auto;
  text-align: center;
}

#lifestream_images li img {
  width:  200px;
  height: 200px;
  border: 1px solid #ccc;
}

#lifestream_image {
  display:none;
}

#lifestream_register {
  display:none;
}

#lifestream_complete {
  display:none;
}

#post_pic {
  display: block;
  margin: 0px auto;
  width:  200px;
  height: 200px;
  border: 1px solid #ccc;
}

#post_msg {
  text-align: center;
```

```
    font-weight: bold;
}

#follow_followee {
  display:none;
  height: 40px;
}

a.signin {
  margin: 8px;
  display: block;
}

ul {
  list-style-type: none;
  padding: 0px;
}

li {
  width: 300px;
  margin: 8px auto;
}

li p.username {
  margin: 6px;
  width: 160px;
  float: left;
}

li a.follow {
  width: 100px;
  float: right;
}
```

code snippet lifestream/app-www-basic/lifestream.css

4. Open the lifestream.js file and replace its contents with the following code, using your own details instead of the boldfaced YOUR_IP_ADDRESS and YOUR_S2_BUCKET_NAME placeholders:

```
document.addEventListener("deviceready", ondeviceready)

var server = 'YOUR_IP_ADDRESS'

var s3prefix = 'https://s3.amazonaws.com/YOUR_S3_BUCKET_NAME/'


var app = null

function ondeviceready(){
  app = new App()
}


function App() {
```

```javascript
var self = this

var imagedata = null

var con = $('#con_lifestream')

var lifestream_images   = $('#lifestream_images')
var lifestream_image    = $('#lifestream_image')
var lifestream_register = $('#lifestream_register')
var lifestream_username = $('#lifestream_username')

var follow_followers = $('#follow_followers')
var follow_following = $('#follow_following')
var follow_search    = $('#follow_search')
var follow_results   = $('#follow_results')
var follow_followee  = $('#follow_followee')

var post_pic = $('#post_pic')
var post_msg = $('#post_msg')


$('#nav_lifestream').click(function(){
  showcon('lifestream')
  showimages( load('images') )
  update()
})

$('#nav_post').click(function(){
  showcon('post')
})

$('#nav_follow').click(function(){
  showcon('follow')
  update()
})

$('#btn_takepic').click(picTake)
$('#btn_upload').click(picUpload)
$('#btn_register').click(register)
$('#btn_search').click(search)


function update() {
  var user = load('user')
  follow_search.val('')
  follow_results.empty()

  http_get(user.username,function(data){
    showfollowers(data.followers)
    showfollows(follow_following,false,data.following)

    save('images',data.stream)
    showimages(data.stream)
  })
}


function search() {
  var query = follow_search.val()
```

```
    http_get('search/'+escape(query),function(data){
      showfollows(follow_results,true,data.list)
    })
}


function picTake(){
  navigator.camera.getPicture(
    function(base64) {
      imagedata = base64
      post_pic.attr({src:"data:image/jpeg;base64,"+imagedata})
    },
    function(){
      post_msg.text('Could not take picture')
    },
    { quality: 50 }
  )
}


function picUpload(){
  var user = load('user')

  if( imagedata ) {
    post_msg.text('Uploading...')

    uploadData(function(data){
      http_post(
        user.username+'/post',
        {picid:data.picid},
        function(data){
          post_msg.text('Picture uploaded.')
          appendimage(username,data.picid)
        }
      )
    })
  }
  else {
    post_msg.text('Take a picture first')
  }
}


function uploadData(win) {
  var padI = imagedata.length-1
  while( '=' == imagedata[padI] ) {
    padI--
  }
  var padding = imagedata.length - padI - 1

  var user = load('user')
  $.ajax({
    url:'http://'+server+'/lifestream/api/user/'+user.username+'/upload',
      type:'POST',
    contentType:'application/octet-stream',
    data:imagedata,
```

```
      headers:{'X-Lifestream-Padding':''+padding,
                'X-Lifestream-Token':user.token},
      dataType:'json',
      success:win,
      error:function(err){
        showalert('Upload','Could not upload picture.')
      },
    })
}


function register() {
  var username = lifestream_username.val()
  if( username && '' != username ) {
    createuser(username)
  }
  else {
    showalert('Registration','Please enter a username.')
  }
}


function createuser(username){
  http_post('register',{username:username},function(data){
    lifestream_register.hide()
    var user = load('user')
    user.username = username
    user.token = data.token
    save('user',user)
    showcon('post')
  })
}


function showimages(images) {
  lifestream_images.empty();
  for( var i = images.length-1; 0 <= i; i-- ) {
    var li =
      lifestream_image.clone()
      .css({display:'block'})
    li.find('span').text(images[i].user)
    li.find('img').attr({src:s3prefix+images[i].picid+'.jpg'})
    lifestream_images.append(li)
  }
}


function appendimage(username,picid) {
  var images = load('images')
  images.push({picid:picid,user:username})
  save('images',images)
}


function showfollowers(followers) {
  follow_followers.empty();
```

```
  for( var i = 0; i < followers.length; i++ ) {
    var li = $('<li>').text(followers[i])
    follow_followers.append(li)
  }
  if( 0 == followers.length ) {
    var li = $('<li>').text('No followers yet.')
    follow_followers.append(li)
  }
}

function showfollows(follows,yes,users) {
  follows.empty();
  for( var i = 0; i < users.length; i++ ) {
    var username = users[i]
    var li
      = follow_followee.clone()
      .css({display:'block'})
    li.find('.username').text(username)
    li.find('.follow')
      .attr({id:'username_'+username})
      .text(yes?'Follow':'Unfollow').click(function(){
        follow(yes,$(this))
      })
    follows.append(li)
  }
  if( 0 == users.length ) {
    var li = $('<li>').text('No follows yet.')
    follows.append(li)
  }
}

function follow(yes,li) {
  var user = load('user')
  var username = /username_(.*)/.exec( li.attr('id') )[1]
  http_post(
    user.username+'/'+(yes?'':'un')+'follow',
    {username:username},
    function(data){
      li.text(yes?'Unfollow':'Follow').click(function(){
        follow(!yes,$(this))
      })
    }
  )
}



function init() {
  var user = load('user')

  if( !user.username ) {
    lifestream_register.show()
  }
  else {
```

```
      update()
    }
}


function http_get(suffix,win) {
  var user = load('user')
  $.ajax(
    {
      url:'http://'+server+'/lifestream/api/user/'+suffix,
      headers:{'X-Lifestream-Token':user.token},
      dataType:'json',
      success:win,
      error:function(err){
        showalert('Network','Unable to contact server.')
      }
    }
  )
}


function http_post(suffix,data,win) {
  var user = load('user')
  $.ajax(
    {
      url:'http://'+server+'/lifestream/api/user/'+suffix,
      type:'POST',
      headers:{'X-Lifestream-Token':user.token},
      contentType:'application/json',
      data:JSON.stringify(data),
      dataType:'json',
      success:win,
      error:function(err){
        showalert('Network','Unable to contact server.')
      }
    }
  )
}


function showalert(title,msg){
  navigator.notification.alert(
    msg,
    function(){},
    title,
    'OK'
  )
}


function showcon(name) {
  if( con ) {
    con.hide()
  }
  con = $('#con_'+name)
```

```
      con.show()
    }


    var cache = {}

    function load(key) {
      return cache[key] || JSON.parse(localStorage[key] || '{}')
    }

    function save(key,obj) {
      cache[key] = obj
      localStorage[key] = JSON.stringify(obj)
    }


    init()
  }
```

Code snippet lifestream/app-www-basic/lifestream.js

5. Start the `server.post.js` script if it is not already running. Your nginx web server should also be running and proxying requests back to the script. (Review the setup instructions for this in Chapter 9 if you need a reminder.)

6. Select Build ➪ Clean All Targets and run the app in the simulator. Verify that the registration page appears as shown in Figure 10-1. In the simulator version of the app, you can register and follow other users. You can't take any pictures because the simulator does not have a camera.

7. Run the app on your physical iPhone device. Register a new user. Return to the simulator and search for and follow your new physical iPhone user. Figure 10-2 shows an example of a follower/following relationship, where the simulator user has followed and is following another user called bob.

FIGURE 10-1　　　　　　　　**FIGURE 10-2**

8. Use your physical iPhone to take and upload a photo. Confirm that the photo appears on the Lifestream tab. Confirm that the photo also appears in the Lifestream tab on the simulator.

9. Repeat steps 7 and 8, using Eclipse, and deploy the app to your Android emulator and physical Android device. Follow the various users from the various devices and confirm that posted photos appear in the correct follower photo streams. Figure 10-3 shows the user `alice`'s app for the scenario where `alice` has taken a photo, and `then` bob has taken a photo. As `alice` follows `bob`, these photos appear in reverse chronological order in `alice`'s photo stream.

FIGURE 10-3

 WARNING *In order for this example to work on your local network, you need to use IP addresses when configuring the web address of your API. For a live system, you of course need to use a domain name. You need to ensure that you also have a live network connection so that you can reach Amazon S3 and* MongoHQ.com.

How It Works

The HTML and CSS code provide the additional user interface elements for this example. This interface combines all the techniques you have learned in the previous chapters.

The `lifestream.js` file has a lot of new code. The start of the file has a lot more jQuery code to hook buttons and tabs to handler functions. The first new function is `update`, which is called whenever the user interface needs to be updated:

```
function update() {
  var user = load('user')
  follow_search.val('')
  follow_results.empty()

  http_get(user.username,function(data){
    showfollowers(data.followers)
    showfollows(follow_following,false,data.following)

    save('images',data.stream)
    showimages(data.stream)
  })
}
```

The update function cleans up any old searches and then sends a request to the server to get the most recent details for the user. The follower/following details and the image stream are then updated with the results. Note that no image data is transferred — only image names. The app constructs a direct image URL reference to your Amazon S3 bucket for the HTML img tags. This means that the app loads the images directly from Amazon, not from your server. This also means that the update call is quite inexpensive, as only a small amount of text data is transferred.

The http_get utility function constructs the correct URL to make an API call. The registration token must be included so that the request can be authenticated:

```
function http_get(suffix,win) {
  var user = load('user')
  $.ajax(
    {
      url:'http://'+server+'/lifestream/api/user/'+suffix,
      headers:{'X-Lifestream-Token':user.token},
      dataType:'json',
      success:win,
      error:function(err){
        showalert('Network','Unable to contact server.')
      }
    }
  )
}
```

The http_post utility function operates in the same way but also sends to the server any JSON data you provide.

showimages, showfollows, and showfollowers are classic jQuery HTML builder functions. A hidden div is used as a template for the items to be inserted, be they images or follower names. This hidden template div is cloned, and then the clone is updated with the content to display. Finally, the clone is inserted into the appropriate HTML element. This cloning approach is much easier to work with, and much less error-prone, than attempting to concatenate HTML strings.

The follow, register, search, and picUpload functions implement the main user-facing actions of the app. Each function calls the server API and updates the user interface with the results.

Posting an image is a two-stage process. First, the image data is uploaded as a stream. When this is completed successfully, a post API call is made to publish the picture out to the followers of the user.

Integrating Social Network Identity

Many users expect to be able to register with an app by using their existing Facebook and Twitter accounts. In this section, you'll learn how to add that functionality to the Lifestream app. With this social network integration in place, the Lifestream app goes from being a learning example to a fully functional "minimum viable product." Go find yourself some venture capitalists!

To support Facebook and Twitter registration, in the following example, you'll be reusing a slightly modified version of your code from Chapter 8. This version uses the OAuth protocol to verify the user's account details and provide the user's username. There is a challenge here: You need to send the user out to a mobile browser to complete the registration and then return the user to your app. You can do this can by using custom URL schemes.

Connecting the Lifestream App to Facebook and Twitter

To enable Facebook and Twitter registration in the Lifestream app, follow these steps:

1. Open the `index.html` file and replace the contents of the `lifestream_register` div with the following:

Available for download on Wrox.com

```html
<div id="lifestream_register">
  <h2>Registration</h2>

  <a target="_blank" id="lifestream_twitter"
     class="signin">
    <img src="twitter.png">
  </a>

  <a target="_blank" rel="external" id="lifestream_facebook"
     class="signin">
    <img src="facebook.png">
  </a>

  <label>Or Create a New Username:</label><br/>
  <input id="lifestream_username"><br/>
  <a id="btn_register" data-role="button">Register</a>
</div>

<div id="lifestream_complete">
  <a id="btn_complete" data-role="button">Complete Registration</a>
</div>
```

code snippet lifestream/app-www-social/index.html

2. Open the `lifestream.js` file and add the following boldfaced lines at the top of the file to support the new Facebook and Twitter login images:

Available for download on Wrox.com

```js
var lifestream_images   = $('#lifestream_images')
var lifestream_image    = $('#lifestream_image')
var lifestream_register = $('#lifestream_register')
var lifestream_username = $('#lifestream_username')
var lifestream_complete = $('#lifestream_complete')
var lifestream_twitter  = $('#lifestream_twitter')
var lifestream_facebook = $('#lifestream_facebook')
```

code snippet lifestream/app-www-social/lifestream.js

3. Scroll down the `lifestream.js` file and add an event handler for the new Complete Registration button:

```
$('#btn_takepic').click(picTake)
$('#btn_upload').click(picUpload)
$('#btn_register').click(register)
$('#btn_search').click(search)
$('#btn_complete').click(complete)
```

code snippet lifestream/app-www-social/lifestream.js

4. Scroll further down and add the new `complete` handler function just after the `register` handler function:

```
function complete() {
  var registration = load('registration')
  http_get('complete/'+registration.token,function(data){
    delete registration.token
    save('registration',registration)
    lifestream_complete.hide()
    createuser(data.username)
  })
}
```

code snippet lifestream/app-www-social/lifestream.js

5. Scroll to the end of the `lifestream.js` file and replace the `init` function with the following code:

```
function init() {
  var user = load('user')
  var registration = load('registration')

  if( registration.token ) {
    lifestream_complete.show()
  }
  else if( !user.username ) {

    function service(btn,kind){
      btn.click(function(){
        registration = load('registration')
        if( !registration.token ) {
          var token = ''+(new Date().getTime())+Math.random()
          save('registration',{token:token})
          lifestream_register.hide()
          lifestream_complete.show()
          btn.attr(
            {href:'http://'+server+'/lifestream/api/user/oauth/'+
                  kind+'/login/'+token}
          ).click()
        }
      })
    }

    service(lifestream_twitter, 'twitter')
```

```
      service(lifestream_facebook,'facebook')

      lifestream_register.show()
   }
   else {
     update()
   }
}
```

code snippet lifestream/app-www-social/lifestream.js

6. To add support for the `lifestream:` URL scheme to your iPhone app, in Xcode, open the `lifestream-Info.plist` file. Add URL types setting, as shown in the boldfaced portion of Figure 10-4. The URL identifier should be your own domain name.

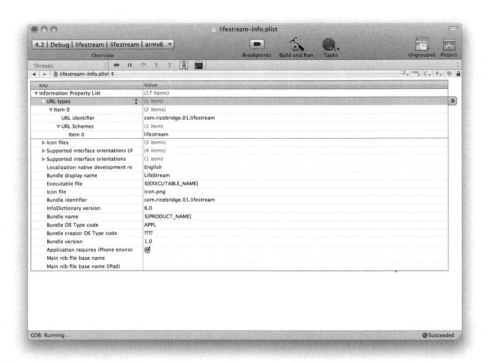

FIGURE 10-4

7. To add support for the `lifestream:` URL scheme to your Android app, edit the `AndroidManifest.xml` file and insert the following boldfaced lines into the `activity` section:

```
<activity ...
  ...

  <intent-filter>
    <action android:name="android.intent.action.VIEW" />
```

```
            <category android:name="android.intent.category.DEFAULT" />
            <category android:name="android.intent.category.BROWSABLE" />
            <data android:scheme="lifestream" android:host="" />
        </intent-filter>
    </activity>
```

8. In the `lifestream/server` folder, copy the `server.post.js` script to a new file called `server` `.social.js`. Insert the following new API function just after the `// API functions` comment near the top of the file:

```
function complete(req,res) {
  var username = oauthstate[req.params.token]
  if( !username ) {
    err400(res)()
  }
  else {
    delete oauthstate[req.params.token]
    common.sendjson(res,{username:username})
  }
}
```

code snippet lifestream/server/server.social.js

9. Also in the `server.social.js` file, add the following Facebook and Twitter OAuth support functions just after the `// utility functions` comment in the middle of the file:

```
// utility functions

var oauthstate = {}

var oauthactions = {
  facebook: {
    login: function(req,res) {
      var redirectUrl =
        oauthclients.facebook.getAuthorizeUrl(
          {redirect_uri:'http://'+config.server+
            '/lifestream/api/user/oauth/facebook/callback', scope:'' })

      var token = req.params.token

      var cookies = new Cookies(req,res)
      cookies.set('lifestream_register',token, {path:'/'})

      res.writeHead( 301, {
        'Location':redirectUrl,
      })
      res.end()
    },

    callback: function(req,res) {
      var parsedUrl = url.parse(req.url, true);
      var cookies = new Cookies(req,res)
```

```
          var token = cookies.get('lifestream_register')

          oauthclients.facebook.getOAuthAccessToken(
            parsedUrl.query.code ,
            {redirect_uri:'http://'+config.server+
             '/lifestream/api/user/oauth/facebook/callback'},
            function( error, access_token, refresh_token ){
              if (!error) {
                res.writeHead( 301, {
                  'Location':'http://'+config.server+
                    '/lifestream/api/user/oauth/facebook/launch'
                })

                request.get(
                  {uri:'https://graph.facebook.com/me?access_token='+
                      access_token},
                  function (err, res, body) {
                    if( !err ) {
                      var json = JSON.parse(body)
                      var username = json.username
                      oauthstate[token] = username
                    }
                    else {
                      util.debug(JSON.stringify(error))
                    }
                  })
              }
              else {
                util.debug(JSON.stringify(error))
              }
              res.end()
            }
          )
        },

        launch: function(req,res) {
          res.writeHead(200)
          res.end( "<script>window.location='lifestream:///'</script>" )
        }
      },

      twitter: {
        login: function(req,res) {
          var token = req.params.token
          var cookies = new Cookies(req,res)
          cookies.set('lifestream_register',token, {path:'/'})

          oauthclients.twitter.getOAuthRequestToken(
            function(
              error,
              oauth_token,
              oauth_token_secret,
              oauth_authorize_url,
              additionalParameters)
```

```
        {
          if (!error) {
            oauthstate[token] = oauth_token_secret

            res.writeHead( 301, {
              "Location":
              "http://api.twitter.com/oauth/authorize?oauth_token="+
                oauth_token
            })
            res.end()
          }
          else {
            res.end( JSON.stringify(error) )
          }
        }
      )
  },

  callback: function(req,res){
    var parsedUrl = url.parse(req.url, true);
    var cookies = new Cookies(req,res)
    var token = cookies.get('lifestream_register')

    oauthclients.twitter.getOAuthAccessToken(
      parsedUrl.query.oauth_token,
      oauthstate[token],
      parsedUrl.query.oauth_verifier,

      function(
        error,
        oauth_token,
        oauth_token_secret,
        additionalParameters)
      {
        if (!error) {
          oauthstate[token] = additionalParameters.screen_name

          res.writeHead( 301,
            { 'Location':
                "http://"+config.server+
                "/lifestream/api/user/oauth/twitter/launch"
            })
          res.end()
        }
        else {
          res.end( JSON.stringify(error) )
        }
      }
    )
  },

  launch: function(req,res){
    res.writeHead(200)
    res.end( "<script>window.location='lifestream:///'</script>" )
```

```
      }
    }
  }

oauthclients = {
  facebook:new oauth.OAuth2(
    config.facebook.keyid,
    config.facebook.secret,
    'https://graph.facebook.com'
  ),
  twitter:new oauth.OAuth(
    'http://twitter.com/oauth/request_token',
    'http://twitter.com/oauth/access_token',
    config.twitter.keyid,
    config.twitter.secret,
    '1.0',
    'http://'+config.server+'/lifestream/api/user/oauth/twitter/callback',
    'HMAC-SHA1',
    null,
    {'Accept': '*/*', 'Connection': 'close', 'User-Agent': 'twitter-js'}
  )

}


function oauthaction(req,res) {
  oauthactions[req.params.service][req.params.action](req,res)
}
```

code snippet lifestream/server/server.social.js

10. To provide the URL end points in the Lifestream API for the Facebook and Twitter
OAuth login functions, add the following boldfaced lines to the `connect` middleware
setup section:

```
        collect('/upload$'),

        connect.router(function(app){
          app.post( prefix+'register', register)
          ,app.get( prefix+'oauth/:service/:action/:token', oauthaction)
          ,app.get( prefix+'oauth/:service/:action', oauthaction)
          ,app.get( prefix+'complete/:token', complete)

          ,app.get( prefix+'search/:query', search)
        }),
```

code snippet lifestream/server/server.social.js

11. Start the `server.social.js` server.

12. On your iPhone or Android device, delete any existing versions of the app. It is important to remove old login details so that you can register again using your Twitter or Facebook account.

13. Rebuild and install your app on your iPhone or Android device. You should see the new registration page with the Facebook and Twitter login buttons, as shown in Figure 10-5. Tap either of the buttons to follow the login process.

14. When you return to your app, tap the Complete Registration button to finish the process. Your username should now be the same as your Facebook or Twitter username.

FIGURE 10-5

WARNING *If you run repeated tests on this code and have to log in repeatedly, you may encounter caching issues. To avoid such problems, log out of Facebook and Twitter before each test so that they do not assume that your app is already authenticated.*

How It Works

To add the Twitter and Facebook login images to `index.html`, you use the same code as in Chapter 8. These images appear only if the user is not yet registered. The `init` method is updated to handle this:

```
function init() {
  var user = load('user')
  var registration = load('registration')

  if( registration.token ) {
    lifestream_complete.show()
  }
  else if( !user.username ) {

    function service(btn,kind){
      btn.click(function(){
        registration = load('registration')
        if( !registration.token ) {
          var token = ''+(new Date().getTime())+Math.random()
          save('registration',{token:token})
          lifestream_register.hide()
          lifestream_complete.show()
          btn.attr(
            {href:'http://'+server+'/lifestream/api/user/oauth/'+
```

```
                    kind+'/login/'+token}
          ).click()
        }
      })
    }

    service(lifestream_twitter, 'twitter')
    service(lifestream_facebook,'facebook')

    lifestream_register.show()
  }
  else {
    update()
  }
}
```

The `service` function sets up the registration process when the user taps either the Twitter or Facebook login button.

You use the following to create a unique registration token:

```
var token = ''+(new Date().getTime())+Math.random()
save('registration',{token:token})
```

Then you hide the registration buttons and show the Complete Registration button:

```
lifestream_register.hide()
lifestream_complete.show()
```

The user won't tap the Complete Registration button just yet, but you need to have it ready for when the user returns from the Twitter or Facebook site.

 NOTE *Chapter 12 has a more advanced OAuth sign-in process that removes the need for the Complete Registration button and the server-side code.*

Finally, you launch the mobile browser and start the OAuth protocol. In order to ensure that your app launches a new mobile browser, the link for the images contains the `target="_blank"` attribute. The code dynamically constructs a URL containing the token and then sends an artificial click to the image button. This is also necessary to get the mobile browser to launch:

```
btn.attr(
  {href:'http://'+server+'/lifestream/api/user/oauth/'+
        kind+'/login/'+token}
).click()
```

The URL containing the token points first at the Lifestream server and is the first HTTP call of the OAuth protocol sequence. (Review the discussion on OAuth in Chapter 8 if you need a quick reminder of how this works.)

On the server side, you use almost the same code as in Chapter 8. The main difference is that the token is stored on the server side. This makes the registration process stateful. In a scalable app with multiple Node instances, you need to store this state in an external system.

Once the OAuth protocol is completed, your `launch` end point is called. In a web app, this will return the start page of the app, in the browser. But you need to return to your app. You do this by using a custom URL scheme.

Custom URL schemes are a special feature of mobile apps. Your app can register a custom scheme (Lifestream uses `lifestream:`), and any time a link is clicked on a website that uses this scheme, your app will be launched to deal with the URL. By registering a custom URL, you can get back to your app by sending to the browser a `script` tag that dynamically loads your app:

```
launch: function(req,res) {
  res.writeHead(200)
  res.end( "<script>window.location='lifestream:///'</script>" )
}
```

When the user is returned to your app, you need to synchronize the app and the server. You do this by submitting a request to the `complete` end point. You can trigger this call when the user taps the Complete Registration button.

The `complete` functions on the client and server then tie everything together. Both the client and server have the token, and they use it to verify the registration. Here's the token handling on the client:

```
function complete() {
  var registration = load('registration')
  http_get('complete/'+registration.token,function(data){
    delete registration.token
    save('registration',registration)
    lifestream_complete.hide()
    createuser(data.username)
  })
}
```

And here's the token handling on the server:

```
function complete(req,res) {
  var username = oauthstate[req.params.token]
  if( !username ) {
    err400(res)()
  }
  else {
    delete oauthstate[req.params.token]
    common.sendjson(res,{username:username})
  }
}
```

The username is set to the same name as the user's username on Facebook or Twitter.

SUMMARY

In this chapter, you pulled together all the different functions that you built separately in the preceding chapters. You created a fully functional mobile app that implements a photo-blogging service. Your app is just like a native app and is deployed to physical devices in the same way. You also built a full cloud-based server platform for your app. Finally, you integrated your app with major social networks so that users can easily register using their existing social networking accounts.

In the next chapter, you'll learn how to use cloud-based commercial services to develop, build, and deploy your apps. You'll also learn about the additional features these commercial services offer and what criteria you can use to decide if and when to use them.

EXERCISES

1. Like more traditional databases, MongoDB also allows you to specify indexes to be built on particular fields. This speeds up query time enormously and is a vital element of any production database. Analyze the queries that are used in the Lifestream server code to determine which indexes you should define. Refer to the documentation at `mongodb.org` for the commands to create an index.

2. When you deploy your app into production, you'll run it on one or more servers. If you are using Ubuntu instances on the Amazon cloud as in the examples in this book, you'll need to ensure that your Node server keeps running at all times and that it restarts if it crashes. Write an `upstart` configuration to do this. Start here: `upstart.ubuntu.com`.

3. Once you deploy an app into production and real people start using it on real devices, weird stuff is going to happen. Your app will fail in all sorts of strange ways. You need to capture these errors so that you can analyze them and work to improve the quality and robustness of your app. MongoDB is a great place to log the errors, but how do you get them, reliably, from the client to your server?

4. The pictures in the Lifestream app's photo stream are shown in reverse chronological order. Extend the app and server so that the photo stream shows what time each picture was taken.

Answers to the Exercises can be found in the Appendix.

▶ WHAT YOU LEARNED IN THIS CHAPTER

TOPIC	KEY CONCEPTS
App API	A useful design approach to building cloud-based mobile apps is to design the API for the app first and then connect the app afterward. This makes development much faster and allows you to test your server-side code in isolation. You also gain a stand-alone API for your app that third parties can use.
Unit testing versus acceptance testing	When you unit test software, you test its functionality without reference to external resources. With acceptance testing, you test software as if you are in an operation environment, and you rely on external resources, such as third-party web services.
Stream buffering	Due to the way in which Node handles incoming data, it is sometimes necessary to create a temporary buffer to store incoming data until you are ready to connect your callbacks. You can do this by using an object that stores the cached data and routes data events to your actual callbacks later. Stream buffering is especially useful when you need to make asynchronous calls, such as database queries, before attaching your data event callbacks.
Redundant data schemas	When you are building large-scale systems, it is more important to store data where you need it for performance reasons than to make sure that there is only one consistent version of the data in the entire system.
Custom URL schemes	It is possible to register a custom URL scheme when you install a mobile application. This allows you to launch your application from a web page when the user is using the mobile web browser.

11

Working with Cloud Development Services

WHAT YOU WILL LEARN IN THIS CHAPTER:

➤ Understanding the different kinds of cloud development services

➤ Using the FeedHenry app development platform

➤ Using the Appcelerator app development platform

➤ Using the appMobi app development platform

In this book, you have learned how to build a cloud-based mobile app from the ground up. You have done everything yourself, including setting up your own Amazon server. You've used the Amazon cloud, but you've still had to do a lot of system administration work yourself. You will often need this level of control, and the knowledge you've gained in this book will be very useful when you need to meet client requirements in a flexible way.

Sometimes, you will not need quite so much control, and it may be more cost-effective to let someone else worry about server configuration. In such cases, you can use prebuilt services in the cloud and focus on building your mobile app. This chapter looks at three commercial vendors that can help you build apps very quickly, by abstracting away many of the details.

It is useful to have a conceptual framework in order to help make a decision about what cloud vendor to use. There are three main types of cloud services:

➤ **Infrastructure-as-a-service** — You get virtual infrastructure software, such as operating systems, databases, and file storage. Amazon and Rackspace are good examples.

➤ **Platform-as-a-service** — You get a prebuilt execution environment for your code, and the service looks after all the infrastructure elements. The Heroku cloud environment for Ruby web apps is the archetypal example here.

➤ **Software-as-a-service** — You do not need to write any code, you just use an online service for a particular purpose, such as email. Gmail and Hotmail are perfect examples.

This book has focused on the first type: infrastructure-as-a-service. Amazon remains the leading company in this area, and familiarity with Amazon's systems is essential knowledge for a web and mobile developer.

The software-as-a-service cloud services are not particularly useful to you as a developer for building apps. While you may need to integrate with cloud services of this kind — for example, social media sites — in general, your interaction with these kinds of services will be more about using their APIs for integration. You've already learned how to use the social media sites for easy user login. In the next two chapters, you'll extend that knowledge to include the use of social media APIs.

So what you really need is the platform-as-a-service offerings. This chapter takes a look at the three leading companies in the JavaScript-based mobile app development space. Other companies provide mobile app development services, such as Rhomobile (which uses Ruby), but they do not support JavaScript as a development language.

What you are looking for from a service like this is a way to reduce the amount of work you have to do to build a production-quality app that integrates with your own and third-party cloud services. You should not need to install any server software. The service should be able to build app binaries that you can submit directly to the app stores. And the service should provide you with pre-built modules for common requirements such as e-commerce, push notifications, and analytics. The service should also provide a place to run your server-side business logic and store your app data in the cloud. Such an ideal service does not yet exist. But if you understand what the three leading services can provide, you will be able to understand the necessary trade-offs between effort, features, and price.

GETTING TO KNOW THE MOBILE APP DEVELOPMENT PLATFORMS

This book has shown you how to develop JavaScript-based mobile apps by using open source tools. But this is not the only option for building mobile apps using JavaScript. A number of commercial offerings have emerged that promise to make your development life easier. It is, of course, entirely possible to build an app using only PhoneGap and open source server software. However, doing this may not be advisable if you need to meet tight deadlines and provide certain levels of postdeployment support. Especially when you are dealing with large clients, or when you need special capabilities such as augmented reality, it is worth considering a commercial development platform.

This chapter takes a look at the commercial mobile and cloud platforms that allow you to build an app using JavaScript. There are other excellent platforms based on other languages, but we don't cover them here because the focus is on using the techniques and skills you have developed in reading this book.

You'll learn about three platforms: FeedHenry, Appcelerator, and appMobi. As a preview, here is a feature comparison table:

FEATURE	FEEDHENRY	APPCELERATOR	APPMOBI
HTML5 defines user interface	YES	NO	YES
JavaScript development	YES	YES	YES
Proprietary API	YES	YES	YES
API Complexity	LOW	HIGH	MEDIUM
Own IDE	YES	YES	NO
Cloud Hosting of Server Code	YES	NO	NO
Prebuilt Cloud Components	NO	YES	YES
Enterprise Support Features	YES	YES	NO
Custom Extensions	YES	YES	YES
User Interface Components	NO	YES	NO
App Management Dashboard	YES	YES	YES
App Analytics	YES	YES	NO

USING THE FEEDHENRY PLATFORM

FeedHenry (www.feedhenry.com) was one of the first companies to offer a production-quality cross-platform app development service using HTML5 as the core technology. Founded in 2007, FeedHenry started with a web app framework and adapted it for mobile uses. In addition to this HTML5 strategy on the client, FeedHenry from the start has offered a cloud-hosting platform that enables you to develop server-side JavaScript business logic. Initially this system was delivered using the Java-based Rhino engine from Mozilla, but FeedHenry now uses Node, which means you can directly apply everything you have learned in this book.

 NOTE Disclaimer: I was the chief technology officer of FeedHenry from 2007 until 2010.

FeedHenry allows you to take advantage of the techniques you have learned in this book to build a mobile app using JavaScript, CSS, and HTML. Whereas Amazon is an infrastructure-as-a-service cloud offering, FeedHenry is a platform-as-a-service offering. This means that with FeedHenry, you do not need to concern yourself with the management and maintenance of your servers. Instead, the FeedHenry system looks after scaling of your apps when load increases and also ensures that your apps remain running at all times. The FeedHenry system is designed so that you only have to focus on the development of your app and don't need to worry about system administration. This means you can build and deploy apps much faster.

Of course, you have to operate within the constraints of the system, and you'll need to determine whether this strategy is appropriate for your needs. The approach is particularly powerful for developing enterprise mobile apps leveraging existing web service end points, as the FeedHenry server side can act as a security and performance management buffer between these end points and the mobile apps, through the use of intelligent caching.

Figure 11-1 shows the main app management dashboard of the FeedHenry service.

FIGURE 11-1

FeedHenry Technology

The core concept of the FeedHenry service is that you should be able to use JavaScript on both the client and the server. FeedHenry also makes sure that you can use the same API on both the client and server and that this API deliberately has a small footprint and is thus easy to learn and use.

On the client side, you can continue to use your favorite JavaScript libraries, such as jQuery and jQuery Mobile, or other libraries that you may prefer. In addition, all the examples in this book will work with FeedHenry, with only minor modifications. The FeedHenry client-side API provides an abstraction for common device and cloud functions. It is similar to the PhoneGap API, and it allows you to perform most of the device interactions you need, such as camera access.

On the server side, you can use your experience with Node to build out your business logic. FeedHenry allows you to deploy your own Node modules, using a sandbox system. You have access to a virtualized machine environment, and you do not have significant limitations on the types of modules you can use. Again, this is a design feature of the system. Because this cloud hosting feature of the FeedHenry service is based on Node, it takes advantage of an event-based architecture, which means you can build robust and high-performance services for your mobile apps. FeedHenry also provides access to a hosted MongoDB database, and you can also access external database services, such as MongoHQ.com or Amazon RDS. The FeedHenry-hosted MongoDB database gives you a high-scale, low-latency data store and is fully integrated into the API. In case you are working in an enterprise software environment, FeedHenry also offers a multi-tenancy architecture that lets you specify multiple kinds of user and access permissions.

If you decide to use the FeedHenry system, you need to consider a number of factors. It is a proprietary system, and when you take full advantage of its features, you are to a certain extent locked in. This is particularly true if you use the FeedHenry API, the cloud database, or the multi-tenancy features. The system is deliberately designed to leverage HTML5. This is great for standards compliance, but it leaves you on your own to build the entire client-side code architecture yourself. FeedHenry provides sample applications that you can clone to get started, but you must essentially start from a blank slate.

FeedHenry is oriented toward enterprise app development. This can be useful for you if you're an independent developer or small development house that has a large company as a client. It means you can rely on the FeedHenry enterprise features such as service-level agreements and 24-hour monitoring and support. If you are looking to build your own apps, you should first consider whether you really need the extensive cloud hosting features, as you will have to pay for them.

The advantages of using the FeedHenry system are that you can reuse your knowledge of HTML5, JavaScript, and CSS right away. You do not even need to learn the FeedHenry API to get started. FeedHenry has an easy-to-use build system hosted in the cloud that does all the hard work of building apps for you. Unlike Appcelerator, discussed next, FeedHenry does not require you to install separate software development kits (SDKs) from Apple or Google. Instead, you can press a button and get an app binary right away, ready for submission to the iPhone App Store and Android Marketplace.

The FeedHenry Development Environment

The primary development environment for FeedHenry is an online IDE. You can build your apps entirely in the cloud, using your web browser, without downloading or installing anything. The IDE has a main dashboard that lists all your apps, an account management area, and a documentation area. Finding your way around is quite easy.

The development area gives you an in-browser code editor, with syntax highlighting for HTML, JavaScript, and CSS. The editor struggles a little bit with very large files, but for the most part is very usable. The editor follows the traditional IDE layout, with a folder-and-file hierarchy on the left and the main code body on the right. In addition, you can see a preview of your app on the left. The FeedHenry system uses your own browser to generate a preview of your app that is fully interactive. This enables a very rapid development cycle because you can see your changes immediately. If the preview is too large, then it automatically pops out of the browser window.

With FeedHenry, you can configure the various build options for your app. In order to create app binaries that you can submit to the app stores, you need to upload your app-signing certificates. FeedHenry stores them securely for you and uses them to build your app in its cloud build system. You are thus freed from the requirement to have a local build environment. In particular, FeedHenry allows you to build iPhone apps without owning a Mac.

Because FeedHenry also offers a cloud hosting platform, it has a debugging section that allows you to review any log entries that your server-side business logic has generated. As with the client-side app development, the aim here is for you to never have to leave the browser IDE. Figure 11-2 shows the code editor area of the IDE.

FIGURE 11-2

FeedHenry is not limited to the online IDE. You can also build your apps locally, using your own development tools. FeedHenry offers a downloadable integration application that lets you manage your apps from your desktop. The integration application is also available as an Eclipse plug-in. Finally, FeedHenry offers GitHub integration (see `http://github.com`), enabling you to pull your app code directly from GitHub.

Deciding to Use FeedHenry

FeedHenry's pricing is structured for enterprise customers. FeedHenry also provides many of the ancillary services that large companies need, such as support and service guarantees.

If you need maximum flexibility, FeedHenry is also a good option. You have the same level of flexibility as if you are using PhoneGap. There are no restrictions on the client-side libraries you can include, and you can use most Node modules. You can export the full source code of your app, and you can customize it in any way you like.

Unlike some of the other services described in this chapter, FeedHenry does not provide many additional components, such as data synchronization or alerting. However, because you have a full server-side cloud hosting platform at your disposal, you can easily integrate with any third-party service that offers a web service interface. Because you can do this from either the client or the server, your integration work is very easy. Your server-side code can even expose its own mini web service API, which is very difficult to do with services that only allow you to execute code on the client.

FeedHenry offers its own analytics solution. It covers all the bases that you would expect, showing you app usage levels, active users, and device details. You can also track the interaction pathways through your app, and this helps you understand which aspects of your app interface are user friendly and which are not. There is also an option to use the Flurry analytics service.

FeedHenry offers extensive device coverage. This book focuses on the two main platforms, iPhone and Android, but FeedHenry also allows you to build apps for Windows Mobile, BlackBerry, and Nokia Web Runtime. There are some challenges supporting platforms beyond iPhone and Android in terms of HTML5 compliance and the requirement to write some platform-specific code. FeedHenry makes this much easier by allowing you to break your app into constituent files that can be customized on a per-platform basis.

USING THE APPCELERATOR PLATFORM

Appcelerator (www.appcelerator.com) was founded in 2006, and with over 1 million developers, is one of the most popular services for cross-platform mobile app development. You develop apps using JavaScript and a proprietary API. This API has the same purpose as the PhoneGap API, but it is considerably deeper and more extensive. The big idea that Appcelerator brings to the table is that you can build your app using only JavaScript — no HTML or CSS is required! Developing with Appcelerator is thus more similar to traditional user interface development, in that you use API calls to build your user interface programmatically. You specify the entire user interface using only JavaScript. If you intend to use the examples in this book on the Appcelerator platform, you will need to do two things: convert the API calls to use the Appcelerator API and replace the HTML/CSS code with user interface–building JavaScript code.

One of the other great things about Appcelerator is that it offers a fully featured IDE similar to Eclipse or Xcode, known as Appcelerator Studio. From within this IDE you can build, test, and deploy your mobile apps.

Appcelerator primarily focuses on mobile app development but also offers a number of vertical cloud modules that provide integration with social media services such as Twitter and Facebook, as well as e-commerce services such as PayPal. It gives you a ready-made software toolkit that lets you provide many commonly requested features in your apps.

When you create an account on the Appcelerator service, you are given access to an online account administration area where you can list your apps, review their analytics charts, and buy access to some of the commercial cloud modules. Figure 11-3 shows the main dashboard.

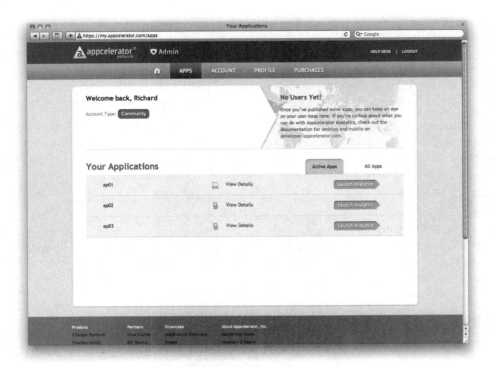

FIGURE 11-3

Appcelerator Technology

The key idea behind Appcelerator is that its JavaScript API calls native Objective-C or Java code for iPhone and Android, respectively. Your Appcelerator app executes your JavaScript code on the mobile device as normal, but the Appcelerator API uses the native device API instead of manipulating an HTML document. The advantage here is that your user interface is built using native interface controls rather than being constructed from HTML and CSS. This gives you a significant performance improvement. Of course, you are making the choice to develop your app using a proprietary API rather than the HTML5 web standard.

The Appcelerator API is extensive and covers everything covered by the PhoneGap project. In the last few chapters, you used the PhoneGap project to build the LifeStream app as a native app. You will find that the Appcelerator API, while different, has a similar feel and set of concepts to PhoneGap. In addition, the Appcelerator API provides other functions, such as Facebook integration, mapping support, and finer-grained access to device capabilities. As a strategic move to gain developer adoption, Appcelerator has made its API open source. You are not limited to the functions Appcelerator provides. You can also use Objective-C or Java to write your own extensions in much the same way as you write plug-ins with PhoneGap.

Unlike FeedHenry, Appcelerator does not provide a cloud hosting service and does not enable you to run your server-side app code in its own cloud. Instead, you have to use a third-party service to do this. The Appcelerator Studio IDE has good integrated support for a number of the major cloud app hosting services. The only problem is that you will have to write your server-side code in Ruby or PHP, rather than JavaScript. As Node app hosting services go mainstream, this should become less of an issue.

Appcelerator provides better performance than embedded HTML due to the fact that its operation is more like that of a native app. The company has also made it really easy to develop apps based on common use cases, such as social media integration or data synchronization, by offering vertical modules inside the API that take care of these functions. It is thus very easy to get started building apps. The excellent IDE also makes development very easy and fluid. The company seems to have considerable momentum behind it and regularly releases updates with expanded features.

Appcelerator does have some disadvantages. There is a long-term industry trend toward HTML5. While you can use HTML5 with Appcelerator by embedding a `WebView` control, doing so negates almost all the advantages of the platform. When you use Appcelerator, you rely on a proprietary API. This API is comprehensive and well designed, but you must nonetheless place a bet on the success of the Appcelerator company rather than the Appcelerator technology. Although the development environment is very easy to use, it has a slow development cycle. In order to test your app, you must build it using the iPhone or Android SDK, and you have to install this alongside the Appcelerator IDE. This introduces an inevitable delay in your code–test–debug work cycle. The lack of support for general-purpose server-side code hosted in the cloud means that you must rely on yet another third party to fully deliver your app. Remember that most apps are not stand-alone but require some level of server-side business logic. Finally, of the three mobile app development platforms covered in this chapter, Appcelerator is the only one that requires you to extensively modify your code from the examples in this book.

The Appcelerator Development Environment

The Appcelerator IDE, called Titanium Studio, is similar to Eclipse. The IDE follows the standard convention of having a tree-based list of your files on the left, the main editor page in the middle, and a console with output at the bottom. You can launch your apps directly by clicking the Run button. You then choose whether to run an Android or iPhone app. You can run an app using an emulator or install it on a device. You can even build release versions and deploy your apps directly to the app stores. This is all very seamless and a really frictionless experience. The development environment offers integration with third-party cloud services such as Heroku, which makes life slightly easier when there is a cloud-hosted server-side component to your app, even if you have to write the business logic in Ruby! Figure 11-4 shows the IDE layout.

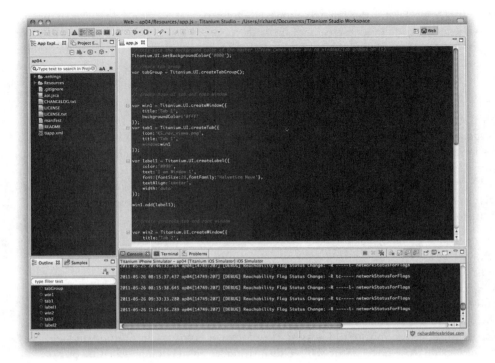

FIGURE 11-4

If you develop apps using Appcelerator, you have to commit yourself to learning the Appcelerator API. This investment of your time makes sense when you can also make use of the additional services that Appcelerator provides. The basic package from Appcelerator is free. However, you have to pay to use the more advanced vertical cloud modules, such as e-commerce integration. When these features are things that you need to build and deploy quickly for a client, using Appcelerator can really help.

Deciding to Use Appcelerator

Appcelerator uses a feature level–based pricing model that is common to many online services. The prices range from free to a few hundred dollars per month. As with FeedHenry, there is also an enterprise pricing structure, which includes professional services. The differences between the options are laid out in an easy-to-understand table at www.appcelerator.com/products/plans-pricing. The price differences are mostly driven by the different types of vertical modules and ancillary services.

Using Appcelerator is not as immediately flexible as using an approach based directly on HTML5. To customize the Appcelerator solution, you need to be able to code in Objective-C or Java. It is not enough to have HTML, CSS, and JavaScript knowledge. On the other hand, because Appcelerator uses native user interface controls and ultimately has access to the native capabilities of the device, your app can have a far more native feel than HTML5-based apps.

Appcelerator provides a basic HTTP client as part of the API that you can use to integrate with third-party web services. The calls to a web service must take place from the device, unlike with FeedHenry, where calls can happen both from the device and from the FeedHenry cloud. Appcelerator does not provide any additional support for third-party integration, and you may find that you need to do more work on the server yourself. The Appcelerator API does provide support for the JSON and XML data formats, which makes web service integration easier.

Appcelerator provides an in-house analytics solution that lets you track how your users are interacting with your app. As well as the standard mobile app analytics, such as device type, session duration, and usage levels, you can also track custom events. The analytics element of the Appcelerator service is quite comprehensive, and while not real-time, is certainly competitive with focused offerings such as Flurry.

In terms of device coverage, Appcelerator focuses on iPhone and Android. This means you cannot as yet build applications of the same quality for other platforms, such as Windows Mobile or BlackBerry. You have to carefully consider the user base for your app as you determine whether Appcelerator is the right app platform for you. If you are an independent developer building a game or utility app, and primarily targeting the Apple App Store and Android Marketplace, then Appcelerator is certainly suitable. If you work for a large company and need to build an app that offers access to your services from a wide range of devices, then Appcelerator may be only part of your solution, and you may need to consider other options for supporting less popular platforms.

USING THE APPMOBI PLATFORM

appMobi (www.appmobi.com) grew out of the efforts of a mobile consulting company to streamline its cross-platform mobile app development efforts. Founded in 2006, appMobi is the end result of a large amount of work developing high-end mobile media applications using HTML5. As a result, the appMobi system is also quite suitable for game development, and the company promotes game development using JavaScript game engines such as ImpactJS and LimeJS. The underlying approach is the same as FeedHenry, using HTML5 to build the user interface, and it provides a JavaScript API for accessing device capabilities. Unlike FeedHenry, but like Appcelerator, appMobi opts for vertical cloud components rather than a general-purpose cloud hosting solution for your server-side business logic. Unlike both of the other services, appMobi does not offer an IDE, as such, but rather has an in-browser app development kit that includes a full-featured test and emulation environment.

As with FeedHenry, the appMobi service builds binary versions of your apps on its servers. This frees you from the requirement to install the iPhone and Android SDKs, which is something that Appcelerator does require. As with the two other platforms, appMobi provides an online account management interface, where you can control your apps and services. Figure 11-5 shows the main dashboard.

FIGURE 11-5

appMobi Technology

In terms of API complexity, appMobi is more complex than the small-footprint FeedHenry, but it is less complex than the Appcelerator kitchen-sink strategy. The API is quite similar to the PhoneGap API, so you should not have too much trouble finding your way around. appMobi takes the more common cross-platform approach of using HTML, CSS, and JavaScript to building apps. This means that, as with FeedHenry, you can reuse most of the code examples from this book.

Like Appcelerator, appMobi offers a suite of cloud services, such as e-commerce integration, push notifications, and analytics. It also provides an interesting service that can auto-update your app by downloading new versions of the static assets. While this is probably not entirely compatible with the Apple developer agreement, which prohibits apps from making drastic post-installation changes, it is certainly a great feature for your Android apps.

The appMobi API contains a fantastic augmented-reality feature. It allows you to show a live feed from the device camera and overlay your own interface elements. This is quite unique in the world of HTML5 apps. If you need an augmented-reality feature, than appMobi is definitely the way to go.

The core benefit of the appMobi approach is that with it, you are building on a standardized technology: HTML5. The appMobi API is quite comprehensive and offers good coverage of device capabilities, such as camera and file system access. Your development code–test–debug work cycle is streamlined because you can test directly in the browser. The appMobi solution has integrated design and a very consistent feel. It gets out of your way and allows you to concentrate on building apps.

The downside to appMobi, as with Appcelerator, is that you must find your own cloud hosting solution for your server-side business logic. While appMobi does provide a number of vertical cloud modules, you still need to use third-party services to build the server-side business logic of the service your mobile app provides. The reliance on HTML5, as with FeedHenry, also has the downside that you must create the user interface of your app yourself. Whereas Appcelerator provides an API for constructing the user interface, when you use HTML5, you must build the interface manually and rely on third-party libraries such as jQuery Mobile for help.

The appMobi Development Environment

You develop apps for appMobi by using your existing code editor and HTML development tools. Unlike with FeedHenry and Appcelerator, there is no appMobi-specific code editor or IDE. However, appMobi does provide you with a downloadable SDK that runs inside your web browser. This is actually a lot more useful than it sounds, and appMobi has built a really great tool. This SDK, known as appMobi XDK, provides an environment to test, manage, and deploy your apps. The app-testing capabilities of the XDK environment far exceed those of appMobi's competitors. For example, you can specify device context, such as orientation in three-dimensional space, geolocation, and network connectivity characteristics. These test capabilities are more advanced than those provided by the native Xcode and Android emulators. If you are building an app that is heavily reliant on environmental context, then the appMobi XDK will almost certainly allow you to develop your app more rapidly. Figure 11-6 shows the XDK main screen.

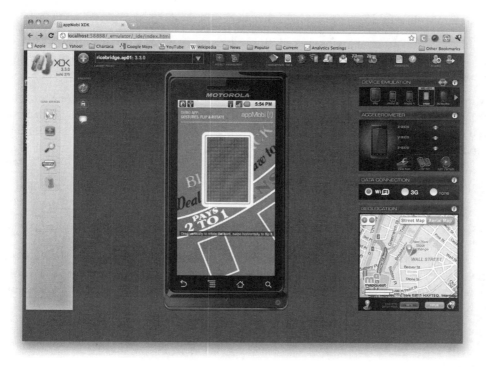

FIGURE 11-6

You need to use your existing development tools when developing on the appMobi platform. Depending on your perspective, this could be a considered an advantage. On the other hand, more integrated environments allow you to manage your entire development process in one place, which can be more efficient. The XDK runs inside a desktop browser, which means very quick turnaround times when testing and debugging. You can also use the built-in browser debugging tools, such as the browser's Developer Console.

Deciding to Use appMobi

The pricing structure for appMobi is based on the concept of resource "blocks," for which you pay a few dollars each per month. Each block buys you a certain amount of capacity — whether bandwidth, storage, log entries, or other resources specific to the particular type of block. This pricing model can become quite expensive under high-volume usage but is suitable if you are a freelance developer with a smaller user base. The appMobi service in general has much less of an enterprise focus than the other two services discussed in this chapter.

The code underlying the appMobi device API is not open source. This means you have less insight into how the system works and less flexibility to tweak it to your needs. However, appMobi does provide a plug-in architecture so that you can extend your apps with native iPhone and Android components if you know Objective-C or Java.

To integrate with third-party cloud services, you need to write your own code to talk to their APIs. In most cases, this means you need to include jQuery or a similar library in your app to make HTTP calls easier. The appMobi API does not provide convenience methods for this purpose.

While appMobi does provide an analytics feature, it is relatively limited. The service allows you to create log entries that you can export. It does not provide a dashboard or summary view of the data. You can log custom events, but you have to parse them out of the log entries yourself.

The primary devices covered by the appMobi platform are iPhone and Android. The appMobi cloud services are also accessible from native apps, including BlackBerry apps. However, this is not very useful for web developers building mobile apps. For practical purposes, you can only build iPhone or Android apps using HTML5 on appMobi.

SUMMARY

This chapter covers the three leading JavaScript-based mobile app development services. It explores the advantages and disadvantages of each service, and you gained an understanding of the capabilities of each platform. You should now be in a position to decide the best strategy for building your next app — whether you need to opt for a lower-level service such as Amazon that gives you more control or whether to make use of prebuilt components and hosting from one of the companies discussed in this chapter.

In the next chapter, you'll learn how to use social media services to enhance the user experience and usefulness of your app. You'll also learn how to introduce viral elements into your app, which can be useful for promotional purposes.

▶ **WHAT YOU LEARNED IN THIS CHAPTER**

TOPIC	KEY CONCEPTS
Cloud service types	The term *cloud development service* covers a wide range of online services and offerings. It is useful to break these down into three broad categories: services that provide infrastructure, services that provide a software platform, and services that provide a vertical user-oriented online service. The key differences are in the level of effort you need to expend to configure and maintain the different kinds of services and the level of customization that you can achieve.
Vertical cloud services	Cloud development service providers often deliver their services as discrete modules of functionality, with different pricing models. These functional modules address various vertical business requirements, such as e-commerce or analytics. Cloud development service providers allow you to pick and choose the set of modules that you need for each app. The benefit is that you do not need to develop the functionality that the module provides, and you don't need to provision the storage or computation resources required.
FeedHenry.com	The FeedHenry mobile cloud service offers a full cloud environment for building mobile apps using HTML5. FeedHenry also offers a server-side code execution platform so you can run your entire service from within FeedHenry. This service is targeted more at enterprise developers and may be suitable if you have a large client.
Appcelerator.com	The Appcelerator service allows you to build mobile apps for iPhone and Android against native user interface components using JavaScript. This is done by providing you with an extensive proprietary API. Appcelerator does not have a general-purpose cloud hosting facility, but it does offer cloud modules to integrate with social media.
appMobi.com	The appMobi environment is very suitable for game development, and this is a quality they promote. While the service does not provide an IDE, it does provide a comprehensive in-browser simulation environment.

12

Going Social!

- ➤ Understanding the Twitter REST API
- ➤ Using the Twitter developer console
- ➤ Using an App Design Process
- ➤ Understanding use case analysis
- ➤ Organizing your code
- ➤ Drawing wire frames
- ➤ Analyzing object dependencies
- ➤ Implementing client-only OAuth
- ➤ Making OAuth API calls
- ➤ Using events to keep your code clean

Social media sites such as Twitter, Facebook, LinkedIn, and even Google are an essential part of the cloud. You need to understand how to use these social cloud services and how to integrate their APIs into your apps. This chapter shows you how to build a social media mobile app.

As with the Amazon API, the APIs provided by the social media sites are large and extensive, and they could fill books all by themselves. This chapter uses the Twitter social media site, http://twitter.com, as the basis for building an app that interacts with social media sites. It assumes that you are familiar with the basic features of Twitter. If you're not, you should register an account and play around a bit.

The Twitter API is a REST-based HTTP API that uses the JSON data format. You have been well prepared by the earlier chapters in this book to deal with this API, and you will find yourself in familiar territory. This chapter focuses on a subset of the Twitter API so that you can examine the implementation of the API integration rather than struggle to learn the details of the API.

In this chapter, you'll build an app to manage your Twitter direct messages. This is especially useful if you have multiple Twitter accounts — and as a developer, you'll likely end up with more than one.

The app you're going to build will be able to sign you in to Twitter, using the OAuth protocol. It will also enable you to get a list of the direct messages you have received and sent. And it will provide you with a list of your followers so you can select people to send new direct messages to.

As you build the app in this chapter, you'll face some challenges. For example, it's expensive running a cloud server; can you build a completely stand-alone app? How will you implement OAuth? Twitter is great, but eventually you'll want to support other social networking sites as well. How can you structure the code for your app so that it is easy to extend without resulting in spaghetti code? This chapter will show you how to deal with these challenges.

Note that the code base for the app in this chapter is pretty big. So far, this book has provided the complete code for all examples and apps. That just isn't possible with this chapter's app; there's too much code to print it all. However, it is all available for download. You should make sure to download the full source so that you can understand the code fully. This chapter does present snippets of the code to help you follow the logic of the code for this app.

Finally, this chapter assumes that you can launch and deploy apps to your device without too much trouble. Review Chapters 9 and 10 if you need some help with this.

USING THE TWITTER API

The Twitter API is one of the easiest social media site APIs to use. It is a well-designed and logical API, and it is thus easy to understand. The part of the API that you will use in this chapter is the HTTP REST interface. Remember from Chapter 6 that REST stands for Representation State Transfer. A REST API allows you to query the state of various logical entities, as defined by the server. Because REST uses the HTTP verbs GET, PUT, POST, and DELETE to communicate changes in the state of these entities, you already know how to interact with the API!

You still need to learn what the Twitter entities are. As you might guess, there are entities for tweets, users, direct messages, and so forth. In the next section, you'll take a look at the most useful ones.

Twitter provides extensive developer documentation at http://dev.twitter.com. As you work through this chapter, you can cross-reference the code and discussion with the official Twitter documentation to get a deeper understanding of how the app in this chapter is implemented.

Another resource you'll find helpful is http://stackoverflow.com. If you have a question about the Twitter API, you'll almost certainly find a good answer there.

For many requests, the Twitter API requires you to authenticate your requests by using OAuth. This means you need to get the user of your app to complete an OAuth sign-in process, and then you need to store the resulting access token. You use this token to cryptographically sign HTTP requests to the API.

NOTE *OAuth introduces quite a bit of complexity, and it can make debugging much more difficult. Review the introduction to the OAuth protocol in Chapter 8 if you need a reminder of how it works.*

To give you a taste for the API, here is an example request:

```
http://api.twitter.com/1/account/verify_credentials.json
```

This request gets the details of the current user. You can use it to get some information about the user of your app, such as his or her Twitter username and avatar image. When you execute this request as an HTTP GET, the Twitter API responds with the following JSON:

```
{
    "notifications": false,
    "profile_text_color": "333333",
    "protected": false,
    "profile_image_url_https": "https://si0.twimg.com/...png",
    "profile_sidebar_fill_color": "DDEEF6",
    "location": null,
    "name": "tonvo",
    "contributors_enabled": false,
    "statuses_count": 0,
    "profile_background_tile": false,
    "default_profile_image": true,
    "utc_offset": null,
    "url": null,
    "id_str": "308459527",
    "following": false,
    "verified": false,
    "favourites_count": 0,
    "profile_link_color": "0084B4",
    "description": null,
    "is_translator": false,
    "created_at": "Tue May 31 13:08:27 +0000 2011",
    "profile_sidebar_border_color": "C0DEED",
    "default_profile": true,
    "follow_request_sent": false,
    "time_zone": null,
    "friends_count": 4,
    "profile_image_url": "http://a0.twimg.com/...png",
    "profile_use_background_image": true,
    "id": 308459527,
    "profile_background_color": "C0DEED",
    "followers_count": 2,
    "screen_name": "tonvo",
    "profile_background_image_url": "http://a0.twimg.com/i.../bg.png",
    "show_all_inline_media": false,
    "listed_count": 0,
    "lang": "en",
    "geo_enabled": false,
    "profile_background_image_url_https": "https://si0.twimg.com/i.../bg.png"
}
```

The following are some of the most interesting fields in this JSON:

- ➤ **id_str** — This is the user's unique identifier.
- ➤ **profile_image_url** — This is the URL of the user's avatar image.
- ➤ **screen_name** — This is the user's Twitter username.

You can see that there is a lot of other data here, but for now, you can ignore all the fields that are not relevant to the functionality you are trying to build.

 WARNING When using JavaScript to work with the Twitter API, always use the id_str field rather than the plain integer id field, as the Twitter ID numbers are too large for JavaScript, and the values will be corrupted.

Working with the Twitter API Usage Limits

The Twitter API is free to use, but with a few restrictions. You need to make sure to follow the "Developer Rules of the Road," as defined by Twitter: https://dev.twitter.com/terms/api-terms. In particular, Twitter does not recommend building yet another Twitter client; rather, it suggests using the Twitter API to extend and enhance existing services.

The API also imposes rate limits. If you try to process too many requests too quickly, the Twitter API will block you. This is not normally an issue when you are building mobile apps that are used by only one user, as each user will get his or her own limit. Be careful with infinite loop bugs, though: If you don't kill the app quickly, you will burn up your request quota! If you are building a server-side component, it can be easy to run up against the limits, and you need to be careful. For the most up-to-date details on rate limiting and to get the specific limit numbers, visit https://dev.twitter.com/docs/rate-limiting.

Using the Entities that the Twitter API Exposes

In order to get an understanding of what is possible with the Twitter API, you need to be familiar with the major logical entities that it exposes. Twitter uses the word "entity" to refer to the individual elements of their feature set, rather than referring to database tables in their system. This section gives you a brief overview of the most useful entities. Each entity has a number of qualifiers that focus on different aspects of the entity. For example, a GET request on /lists/members returns the users in one of your Twitter lists. This is a query on the lists entity, with the members qualifier. You can also add optional parameters to the end of a request; for example, you can add count=100 to return exactly 100 items.

You'll find that most Twitter API requests follow this pattern:

```
/entity/qualifier?optional=parameters
```

These are the major entities in the Twitter API:

- ➤ **statuses** — Tweets and lists of tweets
- ➤ **direct_messages** — Direct messages to and from your account
- ➤ **followers** — Everyone following you
- ➤ **friends** — Everyone you follow
- ➤ **friendships** — Your relationships with other users
- ➤ **users** — Details about users
- ➤ **favorites** — Tweets you have favorited
- ➤ **lists** — Lists of users that you have defined
- ➤ **account** — Details about your account
- ➤ **trends** — Current hot topics on Twitter

Each of these entities will have one or more qualifiers.

There are a few more minor entities, and the API is occasionally extended with new entities. Twitter also provides a search API that has both a REST version and a streaming version. The search API is not used in this book, but you can find all the details on the Twitter developer site.

The Parts You Need

The app that you'll build in this chapter is a direct message manager. To implement the app, you need to access the `direct_messages` entity to send and receive direct messages. You also need the `account` entity to get the details of the user of the app so that you can display the user's avatar. These tasks are both pretty easy.

Getting the list of followers of the user is a little trickier. Although the `followers` entity provides this information, it does so by giving you a list of identifiers only. What you really need is the username and avatar of each user. To simplify the code for this example, you use the `statuses` entity with the `followers` qualifier. This gives you the list of your followers' most recent tweets and includes the followers' details.

To get the 100 most recent direct messages sent to you, you use this:

```
GET http://api.twitter.com/1/direct_messages.json?count=100
```

This returns a JSON array, each element of which contains the full details of each message. The parts you'll use are highlighted in the following example:

```
[
    {
        "sender_id": 20696610,
        "text": "t4",
        "id_str": "3486849671",
        "recipient": {
            ...
        },
```

```
        "created_at": "Mon Jul 11 01:39:34 +0000 2011",
        "recipient_id": 308459527,
        "sender_screen_name": "rjrodger",
        "sender": {
          ...
        },
        "recipient_screen_name": "tonvo",
        "id": 3486849671
      },
      ...
    ]
```

The text field is the text of the message. id_str is a unique identifier for the message. sender_screen_name and recipient_screen_name are the sending and receiving Twitter usernames, respectively. The created_at field contains the date and time of the message. It's not a common date format, and it can't be parsed directly by JavaScript. You'll see later in this chapter how to deal with it.

To get the 100 most recent direct messages that you sent to others, you use the sent qualifier:

```
GET http://api.twitter.com/1/direct_messages/sent.json?count=100
```

The JSON returned is in the same format you saw earlier in this chapter.

To send a message, you use this:

```
POST http://api.twitter.com/1/direct_messages/new.json
{"screen_name":"<recipient>", "text":" ... message text ... "}
```

In this case, you use an HTTP POST verb because you are modifying an entity on the server.

To get the user's username and avatar, you use this:

```
GET http://api.twitter.com/1/account/verify_credentials.json
```

You've already seen this one: It is the first example of the Twitter API shown in the previous section.

Finally, to get your followers, you use this:

```
GET http://api.twitter.com/1/statuses/followers.json
```

If you have a large number of followers, you will need to page through the results and make further requests to get each subset of the full list. You do this by checking for a next_cursor field in the returned JSON result. If it is not zero, then there are more results, and you must resubmit the same request, including the cursor parameter set to the value of next_cursor:

```
GET http://api.twitter.com/1/statuses/followers.json?cursor=next_cursor
```

You will see how to implement this shortly.

When you develop against an HTTP API, you can normally test the API by manually sending requests using the curl command-line utility or even just typing the full request URL into a browser. This manual interaction is much more difficult with an OAuth API, where each request needs a digital signature.

The solution is to use an API console. This is an application or a service that performs all the OAuth for you but still lets you manually type in requests and see the results. The official desktop client for Twitter on the Mac includes a built-in API console. The following example shows you how to use it.

If you are on a PC, you can still follow this example. You can use the Apigee API console service instead (see `http://apigee.com`) — and just ignore the Mac stuff. The user interface is very similar to that of the Twitter client. The Apigee service covers many social media sites, not just Twitter, so it is useful regardless of your development platform.

There's one more thing you need to make this example work: a registered Twitter app. You created one in Chapter 8 for the Lifestream app. If you need to register a new app, you should head over to `http://dev.twitter.com` and click the Create an App link there.

It's time to get your hands dirty! In the following example, you'll try actually using the API.

 NOTE *The direct messaging app used as an example in this chapter requires the Direct Message Read/Write permission. Make sure this check box is selected on the Create an App form when you go to create an app on* `http://dev.twitter.com.`

TRY IT OUT Using the Developer Console

In this example, you'll get a taste of using the developer console. Follow these steps:

1. Install the official Twitter desktop app on your Mac. Do this by opening the desktop Apple App Store and searching for "twitter." The Twitter app is free. You'll know you have the right one when you see the official Twitter bird logo. Once the app is installed, log in with your Twitter user account.

2. Visit `http://dev.twitter.com`, click on your username at the top, and select My Applications. You see a list of your registered applications. Select one or create a new one.

3. On the Details tab for your app, make a note of the Consumer Key and Secret settings, as well as the Access Token and Secret settings.

4. Open the Preferences pane of your Twitter desktop app by selecting Twitter ➪ Preferences.

5. Select the Developer tab. Select the Show Developer Menu check box.

6. On the Developer tab, enter the four values from step 3 for Consumer Key, Secret, Access Token, and Secret. These are all required for OAuth to work.

7. Select Develop ➪ Console. An API console window opens.

8. From the tree menu on the left, choose Direct Messages ➪ Direct Messages. The address bar at the top of the window displays the following:

```
http://api.twitter.com/1/direct_messages.json
```

9. Ensure that the Authenticated option is selected on the leftmost drop-down menu beside the address bar. The HTTP method should be GET.

10. Click in the address bar and press the Return key. The HTTP request is made to the Twitter API, and you should see a result similar to what's shown in Figure 12-1.

FIGURE 12-1

How It Works

The API console performs the OAuth signature generation for you. When you specify a request, the API console creates a valid `Authorization` header and sends that along with your request. To see this, you can use the Wireshark utility (see Chapter 8) to spy on the HTTP request and response from Twitter.

Try out the various entities in the Twitter API to see what happens when you make requests. In particular, try out the entities that you need to implement the direct messaging app. You can cut and paste them directly into the address bar:

```
http://api.twitter.com/1/account/verify_credentials.json
http://api.twitter.com/1/direct_messages.json
http://api.twitter.com/1/direct_messages/sent.json
http://api.twitter.com/1/statuses/followers.json
```

When you develop your own Twitter apps, the console keeps you sane. In your darkest moments of OAuth debugging, you can break out the console and verify that everything works as it should. You can even paste in the exact keys that you are using, and with Wireshark, you can validate your OAuth signatures by comparing the requests you send with the ones the Twitter app sends.

AN APP FOR DIRECT MESSAGES

It is very likely that you'll end up with more than one Twitter account. You'll create testing accounts. You'll create accounts for clients. You'll create accounts for your open source projects and experiments. If you use any of these accounts to interact with other Twitter users, you'll soon end up having to deal with direct messages spread over a number of accounts. Logging in and out of multiple Twitter accounts to check for direct messages becomes a hassle pretty quickly.

You can write a mobile app to solve this problem! Scratching your own itch may just be the best thing about being a developer. In this chapter, you'll build an app that lets you check direct messages from multiple Twitter accounts. But unlike the apps in previous chapters, this app will also be good enough to submit to the Apple App Store and Android Marketplace — which you'll do in Chapter 13.

To build an app of sufficient quality to make it through an app store review process and that you can be proud to put your name to, you need to use a rigorous approach to designing and building the app. You need to get the user interaction model right so that the app is user friendly and easy to use. It should be obvious what to do from the moment the user launches your app. This section takes you through a design and implementation process that will help you get there. You can also use this approach when building apps for your clients or employer.

The direct message helper app you're about to build is called tonvo — a combination of the words *Twitter* and *conversation*. The app lets you do the following:

- ➤ Log in with multiple Twitter accounts
- ➤ Send and receive direct messages
- ➤ See your list of followers (the people you can directly message)

In the next sections, you'll begin to design the app.

The Design Process

The idea of *use case analysis* is a good place to start building your app. A use case describes how someone achieves a goal with software. In the case of the tonvo app, that someone is the user. To build a use case, you first describe the goal and then, in a few short sentences, how that goal is achieved. The use cases are not meant to be a specification but to guide you in developing an app. They help you see what you need to change as you get more feedback from building the app. They are also useful as a communication tool with nontechnical clients.

Tables 12-1 through 12-5 list the use cases for the tonvo app. As you can see, the idea is to keep them short and sweet.

TABLE 12-1: Register Account Use Case

USE CASE	DESCRIPTION
Name	Register Account
Actor	App user
Goal	Log in with Twitter multiple times
How	When the app first launches, there is a Sign In with Twitter button. Click the button, and you can log in with Twitter, using the OAuth process. Once you have authorized the app, your account is registered and stored by the app. You can do this more than once, and a list of your registered Twitter accounts is shown.

TABLE 12-2: Select Follower to Direct Message Use Case

USE CASE	DESCRIPTION
Name	Select Follower to Direct Message
Actor	App user
Goal	Send a direct message to a particular person
How	You are given a list of your followers for each account that you have registered. You can choose a follower to send a direct message to.

TABLE 12-3: View Inbox Use Case

USE CASE	DESCRIPTION
Name	View Inbox
Actor	App user
Goal	Get a list of your most recent direct messages
How	As with an email account, you can see your most recent direct messages, ordered by date. You can tap a message to reply.

TABLE 12-4: Conversation Use Case

USE CASE	DESCRIPTION
Name	Conversation
Actor	App user
Goal	Have a conversation with one of your followers by direct message
How	You can see the history of direct messages between you and a particular follower. You can type in a new message and send it to that person.

TABLE 12-5: Get Updates Use Case

USE CASE	DESCRIPTION
Name	Get Updates
Actor	App user
Goal	Check for new messages and new followers
How	The app does not refresh automatically because that could result in higher bandwidth charges on a cellular network. Instead, you can choose to check for new messages and followers by using the pull-down gesture you use in the official Twitter app. This gesture works as follows: If you are at the top of your inbox and you pull down with your finger, the app starts a refresh operation and puts a "refreshing" message at the top of the inbox. This message disappears when the refresh is complete.

Once you have your use case analysis complete (as well as agreement from your client, if you're developing for someone else), you can move to the next phase of the design process: developing the user flow.

The user flow describes how the user moves between the different page views of the app. To develop the flow, you need to decide what the major page views are and how the transitions between them work. Because the mobile device screen is small, you need to organize your page views into a hierarchy. Getting the structure of this hierarchy right is an important part of making your app easy to use.

The use case analysis helps you identify potential page views:

➤ **Accounts view** — The Register Account use case suggests an Accounts view for the sign-in button and the list of accounts.

➤ **OAuth Sign-in view** — Because the app uses OAuth, there will also be an external view — the Twitter sign-in page (which you can call OAuth Sign-in).

➤ **People view** — The Select Follower to Direct Message use case suggests a page view showing a list of followers — that is, a People view.

➤ **Inbox view** — The View Inbox use case must surely be represented by an Inbox view.

➤ **Conversation view** — Finally, the Conversation use case needs a view for individual one-on-one conversations; you can call this the Conversation view.

Developing views based on the use cases requires a lot of thought and several iterations. It may look like I got it right for this app the first time, but trust me, that is not the case!

Once you have the views, you can define the transitions between them. Again, the use cases provide you with direction. It seems clear that the user needs to be able to go from the Inbox and People views to the Conversation view and that the Conversation view is at a lower level of the hierarchy because you can reach it only by selecting either a person or a message. This means that while the Inbox and People views can have top-level navigation items, the Conversation view cannot have these items. The Accounts view will also need a top-level navigation item, while the OAuth Sign-in view is definitely a sublevel of the Accounts hierarchy. Figure 12-2 diagrams this. The arrows in the figure show the major view transitions.

View Interaction Model

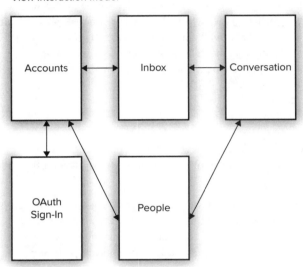

FIGURE 12-2

Once you have the user flow in place, the next step is to create a wire frame for review by your client (or yourself). A wire frame is a visual communication of the appearance and functionality of the app. A wire frame should show, in rough outline, the position of user interface elements. It should also provide a mini storyboard of the user interaction model. Wire frames are very useful for confirming your understanding of an app's requirements. They often shed light on things you have not previously considered. You should consider it a success if you need to iterate on your wire frames a few times to incorporate client feedback. Doing so is much easier than recoding.

> **TIP** Don't use "realistic" wire frames. Nontechnical clients are likely to look at a realistic wire frame and assume that because it "looks" finished, it is. They will not understand why you need to spend another couple of weeks coding. Keep your wire frames as ugly as possible.

One of the best wire framing tools, especially for apps, is the Balsamiq wire framing application. Free and commercial versions are available from `http://balsamiq.com`. Figure 12-3 shows a set of wire frames created using Balsamiq that reflect the use case analysis for the tonvo app. It shows a wire frame of the four main views in the app, including the key user interface elements and how they are positioned relative to each other. Balsamiq allows you to annotate your wire frames with "sticky notes," which helps convey context-specific points. In a wire frame, you can use arrows to show how tapping on one element moves the user from one view to another.

FIGURE 12-3

TIP *It is good idea to print out your wire frames if you are bringing them to a meeting with a client because the physicality of the design on paper will help bring it to life for your client. You can also shuffle the pages to simulate view transitions. This helps to communicate the view hierarchy.*

The wire frame images in Figure 12-3 are very clearly wire frames. The lines look hand-drawn, and the images are just outlines. The informality of the presentation is important because it conveys flexibility. At this stage, it is easy and inexpensive to experiment with different designs, interactions models, and layout positioning.

Getting the Hygiene Factors Right

Building a production-quality app requires you to deal with a large code base. The apps that you have seen in this book so far, even the Lifestream app, are smaller than most of the apps you will build professionally. Commercial apps need to consider all the edge cases, platform differences, and minor client requirements. It's important to approach the code in the right way to manage such large code bases.

The key to building and maintaining software is organizing the code properly. If you can find the right way to break the system into modules, understand the interactions between the modules, and allow scope for new features, then you can achieve high levels of software development productivity.

NOTE *One subject that this book does not cover is continuous integration and testing. These subjects are vitally important, but this book simply doesn't have space to cover everything. If you decide to build apps for a living or need to maintain a suite of apps for your clients or employer, then you will need to put in place a testing system. Ideally, you will have a set of unit tests, acceptance tests, and a build server to run them. The Jasmine testing framework is particularly good:* `http://pivotal.github.com/jasmine`. *So is the Jenkins continuous integration server:* `http://jenkins-ci.org`.

For most of your apps, you will find that there is a core set of functions and common code that you will always need. This code covers things like configuration, user messages, logging and error handling, and network requests. These types of common functionalities are known as *hygiene factors* because you always have to have them.

You can easily recognize hygiene factors because they tend to be orthogonal to the rest of your app, in that it is difficult to assign them to any particular object or module. For example, you use logging all over the place. The best thing to do is place them in their own "utility" module. This module ends up being a motley collection of unrelated code, but it gives you a default place for functions that don't have anywhere else to live. Instead of polluting your global namespace with random function names, you can isolate them inside a single namespace.

NOTE *Namespacing is a useful and easy strategy for code organization. Any time you find yourself with the possibility of the names of things like variables conflicting with each other, or when you have different kinds of things in the one global namespace, explicit namespacing can help you future-proof your code against maintenance problems. You can put all the objects or things that are similar into the same namespace. A namespace can be a containing object, a module, or even just a suitable prefix string. There is very little downside to creating a namespace. If in doubt, you can just use a new one!*

The tonvo app has three namespaces:

➤ The `util` object contains utility functions.

➤ The `conf` object contains configuration settings.

➤ The `text` object contains user interface messages.

In JavaScript it is common to use objects in this way to define namespaces.

In the tonvo app, all the code is placed inside the `tonvo.js` file. The utility code covering the hygiene factors is placed at the top of this file, before any app-specific business logic. The full source code for this app is too long to list in its entirety here; you should download the code so that you can review it fully. The downloadable code includes several variations of the `tonvo.js` file, each containing more and more of the complete code of the app. The smaller versions (with code removed), allow you to focus on specific elements of the design, as an aid to understanding.

Here is the configuration code for the app:

Available for
download on
Wrox.com

```
// Configuration

var conf = {
  network: {
    twitter: {
      key:'YOUR_TWITTER_KEY',
      secret:'YOUR_TWITTER_SECRET',
      authorizeurl:'https://api.twitter.com/oauth/authorize',
      requesturl:'http://api.twitter.com/oauth/request_token',
      accessurl:'http://api.twitter.com/oauth/access_token',
      apibaseurl:'http://api.twitter.com/1/'
    }
  }
}

var text = {
  netfail: 'Network request failed. Please try again.',
  netfailtitle: 'Network Error',
  close: 'Close',
  authfail: 'Sign in request failed. Please try again.',
  authfailtitle: 'Sign In Error'
}

...
```

code snippet tonvo/tonvo-struct.js

This is just a simple JSON data structure, mostly holding OAuth settings. The structure allows you to add other social media networks later, so that in addition to referencing `conf.network.twitter`, you could also have `conf.network.facebook` or `conf.network.linkedin`.

Next up is the initialization code for the app. This code sets up the app objects. It is a good idea to make sure you can easily run your app in the desktop Safari browser, as this is a good environment for development and debugging. However, on desktop Safari, you don't have access to the PhoneGap

API, so the `deviceready` event will never fire. (Jump back to Chapters 9 and 10 if you need a reminder of how PhoneGap works.) Therefore, when debugging in the desktop Safari browser, you need to explicitly call your `init` function to kick-start the app, as shown highlighted here:

```
...
// Initialization

var app = null

document.addEventListener("deviceready", init)

function init() {
  app = new App()
}

$(function(){

  // call init() explicitly if not on a device
  if( !/iPad|iPhone|Android/.test(navigator.userAgent) ) {
    init()
  }
})
...
```

code snippet tonvo/tonvo-struct.js

Now you need all the utility functions. Each of these functions is short and readily understandable. You'll recognize most of this code from earlier chapters. Each function has a comment explaining what it does:

```
...
// Utility

var util = {}

// inject text into sub elements using CSS classnames
util.text = function(elem,textmap) {
  if( elem ) {
    for( var classname in textmap ) {
      elem.find('.'+classname).text(textmap[classname])
    }
  }
}

// log debugging messages to the console
util.log = function() {
  console && console.log( Array.prototype.slice.call(arguments) )
}


// localStorage helper functions
```

```
util.cache = {}
util.load = function(key) {
  return util.cache[key] || JSON.parse(localStorage[key] || '{}')
}
util.save = function(key,obj) {
  util.cache[key] = obj
  localStorage[key] = JSON.stringify(obj)
}


// URL querystring parameter parsing
util.params = function(qs) {
  var params = {}
  var kvpairs = qs.slice(qs.indexOf('?') + 1).split('&')

  for(var i = 0; i < kvpairs.length; i++) {
    var kv = kvpairs[i].split('=')
    params[kv[0]] = kv[1]
  }

  return params;
}


// browser or device alert
util.alert = function(text,title,button) {
  if( navigator.device ) {
    navigator.notification.alert(text,function(){},title,button)
  }
  else {
    alert( text )
  }
}


// On HTTP error, display a notification to the user
util.http_error = function( cb ) {
  return function(jqXHR, textStatus, errorThrown){
    var err = {
      status:jqXHR.status,
      jqXHR:jqXHR,
      textStatus:textStatus,
      errorThrown:errorThrown
    }
    util.log(err)

    util.alert(text.netfail,text.netfailtitle,text.close)

    cb && cb(err,null)
  }
}

// lookup key for user account data
```

```
util.key = function(type,account) {
  return type+'_'+account.network+'_'+account.nick
}

...
```

code snippet tonvo/tonvo-struct.js

You need to be sure to watch out for the following:

➤ The `load` and `save` functions wrap the `localStorage` interface and use a cache object to improve performance.

➤ The `log` function converts its arguments to an array so that they print nicely in the Safari and Xcode debugger consoles.

➤ The `text` function is a convenience function for injecting text into an HTML template.

➤ The `alert` function displays a nicer pop-up when on a device than in the desktop Safari browser.

➤ The `http_error` function dynamically creates an error handler that pops up a message to the user if there is problem with the network connection. This simplifies your error handling throughout the code base.

The Code Structure

Now you're ready to get to the meat of the tonvo app. What objects do you need? There are many design approaches to answering this question. Some people recommend using a full-scale Model–View–Controller (MVC) architecture, which is a common user interface design pattern.

 NOTE *If you are familiar with the MVC architecture and want to use it, your best bet is to use the Backbone library:* http://documentcloud.github.com/backbone. *I have used Backbone on large-scale projects and can highly recommend it. Backbone is complex, however, and describing its use is well beyond the scope of this book.*

For this example, you will use a view-based mini-pattern. This gives you good code organization and means that you can start with code you fully understand. The main objects in this pattern are known as *views*, and each of these view objects is given the job of building and handling a specific part of the user interface.

In the tonvo app, the view objects are responsible for building the user interface views. To determine which objects you need, you should examine the use case analysis and the wire frames, which suggest the following view objects:

➤ `Accounts` — Displays the list of accounts

➤ `People` — Displays the list of people

➤ `Inbox` — Displays the inbox of messages

➤ `Convo` — Displays a conversation

➤ `TopNav` — Handles the navigation menu

What methods should these objects have? Well, you'll need to get each view to render itself when it becomes visible. You'll also need to be able to update the inbox and the list of people whenever the app loads or the user requests a refresh (by pulling down on the Inbox view). There are a few more individual methods, and you'll see them in the next code example.

> **NOTE** *What are methods and members? How are they different from functions and properties? A method is a function that operates on an object. A member variable is a property of an object. In JavaScript, these terms are transplanted from stricter languages such as Java or C#. They are commonly used when talking about JavaScript objects that are used as instances of classes. Of course, JavaScript does not really have classes, but it does have a flexible prototype system that lets you emulate them. Thus, the terms* method *and* member, *when used in a JavaScript context, enable you to document your intention to use objects in a certain way that emulates Java or C#.*

In addition to the view objects, you'll also need some data objects to represent Twitter accounts, people, and messages. JavaScript makes it really easy to create these on-the-fly. You just need to decide on a convention and stick to it. For example, `account` objects consist of two members: `nick` (the username for the account) and `network` (the type of social media network):

```
{nick:'rjrodger', network:'twitter'}
```

You'll also need some business objects to abstract away the interaction with the social networks. A simple pattern consists of manager object, `Social`, that presents a generic social media interface, and an abstract base object, `Network`, from which objects specific to individual networks, such as `Twitter`, can inherit OAuth handling code.

Finally, you'll need an `App` object to coordinate everything and link up all the objects. You've seen an `App` object used before, for the Lifestream app.

To verify this design and to understand it more clearly, you might want to diagram the dependencies between the objects. By working out which objects depend on which other objects, you can make sure your code is well structured. You want to avoid too many cross-dependencies. Objects should operate on a need-to-know basis. This keeps your code clean and reduces the risk of side effects. For example, none of the view objects should know about each other's existence. Instead, the `TopNav` object should coordinate between them. You'll see in a later example how you can use events to make this design work.

Figure 12-4 shows an object dependency graph for the tonvo app. If an arrow points at an object, this means the object it comes from depends on the object pointed to. For example, the `Social` object depends on the `Network` object to do the dirty work of OAuth sign-in.

Object Dependency Graph

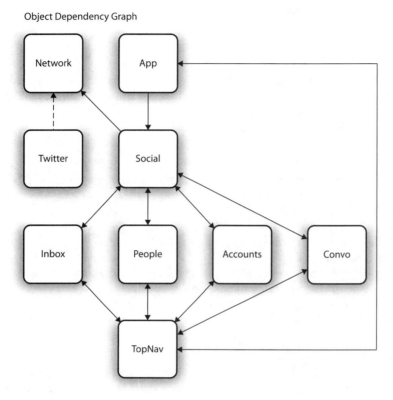

FIGURE 12-4

In the following example, you'll pull together all the elements from the preceding discussion to create an empty tonvo app that has the structure you want but no functionality. You'll then build out the functionality by providing implementations for the empty objects.

Unlike in earlier chapters in this book, the full source code for this example is not listed, as it is too long. Instead, the relevant sections of code are shown and explained. This means you can still read and understand how the app works; you just won't see the full source code on the pages of the book. However, you can download the full source code and review it to understand the complete context of the examples.

The following example shows how to implement the TopNav object so that you can switch between the Inbox, People, and Accounts views. The user interface is built using jQuery Mobile, and the code is based on the Lifestream app so should be quite familiar.

The tonvo app uses some third-party libraries for OAuth and for date parsing. For OAuth, you can visit http://code.google.com/p/oauth and download the JavaScript implementation. There is no convenient package file to download, but you can navigate to the code/javascript folder of the repository (by selecting Source ➪ Browse) and download the oauth.js and sha1.js files. For date parsing, you can download the date.js file from www.datejs.com. You need this library to handle Twitter's date format.

TRY IT OUT Building the tonvo App from the Top Down

Follow these steps to create the tonvo app from the top down:

1. Create a new PhoneGap project called tonvo. Do this in exactly the same way as you did for the Lifestream app in Chapters 9 and 10.

2. Download the full source code and image files for this example from www.wrox.com, and store them in a project folder of your choice.

3. Copy the tonvo-struct.js, tonvo.css, and index.html files from the download into the www folder in the project. Also copy the img folder.

4. Copy the standard jQuery and jQuery Mobile files and folders into the www folder. (Refer to the Lifestream examples in Chapters 9 and 10 for details.)

5. Copy in the oauth.js, sha1.js, and date.js files that you have downloaded separately into the www folder.

6. Open the index.html file and modify the script tag by importing the tonvo.js file to import tonvo-struct.js, as boldfaced in the following code:

```
<script src="jquery.js"></script>
<script src="jquery.mobile.js"></script>
<script src="oauth.js"></script>
<script src="sha1.js"></script>
<script src="date.js"></script>
<script src="tonvo-struct.js"></script>
</head>
```

7. Run the tonvo app in your desktop Safari browser by loading the index.html file. It should present the Accounts view, and there should be no JavaScript errors if you open the Web Inspector.

8. Deploy the tonvo app to your iPhone simulator or Android emulator. The Accounts view should look as shown in Figure 12-5. Again, follow the same procedure as for the Lifestream app (see Chapters 9 and 10).

How It Works

If you review the HTML code for the app in the index.html file, you will see that it uses the same basic structure as the Lifestream app. The HTML uses the jQuery Mobile markup conventions to build the visual appearance of the app. If you review the tonvo.css file, you will see some CSS-style tweaking. This is all very basic HTML and CSS code that produces the user interface you see in the screenshots.

The top navigation structure uses a jQuery Mobile header. As per the wire frames, you can access the Inbox, People, and Accounts views. Also

FIGURE 12-5

note that the id attribute values are namespaced. You'll see this throughout the code. The links are boldfaced in the following code:

```
<div data-role="header" data-position="fixed">
  <div data-role="navbar">
    <ul>
       <li><a id="nav_inbox">Inbox</a></li>
       <li><a id="nav_people">People</a></li>
       <li><a id="nav_accounts">Accounts</a></li>
    </ul>
  </div>
</div>
```

The Inbox view contains two main elements. The first is a hidden div that contains the "refreshing" message. This div is shown whenever the app updates its data over the network by checking for new messages and followers. The second is the list of inbox messages. As in the To-Do List application, the items of the list are constructed by cloning a hidden template, shown boldfaced in the following code:

```
<div id="con_inbox" data-role="content" class="con hide">
  <div id="inbox_refresh" data-role="header" data-theme="b">
    refreshing...
  </div>
  <ul id="inbox_itemlist" data-role="listview">
    <li id="inbox_item_tm" class="hide">
      <a>
      <div class="inbox_item_head">
        <span class="from"></span>
        <span class="name"></span>
        <br />
        <span class="when"></span>
        <img class="network_img">
        <span class="nick"></span>
      </div>
      <div class="subject"></div>
      </a>
    </li>
  </ul>


  <div style="height:480px"></div>
</div>
```

Figure 12-6 shows what the inbox looks like when the app is complete, including some messages that have been downloaded.

The Conversation view shows the direct messages that you have exchanged with a follower on Twitter. When the app is complete, the messages in the input text area for writing a new message will look as shown in Figure 12-7.

FIGURE 12-6   **FIGURE 12-7**

The HTML code to construct the Conversation view uses the same template cloning approach as the Inbox view to insert new messages. The message template is boldfaced in the following code:

```
<div id="con_convo" data-role="content" class="con hide">
  <img id="convo_avatar" />
  <h1 id="convo_other">convo</h1>
  <p style="clear:both">
    <img id="convo_network" />
    <span id="convo_me"></span>
  </p>
  <textarea id="convo_compose"></textarea>
  <a id="convo_send" data-role="button" data-inline="true">send</a>

  <ul id="convo_list">
    <li id="convo_msg_tm" class="convo_msg" class="hide">
      <p class="meta"></p>
      <p class="body"></p>
      <p class="who"><p>
    </li>
  </ul>
</div>
```

The People view shows the list of people you can message. There is a complication here: What if you have hundreds or thousands of followers? The user interface will not easily scroll through that many items, especially if you want to show the avatar image of each follower. You have to find a way to hide most of the followers. There is also a question of how to find the correct person to message from the list.

You can solve both problems by using a top-level list that consists of the first character of the username of each follower. This keeps the main list of items short. When you tap in a character item, it expands to show you all the people whose username starts with that character. This makes it easy to find the right person, and the list is short and performant. Figure 12-8 shows an example.

The code to construct the people list requires three separate kinds of list items. You need a big item to identify the account that has the followers listed. Then you need divider items for the initial characters, and finally you need an item for each person. The first two item types use the jQuery Mobile `data-role="list-divider"` attribute so that they have a different visual appearance from the person items. The items appear as follows, in the order mentioned, in the code:

FIGURE 12-8

```
<div id="con_people" data-role="content" class="con hide">
    <ul id="people_list" data-role="listview" >
      <li id="people_network_tm" class="hide network"
          data-role="list-divider">
        <img class="network">
        <p class="details">
          <span class="nick"></span>
        </p>
      </li>
      <li id="people_divider_tm" class="hide divider"
          data-role="list-divider" data-theme="e">
        <span class="char"></span>
      </li>
      <li id="people_person_tm" class="hide person">
        <img class="avatar">
        <a class="person">
          <p class="details">
            <span class="nick"></span>
            <span class="name"></span>
          </p>
        </a>
      </li>
    </ul>
</div>
```

The Accounts view again uses the "hide and clone" template trick to build the list of Twitter accounts. The Sign In button also appears here:

```
<div id="con_accounts" data-role="content" class="con hide">

  <div id="accounts_login" data-role="collapsible">
    <h3>Account Sign-in</h3>

    <p>
      <a id="accounts_signin_twitter" class="signin">
        <img src="img/twitter.png">
      </a>
    </p>

  </div>

  <div data-role="collapsible">
```

```
        <h3>Your Accounts</h3>
        <ul id="accounts_list" data-role="listview" data-inset="true">
          <li id="accounts_item_tm" class="hide">
            <img class="avatar">
            <p class="details">
              <span class="nick"></span>
            </p>
            <img class="network">
          </li>
        </ul>
      </div>

      <div id="debug"></div>

    </div>
```

You've seen this view already, in Figure 12-5.

The code for this example is quite simple. In addition to the utility code already described, you need to create the App object and set up all the view and business objects. If you review the downloadable code, you'll see that these objects are all empty and have no code in them because this example is focused purely on setting up the code structure of the app.

As per the object dependency graph, the view objects should only have a reference to the Social object, whereas the TopNav object will need to know about each view object so that it can call the render function of the view object to get it to display:

```
    // The main application object
    function App() {
      var self = this

      util.log('app init')


      // set up the social and view objects

      var social = self.social = new Social()

      self.inbox = new Inbox(social)
      self.convo = new Convo(social)
      self.people = new People(social)
      self.accounts = new Accounts(social)

      self.topnav = new TopNav('inbox',self)

      self.topnav.show.accounts()
    }
```

When you run the app on your desktop Safari browser, you should open the Web Inspector and review the logging output. This will show you the progress of the code as it initializes.

The TopNav object dynamically creates a function for each view that causes the view to be displayed. For the Inbox, People, and Account views, a tap handler is attached to the corresponding button in the user interface. The code is as follows:

```
// Manage the top bar navigation buttons
function TopNav(firstcon,app) {
  var self = this

  self.app = app

  self.el = {
    nav: {},
    con: {}
  }

  self.show = {}

  // create a function to display a content view
  function makeshowcon(name) {
    return function() {
      if( self.con ) {
        self.con.addClass('hide')
        self.app[self.name].visible = false
      }

      self.name = name
      self.con = self.el.con[name]
      self.app[name].render()

      self.con.removeClass('hide')
      self.app[name].visible = true
    }
  }

  // set up content views
  for( var cn in {inbox:1,people:1,accounts:1,convo:1} ) {
    self.el.nav[cn] = $('#nav_'+cn)
    self.el.con[cn] = $('#con_'+cn)

    self.show[cn] = makeshowcon(cn)
    self.el.nav[cn].tap( self.show[cn] )
  }
  self.con = self.el.con[ firstcon ]
  self.name = firstcon
}
```

The makeshowcon function performs the dynamic function creation. The function that it returns knows how to hide the currently visible view and then render the new view. This function is then assigned to the show member variable. That is why this line of code in the App object works, despite the fact that no accounts function is explicitly defined:

```
self.topnav.show.accounts()
```

As a coding shortcut, you can iterate the names of the views by making them the property names of a throwaway object:

```
// set up content views
for( var cn in {inbox:1,people:1,accounts:1,convo:1} ) {
```

If you run this version of the app on your mobile device, you'll be able to swap between views by tapping the navigation items at the top.

OAuth Without a Server

The code for the tonvo example app is focused on the Twitter API integration. One of the challenges therefore is to make it completely stand-alone, with no dependency on server-side code. The only servers that the app should talk to are the Twitter API servers.

The implementation of OAuth that you have seen in previous chapters has a server-side component. You need to provide a callback URL to Twitter so that after the user authorizes your app, Twitter can hand you back an access token.

So how can your app, on the user's iPhone or Android device, provide a callback URL to Twitter? You need to use a custom URL scheme. Twitter will happily issue a callback even if the URL does not start with `http`. If you associate a custom URL scheme with your app, mobile Safari will launch your app to deal with any URLs that have the associated scheme. (Refer to Chapter 10 for a reminder of how custom URL schemes work; you created the `lifestream://` URL scheme in that chapter.)

Let's review how this works. The user taps your Sign in with Twitter button. You start the OAuth flow by asking Twitter for a request token. Once you have the request token, you launch the mobile Safari browser and send the user to Twitter, passing along the request token. Twitter then presents the user with a sign-in page to authorize your app. Once the user has authorized your app, Twitter calls your callback URL *by sending an HTTP redirect to the mobile Safari browser.* If the callback URL has a custom URL scheme, Safari will open the associated app — your app. This gives you a chance to parse the access token out of the callback URL, just as you did with the server implementation. This process works for two reasons:

1. Twitter accepts custom URL schemes.
2. Safari launches your app to handle redirects to your custom URL scheme.

Now, how do you get hold of the URL that opened your app? Luckily, PhoneGap makes this easy. You just need to define a special function called `handleOpenURL`. This magic function is called by PhoneGap whenever your app is launched or resumed by your custom URL scheme. The `handleOpenURL` function receives one argument, the string value of the URL. This will contain the OAuth access token; you just need to parse it out. The custom URL scheme used by the app in this example is `tonvo://`.

In the previous example, you downloaded a JavaScript OAuth library, implemented in the files `oauth.js` and `sha1.js`. You'll put these to use now. You'll also fill out the code structure to handle network access to social media APIs. You need to allow yourself the flexibility to handle other social networks in the future. This suggests a simple base class pattern. You have a `Network` object that handles generic things like the OAuth flow. It also provides a standardized interface. You have a `Twitter` object that inherits from the `Network` object and provides Twitter-specific implementations of the standardized methods to get and send direct messages, get the user's followers, and get the user's details. Finally, you have a `Social` object that wraps up the network operations into a clean interface for the rest of the code.

The `Social` object only knows about the standardized interface provided by the `Network` object. The `Social` object never knows that it is dealing with Twitter, say, as opposed to Facebook or LinkedIn. The `Social` object just knows that it has a set of one or more `Network` objects that can perform certain well-defined API actions. This design makes the code extensible.

To implement the client-side OAuth flow, you need to be able to debug properly. Because the OAuth code is tricky to get right, you can't rely on displaying alert messages on your phone. The challenge is that the complete OAuth flow depends on the magic `handleOpenURL` function, which works only if PhoneGap is available, and PhoneGap is available only when you are running on the simulator or an actual device. And then you don't have the Web Inspector to help with debugging.

There are two things you can do. First, you can simulate the `handleOpenURL` function manually in your desktop Safari browser; you'll see how to do this in the example. Second, you can use the Weinre debugger to get a Web Inspector console for your app when it is running on the simulator or physical device. Don't know what Weinre is? Go back and do the exercises for Chapter 9!

TRY IT OUT   Implementing the OAuth Flow

Follow these steps to implement the OAuth flow in your app:

1. Copy the `tonvo-oauth.js` file from the download into the www folder in the tonvo project you created in the previous example.

2. Open `index.html` and modify the `script` tag by importing the `tonvo-struct.js` file to import `tonvo-oauth.js`, as boldfaced below:

```
...
  <script src="date.js"></script>
  <script src="tonvo-oauth.js"></script>
</head>
```

3. Modify the app configuration at the top of the `tonvo-oauth.js` file. Replace the `YOUR_TWITTER_KEY` and `YOUR_TWITTER_SECRET` markers with the consumer key and secret for your app, as displayed on the app details page on the Twitter developer site.

4. Run the tonvo app in your desktop Safari browser by loading the `index.html` file directly. You should see the same empty accounts view as in the previous example.

5. Open the Web Inspector console so that you can observe the logging output.

6. Click on the Sign In with Twitter button. Several lines of logging appear, as in Figure 12-9.

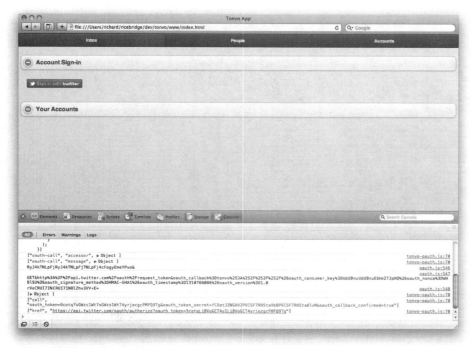

FIGURE 12-9

7. Copy the URL in the last line of logging output, which has the following form:

```
https://api.twitter.com/...?oauth_token=...
```

8. Open a new browser tab, paste in the copied URL, and load the Twitter authorization page. Click the Authorize App button. An error message appears because your desktop Safari browser does not know what to do with `tonvo://` URLs. Twitter displays a redirect page that displays a "Click here to continue" link. Right-click and copy the URL of this link, which is the callback URL.

9. Go back to the browser tab that contains your app. In the Web Inspector console, manually execute the `handleOpenURL` function, providing the copied callback URL as the first argument:

```
handleOpenURL("tonvo://oauth_token=...&oauth_verifier=...")
```

The app completes the OAuth sign-in process and obtains an access token from Twitter. Figure 12-10 shows this process in action. Note the manual call to the `handleOpenURL` function. The app displays the OAuth access key and secret as a JSON string in the Accounts view, as a debugging aid.

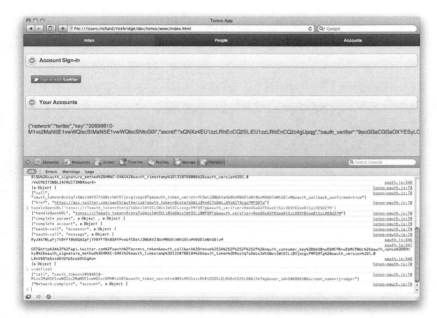

FIGURE 12-10

10. Deploy the app to your simulator or physical device and attempt to repeat the login process. You do not need to copy and paste the authorization token as the code detects that it is running on a mobile device rather than in a web browser. The Twitter authorization page should appear, as shown in Figure 12-11.

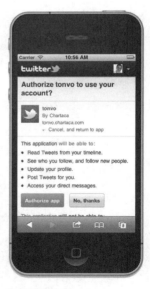

How It Works

To understand the OAuth login process, you need to trace the path through the code. If you review the code in the tonvo-oauth.js file you downloaded, you won't see this path because the code is organized into objects. Most of the code explanations in this book follow the code down the page as it is written. The explanation here, however, jumps around to follow the OAuth flow. When you run the app, you can also follow the flow of execution by observing the copious logging output. I have deliberately left all the log statements in the code so that you can do this.

What happens when you tap the Sign In with Twitter button? Here's the code in the Accounts object that deals with that. The boldfaced line is the one that the tap action activates:

FIGURE 12-11

```
// bind signin functions to signin buttons
for( var n in conf.network ) {
  var signin = self.el.signin[n] = $('#accounts_signin_'+n)
  util.log('signin',n)
  signin.tap(social.makesignin(n))
}
```

In this version of the app, there is only one network configured, Twitter, so this `for` loop executes only once. It finds the button by using a simple naming convention: It looks for an `id` attribute in the form `accounts_signin_<network>`. The event handler function itself is actually constructed dynamically by the `Social` object, via the `makesignin` function:

```
self.makesignin = function(name) {
  var network = self.network[name]
  util.log('makesignin',network,name,self.network)
  var signin = network.makesignin(name)
  util.log(signin)
  return signin
}
```

This code uses the name of the network, in this case the string "twitter", to find the child object of the `Network` object that implements the API for that network. The `network` member variable defines a mapping from network names to implementation objects. In this app, that object is the `Twitter` object.

The `Social` object does not know how to perform an OAuth sign-in. It delegates that to the network-specific instance of the `Network` object by calling the `makesignin` method of that object:

```
var signin = network.makesignin(name)
```

You know this is the `Twitter` object because Twitter is the only social network you've implemented. Here's the complete code of the `Twitter` object, including the `makesignin` method:

```
function Twitter(reqtokens) {
  var self = this

  self.reqtokens = reqtokens
  self.conf = conf.network.twitter


  // create a handler function for user sign in
  self.makesignin = function() {
    return function() {
      var account = {
        network:'twitter'
      }

      self.call(
        account,
        { path:self.conf.requesturl },
        function(err,data) {
          if( err ) return util.log(err);
          self.handleauthorize(err,data,account)
        }
      )
    }
  }
}
Twitter.prototype = new Network()
```

The `Twitter` object is a child object of the `Network` object. You set this up with a line at the bottom:

```
Twitter.prototype = new Network()
```

By doing this, you ensure that the `Twitter` object inherits all the methods of the `Network` object. One of the inherited methods is the `call` method, the basic pattern of which is shown here:

```
self.call(
  ...,
  function(err,data) {
    ...
  }
)
```

This is a general-purpose method that can make calls to OAuth protected URLs. You'll see the code for this method in the next example. For now, you can assume that it just works. Here, you are using it to send the first part of the OAuth flow — getting the request token. The exact request URL comes from the network-specific configuration: `conf.network.twitter`. You saw the code that sets up this configuration in the previous example. You also need to construct an account description object to pass as the first argument to the `call` method. This account description object should have a `network` field set to the name of the network: "twitter".

The `call` object interacts with remote services over the network. In the best asynchronous tradition, and just as with the Node API, you provide a callback function that takes two arguments: The first is an `err` object, which is `null` if everything is okay, and the second is a `data` object, which contains the data returned by the remote server.

How do you deal with the `err` object when it is not `null` when there is an error? As it happens, you've already solved this problem. The `util.http_get` and `util.http_post` utility methods, whose definitions you saw earlier in this chapter, pop up an alert to the user if a network request fails. You just need to make sure you don't attempt to work with empty data. The first line of the callback function ensures this:

```
if( err ) return util.log(err);
```

You'll see this line in most of the callbacks in the code. It is an idiomatic way of exiting from a callback when something has gone wrong. The return value from the `util.log` is not used; this is just a way to get it all neatly on one line at the top of the callback.

The `makesignin` function wraps up all this logic in a dynamic function, which is returned to the `Accounts` object and bound to tap events on the Sign In with Twitter button. When the user taps this button, the dynamic function is executed.

So what do you do with the data when a token request to Twitter is successful? You pass it on to the `handleauthorize` method of the `Network` object, shown boldfaced here:

```
function(err,data) {
  if( err ) return util.log(err);
  self.handleauthorize(err,data,account)
}
```

The `handleauthorize` function is a general-purpose OAuth method of the `Network` object. It understands how to use the request token to construct an authorization URL, which it then redirects the user to so that the user can sign in on the corresponding social media site. It also caches the token secret so that the OAuth callback can be completed. The cache object is the `reqtokens` member variable. If you look closely at the code for the `Twitter` object (shown above), you'll see that- the `reqtokens` cache object is actually a member variable of the `Social` object and is passed in as a construction parameter to the `Twitter` object. The happens so that the `Social` object can look up the request token later, when an OAuth callback comes in, and determine which `Network` object should deal with it.

Here is the code for `handleauthorize`:

```
this.handleauthorize = function(data,account) {
  var networkconf = conf.network[account.network]

  var params = util.params(data)

  // store the token, to be accessed after callback
  this.reqtokens[params.oauth_token] = {
    network:account.network,
    key:params.oauth_token,
    secret:params.oauth_token_secret,
  }

  var href=networkconf.authorizeurl+'?oauth_token='+params.oauth_token
  util.log('href',href)

  if( navigator.device ) {
    window.location.href = href
  }
  // else on browser, manually copy and paste href into new window
}
```

The `util.params` utility function parses out the OAuth token and secret from the data returned by Twitter. This token and secret are then cached in the `reqtokens` object, keyed by the token. As explained earlier, this allows the `Social` object to retrieve this data later.

 NOTE *Why does the code for the* `Network` *object use the* `this` *variable instead of the safer* `self` *variable you've been using up to now? Because it is a superclass. If you set a* `self` *variable, it would point to an instance of the superclass, not to the subclass, which is what you need. To put it another way, the* `this` *refers to the* `Twitter` *object, whereas a* `self` *variable would remain fixed on the* `Network` *object itself.*

A standard OAuth authorization URL is then constructed in the `href` variable, and the user is sent to Twitter by the simple expedient of setting the good old-fashioned `window.location.href` property. When you use the app, this is the point at which the app is moved into the background, Safari moves into the foreground, and you are presented with the Twitter authorization web page.

What if you are testing on the desktop Safari browser? In that case, the `navigator.device` object will not be present because it is created by PhoneGap. In that case, sending a redirect will kill your current instance of the app, and you don't want to do that. Instead, you can just log the authorization URL to the console and then manually copy and paste it into a new browser tab, as you did in the preceding example.

After the user authorizes your app, Twitter will use a redirect to send the user back to your app. As discussed earlier, you use a custom URL scheme to relaunch your app when on a physical device. Otherwise, you must manually complete the process. In both cases, the `handleOpenURL` function is called with the callback URL from Twitter as its first argument.

Here's the implementation of the `handleOpenURL` function:

```
function handleOpenURL(url) {
  util.log('handleOpenURL',url)
  app.social.complete(url)
}
```

As you can see, the real action happens inside the `Social` object:

```
self.complete = function(url) {
  var params = util.params(url)
  util.log('complete params', params, self.reqtokens)
  var account = self.reqtokens[params.oauth_token]
  account.oauth_verifier = params.oauth_verifier
  util.log('complete account', account)

  var network = self.network[account.network]

  if( account ) {
    network.complete(account, function(err,account){
      if( err ) return util.log(err);

      $('#debug').text( JSON.stringify(account) )
    })
  }
}
```

Again, you parse the URL parameters by using `util.params`. You look up the token details in the `reqtokens` cache object. You place all the details, including the `oauth_verifier` value that the callback URL has given you, into an `account` object and you call the `complete` method of the appropriate `Network` implementation object. This method returns by way of a callback in the usual manner. Once it does, you just dump the result onto the screen to verify that everything works, as shown in Figure 12-10. In the final version of the app, you will instead set up a proper user account.

The final `complete` method in the `Network` object looks like this:

```
this.complete = function( account, cb ) {
  var networkconf = conf.network[account.network]

  this.call( account, { path: networkconf.accessurl }, function( err,
```

```
data ) {
  if( err ) {
    util.log(err)
    util.alert(text.authfail,text.authfailtitle,text.close)
    return
  }

  var params = util.params(data)
  account.key = params.oauth_token
  account.secret = params.oauth_token_secret

  util.log('Network.complete','account',account)
  cb( null, account )
})
}
```

What you are doing here is completing the second part of the OAuth protocol flow — using the request token to obtain an access token. The access token is the one you need in order to make API calls.

You use the `call` method as before to make the actual OAuth call, but this time you send the request to the access token URL endpoint (defined in `conf.network.twitter`). If the call returns successfully, you store the access token and secret in the `account` object and send it back to the calling code by using the callback parameter `cb`. If it does not return, you display a special-case error message to the user.

Isn't OAuth fun?

Calling the Twitter API

Now that you have that OAuth access token, you can get some real work done. In the following example, you'll extend the code to make requests to the Twitter API to get the data you need to make the app functional.

The API calls are performed by a set of methods on the `Social` object:

➤ **sendmsg** — Sends a direct message

➤ **getmsgs** — Gets the user's direct messages

➤ **getpeople** — Gets a list of the user's followers

➤ **userdetails** — Gets some details about the user

Because the `Social` object does not know anything about Twitter, it delegates the API calls to methods with the same names on the `Twitter` object. The `Social` object just looks after the housekeeping by organizing and storing the resulting data.

To keep this example manageable, you'll focus on the `getmsgs` method. The other methods work in much the same way as `getmsgs`, and their code is available for review in the downloadable code file.

Getting Data Out of Twitter

In this example, you won't see how to display any results in the app. You'll have to wait for the next example to see how that is done. Instead, you'll use the Web Inspector console to manually execute the `getmsgs` function of the `Social` object to retrieve the user's direct messages. Here's what you do:

1. Copy the `tonvo-api.js` file from the downloadable code into the www folder of the tonvo project.

2. Open `index.html` and modify the `script` tag to import `tonvo-api.js`, as highlighted in the following code:

```
...
  <script src="date.js"></script>
  <script src="tonvo-api.js"></script>
</head>
```

3. Replace the `YOUR_TWITTER_KEY` and `YOUR_TWITTER_SECRET` markers with your consumer key and secret, as in the previous example.

4. Run the tonvo app in your desktop Safari browser and log in with one of your Twitter accounts. This time, the Accounts view updates and displays your username and avatar, as shown in Figure 12-12. (Figure 12-12 shows the iPhone view, but the desktop view is the same.)

5. Open the Web Inspector console so that you can observe the logging output.

6. Execute the following command in the console:

```
app.social.getmsgs()
```

7. Observe the logging output. After a few seconds, you should see a logging entry that looks like this:

```
["inbound-msgs", Array]
```

FIGURE 12-12

8. Expand `Array` by clicking the little arrow to the left of `Array`. You should see a list of the user's direct messages, as shown in Figure 12-13.

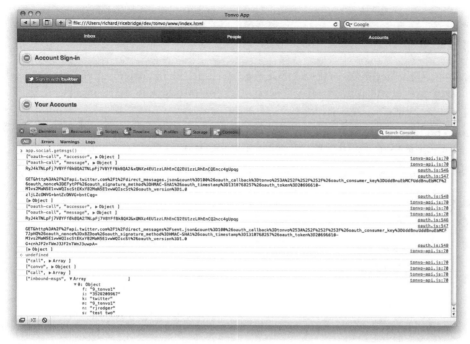

FIGURE 12-13

9. If you inspect the value of the `app.social.inbound` variable, you'll also see a list of the user's direct messages. And you'll find the same list stored in the `localStorage` API, under the `"inbound"` key.

How It Works

You can follow the code path to understand how the API call works. Here is the code for the `app.social.getmsgs` function:

```
self.getmsgs = function() {
  // request concurrently
  for( var i = 0; i < self.accounts.length; i++ ) {
    var network = self.network[self.accounts[i].network]

    // network returns msgs in reverse chronological order
    network.getmsgs( 'inbound', self.accounts[i], function(err,msgs) {
      if( err ) return util.log(err);

      inboundmsgs(msgs)
      util.log('inbound-msgs',self.inbound)
    })

    network.getmsgs( 'outbound', self.accounts[i], function(err,msgs) {
      if( err ) return util.log(err);

      outboundmsgs(msgs)
```

```
            util.log('convo', self.convo)
        })
    }
}
```

This function loops through all the accounts that you have registered. Remember that supporting multiple accounts is a design goal of the app. The list of accounts is maintained in the accounts member variable of the Social object.

For each account, the loop body calls the getmsgs method of the Network object — twice. One call gets inbound messages sent to the user and the other call gets outbound messages sent by the user.

The getmsgs function of the Social object returns a list of message objects via a callback. When you have the list of messages, you call the inboundmsgs and outboundmsgs housekeeping functions. These are rather banal pieces of code that organize and index the messages. You can review them in the code download to see them, if you are interested.

Let's move on to the interesting part, the getmsgs function of the Network object. Here's the code:

```
self.getmsgs = function(direction,account,cb) {

  var subpath = 'inbound'==direction?'':'/sent'

  self.call(account,{
    path:self.conf.apibaseurl+'direct_messages'+subpath+'.json?count='+100,
    jsondata:true
  },function(err,data){
    if( err ) return cb(err);

    var msgs = []
    for( var i = 0; i < data.length; i++ ) {
      var dm = data[i]

      var d = self.twitterdate( dm.created_at )

      var msg = {
        k:'twitter',
        n:account.nick,
        s:dm.text,
        w:d.getTime(),
        i:dm.id_str
      }

      var sender = dm.sender_screen_name
      var recipient = dm.recipient_screen_name

      if( account.nick == sender ) {
        msg.t = recipient
      }
      else {
        msg.f = sender
        msg.m = dm.sender.name
      }
```

```
        msgs.push(msg)
      }

      cb(null,msgs)
    })
  }
```

The `call` method makes an appearance to perform the HTTP request and handle the OAuth signature. You'll see the implementation of that function in a minute.

Let's go back to the `getmsgs` function. This is the URL for inbound messages:

```
http://api.twitter.com/1/direct_messages.json
```

And this is the URL for outbound messages:

```
http://api.twitter.com/1/direct_messages/sent.json
```

There is a little bit of logic at the top of the function to create the right URL, depending on the value of the `direction` parameter. As the result returned by both API calls is the same JSON structure encoding a list of messages, it makes sense to handle both inbound and outbound messages in the same method. This is an example of the Don't Repeat Yourself (DRY) principle discussed on Chapter 2.

When you get the data back, it is a JSON array of objects— one object for each message. These objects are in Twitter's JSON format, which is rather verbose. In order to maximize storage space (you store the message using the `localStorage` API), you need to convert the Twitter message format to a more compact form. Also, if you later add other social networks, this compact format will define a common message schema for your app. The need for this custom conversion is another reason for the inheritance relationship between the `Network` and `Twitter` objects. It hides the accidental custom code from the `Social` object, which does not need to know, and does not care, what the Twitter JSON looks like.

If you examine the code for the other API call functions, you will see that they all follow this basic pattern, shielding the rest of the app from the details of Twitter's API.

Event Consumers and Producers

It's time to complete the tonvo app and produce something that can be submitted to the app stores. You need to handle user input in an effective and responsive way. The key to this is to use custom events instead of function calls.

Using events helps you avoid spaghetti code. The problem with a large code base is that as it grows, you'll find yourself making function calls between and across many objects. If you are not careful, all your objects will end up depending on all your other objects, wrecking the nice dependency design in Figure 12-4.

You can keep your objects separate by moving their communication into events. You can use a basic producer–consumer model to keep things under control. Some objects will produce events, and others will consume them. Multiple objects can produce the same event, and multiple objects can respond to the same event. This makes everything very neat and reduces the amount of knowledge you need to share between objects.

Consider this example: When you call the `getmsgs` function to get the latest direct messages from Twitter, the call takes several seconds to complete. When the data does come in, the user might be in the Inbox view or in the Conversation view. In both cases, you may need to render the view again to display any new messages. If you trigger an `"inbound-msgs"` event when the messages arrive and listen for this event in the `Inbox` and `Convo` objects, you can easily implement this update logic, without worrying about whether you have captured every point in the code where it is needed.

To determine what events you need, you should iterate your design and code a few times. Some events, such as `"inbound-msgs"`, will be obvious from the start. Other events will emerge only as you create the code. It can be useful to maintain a graph that describes the events and shows their producer and consumer objects. Figure 12-14 shows the complete event model for the tonvo app. Remember that you are not expected to design the whole event model before you code, but you are expected to refactor your code into events as you progress.

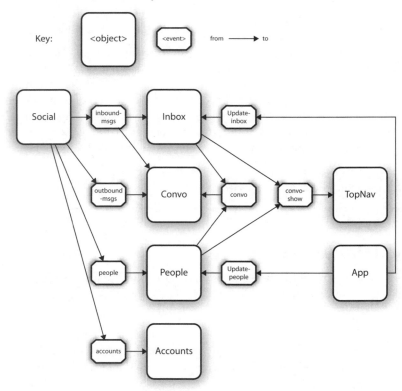

FIGURE 12-14

This diagram shows the events that each object generates and the events that each object responds to. Working from left to right, the `Social` object generates the `"inbound-msgs"`, `"outbound-msgs"`, `"people"`, and `"accounts"` events whenever a call to the Twitter API returns new data that needs to be displayed.

The Inbox, Convo, People, and Accounts objects listen for events relevant to the data they display. When such an event comes in, the corresponding view object renders itself again. The event model means that you do not need to know or care which view is currently displayed to the user. Everything will update automatically, and the user will always see the most recent data as soon as it is available.

The Inbox and People views can cause the Conversation view to be displayed if the user taps a message or a person. The "convo" event lets the Conversation view know that it needs to update itself. However, the Conversation object cannot *display* itself. Only the TopNav object can do that. A separate event, "convo-show", is used to do this. Two events are used here because changing the contents of the Conversation view to display a different conversation is not the same thing as simply displaying the current Conversation view. Keeping separate things separate is a good software design principle that keeps your code flexible.

Finally, the App object needs some events (such as "update-inbox" and "update-people") to force an update of the list of people and messages when the app launches.

To implement custom events, you can co-opt the jQuery event mechanism. You simply attach events to the document object by using the bind function and fire the events by using the trigger function. The Social object is the best place to do this, as it already has a coordinating role. It's also a good idea to namespace the events with a prefix (such as "social-"), in case you want to provide an event interface on another object:

```
function Social() {
  var self = this
  ...

  self.bind = function( eventname, callback ) {
    $(document).bind('social-'+eventname,callback)
  }

  self.trigger = function( eventname ) {
    var args = Array.prototype.slice.call(arguments,1)
    $(document).trigger('social-'+eventname,args)
  }

  ...
}
```

The following example shows how to implement a pull-down updater. This is a common interface feature in mobile apps that display a list of messages. If you pull down on the message list when you are at the top of the list, you trigger an update request, and the app goes out to a server to see if you have any new messages. A "refreshing" message or animation typically appears at the top of the message list for the duration of the update.

The following example also does a good job of showing you how event processing works. When the update completes, it triggers update events that are processed by the Inbox and Conversation views.

As with the other examples in this chapter, the following example covers only a subset of the code base of the app. To see the full implementation of the event model, you'll need to review the full source code from the code download.

TRY IT OUT | **Triggering User Interface Updates**

To implement a pull-down updater in the tonvo app, follow these steps:

1. Copy the `tonvo-full.js` file from the code download into the www folder of the tonvo project.

2. Open `index.html` and modify the `script` tag by importing the `tonvo-api.js` file to import `tonvo-full.js`, as highlighted in the following code:

```
...
  <script src="date.js"></script>
  <script src="tonvo-full.js"></script>
</head>
```

3. Configure the `YOUR_TWITTER_KEY` and `YOUR_TWITTER_SECRET` markers as in the previous examples.

4. Deploy the app to your simulator or physical device.

5. Sign in with one of your Twitter accounts.

6. Go to the Inbox view and pull down on the list. A "Refreshing . . . " message appears, and the list of direct messages updates with any new messages.

7. To observe the logging output for this operation when run on a physical device or the simulator, use the Weinre debugger.

8. Run the app in your desktop Safari browser. Open the Web Inspector console and execute it manually:

```
app.inbox.refresh( {touches:[{clientY:999}]} )
```

How It Works

The `Inbox` object handles the refresh feature. In needs to detect a download pull motion. To do this, it keeps track of the location of any `touchstart` events. It also tracks `touchmove` events. If the Inbox view is at the top of the message list and the `touchmove` event reports a finger position below the `touchstart` event, then a refresh is initiated.

Here's the code to capture the touch events:

```
var startY = 0

document.addEventListener("touchstart", function(e) {
  startY = e.touches[0].clientY
})

document.addEventListener("touchmove", function(e) {
  self.refresh(e)
})
```

This is pretty standard touch event–handling code. (Refer to Chapter 4 if you need a reminder of how this type of code works.)

The `refresh` method of the `Inbox` object implements the math to check for a downward pull. If there is to be a refresh, the `Inbox` object initiates the refresh by triggering the `"update-inbox"` and `"update-people"` events. The `Inbox` object does not make any method calls on any objects other than the `Social` object. There could be many other view objects affected, but you don't need to maintain a list of them in the `Inbox` object. This makes your code much more robust.

Here's the `refresh` method, with the event triggers boldfaced:

```
var refreshing = false

self.refresh = function(e) {
  var wst = self.el.window.scrollTop()
  var curY = e.touches[0].clientY

  var atpagetop = 0 == wst && startY < curY
  if( atpagetop ) {
    e.preventDefault()
  }

  var refresh = atpagetop && !refreshing && self.visible
  util.log(refresh,wst,startY,curY,atpagetop,refreshing,self.visible)

  if( refresh ) {
    refreshing = true
    self.el.refresh.show()
    social.trigger('update-inbox')
    social.trigger('update-people')
  }
}
```

Which objects listen for the `"update-inbox"` and `"update-people"` events? The `Inbox` object itself does this, as does the `People` object. When they receive these events, both objects call appropriate methods of the `Social` object to request an update to the list of messages and people:

```
function Inbox() {
  ...

  social.bind('update-inbox', function(){
    self.update()
  })

  self.update = function() {
    self.dirty = true
    social.getmsgs()
  }

  ...
}

...

function People() {
  ...

  social.bind('update-people', function(){
    self.update()
  })

  self.update = function(cb) {
    self.dirty = true
```

```
      social.getpeople()
  }

  ...
}
```

 NOTE *Yes, the* Inbox *object does trigger one of its own events! This is perfectly okay. The whole idea of events is that objects don't know what triggered them. An object just reacts to the events it says it will react to, regardless of their origin.*

Control now passes to the `getmsgs` and `getpeople` methods of the `Social` object. These methods perform network requests to get new data. When the network requests complete and the new data comes in, these methods trigger their own events (`"inbound-msgs"`, `"outbound-msgs"`, and `"people"`), shown boldfaced:

```
function Social() {
  ...

  self.getmsgs = function() {
    ...

    network.getmsgs( 'inbound', self.accounts[i], function(err,msgs) {
      ...
      self.trigger('inbound-msgs')
    })

    network.getmsgs( 'outbound', self.accounts[i],
    function(err,msgs) {
      ...
      self.trigger('outbound-msgs')
    })

    ...
  }

  self.getpeople = function() {
    ...

    network.getpeople(account,function(err,people){
      ...
      self.trigger('people')
    })

    ...
  }

  ...
}
```

Now control passes back to the Inbox object, which listens for the "inbound-msgs" event. The Convo object is also activated, as it listens for both the "inbound-msgs" and "outbound-msgs" events. Finally, the People object responds to the "people" event. These bindings are shown boldfaced below:

```
function Inbox() {
  ...

  social.bind('inbound-msgs', function(){
    if( refreshing ) {
      refreshing = false
      self.el.refresh.hide()
    }

    self.render()
  })
  ...
}

function Convo() {
  ...

  social.bind('inbound-msgs', function(){
    self.render()
  })

  social.bind('outbound-msgs', function(){
    self.render()
  })
  ...
}


function People() {
  ...

  social.bind('people', function(){
    self.render()
  })

  ...
}
```

This completes the event roundtrip. When you extend this app by adding new features and user interface views, you can use this eventing architecture to keep everything under control and maintainable.

SUMMARY

In this chapter, you took an accelerated tour of creating a complete social networking mobile app. You learned how to interact with the Twitter REST API and also how to structure a professional, large-scale, complex app. In particular, you learned how to take an app concept from initial specification right through to a fully working implementation.

In the next chapter, you'll submit the tonvo app to the Apple App Store and the Android Marketplace. There are a few hoops to jump through, and the next chapter will help you get through them. In particular, you'll learn how to digitally sign your apps for public distribution in the app stores.

EXERCISES

1. The transitions between pages in the tonvo app are instantaneous. Many apps use a sliding transition to animate transitions to make them more pleasing to eye. Use the Firmin library, at `http://extralogical.net/projects/firmin`, to implement sliding transitions by using CSS transforms.

2. If you place the tonvo app in the background and then open it again, it would be nice if the app updated its list of messages and people. Use the PhoneGap `resume` event to implement this functionality.

3. Once you register an account, there is no way to get rid of it in the tonvo app. Remedy this by implementing a swipe gesture on the account items in the Accounts view. Remember that you have to clear out all information associated with the account, not just the account object itself.

4. The Twitter API allows you to delete direct messages. Extend the app to support this feature. Use the swipe gesture to trigger a direct message delete. Review the Twitter API documentation to find the required REST API call.

Answers to the Exercises can be found in the Appendix.

▶ WHAT YOU LEARNED IN THIS CHAPTER

TOPIC	KEY CONCEPTS
Twitter REST API	Each of the major social media sites provides a programmatic API for its services. This allows third-party developers to build apps and enhanced services using the features of the social media site. The APIs are usually free to use but can be rate-limited to prevent abuse. Twitter provides an HTTP API for its services that follows these principles and is also a reasonable implementation of the REST concept.
Software design principles	When designing a complex piece of software, you should take a structured approach to the development of the system. You need to take into account the user interaction model, the need for your client to understand what you are building, and the need to create extensible, clean code. All these pieces come together to produce a successful high-quality app. To achieve this, you should use wire frames, use case analysis, and dependency analysis to build an understanding of how an app will work.
Use case analysis	Use case analysis is a semi-formal method for designing an application. You break down the behavior of the app by looking at it from the perspective of the user. You think about who the user is and about the user's goals and motivations. Use cases describe *what* rather than *how*.
Wire frames	To give your client insight into the layout and behavior of a finished app, you can use wire frames of the user interface. It is important that these drawings be rough so as not to create the impression that they are the final product. Wire frames need to be put through several iterations as they form the basis for discussion of the goals and design of the app.
Object dependencies	The objects in a software system necessarily depend on each other to implement features and functionality. Managing these dependencies is important. If there are too many interconnections, your code will become messy and difficult to maintain. By carefully designing a hierarchy of object dependencies, you can avoid this.
Client-side OAuth	The OAuth protocol was designed for use within web browsers. In order to implement client-side OAuth from within your app that does not rely on a hosted website, you need to use custom URL schemes to force the OAuth callback URL to trigger activation of your app.
Events	Events provide a way to build extensible code that has few internal connections. They enable you to implement your object dependency hierarchy. Objects produce or consume events independently of each other, meaning that the object implementations can be changed and new objects can be added quite easily, as needed.

13

App Stores

WHAT YOU WILL LEARN IN THIS CHAPTER:

➤ Creating icons for your app

➤ Creating a splash screen for your app

➤ Preparing screenshots

➤ Preparing app metadata

➤ Understanding App Store terms and conditions

➤ Building and submitting an iPhone app

➤ Building and submitting an Android app

It is finally time to release your app to the world! For both the iPhone and Android platforms, you register with an online portal to submit and manage your apps. You have to follow specific technical requirements and procedures to produce app binary packages that users can install. This chapter takes you through that process.

Before you perform the build and deploy steps you also need to prepare supplementary materials, such as screenshots, and make certain decisions about your app, such whether it is free or paid. Some preparation in advance will save you time and effort when you are filling in the online forms.

This chapter assumes that you can get your app to the point where you are happy with the quality, and where it is usable by others (you have conducted at least informal usability tests, right?). An assumption is also made that you have spent some time optimizing the code for performance. This is something that you will have to do with all hybrid apps, because it is easy to introduce glitches and pauses in the app user interface if you are not careful with your HTML and JavaScript code.

The tonvo app from Chapter 12 is used as an example in this chapter. It has been submitted to the iPhone App Store and the Android Marketplace, and you can find it by searching for the keyword "tonvo."

You should also ensure that you are using the Xcode version 4 (which was released during the writing of this book) in order to follow the iPhone submission example. The procedure is quite different from Xcode version 3.

WHAT YOU NEED TO PUBLISH YOUR APP

One of the really great things about building your app using HTML5 and PhoneGap is that you can publish an iPhone and Android version from the same code base. This means your app can appear on both the iPhone App Store and Android Marketplace without too much extra effort.

The iPhone and Android versions of your app will diverge when it comes to platform-specific assets such as icons and splash screens. You can make your life a lot easier by setting up a sensible folder structure in advance. Create a single top-level project folder to hold both the iPhone and Android project folders — you might as well call these subfolders `iphone` and `android`, respectively.

To share your HTML, CSS, and JavaScript code directly, create a symbolic link pointing from the Android project `assets` folder to the iPhone project `www` folder:

```
ln -s iphone/www android/assets
```

This means you can edit one canonical version of your code without worrying about accidental versioning. Refer to Chapters 9 and 10 if you need a reminder on the details of setting up Xcode and Eclipse projects.

Although you can maintain a unified code base, you will need to maintain separate project folders. Each platform has different configurations and icon image file requirements, and the separate project folders are a good place to keep these files.

Icons

The icon for your app is the most visible image associated with it, and will appear on the device home screen. Though it is important to have a unique and recognizable icon, it is also important to keep to the icon design guidelines for each platform. Unless you also have graphic design skills, you will need to bring in a graphic designer to get icons with a professional appearance.

You need to provide a number of different icon image files in different sizes. Some are required, and some are optional. The optional sizes are created automatically by resizing the icons you have provided, and this may not always produce the best results. If you have the resources, you should try to provide specific icon versions for each size.

To make this easier, ask your graphic designer to design the icon using a vector-based format, because this enables easy resizing. You should be aware that even vector-based icons may need manual adjustment, especially for smaller icon sizes.

Your app icon will appear in a variety of places — more than you think. In addition to the home screen, your icon is used in the app stores for your app listing, in iTunes in your list of apps, in search results, and in promotional slots if you are lucky enough to be selected as an "app of the day."

What can you do if you don't have access to a graphic designer? You can still produce reasonable icons. The trick is to stick to simple ideas. For example, your icon could just be the name of your app, written using a distinctive decorative font.

The PhoneGap project provides you with a default configuration for your icons, and there is little need to change this. PhoneGap defines a set of icon names to use, and references them in a set of standard folders. You can change the names and folder locations to a certain extent, by modifying the various `plist` files in your iPhone project, or the `AndroidManifest.xml` file, but there is little to be gained from a non-standard configuration.

The image file format used for icons on both the iPhone and Android platforms is the PNG format. More specifically, the color depth should be 24 bit, the images should have no transparency, and the density should be 72 DPI (dots-per-inch). Although your graphic designer may be the one producing the images, it is important that you understand the technical requirements for the images.

When it comes to the iPhone, you will need to produce two versions of some icons, one double the size of the other. This is because the Retina display, introduced with the iPhone 4, has double the number of physical pixels in the screen. Whereas the iPhone 3 had a 320 x 480 pixel screen, the iPhone 4 has a 640 x 960 pixel screen. Apple introduced a special naming convention that ensures the correct version is used. You append the character sequence `@2x` to the end of the filename, before the file type extension. For example, `icon.png` becomes `icon@2x.png`.

Here are the required iPhone icons:

➤ **57 x 57 pixels:** This is the main icon, used on the home screen. The icon file should be saved as `Resources/icons/icon.png` in your iPhone project.

➤ **114 x 114 pixels:** The Retina version of the main icon, saved as `Resources/icons/icon@2x.png` in your iPhone project.

➤ **512 x 512 pixels:** App store icon, in both iTunes and the online app store pages. Save this as `Resources/iTunesArtwork` in your iPhone project. The `.png` extension should be removed for this icon.

In addition to these required icons, you can provide a set of icons for search results and custom document types. The full list, and the most recent updates to the list, are available online from the Apple developer documentation at `http://developer.apple.com`.

The techniques in this book enable you to build iPad applications as well as iPhone applications. The design considerations for iPad are different for smaller devices, and in particular, additional, different, icon sizes are required. The Apple developer documentation is the best place to review these requirements if you are also going to build iPad apps.

Your Android app will also need a home screen icon, known in the Android environment as a "launcher" icon. Due the wide variety of Android devices, you will need to provide three different icon sizes. These sizes correspond to low, medium, and high pixel density Android device screens.

Android launcher icons also need an empty border, because they may be modified for display. This means that the practical size for your icon graphic is actually smaller than the full pixel dimensions of the image. You are restricted to a central square-shaped zone.

Here are the required Android icons:

➤ **72 x 72 pixels:** For high-density displays; however, the usable internal area is 60 x 60 pixels. Save this file as `res/drawable-hdpi/icon.png` in your Android project.

➤ **48 x 48 pixels:** For medium-density displays; however, the usable internal area is 40 x 40 pixels. Save this file as `res/drawable-mdpi/icon.png` in your Android project.

➤ **36 x 36 pixels:** For low-density displays; however, the usable internal area is 30 x 30 pixels. Save this file as `res/drawable-ldpi/icon.png` in your Android project.

➤ **512 x 512 pixels:** Android Marketplace icon. You'll upload this separately when you publish your app, so it does not need to be stored within your Android project folder.

In addition to these required icons, you can specify other optional platform-specific icons, such as icons for menus and the status bar. Refer to the Android developer documentation for the latest details on these at `http://developer.android.com`.

When you create an iPhone or Android project using PhoneGap, default versions of these required icons are created for you. The minimum work necessary to publish your app is to replace the default `.png` files in the project with your own.

Splash Screen

Your app will also require a splash screen. This is a static full-screen image that is displayed while your app is loading. It can be tempting to use the splash screen for promotional content, but a more user-focused approach, and the one recommend by Apple, is to display an "empty" version of your app's main page.

When you do this, your app will appear to load more quickly, because the main page will present itself to the user without delay and then appear to update as the app finishes loading. You can see this behavior when you start the built-in native apps on the iPhone.

The default iPhone splash screen provided by PhoneGap is located at `Resources/splash/Default.png`, and is a 320 x 480 pixel image. You can produce your own splash screen image very easily by simply starting a clean install of your app that has no data, and taking a screen capture. Press the Home button and the Sleep/Wake button at the same time, and a screen capture of the current screen will be saved to the photo album on your iPhone.

For the Retina display on the iPhone 4, you'll need a 640 x 960 pixel image for the splash screen. Either capture this directly as a screen capture if you have an iPhone 4, or take a screenshot on your Mac using the iPhone simulator application. The Retina version should, as usual, be saved with the name `Default@2x.png`.

If your app starts in a landscape, rather than a portrait orientation, you can provide a splash screen for this case by naming your file `Default-Landscape.png`.

Android apps do not normally have splash screens. Instead you are launched directly into the app interface. If you really need one, it is possible to write custom Java code to simulate a splash screen, and you can find some examples on the PhoneGap forums at `www.phonegap.com/community`.

Screenshots and Orientations

When you submit your app to the Apple App Store and the Android Marketplace, you'll need to provide screenshots as part of the upload. These screenshots will be displayed on the details page for your app, and are an opportunity to present your app in its best light.

Your screenshots should of course match the primary orientation that your app is designed for. If your app can support multiple orientations, you should provide screenshots demonstrating that.

You screenshots should show the primary use case for your app. They should tell a story. When you look at them in sequence, they should show the viewer how your app is used and how it can benefit them. Far more people will simply review your screenshots than read your app description text, so they are vital elements in your marketing.

Capturing screenshots on your iPhone is easy. Create the view that you want, and then hold the Home button and Wait/Sleep button at the same time, as noted earlier. If you do not have access to an iPhone 4, you can create retina screenshots using the desktop simulator application that came with Xcode. Open your app in the simulator and grab a rough version that is slightly too large using the Cmd+Shift+4 key combination on your Mac. Then edit the screen capture (which is saved to your desktop as a `.png` file) using an image editor, cropping it down to the correct size (640 x 960 pixels).

 NOTE *If you don't have access to Photoshop for working with images on your Mac, you can download the free SeaShore image editor from* `http://seashore.sourceforge.net`. *This image editor is quite adequate for simple jobs like cropping and resizing. On Windows, try Paint.NET available from* `http://getpaint.net`. *It is also free, and very easy to use. On Linux, your best bet is GIMP, from* `http://www.gimp.org`, *although beware: this application is almost as complex as Photoshop.*

On Android, you can hold the Back key and then also press the Home key after a few seconds to grab a screen capture in much the same way as on the iPhone. The capture will be saved to your photo gallery. However, this feature does depend on the version of Android that you have, and produces images corresponding to the screen size of your device.

For greater flexibility, you can use the Android emulator instead to generate screenshots. This gives you greater control and enables you to generate screenshots for different device sizes. Capture and crop the images using an image editor.

When you are preparing your app for publication, you will need to specify the device orientations that it supports. You do this using the Xcode and Eclipse development environments.

To specify the device orientations that you support for your iPhone app, click your app target (under the TARGETS heading on the left of the main Xcode interface), and then click the Summary tab. You can then visually select the supported orientations by clicking the icons for each one.

For your Android app, you can set the supported orientation by opening the `AndroidManifest.xml` file in Eclipse. Open the Application tab of the manifest editor window, and select the top-level node from the Application Nodes tree on the bottom right. A property editor form appears on the right, containing a Screen Orientation property that you can set.

App Metadata

When you submit your app to the app stores, you'll be asked for various metadata items. You'll need to determine your answers in advance, before you go online and start filling out the forms. A little bit of preparation, especially if you are building an app for a client, will go a long way. Here's what you'll need:

- ➤ **A short textual description:** This should encourage users to download and install your app. Focus on the benefits of your app to the user, rather than simply describing features.

- ➤ **Categories:** You can choose up to two app store categories for your app. Choose wisely. Review the categories in the app store to see where you fit best.

- ➤ **Keywords:** These are relevant for search results.

- ➤ **Supporting websites:** Do you have a website for your app? See Chapter 14 for some ideas.

- ➤ **Promotional graphics and videos:** If you are lucky enough to get selected for premium positioning, you'll need these.

- ➤ **Change log:** A description of changes if you a releasing a newer version of an existing app.

- ➤ **Content rating:** The app store tightly controls apps that contain mature content.

- ➤ **Market geography:** The countries that your app should be available in.

To give your app the best chance for success, and to take maximum advantage of the short launch window when your app appears near the top of the recent releases list, you should take some time to develop these items of metadata.

Working with the App Stores

Unlike mobile web apps, which you can deliver from any web server, apps that are downloaded from the app stores must first be successfully submitted and listed on those app stores. This process is more challenging for iPhone apps, because your app has to pass automated and manual reviews by Apple.

For both app stores you will need to digitally sign your apps. Again, though doing so is more onerous with Apple, you still need to follow essentially the same technical process with Android.

If you are releasing a free app, your life will be much easier. The only significant warranty that you have to provide is that your app complies with U.S. export regulations with respect to cryptography. If your app does use cryptography, you'll need a source of deeper legal and technical knowledge and advice than this author can provide.

If you are releasing a paid app, things can also get interesting. The app stores are continuing to experiment with new business models, and now offer not only one-time app purchases and in-app purchases of digital content, but also regular subscription services. The standard commission for these payment services is 30 percent, in both the Apple App Store and the Android Marketplace. That means that if you sell an app for $10, you will only see $7.

That's the large print. There's also a significant amount of small print, and that small print changes frequently. You will need to make sure that you are happy with the full developer agreements required by the app stores.

Payment terms are typically on a 30-day monthly cycle, so you should factor that into your budgeting. You'll also need to take into account tax issues. You will of course need to pay tax on sales of your app — this is regular income. If you are based outside the U.S., you'll need to submit the appropriate tax forms to the U.S. tax authorities. There may also be sales tax issues depending on your location. In order to sell Android apps, you'll need to sign up for a Google Checkout merchant account, because Android purchases are processed via Google Checkout.

Consider carefully the implications of selling apps directly via the app stores. You may find it easier to produce revenue via in-app advertising rather than direct sales, and you may also find your tax and accounting situation is easier to deal with.

To register with the Android Marketplace, visit `http://developer.android.com`, and click the Publish link on the right menu. You can submit your apps directly to the Android Marketplace, and you do not have to wait for a manual review to have them listed. The next section takes you through the steps required to build your app for release and upload it to the marketplace.

To submit your app to the Apple App Store, you will need to set up an iTunes Connect account, at `http://itunesconnect.apple.com`. This is the portal provided by Apple for content producers, including app developers. The next section takes you through the steps required to get your iPhone app built and released.

The iPhone App Store is more difficult to get into than the Android Marketplace. Apple has a strict review process that includes both automated and manual steps. Typically you will submit your app for review and wait for about two weeks to get approval. Or not. Your app can be rejected, and you will then have to make suitable changes before resubmitting. Be careful here. If you are building an app for a client, you need to make it very clear that you cannot provide any guarantees with regard to this part of the process. Set this expectation from the beginning.

Apple maintains a set of terms and conditions, known as the iOS Developer Agreement, that defines the rules for iPhone apps. These rules include restrictions on access to internal iPhone APIs, "beta" quality apps, trademark infringements, and so on. The documentation on `http://developer.apple.com` explains the full list. If you develop iPhone apps, you will need to stay up-to-date with these rules. Apple enforces them quite strictly.

BUILDING YOUR APP FOR RELEASE

Now it is time to submit your app to the app stores — to "go live." Before you do this, you will need to make sure that you have done final testing, fixed all the bugs you know about, are happy with performance and usability, and have tested on as many physical devices as you have access to. Only once you are happy that you can deliver an application binary of sufficient quality should you proceed to the publishing stage.

To publish your app, you will need to digitally sign it with a distribution certificate. For Android, you can create your own, self-signed, certificate. For iPhone, you'll need to obtain a distribution certificate, in much the same way as you obtain a developer certificate. The following examples will take you through this process.

Let's publish your app!

TRY IT OUT Submitting an iPhone Binary

The basic set of steps you need to perform for publishing an iPhone app are as follows:

1. Register your app.

2. Obtain a distribution certificate.

3. Create a distribution build.

4. Upload and wait for a review.

This example works through these steps in detail. As noted at the start of this chapter, these steps assume you are using Xcode version 4.

1. Register with `http://itunesconnect.apple.com`.

2. Log in to the iTunes Connect site and click the Manage Your Applications link.

3. You'll see an empty dashboard because you don't have any apps yet. Click the Add New App button at the top.

4. You'll see the first page of details that you need to fill out for your app. An example is shown in Figure 13-1.

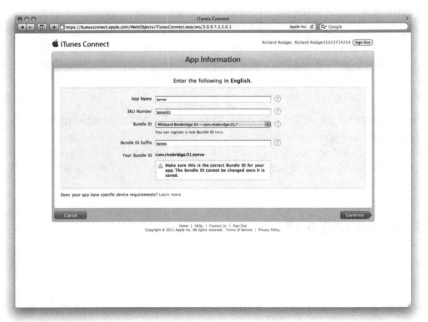

FIGURE 13-1

5. Enter the name of your app (which must be unique), a SKU number (just choose a unique code if your company or client does not use SKU numbers), and the Bundle ID corresponding to your distribution certificate. If you are using a wildcard certificate (these end with the character *), you will also need to supply a unique suffix (as shown in Figure 13-1). When you are ready, click the Continue button.

6. You can now set your app pricing and availability date, as shown in Figure 13-2. You cannot set the price directly, but instead have to choose a pricing tier. Click the Continue button.

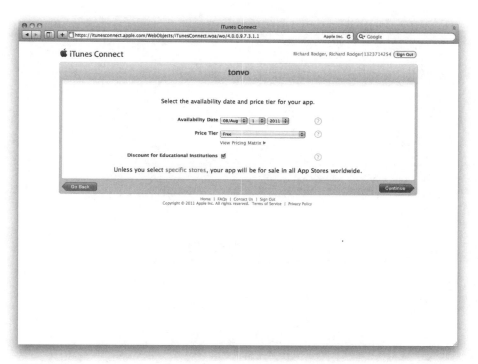

FIGURE 13-2

7. The next page is a long form where you enter all the metadata for your app. Because you've prepared this in advance (right?), just fill in the details. You'll also upload your screenshots and the `iTunesArtwork` icon file here. Figure 13-3 shows the bottom of this page with the screenshots of the tonvo app from Chapter 12 as an example. Click Continue once you are done.

8. You are presented with a summary page for your app, showing its current status as "Prepare for Upload." Click the Ready to Upload Binary button at the bottom. You are asked if your app uses cryptography. Click No if this does not apply to you. You are then taken back to the summary page, which appears as shown in Figure 13-4. You are now ready to build and upload the distribution binary version of your app!

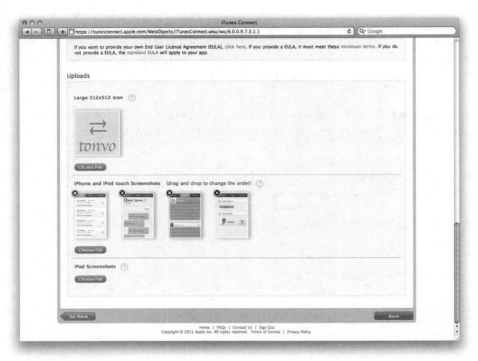

FIGURE 13-3

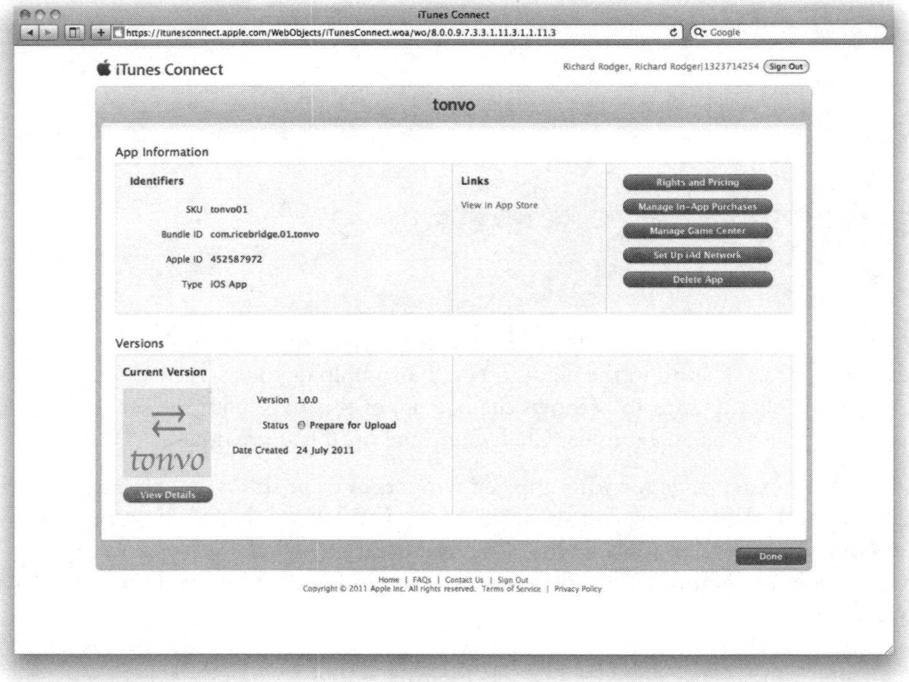

FIGURE 13-4

WARNING *If you forget to click the Ready to Upload Binary button, you will not be able to upload your app. This can be very confusing, because all the app details, such as the name and version, will be correct, but the Xcode uploader will still disclaim any knowledge of your app!*

9. Log in to `http://developer.apple.com` and click the iOS Provisioning Portal link.

10. Click the Distribution tab on the left, and then the Prepare App sub tab at the top. Follow the detailed instructions provided by Apple to obtain a distribution certificate. The procedure is much the same as for development certificates, discussed in Chapter 9.

11. Create, download, and install a Distribution Provisioning Profile using the iOS Provisioning Portal. This enables your Xcode to create distribution builds. The process is again similar to creating, downloading, and installing a Developer Provisioning Profile (see Chapter 9).

12. Open your app project in Xcode, click your app target, and click the Info tab. Make sure that you have the correct settings for your Bundle Identifier and Bundle version (which should be a set of numbers in the format x.y.z). The Bundle Identifier should correspond to your distribution certificate, either fully, or as a wildcard prefix.

13. In Xcode, select the Product / Archive menu option. This triggers a build using your distribution certificate. If the build is successful, the Organizer window opens, showing the Archives tab, as shown in Figure 13-5.

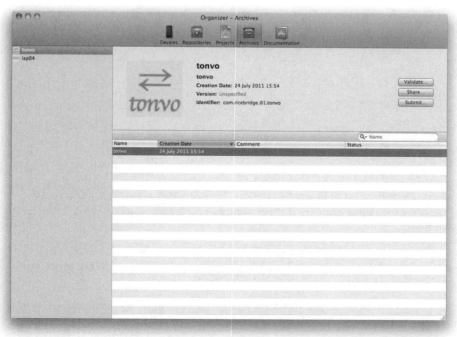

FIGURE 13-5

> **NOTE** *Xcode automatically archives your production builds to* ~/Library/Xcode/ Archives. *You may want to create an independent backup of these binaries.*

14. On the Archives tab of the Organizer window, click the Validate button.

15. You are asked to log in to your iTunes Connect account from within Xcode. Enter your username and password in the dialog window that appears.

16. You are then asked to confirm your app registration details. A dialog window, shown in Figure 13-6, lists your app name and version number, and the signing identity for your distribution certificate. Click Next if everything is correct.

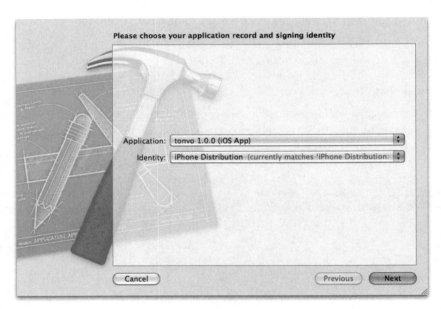

FIGURE 13-6

17. The validation process then runs, and your app is checked against various Apple criteria in an automated manner. An error message appears if there are any problems, which you must resolve before validation will pass.

18. If validation passes, you can now submit your app. Click the Submit button on the Organizer / Archives tab. You are presented with the same dialog sequence as for validation. If there are no errors, your app is uploaded to Apple's servers.

19. Return to the iTunes Connect website. Open the details page for your app. You can now see that the app status has changed to "Upload Received," as shown in Figure 13-7.

FIGURE 13-7

20. Within 24 hours, the status of your app will change to "Waiting For Review." Once your app passes the review, it will go live on to the App Store!

How It Works

You need to have an Apple developer account to use the iTunes Connect site and the iOS Provisioning Portal. If you are building your own apps, you will use your own account. If you are building an app for a client, you will need an account that your client owns. It is not a good idea to maintain client apps from your own account, unless you have a long-term maintenance contract with them.

When you have multiple clients, you will end up with multiple accounts, certificates, and provisioning profiles. Be extremely careful in your management of these files. Make sure you back them up securely. Write down all your passwords (on paper), and keep them safe. When you import certificates and profiles into Xcode, make sure to use the Notes field to keep track of important details about the certificate.

As matter of professional practice you should also ensure that your clients have a copy of their certificates. This will make the transition to a new developer (this can happen for many reasons) much easier for everybody.

When you create your distribution certificate and provisioning profile, it is a good idea to use a wildcard identifier. This means you can use the same certificate and profile for multiple apps, changing only the app suffix. This reduces the amount of work you have to do to keep track of certificates.

Apple requires you to provide a version number for your app. This is also required by the Android Marketplace. The convention is to use a string in the format x.y.z where x, y, and z are integers, typically standing for major, minor, and patch release numbers.

The availability date is the date on which your app will be made available in the app store. You'll mostly want to set this to be as soon as possible, so that the only delay will come from the review process. However, on some occasions you will want to delay the release to coordinate with external events, and you can use the availability date to do this.

If you have built a paid app, you will not be able to set the price directly. Instead, Apple provides a fixed set of pricing tiers. These correspond to set prices in various currencies. A link to the current table of tiers and prices is available as part of the app registration process.

App pricing is very elastic, meaning that lower prices will lead to higher sales volumes, and higher prices will lead to lower sales volumes. You may need to experiment to find the sweet spot that delivers maximum revenue. There is one other thing to take into account: the higher the price, the more scrutiny you will face as part of the review process. If you intend to set a high price for your app, be prepared to deliver a higher quality app as well.

TRY IT OUT | **Submitting an Android Binary**

To publish an Android app, you need to complete these basic steps:

1. Create a signed version.

2. Upload to the Android Marketplace.

3. Provide your app details.

As you can see, the process is slightly less complex than for iPhone apps. On the other hand, you need to pay far more attention to the range of devices you support, due to the wide variety of Android versions.

1. Open your app project in Eclipse, and open the `AndroidManifest.xml` file.

2. Select the Manifest tab in the Manifest editor window, and enter a unique package name for your app. Use the Java reverse-domain name convention: `com.example.appname`. Set the version name to a string in the format X.Y.Z. Set the version code to be an integer value. Start with 1. An example of these settings for the tonvo app from Chapter 12 is shown in Figure 13-8.

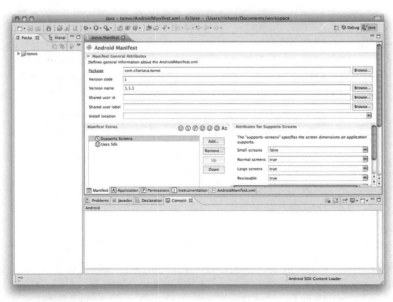

FIGURE 13-8

3. Also on the Manifest tab, specify the screen sizes that you support by using the drop-down menu items on the bottom right.

4. Select the Application tab, and set the `Debuggable` property (which appears in the list on the right) to `false`.

5. Select the Permissions tab. Remove all the permissions your app does not need.

6. Right-click the name of your project in the tree-view on the left, and select the Android Tools / Export Signed Application Package option. An export wizard window appears, as shown in Figure 13-9.

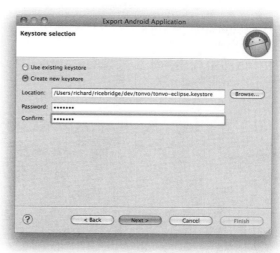

FIGURE 13-9

7. Select the Create New Keystore option. Enter a file location for the keystore file. In Figure 13-9, a location at the top level of the project was chosen. Enter a password for the keystore file. Click Next.

 NOTE *Write down your keystore passwords, on paper. Do it right now. If you are building many different apps for many different clients, you do not want to lose any passwords. I use one of those trendy Moleskine address books. They work very well because the pages are alphabetized:* `http://www.moleskine.com`.

8. Now you need to enter your self-signed certificate details. You should aim to be as accurate as possible. A validity period lasting beyond 2033 is required, and a period of least 25 years is recommended. An example for the tonvo app is shown in Figure 13-10.

9. A signed binary package for your app is now generated. Save this file, which has an `.apk` extension, to a safe place. As with the iPhone, you should back up the binaries that you submit.

10. Go to `http://market.android.com/ publish` and register a developer account. You will need to pay a one-time fee of $25.

FIGURE 13-10

11. Once you have registered, you can log in, and you are presented with an empty dashboard, because you have no apps. Click the Upload Application button.

12. You are presented with a simple dialog window, as shown in Figure 13-11. Select your `.apk` file and upload it.

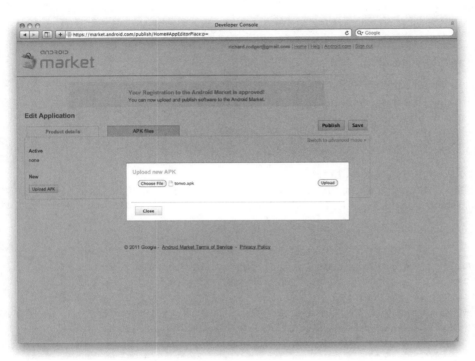

FIGURE 13-11

13. Once your app has uploaded, click the Product Details tab. A long form appears, where you can enter your app metadata (which you have prepared already!). As with the iTunes Connect site, you can upload an icon and a set of screenshots. When you are done, click the Save button.

14. To publish your app, live, to the Android Marketplace, simply click the Publish button! It may take some time for your app to appear in the search results, but you can visit your listing page right way by entering a URL in the following format, replacing com.package.name (highlighted), with the package name of your app:

```
http://market.android.com/details?id=com.package.name
```

15. Your app listing page appears, looking something like Figure 13-12.

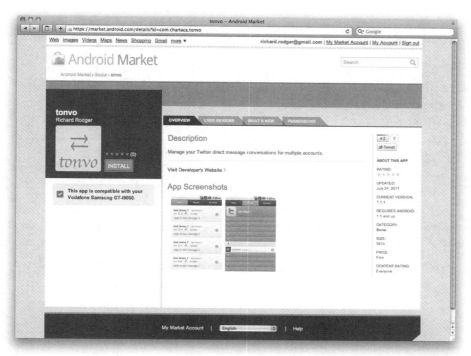

FIGURE 13-12

How It Works

Publishing your Android app is an easy and immediate experience, in contrast to the awkward wait to have your iPhone app reviewed by Apple. On the other hand, the challenge with Android is to produce an app that works on as many devices as possible.

There is no substitute for on-device testing, and you will need to try to get your hands on as many physical Android phones as possible to test. If you are limited in the number of devices that you can get physical access to, your next best option is to use an online testing service, such as http://deviceanywhere.com. This service is relatively expensive because it charges by the minute. You will probably want to pass on this cost to your client, so make it part of your contract from the start.

As important as supporting a wide range of devices is preventing installation on devices where your app will not work. There is no quicker way to get bad reviews than to make your app available to devices that it simply cannot work on. Be careful to set the device parameters tight enough to prevent this. Choose the right API level when you start your Android project, and decide on the screen sizes that you will support in advance.

For your Android app, you need to supply two version numbers: a version *name* and a version *code*. The version name should be a string in the x.y.z format. The version code is an integer value that you have to increase each time you release a new version. It is essentially just a counter.

Because the Android Marketplace does not review apps, the burden is placed on the user to decide if an app is suitable. This means that a fine-grained set of permissions are required for each app to perform the tasks that it needs. For example, you need the `android.permission.INTERNET` permission to make outbound HTTP calls from your app. Choose the minimum set of permissions required. There is no need to request permissions that you do not need; for example, for access to the camera. The PhoneGap Android template includes all permissions by default, so make sure to delete unnecessary permissions from the manifest before publishing your app.

SUMMARY

This chapter took you through the process of preparing, submitting, and publishing your app on the iPhone App Store and the Android Marketplace.

In the next chapter, you move forward to the challenge of getting users to download, install, and use your app!

▶ WHAT YOU HAVE LEARNED IN THIS CHAPTER

TOPIC	KEY CONCEPTS
Launch Icon	This icon is the first point of reference for your app that the user interacts with on a daily basis. This icon is placed on the home screen of the device, and launches your app when touched. You will need to provide multiple versions to satisfy different screen sizes and resolutions.
Splash screen	A static image shown while your app is loading. The best practice is not to use this for promotional content, but rather to enhance the user's perception of the performance of the app by presenting an empty initial page, which then appears to be filled in once the app proper starts.
App Stores	To install your app in their devices, users will visit the Apple App Store or Android Marketplace. Although other services exist to install apps, particularly those that have been "jail-broken" to circumvent built-in security restrictions, these two main app stores are by far the most important when listing your app. Each app store has its own set of guidelines and terms and conditions, and these do change on a regular basis. You will need to familiarize yourself with the official documentation provided by the app stores.
Distribution Signing	To publish your app, you need to digitally sign the binary file so that it can be accepted by the app stores. This requirement ensures that the developer of an app can be identified, and also ensures that the integrity of the app code is protected. This prevents malicious behavior. The requirement to digitally sign your app does introduce an added layer of complication when building and publishing your app, and you should make sure you have set aside time to complete the process in your project schedule.

14

Selling Your App

WHAT YOU WILL LEARN IN THIS CHAPTER:

➤ Determining the right marketing strategy for your app

➤ Working as a freelancer

➤ Using apps to promote your products and services

➤ Selling your own apps as a business

➤ Marketing your app using standard techniques

➤ Marketing your app using techniques that give you an edge

➤ Spending money effectively to market your app

➤ Building a community of loyal fans

Selling your app may be far more difficult than coding it. And you can sell your app in far more ways that just putting a price on it in an app store. You need to take a step back from the keyboard and your development environment and really think about what you — or your company or client — wants to achieve with your app. This is a process. It is something that you refine as you take your app to users and as you see how your app performs out there in the real world. Be prepared to drop your original ideas if the evidence that comes in says to try something else.

Concurrently with building your app, you need to think about how to sell it. This chapter gets you up to speed on the basics and describes a number of strategies and tactics for getting the best return from your development investment. You should read this chapter as a starting point for your sales work. There is at least as much to do in selling your app as there is in building it. Even if you, as a developer, will hand over this work to someone with a marketing or sales background, you still need to know, as an industry professional, how it works.

DETERMINING A MARKETING STRATEGY

Before you jump into random tweeting and ad-buying, you need to determine a strategy for selling your app. You need to do some thinking: Who is the audience for your app? Who will buy your app? Or will you have a free app that is supported by advertising? Who will respond to your ads? Who will want to advertise in your app?

You can answer these general questions by looking at a number of specifics:

➤ **Demographics** — Is your app a game targeted at teenagers? Is it targeted to those only newly introduced to casual games via Facebook? Is it a utility for tech-savvy users? Is it highly targeted at parents with small children? Take some time to think about who will use your app, how much disposable income they have, and how you can reach them.

➤ **Needs** — A game could be an entertaining distraction for the "bored at work" market. A utility app could be a can't-live-without-it productivity tool. Is your app an extension of a website that already has a community? You need to know your users' needs. You may have built a better mousetrap, but that's not so great if nobody needs or wants it.

➤ **The cost of promotion** — Can you reach your audience easily? Or will you need to do lots of advertising? Will users talk about your app? You might have a great app idea, but if you don't have the marketing budget to compete with similar apps, it may be a better idea to build a different app.

➤ **How your app will be used** — Will your app be used for short interactions or deeper, longer sessions? Does your audience have the time to actually use your app? How easy is the app to use? Does its complexity suit your target audience? For example, an app targeted at the seniors market should not rely on background tech knowledge.

Take the time to write down your assumptions. A one-pager is all you need. Explain your assumptions to colleagues, friends, and family members. If most of them don't understand your idea, you're probably on the wrong track. Go back and refine the concept.

 NOTE *Resist the urge to ignore this work and just get straight into coding. It is very easy to waste weeks and months writing beautiful code that no one will ever use. It is best to tackle these big questions up front.*

Once you have come up with some ideas about who your audience is, how they will behave, and how much they will spend, you need to identify some measurements that will prove or disprove your guesses. This is where the real value of the exercise comes into play. The true customer is a fickle thing and changes over time. You need to measure and adjust.

It's important to decide on a key set of metrics that will guide you. You should implement them using an analytics system, such as `flurry.com` or `percentmobile.com`. And you should watch them like a hawk. After you launch your app, do the analytics make your hypothesis stronger or weaker? You should keep adjusting your app to test specific ideas and guesses.

Launching and maintaining a successful app is not a one-shot event. It is a process that continues long after the first version goes live. Many of the most successful apps are not one-hit wonders. The developers of those apps often have a long list of previous apps that you have never heard of. They learned from their earlier mistakes and partial successes. They measured what worked and what didn't. All those little pieces of knowledge and insight feed into later work and ultimately lead to success. The most important strategic decision you can make is to decide to learn from what really happens to your app out there in the wild.

You want to make money from your app. In the following sections, you'll take a closer look at the primary revenue strategies for any app.

Building Apps for Others

Even if you plan to build and sell your own apps, you will almost certainly end up building apps for others. It may even be your main business. The easiest way to make money from mobile apps is to build them on contract for other people or as part of your paid employment. It isn't easy to develop and promote a hit app that sells millions. It may take years of refinement and many apps to get there, and you have to live in the meantime.

Keep this in mind that regardless of whether someone else owns an app you built and it is successful, you will benefit. A portfolio of successful apps is a huge asset to your professional reputation. Always build your apps for success. Even when you are building an in-house app that will be used only by a team of 50 sales representatives, you should build for success. There is no downside to building the best app you can. People in sales have a habit of starting successful businesses, and you just might get a call to build one of them an app that will bootstrap your own business. Keep an eye on the long game and always build professional-quality apps.

Many of your customers will be commissioning you to build their first app. They will not have the depth or breadth of experience in the app industry that you have. As part of your professional service, you have a duty to help them make their app as successful as possible. Don't just execute to their requirements. Rather, bring something extra to the table. Explain to each client the importance of usability, meeting app store guidelines, common conventions for app user interfaces, the economics of cloud hosting, and how to launch and market an app successfully. As you build experience in these things, your knowledge of them may become more valuable than your coding skills. You can provide a lot of value to your clients by guiding them in their decisions.

As you're working with clients, keep in mind that whoever has the gold makes the rules. Ultimately, your client has the final say. Therefore, you need to be careful to choose clients who will not harm your reputation by ignoring your advice. This is not always easy. You can protect yourself by checking out references, reviewing a client's web presence, and talking to people the client has worked with before.

 NOTE *To make sure that your best work pays dividends for you, always ask to include the app in your professional portfolio. No reasonable customer will refuse this.*

As a revenue model for apps, professional services work is the least risky. It is not without some risk, however. All the usual freelancing caveats apply:

➤ Make sure you have a contract, purchase order, or letter of understanding, as appropriate.

➤ For brand-new clients, you absolutely must get a down payment before you start work.

➤ Keep track of your time and invoice properly.

Many clients will look for fixed-price work. In principle, there is nothing wrong with this, but you need to manage the risks. In a fixed-price scenario, you are taking on the bulk of the risk in the project. If there is a huge technical challenge that soaks up your time, it will eat into your profit. Even when a client drags his or her feet about getting requirements and materials to you, you'll still have to meet the deadline. If there is a dependency on other third parties, you may have to absorb low-quality deliveries from others. All these things happen on time-and-materials projects as well, but you charge for your time there, so the impact is not as great.

To mitigate these risks, the best approach is to always offer two prices: your standard time-and-materials day rate and a fixed-price rate with a 50% (or more!) markup. Your estimate for the amount of work is the same, of course. Let's put some numbers on this. Let's say you bill at $1,000 per day on a time-and-materials basis. For a two-week project, you'll charge $10,000. But your fixed-price rate is $1,500 per day, coming in at $15,000 for two weeks. Offer both options to your client and let the client decide on his or her level of risk tolerance.

The other reason for taking this approach is to frame the debate on your terms. By clearly stating the framework in which your prices operate, you remove grounds for misunderstanding and false expectations. By pricing the difference between fixed and time-and-materials work in terms of risk, you make it clear that all software projects are subject to schedule risk, and you force the issue out into the open. This leads to a healthy discussion with your client. If the client does not accept this basis for the pricing, then it is probably best to decline the job, as it is an indicator of further problems down the road because the client is not willing to accept the realities of software development projects.

One final tip for freelance invoicing: You may end up waiting weeks or months to get paid. Always offer a small discount (for example, 2%) for payment within 10 days. This is a marvelous way to get your invoice prioritized. There are also many larger organizations with internal policies that require staff to take advantage of early payment discounts, and this is an excellent and relatively inexpensive way to activate those policies. And it's not really a discount: You did remember to price in slow-payment risk in the first place, didn't you?

Using Apps to Promote Your Business

One-off stories of newly minted app millionaires notwithstanding, the main way existing business and services derive value from mobile apps is by using them to reach new and existing customers. Mobile apps are an excellent promotional strategy for an existing product or service. They offer mobility, convenience to existing customers, and promotion to new potential customers.

This strategy is often the most effective one when apps are not your core business. As with websites, most businesses are now expected to have an app of some sort. Unlike websites, where you can get away with simple brochure-style content, an app for a business needs to provide actual utility for customers. The following sections describe some of the ways you use apps to build you business.

Selling a Subscription-based Service

If your business is Internet based and the primary communication channel is your website, then an app is a natural extension of your service. For example, Twitter provides an app on both iPhone and Android to read and post tweets. Amazon offers its Kindle ebook reader as a mobile app on both platforms. Many new social media startups, such as the Instagram photo sharing service, are offered primarily via an app. In all these cases, the app itself is free, and the user pays for the service via a monthly subscription fee. Online services that have this type of subscription business model need to have an app version of their service, or they cannot compete.

Many more traditional businesses can make use of apps this way as well. Utility companies now offer apps that let you take meter readings. Government offices offer apps that let you pay service charges. Transport companies offer apps that provide up-to-the-minute information on delays and waiting times.

The key challenge for apps following this strategy is that they are not very useful without a subscription to the underlying service. There is no point downloading an app for a power company if you are not a customer. The main focus of the app should be on existing customers. Most functionality will, of necessity, be hidden behind a login screen.

Offering a Useful Free Version of Your App

Strategically, there is an advantage in offering some value for non-subscribers. A limited service, especially an informational one, can be offered without charge. You can allow the user to access the service via your app and encourage sign up afterward. It is important to offer some value. People often install free apps on a whim, and it is very easy to collect a large number of bad reviews and a low star rating in the app stores from users who do not have a subscription and thus have a poor experience with the app.

Promoting Through Your Existing Channels

Promoting a subscriber-based app also requires a fit-for-purpose strategy. It is most effective to use your existing customer communications channels. Promoting the app in your standard advertising runs, on your website, and via your mailing lists will generate far more active users than advertising on mobile channels such as app advertising networks.

Selling In-App Advertising

Free apps can also generate revenue. You can place advertising in your app. This works where your content is compelling enough to generate large amounts of usage. For example, the Angry Birds game on the Android platform is supported by advertising. This strategy is feasible as a primary revenue stream only if you can build up the user base to the required numbers.

Delivering the App as a Premium Service

An alternative revenue strategy is to offer an app as a premium service, where subscribers to your service need to pay extra to use the app. This strategy is much less common and requires your service to be very sticky. If you run an online accounting service targeted at the local laws and regulations for your state or country, this can work. If you have a to-do list application, it won't.

Remember The Milk, a popular to-do list service, was forced to drop premium pricing for its app because it faced too much competition.

Selling In-App Purchases

In-app purchases are a growing and highly effective revenue strategy. Due to the ease of use and impulsive nature of in-app purchases, this can be an easy way to sell additional products and services to existing customers. Many games offer the base version for free and make their money via in-app purchases of additional equipment. The F.A.S.T fighter pilot game is a particularly good example, selling you new fighter jets for a couple dollars each.

For the in-app purchases model to work, you need to make sure that the numbers add up. Don't forget that you will have to hand over 30% of the list price to the app stores. You also need to have a product or service that lends itself to the sale of virtual goods. Content readers or players can work very well under this model. Services that limit usage and offer various levels of premium accounts are also suited. Pizza Hut has found this model to work rather well for pizza deliveries.

Building a Cross-Platform App

When you are using apps to sell your product or service, and the app itself is not the main product, it is important to have a cross-platform strategy. It is less important to be the fastest or the most beautifully designed iPhone app if your existing customers who use Android cannot use your service. Using HTML5-based apps is a real win in this situation because they not only allow you to reach more customers but also reduce your development cost because you have to build only one version.

Selling Your Own Apps

What do you want to do with your life? It's a serious question. Are you going to sell apps for pocket money or to pay the mortgage? You've read the articles about 16-year-olds earning $1 million by creating a novelty app. There's a reason you're reading an article about that, though: It's newsworthy because it's so remarkable. It's a fantasy, not a strategy. App developers who do make a living from apps and who have the occasional minor hit put in a lot of grunt work behind the scenes.

Your strategy should depend on *why* you're going to write apps and sell them. If you're looking to improve your résumé or increase your contracting rates, then you need popular apps that you can release for free. If you're looking to enjoy coding on a new platform and maybe make a bit of cash on the side, by all means put a price on your app and sell it. If you want to make a living out of app development, your approach will need to be very different. You'll need to embrace marketing and sales. The coding and building of your apps will take up less than half your time — and probably less than a quarter of your time, if you're successful. Promoting your app and getting people to buy it will occupy most of your time and headspace.

You need to be honest with yourself: If you're in it for the coding, you may end up short on cash. It's not a huge risk, of course, because you can always go freelance with your mobile skill set. In fact, the ability to easily pick up freelance work will make it quite difficult to be a true app developer living off the sales of your apps. You are going to have to forego certain income now in the hopes of creating a larger income later. This is not for the faint of heart.

Setting the Right Goals for Yourself

It's important to set clear goals and know what you want to do. Maybe you want to earn $100,000 per year at the end of year 2. Or maybe you want to have 10 apps each earning $500 per month. It may be a self-help cliché, but you need to set a SMART (specific, measurable, attainable, realistic, timely) goal before you start. And actually write it down. On paper. As you do, make sure your goal has the following qualities:

- ➤ **Specific** — What apps for what audience?
- ➤ **Measurable** — How much income, per month, do you want?
- ➤ **Attainable** — Consider apps you can build in a month, not in a year.
- ➤ **Realistic** — How will you live in the early days?
- ➤ **Timely** — What will you deliver in the first three months?

Your most important app development tool is not Xcode, or Eclipse, or HTML5, or PhoneGap. It's a spreadsheet. You should create a model of your income and expenditure, and don't forget to include your cloud-hosting costs. You need to work out where you break even and how much of a financial hole you'll dig first.

To realistically plan the development of your apps, you need to assess your skill set. Yes, you can code. But how are your graphic design skills? Users have very high expectations for the visual appearance of apps, and you need to meet those standards. You likely to need the help of a design professional.

Embracing the Marketing Work

An important element in your plan is your target market. Choose customers who have money. This may seem obvious, but it's easy to forget. If your app targets a demographic with little disposable income, then they probably don't even have smartphones! If your niche is too niche, you may meet customer needs exactly — for all 15 people in your global customer base.

Once you launch your app, you need to tend it. You can't just build an app, submit it, and move on the next one. If you do, you'll see some sales just after launch and then almost nothing for the remainder of the app's life. Each app you launch has to be continually marketed and updated. This is where the hard work comes in. You know you can stay up all night coding. Can you stay up all night writing content for a promotional website? You'll learn some of the tactics for promoting your app this way in the next section. As a question of strategy, you need to decide if you can do this.

Finally, remember that there are lots of sales of the top apps but very few sales of everything else. This means that to make money, you need to have a very large number of apps (the so-called long-tail strategy), or you need to focus on promoting one or two apps. You should decide in advance, as this choice will dictate your build process, your audience, and how you set up your app code architecture.

Now that you're ready to make that leap of faith and become a fully fledged app developer, it's time to get tactical. The next section looks at the practical details of how to promote and make money from your apps.

CHOOSING TACTICS FOR PROMOTING YOUR APP

The market for mobile apps is extremely crowded. Getting users to notice you through the noise requires hard work and sustained effort. You'll need to try some or all of the sales and promotional tactics outlined in this section. If you're developing apps for fun, or résumé building, you can be more relaxed in your approach to promotion. But it is still worthwhile promoting your app: Prospective clients or employers will take you a lot more seriously if they heard about your app independently because it was popular.

If you are writing apps as your main business, it's a different story. In order to make the best use of your limited time and resources, you need to track everything you do and how effective it is. You need to spend money and time putting these tactics into play:

➤ Track every penny spent and every minute consumed.

➤ Keep a spreadsheet that tracks your entire investment in your app.

➤ Convert your time into an equivalent daily contracting rate.

➤ Add it all up and monitor your investment on a weekly basis.

There is no point putting money into advertising that does not work. One very painful lesson that you'll learn about marketing is that doubling the amount you spend usually increases sales by only a few percent. You are much better off finding the right marketing channels and putting your money and time into those.

Before you start creating advertising copy text and messaging, and before you start paying for logos and other pieces of creative collateral, you need to know what you are selling. What makes your app unique? Why will people buy it? If, like me, you are an engineer at heart, these questions will make you cringe. They are impossible to answer! That is actually true. You can't answer them by sitting at your desk. You need to get out of the house and talk to people. You need to see people using your app. You need to iterate. By getting many people to try your app in the early stages, before you release it or build up a design concept, you'll gain very valuable information about how other people perceive the app. What they think may be quite different from your perspective. Test users may very well give you your unique selling point in what seems to be a throwaway comment.

 TIP Do not develop in secrecy, "perfecting" your app. You will not know what works in the market. Get out there and find out what really resonates with users.

From the time you spend talking to your trial users, you will develop an idea of your app's uniqueness and what works as a marketing message. There is no point refining this too much. At this point you can go live, release your app, and measure the results. Do the results support your ideas about the app and who uses it? Does the data show something completely different, like an enthusiastic user base you never knew existed? Don't be afraid to refine and refocus after launch.

It's important to have a written marketing plan. For each week until you go live, you should plan out your non-development marketing and promotion activities. You will have far better results with a sustained blogging campaign over many months, where you build up a loyal readership, than with an advertising blitz at the last moment. You should aim to have your users ready to buy when the app comes out, already knowing who you are and what you are building.

It is all too easy to stay in front of code and focus on the engineering. In order to make money from your apps, though, you need to get out there and sell them. The following sections discuss some practical tactics to achieve those sales!

Standard Tactics

You need a website to go with your app. This is easy if you already have a website or service that the app extends. If the app is the primary product, you still need to create a website. This is an alternative place to interact with your users, where they can manage their accounts and get support from you. It also serves as a marketing base for online promotion. Apps that lack a website do not appear professional, even if they have great graphic design.

Your website needs to have a user forum. No matter how easy your app is to use, there will be issues. You want to get to the point where users can help each other. A forum can help with this, and it can also help you build a valuable list of frequently asked questions rather than your own random guesses. The forum is also the place to interact with your serious fans and give them special offers. Maintaining and managing an app forum takes work and time. You need to budget this into your weekly activities. A well-managed forum will pay dividends and is worth building.

Using social media to promote an app is now standard practice. Therefore, you should make sure to have a presence on Twitter and Facebook, and also use niche social media sites such as Quora that might have a more focused audience for your app. Maintaining a social media presence requires a degree of time and effort, and you need to plan for this as well. Your app will not be successful in the long run if you don't stay engaged with your users. At a minimum, you need to provide regular updates to your subscriber base. At the high end, you can establish a powerful personal presence that will help solidify your customer base. If your app is tech focused, you should be sure to take advantage of older forms of social media, such as Google Groups, or Internet Relay Chat, as many of your tech-oriented users will be happier using such means of communication.

In addition, focused marketing-oriented mailing lists can be remarkably effective. Email is still the most-used means of communication on the Internet. Mailing list subscribers are often true fans, and you can get directly into their inboxes. A monthly newsletter can provide tips, tricks, industry news, and useful information about the space where your app resides. And it can link to complementary apps and services. A newsletter with high-quality content like this will create a strong word-of-mouth community for you. By using a service like MailChimp to send mail to your mailing list, you can avoid issues with spam blacklisting and user subscription management. You'll need to budget time for this as well. If your app is successful, or if you have a marketing budget, you can start to outsource some of this work over time. A good marketing person can help you build and retain your active user volume.

 NOTE *You can see that coding will take up less and less of your time as your app becomes more successful. This is what it takes to make a living directly from apps.*

When you are launching your app, you'll need to handle some standard promotional activities. For example, you need to submit your app to all the app directory and review sites, such as www.appstorehq.com and http://bestapps.com. Submitting apps to these sites is a thankless job; if you can afford to outsource it, you should.

You also need to develop a standard short promotional piece for your app, including text and pictures. Then you should create a landing page for each directory to link to. By using separate pages, you can track the effectiveness of each directory. You can also use different versions for A/B testing, where you try out different content on your landing pages. You can then feed this back into the content you use to describe you app on its app store listing.

The other essential players in any successful app launch are the bloggers. You'll need to get bloggers to write about your app. Don't fret about readership. Anyone who maintains even a semi-regular blog has enough readership. The standard approach is to write a polite and short email, explaining the key points of your app and offering a free download so that the blogger can review your app. You can use app store coupons to cover the price of the download for the blogger. Needless to say, choose bloggers that cover topics relevant to your app. There is no magic bullet when it comes to getting coverage from bloggers. You really need to build up your relationships with them individually and over time.

 TIP *Don't expect a very high response rate from bloggers, especially from popular ones, who receive many requests like this. Less popular bloggers may well be flattered and write reviews. These are still valuable and will remain on the web, providing a baseline of traffic to your app and website.*

Getting coverage from traditional media can also be challenging. You need to put out a press release via http://prnewswire.com. If you don't have the budget for this, though, you can send the press releases yourself to media sites that you think are relevant. Make sure that your app web site has a "press kit" — a page with the basic details of your app, who you are, your background story, and a list of previous press releases. Writing effective press releases and getting coverage in traditional media is a book-length subject in itself — and it's worth researching.

You need to submit your app to as many mobile app competitions as you can find. Mobile industry conferences usually have associated competitions. (But beware of those that require high entry fees; they are not normally good value for money.) This has two benefits. First, you might win or even get placed. At the very least, you will appear on the list of entries. Second, you'll get real people looking at your app, evaluating it very critically. You might get very valuable feedback from competition entries. You can reuse your blogger email and directory submission content for your competition submissions. Many also require a YouTube video demonstration of your app. It's worth creating such a video because you can reuse it for other promotional activities. I maintain an up-to-date list of mobile competitions at http://mobileapps.listkitty.com that you might find useful.

If your primary revenue is from app sales rather than advertising or in-app purchases, you need to consider providing a lite version of your app so that users can try it out first. The lite version should have greatly reduced functionality and be limited in various ways. You can use this version to promote the purchase of the full version. Your lite version still needs to be useful, though, or it won't be accepted into the app stores.

> **NOTE** *There is another danger with lite versions: bad reviews. This is a problem that plagues free apps in general and lite versions in particular. Because happy users do not uninstall the app, they do not get the opportunity to rate your app unless they actively return to the app stores to do so. On the other hand, users who are unhappy may rate your app when they uninstall it. Casual users who are just testing your app or who do not have an account with your app's service will necessarily have a reduced user experience and will tend to post bad reviews. So, while a lite version will provide you with a marketing boost, it can be counterproductive. You need to carefully weigh this one: Is your target audience fickle? Do they have a significant need that your app addresses? Be prepared to pull the lite version if things don't go your way.*

The final standard tactic almost does not need to be stated: You need to price your app properly! To do so, you should benchmark your price against the prices of similar apps. If you are too far above or below the expected price, you will damage your profits. Games generally need to be quite inexpensive. Apps that extend an existing service can be more expensive. If your service is unique in some way, or has very high value, then you can push the price above single figures.

Expensive Tactics

If you have a marketing budget, you have extra options when it comes to promoting your app. You need to be careful, however, to measure and track everything you spend money on. It is very easy to spend large amounts on online advertising without getting results. This section provides links to websites that serve as examples of the types of services discussed. Providing these links doesn't imply endorsement of these services. In addition, you need to do your own research to find services that suit your budget and needs.

The primary place to advertise your app is on the app directory sites so you can target users who are actually looking for apps. You can expect to pay hundreds or thousands of dollars per month for advertising a single app, depending on the site.

You can also target high-readership content sites, such as `http://alistapart.com`, especially for iPhone app advertising. For this type of advertising, you really need to use an advertising network such as `http://fusionads.net`. This marketing tactic is very expensive. It makes sense only if you are promoting a brand or have a very clear revenue model.

You can also advertise your app inside other apps. A number of networks offer this service, and it can be quite effective. When you use this tactic, you are advertising to a highly targeted user base of people who are guaranteed to have smartphones. `www.admob.com` is the market leader for this type of advertising. By using this tactic, you can generate a large number of impressions very quickly, so you need to make sure that the rest of your marketing apparatus is ready to handle the influx of potential customers. You also need be prepared to pay handsomely for this type of promotion.

To create a sustained marketing campaign that includes social media and major content sites, you may need to turn to an app promotion agency, such as `www.apalon.com`. Typically, such services offer a range of fixed-price promotional packages that can get you coverage across a range of sites.

This can be a cost-effective way to outsource the grunt work of app promotion — if you have the budget. These agencies have developed media relationships that make them more effective than do-it-yourself efforts at getting placements. This is part of the value they provide.

Finally, depending on your business, you might find it useful to promote your app offline. Traditional media such as newsprint, radio, and TV reach large audiences, and if your company or client is a well-known brand, this can be the right way to reach your users. This works not only on a national scale but also on a local scale. As an app developer, you can suggest this marketing tactic, but implementation is best left to the traditional experts.

Guerrilla Tactics

You're an independent developer, and you have no budget. What do you do? How do get people to buy your app? You need some guerrilla tactics! If you play by the traditional rules, you don't stand a chance. Instead, you should work on the things money can't buy and find ways to make your users love you.

The most important thing you can do for your app is build a community around it. This community consists of an inner circle of loyal fans who will promote your app for free, just because they love it so much. They are surrounded by an outer circle of casual users who are well-disposed toward your app. You need to create this community from the ground up.

One of the ways to lay the foundations for your app community is to recruit test users. You need to personally speak to these users and convince them to give your app a try. You'll be giving them prerelease versions that aren't yet available in the app stores. It is vital in any case to do independent user testing, but you can also use this part of the development process to sow the seeds of your community. You need to keep this group feeling that they are part of something special. You need to be prepared to communicate continuously with them, face to face or over the phone, and you need to be serious about incorporating their feedback. By doing this, you'll create a sense of shared ownership in your app. Community building is a considerable art in itself. There are several books and many blogs on the subject. Do your research, learn the ropes, and bootstrap your fan base.

One of the things that makes your community so valuable is its ability to spread the word about your app. Getting your committed fans to re-Tweet your announcements and like your Facebook status messages is an essential element of online app promotion. You can go further than this, however. It is extremely effective to offer a reward for spreading your message. This reward can be very simple, from entering re-Tweeters into a competition to offering credit for in-app purchases. Be creative in your reward schemes and suit them to your user base and app. By creating an incentive to spread the word, you can greatly increase the amount of buzz your app generates.

You can take the reward tactic to the next level by offering rewards for bug hunters. This may seem dangerous and counterintuitive, but it can actually be hugely successful. The users who find bugs are almost always real users who actually care about your app enough to push into edge cases that contain bugs. Reward them with gift vouchers for the app stores or other appropriate services. For the tech crowd, I've found that `thinkgeek.com` vouchers are very popular. By publicly rewarding bug hunters, you create a feeling of honesty and fair dealing about your app and your business. And you get free quality assurance!

The reward model has many uses. The `dropbox.com` file-sharing utility has become the gold standard for viral marketing using rewards. Take a close look at how this model works. When you refer a friend to Dropbox, and that person signs up via your referral, you benefit by getting extra free storage. But your friend *also* gets some free storage, over and above what he or she would have gotten signing up by themselves. Instead of your referral being perceived as spam, now you are doing your friend a favor. This is an incredibly powerful approach that you can use for your own app.

The key practical element here is to always have a sharing screen in your app. This is a page that is easily accessible — so maybe a top-level menu item — that offers a range of sharing options. You can offer email, SMS, social sharing, social news, and anything else appropriate to your customer base. You should use large and friendly icons from the social sites and make this page easy and intuitive to use. This single page in your app can generate more users than most other forms of promotion.

When someone has received an invitation to download and buy your app, you need to help that person overcome any lingering doubts. This is where your supporting website and online community come into their own. Different users will respond to different types of media. You need to provide an extensive text description of the app and also provide a slideshow walkthrough of the app. You can use a service such as `http://slideshare.net` for this. And you can reuse the video walkthrough that you created for your competition entries here as well. You'll need to get some testimonials from your biggest fans; these really work, even if they can be a little cheesy!

When you sell a digital product, you can expect to encounter piracy. Users with jail-broken and rooted phones can download cracked apps from a number of less-than-innocent websites. This is a fact of life. You can either stay up late at night worrying about lost sales or use this as another marketing challenge. The fact of the matter is that most pirates cannot afford to pay for your app anyway. They are either underage or unable to use credit facilities. But think about it this way: In these times when you have to fight for every ounce of online attention, and for every user, even the pirates have some value. They may persuade their more honest friends to buy your app. They may still rave about it on their blogs if they really like it. They will still bump up your "free" user numbers. And you have every right to market to them. Do not be afraid to make your app "pesterware" so that pirated versions continuously emit pop-ups, asking the user to purchase the real thing. While crackers might get a juvenile kick out of breaking your app copy protection, they have no interest in laboriously recoding it to remove pop-ups. So turn piracy to your advantage, accept that it happens, do not lose any sleep over it, and move on.

One of the most difficult guerrilla tactics is to develop a high-value content blog. There is no magic formula here. This really is at the grunt work end of the scale. However, the dividends from a blog that has a large reader base are enormous and continue for years. You can write about topics that are related to your app and be useful. You should resist the urge to sell your app in every second post. Again, this is a topic on which many books have been written, so read them. My one piece of advice here is that quantity sometimes trumps quality. The more you write, the better you will get. You can never tell which articles will be popular. As a journalist friend once said to me, each article should be "fire and forget." Posting once a week is the absolute minimum.

There's one final guerrilla tactic that's very simple: Promote your app in your email signature. Include a link to your app at the bottom of every email you send. You'll be surprised how effective this is.

SUMMARY

This chapter moves at a fast pace over a wide range of strategies and tactics for selling an app. It is just a starting point, though. By now you should know what you don't know; where to look for more information; and how to start, execute, and run a basic marketing campaign for your app.

Even though you're a developer, you shouldn't be afraid to jump into these marketing activities. You might find that they are more fun than you think. When you experience the thrill from your first sale, you will experience something special and almost addictive. Running a marketing campaign will take you to the next level professionally, and you shouldn't shy away from it. If you approach it logically and methodically, you'll be just fine.

After reading these 14 chapters, you are now ready to build, launch, and sell you own apps; host them in the cloud; and deploy them to multiple device platforms. Open `index.html`, type in `<!DOCTYPE html>`, and get started!

▶ WHAT YOU LEARNED IN THIS CHAPTER

TOPIC	KEY CONCEPTS
Marketing plan	Selling your app requires executing a wide range of disparate activities — and doing so on a consistent and regular basis. Unlike software development estimation, many of these activities are very predictable in terms of time and effort, and this means you can plan for them far more easily. You should put together a written marketing plan for your apps and decide in advance how much time and effort you will devote to the plan. It is important to write it down; there is too much detail to keep in your head.
Freelance work	Freelance work is a great way to earn a living or even to fund your long-term ambitions to live off app development alone. It necessarily involves an element of risk, as your invoices may not get paid on-time, and your clients can keep extending your project scope. You address these risks by being upfront about them with potential clients and building them into your rates.
Guerilla tactics	If you do not have an advertising budget or if your budget is very small, you need to find alternative ways to promote your app. There are many ways of doing this that do not involve spending money. Some, like blogging, involve a time commitment, but others merely require a decision to use them, such as referral programs designed to have viral effects. Do not be afraid to find new ways of promoting your app.
Community building	Creating a community of dedicated fans is the number one way to achieve lasting customers for your app. A loyal fan base will buy all your apps, have no issues with in-app purchases, and support you on social media sites. Although the investment in your community can seem indirect at times, it pays dividends over the long haul.

Exercise Solutions

CHAPTER 1

1. In the `view.html` file, replace this line:

```
tapper.onclick = function() {
```

with this:

```
tapper.ontouchstart = function() {
```

Reload the app in your mobile browser. Tapping still works, and the color changes. Reload the app in your desktop browser. You'll notice that clicking no longer works, and the app only responds to touch events.

2. Add an `onresize` event handler to the JavaScript:

```
window.onresize = function() {
  var tapper = document.getElementById('tapper');
  var landscape = window.innerHeight < window.innerWidth
  tapper.style.width  = ( landscape ? 400 : 300 ) + 'px';
  tapper.style.height = ( landscape ? 200 : 300 ) + 'px';
}
```

This code first obtains a reference to the tapper `div` in the usual way, using `getElementById`. Then it determines whether the mobile device is in landscape orientation by comparing the window width and height. If the window is shorter than it is wide (height < width), then the device must be on its side, in landscape mode.

The code then sets the width and height style values, using the convenient conditional evaluation syntax (<test> ? <test is true> : <test is false>).

3. When you scroll up, the mobile device browser automatically hides the address bar. You can use this behavior to force the address bar to disappear. Even if you scroll up by one pixel, it will still work.

However, it is not quite so simple. First, you need to ensure that the page is in fact scrollable, so you give the page a large height:

```
<style>
  body { margin: 0px; height:1000px; }
  ...
</style>
```

Then you can call the `window.scrollTo` function, with a 0 pixel horizontal scroll and a 1 pixel vertical scroll. You call this function in the `onload` event handler:

```
window.onload = function() {
  setTimeout(function(){ window.scrollTo(0,1)}, 1)
```

But what is the `setTimeout` call for? This is a pure hack to trigger the desired behavior from the internal logic of the mobile web browser, which has been discovered to require this small delay. If you don't introduce the delay, this trick just won't work.

4. To make your app zoomable, simply remove the `maximum-scale=1.0` setting from the `viewport` metatag and set the `user-scalable` setting to `yes`. To start zoomed out, set the `initial-scale` setting to `0.5`, which reduces the size of the app by half:

```
<meta name="viewport" content="user-scalable=yes,initial-scale=0.5" />
```

CHAPTER 2

1. In your `draw-dry.html` file, add these highlighted lines to define the color buttons:

```
...
<body>
<button id="clear">clear</button>
<button id="red" style="color:red">R</button>
<button id="green" style="color:green">G</button>
<button id="blue" style="color:blue">B</button>
<br>
<canvas id="main" width="300" height="300"></canvas>
...
```

In your `draw-dry.js` file, replace the code dealing with the Clear button (just after the `ontouchmove` code) with the following boldfaced refactored and DRY code:

```
...
canvas.ontouchmove = function(event){
    position(event,function(lastx,lasty, newx,newy){
      line(lastx,lasty, newx,newy);
    })
  }

  var buttons = {
```

```
    clear: document.getElementById('clear'),
    red: document.getElementById('red'),
    green: document.getElementById('green'),
    blue: document.getElementById('blue'),
  }

  function setcolor(event) {
    draw.fill = event.target.id;
    draw.stroke = event.target.id;
  }

  buttons.clear.onclick = clear;
  buttons.red.onclick = setcolor;
  buttons.green.onclick = setcolor;
  buttons.blue.onclick = setcolor;

  clear();
}
```

This code uses JSON to define the HTML element for each color button and then uses a common `setcolor` function to change the `draw.fill` and `draw.stroke` color properties. The `id` attributes of the buttons are chosen to match valid color names (`red`, `green`, and `blue`) and are retrieved using `event.target.id`.

2. To save and restore the user's drawing, add Save and Restore buttons that you'll show one at a time. If there is no drawing saved, show the Save button. If a drawing has been saved, show only the Restore button. You can use the CSS `display:none` property value to hide a button. Initially, the Restore button is hidden:

```
...
<button id="clear">clear</button>
<button id="red" style="color:red">R</button>
<button id="green" style="color:green">G</button>
<button id="blue" style="color:blue">B</button>
<button id="save">save</button>
<button id="restore" style="display:none">restore</button>
<br>
<canvas id="main" width="300" height="300"></canvas>
...
```

Update the `draw-dry.js` file to handle the new buttons. This is where your DRY approach starts to pay dividends. It is now easy to add the new buttons in the right place:

```
var buttons = {
  clear: document.getElementById('clear'),
  red: document.getElementById('red'),
  green: document.getElementById('green'),
  blue: document.getElementById('blue'),
  save: document.getElementById('save'),
  restore: document.getElementById('restore'),
}
```

You'll also need a way to save the image in the canvas. You can do this by using the `getImageData` and `putImageData` functions, which extract and insert a rectangular area of image data, respectively:

```
var imagedata

buttons.save.onclick = function() {
  imagedata = context.getImageData(0,0,draw.width,draw.height)
  buttons.save.style.display = 'none'
  buttons.restore.style.display = 'inline'
}

buttons.restore.onclick = function() {
  context.putImageData(imagedata,0,0)
  buttons.save.style.display = 'inline'
  buttons.restore.style.display = 'none'
}

clear()
}
```

Remember to update the visibility of the Save and Restore buttons!

3. You can use the simple HTTP `basic` password-protecting to prevent unwanted access to a site that is under construction. This is not very secure but is normally good enough for ordinary sites. Do not use this method for sensitive material!

In your nginx configuration file on your Amazon server, add the following highlighted lines to your location directive:

```
location /draw {
  alias /home/ubuntu/draw;
  auth_basic            "Restricted";
  auth_basic_user_file  /home/ubuntu/restricted.pwd
}
```

This causes the web browser to display a username and password dialog box with the title "Restricted" when you visit your site. Before you do that, you'll need to set up the username and password.

Create a file called `restricted.pwd` in your `/home/ubuntu` folder on your Amazon server. You can also store this file elsewhere if you have a specific project folder structure. The one place you should not store it is in any folder that will be publicly accessible via nginx!

The `restricted.pwd` file is used to specify the username and passwords to nginx that can access the site. The format of this file is a list of `username:password` entries, one per line. The username is in plain text, and the password is encrypted. This is actually the format of the Apache web server password file, which nginx has adopted.

Creating the encrypted password value is a little awkward. If Apache was previously installed on your system, you may have the `htpasswd` utility installed. If so, use that, like so:

```
htpasswd -c restricted.pwd myclient
```

The username will be *myclient* and you will be prompted for the password.

If you don't have `htpasswd` installed, you can use the following Python language script to print out the encrypted password value and then manually paste it into the file. If you need to install Python first on your Amazon server, use the following command:

```
apt-get install python
```

To generate the encrypted password, run the following command, replacing *thepassword* with your password.

```
python -c "import crypt,random,string;
  print crypt.crypt('thepassword',random.choice(string.letters))"
```

Edit the `restricted.pwd` file so that it looks something like the line below, replacing the encrypted value with the output from the script, and *myclient* with your username:

```
myclient:qsCQhqCZrRpyM
```

Finally, reload the nginx configuration to activate the password protection:

```
nginx -s reload
```

Reload the site in your web browser, and you will be prompted for the username and password: *myclient* and *thepassword*.

4. The `http://github.com` service is a cloud service offering source code hosting using the `git` version control utility. `git` can take a little getting used to, but it is well worth it, as it lets you manage your code in a professional manner. Register with the github.com site, and follow the instructions to get set up.

 WARNING *Github source code repositories are public by default. If you are working on a confidential client project, then you will need to pay for a private repository.*

To deploy your latest work to your server, `cd` into your project folder, and run

```
git add -i
```

This starts the interactive version of `git add`, which is an easy way to find out what files you've changed and now need to deploy to the server. Follow the instructions to select your changed files.

Then commit your changes:

```
git commit -m "a suitable message explaining the changes"
```

Then push your changes up to the github.com service:

```
git push
```

Now log in to your Amazon server. This time, include the -A option to ssh. This brings your Github access keys along for the ride so that you can access your Github repository from the Amazon server.

```
ssh -l ubuntu -A your.amazon.server.com
```

On the server, cd to your project folder, and run:

```
git pull
```

And you're live! There's a lot more to the git utility—be sure to read the tutorials on the Github site.

CHAPTER 3

1. The to-do items have an id property that is set as the creation time, in milliseconds. You can use this to create a new Date object. Prepend the creation date at the point where you add items to the list. Modify the todo.js file by adding the lines in bold:

```
function additem(itemdata) {
  var item = $('#item_tm').clone();
  item.attr({id:itemdata.id});

  var date = new Date(itemdata.id);
  var when = '<small><i>'+(1+date.getMonth())+'/'+date.getDate()+
    ' '+date.getHours()+':'+date.getMinutes()+'</i></small> ';
  item.find('span.text').html(when+itemdata.text);
```

2. You can achieve this effect by using a WebKit animation. In the todo.css file, add the following lines:

```
.appear {
  -webkit-animation-name: appear;
  -webkit-animation-duration: 0.3s;
}
@-webkit-keyframes appear {
  from { -webkit-transform: translateX(100%); }
  to { -webkit-transform: translateX(0); }
}
```

Then, in the todo.js file, modify the swipe event handler with the line in bold:

```
item.swipe(function(){
  var itemdata = item.data('itemdata');
  if( !swipeon ) {
    markitem(item,itemdata.done = !itemdata.done);

    $('#delete_'+itemdata.id).show().addClass('appear');
    $('#add').hide();
    $('#cancel').show();
    swipeon = true;
```

3. To use iScroll, include the `iscroll.js` file in `todo.html` by inserting `<script src="iscroll.js"></script>` before the other `script` tags. Then surround the page `div` in `todo.html` with a `div` that has a defined height. Then give the page `div` an id:

```
<div style="height:435px">
<div id="content" data-role="content">
    ...
</div>
</div>
```

Then add the following lines marked in bold to `todo.js`:

```
$(document).ready(function(){
  scroller = new iScroll('content',{checkDOMChanges:false});
    ...
}
...
function additem(itemdata) {
    ...
  $('#todolist').append(item).listview('refresh');
  scroller.refresh();
```

CHAPTER 4

1. Add the following `div` element to the main `div` with `id="main"` on the `todo.html` page:

```
<div id="online"></div>
```

Next, add some CSS styling for this `div` at the bottom of the `todo.css` file:

```
#online {
  font-face: arial black;
  font-weight: bold;
  width: 310px;
  position: absolute;
  bottom: 5px;
  text-align: right;
  padding: 5px;
  -webkit-opacity: 0.5;
}
```

Finally, edit `todo.js` by adding these lines to bottom of the `$(document).ready` function:

```
$('body').bind('online', showOnline);
$('body').bind('offline', showOnline);
showOnline();
```

Also add this function definition:

```
function showOnline() {
  $('#online').text( navigator.onLine ? 'online' : 'offline' );
}
```

Don't forget to increase the version number in the `todo.manifest` file before you reload.

2. Add a new variable to store the orientation of the images:

```
var images = [];
```

In the event handler for `touchend`, insert the following code just before the `setTimeout` call at the end of the function:

```
images[lastimgI] = $.extend({},current);
current = images[imgI] = (images[imgI] || $.extend({},{
  ydeg:0, xdeg:0, zdeg:0,
  w:img.width(), h:img.height(),
}));
rotate();
```

This code uses the jQuery `extend` method to copy all the properties of the previous image into a new object that is stored in the `images` array. The current image is then updated with its previously stored orientation. The `||` operator is used to check whether the previous orientation has been stored yet, and if not, it sets the default orientation.

This code will work just fine except for one problem. In the sample code, a swipe is defined as a quick movement over at least 160 pixels in under 500 milliseconds. However, image rotation can still occur in these 500 milliseconds, which means the image orientation is inadvertently changed when the user swipes. A more suitable definition in this case is to use the speed of finger movement. Here is the new definition of the `isSwipe` function:

```
function isSwipe(e) {
  var duration = new Date().getTime()-start.when;
  var xdist    = Math.abs(current.x - start.x);
  return ( duration / xdist ) < 3;
}
```

If the ratio of duration to distance is less than 3, which is approximately 500 divided by 160, consider the movement to be a swipe.

3. Add the following line, marked in bold, to the HTML of the `map.html` file:

```
<input type="button" onclick="findme()" value="Find Me">
<input type="button" onclick="mark()" value="Mark">
<div id="loc"></div>
```

Next, add a top-level variable to hold the marker object:

```
var map;
var marker;
```

Add the following lines at the end of the `onload` function to create the marker object:

```
marker = new google.maps.Marker({
  animation: google.maps.Animation.BOUNCE,
});
```

Finally, provide the `mark` function:

```
function mark() {
  marker.setPosition(map.getCenter());
  marker.setMap(map);
  google.maps.event.addListener(marker, 'click', function(){
    marker.setMap(null);
  });
}
```

CHAPTER 5

1. There are three approaches you can use to print a JSON-formatted object description. First, you can just format the object to a JSON string directly using `JSON.stringify`:

```
console.log( JSON.stringify( myobject) )
```

Unfortunately, this does not work when your object contains circular references (when an object references itself). To solve that problem you can use the built-in function `console.dir`, which handles the circular references:

```
console.dir( myobject )
```

For the purposes of debugging, it is sometimes easier to review nicely-formatted and syntax-colored output. The `eyes` modules provides this functionality. It is similar to `console.dir`, but the output is much easier to understand, especially with large objects. Use `npm install eyes` to install.

```
var eyes = require('eyes')
eyes.inspect( myobject )
```

2. You can query the collections in your database using the MongoDB command-line environment, which you start with the `mongo` command. To query a collection, you use the command format `db.<name>.find(<query>)`, where `<name>` is the name of the collection and `<query>` is a JSON object that describes the query. To verify that your database has the correct last count for your app, use the Safari Web Inspector tool to find the app `id` value under the Storage > Local Storage tab. Copy this value and use it to query the database. The `id` value will be a number (for example, 163938349). You can then use this in the following query, which should print the JSON documents for each metric associated with your app `id`:

```
mongo todo
> db.last.find({id: '163938349'})
{ "_id" : ObjectId("4dcfafd33850e9093d3ed483"), "id" : "163938349",
  "kind" : "total", "sec" : 1305456642, "val" : 2 }
{ "_id" : ObjectId("4dcfafd33850e9093d3ed484"), "id" : "163938349",
  "kind" : "done", "sec" : 1305456642, "val" : 1 }
{ "_id" : ObjectId("4dcfafd33850e9093d3ed485"), "id" : "163938349",
  "kind" : "notdone", "sec" : 1305456642, "val" : 1 }
```

3. To determine which indexes you'll need, you examine your code and see what queries it makes. In the `collect.js` script, the `initEntry` function does an upsert, using the `id` and `kind` properties of objects in the `last` collection. This is your first index:

```
mongo todo
> db.last.ensureIndex({id:1,kind:1},{unique:true,background:1})
```

You also define this index as unique. There should only be one `last` entry for each metric for each app. And you set it up to build in the background so that it does not block the application. The `saveEntry` function can also make use of this index.

The `agg` collection also needs an index. In this case, the time slots are uniquely identified by metric, period, and index:

```
> db.agg.ensureIndex({kind:1,period:1,index:1},{unique:true,background:1})
```

4. You can use the `nginx upstream` directive to distribute the load evenly between a set of Node processes on multiple servers:

```
http {
  ...
  upstream myapp {
    server hostnameA:3000;
    server hostnameB:3000;
    server hostnameC:3000;

  }
  ...
}

location /myapp/mypath/ {
  proxy_pass http://myapp/mypath/;
}
```

This configuration sends requests in round-robin fashion to each of the three servers `hostnameA`, `hostnameB`, and `hostnameC`, one after the other. Make sure your Amazon security group configuration allows your `nginx` server to access the specified port on the Node process machines.

CHAPTER 6

1. Use the `uuid` Node module, available at: `https://github.com/broofa/node-uuid`. Download the `uuid.js` file and place it in the `todosync/public` folder. Then add a reference to it in `todo.html`:

```
<script src="jquery.js"></script>
<script src="jquery.mobile.js"></script>
<script src="uuid.js"></script>
```

Then use it to generate identifiers, by modifying the `makeid` function in the `todo.js` file:

```
function makeid() {
  return uuid()
}
```

2. In the `api.js` script, the `getapp` function already knows how to generate a list of all the to-do items for an app, so you can reuse it. First, make the `:itemid` query parameter optional, by suffixing it with a `?` character:

```
app.get('/todo/sync/api/app/:appid/item/:itemid?',
  function(req,res,next){
    api.getitem( sendjson(res), req.params.appid, req.params.itemid )
  }
)
```

Then modify the `getitem` function to reuse the `getapp` function. If there is no `itemid`, call `getapp`, and return the list of items found inside the result from `getapp`. You can make use of a custom callback that takes the place of the `jsonout` function. This custom callback pulls the item list out of the `getapp` results. The `getapp` function itself is unaffected:

```
self.getitem = function( jsonout, appid, itemid ) {
  if( itemid ) {
    var itemname = appid+'_'+itemid
    getsdb().getItem('todo_item',itemname, err500(jsonout,function(itemres){
      ...
    }))
  }
  else {
    self.getapp(function(appres){
      jsonout(appres.items)
    },appid)
  }
}
```

code snippet todosync/api-list.js

You can test this new feature by using the command line interface:

```
node api-list.js debug getitem <appid>
```

3. First, add an input text field to the to-do item HTML elements. Here's how:

```
<div id="tm">

  <li id="item_tm">
    <span class="check"> </span>
    <span class="text"></span>
```

```
    <input type="text" class="edit" style="display:none"/>
  </li>

  <div id="delete_tm" class="delete">Delete</div>

</div>
```

code snippet todosync/public/todo-text.html

This text field is not shown at first, and it becomes visible only when the user taps on the to-do item text.

Next, you need to distinguish between taps in the done/not-done check box and taps on the item text. Go to the additem function and change the target of the tap event handler:

```
// was: item.tap(function(){
item.find('span.check').tap(function(){
```

At the top of the additem function, add the following event-handling code for taps on the item text.

```
function additem(itemdata,nosave) {
  var item = $('#item_tm').clone()
  item.attr({id:itemdata.id})

  var itemtext = item.find('span.text')
  itemtext.text(itemdata.text).tap(function(){
    var edit = item.find('input.edit')
    itemtext.hide()

    function updatetext() {
      itemdata.text = edit.val()
      itemdata.updated = new Date().getTime() + serveroffset
      itemtext.text(itemdata.text)
      edit.hide()
      itemtext.show()
      saveitemdata(items)
      uploaditem(itemdata)
    }

    edit.val(itemdata.text).show().focus().blur(updatetext).tap(updatetext)
  })

var delbutton = $('#delete_tm').clone().hide()
  item.append(delbutton)
```

code snippet todosync/public/todo-text.js

This handler makes the input text field visible, and if the text changes, it uploads the new item text. Notice that this update function is attached not only to the tap handler but also to the blur event handler. This ensures that the handler is called when the user taps the Done button on the iPhone keyboard. Notice also that the solution makes good use of jQuery function chaining to keep the code short and sweet.

4. The obvious place to start is the point at which items are deleted. Add the following code to delete the item from the server:

```
delbutton.attr('id','delete_'+itemdata.id).tap(function(){
  ...
  if( navigator.onLine ) {
    sendjson(
      'DELETE','sync/api/app/'+appinfo.id+'/item/'+itemdata.id
    )
  }
  ...
```

What about the offline case? If the app is offline, you need to keep a record of the delete operations so that you can send them to the server when the app comes online. The `localStorage` API is the obvious choice:

```
if( navigator.onLine ) {
    sendjson(
      'DELETE','sync/api/app/'+appinfo.id+'/item/'+itemdata.id
    )
  }
  else {
    var deleted = JSON.parse(localStorage.deleted || '[]')
    itemdata.updated = new Date().getTime() + serveroffset
    deleted.push(itemdata)
    localStorage.deleted = JSON.stringify(deleted)
  }
```

code snippet todosync/public/todo-del.js

Whenever the `syncitems` function runs, you need to act on these pending delete operations. You should ensure that the delete operations run first, to avoid unnecessarily updating any deleted items.

You can't just delete all the items in the delete list. You need to check each one against the most recent list from the server. If the server version is more recent, it means that the local delete operation occurred earlier than a remote update. Therefore, the local delete is not the most recent operation and has effectively been undone remotely. So you should not delete the item but rather apply the more recent remote update. Here's the code to add near the top of the `syncitems` function:

```
function syncitems(serveritems) {
  ...

  var servermap = {}
  serveritems.forEach(function(item){
    servermap[item.id] = item
  })

  var deleted = JSON.parse(localStorage.deleted || '[]')
  deleted.forEach(function(delitem){
    if( servermap[delitem.id] ) {
```

```
      if( delitem.updated < servermap[delitem.id].updated ) {
        additem( servermap[delitem.id] )
      }
      else {
        sendjson(
          'DELETE','sync/api/app/'+appinfo.id+'/item/'+delitem.id
        )
      }
    }
  })
  localStorage.deleted = '[]'
```

```
serveritems.forEach(function(serveritem){
  ...
```

Done? No, not yet! There may have been some remote deletes. You need to remove these items from your local app. How do you detect remote deletes? If a local item is not in the list of items from the server and not a new local upload, it must have been deleted remotely. You need to remove that item from your local item storage and from the user interface of the app. You place this logic at the bottom of the syncitems function, where you have access to all the information you need:

```
  ...
  localStorage.uploads = '[]'

  localitems.forEach(function(localitem){
    if( !servermap[localitem.id] &&
        !newitems[localitem.id] &&
        !existingitems[localitem.id]
    ) {
      $('#'+localitem.id).remove()
      for( var i = 0; i < items.length; i++ ) {
        if( localitem.id == items[i].id ) {
          items.splice(i,1)
        }
      }
    }
  })
  saveitemdata(items)

}
```

CHAPTER 7

1. Copy the scroll-is.css file from the downloadable code for this chapter, and create a new file called scroll-slide.css. Modify the contents of the file, adding the boldfaced lines:

```
div {
  padding: 0px !important;
}

ul, p {
```

```
    margin: 0px !important;
}

div.content {
  display: none;
  -webkit-backface-visibility: hidden;
  -webkit-animation-duration: .2s;
  -webkit-animation-name: inbound;
}

@-webkit-keyframes inbound {
  from {
    -webkit-transform: translateY(100%);
  }
  to {
    -webkit-transform: translateY(0);
  }
}
```

Modify the `scroll-is.html` file to reference this new CSS file:

```
<head>
  ...
  <link rel="stylesheet" href="jquery.mobile.css" />
  <link rel="stylesheet" href="scroll-slide.css" />
  ...
</head>
```

When you transition between tabs, you will now see the new tab content sliding in from the bottom of the screen. This is achieved using only CSS. An animation is defined using the `@-webkit-keyframes` syntax. This animation places the content at the bottom of the screen by setting the Y position to be 100% of the height of the element. The animation then moves the Y position back to 0, which slides the content up the screen. The `div.content` element contains additional CSS rules to control the animation.

2. The iScroll library provides you with a range of settings to fine-tune its operation. Set the `vScrollbar` setting to `false` to hide the simulated scrollbar, and set the `momentum` setting to `false` to make the scrollable area respond in a linear fashion:

```
scrollers[current] = new iScroll("content_"+current,{
  hscroll:false,
  vScrollbar:false,
  momentum:false
})
```

3. You can create links to the iTunes Store App using the iTunes Link Maker website. Start with the FAQ page: `http://www.apple.com/itunes/linkmaker/faq`. When you embed these links in your app, tapping on them will launch the user into the iTunes application. The iTunes application is not available on Android devices, and the link will simply take you to the iTunes website.

4. You can use the `onPullDown` event from the iScroll library to implement this functionality. Create a new set of files called `scroll-refresh.css`, `scroll-refresh.js`, and

scroll-refresh.html by copying the scroll-is.* files. These files are also available in the downloadable code for this chapter.

In the scroll-refresh.html file, add an enclosing div around the scrollable list content example. The iScroll library inserts a message div as the first element of the scrollable content, and you don't want it inserted into the content list items:

```
<div id="content_scroll" class="content">
  <div>
  <ul data-role="listview">
    <li>a</li><li>b</li><li>c</li><li>d</li>
    ...
    <li>Y</li><li>Z</li>
  </ul>
  </div>
</div>
```

In the scroll-refresh.js file, add a handler for the onPullDown event and set pullToRefresh to true. Do this only on the content for the scroll example. Use a counter variable to create test content for the new list items that you add to the list each time the user pulls down on the scrollable area:

```
var counter = 0
function refresh() {
  var content = $("#content_"+current)
  if( !scrollers[current] ) {

    var config = { hscroll:false }
    if( 'scroll' == current ) {
        config.pullToRefresh='down'
        config.onPullDown = function () {
        counter++
        var ul = $('#content_'+current+' ul')
        ul.prepend(
          '<li class="ui-li ui-li-static ui-body-c">'+counter+'</li>'
        )
        setTimeout(function(){
          scrollers[current].refresh()
          scrollers[current].scrollTo(0,0,50,false)
        },50)
      }
    }
    scrollers[current] = new iScroll("content_"+current,config)
  }

  content.height( $('body').height() - header.height() - footer.height() - 4 )
  scrollers[current].refresh()
}
```

You use the jQuery prepend function to insert the new list items at the top of the list. You also need to set the correct jQuery Mobile list item styles manually, as they are set automatically only on elements that exist when the page first loads. You can see which styles to set on an element by using the Safari web development tools to inspect the element classes.

You use `setTimeout` to call the iScroll refresh. This ensures that the browser has completed the element updates to the list before iScroll refreshes. It also prevents incorrect scrolling behavior.

When you pull down on the list, iScroll presents a short message indicating that the list is updating, as shown in Figure A-1.

FIGURE A-1

CHAPTER 8

1. To perform a delete operation using the knox Node module, you call the `del` function. This function is very simple to use because you do not have to worry about streaming data. Copy the `s3-put.js` file and replace the call to `fs.stat` with the following code:

Available for
download on
Wrox.com

```
client.del(testfile).on('response', function(res){
  console.dir(res.statusCode);
}).end();
```

code snippet server/s3-del.js

2. Copy the `public/twitter.html` file to `public/linkedin.html` and replace the test `twitter` with `linkedin` where it occurs. The downloadable code for this chapter includes a LinkedIn sign-in icon that you can use.

```
<a href="http://YOUR_IP_ADDRESS:3003/oauth/linkedin/login?1">
  <img src="linkedin.png">
</a>
```

Next, copy the `server/twitter.js` script to `server/linkedin.js`. Modify the script by replacing all occurrences of the string "twitter" with the string "linkedin". You'll also need to modify the configuration of the `oauthclient` object:

Available for
download on
Wrox.com

```
var oauthclient = new oauth.OAuth(
  'https://api.linkedin.com/uas/oauth/requestToken',
  'https://api.linkedin.com/uas/oauth/accessToken',
  keys.linkedin.keyid,
  keys.linkedin.secret,
  '1.0',
  'http://YOUR_IP_ADDRESS:3003/oauth/linkedin/callback',
  'HMAC-SHA1',
  null,
  {'Accept': '*/*', 'Connection': 'close', 'User-Agent': 'linkedin-js'}
```

```
)
...
        oauthclient.getOAuthRequestToken(
          ...

            res.writeHead( 301, {
              "Location":
              "https://www.linkedin.com/uas/oauth/authenticate?oauth_token="
                + oauth_token
            })
            res.end()
```

code snippet server/linkedin.js

Finally, you'll need to add the LinkedIn keys to your `server/keys.js` file. To get your LinkedIn keys, register on the LinkedIn developer site and create an application. You'll be able to get the keys from the application settings page.

```
exports.keyid  = 'YOUR_AWS_KEY_ID'
exports.secret = 'YOUR_AWS_SECRET_KEY'

exports.twitter  = {
  keyid:'YOUR_TWITTER_KEY_ID', secret:'YOUR_TWITTER_SECRET'
}
exports.facebook = {
  keyid:'YOUR_FACEBOOK_KEY_ID', secret:'YOUR_FACEBOOK_SECRET'
}
exports.linkedin = {
  keyid:'YOUR_LINKEDIN_KEY_ID', secret:'YOUR_LINKEDIN_SECRET'
}
```

code snippet server/keys.js

3. At the top of the `twitter.js` file, add the following lines of code to use the memcached module:

```
var memcached = new Memcached("127.0.0.1:11211")
var expires   = 3600
```

After you get the request token, store the token secret using `memcached` (as shown here in bold):

```
        oauthclient.getOAuthRequestToken(
          function(
            error,
            oauth_token,
            oauth_token_secret,
            oauth_authorize_url,
            additionalParameters)
          {
            if (!error) {
              memcached.set(
```

```
        oauth_token,
        oauth_token_secret,
        lifetime,
        function(err,result){
```

code snippet server/twitter-memcache.js

When you need to retrieve the token, get it from memcached (as shown here in bold):

```
app.get('/oauth/twitter/callback',function(req,res,next){
  var parsedUrl = url.parse(req.url, true);
  var oauth_token = parsedUrl.query.oauth_token;

  memcached.get( oauth_token, function(err,oauth_token_secret){
    oauthclient.getOAuthAccessToken(
      oauth_token,
      oauth_token_secret,
      parsedUrl.query.oauth_verifier,
```

4. Install Redis by following the instructions on `http://redis.io`. Start the Redis server, again as per the included instructions. As with memcached, you can run it as a command-line process.

Install the `redis-node` module using npm:

```
sudo npm install redis-node
```

Next copy the `server/twitter-memcache.js` script to `server/twitter-redis.js`. Replace the memcached set up line with:

```
var connect = require('connect')
var oauth   = require('oauth')
var url     = require('url')
var redis   = require("redis-node");


var redisclient = redis.createClient();

var keys = require('./keys.js')

var oauthclient = new oauth.OAuth(
  ...
```

code snippet server/twitter-memcache.js

Replace the memcached `get` and `set` calls with Redis `get` and `set` calls:

```
        redisclient.set(
          oauth_token,
          oauth_token_secret,
```

```
                         function(err,result){

...


        redisclient.get( oauth_token, function(err,oauth_token_secret){
          oauthclient.getOAuthAccessToken(
            oauth_token,
            oauth_token_secret,
            parsedUrl.query.oauth_verifier,
```

Run the script and login as usual. Don't forget to increment the counter in the `public/twitter.html` file:

```
<a href="http://YOUR_IP_ADDRESS:3003/oauth/twitter/login?X">
```

CHAPTER 9

1. To send test versions of your iPhone app to clients, you'll need to use *Ad Hoc* distribution. This is the form of distribution that Apple recommends for client testing. Apps generated using Ad Hoc distribution will function correctly with Apple's cloud services, such as Push Notifications. This means they can be fully tested by your clients. Follow these steps to get your test app onto a client's physical iPhone:

1. You'll need the UDID of your client's iPhone. If your client has several staff members who all want to test the app, you'll need UDIDs from all of them. Ask your client to connect their iPhone to iTunes on their computer.

2. Ask your client to select their iPhone from the Device tab in iTunes. On the Summary page, ask them to click on the Serial Number value. When you do this, the serial number changes to the UDID. Choose the Edit ➪ Copy menu option. Ask your client to paste the UDID into an email and email it to you.

3. Create a distribution certificate (not a development certificate) by following the instructions on the How To sub-tab of the Certificates tab on the iOS Provisioning Portal.

4. Create a new ad hoc provisioning profile by clicking the New Profile button on the Distribution sub-tab of the Provisioning tab. Select Ad Hoc as the distribution method. Important: remember to include all the UDIDs for the client iPhones in the list of UDIDs for this profile.

5. Download and install your ad hoc provisioning profile by double-clicking on it.

6. In Xcode, change the project settings of your app to use your ad hoc provisioning profile. Do this in the Code Signing section of the Build Settings page. Refer to the detailed and up-to-date online PhoneGap documentation if you need guidance here.

7. In Xcode, set the build target to be a device, not the simulator, by choosing a device option from the Build Scheme drop-down menu in the top bar of the project window.

8. Select the Build ⇨ Build and Archive menu option. This creates an archive file for your app.

9. Select the Window ⇨ Organizer menu option. Click the Archive tab. Your app will appear in the list of app archives. Select your app and click Share. Follow the instructions to generate and save an `ipa` file. The `ipa` file includes not only your app binary package, but also the ad hoc provisioning profile.

10. Email the `ipa` file to your client as an email attachment.

11. Instruct your client to install the `ipa` file on their device. They can do this by using iTunes. Ask your client to start iTunes and connect their iPhone.

12. Ask your client to drag the `ipa` file onto the Library tab in iTunes. This installs the app into iTunes.

13. Ask your client to sync their iPhone with iTunes, This installs your test app on their physical device, and they can now test it.

2. The weinre debugger repurposes the debug console from Safari and connects it to your mobile web or PhoneGap app running on the simulator or physical device. The weinre debugger uses a Java server running on your desktop machine to do this. It will work for both iPhone and Android.

1. If you are using Linux or Windows, download the `jar` version of weinre, and run it from the command line, like so:

```
java -jar path/to/weinre.jar --boundHost YOUR_IP_ADDRESS
```

If you are using a Mac, download the Mac application instead. Run the application, and then exit it. If you look in your home folder, you'll see that weinre has created a new subfolder called `.weinre`. Create a new file called `server.properties` inside the `.weinre` folder. Insert the following setting into the file, and save it:

```
boundHost=YOUR_IP_ADDRESS
```

2. Restart the weinre app.

3. The `boundHost` configuration setting is important. You need to set this to the IP address of your desktop machine so that your physical device can find the weinre server. Insert the following script tag into head element of the index.html file of your app:

```
<script src="http://YOUR_IP_ADDRESS:8080/target/target-script-min.js"></script>
```

The JavaScript in this file monitors your running application, connecting it to the weinre server, which then connects it to the debug console.

4. In the weinre application on your desktop, click the Remote tab at the top, and then select your device or simulator from the list of targets shown. This connects everything.

You can now use the Elements, Resources, Timeline, and Console tabs just as you do in the Safari developer console. This is invaluable for solving tricky bugs that occur only on the device.

3. In order to annotate the photo image, you need to copy its contents into a canvas element, write the text with the date, time, and compass direction, and then extract the image data from the canvas.

There's one other complication you need to take care of. You need to create a canvas of the correct, original size of the photo. The photo is displayed using a 200 by 200 pixel square in the app user interface, so you can't use the width and height of this img tag. Instead, you'll need to create a new hidden img tag to read the true width and height from. You'll also need to hide the canvas element. Add these two highlighted lines to your index.html file:

```html
<div id="con_post" data-role="content">
  <a id="btn_takepic" data-role="button">Take Picture</a>
  <img id="post_pic" />
  <a id="btn_upload" data-role="button">Upload Picture</a>
  <p id="post_msg"></p>

  <img id="work_pic" style="display:none"/>
  <canvas id="work_sheet" style="display:none"></canvas>

</div>
```

code snippet lifestream/app-www-annotate/index.html

In your lifestream.js file, you'll need to create references to these elements in the App object, so that you can access them later:

```js
var work_pic = $('#work_pic')
var work_sheet = $('#work_sheet');
```

Then, when the user takes a photo, you'll need to store it twice, once in the smaller, visible, 200 by 200 pixel img tag, and again in the hidden img tag. Then you'll need to annotate the hidden image. Here are the changes in the getPicture handler:

```js
navigator.camera.getPicture(
  function(base64) {
    imagedata = base64
    post_pic.attr({src:"data:image/jpeg;base64,"+imagedata})

    work_pic.attr({src:"data:image/jpeg;base64,"+imagedata})
    annotate()

  },
```

As you've probably guessed by now, the real work happens in the annotate function, which you place inside the App object:

```js
function annotate() {
  function inserttext(heading) {
    var direction = ''
    if( null != heading ) {
      heading = Math.floor((heading+22.5)/45) % 8;
      var directions = [
```

```
          'North','North East',
          'East','South East',
          'South','South West',
          'West','North West'
      ];
      direction = directions[heading];
  }

  var width = work_pic.width();
  var height = work_pic.height();

  work_sheet[0].width  = width;
  work_sheet[0].height = height;

  var context = work_sheet[0].getContext('2d');
  context.drawImage(work_pic[0],0,0,width,height);

  context.font = "bold 48px sans-serif";
  context.fillStyle = "rgb(255,0,0)";
  context.fillText(''+new Date().toISOString(), 10, height-200);

  if( direction ) {
    context.fillText('Facing: '+direction, 10, height-100);
  }

  var imagesrc = work_sheet[0].toDataURL('image/jpeg');
  post_pic.attr({src:imagesrc});
  imagedata = imagesrc.substring("data:image/jpeg;base64,".length);
}

navigator.compass.getCurrentHeading(
    function(heading){
      inserttext(heading);
    },
    function(){
      inserttext(null);
    },
    {}
  );
}
```

---

code snippet lifestream/app-www-annotate/lifestream.js

The `navigator.compass.getCurrentHeading` function (highlighted) kicks things off. You pass a success function and a failure function. If the compass heading cannot be read, then you can still annotate with the date and time. If it can be read, then PhoneGap gives you a heading in degrees, where 0 degrees represents North, 90 degrees represents East, and so on.

The `inserttext` function first converts the numeric heading (if available) from degrees to more familiar directions such as North, North East, East, and so on. It does this by dividing the 360 degrees in a circle into 45 degree segments. The heading is divided by 45 and the answer is then taken modulo 8 (as there are eight 45s in 360), which gives an index offset into an array containing the direction names, in clockwise order.

The heading needs to be adjusted by half of 45 degrees (22.5) because half of the North segment is in the range 337.5 to 360.

Next, you get the true width and height of the picture that was taken. It is important to get the true values as different devices create photos with different dimensions. Because the work_pic img tag has no defined size, it takes on the full size of the photo image.

Using these dimensions, you set the width and height of the canvas tag. Notice that you need to use a reference to the underlying DOM element, not the jQuery wrapper. Do this by using [0] on the jQuery wrapper. This works because jQuery wrappers provide a natural array interface to the DOM elements they contain. In this case, only one element, the underlying canvas tag, is contained in the work_sheet wrapper.

With the width and height set, you can use the drawImage function to draw the contents of the photo image onto the canvas. As is normal with canvas elements, you do this using a context object. You use the context object to add the textual annotations (in a large red font) to the image, inserting the date and time, and the direction, if available.

When you are done, you use the toDataURL function to get the image data as a base64 string. One you have this, you are back in familiar territory, and you can reset the small visible image data to use the annotated photo. Everything proceeds as normal from here, and when the user uploads their photo to Amazon, it will have the annotation embedded within it.

4.   You follow these steps:

1.   First, you provide a ul tag on the Lifestream content div in the index.html file:

```html
<div id="con_lifestream" data-role="content">
    <ul id="lifestream_images">
    </ul>
</div>
```

code snippet lifestream/app-www-photolist/index.html

2.   You also need some styling for the image list, so you add these lines to the lifestream.css file:

```css
#lifestream_images {
  list-style-type: none;
  width: 100%;
}

#lifestream_images li {
  display: block
  margin:  8px auto;
}

#lifestream_images li img {
  width:   200px;
  height:  200px;
  border: 1px solid #ccc;
}
```

code snippet lifestream/app-www-photolist/lifestream.css

3. Next, you add the code to support this functionality to the `lifestream.js` file and add a reference to the `ul` tag:

```
var lifestream_images = $('#lifestream_images')
```

4. Then you call a `showimages` function (highlighted below) to show the images when the user taps the Lifestream tab:

```
$('#nav_lifestream').click(function(){
  showcon('lifestream')
  showimages()
})
```

5. When a picture is successfully uploaded, you add it to the list of images:

```
success:function(data){
  post_msg.text('Picture uploaded.')

  appendimage(data.picid)
},
```

6. Then you add these image-management functions to the `App` object:

Available for download on Wrox.com

```
function appendimage(picid) {
  var images = loadimages()
  images.unshift({picid:picid})
  localStorage.images = JSON.stringify(images)
}

function loadimages() {
  return JSON.parse(localStorage.images || '[]')
}

function showimages() {
  lifestream_images.empty();
  var images = loadimages()
  console.log(images)
  for( var i = 0; i < images.length; i++ ) {
    var li = $('<li>')
    var img = $('<img>').attr({src:s3prefix+images[i].picid+'.jpg'})
    li.append(img)
    lifestream_images.append(li)
  }
}
```

code snippet lifestream/app-www-photolist/lifestream.js

7. Finally, at the end of the `App` object block, you call the `showimages` function when the app starts to show the current list of images:

```
showimages()
```

CHAPTER 10

1. Here are the results of the code analysis to determine the types of queries the Lifestream server code makes:

MongoDB Queries by Function

FUNCTION	COLLECTION	FIELD
Followop	user	username
Search	user	username
Register	user	username
Finduser	user	username
Auth	user	token

As you can see, there is a strong case for defining a database index on the username field of the user collection, as it is used frequently. To create the index, log in to your MongoDB database using the mongo command line client, and issue the command:

```
db.user.ensureIndex({username:1}, {unique:true});
```

This index is also unique, which makes sense for usernames.

The token field is also queried. Is it worth creating an index? The answer is yes, because this field is queried for nearly every operation to authenticate user requests. In the example code, the authentication token is stored directly in the user table. In a production setting, you would probably want to put these tokens into their own table. In either case, the index creation statement is:

```
db.user.ensureIndex({token:1});
```

In this case, there is no need for a unique index, as the token UUIDs are generated in a way that makes them unique for the next few millennia at least.

2. The upstart service provides Ubuntu systems with an easy way to configure long-running processes. In particular, it has the nice feature that it can restart a service if it goes down. To control your Node service using upstart, become root using:

```
sudo -s
```

and then create a file called /etc/init/my-node-server.conf, and save the following in it:

```
description "my-node-server"
author   "username"

pre-start script
```

```
 mkdir -p /var/log/my-node-server
 touch /var/log/my-node-server/stdout.log
 chmod a+r /var/log/my-node-server/stdout.log
end script

start on runlevel [2345]
stop on runlevel [!2345]

respawn
respawn limit 999 1

exec sudo -u username /usr/local/bin/node /path/to/my-node-server.js
  >> /var/log/my-node-server/stdout.log 2>&1
```

Now you can start and stop your node server using:

```
sudo start my-node-server
sudo stop my-node-server
```

There's one more thing. After you deploy a new version of your server code, you can get it to restart by simply killing the existing server:

```
sudo killall node
```

The upstart service will automatically restart your server!

3. The challenge with error logging is to ensure that the data arrives at your server even if the client has entered a severely corrupt state. One of the most reliable things in the HTTP protocol is sending a GET request. What you need to do is embed your error description into a GET request. In your client code, place this function inside the very first script tag in your head element (which ensures it is always available):

```
<script>
function logerror() {
  try {
    var desc = JSON.stringify({
      when:new Date(),
      userAgent:navigator.userAgent,
      args:Array.prototype.slice.call(arguments)
    })
    new Image().src = '/api/log/error?desc='+escape(desc)
  }
  catch( e ) {
    console.log && console.log(e)
  }
}
</script>
```

Whenever an error occurs, call this function with arbitrary arguments describing the error. Enclose major sections of code in a top level try-catch block, and call this function to log top level errors.

The function creates a GET request for an image that does not exist, embedding the JSON description of the error as a URL encoded value.

On the server side, add a connect middleware function to listen for these client errors, and place in the call-handling flow as highlighted in the server.js file:

```
server = connect.createServer(
  connect.logger(),
  collect('/upload$'),

  clienterror(),

  connect.router(function(app){
    app.post( prefix+'register', register)
```

Implement the clienterror function as follows:

```
function clienterror() {
  return function(req,res,next){
    if( '/lifestream/api/log/error?desc=' == req.url.substring(0,31) ) {
      res.writeHead(200)
      res.end()

      var desc = {}

      var report = JSON.parse(unescape(req.url.substring(31)))
      console.dir(report)

      mongo.coll(
        'clienterror',
        function(coll){
          coll.insert(report)
        })
    }
    else {
      next()
    }
  }
}
```

This function performs a hard-coded check against each inbound HTTP request to see if it is a client error to be logged. If so, the JSON-encoded error description is decoded and saved to the clienterror collection in the MongoDB database.

4. You need to add the posting date as a data field in the objects stored in the user's picture stream. On the server, you replace the post function with the following code, where the highlights show the support for the posting date:

```
function post(req,res) {
  var merr = mongoerr400(res)

  var picid    = req.json.picid
```

```
var username = req.params.username
var now       = new Date()

finduser(true,['followers'],req,res,function(user,coll){
  append(username,username,picid,now,coll,merr,function(){
    common.sendjson(res,{ok:true})

    var followers = user.followers
    function appendfollower(fI) {
      if( fI < followers.length ) {
        append(followers[fI],username,picid,now,coll,merr,function(){
          appendfollower(fI+1)
        })
      }
    }
    appendfollower(0)

  })
})

}
```

You also need to add date support to the `append` function:

```
function append(touser,fromuser,picid,when,coll,merr,cb) {
  coll.findOne(
    {username:touser},
    {fields:['stream']},

    merr(function(user){
      var stream = user.stream

      coll.update(
        {username:touser},
        {$push:{stream:{picid:picid,user:fromuser,when:when}}},
        merr(function(){
          ...
```

Finally, in the `lifestream.js` file in the app, you use the following `showimages` function, which grabs the time as a substring from the data returned by the server:

```
function showimages(images) {
  lifestream_images.empty();
  for( var i = images.length-1; 0 <= i; i-- ) {
    var whenstr = images[i].when.substring(11,16)
    var li =
      lifestream_image.clone()
      .css({display:'block'})
    li.find('span').text( images[i].user + ' ' + whenstr )
    li.find('img').attr({src:s3prefix+images[i].picid+'.jpg'})
    lifestream_images.append(li)
  }
}
```

CHAPTER 12

1. Download the `firmin.js` script from the Firmin library website, `http://extralogical.net/projects/firmin`. Add a script reference to your `index.html` file:

```
<script src="firmin.js"></script>
```

Add some extra style settings to the CSS:

```css
div { -webkit-transform:translate3d(0,0,0); }

div.con {
  position: absolute;
  top: 36px;
  left: 0px;
  width: 290px;
  background: #eee;
  min-height:1024px;
}
```

The `-webkit-transform:translate3d(0,0,0);` rule is important. It ensures that your animations will be hardware accelerated. This rule works because it triggers WebKit to use a separate internal graphics layer for each `div`. These layers are then composited together, using a hardware-accelerated algorithm. The result: smooth slide transitions.

Replace the `makeshowcon` function in the `TopNav` object with the following version, where the Firmin library call is shown highlighted:

```javascript
// create a function to display a content view
function makeshowcon(name) {
  return function(e) {
    if( self.app[name].visible ) return;

    if( self.con ) {
      console.log('oldcon',self.con)
      var oldcon = self.con
      oldcon.css({'z-index':100})
      self.app[self.name].visible = false
    }

    self.name = name
    self.con = self.el.con[name]
    self.app[name].render()

    self.app[name].visible = true
    self.con.removeClass('hide').css({'z-index':200})

    Firmin.translateX(self.con[0],320).translateX(0,'0.4s',function(){
      oldcon && oldcon.addClass('hide')
    })
  }
}
```

2. PhoneGap provides two events to let you know when your app moves into and out of the background: `pause` and `resume`. They occur when the user opens a new app while your app is running. Amend the `init` function as follows to listen for the `resume` event:

```
function init() {
  app = new App()
  document.addEventListener("resume", app.resume, false);
}
```

Add the new `resume` method to the `App` object:

```
function App() {
  ...

  self.resume = function() {
    util.log('resuming...')
    social.trigger('update-inbox')
    social.trigger('update-people')
  }

  ...
}
```

Here you are leveraging the eventing architecture to trigger updates when the app resumes.

3. To delete an account, add a `swipe` event handler to the account items:

```
function Accounts(social) {
  ...

  self.render = function() {
    ...

    for( var i = 0; i < social.accounts.length; i++ ) {
      var account = social.accounts[i]

      var item = self.el.item_tm.clone()
      ...

      item.swipe(function(i){
        return function(){
          var account = social.accounts[i]

          navigator.notification.confirm(
            'Remove '+account.nick+' ('+account.network+') from this app?',
            function(index){
              if( 0 == index ) {
                social.clear(account)
              }
            },
            'Remove Account',
            ['Remove','Keep'])
        }
      }(i))
    }
  }
}
```

This code uses the PhoneGap notification API, covered in Chapter 9, to present a nicely formatted confirmation pop-up to the user. If the user confirms the account deletion, you call the `clear` method of the `Social` object. The `clear` method needs to delete from `localStorage` not only the account but also all messages and people associated with the account. You can cheat and just delete *all* the messages and people in the app's cache variables. Then you trigger an update:

```
self.clear = function( account ) {
  var acc = self.findaccount( account.nick, account.network )
  self.accounts.splice( acc.index$, 1 )

  util.save('accounts',{accounts:self.accounts})

  var key = util.key('people',account)
  util.save(key)

  self.inbound = []
  self.convo = {}

  self.trigger('accounts')

  if( 0 < self.accounts.length ) {
    self.getmsgs()
    self.getpeople()
  }
  else {
    util.save('inbound',{inbound:self.inbound})
    util.save('convo',self.convo)
    self.trigger('inbound-msgs')
    self.trigger('outbound-msgs')
    self.trigger('people')
  }

  self.getmsgs()
  self.getpeople()
}
```

You also need to alter the `findaccount` convenience method in the `Social` object to keep a record of the array index of each account. This is used by the `clear` method. Since this is accidental metadata rather than a core attribute of an account, you should use a variable name suffixed with $ to indicate its inferior status:

```
// find an account object by nick and network
self.findaccount = function(nick,network) {
  var account = null
  for( var i = 0; i < self.accounts.length; i++ ) {
    var acc = self.accounts[i]
    if( acc.nick == nick && acc.network == network ) {
      account = acc
      account.index$ = i
      break
    }
  }

  return account
}
```

4. Amend the `displaymsg` method of the `Inbox` object to add a `swipe` event handler to each message:

```
self.displaymsg = function( msg ) {
  var item = self.el.msg_tm.clone()
  item.css({float:msg.f?'right':'left'})
  util.text(item,{
    meta: ''+new Date(msg.w).toString('ddd HH:mm'),
    body: msg.s,
    who: (msg.f || msg.n)
  })
  self.el.list.prepend(item)

  if( !msg.f ) {
    item.swipe(function(){
      var remove = confirm('Delete this message?')

      if( remove ) {
        social.delmsg(self.account,msg.i)
        self.convo.splice(msg.index$,1)
        util.save('convo',social.convo)
        self.dirty = true
        self.render()
      }
    })
  }
}
```

Then you need a `delmsg` method on the `Social` object:

```
self.delmsg = function(account,msgid) {
  var network = self.network[account.network]

  network.delmsg( account, msgid, function(err,msgs) {
    if( err ) return util.log(err);
  })
}
```

Finally, you need an actual implementation in the `Twitter` object:

```
self.delmsg = function( account, msgid, cb ) {
  self.call(account,{
    path:self.conf.apibaseurl+'direct_messages/destroy/'+msgid+'.json',
    method:'DELETE',
    jsondata:true
  },function(err,data){
    if( err ) return cb(err,null);
    cb(null,data)
  })
}
```

INDEX

Symbols

: (colon), JavaScript key/value pairs, 8

, (comma), JavaScript literal data structures, 8

. (dot), bucket names, 240

; (semi-colon), indentation, 188

\ (backslash), JavaScript, 10

{} (curly brackets), callback functions, 83

- (dash), bucket names, 240

$ (dollar sign)
   JavaScript variables, 79
   jQuery, 79, 81
   jQuery Mobile, 84
   metadata, 502
   simpledb, 187

(hash mark)
   comments, 114
   direct hashing, 264
   iScroll, 222
   jQuery, 81

() (parentheses), callback functions, 83

| (pipe character), grep, 65

"" (quotes-double), JavaScript, 10

' ' (quotes-single), JavaScript, 10

[] (square brackets), dot notation, 11

_ (underscore), bucket names, 240

A

-A, 476

acceptance testing, 317, 327–328, 332–333, 336, 345

accept.follow.js, 335, 336
   accept.post.js, 341

accept.mongo.js, 325, 327, 335

accept.post.js, accept.follow.js, 341

Access Control List (ACL), 244

access keys, Amazon SimpleDB, 243

account, 391, 405, 420

Accounts, 397, 404, 412, 427
   hide and clone template, 410
   makesignin, 418
   OAuth, 415

accounts, 412
   Social, 424

"accounts", 426

accounts_signin_<network>, 417

ACL. *See* Access Control List

acl, 244

action, 52

activatesave, 102

activity, 360

activity logging, 257

Ad Hoc, 490

additem, 102, 107, 482

$addToSet, 336

advertising, 459

agg, 160–161

ajax
   jQuery, 164, 295, 304
   sendjson, 166

alert, 404

alestic.com, 53, 56

Amazon Elastic IP Service, 65

Amazon Machine Image (AMI), 53

Amazon S3, 53
   adding content, 240–245
   architecture, 236–237
   buckets, 236, 238–240
   callback functions, 243
   content storage, 236–247
   event handlers, 244–245
   getting content, 245–247
   HTTP, 244
   memory, 244
   objects, 236
   setting up, 238–240
   storing pictures, 306–310

Amazon SimpleDB, 53, 180–182
   access keys, 243
   API, 181–182
   Code, 185
   Message, 185
   metadata, 186, 195
   tracer bullets, 183–188

Amazon Web Services (AWS), 4, 52–67
   Amazon S3, 237, 238

Amazon Web Services (*continued*)
  Amazon SimpleDB, 180
  DNS, 65
  geography, 54
  public private key pairs, 64
  security groups, 60
  Ubuntu, 60
AMI. *See* Amazon Machine
  Image
Android
  Appcelerator, 379
  appMobi, 381
  HTML5, 436
  hybrid native apps,
    283–288
  icons, 437–438
  Java, 2
  JavaScript, 283
  jQuery Mobile, 88
  launcher icons, 437–438
  Marketplace, 441
  mobile web apps, 72,
    77–78
  nginx, 122
  orientations, 440
  PhoneGap, 283, 288, 436
  pixels, 438
  RAM, 287
  screenshots, 439
  SDKs, 3, 283
  self-signed certificates, 442
  splash screens, 438
  submitting binary for,
    448–452
  todo.html, 97
  Twitter, 413
  video, 226
  Virtual Device, 287
  WebKit, 20–21, 72
AndroidManifest.xml, 360
android.permission.
  INTERNET, 452
animation effects
  jQuery, 82
  WebKit, 123, 476

anonymous callback functions,
  16, 46
anonymous event handler, 38
Apache, 474
//API functions, 361
api-cmdline.js, 189–194,
  202
Apigee API, 393
Api.getapp, 196
api.js, 199–200
  getapp, 481
apk, 288
App, 405, 412
  HTML, 302
apps. *See also specific apps and
  app types*
  cross-platform, 460
  free versions of, 459
  as premium service,
    459–460
  selling, 455–468
    building for others,
      457–458
    for business promotion,
      458–460
    marketing strategy,
      456–461
    promotion tactics,
      462–467
    your own apps,
      460–462
app ID, 276
app stores, 435–452
  building app for release,
    441–452
  icons, 436–438
  metadata, 440
  orientations, 439–440
  screenshots, 439–440
  splash screens, 438–439
  working with, 440–441
Appcelerator, 377–381
  development environment,
    379–380
  technology, 378–379

append(para), 81
appendfollower, 344
Apple App Store, 441
application/json, 166
application/octet-stream,
  304
Applications, 26
applookup.com, 230
appMobi, 381–384
  development environment,
    383–384
  technology, 382–383
  XDK, 383–384
app.social.inbound, 423
apt-get
  Debian Advanced Packaging
    Tool, 60, 62
  memcached, 258
  MongoDB, 146
  nginx, 64–65
arc, 33, 39
  dot, 51
  fillStyle, 43
arcs, 33
architecture, 177–180
  Amazon S3, 236–237
  Lifestream app, 316–317
  shared-nothing, 257
Array, 140, 422
arrays, JavaScript, 10
  literal data structures, 8
assets/www, 286
asynchronous messaging system,
  256
attr, 81
Audacity, 223
audio, 222–226
audio, HTML5, 222
Auth, 496
auth
  finduser, 331
  middleware, 331, 343
authentication, MongoDB, 321
AWS. *See* Amazon Web
  Services

B

backbutton, 289
Balsamiq, 399
"bar", 259
/bar, 144
base64, 295
   Node, 342
BatchPutAttributes, 182
beginPath, 33, 43, 51
bin, 288
bind, 427
BlackBerry, 381
blogs, 467. *See also* Lifestream
  app
body, 10, 13
   innerHTML, 15
$('body'), 81
boundHost, 491

, 15
Brewer, Eric, 180
browser launching, 230
buckets
   Amazon S3, 236, 238–240
   knox, 243
   Lifestream app, 238–240
   UUID, 240
Buffer, 305
Build and Run, 280, 283
buttons, jQuery Mobile,
  90–91

C

cache, 112–115
  complex objects, 265–271
  hit, 260
  in-memory, 256
    shared-nothing
     architecture, 257
  large-scale apps, 258–271
  miss, 260
  multiple servers, 260–265
  reqtokens, 419
  size limits, 113

status, 115
version number, 114
call
  HTTP, 425
  OAuth, 421
callback, 17
  callme, 46
callback functions
  () (parentheses), 83
  action, 52
  Amazon S3, 243
  anonymous, 16, 46
  DRY, 46
  getCurrentPosition, 72
  JavaScript, 15–17
  jQuery, 81
  MongoDB, 148, 173
  moves, 51
  Node, 141
  position, 52, 73
  router, 144
  simpledb, 185–186
callback(), 17
canvas, 42, 492
  clear, 43
  context, 33
  document
   .getElementById, 32
  head, 38
  HTML5, 32
  img, 32
  JavaScript, 33
  touch-sensitive drawing
   app, 32
  WebKit, 32
canvastop, 44
CAP. *See* consistency,
  availability, partition
  tolerance
cap, 50
Cascading Style Sheet (CSS), 2–3
  Appcelerator, 377, 378
  appMobi, 382
  FeedHenry, 373, 375
  head, 38

HTML5, 72
jQuery Mobile, 90
left, 123
leftout, 123, 126
overflow:scroll, 212
PhoneGap, 275
pixels, 125
properties, 83
rightout, 123, 126
symbolic links, 436
top, 123
user accounts, 356
@-webkit-keyframes,
  485
-webkit-transform, 127
www, 282
z-index, 220
cd, 476
  draw, 66
CDN. *See* Content Delivery
  Network
center, 127
changedTouches, 116
check, 90
CHECKING, 115
Chrome. *See* Google Chrome
classes, JavaScript, 405
class="scroller", 217
clear
  canvas, 43
  draw, 50
  localStorage, 502
  paths, 43
  Social, 502
clear(), 45
clearButton, 45
clearWatch, 74
click, 15
  event handlers, 95
clienterror, 498
clientX, 42, 44
  touches, 117
clientY, 42, 44
  touches, 117
clone, 101

closePath, 33, 43, 51
closures, 20
cloudkick.com, 61
Code, 185
code editors
    draw.js, 40–41
    JavaScript functions, 12
code-signing, 276–283
collect
    dynamic functions, 331
    middleware, 330
    POST, 330
    server.post.js, 340
collections, 145
    MongoDB, 160–164
collect.js, 166, 172, 480
color
    fillStyle, 43
    hex, 24
    id, 473
    JavaScript, 22–25
command-line
    MongoDB, 479
    To-Do List app, 188–196
comments, 114
common, 158
common.js, 158, 202, 332
    HTTP, 328
    initEntry, 163
    JSON, 328
    Lifestream app, 319
    MongoDB, 328
common.readjson, 330
complete, 367
    Network, 420
con, 302
conf, 401
config.js, 317, 318, 328
config.max_stream_size, 344
conf.network.twitter, 418
connect
    HTTP, 144

middleware, 330–331, 364, 498
    Node, 142–144, 252
    URL, 159, 334
connectserver.js, 142–143
consistency
    availability, partition tolerance (CAP), 180
    eventual, 180, 237
consistent hashing, 264
consistent:false, 186
console.dir, 243, 479
console.log, 140, 141
Content Delivery Network (CDN), 80
content storage, Amazon S3, 236–247
Content-Length, 244
contentType
    application/json, 166
    application/octet-stream, 304
Content-Type, 144
context, 494
    canvas, 33
    stroke, 39
continuous integration, 400
Conversation view, 397, 427
Convo, 405, 431
cookies, 328
coords, 73
create, 195
created_at, 392
CreateDomain, 181, 187
createDomain, 187
createReadStream, 244
createWriteStream, 246
Crockford, Douglas, 20
cross-platform, 5
    apps, 460
CSS. See Cascading Style Sheet
css, 81
cssAncestorSelector, 229
curl

databases, 179
    HTTP, 392
    Node, 159, 201
    POST, 159
current, 124
cursor, 150, 392
    each, 329
Cygwin, 3, 61
    Node, 138

D

data-*, 84
    jQuery Mobile, 90
data objects, 405
databases, 179–180. See also MongoDB
data-icon, 90
data-position="fixed", 215
data-role, 97
data-role="list-divider", 410
dataType, 166
Date, 140
    getTime, 172
    id, 476
deadlocks, 137
Debian Advanced Packaging Tool, apt-get, 60, 62
'debug', 185
debugging
    OAuth, 389, 415
    weinre, 491
declaration, 14
declarations
    HTML5, 37
    JavaScript functions, 14
declarative programming, 84
    div, 101
DELETE
    HTTP, 388
        api-cmdline.js, 202
    REST, 179
    REST, 237

delete, 107
DeleteAttributes, 182
DeleteDomain, 181
delitem, 196
delmsg, 503
developer console, Twitter, 393–395
developer profile, 277
development certificate, 276
    Xcode, 277
development phase, hybrid native apps, 276
development services, 371–384
device, 289
device orientation, 74–76
deviceready, 289, 402
    PhoneGap, 294
direct hashing, 264
direct message app
    code structure, 404–413
    design process, 395–399
    events, 425–431
    hygiene factors, 399–404
    JavaScript, 407
    jQuery, 407
    jQuery Mobile, 406, 407
    OAuth, 413–421
    PhoneGap, 407
    Twitter, 395–432
direction, 425
direct_messages, 391
display: none, 102
displaymsg, 503
display:none, 473
distribution certificate, iPhone, 442
distribution phase, hybrid native apps, 276
div, 22
    audio, 226
    class="scroller", 217
    clone, 101

data-role, 97
declarative programming, 101
document
    .getElementById, 24
getElementById, 471
Google Maps, 127
HTML, 123, 127, 357
id, 477
id="main", 477
Inbox, 408
jQuery Mobile, 89, 90
onclick, 24
span, 101
style, 24
todo.css, 98
todo.html, 99, 103
divs
    HTML, 302
    showcon, 303
dmg, 26
DNS, 60, 65
<!DOCTYPE html>, 10, 23, 37
    HTML5, 88
    jQuery Mobile, 88
document, 140
    bind, 427
Document Object Model (DOM)
    Google Maps, 130
    HTML, 79
    JavaScript, 10, 79
    PhoneGap, 294
document.getElementById
    canvas, 32
    div, 24
    null, 11
document.onload, 80
$(document).ready, 477
DOM. See Document Object Model
DomainMetadata, 181
domains, 180

done, 102
Don't Repeat Yourself (DRY), 46–52
    callback functions, 46
    if else, 102
    JavaScript, 46–47
    JSON, 50, 425
dot, 43, 44
    arc, 51
dot notation, 11
DOWNLOADING, 115
draw
    cd, 66
    clear, 50
    moves, 51
    nginx, 67
draw-dry.html, 472
draw-dry.js, 473
draw.fill, 50, 473
draw.html, 66
draw.js, 66
    code editors, 40–41
draw.stroke, 473
dropbox.com, 467
DRY. See Don't Repeat Yourself
dynamic, 19
dynamic functions
    collect, 331
    JavaScript, 18–20

E

-e, 163
each, 329
EBS. See Elastic Block Service
EC2. See Elastic Compute Cloud
Eclipse, 288
    Appcelerator, 377
Elastic Block Service (EBS), 53, 60

Elastic Compute Cloud (EC2)
    instances, 53, 54–61
        public private key pairs,
          56
        Ubuntu, 56
    storage system, 236
`else`, 102
`end`, 244
`enhanced`
    `iscroll.js`, 217
    MPEG4, 229
entities, Twitter, 390–391
`err400`, 331
`error`, 268
    `null`, 186, 259
error logging, 497
events
    direct message app,
      425–431
    gesture, 118–127
      rotation, 124
      zoom, 125
    `Inbox`, 430
    jQuery, 427
    Node, 137
    PhoneGap, 501
    touch, 115–127
      jQuery Mobile, 117–118
      Node, 137
      WebKit, 115–116
event handlers
    Amazon S3, 244–245
    HTML, 95
    jQuery, 82–83, 95, 294
    MongoDB, 148
    Node, 137
    `preventDefault`, 124
`event.target.id`, 473
eventual consistency, 180
    Amazon S3, 237
expression, 14
expressions, 14
`extend`, 478

`eyes`, 479
    JSON, 183
    `npm`, 185

F

Facebook
    `index.html`, 365
    Lifestream app, 357–367
    OAuth, 255, 364
    `service`, 366
    signing in, 253–255
    URL, 255
`fadeIn`, 82
`fail`, 194
fault-tolerant systems, 257
`favorites`, 391
FeedHenry, 373–377
    development environment,
      375–376
    technology, 374–375
`fill`, 33, 43
    `path`, 51
`fillStyle`, 33
    `arc`, 43
    `color`, 43
`find`, 150
`findaccount`, 502
`findAndModify`, 164
`Finduser`, 496
`finduser`, 329, 330
    `auth`, 331
Firebug, 20
firewalls, 58
`firmin.js`, 500
Flash, 222
Flot, 167
`flurry.com`, 456
`follow`, 268, 270, 336, 357
`FollowAPI`, 268
`FollowDB`, 268
`followers`, 316, 343, 391
`following`, 316

`Followop`, 496
`followop`, 336
`fontsize`, 83
`"foo"`, 259
`/foo`, 144
`for`, 81
    `appendfollower`, 344
    jQuery Mobile, 91
    Twitter, 417
free versions of apps, 459
`friends`, 391
`friendships`, 391
`fromx`, 44
`fromy`, 44
`fs`
    `createReadStream`, 244
    Node, 243
`fs.stat`, 487
`function`, 14
`$(function(){...})`, 220
functions. *See also* callback
    functions
    chaining, jQuery, 102
    dynamic
      `collect`, 331
      JavaScript, 18–20
    generator, 215
    JavaScript, 7–20
      code editors, 12
      declarations, 14
      expressions, 14
      variables, 45
    sin, 125, 126
    tap, 215

G

garbage collection, 137
generations, 137
generator function, 215
geography
    Amazon S3, 236
    AWS, 54

Geolocation API, 72–74, 131
gesture events, 118–127
    rotation, 124
    zoom, 125
gesturechange, 118
    rotation, 125
    scale, 126
    zoom, 126
gestureend, 118
gesturestart, 118
GET, 144
    HTTP, 137, 159, 346, 388, 497
        api-cmdline.js, 202
        REST, 179
    JSON, 498
    REST, 237
get, 144, 332
    Redis, 489
getapp, 195
    api.js, 481
GetAttributes, 182
getAuthorizeUrl, 255
getCurrentPosition, 72
getElementById, 471
getImageData, 474
getItem, 195
    result, 186
getitem, 195, 481
    memcached, 265
getmsgs, 421, 422
    Network, 424
    Social, 424, 430
getOAuthRequestToken, 252
getorientation, 76
getpeople, 421
    Social, 430
getTime, 172
GIMP, 439
Git, 65
git add, 475
github.com, 142, 376, 475

global positioning system (GPS), 73
global variables, 19
Google Analytics, 136
Google Checkout, 441
Google Chrome, 136
    JavaScript literal data structures, 9
Google Docs, 136
Google Maps, 73, 127–131
    div, 127
    DOM, 130
    JSON, 130
    launching, 231
    zoom, 128–131
Google V8 JavaScript, 136–137
GPS. See global positioning system
grep, 65
Group Name, 58

H

H.264 codec, 227
h264aac, 229
handle, 332
handleauthorize
    Network, 418, 419
    OAuth, 419
handleOpenURL, 413, 414, 415, 420
handletab, 215, 220
hashing, 264
HEAD, 237
head, 23
    canvas, 38
    CSS, 38
    JavaScript, 38
    script, 497
    viewport, 37
height, 50
hex, 24
hide, 82

hide and clone template, 410
/home/ubuntu, 474
horizontal scaling, 256
href
    jQuery Mobile, 90
    OAuth, 419
hscroll:false, 221
HTML
    App, 302
    Appcelerator, 377, 378
    appMobi, 382
    attr, 81
    div, 123, 127, 357
    divs, 302
    DOM, 79
    event handlers, 95
    FeedHenry, 373
    gesture events, 123
    img, 357
    index.html, 407
    iScroll, 220
    jQuery, 80, 357
    jQuery Mobile, 84, 91, 97, 407
    JSON, 473
    log, 404
    MIME, 114
    PhoneGap, 275
    pixels, 125
    select, 91
    symbolic links, 436
    templates, 404
    user accounts, 356
    user experience, 212
    video, 229–230
    www, 282
html, 23, 81
    nginx, 28
HTML5, 2–3
    advantages, 5–6
    Android, 436
    Appcelerator, 379, 380
    appMobi, 381, 382–383

HTML5 (*continued*)
audio, 222
cache, 112
canvas, 32
CSS, 72
declarations, 37
<!DOCTYPE html>, 88
FeedHenry, 375
Geolocation API, 72–74, 131
hybrid native apps, 2
iPhone, 436
JavaScript, 6, 72
localStorage, 106
native apps, 4
nginx, 27
user experience, 211
video, 226
WebKit, 72
htpasswd, 474
HTTP
Amazon S3, 237, 240–241, 244
Appcelerator, 381
call, 425
common.js, 328
connect, 144
curl, 392
databases, 179
DELETE
api-cmdline.js, 202
REST, 179
EC2 instances, 58
GET, 137, 159, 346, 388, 497
api-cmdline.js, 202
REST, 179
helper modules, 328
JSON, 144, 498
large scale apps, 257
MongoDB, 329
nginx, 152
Node, 138, 141

OAuth, 366
POST, 330, 346, 392
api-cmdline.js, 202
REST, 179
SOAP, 178
post, 343
PUT
api-cmdline.js, 202
REST, 179
req, 329
REST, 178, 288, 387
Safari, 413
Twitter, 413
Wireshark, 394
http, 140
knox, 244
http://, 230
http_error, 404
http_get, 357
http_post, 357
Human Interface Guidelines, 131
hybrid native apps, 273–311
Android, 283–288
code-signing, 276–283
development phase, 276
distribution phase, 276
HTML5, 2, 5
iPhone, 275–283
PhoneGap, 3, 274
using device features, 288–294
hygiene factors, 399–404

I

-i, 64
icons, 131–132, 436–438
Android, 437–438
iPhone, 437
PhoneGap, 437
pixels, 437–438

id
accounts_signin_<network>, 417
attr, 81
color, 473
Date, 476
div, 477
itemdata, 101–102
item_tm, 102
jQuery, 81
jQuery Mobile, 89, 90, 91
MongoDB, 160
onclick, 45
#id, 90
IDE
Appcelerator, 377, 379
appMobi, 381
FeedHenry, 375–376
idempotent operations, 179
identifier, 117
IDLE, 115
id="main", 123
div, 477
id_str
JSON, 390
message.sender_screen_name, 392
if, 329
else, 102
ifconfig, 28
IIS. *See* Internet Information Server
imagedata, 303
images, 89, 478
jQuery Mobile, 290
img, 492
canvas, 32
HTML, 357
src, 303
imgI, 123
in-app advertising, 459
in-app purchases, 460
"inbound", 423

Inbound Rules, 58
inboundmsgs, 424
"inbound-msgs", 426
   Convo, 431
   Inbox, 431
Inbox, 405, 427
   displaymsg, 503
   div, 408
   events, 430
   "inbound-msgs", 431
   refresh, 428
   Social, 428–429
   touchmove, 428
   touchstart, 428
inc update, 164
incr, 269
index, 160
index.html, 279, 290, 492
   Facebook, 365
   HTML, 407
   Open in Text Editor, 286
   PhoneGap, 282
   Safari, 414
   script, 422
   Twitter, 365
   www, 346
infrastructure-as-a-service, 371
init, 365
initapp, 166
initEntry, 480
   common.js, 163
   last, 163
initialization code, 401–402
in-memory cache, 256
   shared-nothing architecture, 257
innerHTML, 11
   body, 15
   JavaScript callback functions, 17
input, 91
inserttext, 493
instances, EC2, 53, 54–61

public private key pairs, 56
   Ubuntu, 56
Internet Information Server (IIS), 27
Internet Protocol (IP), 28
   memcached, 263
iOS Developer Agreement, 441
iOS Provisioning Portal, 276, 447
IP. *See* Internet Protocol
ipa, 491
iPhone
   Ad Hoc, 490
   App Store, 441
   Appcelerator, 379
   appMobi, 381
   distribution certificate, 442
   HTML5, 436
   hybrid native apps, 275–283
   icons, 437
   jQuery Mobile, 88
   Mac OS X, 3
   mobile web apps, 72, 76–77
   nginx, 122
   Objective-C, 2
   orientations, 439
   overflow:scroll, 222
   PhoneGap, 436
   pixels, 437
   plist, 437
   screen width, 302
   screenshots, 439
   submitting binary for, 442–448
   todo.html, 97
   Twitter, 413
   UDID, 490
   video, 226, 229
   WebKit, 72
   Xcode, 277, 445–446
iScroll
   onPullDown, 485
   script, 477
   scrolling, 219

   setTimeout, 487
   user experience, 216–222
   vScrollbar, 485
   wrappers, 217
iscroll.js, 217
isSwipe, 478
itemdata, 101–102
$ItemName, 187
items, 107
item_tm, 102
iTunes Connect, 446–447
iTunes Link Maker, 485
iTunes Store App, 485

J

jar, 288
Jasmine, 400
Java
   Android, 2
   Appcelerator, 378
   jar, 288
   splash screen, 438–439
   wrappers, 288
JavaScript, 2–3
   Android, 283
   Appcelerator, 377, 378
   appMobi, 382
   arrays, 10
   callback functions, 15–17
   canvas, 33
   classes, 405
   color, 22–25
   direct message app, 407
   DOM, 10, 79
   DRY, 46–47
   dynamic functions, 18–20
   FeedHenry, 373, 374
   functions, 7–20
      code editors, 12
      declarations, 14
      expressions, 14
      variables, 45

JavaScript (*continued*)
  gesture events, 123
  Google V8, 136–137
  head, 38
  HTML5, 6, 72
  iScroll, 219
  jQuery, 78–83
  JSON, 107
  key/value pairs, properties, 10–11
  literal data structures, 7–12
  namespaces, 401
  Node, 136–141, 317
  onresize, 471
  PhoneGap, 275, 289
  server-side, 4, 136–150
  splice, 107
  Twitter, 390
  variables, $ (dollar sign), 79
  window.onload, 42
  www, 282
JavaScript Object Notation (JSON), 8, 12
  Appcelerator, 381
  common.js, 328
  DRY, 50, 425
  eyes, 183
  GET, 498
  Google Maps, 130
  HTML, 473
  HTTP, 144, 498
  http_post, 357
  id_str, 390
  JavaScript, 107
  MongoDB, 135, 144–145, 164
  Node, 144
  OAuth, 401, 415
  objects, 479
  POST, 331
  profile_image_url, 390
  properties, 50
  REST, 178

screen_name, 390
To-Do List app, 106
Twitter, 387, 389, 425
upload, 345
join, 50

, 15
  JavaScript callback functions, 17
Joyent, 6
jp-*, 226
jPlayer, 223, 226
jqmob.html, 85
  Safari, 87
jQuery
  $ (dollar sign), 79, 81
  ajax, 164, 295, 304
  animation effects, 82
  callback functions, 81
  dataType, 166
  direct message app, 407
  document.onload, 80
  events, 427
  event handlers, 82–83, 95, 294
  extend, 478
  FeedHenry, 374
  function chaining, 102
  HTML, 80, 357
  JavaScript, 78–83
  originalEvent, 116
  prepend, 486
  touchstart, 123
  wrappers, 494
jQuery Mobile, 72, 83–91
  Android, 88
  buttons, 90–91
  data-role="list-divider", 410
  direct message app, 406, 407
  FeedHenry, 374
  generator function, 215
  HTML, 84, 91, 97, 407

images, 290
iPhone, 88
page transitions, 216
scrolling, 89, 215
swipe, 107
tap, 95
tap function, 215
touch events, 117–118
uncompressed versions, 84
user experience, 212–216
jquery.js, 83, 88
jquery.min.js, 83
jquery.mobile.css, 85, 89
jquery.mobile.js, 88
JSON. *See* JavaScript Object Notation
JSON, 106
json, 330
  req, 331
jsonout, 194, 196, 481
JSON.parse, 196
JSON.stringify, 12, 106, 479

K

Karlton, Phil, 265
Keychain Access, 276
keypress, 15
keys.js, 243, 248, 328
key/value pairs, JavaScript literal data structures, 8
  properties, 10–11
KHTML, 20
kind, 160
knox, 241
  buckets, 243
  http, 244
  put, 244

L

label, 91
'landscape', 76

landscape orientation, 438
large-scale apps, 255–271
   cache, 258–271
last
   initEntry, 163
   MongoDB, 160
lastx, 42, 44, 45
   position, 52
lasty, 42, 44, 45
   position, 52
launch, 367
launcher icons, Android, 437–438
launching apps, 230–232
left, 123
leftout, 123, 126
libs, 286
Lifestream app, 235–271,
   294–311, 315–368
   adding content, 240–245
   Amazon S3, 236–247,
      306–310
   architecture, 316–317
   buckets, 238–240
   cache, 258–271
      complex objects,
         265–271
   completing, 345–367
   enabling user following,
      333–336
   Facebook, 253–255, 357–367
   getting content, 245–247
   MongoHQ, 317
   nginx, 355
   OAuth, 318
   server, 317–345
   signing in, 247–255
   social networking, 357–367
   Twitter, 248–252, 357–367
   uploading pictures,
      295–306, 336–345
   URL, 341, 364
   user accounts, 346–357
   Xcode, 346

line
   fromx, 44
   fromy, 44
   lineTo, 51
   moveTo, 51
   ontouchmove, 44
lineCap, 33, 43
lineJoin, 33, 43
lineTo, 34, 39, 44
   line, 51
lineWidth, 33
LinkedIn, 247, 387,
   487–488
Linux, 3
   ifconfig, 28
   IP, 28
   MongoDB, 146
   nginx, 26
   Node, 138
#list, 90
listapp, 195
ListDomains, 181
listen, 141
lists, 391
literal data structures,
   JavaScript, 7–12
literal object notation, 11
load, 404
load balancer, 256
   shared-nothing architecture,
      257
loaditemdata, 167
loaditems, 107
loaduser, 329
localhost, 28
localStorage, 404, 483
   clear, 502
   HTML5, 106
   "inbound", 423
   Twitter, 425
location.reload, 115
log, 13
   HTML, 404

low-friction deployment, 5
$lte, 164

M

Mac OS X
   IP, 28
   iPhone, 3
   nginx, 26
   Node, 138
MacPorts, 26
mail app launching, 231
main, 10, 11, 13
make, 19
makeid, 481
makeshowcon, 412, 500
makesignin, 417
   Accounts, 418
map.html, 478
mark, 479
marketing strategy, 456–461
markitem, 102, 107
Math.sin, 125, 126, 140
maximum-scale=1.0, 472
members, 405
memcached, 258–260
   getitem, 265
   IP, 263
   multiple servers, 260–265
   RAM, 260
   setitem, 265
memcached incr, 269
memcache-followers.js,
   266–268
memcache.js, 258–259
memcache-multi.js, 261–263
memory
   Amazon S3, 244
   in-memory cache, 256, 257
   RAM
      Android, 287
      memcached, 260
menubutton, 289

Message, 185

message.sender_screen_
name, 392

metadata, 440

$ (dollar sign), 502

DomainMetadata, 181

metadata, 186, 195

metatags, 3

viewport, 23–24, 37

methods, 405

metrics, 456

middleware, 142, 144

auth, 331, 343

collect, 330

connect, 330–331, 364,
498

MIME, 114

mime.types, 112

nginx, 113, 114

minification, 83

minus, 90

mobile web apps, 2, 71–109

Android, 77–78

development platforms,
372–373

device orientation, 74–76

iPhone, 76–77

To-Do List app, 91–107

user location, 72–74

uses, 71–72

Model-View-Controller (MVC),
404

Moleskine, 449

momentum, 485

MongoDB, 60, 144–150

authentication, 321

callback functions, 148, 173

clienterror, 498

collections, 160–164

command-line client, 479

common.js, 328

event handlers, 148

FeedHenry, 375

findAndModify, 164

HTTP, 329

JSON, 135, 144–145, 164

last, 160

$lte, 164

memcached, 258

$pull, 344

total, 173

mongodb, 146

MongoHQ

FeedHenry, 375

Lifestream app, 317

user, 328

mongo.js, 146–147, 148

Monitoring tab, 60

moves, 51

moveTo, 34

line, 51

paths, 44

MPEG4, 226

enhanced, 229

multiple cache servers, 260–265

MVC. See Model-View-
Controller

myarray, 10, 12

myobject, 12

N

:name, 159

<name>, 50

namespaces, 400

JavaScript, 401

native apps, 2

HTML5, 4

URL schemes, 230

navigator.accelerometer,
289

navigator.camera, 289

navigator.camera
.getPicture, 295

navigator.compass
.getCurrentHeading, 493

navigator.device, 420

navigator.geolocation, 72

navigator.notification, 289

navigator.notification
.alert, 294

navigator.notification
.beep, 294

navigator.notification
.confirm, 294

navigator.onLine, 166

Network, 414, 417

complete, 420

getmsgs, 424

handleauthorize, 418,
419

this, 419

network, 405, 417

next_cursor, 392

nginx, 24–29

apt-get, 64–65

draw, 67

HTML5, 27

HTTP, 152

Lifestream app, 355

Node, 152

UNIX, 65

warning messages, 66

nginx

Android, 122

iPhone, 122

mime.types, 113, 114

nginx location, 158

nginx.conf, 199

nginx location, 158

nginx -s, 87

nginx -s reload, 97

nginx upstream, 480

nginx.conf, 87, 97, 112

nginx, 199

nick, 405

Node

base64, 295, 342

Buffer, 305

callback functions, 141
connect, 142–144, 252
curl, 159, 201
-e, 163
events, 137
event handlers, 137
FeedHenry, 375
fs, 243
HTTP, 138, 141
JavaScript, 136–141, 317
JSON, 144
memcached, 258
modules, 140
nginx, 152
oauth, 248
package manager,
    141–144
require, 304
server, 6
simpledb, 185
threads, 137
touch events, 137
upload, 345
URL, 158
uuid, 310, 480
node-uuid, 166
npm, 142, 318
    eyes, 185
    simpledb, 185
npm install, 300
null
    delete, 107
    document
        .getElementById, 11
    error, 186, 259
    user, 329

O

OAuth
    Accounts, 415
    call, 421
    debugging, 389, 415

direct message app,
    413–421
Facebook, 255, 364
handleauthorize, 419
href, 419
HTTP, 366
JSON, 401, 415
launch, 367
Lifestream app, 318
Sign-in view, 397
Social, 417
Twitter, 247–248, 364, 388,
    393
URL, 418
Wireshark, 252
without server, 413–421
oauth, 247, 316
    getAuthorizeUrl, 255
    Node, 248
oauthclient, 252
oauth.js, 414
oauth_token_secret, 252
oauth_verifier, 420
objects
    Amazon S3, 236
    data, 405
    JSON, 479
    views, 405
Objective-C
    Appcelerator, 378
    iPhone, 2
    PhoneGap, 282
OBSOLETE, 115
offsetTop, 42
oncached, 115
onchecking, 115
onclick, 15, 18
    clearButton, 45
    div, 24
    id, 45
    touch-sensitive drawing app,
        32
ondownloading, 115

onerror, 115
onkeypress, 15
onload, 11, 38, 478
onmousemove, 32
onnoupdate, 115
onobsolete, 115
onprogress, 115
onPullDown
    iScroll, 485
    pullToRefresh, 486
onresize, 471
ontouchmove, 32, 39
    line, 44
    scrolling, 42
ontouchstart, 32, 39, 45
    preventDefault, 44
onupdateready, 115
Open in Text Editor, 286
openssh.com, 64
orientations, 439–440
    Android, 440
    device, 74–76
    iPhone, 439
    splash screen, 438
originalEvent, 116
outboundmsgs, 424
"outbound-msgs", 426
    Convo, 431
outstream, 246
overflow:scroll
    CSS, 212
    iPhone, 222

P

'p', 81
<p>, 81
package manager, 141–144
page transitions, 216
pageX, 117
pageY, 117
Paint.NET, 439
parseInt, 83

passwords, 474, 475
path, 51
paths, 33
    clear, 43
    moveTo, 44
pause, 289, 501
People, 397, 404, 409, 427, 429
"people", 426
percentmmobile.com, 456
period, 160
PhoneGap
    Android, 283, 288, 436
    Appcelerator, 377, 378
    deviceready, 294
    direct message app, 407
    DOM, 294
    events, 501
    FeedHenry, 374
    hybrid native apps, 3, 274
    icons, 437
    index.html, 282
    iPhone, 436
    JavaScript, 289
    navigator.device, 420
    Objective-C, 282
    Safari, 401–402
    splash screen, 438
    wrappers, 5
phonegap.jar, 286, 288
phonegap.js, 290
photo-blogging app. See
    Lifestream app
Photoshop, 439
picTake, 303
pictures
    storing, Amazon S3,
        306–310
    uploading, Lifestream app,
        295–306, 336–345
picUpload, 304, 357
pingdom.com, 61
pixels
    Android, 438
    CSS, 125

HTML, 125
    icons, 437–438
    iPhone, 437
platform-as-a-service, 371
    FeedHenry, 373
plist, 437
plus, 90
PNG format, 437
'portrait', 76
portrait orientation, 438
position
    callback functions, 52, 73
    coords, 73
    lastx, 52
    lasty, 52
POST, 144
    collect, 330
    curl, 159
    HTTP, 330, 346, 388, 392
        api-cmdline.js, 202
        REST, 179
        SOAP, 178
    JSON, 331
post, 144, 332
    HTTP, 343
        stream, 343
pre, 14
premium service, app as,
    459–460
prepend, 486
preventDefault
    event handlers, 124
    ontouchstart, 44
profile_image_url, 390
properties
    CSS, 83
    JavaScript key/value pairs,
        10–11
    JSON, 50
provisioning profile, 277, 281
ps, 65
Public DNS, AWS, 60
public private key pairs
    AWS, 64

EC2 instances, 56
$pull, 344
pullToRefresh, 486
push, 10, 14
PUT, 244
    HTTP, 388
        api-cmdline.js, 202
        REST, 179
    REST, 237
put, 196
    knox, 244
putapp, 195
PutAttributes, 181
putImageData, 474
putItem, 186
putitem, 196
PuTTY, 64
Python, 475

R

race conditions, 137
Rackspace, 6
RAM
    Android, 287
    memcached, 260
rapid development, 5
readjson, 158, 159
realistic wire frames, 398
rect, 33
Redis, 489
refresh, 90, 220–221
    Inbox, 428
Register, 496
register, 316, 330, 357
registered device, 276
    Xcode, 277
remove, 107
render, 411
Representation State Transfer
    (REST), 178–179
    Amazon S3, 237
    HTTP, 288, 387

Twitter, 387
URL, 179
req
    HTTP, 329
    json, 331
req.params.name, 159
reqtokens, 420
    cache, 419
Request, 140, 144
request, 328
Request Instances Wizard, 56
require, 304
require('http'), 140
research, 316
resources, 182
Response, 140, 144
Response.end, 141
REST. *See* Representation State Transfer
Restore button, 473
restricted.pwd, 474, 475
result, 186
resume, 289, 501
Retina, 438
return, 243
rightout, 123, 126
root, 300
root user, 64
rotate, 125
rotation
    gesture events, 124
    zoom, 126
rotation, 118, 125–126
    gesturechange, 125
round-robin algorithm, 257
router, 144
rubber-band effect, 294

S

S3. *See* Amazon S3
s3-get.js, 246
s3-put.js, 243, 246, 487

Safari
    alert, 404
    Dev Center, 21
    HTTP, 413
    index.html, 414
    jqmob.html, 87
    PhoneGap, 401–402
    todo.html, 97, 100
    view.html, 24
    Web Inspector, 21, 411, 415
        MIME, 114
    WebKit, 3, 20–21
Save button, 473
saveEntry, 163, 404
saveitems, 107
saveon, 102
scalability, databases, 180
Scalable Vector Graphics (SVG), 32
scale, 118
    gesturechange, 126
schema, 145
    Amazon SimpleDB, 181
scope, JavaScript functions, 19
scp, 66
screen_name, 390
screenshots, 439–440
screenX, 117
screenY, 117
script, 11, 24
    head, 497
    index.html, 422
    iScroll, 477
    iscroll.js, 217
    src, 290
    URL, 367
scrollers, 220
scrolling
    data-position="fixed", 215
    iScroll, 219
    jQuery Mobile, 89, 215
    ontouchmove, 42

scroll-is.css, 484
scroll-slide.css, 484
sdberr, 194
SDKs. *See* software development kits
Search, 496
search, 357
searchbutton, 289
SeaShore, 439
sec, 160
security groups, 60
SELECT, 195
Select, 182
select, 91
self, 419
self-signed certificates, 442
sendjson, 158, 159
    ajax, 166
    timesync, 203
sendmsg, 421
sendstats, 167
    navigator.onLine, 166
server, 141
server offset, 197
server.follow.js, 333, 336, 337
server.js, 317
server.*.js, 328
server.mongo.js, 328, 336
server.post.js, 337, 339, 355, 361
    collect, 340
server-side JavaScript, 4, 136–150
server.social.js, 361
service, 366
set, 489
$set, 149
setitem, 265
setTimeout, 472
    iScroll, 487
    touchend, 478
sha1.js, 414
shared-nothing architecture, 257

show, 412
showcon, 303
showfollowers, 357
showfollows, 357
showimages, 357, 495
Sign In button, 410, 413
signing in, 247–255
    Facebook, 253–255
    Twitter, 248–252
Simple Object Access Protocol
    (SOAP), 178
    Amazon S3, 237
Simple Storage Service (S3). *See*
    Amazon S3
SimpleDB. *See* Amazon
    SimpleDB
simpledb, 182–188
    callback functions,
        185–186
    Node, 185
    npm, 185
sin function, 125, 126
size, 50
slideshare.net, 467
slideUp, 82, 102
SMS launching, 230
SOAP. *See* Simple Object Access
    Protocol
Social, 414
    accounts, 424
    clear, 502
    delmsg, 503
    getmsgs, 424, 430
    getpeople, 430
    Inbox, 428–429
    OAuth, 417
social networking, 387–432.
    See also Facebook; LinkedIn;
    Twitter
    Lifestream app, 357–367
software development kits
    (SDKs)
    Android, 3, 283

FeedHenry, 375
    iPhone, 3
software-as-a-service, 372
someText, 17
span, 101
splash screen, 131–132
    Android, 438
    Java, 438–439
    landscape orientation, 438
    portrait orientation, 438
splice, 107
src
    img, 303
    script, 290
SSH, 64
    EC2 instances, 58
    Node, 138
ssh, 66
    -A, 476
    -i, 64
.ssh, 64
stackoverflow.com, 37
standards compliant, 5
star, 90
start, 123
startup screens, 131–132
startupdeathclock.com, 76,
    77
stat, 243
status, 115
statuses, 391
stick sessions, 257
stream, 316
    config.max_stream_
        size, 344
    post, 343
    user, 343
StreamBuffer, 345
stroke, 33, 43, 44, 50
    context, 39
    path, 51
strokeStyle, 33, 43
style, 24

subscription-based services,
    459
Subversion, 65
sudo, 64
sudo -s, 142
superclass, 419
SVG. *See* Scalable Vector
    Graphics
swapCache, 115
swipe, 118, 501, 503
    jQuery Mobile, 107
swipe gesture, 126–127
swipeleft, 118
swiperight, 118
symbolic links, 283, 436
syncitems, 483, 484

T

tap, 117
    event handlers, 95
    jQuery Mobile, 95
tap function, 215
taphold, 117
target, 117
target="_blank", 366
targetTouches, 116
templates
    hide and clone, 410
    HTML, 404
    Xcode, 282
text, 392, 401
    itemdata, 102
text/html, 114
text/plain, 141
thinkgeek.com, 466
this, 83
    Network, 419
threads, 137
throw, 243
thundering herd problem, 260,
    264

time synchronization,
196–198
timesync, 202
    sendjson, 203
toDataURL, 494
To-Do List app, 91–107
    cache, 112–113
    in cloud, 182–208
    cloud analytics, 150–174
    command-line, 188–196
    icons, 131–132
    items, 107
    JSON, 106
    saving, 103–107
    startup screen, 131–132
    synchronizing, 203–208
    time synchronization,
    196–198
    updating, 164–167
    web service, 198–203
todo.css, 92, 93–94
    div, 98
todo.html, 93, 95–96, 112
    Android, 97
    div, 99, 103
    iPhone, 97
    Safari, 97, 100
    ul, 99
todo.js, 92, 94, 99–100, 165,
476
todo.manifest, 112, 113
token, 316, 330
tonvo. *See* direct message app
top, 123
TopNav, 405, 406, 427
    views, 412
total, 173
totalinperiod, 173
touch events, 115–127
    jQuery Mobile, 117–118
    Node, 137
    WebKit, 115–116
touchcancel, 116

touchend, 116
    setTimeout, 478
touches, 116, 117
touch.html, 122
touchmove, 116, 125
    Inbox, 428
touch-sensitive drawing app,
32–52
    DRY, 46–52
    finger touches, 39–45
touchstart, 116
    Inbox, 428
    jQuery, 123
tox, 44
toy, 44
tracer bullets, 34–36, 152–160
    Amazon SimpleDB,
    183–188
transactions, 180
trends, 391
trigger, 427
Twitter
    for, 417
    Android, 413
    developer console,
    393–395
    direct message app,
    395–432
    entities, 390–391
    HTTP, 413
    index.html, 365
    iPhone, 413
    JavaScript, 390
    JSON, 387, 389, 425
    Lifestream app, 357–367
    localStorage, 425
    OAuth, 247–248, 364, 388,
    393
    REST, 387
    service, 366
    signing in, 248–252
    URL, 413
    usage limits, 390

U

Ubuntu, 26
    AWS, 60
    EC2 instances, 56
    Node, 138
    upstart, 496
UDID, 276–277
    iPhone, 490
    Xcode, 277
ul
    remove, 107
    todo.html, 99
UNCACHED, 115
unfollow, 336
unique identifiers, 166
unit testing, 317, 328, 400
universally unique identifier
    (UUID), 240, 310
UNIX, 65
update, 149, 356–357
"update-inbox", 427, 428, 429
"update-people", 427, 428,
    429
UPDATEREADY, 115
upload, 343
    JSON, 345
    Node, 345
upserts, 163
upstart, 496
URL
    connect, 159, 334
    customized, 413
    Facebook, 255
    http_get, 357
    Lifestream app, 341, 364
    :name, 159
    Node, 158
    OAuth, 418
    REST, 179
    scheme, 230
    script, 367
    Twitter, 413

url, 328
use case analysis, 395
user, 268
    MongoHQ, 328
    null, 329
    stream, 343
user accounts
    CSS, 356
    HTML, 356
    Lifestream app, 346–357
user experience, 211–234
    iScroll, 216–222
    jQuery Mobile, 212–216
user flow, 397
user sessions, 257
userdetails, 421
username, 316
:username, 316
usernames, 474
;username/follow, 316
username:password, 474
:username/post, 317
:username/stream, 317
:username/unfollow, 317
:username/upload, 317
users, 391
user-scalable, viewport, 472
util, 141, 401
    common, 158
util.debug, 141
util.http_get, 418
util.http_post, 418
Utilities, 26
//utility, 339
//utility functions, 361
util.log, 418
util.params, 419, 420
UUID. *See* universally unique identifier
uuid, 310, 480

V

val, 160, 161
variables, JavaScript
    $ (dollar sign), 79
    dynamic functions, 19
    functions, 45
version number, cache, 114
vertical cloud services, 377, 380, 381, 383
vertical scaling, 256
video, 226–230
video, 226
view.html, 471
    nginx, 28
    Safari, 24
view.js, 172
viewport
    head, 37
    metatags, 23–24, 37
    user-scalable, 472
    zoom, 24, 37
views, 397
    objects, 405
    TopNav, 412
    wire frames, 404–405
vScrollbar, 485
-vv, 258

W

W3C, 73, 114
waitForSomething, 17
watchPosition, 73–74
web, 58
Web Inspector. *See* Safari
web service
    Amazon S3, 237
    To-Do List app, 198–203
WebKit
    Android, 20–21, 72
    animation effects, 123, 476
    canvas, 32
    HTML5, 72
    iPhone, 20–21, 72
    JSON, 106
    Safari, 3, 20–21
    touch events, 115–116
@-webkit-keyframes, 485
-webkit-transform, 123, 125, 127
WebView, 5
weinre, 491
width, 50
win, 186, 194
    incr, 269
window, 38
window.applicationCache, 115
window.location.href, 419
window.onload, 24
    JavaScript, 42
window.onorientationchanged, 76
window.onresize, 74, 76
window.orientation, 74
Windows, 3
    IP, 28
    nginx, 26
Windows Mobile, 381
window.scrollTo, 472
wire frames, 398, 399
    views, 404–405
Wireshark, 179
    HTTP, 394
    OAuth, 252
work_pic img, 494
wrappers
    iScroll, 217
    Java, 288
    jQuery, 494
    PhoneGap, 5
write, 244, 246
write-through cache, 260